Core Reference

PROGRAMMING
MICROSOFT® OFFICE
ACCESS 2003

Rick Dobson

PUBLISHED BY
Microsoft Press
A Division of Microsoft Corporation
One Microsoft Way
Redmond, Washington 98052-6399

Library of Congress Cataloging-in-Publication Data [pending.]
Dobson, Rick, 1944-
        Programming Microsoft Office Access 2003 (Core Reference) / Rick Dobson.
              p. cm.
        ISBN 0-7356-1942-5
        1. Microsoft Office   I. Title.

        HF5548.4.M525D63   2003
        005.75'65--dc21   2003050982

Printed and bound in the United States of America.

1 2 3 4 5 6 7 8 9   QWE   8 7 6 5 4 3

Distributed in Canada by H.B. Fenn and Company Ltd.

A CIP catalogue record for this book is available from the British Library.

Microsoft Press books are available through booksellers and distributors worldwide. For further information about international editions, contact your local Microsoft Corporation office or contact Microsoft Press International directly at fax (425) 936-7329. Visit our Web site at www.microsoft.com/mspress. Send comments to *mspinput@microsoft.com*.

Active Directory, ActiveX, FoxPro, FrontPage, IntelliSense, JScript, Microsoft, Microsoft Press, MSDN, the .NET logo, Outlook, PivotChart, PivotTable, PowerPoint, VGA, Visual Basic, Visual C++, Visual InterDev, Visual Studio, Windows, Windows NT, Windows Server, and the Windows logo are either registered trademarks or trademarks of Microsoft Corporation in the United States and/or other countries. Other product and company names mentioned herein may be the trademarks of their respective owners.

The example companies, organizations, products, domain names, e-mail addresses, logos, people, places, and events depicted herein are fictitious. No association with any real company, organization, product, domain name, e-mail address, logo, person, place, or event is intended or should be inferred.

Acquisitions Editor: Anne Hamilton
Project Editor: Dick Brown
Technical Editor: Jack Beaudry
Desktop Publisher: Gina Cassill

Body Part No. X09-69388

Table of Contents

Acknowledgments

Several communities helped make this book available to you. I'll start by thanking the staff at Microsoft Press. My acquisitions editor, Anne Hamilton, used her business acumen and cheery attitude to help me keep my eye on the prize—writing a timely book that serves the needs of busy Microsoft Access developers. My lead editor, Dick Brown, showed real concern for producing a book that gives developers the right information in a way that is easy to grasp. He was backed by two great supporting editors, Jack Beaudry and Brenda Pittsley, both of whom raised questions and smoothed the text to be clearer and more informative.

For each book I write, I seek out Microsoft program and product managers who help ensure that I cover the correct topics in the best way. For this book, I am especially honored to list Bill Ramos, a lead program manager for Access and Microsoft Excel. Other members of the Microsoft Access team who provided valuable insight and direction were Tim Getsch, Mike Wachal, and Sanjay Jacob.

I also want to thank the many readers who provided feedback on previous editions of this book and on my national seminar tours. Your feedback helps me to know what you value the most and to identify content that needs improvement. To provide feedback on this book, please leave a comment in the Guest Book at *www.programmingmsaccess.com*.

Finally, you would not be reading any of this if it were not for the loving, encouraging, and motivating support of my wife, Virginia Dobson. She backed me up when I accepted my first contract to write a book for Microsoft Press back in 1998. Her support has remained steadfast through this, my fifth title with Microsoft Press, for which she proofed much of the content before its initial submittal to Microsoft Press and did page proofs for all chapters before they went to the printer.

I appreciate all those listed above, yet it is the sustenance and divine guidance that I receive through my faith in God that enables me to compose the words and code samples in this book. Thank you, Jesus!

Introduction

This book aims to help experienced Access developers be as productive as possible using features introduced or upgraded with Microsoft Access 2003. Many of the techniques and code samples presented here also apply to Access 2002 and Access 2000. Reading this introduction will help you decide whether *Programming Microsoft Office Access 2003* will be relevant to your needs as a developer.

Who Should Read This Book

Programming Microsoft Office Access 2003 will aid developers who work with all recent versions of Access, including Access 2003, Access 2002, and Access 2000. Those who are migrating to Access 2003 from Access 97 or an earlier version will also benefit from the lessons contained here. Feedback from two previous books on programming Access and four national seminar tours that addressed the needs of Access and other database developers sharpened the book's focus. Professional Access developers said they want help for real problems that is short and to the point. Therefore, this book is chock-full of code samples you can adapt to apply to real-world problems for which your clients seek solutions.

This book represents a conscious attempt to provide content that will make a difference for Access developers. Browse the table of contents for a heading that addresses a question you face. Chances are you'll find one or more relevant code samples. The code is accompanied by clear, concise commentary to help you modify samples to solve your clients' precise needs. For example, you'll find expanded coverage of user-level security. This powerful mechanism for securing Access databases in multiuser solutions eludes many beginning Access developers, but here you will find step-by-step instructions and detailed code samples that make it easy to automate the administration of user-level security.

Developers also are commonly interested in learning techniques for locking clients out of the proprietary code. You want clients to benefit from your solution—without being able to steal your intellectual property. Creating .mde and .ade files is an easy solution to this objective, but it is a solution with important limitations. Therefore, this book describes ways to block users from going behind a Welcome menu that you make available when an application opens. These techniques vary from those that are simple to apply to others that are exceedingly robust and can block even the most determined attempts to access your proprietary code.

Because Jet is in maintenance mode, many professional Access developers seek to become comfortable with SQL Server as a means of creating new Access solutions. Therefore, coverage of Access projects and Access/SQL Server interoperability has been expanded from previous editions of this book. This edition includes three chapters devoted to empowering you to create great Access solutions with a SQL Server database server, including the one that ships with Office 2003.

Finally, this book presents improvements introduced or refined with Access 2003. XML capabilities are upgraded throughout the Office 2003 components, including Access 2003. In order to take advantage of this functionality using either Access database files or Access projects, however, you need a grasp of what XML is, what it's good for, and what it can do for the solutions you create with Access. That's why this book devotes a whole chapter to XML. Another important set of new features involves Macro Security and the Jet SandBox—these technologies combine to secure your Access solutions within organizations. The rationale behind these new feature sets is explained here along with an explanation of how to manage them for the best advantage of your clients.

Organization of the Book

This book spans 15 chapters, all of which focus directly on the needs of experienced Access developers. You begin with several chapters dwelling on ADO programming techniques for data access, data maintenance, and data definition. Next, you shift focus to client interface issues in chapters on Access forms, reports, PivotTables, PivotCharts, and interoperability with other Office 2003 components. The book closes with a series of chapters that generally address multiuser issues, including database security, building solutions for SQL Server databases, making Access data available via Web solutions, and sharing data from Access solutions with others using XML.

This edition of *Programming Microsoft Office Access* includes four bonus sections accessible from the Web, exclusively for owners of this book. This bonus content extends core content within the book. For example, the chapter titled "Access Does the Web" drills down on data access pages and Office Web Components, while the bonus material describes how to make Access data available over the Web via Active Server Pages. Each reference to a bonus Web-based section includes an access URL.

The ADO coverage starts with a pair of chapters on data access techniques. Chapter 1 presents the basics of data access, including how to make a connection to a database and how to open a recordset on a table, query, or SQL string. This chapter thoroughly explains recordsets by showing you how to sort, find, seek, and filter a recordset. In addition to data access issues, you'll also learn the basics of ADO syntax for inserting rows, updating column values, and deleting rows. Chapter 2 presents more advanced ADO issues, including how to use parameters. Probably the most compelling topic in Chapter 2, parameters offer a powerful means for developers to enable dynamic data access. Parameters also can be used to make procedures for modifying recordsets reusable with new data supplied by users at run time.

The next two chapters address data definition issues that enable you to build tables and queries programmatically. These chapters offer developers a powerful means of documenting their database objects in ADO and JET SQL code. This capability is essential if you need to enable users to create tables or queries through your applications.

Chapter 5 is all about creating custom solutions with forms. A major focus here is how to programmatically populate the *RecordSource* and *Recordset* properties of forms. This emphasis equips you with the skills you need to reuse your forms with different data sources. By using the principles and adapting the samples covered in this chapter, you can reduce the number of forms necessary for applications and create solutions that are more efficient to maintain.

Next, you learn how to create static and dynamic reports. After covering essential built-in report design capabilities, Chapter 6 demonstrates code samples that illustrate how to add flexibility to the built-in Access report feature set.

Chapter 7 explores the capabilities of PivotTables and PivotCharts in Access 2003. PivotTables and PivotCharts gained popularity in Microsoft Excel. Their incorporation into Access provides Access developers a means of serving financial and operational analysts who use PivotTables and PivotCharts to support strategic and tactical decision-making.

Chapter 8 and Chapter 9 primarily demonstrate a means of extending built-in Access capabilities through the Microsoft Office 2003 Objects model and other Office 2003 components. With each successive version of Access, Access developers gain powerful new ways to serve their clients just by plugging in references to other object models. For example, Chapter 9 presents a series of code samples that demonstrate how to share data between Access and Excel, Outlook, or Word. Chapter 8, meanwhile, imparts the same approach for objects, such as the *CommandBar* object, from the Office 2003 Objects model.

Chapter 8 further presents samples that demonstrate how to secure your code by severely restricting the ability of users to open the Database window.

Moving on, Chapter 10 considers database security from multiple perspectives. First, it provides an overview of traditional database security issues. Second, it reviews user-level security concepts before presenting steps for manually implementing and managing user-level security. Third, the chapter presents code samples that illustrate how to manage all the important features of user-level security. The commentary associated with these samples provides direction for readily managing user-level security in your own custom applications. The chapter closes with an introduction to two relatively new security features—the Jet SandBox and Macro Security. The Jet SandBox appeared in earlier Access versions as a non-default feature for protecting computers running Access applications. In Access 2003, the Jet SandBox is in force by default. Its operation has been upgraded for easier protection of computers running Access applications within an enterprise. With Access 2003, the Macro Security feature available in Excel and Word since Office 2000 has been adapted to protect Access users from viruses. In addition, Macro security within Access 2003 interacts with the Jet SandBox. Chapter 10 describes and illustrates these two security innovations.

One of the most exciting capabilities of Access 2003 is its ability to build and manage Microsoft SQL Server 2000 solutions through Access projects. Chapter 11, Chapter 12, and Chapter 13 systematically explore how to tap the power of Access projects. Chapter 11 reviews all the major SQL Server database objects, as well as how to create and manage them from Access projects. Chapter 12 shows how to use SQL Server database objects with Access forms and includes special content describing exclusive Access form features for SQL Server databases. Chapter 13 examines SQL Server database security, which differs substantially from Access database files security.

Chapter 14 and Chapter 15 demonstrate different means of sharing data from Access databases and Access projects with others. Chapter 14 focuses on data access pages and Office 2003 Web Components. The book's coverage of these topics includes both graphical and programmatic techniques. Chapter 15 reviews XML syntax and technologies as a basis for demonstrating how to use them with Access 2003. You'll learn what XML is good for and how to put it to work in Access solutions.

To enhance and inform future editions of this book, I encourage you to visit *http://www.programmingmsaccess.com* and sign the Guest Book to share your feedback about the content herein after you are finished.

Installing and Using the Samples and Demo Files

To download the sample files from the book's Companion Content page on the Web, visit *http://www.microsoft.com/mspress/books/6768.asp.*

To access the sample files and the links to other resources, click Companion Content in the More Information menu box on the right side of the page. This will load the Companion Content Web page, which includes links for downloading the sample files and connecting to Microsoft Press Support. The download link opens a Web package executable file containing a license agreement. To copy the sample files onto your hard disk, click the link to run the executable and then accept the license agreement. The sample files will be copied by default to the C:\Access11Files folder. During the installation process, you'll be given the option of changing the destination folder.

Support Information

Every effort has been made to ensure the accuracy of the book and its companion content. Microsoft also provides corrections for books through the World Wide Web at the following address:

http://www.microsoft.com/mspress/support/

In addition to sending feedback directly to the authors, if you have comments, questions, or ideas regarding the presentation or use of this book or the companion content you can send them to Microsoft using either of the following methods:

Postal Mail

Microsoft Press
Attn: Programming Microsoft Office Access 2003 (Core Reference) Editor
One Microsoft Way
Redmond, WA 98052-6399

E-Mail

mspinput@microsoft.com

Please note that product support isn't offered through the above mail addresses. For support information regarding Visual Studio .NET 2003, go to *http://msdn.microsoft.com/vstudio/*. You can also call Standard Support at (425) 635-7011 weekdays between 6 a.m. and 6 p.m. Pacific time, or you can search Microsoft Help and Support at *http://support.microsoft.com/support.*

System Requirements

The samples in this book require Access 2003 from the Office 2003 suite. All samples were tested on a computer with the Windows XP Professional operating system. To run samples from chapters with content on SQL Server (Chapters 11–13), you need a copy of SQL Server 2000. In most cases, you will be able to use the MSDE 2000 version that ships with Office 2003. The sample materials for these chapters include databases that you can attach to your SQL Server instance. Those using MSDE 2000 will be unable to run a few samples that rely on the pubs database, as that database does not ship with MSDE 2000. However, if you obtain Microsoft Visual Studio Tools for Office, you also get a version of SQL Server that includes the sample pubs database. Chapter 14 requires Microsoft FrontPage 2003 and an IIS for Windows 2000 or Windows XP. FrontPage 2003 is available as a standalone component; it is not a part of any Office 2003 suite. IIS is a Web server available as an accessory that you can install on any computer running Windows XP Professional, Windows Server 2003, or any version of Windows 2000.

1

Data Access Models: Part I

Microsoft Access 2003 supports two data access models: the traditional Data Access Objects (DAO) and ActiveX Data Objects (ADO). ADO is part of the Microsoft Data Access Components (MDAC), which initially targeted universal data access. DAO targets just the Jet database engine. DAO was the exclusive data access model for Access developers from Access 1.0 through Access 97. Therefore, it is finely tuned to the Jet database engine. This feature is both a strength and a weakness. While DAO can still perform a few selected tasks for the Jet engine that are impossible or very difficult to do with ADO, accessing data from sources other than Jet using DAO can be very awkward or impossible, depending on the context.

Access 2000 was the first Access version to support ADO for data access to Jet as well as to other databases. ADO is a separate technology from Microsoft Access, but Access interoperates well with it. With Access 2002 and Access 2003, Microsoft improved on past functionality and added new capabilities to ADO programming. Instead of being based on a single database engine (such as DAO), ADO uses a common programming model to access data universally. It relies on OLE DB providers for low-level links to data sources. OLE DB technologies eventually will make their ODBC predecessors obsolete, much as ADO will replace DAO. In fact, the MDAC Road Map (*http://msdn.microsoft.com/library/default.asp?url=/library/en-us/dnmdac/html/data_mdacroadmap.asp*) already describes DAO as an obsolete data access technology. This means that the current 3.6 version of DAO will not be updated in the future. The road map advises against building new systems with obsolete technologies and encourages migrations to ADO or ADO.NET for any modifications of existing applications. The road map describes ADO.NET as an evolutionary progression from ADO. ADO.NET is the data component for the .NET Framework, Microsoft's next-generation application development environment. See my *Programming*

1

Microsoft Visual Basic .NET for Microsoft Access Databases (Microsoft Press, 2002) book for numerous code samples illustrating the use of ADO.NET with Access .mdb files.

ADO was conceived as a universal data access language, and it is highly suitable for developing solutions based on the Web or on a LAN (local area network). DAO does not process data when used in a Web-based solution. Because of its limited scope and obsolete status, DAO does not play a significant role in this book. For information on DAO code, see the online documentation for Access and Microsoft's Support Online (*http://support.microsoft.com/*). Click the Searchable Knowledge Base link for documents that discuss typical problems and their associated workarounds. Many of the articles include DAO code samples.

The subject of data access models is vast. To make this discussion more digestible, I've broken it into two chapters. This chapter and Chapter 2 focus primarily on data access for Jet with the ADO object model. The two chapters also include some coverage of ADO with other database engines, particularly with Microsoft SQL Server. Numerous programming samples show you how to accomplish typical database chores.

This chapter begins with an overview of ActiveX Data Objects and then moves on to discuss the Connection, *Recordset,* and *Field* objects. This chapter aims to convey a basic understanding of the kinds of roles each object plays, as well as how to code the objects. In Chapter 2, you will learn about the *Command* and *Parameters* objects and the *Errors* collection. Chapter 2 also devotes considerable attention to demonstrating the features of the ADO *Record* and *Stream* objects. Chapter 2 closes with a review of ADO event programming techniques. Later chapters build on the information presented in Chapter 1 and Chapter 2 and cover advanced data topics, such as database replication, remote database access, and multiuser security.

ADO Overview

This section presents an overview of ADO features used in Access development efforts. Subsequent sections will build on this foundation and demonstrate data access development techniques.

ADO Components for Microsoft Access Developers

Microsoft Access developers are likely to reference any of three separate ADO object models: the ADODB library, the ADOX library, and the JRO library. However, I will use the term ADO to refer collectively to all three models.

- The ADODB library is a small, lightweight library that contains core objects and offers the basics for making connections, issuing commands, and retrieving recordsets; it also enables recordset navigation. You can use this library to perform basic database maintenance tasks, such as modifying, adding, and deleting records. Most of the library elements apply to other databases as well as Access databases.

- The ADOX library supports data definition language and security issues. It offers objects that let you examine and control a database's schema. For example, it lets you create tables and relations. The model includes support for referential integrity and cascading updates and deletes. It also offers the *Procedures* and *Views* collections, as well as the *Users* and *Groups* collections for user-level database security. Many features of the ADOX library especially target Microsoft Access database files. For example, Access developers programming data definition tasks for SQL Server databases are likely to find the SQL-DMO library more suitable than the ADOX library.

- The JRO library enables Jet database replication. Database replication is especially important for applications built with Access database files (.mdb files), because this capability can vastly extend their availability. This library is exclusively for Access database files. (For more information, see Chapter 13 in the previous edition of this book, which covered database replication in depth, including how to program replication via JRO.)

As mentioned in the chapter introduction, ADO has been readily available to Access developers since Access 2000. The following ADO version numbers correspond to MDAC versions. The ADO 2.1 version was widely available with the release of Access 2000. The 2.5 and 2.6 versions were current versions around the time of the release of Access 2002. Installing MSDE 2000 also installs ADO 2.6 on a computer. Access developers programming data access for any version of SQL Server 2000 require at least ADO version 2.6. The Microsoft Access team thoroughly tested Access 2003 with Windows XP, which includes the 2.7 version of the ADODB and ADOX libraries and the 2.6 version of the JRO library. This book uses the ADO libraries released with Windows XP. The most recently updated version of the JRO library shipped with the MDAC 2.6, but the other two ADO libraries were updated in the MDAC 2.7 version.

> **Note**   Choosing a library version isn't always as simple as picking the reference with the highest version number. For example, if you need the same application to run on multiple machines, which have ADO versions 2.5 through 2.7, you should use the 2.5 version to eliminate the possibility of a failure due to a missing reference on computers without the 2.6 or 2.7 version of the ADODB library. Alternatively, you can upgrade the ADO version on machines running the 2.5 or 2.6 versions. This latter approach is especially appealing when some of your machines require an ADO version with a higher number, such as the 2.6 version for interfacing with SQL Server 2000. You can obtain information about how to download ADO libraries as part of various MDAC versions from www.microsoft.com/data/download.htm.

If you start a new blank database with Access 2003, the Access database file will have a reference to a version of the ADODB library. The version will depend on what is installed on your computer. If you have more than one version of the ADODB library, Access 2003 creates a reference to the earliest ADODB library version. Depending on what is installed on a computer, this might not be the most recent version of the ADODB library. Therefore, you might need to re-specify the reference to the ADODB library if you want a version other than the earliest release. A blank Access 2003 database does not initialize references to either the ADOX or JRO libraries. In addition, the sample Northwind database file ships with a reference to the DAO 3.6 library. If you want to program this sample database with ADO, you must add a reference to one or more of the appropriate ADO libraries.

You can manually specify references to the ADO libraries from the Visual Basic Editor (VBE) of an Access database file. Choose Tools, References, and then select the ADO libraries that you want your application to reference. Figure 1-1 shows the References dialog box with all three ADO libraries selected. The reference to the Microsoft ActiveX Data Objects 2.7 Library is for the ADODB library. The next reference to the Microsoft ADO Ext. 2.7 for DDL and Security is for the ADOX library. The last reference to the Microsoft Jet and Replication Objects 2.6 Library is for the JRO library.

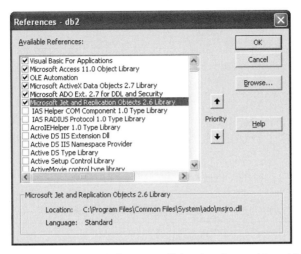

Figure 1-1   The References dialog box is used to add ADO libraries to an application.

Although the ADODB library reference installs by default, users can remove the reference from their workstation settings. You should account for this in your applications by either issuing a warning about installing the ADODB library when it is needed or by creating the reference programmatically. You can create references programmatically using the *References* collection in the Access library. You also can use the *References* collection to verify the ADO library references on a workstation.

OLE DB Providers and ADO Object Model Summary

OLE DB providers make ADO powerful by providing a consistent programming interface for different data sources. Providers operate in a consumer-provider framework. A consumer application—for example your procedure in an Access application—references an OLE DB provider. The data or service provider then assumes control and implements some capability as specified by the syntax for referencing the OLE DB provider. After the provider completes its task, control returns to the consumer application. Depending on the provider and the syntax you use, your procedure can open a connection to a data source, expose a subset of rows from the data source, or save a subset of rows from a data source to a local file.

There are two broad categories of OLE DB providers: data providers and service providers. Data and service providers offer easy ways to extend the kinds of data sources that you can reach with ADO programs. For example,

ADO offers a variety of OLE DB data providers for traditional databases, including those for Jet, SQL Server, Oracle, and general ODBC data sources. In addition, Microsoft makes available other data providers that enable Access 2003 developers to process such nontraditional sources as pages and folders at a Web site. Just as with ODBC drivers, you can obtain OLE DB data providers from Microsoft or third-party sources. Table 1-1 lists selected OLE DB providers available from Microsoft, along with a brief description of when to use each one. Service providers extend how ADO can work with data through providers such as the Microsoft Cursor Service for OLE DB and the Microsoft OLE DB Persistence Provider.

Table 1-1   Selected Microsoft-Supplied OLE DB Providers

Provider Name	Description
OLE DB Provider for Microsoft Jet	Use this data provider to connect to Jet 4 databases and to data from Corel Paradox, dBASE, Microsoft Excel, Microsoft FoxPro, and other ISAM data sources.
Microsoft OLE DB Provider for SQL Server	Use this data provider to connect to databases on SQL Server.
Microsoft OLE DB Provider for Oracle	Use this data provider to connect to Oracle 7.3 and Oracle 8 databases.
Microsoft OLE DB Provider for ODBC	Use this data provider to connect to any ODBC-compliant data source for which you do not have a more specific OLE DB provider.
Microsoft OLE DB Persistence Provider	Use this service provider for saving data to a local file from ADO objects and for retrieving data from local files for storage in ADO objects.
Microsoft Cursor Service for OLE DB	Use this service provider to expand the functionality of native cursors for a service provider. For example, the Cursor Service for OLE DB can dynamically construct an index to speed searches with the *Find* method for ADO recordsets and allow specification of sort criteria for recordsets.
Microsoft OLE DB Provider for Internet Publishing	Use this data provider to access resources served by Microsoft FrontPage and Microsoft Internet Information Services (IIS). This provider enables you to manipulate and open Web site pages programmatically from an Access application.

A major objective for linking to OLE DB providers is to implement data access through the properties, methods, and events of ADODB objects. See the latest version of the ADODB library objects, shown in Figure 1-2. The chart depicts major collection objects along with nested collections and objects. The main object collections are *Connections, Commands, Recordsets, Records*, and *Streams*. Each of these major collections consists of individual objects. So a *Connections* collection consists of one or more *Connection* objects. Selected object collections nest hierarchically within the major objects. For example, a *Command* object can have a *Parameters* collection populated by one or more *Parameter* objects. The parameters for a command allow your application to specify the behavior of the command at run time. This chapter and the next will drill down on selected ADODB objects, along with their properties, methods, and events that are important for typical data access tasks.

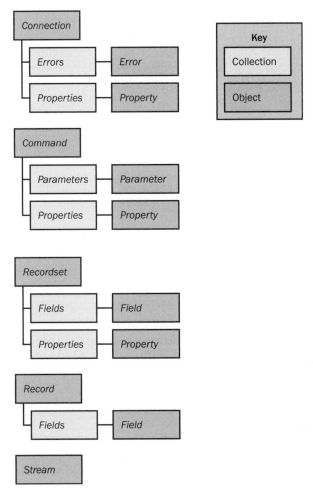

Figure 1-2   The ADODB object library.

The Connection Object

The *Connection* object establishes a link to a database. You use a *Connection* object implicitly or explicitly when you work with a database. When you explicitly create this object, you can efficiently manage one or more connections and reassign the roles that these connections serve in an application. Implicitly creating a *Connection* object shortens your code, but each new object created with an implicit connection consumes more resources. If your application has only one or two objects, each requiring its own connection, implicit connections might be best. ADO lets you choose how to create and manage connections as you see fit.

Unlike DAO, ADO is a universal data access language, so not all ADO properties, methods, or even data types are appropriate for the Jet engine. There is, however, a special OLE DB provider for Jet 4. Microsoft introduced this provider with Access 2000, and it is still available for use with Access 2003. Since *Connection* objects critically depend on provider specifications, the ability to set a *Connection* parameter that references the Jet 4 provider is valuable. This custom provider allows ADO to reflect many of the special strengths that Jet offers. When you refer to an Access database in another file, you might want to include a *Data Source* parameter, which points to the physical location of a database that is not in the current project.

Connecting to Jet Databases

The following simple code sample, *OpenMyDB*, opens the Northwind database. Like all the samples in this chapter, the code is available from the sole module in the Chapter01.mdb file, which is available in this book's companion content (see the Introduction for a URL designating the location of this content). Notice that a *Dim* statement declares and creates a reference to *cnn1* as a *Connection* object from the ADODB library. The use of the *Open* method on *cnn1* makes the database available to the rest of the procedure. The *Provider* and *Data Source* parameters appear within a single set of double quotes. These two parameters are delimited from each other via a semicolon. The *Provider* parameter points to the Jet 4 OLE DB provider, and the *Data Source* parameter points to the physical location of the Northwind database.

> **Note**   Using ADODB as a prefix in declarations for classes from the ADODB library is good programming practice. The convention explicitly names the source library for the class name.

```
Sub OpenMyDB()
Dim cnn1 As New ADODB.Connection
Dim rst1 As ADODB.Recordset

'Create the connection
cnn1.Open "Provider=Microsoft.Jet.OLEDB.4.0;" & _
    "Data Source=C:\Program Files\Microsoft Office" & _
    "\Office11\Samples\Northwind.mdb;"

'Create recordset reference, and set its properties
Set rst1 = New ADODB.Recordset
rst1.CursorType = adOpenKeyset
rst1.LockType = adLockOptimistic

'Open recordset, and print a test record
rst1.Open "Customers", cnn1
Debug.Print rst1.Fields(0).Value, rst1.Fields(1).Value

'Clean up objects
rst1.Close
cnn1.Close
Set rst1 = Nothing
Set cnn1 = Nothing

End Sub
```

After creating a reference to the connection, the code instantiates a *Recordset* object. Instantiating an object reference makes it available for use within the procedure. Next, the procedure assigns values to a couple of properties for the recordset. The next-to-last block of code opens the recordset and prints a couple of fields from the current record when the recordset initially opens. The *Open* method for a *Recordset* object can reference a connection to a database and some source of records in the database. The previous code selects all of the records from the *Customers* table in a database. The *cnn1* variable specifies the database as the Northwind.mdb file.

Although object references declared within a procedure normally go out of scope when the procedure closes, it is good programming practice to close objects and set them to *Nothing* before exiting a procedure. The preceding code sample applies this practice for the *rst1* and *cnn1* variables in its last four lines. By setting an object reference to *Nothing*, you formally release the object's memory. This practice can help avoid memory leaks, which can slow an application. If objects do not close successfully when your application exits a procedure, the memory remains reserved for the object. After repeatedly running a procedure, these memory reservations can slow down your application. The following sub procedure, *OpenFast*, also opens a recordset based on the *Customers* table in the Northwind Access database file and prints the first record. However, it uses fewer lines of code and the code is less complicated than the preceding sample. This is because this sample implicitly creates a connection and accepts more default settings.

```
Sub OpenFast()
Dim rst1 As ADODB.Recordset

'Less code, but potentially greater resource consumption.
Set rst1 = New ADODB.Recordset
rst1.Open "Customers", "Provider=Microsoft.Jet.OLEDB.4.0;" & _
    "Data Source=C:\Program Files\Microsoft Office\" & _
    "Office11\Samples\Northwind.mdb;"
Debug.Print rst1.Fields(0), rst1.Fields(1)

'Clean up objects.
rst1.Close
Set rst1 = Nothing

End Sub
```

Since there is no explicit connection, the *OpenFast* procedure does not need to declare and instantiate a *Connection* object (and therefore doesn't have to open or close such an object). As you can see, the *Open* method for a *Recordset* object can include the essential connection information of a provider and a data source. Calling the *Open* method on a *Recordset* object instead of a *Connection* object requires only one additional parameter—the source for the recordset, which is the *Customers* table. The *Open* method relies on the default *CursorType* and *LockType* settings, which are, respectively, forward-only and read-only. These settings provide for very fast operations, but they do not offer as much functionality as other cursor types. Nevertheless, if the default *Cursor-Type* and *LockType* settings suit your needs and let you turn your attention to other aspects of application development, they might be the best choice.

You can specify a connection to the current Access database file with the syntax *CurrentProject.Connection*. If your current database file has a table, a query, or a linked table named *Customers*, you can rewrite the *OpenMyDB* sample so that *cnn1* points at *CurrentProject.Connection*. This eliminates the need to instantiate a new *Connection* object since you are using the existing one for the current database. The *OpenMyDBLinkedTable* procedure illustrates the syntax for the Chapter01.mdb file with a linked table named *Customers* pointing at the Northwind database. Notice that the sample uses a variable named *cnn1*, which it declares as a *Connection* object. This declaration is optional since the sample could also specify *CurrentProject.Connection* instead of *cnn1* as the *Connection* parameter for the recordset's *Open* method. In any event, there is no need to set *cnn1* to *Nothing* because it was never instantiated as a *Connection* object. The *cnn1* variable merely points at the current database.

```
Sub OpenMyDBLinkedTable()
Dim cnn1 As ADODB.Connection
Dim rst1 As ADODB.Recordset

'Point cnn1 at the CurrentProject
Set cnn1 = CurrentProject.Connection

'Create recordset reference, and set its properties.
Set rst1 = New ADODB.Recordset
rst1.CursorType = adOpenKeyset
rst1.LockType = adLockOptimistic

'Open recordset, and print a test record.
rst1.Open "Customers", cnn1
Debug.Print rst1.Fields(0).Value, rst1.Fields(1).Value

'Clean up objects.
rst1.Close
Set rst1 = Nothing

End Sub
```

The *ReuseAConnection* sub procedure shown next illustrates a couple of ADO programming features not yet covered and reinforces several others. This sample assumes the availability of a copy of the Northwind database named Northwind_backup.mdb in the same default folder as the Northwind database. The best way to discover what the sample offers is to step through it (for example, with the Step Into button on the Debug toolbar). First, the sample demonstrates how to reuse a *Connection* object (or any other ADO object). You must close an object before you can reset its properties so that the object can serve another purpose, such as connecting to a different database. If you step through the sample, you'll see that the code generates and traps a 3705 run-time error. The code in the error trap closes the *cnn1* connection so that the procedure can reuse the object reference to connect to another database.

> **Note**   It is more efficient to re-use an existing connection object than it is to open a new one for every recordset or command. There are two reasons for this. First, opening a new connection is a relatively long process, so re-using an existing connection saves time. Second, minimizing the number of connections to an Access database improves its ability to respond to requests expeditiously. You can think of each connection as simulating a new user.

```
Sub ReuseAConnection()
Dim cnn1 As ADODB.Connection
On Error GoTo connTrap

'Assign the connection reference
Set cnn1 = New ADODB.Connection


'Use Jet provider to connect to Northwind
cnn1.Open "Provider=Microsoft.Jet.OLEDB.4.0;" & _
    "Data Source =C:\Program Files\Microsoft Office\" & _
    "Office11\Samples\Northwind.mdb;"
'Run initially with the next statement commented;
'then rerun with the next statement uncommented
'cnn1.Close

'Incrementally builds connection string.
'Forces error when the Connection object is already open.
cnn1.ConnectionString = "Provider=Microsoft.Jet.OLEDB.4.0;"
cnn1.ConnectionString = cnn1.ConnectionString & _
    "Data Source =C:\Program Files\Microsoft Office\" & _
    "Office11\Samples\Northwind_backup.mdb;"
cnn1.Open

connExit:
'Close any connection still open before exiting
cnn1.Close
Set cnn1 = Nothing
Exit Sub

connTrap:
If err.Number = 3705 Then
'Close an open connection for its reuse
    Debug.Print "Closing cnn1"
    cnn1.Close
    Resume
Else
    Debug.Print err.Number; err.Description
    Debug.Print cnn1.Provider
    Debug.Print cnn1.Provider; cnn1.ConnectionString
End If

End Sub
```

The *ReuseAConnection* sub procedure demonstrates another point worthy of your attention. The *cnn1* declaration includes an ADODB prefix before *Connection*. As noted previously, this is good programming practice. This is especially true when a VBA project has references to both the DAO and ADODB libraries. Since both libraries contain classes with the same name, you might end up with an object based on the wrong class if you do not use the library prefix in your declaration. As you work with more and more references (an easy way to expand the capabilities of your applications), it becomes increasingly desirable to use library name prefixes. The chance of your libraries having identical names for different classes increases as you reference more libraries.

If you are inexperienced with VBA programming, take note of the syntax for declaring an error trap. Just like events, errors happen. In many cases, these errors do not necessarily indicate a problem with the code in a solution (other than the need for more code for an error trap). Error traps give your solutions a way to dynamically adapt to run-time errors, which are not typically caused by failures in your code but by an inappropriate environment for your application. The *ReUseAConnection* sample illustrates use of the *Resume* statement without an argument. When used like this, the statement transfers control back to the point that raised the error.

> **Note**   It is often a good practice to *not* close and remove objects when you detect an error. This is because run-time errors can result from an unanticipated problem associated with the instantiation, closing, or opening of object references. If such an error occurs, looping to a code segment that attempts to close a non-instantiated object can generate an infinite loop.

Connecting to Non-Jet Databases

The next code sample, *OpenMySQLDB*, demonstrates two additional points about the behavior of the *Connection* object.

- First, this sample shows how to connect to a SQL Server database instead of a Jet database. In this case, the database is the NorthwindCS database, a SQL Server database shipping with generally the same tables, queries, forms, reports, and data access pages as those in the Northwind Access database file. You can find more information on the NorthwindCS database in the "Sample Databases" section of Chapter 11.

- Second, this sample highlights how similarly ADO programs for two entirely different database types. In both this sample and the *OpenMyDB* sample, you declare, instantiate, and open a *Connection* object in like ways. The major difference is the connection string, which is always unique for individual data providers. This sample then instantiates a recordset, assigns it property settings, and uses the connection as a parameter for the recordset's *Open* method. This code is identical in the two procedures—despite the fact that the earlier sample references a file-server database and this one references a client/server database.

> **Note**   If you do not have the NorthwindCS database installed on the SQL Server to which you can connect, consider referencing a database other than the NorthwindCS database. For example, a SQL Server Northwind database has shipped with all versions of SQL Server since SQL Server 7. This database has the same tables as the NorthwindCS database. If you use a database other than the SQL Server Northwind database, it is likely that you will have to change the reference to the *Customers* table in the line of code invoking the *Open* method for *rst1*.

```
Sub OpenMySQLDB()
Dim cnn1 As Connection
Dim rst1 As Recordset
Dim str1 As String

'Create a Connection object after instantiating it,
'this time to a SQL Server database.
Set cnn1 = New ADODB.Connection
str1 = "Provider=SQLOLEDB;Data Source=CabSony1;" & _
    "Initial Catalog=NorthwindCS;User Id=sa;Password=password;"
cnn1.Open str1

'Create recordset reference, and set its properties.
Set rst1 = New ADODB.Recordset
rst1.CursorType = adOpenKeyset
rst1.LockType = adLockOptimistic

'Open recordset, and print a test record.
rst1.Open "Customers", cnn1
Debug.Print rst1.Fields(0).Value, rst1.Fields(1).Value

'Clean up objects.
rst1.Close
cnn1.Close
Set rst1 = Nothing
Set cnn1 = Nothing

End Sub
```

The *Provider* parameter in the preceding sample points at the SQLOLEDB provider. This is the ADO data provider specifically designed for SQL Server databases. When connecting to a SQL Server database, you must designate the server name, which is CabSony1 in this case, and the database name. If you know your application will be running against a SQL Server on the same computer as your application, you can use (local) or localhost as the server name. As mentioned, this sample connects to the NorthwindCS database. The designation of a user identification and password depends on the type of authentication your SQL server uses. If your application uses SQL Server authentication, you must specify the user ID and password. If the SQL server for an application uses Windows NT authentication, you do not need to specify a user ID and password in your connection string. If your application ever runs on a Windows 98 computer or a computer disconnected from an office, department, or enterprise server, SQL Server authentication is a necessity. This is because your application will not necessarily have Windows NT or Windows 2000 available to authenticate the identification of users when it runs.

The call to the *Open* method for the *Connection* object in the preceding sample uses a string variable rather than a string constant as an argument. By assigning a different value to the string variable, you can connect to a different server or database. In addition, you can specify either SQL Server or Windows integrated security, which is based on either Windows NT or Windows 2000 logins. For example, the following connection string illustrates the syntax for specifying a connection to the Northwind database on the local server with Windows integrated security. In order for this to work, you must have a SQL Server instance on the local computer and you must have logged on to the workstation with a user ID and password that maps to a SQL Server login with *Select* permission for the *Customers* table in the NorthwindCS database. A complete procedure named *OpenMySQLDBIntegrated* illustrating the application of the connection string below is available in Chapter01.mdb. See Chapter 10 for more coverage of SQL Server security.

```
"Provider=SQLOLEDB;Data Source=localhost;" & _
    "Initial Catalog=NorthwindCS;Integrated Security=SSPI"
```

The rich diversity of ways in which ADO enables applications to connect to remote data sources is one of its major strengths. The *ThreeWaysToConnect-Remotely* procedure highlights three different syntaxes for connecting to remote databases. This sample extends the earlier discussion about connecting to remote databases by contrasting the SQLOLEDB provider with the OLE DB provider for ODBC data sources as well as a DSN.

```
Sub ThreeWaysToConnectRemotely()
Dim cnn1 As ADODB.Connection
On Error GoTo connTrap
```

(continued)

```
'Assign the connection reference
Set cnn1 = New ADODB.Connection

'A connection based on SQLOLEDB

With cnn1
    .Provider = "SQLOLEDB"
    .ConnectionString = "data source = CabSony1;" & _
        "user id = sa; Password=password; initial catalog =Pubs"
    .Open
End With
cnn1.Close

'Use connection string parameters with MSDASQL provider.
'Notice syntax difference from MSDASQL and SQLOLEDB providers.
cnn1.Open "Provider=MSDASQL;Driver=SQL Server;" & _
    "Server=CabSony1;Database=Pubs;uid=sa;pwd=password;"
cnn1.Close

'Designation of the provider, or even the user ID and password,
'might not be necessary with a DSN
cnn1.Open "DSN=Pubs;"
'The following close, in combination with the next one,
'raises a 3704 error number
cnn1.Close

connExit:
'Close any connection still open before exiting
cnn1.Close
Set cnn1 = Nothing
Exit Sub

connTrap:
If err.Number = 3704 Then
'The connection is already closed; skip close method
    Resume Next
Else
'Unanticipated run-time error
    Debug.Print err.Number; err.Description
    Debug.Print cnn1.Provider; cnn1.ConnectionString
End If

End Sub
```

All three examples in the *ThreeWaysToConnectRemotely* procedure connect to the Pubs database on a server named "CabSony1". The Pubs database ships with all versions of SQL Server. The first connection uses the SQLOLEDB provider. Consider using this provider whenever you connect to a SQL Server database. The second example in the code reveals the correct syntax for using the

MSDASQL provider, the default ADO provider. If you omit the provider name from a connection string, ADO uses this provider. This provider is appropriate for databases that do not have a specific OLE DB data provider. The third example in the procedure uses a data source name (DSN) to designate the connection string. This technique is very popular when using ADO on a Web server and in some large organizations that push the DSN onto each computer on a network. Create a System DSN with the ODBC Data Source Administrator. You can reach this administrator through the Control Panel or the Administrative Tools icon within the Control Panel. The sample explicitly specifies a user ID and password for the first two connections, but it buries the user ID and password (along with other connection string elements) in the DSN for the third connection.

> **Note**   You can readily hide the user ID and password with either of the first two approaches. First, VBA offers you the opportunity to lock projects for viewing except by those users with a password. Second, you can convert your .mdb file to an .mde format. This process removes all editable code. Both approaches receive more coverage in Chapter 10.

The Mode Property

By default, the *Connection* object's *Open* method creates a database for shared access. However, you can set the *Connection* object's *Mode* property to any of eight other settings that grant various degrees of restricted access to a database. These mode settings for *Connection* objects pertain generally to recordsets and commands that inherit *Connection* object settings through their *ActiveConnection* property. Additionally, when you open a *Recordset* object on a *Command* object, the *Recordset* object inherits the mode setting that applies to the command. *Record* and *Stream* objects, like *Connection* objects, have a *Mode* argument for their *Open* methods.

The following pair of procedures shows the impact of the read-only mode setting on the ability to update a recordset. Depending on the value of a conditional compiler constant named *varPermitError*, the procedure opens the Northwind database in either the default shared mode or read-only mode. Since the procedure attempts to update the *Customers* table in the Northwind database, opening the database in read-only mode forces a run-time error. Setting the *varPermitError* constant to *True* causes the error by setting the *Mode* property for *cnn1* to read-only mode. The recordset inherits this setting through its *ActiveConnection* property. An error trap catches the error and shuts downs the program gracefully with a custom error message. The *OpenLookOnly* procedure manages the overall process, and the *EncodeMode* procedure returns a string with the name of the enum member corresponding to the *Mode* property setting.

```
Sub OpenLookOnly()
On Error GoTo LookOnlyTrap
Dim cnn1 As New ADODB.Connection
Dim rst1 As ADODB.Recordset
Dim varPermitError As Variant

'Set varPermitError to True to generate
'error from Mode property restriction.
#Const varPermitError = True

'Instantiate a Connection object and
'conditionally set it to read-only data access.
Set cnn1 = New ADODB.Connection
#If varPermitError = True Then
    cnn1.Mode = adModeRead
#End If

'Open the Connection object.
cnn1.Open "Provider=Microsoft.Jet.OLEDB.4.0;" & _
    "Data Source=C:\Program Files\Microsoft Office\" & _
    "Office11\Samples\Northwind.mdb;"

'Use the next line to determine the default mode setting.
Debug.Print EncodeMode(cnn1.Mode)
Set rst1 = New ADODB.Recordset
rst1.ActiveConnection = cnn1
rst1.Open "Customers", , adOpenKeyset, adLockOptimistic, adCmdTable

'An adModeRead setting for cnn1.Mode causes an error in this
'procedure when you execute the next two lines.
rst1.Fields("CustomerID") = "xxxxx"
rst1.Update
Debug.Print rst1.Fields("CustomerID")

LookOnlyExit:
'Clean up objects.
rst1.Close
cnn1.Close
Set rst1 = Nothing
Set cnn1 = Nothing
Exit Sub

LookOnlyTrap:
If err.Number = -2147217911 Then
```

```
'Error -2147217911 signals an attempt to edit a database open
'in read-only mode.
    MsgBox "Forced error by attempt to update with a " & _
        "read-only connection.", vbInformation, _
        "Programming Microsoft Access 2003"
    Resume LookOnlyExit
Else
'Another unanticipated error occurred.
    Debug.Print err.Number; err.Description
    MsgBox "View Immediate window for error diagnostics.", _
        vbInformation, "Programming Microsoft Access 2003"
End If

End Sub

Function EncodeMode(cnn1Mode As Long) As String

'Decode Mode setting and return corresponding enum member value.
Select Case cnn1Mode
    Case 0
        EncodeMode = "adModeUnknown"
    Case 1
        EncodeMode = "adModeRead"
    Case 2
        EncodeMode = "adModeWrite"
    Case 3
        EncodeMode = "adModeReadWrite"
    Case 4
        EncodeMode = "adModeShareDenyRead"
    Case 8
        EncodeMode = "adModeShareDenyWrite"
    Case 12
        EncodeMode = "adModeShareExclusive"
    Case 16
        EncodeMode = "adModeShareDenyNone"
    Case 4194304
        EncodeMode = "adModeRecursive"
End Select

End Function
```

Running the *OpenLookOnly* procedure with *varPermitError* equal to any value other than *True* opens the recordset in shared mode. This setting permits you to modify the value of table cells in the database. The first time you run the procedure it succeeds, unless you previously created a customer with a *CustomerID* field value of *"xxxxx"*. The procedure fails the second time you run it because it attempts to create a duplicate value for the primary key field. The

RestoreFirstCustomerID procedure, found in Chapter01.mdb, replaces the *"xxxxx" CustomerID* value with the original *"ALFKI"* value, which is the original *CustomerID* field value for the first customer in the table.

The *EncodeMode* procedure translates the numeric value of the *Mode* property setting into the name of the *ConnectModeEnum* member matching the value. The procedure uses a *Select Case* statement to perform the translation. Table 1-2 lists the member names and their matching values. While the procedure does not return the actual value of the *Mode* property setting, the *ConnectModeEnum* member name is more meaningful output in the Immediate window from the *OpenLookOnly* procedure.

Besides demonstrating the impact of mode settings, the *OpenLookOnly* procedure is noteworthy for at least one other reason. The recordset *Open* method includes a parameter after the cursor-type setting of *adLockOptimistic*. This is the first sample to show this optional *Open* method parameter. In fact, the parameter has the name *Options*. You designate a value for the parameter with intrinsic constants that are members of either the *CommandTypeEnum* or the *ExecuteOptionEnum* enums. The Object Browser in VBE can help you with the member names and values of enums. The *Options* parameter can designate the type of source for a recordset and indicate how the recordset returns records (for example, synchronously or asynchronously). In the case of the *OpenLookOnly* procedure, the *Options* parameter of *adCmdTable* instructs the *Open* method to treat the first parameter designating *Customers* as a table accessed via a SQL query.

> **Note** Intrinsic constants are constants supplied by Microsoft applications and technologies, such as Access, VBA, ADO, and DAO. These constant names represent numeric or string values. Sets of related intrinsic constants comprise enums, such as the *CommandTypeEnum* or the *ExecuteOptionEnum*. By selecting a library and clicking <globals> in the Object Browser, you can list the full set of intrinsic constants associated with a library. Searching for a particular intrinsic constant with the Object Browser will reveal the enum to which an intrinsic constant belongs.

Table 1-2 describes the nine constants you can use to set a connection's *Mode* property. These constants control the type of editing that one or more users can do through a connection to a database.

Table 1-2   ConnectModeEnum Members

Constant	Value	Behavior
adModeUnknown	0	Permissions not set or determined
adModeRead	1	Read-only permission
adModeWrite	2	Write-only permission
adModeReadWrite	3	Read/write permission
adModeShareDenyRead	4	Prevents others from opening record source with read permissions
adModeShareDenyWrite	8	Prevents others from opening record source with write permissions
adModeShareExclusive	12	Prevents others from opening the connection
adModeShareDenyNone	16	Shared access (default)
AdModeRecursive	4194304	Can propagate share-deny restrictions to children of the current record

The *OpenSchema* Method

The *Connection* object's *OpenSchema* method lets an application browse the objects in the collections available through a connection without the requirement of creating a reference to the ADOX library and enumerating the elements in a collection. The output from the *OpenSchema* method for an Access database file provides information about the design of a database, such as the names of user-defined tables, its queries, and even details such as column and table validation rules. The specific details depend on how a given OLE DB provider implements the general capabilities of the method. For additional details on the scope of this method see the ADO210.chm Help file. Then, click the SchemaEnum link for additional help.

> **Note**   If you go to the SchemaEnum Help page in the ADO Help file (ADO210.chm), you will notice that the hyperlinks in the *Description* column do not work. The links work only from a Web page at the Microsoft Developer Network (MSDN) site. Open your browser to *http://msdn.microsoft.com/library/default.asp?url=/library/en-us/ado270/htm/mdcstschemaenum.asp* for a version of the page with working hyperlinks in the *Description* column. By the way, the linked pages provide detailed information about the field names for the recordset returned by the *OpenSchema* method.

The following code uses the *OpenSchema* method with the Jet 4 provider to list the user-defined tables available from a connection. These tables appear in the Database window when you select Tables from the Objects bar (and the default option of not showing system tables prevails). The procedure starts by declaring a connection and a recordset. The connection acts as the source for the output from the *OpenSchema* method. The recordset holds the output from the *OpenSchema* method. The argument for the *OpenSchema* method indicates that the method returns a rowset of all tables in the data source designated in the connection. By filtering the rows returned by the method, the procedure prints just the names of user-defined tables.

```
Sub OpenSchemaTableTables()
Dim cnn1 As ADODB.Connection
Dim rst1 As ADODB.Recordset

'Connect to the Northwind database
Set cnn1 = New ADODB.Connection
cnn1.Open "Provider=Microsoft.Jet.OLEDB.4.0;" & _
    "Data Source= C:\Program Files\Microsoft Office\" & _
    "Office11\Samples\Northwind.mdb;"

Set rst1 = cnn1.OpenSchema(adSchemaTables)

'Print just tables; other selection criteria include
'TABLE, ACCESS TABLE, and SYSTEM TABLE
Do Until rst1.EOF
    If rst1.Fields("TABLE_TYPE") = "TABLE" Then
        Debug.Print "Table name: " & _
            rst1.Fields("TABLE_NAME")
    End If
    rst1.MoveNext
Loop

'Clean up objects
rst1.Close
cnn1.Close
Set rst1 = Nothing
Set cnn1 = Nothing

End Sub
```

New Access developers, and perhaps some experienced ones, might be surprised to learn that some types of queries can also be considered as tables. For example, you can use the *OpenSchema* method to discover the names of all stored queries that return rows and do not depend on parameters in an Access database file. Access database files typically refer to this type of query as a view.

The following code sample is a simple adaptation of the preceding one; it enumerates all the views in a connection. A view is a stored query that returns rows without requiring parameter values at run time.

```
Sub OpenSchemaTableViews()
Dim cnn1 As ADODB.Connection
Dim rst1 As ADODB.Recordset

'Connect to the Northwind database
Set cnn1 = New ADODB.Connection
cnn1.Open "Provider=Microsoft.Jet.OLEDB.4.0;" & _
    "Data Source= C:\Program Files\Microsoft Office\" & _
    "Office11\Samples\Northwind.mdb;"

Set rst1 = cnn1.OpenSchema(adSchemaTables)

'Print just views; other selection criteria include
'TABLE, ACCESS TABLE, and SYSTEM TABLE

Do Until rst1.EOF
    If rst1.Fields("TABLE_TYPE") = "VIEW" Then
        Debug.Print "View name: " & _
            rst1.Fields("TABLE_NAME")
    End If
    rst1.MoveNext
Loop

'Clean up objects
rst1.Close
cnn1.Close
Set rst1 = Nothing
Set cnn1 = Nothing

End Sub
```

The information provided by the *OpenSchema* method can be substantially richer than just the names of tables within a database. Examine members of the *SchemaEnum* to discover the valid arguments for the *OpenSchema* method. You use an enum member to specify a domain about which to gather schema-based information and then examine the column names for the rowset returned by the method to retrieve the detailed information available for that category. These columns vary according to the enum member.

The *OpenSchemaConstraints* sub procedure that appears next uses the *adSchemaCheckConstraints* argument value to return the set of validation rules in an Access database file. Before listing information in individual rows from the rowset returned by the method, the procedure shows the syntax for enumerating the field column names. As you can see, the columns are zero-based. You can use this enumeration to help decide which detailed information you want to examine. The sample that follows lists the *CONSTRAINT_NAME*, *CHECK_CLAUSE*, and *Description* columns. Some additional code in the sample spaces the string data for columns evenly across the Immediate window. I will review the logic to achieve this result after we examine the procedure's output.

```
Sub OpenSchemaConstraints()
Dim cnn1 As ADODB.Connection
Dim rst1 As ADODB.Recordset
Dim int1 As Integer
Dim int2 As Integer
Dim i As Integer

'Connect to a backup of the Northwind database with a
'clean set of constraints
Set cnn1 = New ADODB.Connection
cnn1.Open "Provider=Microsoft.Jet.OLEDB.4.0;" & _
    "Data Source= C:\Program Files\Microsoft Office\" & _
    "Office11\Samples\Northwind.mdb;"

'Open the constraints in the database
Set rst1 = cnn1.OpenSchema(adSchemaCheckConstraints)

'Demonstrate syntax for enumerating the column names
'in the recordset returned by the OpenSchema method;
'the columns vary depending on the method's parameter
For i = 0 To rst1.Fields.Count - 1
    Debug.Print rst1.Fields(i).Name
Next i

'Find the length of each of the first two columns
int1 = FindTheLongest(rst1, "CONSTRAINT_NAME") + 1
rst1.MoveFirst
int2 = FindTheLongest(rst1, "CHECK_CLAUSE") + 1
rst1.MoveFirst

'Print contraint names, expressions, and descriptions
Do Until rst1.EOF
    Debug.Print rst1(2) & String(int1 - Len(rst1(2)), " ") & _
        rst1(3) & String(int2 - Len(rst1(3)), " ") & " " & rst1(4)
    rst1.MoveNext
Loop

'Clean up objects
rst1.Close
cnn1.Close
```

```
Set rst1 = Nothing
Set cnn1 = Nothing

End Sub


Function FindTheLongest(rst1 As ADODB.Recordset, _
    FieldIndex As String) As Integer
Dim Length As Integer

'Loop to return longest string in a field
Do Until rst1.EOF
    Length = Len(rst1.Fields(FieldIndex))
    If Length > FindTheLongest Then
        FindTheLongest = Length
    End If
    rst1.MoveNext
Loop

End Function
```

The output from the *OpenSchemaConstraints* procedure appears in Figure 1-3. It begins by listing the names for the five columns from the *OpenSchema* method called with an *adSchemaCheckConstraints* argument. Next, the output shows the constraints for the columns within the Access Northwind database file. The procedure succinctly provides that information by listing the table and column of each constraint along with the expression governing the input for a column.

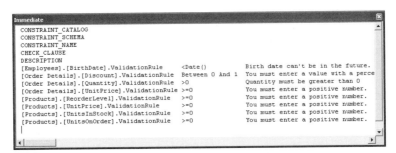

Figure 1-3   The Immediate window output from the *OpenSchema-Constraints* procedure.

Multicolumn string data of uneven lengths do not normally appear in neat columns within the Immediate window. The arrangement of columns is typically uneven because the length of a string in any column usually varies from row to row. This can make the results difficult to read. However, the preceding code sample circumvents this difficulty by padding each string after using a function procedure to determine the longest string in a field within a recordset. The main procedure spaces columns of string data evenly across the Immediate window, based on the longest strings in the *CONSTRAINT_NAME* and *CHECK_CLAUSE* columns.

If you are working with very large result sets from the *OpenSchema* method, you might find it valuable to filter directly with the *Criteria* argument for the OpenSchema method. Use an *Array* function to specify the appropriate criterion for each argument from the return set. Search for the q186246 article at the support.microsoft.com site for more detail, including code samples implementing this approach for both Access and SQL Server databases. The *OpenSchemaTablesWithArray* procedure demonstrates applying this technique to the first sample in this section. The use of the *Criteria* argument syntax removes the need for an *If* statement within a *Do* loop. However, the cost of this benefit is a requirement to use the *Array* function. This, in turn, demands a grasp of how to specify the field criteria arguments for the *Array* function in this context. Some readers will find the *Array* function a worthwhile improvement, but others are likely to find the *If…Then* statement a more natural way to code the solution. This section presents both approaches so you can choose the one you prefer.

```
Sub OpenSchemaTableTablesWithArray()
Dim cnn1 As ADODB.Connection
Dim rst1 As ADODB.Recordset

'Connect to the Northwind database.
Set cnn1 = New ADODB.Connection
cnn1.Open "Provider=Microsoft.Jet.OLEDB.4.0;" & _
    "Data Source=C:\Program Files\Microsoft Office\" & _
    "Office11\Samples\Northwind.mdb;"

'Query for user-defined tables with Criteria argument
'specified as an array
Set rst1 = cnn1.OpenSchema(adSchemaTables, _
    Array(Empty, Empty, Empty, "Table"))

'Print just tables; other selection criteria include
'TABLE, ACCESS TABLE, and SYSTEM TABLE.
Do Until rst1.EOF
    Debug.Print "Table name: " & rst1("TABLE_NAME")
    rst1.MoveNext
Loop

'Clean up objects.
rst1.Close
```

```
cnn1.Close
Set rst1 = Nothing
Set cnn1 = Nothing

End Sub
```

The Recordset Object

As you've seen, a recordset is a programmatic construct for working with records. You can base your records on a table, a row-returning query stored in the current project or in another database file, a SQL statement, or on a command that returns rows. What you can do with a recordset depends on its OLE DB provider and on native data source attributes for the *Connection* object or connection string associated with the recordset's *ActiveConnection* property.

While you can extract recordsets using other objects, such as connections and commands, the *Recordset* object's rich mix of properties and methods make it a natural choice for doing much of your rowset processing. You can use recordsets to perform multiple actions against a set of rows: you can navigate between rows; print all or some of their contents; add, revise, and delete records; find records; and filter records to select one row or any subset of rows from a full recordset. There are two methods for finding records: *Find* and *Seek*. They offer related but not identical benefits, and they have contrasting requirements. Historically, recordsets are non-persistent objects—they normally exist only while they are open in a program. Access 2003 allows developers to persist recordsets to disk and then reopen them later.

Selected Recordset Properties

This section will introduce you to recordsets by describing some of their properties. I will briefly review a few properties of the *Recordset*. Use the Object Browser in the VBE to survey the full range of recordset properties and to further explore the properties that this section summarizes.

A recordset's *ActiveConnection* property lets your application tap an open connection to support a recordset. You can set this property after instantiating the object reference for the recordset. However, the recordset must be closed (or not open yet). Using this property simplifies your *Open* method statement for the recordset. Setting the recordset's *ActiveConnection* property to a previously opened *Connection* object eliminates the need for including a connection string as part of the recordset's *Open* method statement. When you set the *ActiveConnection* property before invoking the *Open* method, you do not even need to reference an existing connection in the *Open* method statement. In that case, the *Connection* object is implicitly created for you.

The cursor type is among the most basic features of a recordset. Use the *CursorType* property to designate a cursor for a recordset. The property setting determines the ways you can navigate through the recordset, the visibility of changes by other users, and the types of locks that you can impose on its records. ADO supports four cursor types:

- **Dynamic**   This type of cursor lets users view changes to a data source made by other users. It enables recordset maintenance functions such as adding, changing, and deleting records, and it permits bidirectional navigation around a database. Users can see all changes to a database made by other users. Assign an intrinsic constant of *adOpenDynamic* to the *CursorType* property to specify this type of cursor.

- **Keyset**   This cursor has many of the properties of a dynamic cursor, except it does not offer immediate access to records added by other users. Records deleted by other users are inaccessible, but they appear in the recordset with a marker. Invoke a recordset's *Requery* method to view records added by other users and to clear the deleted markers for records removed by other users. Assign an intrinsic constant of *adOpenKeyset* to the *CursorType* property to designate this type of cursor.

- **Static**   This cursor is a snapshot of a recordset at a particular point in time. It allows bidirectional navigation. Changes to the database by other users are not visible. This type of cursor is suitable when you do not need information about updates by other users, such as reports from a specific moment in time. Use an intrinsic constant setting of *adOpenStatic* to create this type of cursor.

- **Forward-only**   Sometimes called the fire-hydrant cursor, this type moves in one direction only and can speed up cursor performance. This is the default ADO cursor type. If you need another type of cursor, you must set the *CursorType* property before opening the recordset. If you are changing a recordset's cursor type back to the default setting, assign *adOpenForwardOnly* to its *CursorType* property.

Note   Developers migrating from DAO might be surprised to learn that the keyset cursor is not the default ADO cursor type. You must explicitly designate *adOpenKeyset* as the *CursorType* property if your application requires a keyset cursor.

The *LockType* property interacts with the cursor type because it controls how users can manipulate a recordset. One lock-type setting (*adLockReadOnly*) specifically matches forward-only cursors. That is, specifying *adLockReadOnly* implies a setting of *adOpenForwardOnly* for a cursor's *CursorType* property. The *adLockReadOnly LockType* property setting is the default lock type. Table 1-3 describes the four possible settings for the *LockType* property. The *adLockBatchOptimistic* setting is used specifically for transmitting a batch of changes from a disconnected recordset to a database.

Table 1-3   LockTypeEnum Members

Constant	Value	Behavior
adLockUnspecified	–1	Only for use with recordset clones. One of two possible clone lock-type settings; the other is *adLockReadOnly*.
adLockReadOnly	1	Read-only access (default).
adLockPessimistic	2	Locks a record as soon as a user chooses to start editing it.
adLockOptimistic	3	Locks a record only when a user chooses to commit edits back to the database.
adLockBatchOptimistic	4	Allows edits to a batch of records before an attempt to update a remote database from the local batch of records; use with the *UpdateBatch* method to propagate changes to a local cache back to a remote server.

Note   A recordset's *CursorType* property setting interacts with its lock-type setting with lock type taking precedence over cursor type. If you designate a forward-only cursor type with a lock type other than read-only (*adLockReadOnly*), ADO overrides your *CursorType* setting. For example, ADO automatically converts a forward-only cursor type to a keyset cursor type if you designate optimistic locking.

ADO supports two ways to update data in a data source. When you specify an *adLockOptimistic* or *adLockPessimistic* setting for the *LockType* property, your application immediately updates a record whenever it invokes the *Update* method for a recordset. By using the *adLockBatchOptimistic* intrinsic constant for the *LockType* property, your application can save up changes to one or more records until the application issues an *UpdateBatch* method for a recordset. The

UpdateBatch method then transfers all changes from a local record cache to disk. If the update does not succeed because of conflicts between the recordset's base row values and the corresponding values of the data source on disk, ADO generates a run-time error. Use the *Errors* collection to view warnings and the *Filter* property with an *adFilterAffectedRecords* setting to locate records with conflicts.

Use the *CursorLocation* property to invoke the Cursor Service for OLE DB. Set the *CursorLocation* property to the *adUseClient* intrinsic constant for a *Recordset* object or a *Connection* object. The *CursorLocation* property also enables the *Seek* method. You cannot use the *Seek* method to search a recordset unless its *CursorLocation* property equals the *adUseServer* intrinsic constant.

The *Sort* property for a recordset can affect the results of both the *Find* and *Move* methods. (See the "Finding Records" and "Seeking Records" sections in this chapter for more on these methods.) Through the *Sort* property, you can designate one or more fields that can determine the order in which rows display. The *Sort* property setting allows specification of an ascending or descending order for any field. The default is ascending order. The *Sort* property settings do not physically rearrange the underlying rows—they merely determine the order in which a recordset makes its rows available.

The *Filter* property for a recordset defines a subset of the rows from an existing recordset. Although this property has specialized applications for database synchronization and batch updating of a remote data source, it can also be a simple alternative to defining a new recordset based on a SQL statement or other source. If you already have a recordset and you need only a subset for another purpose, this property can serve admirably. Filter rules can contain compound as well as simple criteria statements. Set a *Filter* property to *adFilterNone* to remove a filter setting from a recordset and restore the full set of original values.

Selected Recordset Methods

Recordset methods complement recordset properties as a means of manipulating the values in a recordset. This section offers a brief review of selected methods and will give you a general idea of the kinds of functions that methods enable you to perform with recordsets. Use the Object Browser to survey the total set of recordset methods. You can get detailed help for any method by clicking the Help button in the Object Browser window.

The recordset's *Open* method is one common route for making a recordset available in a procedure. The source argument is the most critical one for this method. It designates the data source on which the method patterns the object that it opens. Typical options for the source argument include a table, a stored query, a SQL statement, a *Command* object, or a saved recordset file. Access 2003 additionally makes available the option of a URL or a *Stream* object as a potential source for a recordset. You can use the *Open* method's *Options* argument to designate the source type when you open a recordset. However, when designating a *Stream* object as the source for a recordset, you should not designate any other parameters.

Several methods enable recordset navigation. These navigation methods also allow you to specify the current record in a recordset, which is necessary or desirable for certain methods, such as the *Find* method. These four methods reflect functionality comparable to that of a standard built-in bound form:

- **MoveFirst**   This method changes the current record position to the first record in a recordset. The order of records depends on the current index or, if no index exists, on the order of entry. This method functions with all cursor types. Its use with forward-only cursors can force a reexecution of the command that generated the recordset.

- **MoveLast**   This method establishes the last record in a recordset as the current record position. It requires a cursor type that supports backward movement or at least movement based on bookmarks. Using this method with a forward-only cursor generates a run-time error.

- **MoveNext**   This method relocates the current record position one record forward (that is, in the direction of the recordset's final record). If the current record position is the last record, the recordset's end-of-file (*EOF*) property is set to *True*. If this method is called when the recordset's *EOF* property is already *True*, a run-time error results.

- **MovePrevious**   This method sends the current record position one record backward. If the current record position is the first record, the recordset's *BOF* property is set to *True*. If this method is called when the recordset's *BOF* property is already *True*, a run-time error results. This method also generates a run-time error if you use it with a forward-only cursor type.

The *Move* method works differently from the other four recordset navigation methods because it can move the current record position a variable number of records in either direction. You use a positive argument to indicate movement toward the last record and a negative argument to specify movement toward the first record. If a move will extend beyond the first or last record, the *Move* method sets the recordset's *BOF* or *EOF* property to *True*. If that property is already *True*, the *Move* method generates a run-time error. Movement is relative to the current record unless you specify a *Start* parameter, in which case you specify movement from the first or last record.

You can enhance the *Move* method's performance in a couple of ways by using it with a recordset's *CacheSize* property set to greater than the default value, which is 1. *CacheSize* settings cause ADO to store a fixed number of records in the local workstation's memory. Because it is much faster to retrieve records from local memory than from a provider's data store, you can speed record navigation by using a larger cache size. With a forward-only cursor and a larger cache size, you can actually enable backward scrolling as well as forward scrolling. If your cache setting is equal to the number of records in a recordset, you can scroll the full extent of the recordset in both directions. The *CacheSize* property does not enable backward scrolling within the cache with the *MovePrevious* method when using a forward-only cursor. However, you can use the *Move* method with a negative argument to achieve backward scrolling.

The recordset's *Find* method searches for the first record that matches a specified selection criterion. While this method bears a striking similarity to a collection of *Find* methods in Access 97 and earlier Access versions, the Access 2003 version of *Find* has a different syntax and behavior. Rather than attempt to map the similarities and differences, you should simply learn the syntax and behavior of the new version.

The new *Find* method takes as many as four arguments. The first argument is required and is the criterion for the search. Its syntax follows that of SQL statement *WHERE* clauses. If you do not specify any other arguments, the method searches from the current record through the last record to find a record that matches the criterion. Once the method finds a match, you must explicitly move off that record to find a subsequent match in the recordset. If there is no match, the method sets the recordset's *EOF* property to *True*. See the online help for a description of the remaining three optional arguments. The ADO event programming sample you will see in Chapter 2 illustrates the use of these other *Find* arguments. Several requirements govern the operation of the *Find* method. You must set the current record in a recordset before invoking the *Find* method. The only required argument for the *Find* method is a criterion indicating what to search for. You can only search for a value in a single field at a time. The default start location for a search in a recordset is the current row. You can also specify the starting row by using the method's arguments. This approach removes the need to reposition the current row. Otherwise, you must set the current record in a recordset before invoking the *Find* method. You can use one of the *Move* method variations to set the current record. If the *CursorLocation* property is *adUseClient*, the *Find* method can dynamically create indexes for fields that do not have an index specified in the recordset source. These are dynamic indexes that do not permanently update the source for a recordset.

> **Note**   Although the *Find* method works only for one field at a time, ADO readily permits the development of subsets from a data source based on two or more fields. For example, you can open a recordset using a *Select* statement with compound criteria or filter an existing recordset with compound criteria.

The *AddNew* method inserts a new record into a recordset. After you invoke the method, you set the values for the fields in a new row that you want to add. Then you either move off the record using a *Move* method or you call the *Update* method while still on the row. (You can modify the values in a field using a similar pair of techniques. You update fields by assigning them new values, and then you move off the record. Alternatively, you can remain on an edited record as long as you call the *Update* method. You can delete a record by simply navigating to it and then invoking the *Delete* method. The deleted record remains current until you move away from it.)

The *GetRows* method copies a recordset's contents from disk to an array in memory. This can make retrieving recordset values much faster since an application can gather data from memory rather than reading it from a disk storage device. Optional parameters enable you to specify subsets of an original recordset for copying into memory. You can designate a starting row to indicate when to start copying records, and you can designate which columns to include in the memory-based version of a recordset.

The *GetString* method enables you to return rows from a recordset as a sequence of text lines. This method is especially convenient for displaying values from a recordset in the Immediate window. Use *GetString* so that you don't need a loop to pass a group of rows from a recordset to the Immediate window. Optional parameters let you restrict the number of returned rows as well as the row and column delimiters for the values from a recordset. You can also designate a special value to represent fields with *Null* values.

Printing Recordset Rows

Printing recordset values to the Immediate window is a good tutorial for processing recordsets. As you first start to work with ADO recordsets, you will frequently be interested in testing whether you populated them with the intended values. The following procedure, *EasyLoop*, successively prints all the rows of a recordset. A loop passes through all the records and prints the first two fields of each record, *CustomerID* and *CompanyName*.

```
Sub EasyLoop()
Dim rst1 As ADODB.Recordset

'Instantiate and open recordset
Set rst1 = New ADODB.Recordset
With rst1
    .ActiveConnection = "Provider=Microsoft.Jet.OLEDB.4.0;" & _
        "Data Source=C:\Program Files\Microsoft Office\" & _
        "Office11\Samples\Northwind.mdb;"
    .Open "Customers", , , , adCmdTable
End With

'Loop through recordset
Do Until rst1.EOF
    Debug.Print rst1.Fields(0), rst1.Fields(1)
    rst1.MoveNext
Loop

'Clean up objects
rst1.Close
Set rst1 = Nothing

End Sub
```

Notice that the procedure has three parts. First, it declares and instantiates a recordset before opening the recordset based on the *Customers* table. This table is the source for the recordset. The *ActiveConnection* property setting points the recordset at the database containing this table. The *Open* method for the *Recordset* object makes the rows of the source available to the procedure. Notice there are three vacant parameter spaces between the recordset's source and the *Options* parameter, *adCmdTable*. Since the statement specifies an *Options* parameter, it must include placeholders for the intervening parameters of the *ActiveConnection*, *CursorType*, and *LockType* properties. The procedure uses an assignment statement for the recordset's connection property, which is then used as the default value for the *ActiveConnection* parameter in the *Open* method and the *Connection* object is implicitly created. By not including values for the *CursorType* and *LockType* settings, the procedure accepts the default values of *adOpenForwardOnly* and *adLockReadOnly*.

Note The *EasyLoop* sample and other samples in this book use the traditional approach of declaring and instantiating a recordset in two separate statements. This approach has merit in procedures with many lines of code because it allows deferral of the instantiation cost until you need the *Recordset* object in a procedure. However, for short procedures with just a few lines of code (as is typical of many applications), there is no substantial penalty to declaring and instantiating with a single line of code, such as `Dim rst1 as New ADODB.Recordset`. The same coding guidelines apply to declaring and instantiating other ADO objects. Using a single statement to replace two statements is frequently a benefit to developers.

The second part of the procedure loops through all the rows in the recordset while printing the first and second field values in each row to the Immediate window. The sample uses a *Do* loop to navigate through the recordset until reaching an *EOF* flag after the last record. The *MoveNext* method advances the cursor one row with each pass through the loop. The code demonstrates how to reference fields by their index number. The reference to the *Fields* collection for a recordset is not strictly necessary. For example, you can replace `rst1.Fields(0)` with `rst1(0)`. If you know the field names and prefer to use them, you can replace the column index numbers with names, such as *rst1.Fields("CustomerID")* or *rst1("CustomerID")*.

The third part of the procedure merely closes the *Recordset* object and sets its reference to *Nothing*. There is no need to close a *Connection* object since the code sample assigns a connection string rather than a *Connection* object to the recordset's *ActiveConnection* property.

One weakness of the *EasyLoop* procedure is that it prints only the values of the fields you specifically request. The *EasyLoop2a* procedure that follows circumvents this difficulty. No matter how many fields the data source for a recordset has, the procedure automatically prints all of them. In addition, it labels each value with its field name. The main trick to iterating through all the fields is to include a *For...Each...Next* loop inside the *Do* loop. The *For...Each...Next* loop iterates through the *Fields* collection for each row in the recordset while constructing a string that includes the field name and value for each field in the row. After passing through all the fields in the row, the code sample uses the *Left* function to trim the trailing two characters, which are the field delimiters added inside the *For...Each...Next* loop.

```
Sub EasyLoop2a()
Dim rst1 As ADODB.Recordset
Dim fldMyField As ADODB.Field
Dim strForRow As String

'Instantiate and open recordset
Set rst1 = New ADODB.Recordset
rst1.Open "customers", "Provider=Microsoft.Jet.OLEDB.4.0;" & _
    "Data Source= C:\Program Files\Microsoft Office\" & _
    "Office11\Samples\Northwind.mdb;"

'Loop through recordset and fields within rows
Do Until rst1.EOF
    strForRow = ""
    For Each fldMyField In rst1.Fields
        strForRow = strForRow & _
            fldMyField.Name & " = " & fldMyField.Value & "; "
    Next fldMyField
    strForRow = Left(strForRow, Len(strForRow) - 2)
    Debug.Print strForRow & vbCrLf
    rst1.MoveNext
Loop

'Clean up objects
rst1.Close
Set rst1 = Nothing

End Sub
```

Figure 1-4 shows the last two rows of output. You can scroll right in the Immediate window to view the whole record, but it would be more convenient if you could see the whole record without having to scroll the window.

Figure 1-4 The Immediate window output from the *EasyLoop2a* procedure.

The following adaptation of the preceding code sample breaks the line for a row into lines of about 60 characters. An *If…ElseIf* statement inserts as many as four *vbCrLf* dividers into each line for a customer. We cannot use a *Select…Case* statement in this situation because the condition is a compound one based on independent numeric and *Boolean* values. The procedure resets the *Boolean* values to their default values of *False* after processing each customer.

```
Sub EasyLoop2b()
Dim rst1 As ADODB.Recordset
Dim fldMyField As Field
Dim strForRow As String
Dim bolGT60 As Boolean
Dim bolGT120 As Boolean
Dim bolGT180 As Boolean
Dim bolGT240 As Boolean

'Instantiate and open recordset
Set rst1 = New ADODB.Recordset
rst1.Open "customers", "Provider=Microsoft.Jet.OLEDB.4.0;" & _
    "Data Source= C:\Program Files\Microsoft Office\" & _
    "Office11\Samples\Northwind.mdb;"

'Loop through recordset and fields with rows.
'Insert vbCrLf after exceeding each multiple of 60 characters.
Do Until rst1.EOF
    strForRow = ""
    bolGT60 = False
    bolGT120 = False
    bolGT180 = False
    bolGT240 = False
    For Each fldMyField In rst1.Fields
        strForRow = strForRow & _
            fldMyField.Name & " = " & fldMyField.Value & "; "
        If Len(strForRow) > 60 And bolGT60 = False Then
            strForRow = strForRow & vbCrLf
            bolGT60 = True
        ElseIf Len(strForRow) > 120 And bolGT120 = False Then
            strForRow = strForRow & vbCrLf
            bolGT120 = True
        ElseIf Len(strForRow) > 180 And bolGT180 = False Then
            strForRow = strForRow & vbCrLf
            bolGT180 = True
        ElseIf Len(strForRow) > 240 And bolGT240 = False Then
            strForRow = strForRow & vbCrLf
            bolGT240 = True
        End If
    Next fldMyField
    strForRow = Left(strForRow, Len(strForRow) - 2)
    Debug.Print strForRow & vbCrLf
    rst1.MoveNext
Loop

'Clean up objects
rst1.Close
Set rst1 = Nothing

End Sub
```

Figure 1-5 shows the improvement in the formatting of the output to the Immediate window.

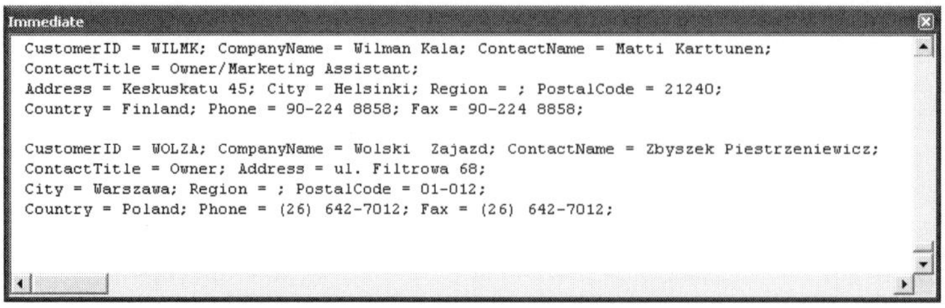

```
Immediate                                                                    ☒
CustomerID = WILMK; CompanyName = Wilman Kala; ContactName = Matti Karttunen;
ContactTitle = Owner/Marketing Assistant;
Address = Keskuskatu 45; City = Helsinki; Region = ; PostalCode = 21240;
Country = Finland; Phone = 90-224 8858; Fax = 90-224 8858;

CustomerID = WOLZA; CompanyName = Wolski  Zajazd; ContactName = Zbyszek Piestrzeniewicz;
ContactTitle = Owner; Address = ul. Filtrowa 68;
City = Warszawa; Region = ; PostalCode = 01-012;
Country = Poland; Phone = (26) 642-7012; Fax = (26) 642-7012;
```

Figure 1-5   The Immediate window output from the *EasyLoop2b* procedure.

Looping is an easy way to perform an operation on the rows and columns within a recordset. However, it is not the most efficient way to retrieve field values from a recordset. The *NoEasyLoop* procedure that follows uses the *GetString* method to retrieve and print all the fields from the first five rows of a recordset in one step:

```
Sub NoEasyLoop()
Dim rst1 As ADODB.Recordset

'Instantiate and open recordset
Set rst1 = New ADODB.Recordset
rst1.Open "customers", _
    "Provider=Microsoft.Jet.OLEDB.4.0;" & _
    "Data Source= C:\Program Files\Microsoft Office\" & _
    "Office11\Samples\Northwind.mdb;"

'Print records without a loop
Debug.Print rst1.GetString(adClipString, 5, "; ")

'Clean up objects
rst1.Close
Set rst1 = Nothing

End Sub
```

The *GetString* method returns a recordset as a string. It can take up to five arguments; the code uses three of those arguments. According to the documentation, you must designate the *adClipString* constant as the first argument in order to assign values to the other optional arguments, which designate the column delimiters, row delimiters, and expressions for *Null* values. The second argument specifies the number of recordset rows to return. The preceding code sample requests the return of five rows. Leaving the second argument blank tells the method to return all the rows in the recordset. The third argument in the code sample designates a semicolon followed by a space as the column delimiter. The default column delimiter is a tab. The fourth and fifth arguments, neither of which appears in the code, specify a row delimiter and a representation for *Null* values. The default values for these arguments are a carriage return and a zero-length string.

> **Note**   You can omit assigning a value of *adClipString* to the first argument and still specify values for row and column delimiters, as well as representations for *Null* values.

The *GetString* method replaces a pair of nested loops. If the defaults are acceptable, you can use the method without any arguments. This makes for a simple way to extract values from a recordset. Although nested loops are the intuitive way to retrieve values from a recordset, the *GetString* method can achieve a similar result in a single line of code.

Another method, *GetRows*, offers several benefits when retrieving recordset values. First, it captures the recordset values to memory in an array. This makes it possible to delete a *Recordset* object and still work with its values. At the very least, this reduces the resource load of an application. In Web applications where a server collects the data for many users, this advantage can be important. Second, you can achieve performance gains by working with an array in memory rather than on disk. These gains depend on the recordset being sufficiently small to fit in physical memory. Third, the ADO *GetRows* method syntax lets you specify the number of rows to retrieve, the row from which to start retrieving, and the fields to retrieve from each row. Because you are storing the recordset values in memory, you should include just the minimum set of rows and fields necessary for your needs.

In using the *GetRows* method, you must literally reorient your way of thinking about the data in a recordset. This is because *GetRows* transposes the rows and columns from disk storage to a two-dimensional *Variant* array. When you declare the *Variant* array for the method's results set, you do not need to specify the number of rows or columns for the array. However, when retrieving data from the array, you must remember that recordset rows populate columns (instead of rows) in the *Variant* array.

The *GettingRows* procedure shown next demonstrates a couple of approaches to retrieving recordset contents with the *GetRows* method. The first application invokes the method with no arguments. This approach reveals just how simple it is to capture a recordset to memory with the *GetRows* method. The syntax for this approach copies all the rows and all their columns from disk to memory. The loop for printing values to the Immediate window shows the syntax for iterating through copied recordset rows as columns in the array.

```
Sub GettingRows()
Dim rst1 As ADODB.Recordset
Dim varArray As Variant
Dim int1 As Integer

'Instantiate and open recordset
Set rst1 = New ADODB.Recordset
rst1.Open "customers", "Provider=Microsoft.Jet.OLEDB.4.0;" & _
    "Data Source= C:\Program Files\Microsoft Office\" & _
    "Office11\Samples\Northwind.mdb;"

'Copy all rows with all columns to varArray in memory
varArray = rst1.GetRows

'Loop through array based on recordset, printing first two fields
For int1 = 0 To UBound(varArray, 2)
    Debug.Print varArray(0, int1), varArray(1, int1)
Next int1

'Restore the pointer to the first record, and copy
'the first five rows with CustomerID and CompanyName
'fields into varArray in memory
rst1.MoveFirst
varArray = rst1.GetRows(5, , _
    Array("CustomerID", "CompanyName"))

'Loop through array based on recordset
For int1 = 0 To UBound(varArray, 2)
    Debug.Print varArray(0, int1), varArray(1, int1)
Next int1

'Clean up objects
rst1.Close
Set rst1 = Nothing

End Sub
```

The second application of the *GetRows* method in the *GettingRows* procedure demonstrates just how easy it is to specify a subset of the rows to copy to memory. The code instructs the ADO interpreter to copy only five rows from disk to memory. These rows are from the top of the recordset because the use of the *MoveFirst* method precedes the use of the second *GetRows* method. By default, the *GetRows* method copies records starting from the current row. However, you can designate a bookmark for another record as the second argument if you want the method to start from a location other than the current row. The second application of *GetRows* also illustrates how to use the built-in *Array* function to specify a subset of fields to copy from disk to memory. In particular, it copies just the *CustomerID* and *CompanyName* column values from the *Customers* table.

> **Note**   Often you will want to start copying with the *GetRows* method from the first row, even when the current row has a different position. In this situation, use the intrinsic constant *adBookmarkFirst* for the method's second parameter to point to the first row.

Adding, Editing, and Deleting Records

The preceding set of samples for printing recordsets all accepted the default settings for the *CursorType* and *LockType* properties. Recall that the default settings are forward-only and read-only. In other words, you cannot change existing rows in a recordset or add new ones with these default settings. When all you want to do is print recordset values, these property settings are fast and efficient. However, by overriding these default settings to change the cursor type to keyset with optimistic locking, you can readily modify the field values within the rows of a recordset. Because the samples in this section all modify recordsets, they all use these non-default settings.

> **Note**   All the samples in this section use optimistic locking for adding, editing, and deleting records. Either optimistic or pessimistic locking is necessary with a keyset cursor. Optimistic locking offers slightly better throughput along with the risk of concurrency violations when two users attempt to modify a record at the same time. ADO returns an error that permits you to detect this kind of error and respond accordingly, such as to resubmit the change that generated the concurrency violation. If you prefer, change the optimistic locking to pessimistic locking to remove the possibility of concurrency violations.

Adding a Row

One way to modify a recordset is by adding a new row of field values. The *AddAShipper* function procedure shown next demonstrates an approach to this task using the *AddNew* method for an ADO recordset. The sample applies this method to a recordset based on the *Shippers* table in the Northwind database. This table has an *AutoNumber* field named *ShipperID* and two string fields named *CompanyName* and *Phone*. Since Access automatically assigns *Auto-Number* field values, the procedure only has to assign values to the *CompanyName* and *Phone* fields. The procedure inserts these assignments between a statement that invokes the *AddNew* method and another one that launches the *Update* method.

```
Function AddAShipper()
Dim rst1 As ADODB.Recordset

'Set your cursor so that it is not read-only
'in order to add a row
Set rst1 = New ADODB.Recordset
rst1.ActiveConnection = "Provider=Microsoft.Jet.OLEDB.4.0;" & _
    "Data Source= C:\Program Files\Microsoft Office\" & _
    "Office11\Samples\Northwind.mdb;"
rst1.Open "Shippers", , adOpenKeyset, adLockOptimistic, _
    adCmdTable

'Invoke the AddNew method
With rst1
    .AddNew
        .Fields("CompanyName") = "Access 2003 Delivers"
        .Fields("Phone") = "(555) 123-4567"
    .Update
End With

'Return ShipperID of new shipper
AddAShipper = rst1("ShipperID")

'Clean up objects
rst1.Close
Set rst1 = Nothing

End Function
```

Because the *AddAShipper* sample uses a function procedure, it can return a value, such as the *ShipperID* value that Access assigns automatically. This *AutoNumber* field is the primary key for the *Shippers* table. If your application inserts records into both a main table and a related table, such as *Orders* and *Order Details*, the *AutoNumber* primary key field value from the main table would be essential for setting the foreign key values in the related table.

Deleting a Row

Another task that you likely will want to perform with recordsets is deleting records. The following pair of procedures shows one approach to this task. While this approach might not be optimal in some respects, it has the benefit of not requiring any special SQL syntax or even advanced ADO functionality. Basically, you loop through a recordset until you find a match. Then, you just delete the matching record.

The code sample in the *CallDeleteARecordsetRow* and *DeleteARecordsetRow* procedures lets a user specify any field as a criterion for the row to delete. If a recordset contains multiple rows with the same field value, it deletes just the first of these rows. The *CallDeleteARecordsetRow* procedure includes the code to delete a row based on *CompanyName*, *Phone*, or *ShipperID* field values. The sample leaves commented only the syntax for deleting a row based on *Phone*.

```
Sub CallDeleteARecordsetRow()
Dim rst1 As ADODB.Recordset
Dim int1 As Integer

'Set your cursor so that it is not read-only
'in order to delete
Set rst1 = New ADODB.Recordset
rst1.ActiveConnection = "Provider=Microsoft.Jet.OLEDB.4.0;" & _
    "Data Source= C:\Program Files\Microsoft Office\" & _
    "Office11\Samples\Northwind.mdb;"
rst1.Open "Shippers", , adOpenKeyset, adLockOptimistic, _
    adCmdTable

'Delete a shipper indexed by CompanyName or Phone
DeleteARecordsetRow rst1, "CompanyName", "Access 2003 Delivers"
'DeleteARecordsetRow rst1, "Phone", "(555) 123-4567"

'Requery recordset to clear row marked for deletion
rst1.Requery

'Delete a shipper indexed by ShipperID
'six seconds after adding it
int1 = AddAShipper()
DoLoopForSeconds 6
DeleteARecordsetRow rst1, "ShipperID", int1

'Clean up objects
rst1.Close
Set rst1 = Nothing

End Sub
```

(continued)

```
Sub DeleteARecordsetRow(rst1 As ADODB.Recordset, _
    FieldName As String, FieldValue As Variant)

'Designate rst1 as repeated value in
'With...End With statement
With rst1
'Loop through recordset to find target
'field value for selected field
    Do Until .EOF
        If .Fields(FieldName) = FieldValue Then
            .Delete
            Exit Do
        End If
        .MoveNext
    Loop
End With

End Sub

Sub DoLoopForSeconds(n As Integer)
Dim Begin As Date

'Setup for Do loop
Begin = Now()
Debug.Print "Time before loop: " & Begin

'Loop until n seconds from begin time
Do
    If DateDiff("s", Begin, Now()) >= n _
        Then Exit Do
Loop

'Print end time and beep
Debug.Print "Time after loop: " & Now()
Beep

End Sub
```

The calling procedure, *CallDeleteARecordsetRow*, passes a recordset, field name, and a field value. The called procedure, *DeleteARecordsetRow*, loops through the recordset. If the loop uncovers a row with a field value that matches the input parameters, it deletes the row and exits the loop. After the deletion, the calling procedure invokes the *Requery* method for the recordset to synchronize its copy with the one in the database.

The sample enables you to delete a recordset row based on the *ShipperID* field by adding a new row and saving the *ShipperID* value for that new row. It does this by saving the return value of the *AddAShipper* function procedure in a memory variable named *int1*. Then, it uses the value of that memory variable as an argument when it calls *DeleteARecordsetRow*. This aspect of the sample demonstrates how to use the value of an automatically added primary key to control another action. In this case, the other action is to delete a row, but it could just as easily be to insert rows in a related table. The sample launches a six-second pause between adding a new row and attempting to delete it (based on *ShipperID*) with the help of a call to the *DoLoopForSeconds* procedure. This pause is necessary to allow the added row to update the Access database.

The *DoLoopForSeconds* procedure includes a *Do* loop without conditions for the *Do* or *Loop* keywords. Instead, the loop exits when the current time is *n* seconds or beyond the time just before entering the loop. A *DateDiff* function computes the difference between the loop start time and the current time within the loop in seconds. The procedure beeps to mark the end of the *n*-second interval.

Editing a Row

The third sample in this section demonstrates how to update an existing field value in a recordset row with a new field value. The calling procedure, *CallUpdateAFieldValue*, calls four procedures in this sample.

- The first call is to the *AddAShipper* function to add a new row to the *Shippers* table for editing.

- Another call to the *DoLoopForSeconds* procedure pauses for the database to perform the insert.

- Next, *CallUpdateAFieldValue* passes four arguments to the *UpdateAFieldValue* procedure. In this case, the passed parameters are the recordset, the name of the field to update, and the old and new field values. The *UpdateAFieldValue* procedure loops through the recordset's rows until it finds a match. Then it assigns the new field value and invokes the *Update* method for the recordset. This commits the changed value to disk. After performing the update, the sub procedure exits the loop and restores control to the calling routine. If multiple records have field values that match the *OldFieldValue* input parameter, the sub procedure updates just the first record. You can update all the rows with matching values by removing the *Exit Do* statement inside the loop.

- A final call to the *DeleteARecordsetRow* procedure removes the row from the *Shippers* table with the *CompanyName* field value updated by the *UpdateAFieldValue* procedure.

```
Sub CallUpdateAFieldValue()
Dim rst1 As ADODB.Recordset
Dim int1 As Integer

'Set your cursor so that it is not read-only
'in order to udpate a record.
Set rst1 = New ADODB.Recordset
rst1.ActiveConnection = "Provider=Microsoft.Jet.OLEDB.4.0;" & _
    "Data Source= C:\Program Files\Microsoft Office" & _
    "\Office11\Samples\Northwind.mdb;"
rst1.Open "Shippers", , adOpenKeyset, adLockOptimistic, _
    adCmdTable

'Add new row and wait 6 seconds for database to update table.
int1 = AddAShipper()
DoLoopForSeconds 6

'Call updating routine, and pass it update info.
UpdateAFieldValue rst1, "CompanyName", "Access 2003 Delivers", _
    "Access 2003 Delivers More"

'Delete updated version of inserted row to restore
'the Shippers table.
DeleteARecordsetRow rst1, "CompanyName", "Access 2003 Delivers More"

'Clean up objects.
rst1.Close
Set rst1 = Nothing

End Sub


Sub UpdateAFieldValue(rst1 As ADODB.Recordset, _
    FieldName As String, _
    OldFieldValue As Variant, _
    NewFieldValue As Variant)

'Designate rst1 as repeated value in
'With...End With statement
With rst1
'Loop through recordset to find target
'field value for selected field
    Do Until .EOF
        If .Fields(FieldName) = OldFieldValue Then
            .Fields(FieldName) = NewFieldValue
            .Update
            Exit Do
        End If
```

```
        .MoveNext
    Loop
End With

End Sub
```

Finding Records

Another common task with a recordset is to find one or more records that meet specified criteria. Access offers several approaches to this task. Before Access 2000, many developers used one or more variations of the Find method in DAO. Access 2000 introduced a single Find method for ADO that consolidates the functionality of multiple DAO Find methods. If your applications used the earlier *Find* methods, you can achieve the same results with the consolidated method in Access 2000. Access 2003 has new *Find* method capabilities unavailable to Access developers with Access 2000.

> **Note**   The *Find* method, along with the *Seek* method and *Filter* property, allows you to re-use an existing recordset rather than create a new recordset to recover rows your application needs. It is generally more efficient to re-use an existing recordset than to declare, instantiate, and open a new one.

The following code shows a simple application of the *Find* method that searches for a record with a customer ID that begins with the letter D. When it finds a record matching its criteria, the method relocates the current record to that location. The code prints the *CustomerID*, *ContactName*, and *Phone* fields to confirm exactly which record matches the criterion.

```
Sub FindAMatch()
Dim rst1 As Recordset

'Instantiate and open recordset
Set rst1 = New ADODB.Recordset
rst1.ActiveConnection = _
    "Provider=Microsoft.Jet.OLEDB.4.0;" & _
    "Data Source= C:\Program Files\Microsoft Office" & _
    "\Office11\Samples\Northwind.mdb;"
rst1.Open "Customers", , adOpenKeyset, adLockPessimistic, _
    adCmdTable
```

(continued)

```
'Find the first row with a CustomerID beginning with D,
'and print the result
rst1.Find ("CustomerID Like 'D*'")
Debug.Print rst1("CustomerID"), rst1("ContactName"), rst1("Phone")

'Clean up objects
rst1.Close
Set rst1 = Nothing

End Sub
```

One drawback to the *FindAMatch* procedure is that it searches for a single match to the criteria and then stops immediately after finding it. The code that follows, which shows the *FindAMatch2* procedure, discovers all the records that match the criterion statement. This simple application reveals more of the flexibility of the *Find* method:

```
Sub FindAMatch2()
Dim rst1 As Recordset

'Instantiate and open recordset
Set rst1 = New ADODB.Recordset
rst1.ActiveConnection = _
    "Provider=Microsoft.Jet.OLEDB.4.0;" & _
    "Data Source= C:\Program Files\Microsoft Office" & _
    "\Office11\Samples\Northwind.mdb;"
rst1.Open "Customers", , adOpenKeyset, _
    adLockPessimistic, adCmdTable

'Open an infinite loop for all records matching
'the criterion
Do
    rst1.Find ("CustomerID Like 'D*'")
    If rst1.EOF Then
'Exit the procedure when no more matches exist
        Exit Do
    End If
    Debug.Print rst1.Fields("CustomerID"), rst1("ContactName"), _
        rst1("Phone")
    rst1.MoveNext
Loop

'Clean up objects
rst1.Close
Set rst1 = Nothing

End Sub
```

The trick to finding all the records that match the search criterion is to embed the *Find* method in an infinite *Do* loop. When the *Find* method sets the recordset's *EOF* property to *True*, there are no additional matching records. In this case, the code executes an *Exit Do* statement to exit the loop. As long as *Find* keeps discovering new matches, the procedure prints *CustomerID*, *ContactName*, and *Phone* fields in the Immediate window. After printing a matching record, the procedure advances the current record by one. Without this, the *Find* method would repeatedly return the same record.

One innovation available to those using Access 2003 is the dynamic index capability of the Cursor Service. Access 2003 ships natively with an ADO version that supports dynamic indexes. To speed the operation of the *Find* method, developers can create dynamic indexes on the fly for record sources that do not have an index on a search field. Creating a dynamic index is a two-step process. First, assign the *adUseClient* intrinsic constant to the recordset's *CursorLocation* property. Second, set the *Optimize* property to *True* in the *Properties* collection so that the field will gain the dynamic index. The index goes out of scope when you close the procedure, but you can force the index's removal by setting the field's *Optimize* property to *False*.

Note   You can acquire the dynamic index feature in Access 2000 by installing a more recent ADO version than the one that initially shipped with Access 2000.

The following pair of procedures demonstrates how to use a dynamic index to speed the search for all the customers from a particular country. The first procedure, *CallFindCustomersInACountry*, assigns a search string value and passes it to the second procedure, *FindCustomersInACountry*. Notice that the sample code uses a pound sign (#) to delimit the country string within the criterion string. With Access 2003, you can use either # or an apostrophe (') for this purpose.

Before opening a recordset on the *Customers* table, the second procedure turns on the Cursor Service by setting the *CursorLocation* property to *adUseClient*. Then after the recordset is open, the procedure sets the *Country* field's *Optimize* priority to *True*. This causes the creation of the index. Next, the procedure performs a normal search to find all the customers from the country designated by *strCriterion*. In the cleanup process for the procedure, there is nothing special you need to do with the index. It goes out of scope automatically.

```
Sub CallFindCustomersInACountry()
Dim strCriterion As String

'Set string for country criterion, and pass it
'to the routine to do the search
strCriterion = "Country = #USA#"
FindCustomersInACountry strCriterion

End Sub


Sub FindCustomersInACountry(strCriterion As String)
Dim rst1 As ADODB.Recordset
Dim int1 As Integer

'Instantiate and open recordset; invoke the Cursor Service by
'setting the CursorLocation property to adUseClient
Set rst1 = New ADODB.Recordset
With rst1
    .ActiveConnection = _
        "Provider=Microsoft.Jet.OLEDB.4.0;" & _
        "Data Source= C:\Program Files\Microsoft Office" & _
    "\Office11\Samples\Northwind.mdb;"
    .CursorLocation = adUseClient
    .Open "customers", , adOpenKeyset, _
        adLockPessimistic, adCmdTable
End With

'Create a dynamic index on Country
rst1.Fields("Country").Properties("Optimize") = True

'Find the longest ContactName field, and add one to it
int1 = FindTheLongest(rst1, "ContactName") + 1

'Open an infinite loop for all records matching
'the criterion
rst1.MoveFirst
Do
    rst1.Find (strCriterion)
    If rst1.EOF Then
'Exit the procedure when no more matches exist
        Exit Sub
    End If
    Debug.Print rst1.Fields("CustomerID"), rst1("ContactName") & _
        String(int1 - Len(rst1("ContactName")), " ") & " " & rst1("Phone")
    rst1.MoveNext
Loop
```

```
'Clean up objects
rst1.Close
Set rst1 = Nothing

End Sub
```

Seeking Records

The *Seek* method is another recordset method that can facilitate finding records in a record source. This method is exclusively used for recordsets that specify a table as their source. In addition, you must set the recordset *Open* method's *Options* parameter to *adCmdTableDirect*, instead of setting it to *adCmdTable* or leaving it blank. Furthermore, the table serving as a record source must have an index on the field or fields that your application searches to find matches for criterion values. ADO does not offer built-in support for creating dynamic indexes for the *Seek* method, but your application can programmatically create an index using the ADOX library for Jet and the SQL-DMO library for SQL Server. The *Seek* method also requires a server-side cursor. Using any value other than *adUseServer* for a recordset's *CursorLocation* property disables the method.

> **Note**   The *Seek* method is not a core ADO data access feature. ADO providers can offer it as an option. For example, the Jet provider enables the *Seek* method, but the SQL Server provider does not. In addition, the Jet provider makes the *Seek* method available only when you open a recordset properly. Use the recordset *Supports* method with *adSeek* as an argument to return a *Boolean* indicating whether a provider offers the *Seek* method. To seek on an index, apply the method to a recordset after opening it.

The *Seek* method searches for a key value or values, and it optionally takes a *SeekOption* parameter that can guide the operation of the method. If the index for the *Seek* method has just one column, you can specify only a single criterion value. If the index for a recordset relies on multiple columns, use an *Array* function to specify values for all the columns in the index. This capability to search concurrently on multiple columns is one feature distinguishing the *Seek* method from the *Find* method. The *Seek* method makes available the recordset in the order of the index and positions the current record at the first record matching the criteria.

You can refine the search behavior of the *Seek* method with some settings for its *SeekOptions* parameter using a member from the *SeekEnum*. The *Seek-Options* setting appears immediately after the key value or values for a *Seek* method. The syntax for the *Seek* method with both key values and *SeekOptions* is *rst.Seek <Keyvalues>, <SeekOptions>*. Table 1-4 lists the *SeekEnum* members with their values and behavior.

Table 1-4   Intrinsic Constants for the SeekEnum

Constant	Value	Behavior
adSeekFirstEQ	1	Seek the first record on the index or indexes matching the key value or values.
adSeekLastEQ	2	Seek the last record on the index or indexes matching the key value or values.
adSeekAfterEQ	4	Seek the first record (or the one after it when no match exists) on the index or indexes matching the key value or values.
adSeekAfter	8	Seek the first record after that potential match to the key value or values on the index or indexes.
adSeekBeforeEQ	16	Seek the first record (or the one before it when no match exists) on the index or indexes matching the key value or values.
adSeekBefore	32	Seek the first record before a potential match to the key value or values on the index or indexes.

The *SeekingUnShippedOrders* procedure that follows illustrates three ways to use the *Seek* method. Before actually invoking the *Seek* method, your application must properly prepare the recordset. First, assign the *Index* property so that it contains the values for which you want to search. Second, open the recordset with the *adCmdTableDirect* setting for the *Options* parameter. Third, ensure the *CursorLocation* property has a setting of *adUseServer*. This is the default setting, so you don't need to assign the property a setting unless your application has changed its default setting. The following procedure demonstrates the first two steps. The third step is not necessary in this sample.

```
Sub SeekingUnshippedOrders()
Dim rst1 As ADODB.Recordset

'Instantiate and open recordset; Seek method requires
'index assignment, adCmdTableDirection Open option, and
'adUserServer setting for CursorLoction (default)
Set rst1 = New ADODB.Recordset
```

```
rst1.ActiveConnection = _
    "Provider=Microsoft.Jet.OLEDB.4.0;" & _
    "Data Source= C:\Program Files\Microsoft Office" & _
    "\Office11\Samples\Northwind.mdb;"
rst1.CursorType = adOpenKeyset
rst1.LockType = adLockOptimistic
rst1.Index = "ShippedDate"
rst1.Open "Orders", , , , adCmdTableDirect

'Print first order not shipped
rst1.Seek Null, adSeekFirstEQ
Debug.Print rst1("OrderID"), rst1("OrderDate")

'Print last order not shipped
rst1.Seek Null, adSeekLastEQ
Debug.Print rst1("OrderID"), rst1("OrderDate")

'Print all orders not shipped
rst1.Seek Null
Do
    Debug.Print rst1("OrderID"), rst1("OrderDate")
    rst1.MoveNext
Loop Until IsNull(rst1("ShippedDate")) = False

'Clean up objects
rst1.Close
Set rst1 = Nothing

End Sub
```

The first two instances of the *Seek* method in *SeekingUnShippedOrders* both demonstrate the syntax for the *Keyvalues* and *SeekOptions* parameters. The first instance of the *Seek* method sets the cursor at the first record in the *Orders* table that is unshipped. This record has the order ID 11008. The steps for opening the *rst1* recordset on the *Orders* table arrange the records in order on the *ShippedDate* index, so that the special ordering indicated by the *Seek* method's *Keyvalues* and *SeekOptions* parameters will work. The second instance of the *Seek* method in the *SeekingUnShippedOrders* procedure sets the cursor at the last *Orders* table record with a *Null* value for the *ShippedDate* field. This record has the order ID 11077. The third instance of the *Seek* method in the preceding procedure searches for all unshipped orders without specifying a *SeekOptions* setting. Its following *Do* loop iterates through the reordered recordset to print the *OrderID* field and *OrderDate* field for each record with a *Null ShippedDate* field value.

The *SeekWith2IndexValues* procedure demonstrates the syntax for designating a seek for two criterion values: the *OrderID* and *ProductID* fields of the primary key for the *Order Details* table. The procedure also demonstrates how to reuse a *Recordset* object. In the first use of the *rst1* recordset, the procedure searches for all line items matching an *OrderID* input by the user. The procedure uses an *InputBox* function nested inside a *CInt* function to permit a user to input an *OrderID* field value. It then returns the *OrderID* and *ProductID* for the line items associated with that record. This first seek relies on the *OrderID* index for the *Order Details* table.

```
Sub SeekWith2IndexValues()
Dim rst1 As ADODB.Recordset
Dim int1 As Integer
Dim int2 As Integer
Dim int3 As Integer

'Instantiate and open recordset; Seek method requires
'index assignment, adCmdTableDirection Open option, and
'adUserServer setting for CursorLocation (default)
Set rst1 = New ADODB.Recordset
rst1.ActiveConnection = _
    "Provider=Microsoft.Jet.OLEDB.4.0;" & _
    "Data Source= C:\Program Files\Microsoft Office" & _
    "\Office11\Samples\Northwind.mdb;"
rst1.CursorType = adOpenKeyset
rst1.LockType = adLockOptimistic
rst1.Index = "OrderID"
rst1.Open "Order Details", , , , adCmdTableDirect

'Search for a user-specified OrderID;
'save OrderID and ProductID of order's last line item
int1 = CInt(InputBox("Input OrderID: "))
rst1.Seek int1
Do Until rst1("OrderID") <> int1
    Debug.Print rst1("OrderID"), rst1("ProductID")
    rst1.MoveNext
    If rst1.EOF Then Exit Do
Loop
rst1.MovePrevious
int2 = rst1("OrderID")
int3 = rst1("ProductID")

'Close and reopen Order Details to seek
'last line item in the order
rst1.Close
rst1.Index = "PrimaryKey"
rst1.Open "Order Details", , , , adCmdTableDirect
```

```
rst1.Seek Array(int2, int3)
Debug.Print rst1("OrderID"), rst1("ProductID"), _
    FormatCurrency(rst1("UnitPrice")), _
    rst1("Quantity"), FormatPercent(rst1("Discount"), 0)

'Clean up objects
rst1.Close
Set rst1 = Nothing

End Sub
```

The second instance of the *Seek* method in the *SeekWith2IndexValues* procedure seeks the last item for the *OrderID* that a user inputs. At the conclusion of the first *Seek* instance, the procedure saves the *OrderID* and *ProductID* field values for the last line item in the order a user referenced. Then the procedure closes the recordset to assign a new index. The index is the primary key that relies on both *OrderID* and *ProductID*. Next, the procedure reopens the recordset. The new index is critical for permitting the use of a compound criterion that includes values for both the *OrderID* and *ProductID* field values. Notice the use of the *Array* function for indicating more than one key value. The cursor points to the record in the recordset for the line item sought. The procedure prints it while formatting the *UnitPrice* and *Discount* columns.

Filtering Records

The *Find* method can go through a recordset sequentially and disclose matches one at a time. The method does not create another version of the recordset that contains all the records that match the criterion values. When you need a new or alternate recordset containing just the matches, your application needs a different approach. The *Seek* method offers a partial solution to this *Find* method deficiency, but the *Seek* method has special requirements that restrict its applicability, such as the need for an index. In addition, the *Seek* method does not truly exclude non-matching records. It merely positions the current record at the first matching record.

The recordset *Filter* property offers a second solution to the *Find* method's inability to return a subset of a recordset based on one or more fields. This property lets you designate a simple criterion for a field, and it returns a filtered version of the original recordset with only those records that match the criterion value or values. By setting the *Filter* property to any of a series of constants instead of to a criterion string, you can achieve special effects for database replication or for updating a remote data source. One filter constant, *adFilterNone*, removes the filter setting from a recordset and restores the original rowset. The *Filter* property also resolves another shortcoming of the *Find* method: it can select records based on more than one field value. Furthermore, it does not require an index to accomplish this goal, as does the *Seek* method.

The following two procedures filter a recordset based on the *Customers* table in the Northwind database. The *FilterRecordset* procedure manages the overall use of the *Filter* property, prints the results set, clears the filter, and then prints the results set again. The *FilterRecordset* procedure relies on the *FilterLikeField* function. This custom function manages the setting of the *Filter* property based on parameters passed to it by the *FilterRecordset* procedure, and it returns the filtered recordset.

```
Sub FilterRecordset()
Dim rst1 As ADODB.Recordset

'Instantiate and open recordset
Set rst1 = New ADODB.Recordset
rst1.ActiveConnection = "Provider=Microsoft.Jet.OLEDB.4.0;" & _
    "Data Source= C:\Program Files\Microsoft Office" & _
    "\Office11\Samples\Northwind.mdb;"
rst1.Open "Customers", , , , adCmdTable

'Filter recordset, and print filtered result
Set rst1 = _
    FilterLikeField(rst1, "CustomerID", "D*")
Debug.Print rst1.GetString

'Restore recordset, and print restored result
rst1.Filter = adFilterNone
Debug.Print rst1.GetString

'Clean up objects
rst1.Close
Set rst1 = Nothing

End Sub


Function FilterLikeField(rst1 As ADODB.Recordset, _
strField As String, strFilter As String) As ADODB.Recordset

'Set a filter on the specified Recordset object, and then
'return the filtered recordset
rst1.Filter = strField & " LIKE '" & strFilter & "'"
Set FilterLikeField = rst1

End Function
```

The *FilterRecordset* procedure starts by creating and opening the *rst1* recordset. Next, it applies a filter by calling the *FilterLikeField* function, which takes three arguments and returns a filtered recordset based on them. *Filter-Recordset* assigns the filtered return set to *rst1* and prints the filtered recordset to confirm the result.

The arguments to *FilterLikeField* include *rst1*, a field name on which to filter records, and a filter criterion value, which can include any legitimate expression for the Like operator used by *FilterLikeField*. *FilterRecordset* passes *D** to find just the records that have a *CustomerID* beginning with the letter *D*. The *Filter* property does not restrict you to filtering with the *LIKE* operator. Other acceptable operators include <, >, <=, >=, <>, and =. You can also include *AND* and *OR* operators in your criteria expressions to combine two or more criteria expressions based on the other legitimate operators.

The *Filter* property restricts your criteria expressions to those of the form *<FieldName> <Operator> <Value>*. However, some *Filter* intrinsic constants that are members of the *FilterGroupEnum* enum enable special uses of the property. The *FilterRecordset* procedure uses the *adFilterNone* constant to restore a recordset by removing its filters. You can also use other *Filter-GroupEnum* enum members to resolve conflicts associated with performing a batch update against a remote data source.

The following pair of procedures demonstrates just how easy it is to filter on multiple criterion fields. You can compound simple filter phrases, such as *"Country='USA'"*, with *AND* and *OR* operators. This capability permits you to filter a recordset on more than one field. You can also group criteria expressions with parentheses and then link them with *AND* and *OR* operators for the construction of complex compound criteria. This next sample shows a compound criteria expression that does not require parentheses.

The sample demonstrating compound filters uses two procedures. The first procedure, *CallFilterOnCountryAndCity*, sets the criteria strings for both country and city, the two filter fields for the *Customers* table. Then the sample calls *FilterOnCountryAndCity*, the procedure that applies the filter, and it saves a reference to the filtered recordset. The main procedure concludes by printing selected fields. Before printing field values, however, it uses the *FindTheLongest* function procedure to determine the longest length for each of two fields.

```
Sub CallFilterOnCountryAndCity()
Dim rst1 As ADODB.Recordset
Dim strCountry As String
Dim strCity As String
Dim int1 As Integer
Dim int2 As Integer
```

(continued)

```
'Set Country and City criteria
strCountry = "USA"
strCity = "Portland"

'Call Filter routine, and store reference to
'filtered return set
Set rst1 = FilterOnCountryAndCity(strCountry, strCity)

'Get the longest lengths for the
'ContactName and CompanyName fields
int1 = FindTheLongest(rst1, "ContactName") + 1
rst1.MoveFirst
int2 = FindTheLongest(rst1, "CompanyName") + 1

'Print selected fields from filtered recordset
rst1.MoveFirst
Do Until rst1.EOF
    Debug.Print rst1("ContactName") & _
        String(int1 - Len(rst1("ContactName")), " ") & _
        rst1("CompanyName") & _
        String(int2 - Len(rst1("CompanyName")), " ") & _
        rst1("City"), rst1("Country")
    rst1.MoveNext
Loop

'Clean up objects
rst1.Close
Set rst1 = Nothing

End Sub


Function FilterOnCountryAndCity(strCountry As String, _
    strCity As String) As ADODB.Recordset
Dim rst1 As ADODB.Recordset

'Instantiate and open recordset
Set rst1 = New ADODB.Recordset
rst1.ActiveConnection = "Provider=Microsoft.Jet.OLEDB.4.0;" & _
    "Data Source= C:\Program Files\Microsoft Office" & _
    "\Office11\Samples\Northwind.mdb;"
rst1.Open "Customers", , adOpenKeyset, adLockOptimistic, adCmdTable

'Set Filter property
rst1.Filter = "Country = '" & strCountry & _
    "' AND City = '" & strCity & "'"
```

```
'Return filtered recordset
Set FilterOnCountryAndCity = rst1

End Function
```

Persisting Recordsets

By using the *Save* method, you can persist a recordset. Later, with the *Open* method and the MSPersist provider, you can open a saved recordset. This capability serves a couple of requirements particularly well. First, it comes in handy when you need to take a snapshot of a record source for viewing later on a computer disconnected from the data source for the records. Second, when remote server access is either slow or unreliable, using a saved recordset based on a record source from a remote server gives an application fast, reliable data access. This is especially convenient for read-only record sources. In either context, you can modify a saved record source and later update the remote source with the *UpdateBatch* method.

You can persist a recordset's contents with either of two formats, a proprietary format or an XML format. Designate your preferred format with a member of the *PersistFormatEnum* enum in the statement using the *Save* method. Saving a file in XML format enables another application to open and view the recordset's data. The *Open* method, which inserts the file's contents into a recordset, works equally well with either format. For example, you can readily view the saved XML file in the Microsoft Internet Explorer browser included with Office 2003. Internet Explorer allows you to view the XML tags and data. The proprietary format is not so easy to view natively. However, users can readily open a file in the proprietary format and then examine its contents in the recordset in which the *Open* method deposits the file's contents.

> **Note**   While the XML format used by the recordset's *Save* method is not fully compatible with the latest industry standard (*http://www.w3.org /TR/REC-xml*), it is nevertheless tagged text that you can read in a browser or Notepad. This readability feature makes XML an especially desirable format for sharing data with others.

The following sample opens a recordset on the *Shippers* table from the Northwind database on the C share of a remote computer named ccs1. Notice from the path specified in the *Data Source* parameter for the connection string argument that the original data source is an Access 2002 database file (you can readily open Access 2002 and Access 2000 database files from Access 2003). The procedure saves the recordset based on the connection to a drive on the local computer. The *Save* method designates an XML file format by using the *adPersistXML* intrinsic constant. Specifying the *adPersistADTG* intrinsic constant saves the recordset in the proprietary format.

```
Sub SaveAccessDBRecordSource()
On Error GoTo SaveAccessDB_Trap
Dim cnn1 As ADODB.Connection
Dim rst1 As ADODB.Recordset
Dim varLocalAddress As Variant

'Create the connection
Set cnn1 = New ADODB.Connection
cnn1.Open "Provider=Microsoft.Jet.OLEDB.4.0;" & _
    "Data Source=\\ccs1\c\Program Files\Microsoft Office\" & _
    "Office11\Samples\Northwind.mdb;"

'Open recordset on Shippers table in the copy of
'Northwind.mdb on a machine named ccs1
Set rst1 = New ADODB.Recordset
rst1.Open "Shippers", cnn1, adOpenKeyset, adLockOptimistic, adCmdTable

'Specify a local address for the recordset based on Shippers table,
'and save the recordset in XML format to that address
varLocalAddress = "C:\Office11Files\Chapter01\ShippersFromCcs1.xml"
rst1.Save varLocalAddress, adPersistXML

SaveAccessDB_Exit:
rst1.Close
Set rst1 = Nothing
cnn1.Close
Set cnn1 = Nothing
Exit Sub

SaveAccessDB_Trap:
If err.Number = 58 Then
'Kill the temporary file of table data because it already exists,
'and resume writing to the file
    Kill varLocalAddress
    Resume
Else
    MsgBox "Procedure failed with an error number = " _
        & err.Number & ", " & vbCrLf & "and an " & _
        "error description of """ & _
```

```
        err.Description & """" & ".", vbInformation, _
        "Programming Microsoft Access 2003"
End If

End Sub
```

The sample's error trap is slightly more robust than necessary, but you will typically need an error trap with a procedure that saves a recordset to a file. This is because you will generate a run-time error if you attempt to save a recordset over an existing file. Since the number for this specific error is 58, the sample kills the old version of the file and resumes executing the line of code with the *Save* method.

Figure 1-6 shows the saved file open in Internet Explorer. Notice that the XML tags show the schema information, such as data type and length for recordset fields, as well as the data for the file's contents.

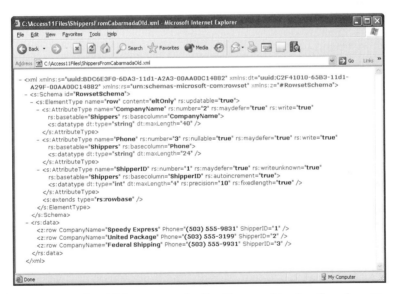

Figure 1-6   The XML contents for the file saved by the *SaveAccess-DBRecordSource* procedure, as seen from Internet Explorer.

The *OpenSavedRecordset* sample that appears next illustrates the syntax for opening and browsing the contents of the file saved in the previous code sample. After declaring and instantiating a recordset, the procedure invokes the recordset's *Open* method. The source for the *Open* method is the path and file-name for the recordset saved previously. In order to use the *Open* method this way, you must designate MSPersist as the provider for the connection argument. Notice that the *Options* argument is *adCmdFile*. I include this just to remind you of the general usefulness of specifying an *Options* argument. In this particular case, the argument is not necessary since ADO assumes an *adCmd-File* argument when you designate MSPersist as the provider.

After opening the file as a recordset, the code sample loops through the columns of each row as it prints the field name and value of each element in the recordset. With this simple code, you can open the local file and view its contents even when you are disconnected from the original version of the *Shippers* table on the ccs1 computer.

```
Sub OpenSavedRecordset()
Dim rst1 As ADODB.Recordset
Dim int1 As Integer

'Instantiate recordset, and open from file with Persistence provider
Set rst1 = New ADODB.Recordset
rst1.Open _
    "C:\Access11Files\Chapter01\ShippersFromCcs1.xml", _
    "Provider=MSPersist;", _
    , , adCmdFile

'Loop through all rows; with each row loop through all columns
Do Until rst1.EOF
    For int1 = 0 To rst1.Fields.Count - 1
        Debug.Print rst1.Fields(int1).Name, rst1(int1)
    Next int1
    rst1.MoveNext
Loop

'Clean up objects
rst1.Close
Set rst1 = Nothing

End Sub
```

As developers, we can use this technology to empower employees who must travel, enter data on a disconnected recordset, and then update the connected recorded source when they return to the office. By using the recordset's *UpdateBatch* method along with the ability to persist recordsets, you can readily meet this need. The *SaveEditInsertShippersAtNorthwindCS* procedure demonstrates the syntax that can help you empower "road warrior" employees. The sample creates a local recordset based on the *Shippers* table in the NorthwindCS database on the cab2000 SQL Server. (Recall that the NorthwindCS database ships with Microsoft Office.) Then the procedure saves this recordset to a local drive.

```
Sub SaveEditInsertShippersAtNorthwindCS()
On Error GoTo EditInsertCS_Trap
Dim cnn1 As ADODB.Connection
Dim rst1 As ADODB.Recordset
Dim varLocalAddress As Variant

'Local address for saved recordset
varLocalAddress = "C:\Access11Files\Chapter01\ShippersFromCab2000.xml"

'Instantiate and open a recordset
Set rst1 = New ADODB.Recordset
rst1.Open "SELECT ShipperID, CompanyName, Phone FROM Shippers", _
        "Provider=SQLOLEDB;Data Source=cab2000;User Id=sa;" & _
        "Password=password;Initial Catalog=NorthwindCS;", _
        adOpenDynamic, adLockOptimistic, adCmdText

'Persist the recordset to disk as an XML file; this saves it
'based on the Shippers table in the NorthwindCS database on the
'cab2000 server
Kill varLocalAddress
rst1.Save varLocalAddress, adPersistXML

'Open the XML file locally
Set rst1 = New ADODB.Recordset
rst1.Open varLocalAddress, "Provider=MSPersist;", , , adCmdFile

'Find a record, and edit it in the local cache
rst1.Find "CompanyName = 'Federal Shipping'"
If rst1.EOF Then
    Debug.Print "Name not found."
    Exit Sub
End If
rst1("CompanyName") = "Federal Shippers"
rst1.Update

'Add a record to the local cache
rst1.AddNew
    rst1("CompanyName") = "CAB Movers"
    rst1("Phone") = "(555) 234.5678"
rst1.Update

'After committing the edit locally, connect to the remote
'data source and update the remote source
Set cnn1 = New ADODB.Connection
cnn1.Open "Provider=SQLOLEDB;Data Source=cab2000;User Id=sa;" & _
        "Password=password;Initial Catalog=NorthwindCS;"
rst1.ActiveConnection = cnn1
rst1.UpdateBatch
```

(continued)

```
EditInsertCS_Exit:
'Clean up objects
rst1.Close
Set rst1 = Nothing
cnn1.Close
Set cnn1 = Nothing
Exit Sub

EditInsertCS_Trap:
If err.Number = 53 Then
'Tried to kill a file that doesn't exist, so simply resume
    Resume Next
ElseIf err.Number = 58 Then
'Kill the temporary file of table data if it already exists,
'and resume writing to the file
    Kill varLocalAddress
    Resume
Else
    MsgBox "Procedure failed with an error number = " _
        & err.Number & ", " & vbCrLf & "and an " & _
        "error description of """ & _
        err.Description & """" & ".", vbInformation, _
        "Programming Microsoft Access 2003"
End If

End Sub
```

A traveling employee can use this file-based version of a recordset to edit existing data and enter new data. The code sample simulates these tasks programmatically. The application of the *Update* method commits the changes to the recordset's local cache, but another *Save* method can transfer those updates from memory to the disk-based version of the local recordset.

After returning from the field, employees will want to update the database at headquarters with entries made while on the road. An employee can accomplish this objective by running a program you prepare that opens the file-based version of the recordset, connects the recordset to the server at headquarters, and invokes the *UpdateBatch* method for the local recordset. The *UpdateBatch* method, along with the recordset *Filter* property, enables developers to reconcile conflicts when they occur. See the Access Help files for more detail on conflict-resolution issues. Another especially useful resource for advanced technical questions is the Search capability at the *http://msdn.microsoft.com/office* site. For example, a search for "UpdateBatch Filter" returns a topic titled "Detecting and Resolving Conflicts," which includes a code sample demonstrating the syntax for detecting and resolving conflicts with the *UpdateBatch* method.

> **Note**   If you run the same procedure as *SaveEditInsertShippersAt-*
> *NorthwindCS*, except for updating its connections so that it initially
> opens and later updates the Access Northwind database file, it will fail.
> The precise error description is "Cannot update 'ShipperID'; field not
> updateable." The solution to this problem for Access database files is
> to construct the initial file-based recordset without primary keys that
> have an *AutoNumber* data type. Use a SQL statement as your source
> for the saved recordset to accomplish this. This book's companion
> content includes a sample procedure, *SaveEditInsertShippersAt-*
> *Northwind*, with the detailed code to perform this task.

Sorting Recordsets

Many database applications benefit from a sorted recordset. Therefore,
Microsoft added a *Sort* property to ADO recordsets. This is a very natural property for Access developers to use. Simply set the *Sort* property for a recordset to
the list of field names on which you want the recordset sorted. Represent the
field names as a comma-delimited string. The default sort order is ascending.
However, you can explicitly set an ascending sort order for any field by trailing
the field name with a blank followed by the *ASC* keyword. Replace the *ASC*
keyword with *DESC* if you want a recordset sorted in descending order on the
values within a field.

In order for *Sort* property assignments to operate, you must assign the
adUseClient intrinsic constant to the recordset's *CursorLocation* property. ADO
takes advantage of user-defined indexes for tables when sorting recordsets.
When no user-defined indexes exist, ADO constructs a temporary index to help
speed the sorting of recordset rows on a field. You can clear any special sort
(and delete temporary indexes that are automatically constructed) by assigning
an empty string to the *Sort* property. You can also dynamically rearrange the
order of rows within a recordset by designating a modified string of field names
for the recordset's *Sort* property.

The following code sample demonstrates how to set the *Sort* property,
while revealing the syntax for most of its typical uses. The sample begins by creating a recordset based on the *Customers* table. Notice that the sample assigns
the *adUseClient* intrinsic constant to the recordset's *CursorLocation* property. It
is essential for the *CursorLocation* property to have this setting (without this setting, the *Sort* property assignments fail at run time). Recall, however, that *adUse-*
Client is the default *CursorLocation* property. Therefore, unless you changed the
default setting, you do not have to make the explicit assignment.

The procedure prints an excerpt of columns for the first five records in the currently sorted version of the recordset four different times. The first set of five records shows the default order, which is the order of the primary key or the order of entry for rows if no primary key exists. You don't need to set the *Sort* property to return records in this order (unless you are clearing a prior sort setting). The second set of five records sorts in ascending order on the *City* field values. To impose this order, the procedure merely assigns the string *"City"* to the *Sort* property. The next set of five records also sorts records on *City* field values, but in descending order. The *Sort* property setting for this order merely trails the field name by a space and the *DESC* keyword. The final sort order is by *City* field values within *Country* field values. Place the outer sort key, *Country*, first in the string for the *Sort* property so that the *City* field values appear in ascending order within each country.

```
Sub SortCustomersDefaultCityUpDown()
Dim rst1 As ADODB.Recordset
Dim int1 As Integer
Dim int2 As Integer
Dim int3 As Integer
Dim int4 As Integer

'Instantiate and open recordset based on customers;
'set CursorLocation to adUseClient to support sorting
Set rst1 = New ADODB.Recordset
rst1.CursorLocation = adUseClient
rst1.Open "Customers", "Provider=Microsoft.Jet.OLEDB.4.0;" & _
    "Data Source= C:\Program Files\Microsoft Office" & _
    "\Office11\Samples\Northwind.mdb;"

'Find and save maximum length of CustomerID, CompanyName,
'and ContactName fields
int2 = FindTheLongest(rst1, "CustomerID") + 1
rst1.MoveFirst
int3 = FindTheLongest(rst1, "CompanyName") + 1
rst1.MoveFirst
int4 = FindTheLongest(rst1, "ContactName") + 1

'Print records in default order
rst1.MoveFirst
Debug.Print "Default Order" & vbCr
For int1 = 1 To 5
    Debug.Print rst1("CustomerID") & _
        String(int2 - Len(rst1("CustomerID")), " ") & _
        rst1("CompanyName") & _
        String(int3 - Len(rst1("CompanyName")), " ") & _
        rst1("ContactName") & _
        String(int4 - Len(rst1("ContactName")), " ") & _
        rst1("Phone"), rst1("City"), rst1("Country")
```

```
        rst1.MoveNext
Next int1


'Sort by City and print
rst1.Sort = "City"
rst1.MoveFirst
Debug.Print String(2, vbCr) & "Order by City Ascending" & vbCr
For int1 = 1 To 5
    Debug.Print rst1("CustomerID") & _
        String(int2 - Len(rst1("CustomerID")), " ") & _
        rst1("CompanyName") & _
        String(int3 - Len(rst1("CompanyName")), " ") & _
        rst1("ContactName") & _
        String(int4 - Len(rst1("ContactName")), " ") & _
        rst1("Phone"), rst1("City"), rst1("Country")
    rst1.MoveNext
Next int1

'Sort by descending City order and print
rst1.Sort = "City DESC"
rst1.MoveFirst
Debug.Print String(2, vbCr) & "Order by City Descending" & vbCr
For int1 = 1 To 5
    Debug.Print rst1("CustomerID") & _
        String(int2 - Len(rst1("CustomerID")), " ") & _
        rst1("CompanyName") & _
        String(int3 - Len(rst1("CompanyName")), " ") & _
        rst1("ContactName") & _
        String(int4 - Len(rst1("ContactName")), " ") & _
        rst1("Phone"), rst1("City"), rst1("Country")
    rst1.MoveNext
Next int1

'Sort by City within Country and print
rst1.Sort = "Country, City"
rst1.MoveFirst
Debug.Print String(2, vbCr) & _
"Order by Country Ascending, City Ascending" & vbCr
For int1 = 1 To 5
    Debug.Print rst1("CustomerID") & _
        String(int2 - Len(rst1("CustomerID")), " ") & _
        rst1("CompanyName") & _
        String(int3 - Len(rst1("CompanyName")), " ") & _
        rst1("ContactName") & _
        String(int4 - Len(rst1("ContactName")), " ") & _
        rst1("Phone"), rst1("City"), rst1("Country")
    rst1.MoveNext
Next int1
```

(continued)

```
'Clean up objects
rst1.Close
Set rst1 = Nothing

End Sub
```

You can combine the *Sort* property for recordsets with other Access programming features to achieve useful results that are difficult to obtain programmatically any other way. For example, it is easy to list all the tables in an Access database file with any number of properties sorted however you need. The *OpenSchema* method for the *Connection* object returns recordsets with fields describing classes of objects within a database. This chapter demonstrated how to use this method earlier, but it did not show you how to customize the order of the output. This section demonstrates how to use the *Save* and *Open* methods in combination with the *Sort* property to arrange *OpenSchema* output to suit your needs.

When used with a parameter set to *adSchemaTables*, the *OpenSchema* method outputs a recordset of table properties with information ordered by table name. However, this list mixes information about all types of tables in rows adjacent to one another. Therefore, it is difficult to find information about a particular user-defined table, view, or system table. Figure 1-7 shows the output to the Immediate window from a VBA program that sorts tables by table name, within table type. Along with the other two columns, this feature makes it easy to look up when a table was last modified or created.

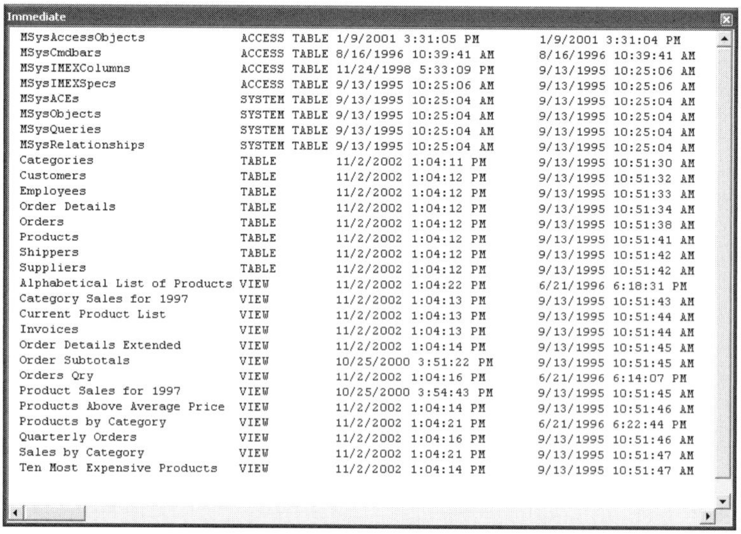
Immediate

MSysAccessObjects	ACCESS TABLE	1/9/2001 3:31:05 PM	1/9/2001 3:31:04 PM
MSysCmdbars	ACCESS TABLE	8/16/1996 10:39:41 AM	8/16/1996 10:39:41 AM
MSysIMEXColumns	ACCESS TABLE	11/24/1998 5:33:09 PM	9/13/1995 10:25:06 AM
MSysIMEXSpecs	ACCESS TABLE	9/13/1995 10:25:06 AM	9/13/1995 10:25:06 AM
MSysACEs	SYSTEM TABLE	9/13/1995 10:25:04 AM	9/13/1995 10:25:04 AM
MSysObjects	SYSTEM TABLE	9/13/1995 10:25:04 AM	9/13/1995 10:25:04 AM
MSysQueries	SYSTEM TABLE	9/13/1995 10:25:04 AM	9/13/1995 10:25:04 AM
MSysRelationships	SYSTEM TABLE	9/13/1995 10:25:04 AM	9/13/1995 10:25:04 AM
Categories	TABLE	11/2/2002 1:04:11 PM	9/13/1995 10:51:30 AM
Customers	TABLE	11/2/2002 1:04:12 PM	9/13/1995 10:51:32 AM
Employees	TABLE	11/2/2002 1:04:12 PM	9/13/1995 10:51:33 AM
Order Details	TABLE	11/2/2002 1:04:12 PM	9/13/1995 10:51:34 AM
Orders	TABLE	11/2/2002 1:04:12 PM	9/13/1995 10:51:38 AM
Products	TABLE	11/2/2002 1:04:12 PM	9/13/1995 10:51:41 AM
Shippers	TABLE	11/2/2002 1:04:12 PM	9/13/1995 10:51:42 AM
Suppliers	TABLE	11/2/2002 1:04:12 PM	9/13/1995 10:51:42 AM
Alphabetical List of Products	VIEW	11/2/2002 1:04:22 PM	6/21/1996 6:18:31 PM
Category Sales for 1997	VIEW	11/2/2002 1:04:13 PM	9/13/1995 10:51:43 AM
Current Product List	VIEW	11/2/2002 1:04:13 PM	9/13/1995 10:51:44 AM
Invoices	VIEW	11/2/2002 1:04:13 PM	9/13/1995 10:51:44 AM
Order Details Extended	VIEW	11/2/2002 1:04:14 PM	9/13/1995 10:51:45 AM
Order Subtotals	VIEW	10/25/2000 3:51:22 PM	9/13/1995 10:51:45 AM
Orders Qry	VIEW	11/2/2002 1:04:16 PM	6/21/1996 6:14:07 PM
Product Sales for 1997	VIEW	10/25/2000 3:54:43 PM	9/13/1995 10:51:45 AM
Products Above Average Price	VIEW	11/2/2002 1:04:14 PM	9/13/1995 10:51:46 AM
Products by Category	VIEW	11/2/2002 1:04:21 PM	6/21/1996 6:22:44 PM
Quarterly Orders	VIEW	11/2/2002 1:04:16 PM	9/13/1995 10:51:46 AM
Sales by Category	VIEW	11/2/2002 1:04:21 PM	9/13/1995 10:51:47 AM
Ten Most Expensive Products	VIEW	11/2/2002 1:04:14 PM	9/13/1995 10:51:47 AM

Figure 1-7 Program output from the *SortedTableTypes* procedure, showing a list of tables sorted by table name within table type from the Northwind Access database file.

The following pair of procedures generate the output shown in Figure 1-7. While this listing is slightly long, you are already familiar with all the techniques that it integrates. The calling procedure, *CallSortedTableTypes*, designates a string that points at a database file and passes that string to the second procedure, *SortedTableTypes*. You can get a listing like the one in Figure 1-7 for any Access database file, just by changing the string.

The second procedure generates a recordset about the tables in a database file by invoking the *OpenSchema* method with the *adSchemaTables* intrinsic constant as an argument. You cannot sort the output from the *OpenSchema* method because it sets the *CursorLocation* property to *adUseServer*. Therefore, the procedure saves the recordset and opens it again. This two-step process creates a version of the recordset with a *CursorLocation* property equal to *adUseClient*. In addition, the process yields a local version of the recordset for future use (for example, when you are disconnected from the computer with the database file). After changing the *CursorLocation* property setting, the procedure just needs to set the *Sort* property and print the results to the Immediate window. By specifying *TABLE_TYPE* before *TABLE_NAME*, the procedure forces the output to show table names sorted alphabetically within the table type.

```
Sub CallSortedTableTypes()
Dim str1 As String


'Specify database for which to generate a sorted list of tables
str1 = "Provider=Microsoft.Jet.OLEDB.4.0;" & _
    "Data Source= C:\Program Files\Microsoft Office" & _
    "\Office11\Samples\Northwind.mdb;"

'Call sub procedure to create sorted list of tables
SortedTableTypes str1

End Sub



Sub SortedTableTypes(str1 As String)
On Error GoTo SortedTableTypes_Trap
Dim cnn1 As ADODB.Connection
Dim rst1 As ADODB.Recordset
Dim rst2 As ADODB.Recordset
Dim int1 As Integer
Dim int2 As Integer

'Instantiate and open connection
Set cnn1 = New ADODB.Connection
cnn1.Open str1
```

(continued)

```
'Save tables report in rst1
Set rst1 = cnn1.OpenSchema(adSchemaTables)

'Since OpenSchema returns a server-based cursor, save original
'returned recordset and reopen saved data with a new recordset;
'the new recordset has a local cursor that you can sort
rst1.Save "C:\Access11Files\Chapter01\SortedTables.adtg", adPersistADTG
Set rst2 = New ADODB.Recordset
rst2.Open "C:\Access11Files\Chapter01\SortedTables.adtg ", "Provider=MSPersist"

'Sort copied data by table name within table type
rst2.Sort = "TABLE_TYPE, TABLE_NAME"

'Compute maximum length of TABLE_NAME and TABLE_TYPE columns
int1 = FindTheLongest(rst2, "TABLE_NAME") + 1
rst2.MoveFirst
int2 = FindTheLongest(rst2, "TABLE_TYPE") + 1
rst2.MoveFirst

'Loop through sorted results set from OPENSCHEMA query,
'and print selected columns
Do Until rst2.EOF
    Debug.Print rst2.Fields("TABLE_NAME") & _
        String(int1 - Len(rst2("TABLE_NAME")), " ") & _
        rst2.Fields("TABLE_TYPE") & _
        String(int2 - Len(rst2("TABLE_TYPE")), " ") & _
        rst2.Fields("DATE_MODIFIED"), _
        rst2.Fields("DATE_CREATED")
    rst2.MoveNext
Loop

SortedTableTypes_Exit:
rst1.Close
rst2.Close
cnn1.Close
Set rst1 = Nothing
Set rst2 = Nothing
Set cnn1 = Nothing
Exit Sub


SortedTableTypes_Trap:
If err.Number = 58 Then
'Kill the temporary file of table data if it already exists,
'and resume writing to the file
    Kill "C:\Access11Files\Chapter01\SortedTables.adtg "
    Resume
Else
```

```
    MsgBox "Procedure failed with an error number = " _
        & err.Number & ", " & vbCrLf & "and an " & _
        "error description of """ & _
        err.Description & """" & ".", vbInformation, _
        "Programming Microsoft Access 2003"
    Resume SortedTableTypes_Exit
End If

End Sub
```

The *Field* Object

A field is a column of data containing entries with the same data type. In the ADODB library, the *Fields* collection used to belong exclusively to recordsets, and its members are *Field* objects. *Field* objects have properties and methods for storing and retrieving data. With Access 2002 and Access 2003, the *Fields* collection also became a member of the *Record* object. This expands the scope of a field beyond relational database models so that it can also embrace the parent-child model suitable for working with child files as members of parent folders.

Recordsets use a *Field* object's *Value* property to display the contents of a column in the current record. Many of the other *Field* properties contain metadata about the data in a record. The *Name* property is a handle by which your applications can reference a field. The *DefinedSize* property characterizes the maximum size of a field (in characters for *Text* fields). The *ActualSize* property is the actual length (in bytes) of the contents of a *Field* object's value. The *Attributes* property contains an array of information features about a field. It can indicate whether a field's value is updateable or whether it can contain *Nulls*.

> **Note**   The *DefinedSize* and *ActualSize* properties use different measurements for *Text* fields. *DefinedSize* is the maximum number of characters in the field, and *ActualSize* is the number of bytes in the field. Since a *Text* field with Jet 4 represents characters with 2 bytes each, its *ActualSize* value can be up to twice the *DefinedSize* value. For numeric fields, and *Text* fields in databases that represent characters using a single byte (for example, a Jet 3.51 database), this difference does not exist. If you are migrating from Access 97 to Access 2003, you are probably using Jet 3.51. Therefore, you should be especially sensitive to this distinction.

The *GetChunk* and *AppendChunk* methods of the *Field* object facilitate the processing of large text or binary data fields in smaller chunks that fit into memory more conveniently. You use the *GetChunk* method to bring a portion of a large field into memory. The *Size* argument specifies the number of bytes to retrieve in one invocation of the *GetChunk* method. Each uninterrupted, successive invocation of the method starts reading new data from where the previous one finished. The *AppendChunk* method lets you construct a large text or binary data field in chunks from memory. Like the *GetChunk* method, *AppendChunk* writes new data into a field from where the previous *AppendChunk* method finished. To use either method correctly, a *Field* object's *adFldLong* bit in the *Attributes* property must be set to *True*.

Name and *Value* Properties

The following pair of procedures demonstrates an application for the *Name* and *Value* properties of the *Field* object. The application enumerates the field names and values in any row of any table in any database. The first procedure, *CallFieldNameValue*, passes information that points at a row in a table of a data base. The called procedure, *FieldNameValue*, constructs a single-record recordset based on the passed arguments. It then enumerates the field names and values for the row in the recordset.

Two alternate sets of passed arguments appear in first procedure. The set without comment markers is for a string criterion, such as the *CustomerID* field in the *Customers* table. The set with comments is for a numeric criterion, such as the *ShipperID* field in the *Shippers* table. Both sets rely on the Northwind database, but you can freely change all these arguments to specify the field names and values in any particular row of any table within any database. The value for *str3* should be the name of a field that has a unique value for each row in the table, such as a primary key. The *var1* variable should contain a string value or a number value for the field denoted by *str3*.

```
Sub CallFieldNameValue()
Dim str1 As String
Dim str2 As String
Dim str3 As String
Dim var1 As Variant

'Specify data source for field name
'and value data
str1 = "Provider=Microsoft.Jet.OLEDB.4.0;" & _
    "Data Source= C:\Program Files\Microsoft Office" & _
    "\Office11\Samples\Northwind.mdb;"
```

```
'Denote a specific record source
'within the data source
str2 = "Customers"
'str2 = "Shippers"

'Designate a criterion field (str3) and a criterion
'value (str4) for picking a particular row from
'the record source
str3 = "CustomerID"
var1 = "BONAP"
'str3 = "ShipperID"
'var1 = 2

'Call the procedure to enumerate field names
'and values
FieldNameValue str1, str2, str3, var1

End Sub


Sub FieldNameValue(str1 As String, _
    str2 As String, str3 As String, _
    var1 As Variant)
Dim cnn1 As ADODB.Connection
Dim rst1 As ADODB.Recordset
Dim str5 As String
Dim fld1 As ADODB.Field

'Open connection and recordset
Set cnn1 = New ADODB.Connection
cnn1.Open str1
Set rst1 = New ADODB.Recordset
rst1.ActiveConnection = cnn1
If IsNumeric(var1) Then
    str5 = "SELECT * FROM " & str2 & _
        " WHERE " & str3 & "=" & var1
Else
    str5 = "SELECT * FROM " & str2 & _
        " WHERE " & str3 & "='" & var1 & "'"

End If
rst1.Open str5, , , , adCmdText

'Report field names and values for record
For Each fld1 In rst1.Fields
    Debug.Print fld1.Name, fld1.Value
Next fld1

End Sub
```

The second procedure uses a SQL string to designate the source for the single-row recordset. It selects all the rows from any table where the field value in *str3* equals the value of the *var1* memory variable. After constructing the recordset, a *Do* loop passes through each field for the first row in the recordset. When you use a primary key value in the *WHERE* clause of the *SELECT* statement for the source of the recordset, the first row will be the only row in the recordset. On each iteration, the loop prints the *Name* and *Value* properties for one field.

The *Type* Property

A *Field* object's *Type* property indicates the kind of data it can contain. This property returns one of the data type constants in the *DataTypeEnum* values range. You can view these options in the Object Browser for the ADODB library. Figure 1-8 shows these constants in the Object Browser screen. By selecting the type for a field, you can determine legitimate values for its *Value* property.

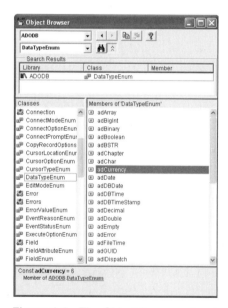

Figure 1-8   The Object Browser showing a selection of data type constants for defining fields.

Printing Field Data Types

The following two procedures work together to process data type constants with ADO. The *FieldNameType* procedure opens a recordset based on the *Orders* table in the Northwind database. This table has a reasonable variety of data types, so it makes a nice case study for examining data types. After opening a recordset, the procedure loops through the fields in the recordset and prints each *Field* object's name and type. The *FieldType* function translates the numeric constant's value to a string that represents the constant's name. The *adCurrency* constant has a value of 6, for example, as shown in Figure 1-8. The *FieldType* function decodes the value 6 to the string *"adCurrency"*. The *FieldNameType* procedure then prints each field's name and data type constant name.

```
Sub FieldNameType()
Dim cnn1 As ADODB.Connection
Dim rst1 As ADODB.Recordset
Dim fld1 As ADODB.Field
Dim str1 As String

'Open connection and recordset
    str1 = "Provider=Microsoft.Jet.OLEDB.4.0;" & _
        "Data Source= C:\Program Files\Microsoft Office" & _
    "\Office11\Samples\Northwind.mdb;"
    Set cnn1 = New ADODB.Connection
    cnn1.Open str1
    Set rst1 = New ADODB.Recordset
    rst1.ActiveConnection = cnn1
    rst1.Open "orders", , , , adCmdTable

'Report field names and types for record
    For Each fld1 In rst1.Fields
        Debug.Print "  Name: " & fld1.Name & vbCr & _
            "  Type: " & FieldType(fld1.Type) & vbCr
    Next fld1
End Sub


Public Function FieldType(intType As Integer) As String
    Select Case intType
        Case adVarWChar
            FieldType = "adVarWChar"
        Case adCurrency
            FieldType = "adCurrency"
        Case adInteger
            FieldType = "adInteger"
        Case adDate
            FieldType = "adDate"
        Case Else
            FieldType = "Not determined"
    End Select
End Function
```

You can easily run *FieldNameType* and *FieldType* against recordsets based on other data sources than the *Orders* table, but the *FieldType* function checks only for the four data types in the *Orders* table. When you use a record source other than the *Orders* table, you might encounter a data type other than the four in the list. In this case, the *Type* field in the report will be "Not determined". You can fix this problem by determining the value of the field. You can do this by putting a breakpoint on the *Debug.Print* statement inside the *Do* loop in the *FieldNameType* procedure. You examine the value of *fld1.Type* for a field whose type doesn't display and then match that constant value against the constant names in the Object Browser for *DataTypeEnum*. (See Figure 1-8.) Finally, you amend the *Select Case* statement in the *FieldType* procedure to decode the new constant.

Note   Place your cursor over an expression or memory variable to determine its value at a breakpoint. You can also track the values of expressions and memory variables in the Watch window.

Creating Fields for a Recordset

Using the *Fields* collection *Append* method, you can create fields for a recordset. In addition, your applications can assign values to those fields. Because it is possible to persist recordsets, you can save recordsets that your applications create on the fly to hold data originally stored as a disconnected recordset. You can leave the recordset on the workstation used to create it or transfer it later to a network-based database for sharing by many users.

The following procedure, *CreateRecordset*, demonstrates the key elements of this approach. First, the procedure instantiates an empty recordset. The procedure uses the *Append* method to populate the empty recordset with fields. As you can see, the procedure assigns the minimum number of *Append* arguments. These include the field name and data type. When you specify a string data type, such as *adVarWChar*, you must also designate its maximum length—ADO terminology calls this the *DefinedSize* argument. Use the third positional argument to specify a field's *DefinedSize*. After defining the schema for the recordset, the procedure moves on to populating its two fields with two rows of data. Then it echoes the data to the Immediate window to confirm the data entry operation. Finally, the procedure persists the recordset to a file using the proprietary Microsoft format. So long as the data is exclusively for reading by the recordset's *Open* method, there is no compelling factor that establishes a preference for either of the two formats available with the *Save* method.

```
Sub CreateRecordset()
On Error GoTo CreateRecordset_Trap
Dim rst1 As ADODB.Recordset
Dim strPath As String
Dim strFileName As String
Dim str1 As String

'Instantiate a recordset
Set rst1 = New ADODB.Recordset

'Specify recordset field name and data type.
'Append to recordset object.
rst1.Fields.Append "LastName", adVarWChar, 10
rst1.Fields.Append "ContactID", adInteger

'Add rows to the recordset
rst1.Open
With rst1
    rst1.AddNew
        rst1("LastName") = "Dobson"
        rst1("ContactID") = 9
    rst1.Update
    rst1.AddNew
        rst1("LastName") = "Edelstein"
        rst1("ContactID") = 10
    rst1.Update
End With

'Echo new contact data to Immediate window
rst1.MoveFirst
Do While Not rst1.EOF
    Debug.Print rst1("LastName") & _
        " " & rst1("ContactID")
    rst1.MoveNext
Loop

'Specify path and file to hold persisted recordset,
'and save recordset to it
strPath = "C:\Access11Files\Chapter01"
strFileName = "NewContactData.adtg"
str1 = strPath + strFileName
rst1.Save str1, adPersistXML

CreateRecordset_Exit:
rst1.Close
Set rst1 = Nothing
Exit Sub
```

(continued)

```
CreateRecordset_Trap:
'Kill previous version of file to hold
'persisted recordset if it exists already
'Otherwise, present error info in a message box.
If err.Number = 58 Then
    Kill str1
    Resume
Else
    MsgBox "Procedure failed with an error number = " _
        & err.Number & ", " & vbCrLf & "and an " & _
        "error description of """ & _
        err.Description & """" & ".", vbInformation, _
        "Programming Microsoft Access 2003"
    Resume CreateRecordset_Exit
End If

End Sub
```

Persisting Quarterly Totals to a Text File

The concluding sample for this section illustrates how to perform a common task that builds on and extends several techniques presented throughout this chapter. The sample prepares a text file with the total extended price for each order from the Access Northwind database. The text file also groups orders by quarter and inserts the total extended price of all orders after the orders for each quarter. This sample illustrates common tasks because it demonstrates techniques for grouping and aggregating. In addition, it builds on techniques presented throughout this chapter because it works with *Recordset* and *Field* objects. The sample extends the approaches presented in this chapter because it persists row values via the *FileSystemObject* instead of the *Save* method for a *Recordset* object. The *FileSystemObject* can persist a file as a series of text lines that are easier for humans to read than the XML output that the *Save* method generates. This is because XML requires text to be bound by tags that can interrupt the easy reading of the contents within a file.

The sample partially relies on two tables linked to the Northwind database. In addition, the sample builds a query based on the linked tables that join the *Orders* and *Order Details* tables by *OrderID*. The query, which is available as *Query1* in Chapter01.mdb, exposes the *OrderID* and *OrderDate* columns from the *Orders* table along with the *UnitPrice*, *Quantity*, and *Discount* columns from the *Order Details* table. I built *Query1* with the Query Designer so that I could copy the SQL string in the query's SQL View to the procedure. Chapter 4 equips you with the background to prepare queries like the one in *Query1* but without the need for the Query Designer.

The sample procedure uses two *Recordset* objects. The first recordset uses the SQL statement from *Query1* as a source; this is the sole reason for *Query1* and its two linked tables in the application. This recordset is the base data for computing the extended price by query. The recordset contains one row per line item. Line items within the recordset are grouped by *OrderID* value. Furthermore, the recordset rows are sorted by *OrderID*, which corresponds with the *OrderDate*. The second recordset is a custom recordset built without a source. This recordset, *rst2*, has three fields that the application appends to the recordset and then populates with values. The initial round of values is based on aggregations of the extended price for the line items within an order. A second pass through *rst2* develops the quarterly totals along with a little formatting—namely, some blank lines around each quarterly total and marking extended prices as currency.

The sample persists the recordset with the quarterly totals in a file named report.txt. The excerpt shows the last few order totals from the third quarter of 1996 and the first few order totals from the fourth quarter of 1996. Between the close of the third quarter and the start of the fourth quarter is the total of extended prices for orders in the third quarter.

The following procedure starts by opening a connection to the Northwind database and basing *rst1* on the SQL string for *Query1*. The local query is used only to create a SQL string. After opening *rst1*, the procedure declares and instantiates the second recordset, *rst2*, and appends three fields to it for the *OrderID*, *OrderDate*, and *OrderTotal* columns that appear in Figure 1-9. The sample opens the second recordset after specifying the name and data type for each of its three fields.

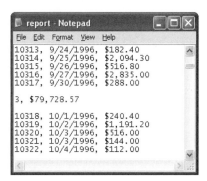

Figure 1-9 An excerpt from the report.txt file showing grouping and aggregation by quarter.

Next, the procedure declares two variables to help compute the total of extended prices for the line items within each order. The application can tell when an order ends by detecting when the *OrderID* value for the current row is different from the last row. A *Do* loop with an *If* statement and three clauses computes the order totals for the second recordset and navigates from one row to the next in the first and second recordsets. Because the procedure detects a new order only when it is past the last row in an order, the procedure needs a special mechanism for retrieving the order total for the last order. By definition, there are no additional rows following the last row in the first recordset. The procedure retrieves the total extended price for the final order by detecting an *EOF* property for the first recordset.

After computing the order totals in *rst2* with the first *Do* loop, a second *Do* loop takes control. This second loop passes through the rows of the second recordset to group the orders by quarter and insert a total extended price for each quarter. While the role of the second loop is different from the first one, its structure is strikingly similar. This second *Do* loop writes the rows from *rst2* to the report.txt file. The application also writes the quarterly totals to the same file. Again, the loop uses an *EOF* to signal a need to process the last row.

The sample uses very basic *FileSystemObject* programming methods to create and populate the report.txt file. It instantiates *fs* as a *FileSystemObject* instance with the *CreateObject* function. This function takes as its argument the class name *Scripting.FileSystemObject*. Next, the procedure invokes the *Create-TextFile* method to create a new instance of the report.txt file. The *True* argument for the method enables overwriting of any existing file with the same name in the same path. The application represents the file within the program with a variable named report_txt. The *Writeline* method for the file transfers a string expression to a line within the file. As with any objects, it is good programming practice to close objects and set them to *Nothing*. The sample application illustrates how to do this for the variables representing the text file and *FileSystemObject* instance at the beginning of its clean-up section.

```
Sub PersistQuarterlyOrderTotals()

Dim str1 As String
Dim cnn1 As New ADODB.Connection
Dim rst1 As New ADODB.Recordset
Dim str2 As String
Dim OrderTotal As Currency
Dim LstQtr As Integer

'Open connection
str1 = "Provider=Microsoft.Jet.OLEDB.4.0;" & _
    "Data Source=C:\Program Files\Microsoft Office\" & _
    "Office11\Samples\Northwind.mdb;"
cnn1.Open str1
```

```
'Specify a SQL string for the rst1 recordset
str2 = "SELECT Orders.OrderID, Orders.OrderDate, " & _
    "[Order Details].UnitPrice, " & _
    "[Order Details].Quantity, " & _
    "[Order Details].Discount " & _
    "FROM Orders INNER JOIN [Order Details] " & _
    "ON Orders.OrderID = [Order Details].OrderID;"

'Open Order Details table with
'the firehose cursor in the rst1 recordset
rst1.Open str2, cnn1

'Declare and instantiate rst2 for
'order totals, date, and ID
Dim rst2 As New ADODB.Recordset
rst2.Fields.Append "OrderID", adInteger
rst2.Fields.Append "OrderDate", adDBDate
rst2.Fields.Append "OrderTotal", adCurrency

'Open rst2 so you can populate it with records
rst2.Open

Dim LstOrderID As Long
Dim LstOrderDate As Date

'Marker values for the current order
LstOrderID = rst1(0)
LstOrderDate = rst1(1)

'Compute order totals in the rst2 recordset
'based on order details in the rst1 recordset
Do
    If rst1.EOF Then
'Write last record
        rst2.AddNew
            rst2("OrderID") = LstOrderID
            rst2("OrderDate") = LstOrderDate
            rst2("OrderTotal") = OrderTotal
        rst2.Update
        Exit Do
    ElseIf rst1(0) = LstOrderID Then
'Continue computing OrderTotal for current order
        OrderTotal = OrderTotal + _
            (rst1("UnitPrice") * _
            rst1("Quantity") * _
            (1 - rst1("Discount")))
    ElseIf rst1(0) <> LstOrderID Then
'Write record for current order, and set up
```

(continued)

```
'for processing the next order
        rst2.AddNew
            rst2("OrderID") = LstOrderID
            rst2("OrderDate") = LstOrderDate
            rst2("OrderTotal") = OrderTotal
        rst2.Update
        OrderTotal = (rst1("UnitPrice") * _
            rst1("Quantity") * _
            (1 - rst1("Discount")))
        LstOrderID = rst1(0)
        LstOrderDate = rst1(1)
    End If
    rst1.MoveNext
Loop

'Prepare file for output
Set fs = CreateObject("Scripting.FileSystemObject")
Set report_txt = _
    fs.CreateTextFile("C:\Access11Files\Chapter01\Report.txt", True)

'Set current record to first record
rst2.MoveFirst

'Assign values to initialize computations
'for report file
LstQtr = DatePart("q", rst2("OrderDate"))
OrderTotal = 0

'Compute quaterly order totals and write individual
'order totals as well as quarterly order totals to
'the report.txt file in the C:\Access11Files\Chapter01 folder
Do
    If rst2.EOF Then
        report_txt.writeline ("")
        report_txt.writeline (LstQtr & _
            ", " & Format(OrderTotal, "Currency"))
        report_txt.writeline ("")
        Exit Do
    ElseIf DatePart("q", rst2(1)) = LstQtr Then
        OrderTotal = OrderTotal + rst2("OrderTotal")
        report_txt.writeline (rst2("OrderID") & _
            ", " & rst2("OrderDate") & ", " & _
            Format(rst2("OrderTotal"), "Currency"))
    Else
        report_txt.writeline ("")
        report_txt.writeline (LstQtr & ", " & Format(OrderTotal, "Currency"))
        report_txt.writeline ("")
        OrderTotal = 0
```

```
            LstQtr = DatePart("q", rst2("OrderDate"))
            OrderTotal = OrderTotal + rst2(2)
            report_txt.writeline (rst2("OrderID") & _
                ", " & rst2("OrderDate") & ", " & _
                Format(rst2("OrderTotal"), "Currency"))
        End If
        rst2.MoveNext
Loop

'Clean up
report_txt.Close
Set report_txt = Nothing
Set fs = Nothing
rst2.Close
Set rst2 = Nothing
rst1.Close
Set rst1 = Nothing
cnn1.Close
Set cnn1 = Nothing

End Sub
```

Summary

This is the first of two chapters that focus on ADO data access issues for Access developers. As such, the chapter aims to achieve two primary objectives. First, it introduces ADO as a tool for data access. The goal is to convey a general understanding of the benefits that ADO brings to data access. Second, the chapter introduces three classes of ADO objects (*Connection*, *Recordset*, and *Field*) and drills down on the properties and methods of each type of object. The goals for this second objective are to provide a detailed grasp of the capabilities of each kind of object as well as convey a working knowledge of how to program the objects.

2

Data Access Models: Part II

This is the second of two chapters covering data access models. As I mentioned at the beginning of Chapter 1, the topic of data access models is extensive, which is why I've broken it into two chapters. Chapter 1 presents you with an overview of ActiveX Data Objects (ADO) and examines the *Connection*, *Recordset*, and *Field* objects. In this chapter, you'll learn about the *Command* and *Parameter* objects and the *Errors* collection. I'll also show you several techniques for managing access to the files on a Web server, demonstrate the features of the relatively new *Record* and *Stream* ADO objects, and explore further the new functionality of the *Recordset* object.

Command and *Parameter* Objects

The *Command* object within the ADODB library delivers three major benefits. First, it can be used to perform a select query to return a set of rows from a data source. Second, it can be used to execute a parameter query so that users can input run-time search criteria. And finally, it supports action queries against a data source to perform operations such as updating, deleting, and adding records.

You must designate a *Connection* object on which to run a command. You can either implicitly create a *Connection* object when you specify a command or explicitly assign an existing *Connection* object to a command. These are the same options as you have for recordsets.

The *CommandTimeout* property determines how long ADO waits for the execution of a command to conclude. This property takes a *Long* value that specifies the maximum wait time in seconds. The default value for this property is 30 seconds. If the timeout interval elapses before the *Command* object completes execution, ADO cancels the command and returns an error. The *Connection* object also supports a *CommandTimeout* property. Although this property has the same name as the *CommandTimeout* property of the *Command* object, it is independent of that property; the *Command* object's *CommandTimeout* property does not inherit the setting of the *Connection* object's *CommandTimeout* property.

> **Note**   When a *Command* object's *CommandTimeout* setting is important to your application, make sure it's compatible with the *Connection* object's *CommandTimeout* setting. For example, the default *Command* object's timeout setting is 30 seconds, but the default *Connection* object's timeout setting is 15 seconds. Therefore, if a workstation using your application does not make a connection within 15 sections, it will never have an opportunity to use the *Command* object.

There are actually several types for the *Command* object. The *CommandType* property sets the type of the *Command* object and lets ADO know how to interpret the object's *CommandText* property. You can base your command on a SQL statement, a table, or a stored procedure by setting the *CommandType* property to one of the values shown in Table 2-1. When working with an Access database, a stored procedure is equivalent to either a stored action query or a stored select query with parameters. Basing your command on a SQL statement keeps your query out of the Database window, although performance isn't as good as basing the command on a stored query.

Table 2-1   Intrinsic Constants for the *CommandTypeEnum*

Constant	Value	Behavior
adCmdUnspecified	−1	Informs ADO that no *CommandText* property setting exists. Do not use this setting with the OLE DB provider for AS/400 and VSAM or the OLE DB provider for DB 2.
adCmdText	1	Lets you run a command based on a SQL statement, a stored procedure, or even a table. Usually, you reserve this setting for a SQL statement. This is the only legitimate setting for the OLE DB provider for AS/400 and VSAM or the OLE DB provider for DB 2.

Table 2-1   Intrinsic Constants for the *CommandTypeEnum*

Constant	Value	Behavior
adCmdTable	2	Bases the return set on a previously designed table. Returns all columns from a table based on an internally generated SQL statement.
adCmdStoredProc	4	Runs a command based on text for a stored procedure.
adCmdUnknown	8	Informs ADO that there is no specification of the type of command. This is the default, except when MSPersist serves as the provider.
adCmdFile	256	Evaluates a source argument for a recordset's *Open* method based on the filename for a persistent recordset. This is the default when MSPersist is the provider. This setting is not appropriate for *Command* objects.
adCmdTableDirect	512	Evaluates a command as a table name. Returns all columns in a table without any intermediate SQL code. Use with the *Seek* method for a recordset.

The default setting for the *CommandType* property is *adCmdUnknown*. Changing the *CommandType* property from its default setting can speed up the operation of a command by reducing the need for ADO to call your provider to properly interpret a command's *CommandText* setting.

> **Note**   You can further improve the performance of commands that do not return records (such as action queries) by adding *adExecuteNo-Records* to a command's *CommandType* specification. Be sure to always use *adExecuteNoRecords*, which has the value 128, with another setting, as shown here:
>
> ```
> cmd1.CommandType = adCmdText + adExecuteNoRecords
> ```

The *CommandText* setting lets you designate what the command should do. You can assign a SQL string to define an operation for the command to perform. Use SQL syntax compatible with the provider for your command's *ActiveConnection* setting. You can also set the *CommandText* property to the name of a stored query or the name of a table. You should update the *CommandType* property to synchronize it with the setting of the *CommandText* property. For example, if a *CommandText* property points at a stored action query, designate *adCmdStoredProc* for the *CommandType* property.

If an application stays open for extended periods of time during which it executes a command repeatedly, you can improve the command's performance by using the *Prepared* property with a SQL statement. If the *Prepared* property is set to *True*, the SQL statement is compiled and saved on the database server the first time the statement is used. This slows the first execution of the command but speeds up subsequent ones.

The *Execute* method for a *Command* object invokes the code behind the *Command* object (for example, a stored query or a SQL statement). You can specify up to three optional arguments for the *Execute* method. The first argument allows the *Command* object to tell the procedure invoking it how many records it has affected. This argument pertains exclusively to action queries with Jet data sources or stored procedures on other types of databases, such as Microsoft SQL Server. (Use the *RecordCount* property on the resulting recordset to determine the number of records returned by a row-returning select query.) The second argument is a *Variant* array containing parameters to drive the command. This approach to designating parameters is for input parameters only. The third argument tells ADO how to evaluate the source. This argument can be any appropriate *CommandTypeEnum* member listed in Table 2-1, possibly combined with the *adExecuteNoRecords* intrinsic constant.

The *Command* object's *CreateParameter* method creates a new parameter for a command. After creating the parameter, you can use the *Append* method to add the parameter to the *Parameters* collection of a command. When running a parameter query, you must assign a value to the parameter. Using the *CreateParameter* method works for input parameters, output parameters, and return values from stored procedures. You can also make programs interactive at run time by using input from a user in a SQL string expression as the CommandText property for a Command object or the source argument for the Open method of a Recordset object. While many Access developers may find it somewhat more complicated to code parameters than SQL string expressions, I generally prefer working with parameters because it is more robust and secure. When invoking a Command object with parameters, the syntax automatically assures the input variable is of the right data type. Using a SQL string expression does not automatically provide such assurances. In addition, using parameters is more secure than using string inputs from users for a SQL string expression. This is because a user can input a constant string value that extends the SQL statement to perform tasks not originally intended for an application. This security issue is especially relevant to client/server databases with rich SQL languages, such as SQL Server.

> **Note**   You can specify parameter values using either an array as an argument for the *Execute* method of a *Command* object or with parameter value assignment statements before invoking the *Execute* method. The *Array* argument for the *Execute* method overrides any prior settings for your parameter values. Output parameters do not return valid values in the *Array* argument for the *Execute* method. This issue only pertains to databases that can return output parameters. Jet is not such a database; SQL Server does offer output parameters.

Creating a Recordset with a Select Query

One of the most straightforward tasks you can perform with a *Command* object is to create a recordset based on a select query. The *Execute* method of the *Command* object runs the select query and returns the resulting recordset. The *SelectCommand* procedure that follows shows how to do this. This procedure has two parts: the first part creates the *Command* object and a connection for it to relate to a database, and the second part processes a recordset returned from the *Command* object.

> **Note**   Before running the following procedure, make sure that *MyTable* in the Chapter02.mdb sample file contains some data (The Chapter02.mdb file is included with the companion content for this book). If the file is empty, run the *InsertRecords* procedure to populate *MyTable* with values automatically.

```
Sub SelectCommand()
Dim cmd1 As ADODB.Command
Dim rst1 As ADODB.Recordset
Dim str1 As String
Dim fld1 As ADODB.Field

'Define and execute command
Set cmd1 = New ADODB.Command
With cmd1
    .ActiveConnection = CurrentProject.Connection
    .CommandText = "SELECT MyTable.* FROM MyTable"
    .CommandType = adCmdText
End With
```

(continued)

```
'Set rst1 to the recordset returned by the command's
'Execute method, and print the recordset
Set rst1 = cmd1.Execute
Do Until rst1.EOF
    str1 = ""
    For Each fld1 In rst1.Fields
        str1 = str1 & fld1.Value & vbTab
    Next fld1
    Debug.Print str1
    rst1.MoveNext
Loop

'Clean up objects
rst1.Close
Set fld1 = Nothing
Set rst1 = Nothing
Set cmd1 = Nothing

End Sub
```

The first part of the procedure declares *cmd1* as a *Command* object and then sets three critical properties. Every command must have an *ActiveConnection* property in order to run against a database. The *Command* object in this sample relies on a SQL statement to represent its select query. The third assignment in the *With...End With* block sets the *CommandType* property to *adCmdText*. You can substitute a saved query for the SQL statement, as shown in the following example:

```
.CommandText = "CustomerID"
.CommandType = adCmdStoredProc
```

The second part of the procedure saves a reference to the recordset returned by the *Execute* method. This is necessary if you want to view the rows returned by the SQL string in the *CommandText* property because commands offer no methods for navigating through a recordset. Notice that you don't need to instantiate the *Recordset* object before assigning the return from the command's *Execute* method to it. The assignment instantiates the *Recordset* object. After saving a reference to the result, the procedure prints each record in the recordset with tab delimiters (*vbTab*) between fields in the Immediate window. The procedure can handle any number of columns in any number of rows.

Creating a Recordset with a Parameter Query

The following code demonstrates the syntax for a parameter query. This procedure also has two major parts to its design. The parameter query in the first part has some extra lines of ADO code and a different SQL statement syntax from that of the previous select query. The second part of this procedure, which assigns the result of the command to a recordset and prints the recordset, is the same as that of the previous select query.

```
Sub ParameterQCommand()
Dim cmd1 As ADODB.Command
Dim rst1 As ADODB.Recordset
Dim str1 As String
Dim fld1 As ADODB.Field
Dim prm1 As ADODB.Parameter
Dim int1 As Integer

'Create and define command
Set cmd1 = New ADODB.Command
With cmd1
    .ActiveConnection = CurrentProject.Connection
    .CommandText = "Parameters [Lowest] Long;" & _
        "SELECT Column1, Column2, Column3 " & _
        "FROM MyTable " & _
        "WHERE Column1>=[Lowest]"
    .CommandType = adCmdText
End With

'Create and define parameter
Set prm1 = cmd1.CreateParameter("[Lowest]", _
    adInteger, adParamInput)
cmd1.Parameters.Append prm1
int1 = Trim(InputBox("Lowest value?", _
    "Programming Microsoft Access 2003"))
prm1.Value = int1

'Open recordset on return from cmd1 and print
'the recordset
Set rst1 = cmd1.Execute
Do Until rst1.EOF
    str1 = ""
    For Each fld1 In rst1.Fields
        str1 = str1 & fld1.Value & vbTab
    Next fld1
    Debug.Print str1
    rst1.MoveNext
Loop

'Clean up objects
rst1.Close
Set fld1 = Nothing
Set rst1 = Nothing
Set cmd1 = Nothing

End Sub
```

The SQL statement syntax uses a *Parameters* declaration line that specifies the parameter's name and data type. The *WHERE* clause should also reference one or more parameters so that the parameters can affect the results set. By themselves, these adjustments to the SQL syntax statement are not sufficient to make the parameter query work—you must create the parameter and append it to the command using ADO code.

To create the parameter, invoke the *CreateParameter* method. The previous code uses three arguments with the *CreateParameter* method. The first one names the parameter, the second designates a data type for the parameter, and the third declares the input/output direction for the parameter. The *adParamInput* intrinsic constant is actually the default that declares the parameter an input to the query. Other constants let you designate output, input/output, and return value parameters. These other parameter types are appropriate for databases other than Jet, such as SQL Server. After creating a parameter, you must append it to the *Parameters* collection of the command.

> **Note** When creating a string parameter with the *CreateParameter* method, you must specify the number of characters after designating the data type. The parameters denoting the number of characters should designate the largest possible size for a parameter. For example, if the *DefinedSize* of a field corresponds to a text data type column of up to 10 characters, then denote 10 as the number of characters for the parameter. It is not necessary to designate the length of numeric data types.

After adding a parameter, you must assign a value to it to make the command's parameter query function properly. The previous code uses an *InputBox* function to gather input from a user. The procedure then invokes the *Command* object's *Execute* method in an assignment statement to save a reference to the resulting recordset so that it can be printed.

Deleting Records

As mentioned earlier, you can use the *Command* object to delete, update, and add records to a data source. *Command* objects offer a programmatic means to maintain a data source. The *DeleteARecord* and *DeleteAllRecords* procedures that follow prune records from a record source, such as the *MyTable* table in

Chapter02.mdb. The *DeleteARecord* procedure removes at most a single row from the table with the *Column1* value equal to 13. The *DeleteAllRecords* procedure removes all rows from the table no matter what values they have. These samples designate the record source and the criteria for selecting records using a SQL *DELETE* statement.

With the Microsoft Access Database window's query designer, you can graphically design a query and then copy the code from the query's SQL view to the *CommandText* property of a command. Normally, it is possible to improve the readability of the SQL code from the Access query designer by editing it slightly. For example, examine the SQL statement for extra parentheses that you can remove. If your query operates on a single table, you can remove the table prefix shown before field names. Compare for readability the following SQL statements with those that you generate automatically with the Access query designer.

```
Sub DeleteARecord()
Dim cmd1 As ADODB.Command

Set cmd1 = New ADODB.Command

With cmd1
    .ActiveConnection = CurrentProject.Connection
    .CommandText = "DELETE Column1 FROM " & _
        "MyTable WHERE Column1=13;"
    .CommandType = adCmdText
    .Execute
End With

End Sub


Sub DeleteAllRecords()
Dim cmd1 As ADODB.Command

Set cmd1 = New ADODB.Command

With cmd1
    .ActiveConnection = CurrentProject.Connection
    .CommandText = "DELETE * FROM MyTable"
    .CommandType = adCmdText
    .Execute
End With

End Sub
```

Inserting Records

When you develop an application, you might want to delete all the records from a table and then reset its contents. The *InsertRecords* procedure, shown next, uses the *Command* object to stock a table with values. You can use this procedure in conjunction with the *DeleteAllRecords* procedure to refresh a table with a small base set of records.

```
Sub InsertRecords()
Dim cmd1 As ADODB.Command

Set cmd1 = New ADODB.Command

With cmd1
    .ActiveConnection = CurrentProject.Connection
    .CommandText = "INSERT INTO MyTable(Column1, " & _
        "Column2, Column3) VALUES (1,2,'3')"
    .CommandType = adCmdText
    .Execute
    .CommandText = "INSERT INTO MyTable(Column1, " & _
        "Column2, Column3) VALUES (4,5,'6')"

    .Execute
    .CommandText = "INSERT INTO MyTable(Column1, " & _
        "Column2, Column3) VALUES (7,8,'9')"

    .Execute
    .CommandText = "INSERT INTO MyTable(Column1, " & _
        "Column2, Column3) VALUES (10,11,'12')"

    .Execute
    .CommandText = "INSERT INTO MyTable(Column1, " & _
        "Column2, Column3) VALUES (13,14,'15')"

    .Execute
    .CommandText = "INSERT INTO MyTable(Column1, " & _
        "Column2, Column3) VALUES (16,17,'18')"

    .Execute
End With

End Sub
```

The general elements of the *InsertRecords* procedure are shared with other applications of the *Command* object and do not depend on the design of a particular table. You must create a reference to the *Command* object and set its

ActiveConnection property. Three lines are required for each row that you add to a recordset: the *CommandText* property setting, which indicates what the command will do; the *CommandType* property setting, which designates the format of the instruction; and the *Execute* method, which launches the addition of the new record. You can repeat these three lines for each row added to the data source (though you don't need to reset *CommandType* unless you are changing the type). If you specify an updateable dynaset as the target, these steps can concurrently add records to two or more tables at the same time. When you add records to a table, you must consider the field data types. In the previous code, the *CommandText* settings are tailored specifically for the structure of the *MyTable* table. You can determine the data types for the columns in *MyTable* by running the *FieldNameType* sub procedure described at the end of Chapter 1. Just change the connection string so that it points to the Access database file holding *MyTable*, Chapter02.mdb. If *MyTable* is in the current database, you can denote the connection with the expression *CurrentProject.Connection*. The first two columns in *MyTable* have *Long Integer* data types, and the third column has a *Text* data type.

The syntax of the *CommandText* SQL statement in this sample has three parts. (This syntax is not available from the SQL view of the Access query designer.) First, the statement uses the *INSERT INTO* keyword, which is followed by the name of the data source to which you want to add records. Second, it takes the optional step of listing the field names for which it submits values. If you do not list the field names, the values in the next step will be appended in sequential order, which could be a problem if the data source design changes over time. Third, the *VALUES* keyword appears before the field values for the new record.

You will frequently want to add a new row to a table with some values that you acquire from another source, such as a form. The following code shows two procedures. The first procedure assigns values to three string variables and invokes the second procedure, which actually inserts the values into the table. In actual practice, you can assign the strings in the first procedure's value from a form or even with an *InputBox* function. The second procedure splices the string values into the *INSERT INTO* SQL statement. While we could make this more complicated by using parameters, this simple design gets the job done. Invoking a parameter query lets users type input values for the parameters (for example, with an *InputBox* function). The simple design of the following procedure uses string data types for all fields on input and then splices them into the *INSERT INTO* statement so that strings for numeric fields become numbers and others remain strings.

```
Sub CallInsertARecord()
Dim str1 As String
Dim str2 As String
Dim str3 As String

str1 = "19"
str2 = "20"
str3 = "21"

InsertARecord str1, str2, str3

End Sub

Sub InsertARecord(str1 As String, _
    str2 As String, str3 As String)
Dim cmd1 As ADODB.Command

Set cmd1 = New Command

With cmd1
    .ActiveConnection = CurrentProject.Connection
    .CommandText = "INSERT INTO MyTable(Column1, " & _
        "Column2, Column3) VALUES (" & str1 & "," & _
        str2 & ",'" & str3 & "')"
    .CommandType = adCmdText
    .Execute
End With

End Sub
```

Updating Values

The *OddToEven* and *EvenToOdd* procedures that follow update the data source values of *Column1* using the *Command* object. Make sure that *MyTable* has row values before running the procedures in this section. If *MyTable* does not have row values, invoke both the *InsertRecords* procedure and the *CallInsert-ARecord* procedure.

Notice from the *InsertRecords* procedure that the *Column1* values alternate between odd and even numbers. The first row has the value 1 in *Column1*, and the second row has the value 4 in *Column1*. The rows of *Column1* continue to alternate between odd and even values throughout *MyTable*. The procedures in this next code sample use this information to manage the contents of the table.

```
Sub OddToEven()
Dim cmd1 As ADODB.Command
Dim intRowsChanged As Integer

Set cmd1 = New ADODB.Command

With cmd1
    .ActiveConnection = CurrentProject.Connection
    .CommandText = "UPDATE MyTable SET Column1 = " & _
        "Column1+1 WHERE ((-1*(Column1 Mod 2))=True)"
    .CommandType = adCmdText
    .Execute intRowsChanged
    MsgBox intRowsChanged & " rows were affected.", _
        vbInformation, "Programming Microsoft Access Version 2003"
End With

End Sub

Sub EvenToOdd()
Dim cmd1 As ADODB.Command
Dim intRowsChanged As Integer

Set cmd1 = New ADODB.Command

With cmd1
    .ActiveConnection = CurrentProject.Connection
    .CommandText = "UPDATE MyTable SET Column1 = " & _
        "Column1-1 WHERE ((-1*(Column2 Mod 2))=False)"
    .CommandType = adCmdText
    .Execute intRowsChanged
    MsgBox intRowsChanged & " rows were affected.", _
        vbInformation, "Programming Microsoft Access Version 2003"
End With

End Sub
```

The overall design of these procedures should be familiar to you by now. The most significant difference between these code samples and the ones you saw earlier in the chapter is in the syntax of the SQL statement for the *CommandText* property. In this case, you can easily derive that general syntax from the Access query designer. The *WHERE* clause in the *OddToEven* procedure selects records where the *Column1* value is odd. The *UPDATE* part of the syntax adds 1 to the value to convert it from an odd number to an even number. The statement invoking the *Execute* method takes advantage of the method's first argument to determine the number of rows that the command changes. A simple *MsgBox* function reports the result to the user.

The *EvenToOdd* procedure reverses the effect of running the *OddToEven* procedure. The latter procedure examines the entry in *Column2* to determine whether it should subtract 1 from the value in *Column1*. When the entry in *Column2* is not odd, the SQL statement operates on the value in *Column1*. This restores the entries in *Column1* to their initial values if *EvenToOdd* runs immediately after the *OddToEven* procedure.

The *Errors* Collection

The *Errors* collection lets you trap some but not all errors that occur in an ADO application. The members of this collection let you examine errors returned from an OLE data provider. A single error condition can return multiple errors, each of which causes a new *Error* object to be placed in the *Errors* collection. Some errors cause a program termination; others do not. A new failure automatically clears the *Errors* collection of all previous errors. ADO errors, as opposed to data provider errors, enter the Visual Basic for Applications (VBA) *Err* object rather than the *Errors* collection. The *Errors* collection is most appropriate for handling connection-based errors returned from a remote database through the database's OLE data provider. Because the *Errors* collection belongs to the *Connection* object, you need an explicit *Connection* object to examine errors returned by a data provider.

> **Note**   The members of *ErrorValueEnum* represent a complete list of ADO errors. You can learn more about these errors from the Object Browser.

Error Object Properties

The *Error* objects in the *Errors* collection have six properties to help you gather more information so that you can respond to them with program logic. The *Number* and *Description* properties parallel those for the *Err* object that you've already seen in VBA error traps. The *Error* object's *Number* and *Description* properties complement one another. The *Number* property returns a unique number that identifies an error, and the *Description* property returns a brief string that describes the error. The *NativeError* property offers a provider-specific error code. If you often work with a particular provider, this property might provide useful information about how to resolve an error. The *Source* property names the object or application that originated the error. The *SQLState* property can contain error messages originating from the database server to which you submit your request concerning errors in your SQL statement syntax. Providers can also return *HelpFile* and *HelpContext* properties for error objects. Since these properties work together, I count them as one property. Furthermore, *HelpFile* and *HelpContext* are not always available. A zero-length string for an error's *HelpFile* property signals that the two properties are not available.

Generating and Trapping *Error* and *Err* Objects

The *OpenLookOnlySQLErrors* procedure shown next is an adaptation of the *OpenLookOnly* procedure in Chapter 1 that reveals the impact of the *Connection* object's *Mode* property. This update uses a connection to a computer running SQL Server instead of a local Jet database, and it includes advice in comments on how to create various errors. Implementing these errors and stepping through the procedure will help you understand how the ADO *Errors* collection and the VBA *Err* object complement one another. A read-only setting for the procedure (as it appears here) generates an error when you attempt to update a database. Interestingly, this error does not become part of the *Errors* collection. You can confirm this by stepping through the *OpenLookOnlySQL-Errors* procedure. The *Err* object traps the error instead.

> **Note**   Database connection errors that generate *Error* objects propagate through to the VBA *Err* object. For example, the last member of the *Errors* collection also appears in the *Err* object. This confirms that one or more provider errors propagate to both the *Errors* collection and the VBA *Err* object. When the *Err* object does not provide sufficient context for you to fix an error, use the *Errors* collection for more detail on the cause of the error.

```
Sub OpenLookOnlySQLErrors()
Dim cnn1 As Connection
Dim rst1 As Recordset
Dim errLoop As Error, intInErrors As Integer
On Error GoTo LookOnlyTrap

'This sample assumes you have NorthwindCS on the CabSony1
'SQL Server instance or whatever other instance you use
```

(continued)

```
'in place of it
Set cnn1 = New ADODB.Connection
cnn1.Mode = adModeRead
cnn1.Open "Provider=sqloledb;Data Source=CabSony1;" & _
    "Initial Catalog=NorthwindCS;User Id=sa;Password=password;"

'Spell NorthwindCS incorrectly to force VBA error only
'cnn1.Open "Provider=sqloledb;Data Source=CabSony1;" & _
    "Initial Catalog=NorthwindsCS;User Id=sa;Password=password;"

'Spell sqloledb incorrectly to force VBA and provider error
'cnn1.Open "Provider=sqloledbs;Data Source=CabSony1;" & _
    "Initial Catalog=NorthwindCS;User Id=sa;Password=password;"

'Manually stop SQL Server to force VBA and provider error

'Spell user ID incorrectly to generate VBA and provider errors
'cnn1.Open "Provider=sqloledb;Data Source=CabSony1;" & _
    "Initial Catalog=NorthwindCS;User Id=sas;Password=password;"

Set rst1 = New ADODB.Recordset
rst1.ActiveConnection = cnn1
'Spell rst1 incorrectly to force a 424 VBA error
'Spell cnn1 as cnn to force a 3001 VBA error
'rst.ActiveConnection = cnn1
'rst1.ActiveConnection = cnn

'Spell table name as "Customer" to force VBA and provider
'error that equals -2147217900
rst1.Open "Customers"
'rst1.Open "Customer"

'adModeRead setting for cnn1.Mode causes a VBA error
'of 3251 here; remove cnn1.Mode line to enable updates
rst1.Fields("CustomerID") = "xxxxx"
rst1.Update
Debug.Print rst1.Fields("CustomerID")
rst1.Close

LookOnlyTrap:
'Loop through and print provider errors
For Each errLoop In cnn1.Errors
Debug.Print errLoop.Number, errLoop.Description
Next errLoop

'Print VBA Err object
Debug.Print err.Number, err.Description

End Sub
```

Review the comments throughout the program to see how to generate a selection of errors that creates ADO errors exclusively for the *Err* object or provides errors for both the *Err* object and the *Errors* collection. Commenting the first *Open* method and removing the comment marker from the second use of the *Open* method generates an attempt to link to an invalid database. (The *Initial Catalog* parameter spells the database name incorrectly.) This flaw causes a provider error that populates the *Errors* collection and writes the same error number and message to the VBA *Err* object.

Recordsets, *Records*, *Streams*, and the Web

The ADO *Record* and *Stream* objects are particularly well suited for working with nonrelational data, such as files in directories and content in electronic mail systems. In addition, the OLE DB Provider for Internet Publishing extends these capabilities for accessing and manipulating files and Web folders at a Microsoft FrontPage Web site. These innovations permit Access 2003 database developers to access and manipulate these nontraditional data sources with only minor extensions to the way they work with relational databases. This section examines how to use records, streams, and recordsets to navigate through the files in Web folders at URLs.

> **Note**   A Uniform Resource Locator (URL) designates the location of a resource, such as a text file or a binary file on a local or networked computer. Although the concept of URLs emerged from use of the Internet, it has evolved into a broader method for specifying the location of resources on networked computers.

A *Record* object can point directly at an absolute URL, a combination of a relative and an absolute URL, or the current row in a recordset. (I'll define absolute and relative URLs in a moment.) When a record points at the current row of a recordset, that row is a node in a hierarchical system, which can be the files and folders of a URL.

URLs can have as many as four parts: scheme, server, path, and resource. The scheme specifies a means of reaching a resource. When working on the Internet or an intranet, you will commonly use the http: scheme. The http designation stands for Hypertext Transfer Protocol. The server references the name of the computer hosting the resource; this will often be a Web server. The path is the sequence of directories on the server that leads to the target resource. You can optionally include the resource within the path or specify it separately as the resource component of a URL.

As I hinted at earlier, there are two kinds of URLs: absolute and relative. An absolute URL designates the full location for a resource, from the scheme to the target resource. A relative URL typically will not contain the URL scheme or server, and it divides the URL into two parts, the second of which can vary. The first part of a relative URL is its base part. If all the files your application uses as resources reside in a single folder on a server that you access via the http protocol, your base URL might appear as */pathtomyfolder/*. This is considered a partial absolute URL. The filenames in the target resource can serve as the second, variable portion of the URL. You can isolate more than the resource targets in the variable portion of a URL. For example, if your application draws information from several folders in a Web server's root, you can include these folders in the variable portion of a URL. A system using relative URLs can locate resources by concatenating the base and variable portions of a URL with a standard scheme and server.

You can use URLs as inputs for the *Source* and *ActiveConnection* arguments for records and recordsets. For example, a recordset opened for a relative URL can designate the base portion of the URL for *ActiveConnection* and the variable portion for *Source*. When using absolute or relative URLs to specify what a recordset connects to, use *adCmdTableDirect* as the *Options* argument. Your statement using the recordset *Open* method can appear as follows:

```
rst1.Open <variableURL>, <baseURL>, , , adCmdTableDirect
```

The *Record* object also has an *Open* method, but this object features a tailored set of arguments that targets file access on the Web. In addition to the *Source* and *ActiveConnection* arguments, other specialized arguments facilitate the use of the *Record* object's *Open* method with Web files and folders. For example, the *Record* object's *Open* method includes arguments for creating Web folders when none exist for a URL specified by the *Source* and *ActiveConnection* arguments. Alternatively, you can force a failure if a URL points to a path or resource that does not exist. In addition, other *Open* method arguments let you designate a username and password for gaining access to a secure URL. Furthermore, the *Record* object has a *ParentURL* property that can expose the next highest node in a file hierarchy and a *GetChildren* property that returns a recordset representing the files and subdirectories within the URL for the current record.

A stream is an ADO object that resides in memory. It can store the contents of a saved file read from a disk. You can use a stream to access and manipulate the contents of these saved files with ADO programming. Streams are very flexible. For example, they enable you to work with both text and binary files. You can open a stream on objects such as a record or a binary large object (BLOB) field in a recordset. *Stream* objects offer different methods for reading the contents of binary and text files. Invoke the *Read* method to get at a specified number of bytes from a binary *Stream* object or the *ReadText* method to extract characters from a text *Stream* object. You can read text files in any number of characters you specify, one line at a time, or a whole file at a time. You can also persist streams to files and load them from files. You use Uniform Naming Convention (UNC) format to specify file locations.

Printing Web Folder Contents

A relatively easy way to begin understanding how to process the contents of a URL with records and recordsets is to print the contents of a Web folder. The *PrintFolderContents* procedure shown here demonstrates a straightforward approach to printing the contents of two Web folders. The sample demonstrates how to use the *Record* object to point at a node in the directory for a Web site. It starts by referencing the root directory for the CabSony1 Web server. After printing the contents of that folder, the code reorients its attention to the PMA11 Web site on the CabSony1 server. Then it applies the same technique for printing the contents of the Web site's folder.

```
Sub PrintFolderContents()
Dim rec1 As ADODB.Record
Dim rst1 As ADODB.Recordset

'Instantiate record and recordset objects
Set rec1 = New Record
Set rst1 = New Recordset

'Specify the URL over which the record applies
'Open the record only if it exists
rec1.Open "", "URL=http://CabSony1/", adModeRead, _
    adOpenIfExists Or adCreateCollection

'Return the files and subdirectories
'in rec1 to rst1
Set rst1 = rec1.GetChildren

'Print the first field's values in the recordset; this
'value matches its representation at a node in the file
'directory tree
'These results are for the server's root directory
Debug.Print "Server root directory contents:"
Do Until rst1.EOF
```

(continued)

```
        Debug.Print rst1(0).Value
        rst1.MoveNext
Loop

'Close recordset and record objects for reuse
'with the directory for the PMA11 site
rst1.Close
rec1.Close
rec1.Open "", "URL=http://CabSony1/PMA11", adModeRead, _
    adOpenIfExists Or adCreateCollection
Set rst1 = rec1.GetChildren

'Print the first field's values in the recordset; this
'value matches its representation at a node in the file
'directory tree
'These results are for the PMA11 site's root directory
Debug.Print vbCrLf & String(10, "_") & vbCrLf
Debug.Print "PMA11 site root directory contents:"
Do Until rst1.EOF
    Debug.Print rst1(0).Value
    rst1.MoveNext
Loop

'Clean up objects
rst1.Close
rec1.Close
Set rst1 = Nothing
Set rec1 = Nothing

End Sub
```

The procedure starts by declaring and instantiating both a record and a recordset. These two objects work together to allow the sample to enumerate the contents of a Web folder. After instantiating the *rec1* object, the procedure invokes the *Open* method for the *Recordset* object. This sample references the first four arguments for the *Open* method. (Refer to Access 2003 Help for the complete list of *Open* method arguments; for example, click anywhere in the *Open* keyword and press F1.) The leading *Source* argument is an empty string because the second argument, *ActiveConnection*, fully specifies the Web address for the CabSony1 server. This server resides on the local intranet in my office. (You cannot access it from the Internet.) To run this sample in your office, replace the server name CabSony1 with the name of another Internet Information Services (IIS) 5.x server that is locally available. The third argument, *Mode*, grants read-only permission for the directory node. The fourth argument, *CreateOptions*, uses two intrinsic constants to indicate its objective. When used together, the *adOpenIfExists* constant and the *adCreateCollection* constant open the record to an existing directory node.

After the code opens the record to the directory node, the record will contain information about the node. The next sample you will see explores this information further. At this point, the current sample does not directly expose the files and folders of the current node. Invoke the *GetChildren* method against the *rec1* object to return a recordset with a row for each file and folder at the current node, which is the root directory of the cab2000 Web server in the sample.

The recordset created by the *GetChildren* method contains many fields of information about the individual files and folders at a directory node. You can discover the names and values of these fields as you would for any recordset. For example, the *PrintFolderContents* sample uses a *Do* loop to print the first field value in the current row for the recordset returned by the *GetChildren* method. Each field's value contains the name of one file or folder at the directory node to which the recordset points.

After printing the names for files and folders at the server's root directory, the sample closes the *rec1* and *rst1* objects to prepare for their reuse with another directory. Then the code opens the *rec1* object to the PMA11 directory at the Web server. This is the folder for a FrontPage Web site with the same name (PMA11). The sample then repeats the code for printing the names of the files and folders at a Web site. Figure 2-1 shows the sample output from the procedure. The root directory listing contains files, such as iisstart.asp and localstart.asp, that are typical for any IIS root folder. In addition, the root directory listing includes a folder named PMA11. The PMA11 directory listing contains folders, namely, _private and images, and a file, Default.htm. FrontPage 2003 routinely creates these folders and files for new Web sites.

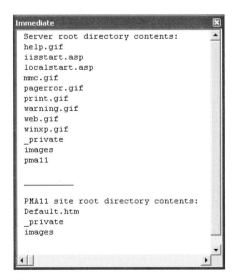

Figure 2-1   Representative output from running the *PrintFolderContents* procedure.

Printing the Properties for Web Folder Contents

Opening either a record or a recordset with a URL designated for the *Source* or *ActiveConnection* argument creates a set of resources that provide metadata about the URL contents. For example, a recordset provides 20 fields of metadata about its URL resource. A record offers 30 fields of metadata about its URL. These fields act as properties for the URL contents. You can use these fields to gather valuable information programmatically about the files and folders within a URL. To enumerate the field names for records and recordsets based on URLs, you can adapt the code from the section "The *Field* Object" at the end of Chapter 1. Use the field properties discussed in that section to discover more information (such as data type and actual size) about the recordset and record resources available for URL file and folder contents.

The *OpenRecordWithRecordsetSource* procedure that follows illustrates how to use selected fields for recordsets and records based on URLs. The procedure has three parts. First, it begins by opening a recordset based on the root directory for the PMA11 Web site. As mentioned previously, this Web site is on my office intranet. In this part of the code, the procedure also prints selected information about the first row in the recordset. Second, the procedure opens a record based on the recordset's first row. Again, the procedure prints selected information about the row, but this time it prints from the record based on the recordset's current row. Third, the procedure moves the current row in the recordset to the second row. Then it opens a record based on this new row, and it prints some information about the row again. After the object and variable declarations, the *OpenRecordWithRecordsetSource* procedure instantiates both recordset and record object references (namely, *rst1* and *rec1*). The next two lines confirm the syntax for opening a recordset based on a URL. The URL points to a FrontPage 2003 Web site that contains the initial setup files and folders after its creation. The recordset contains a single row for each file and folder in the root directory of the PMA11 Web site.

The next block of code completes the first part of the procedure. This block prints selected data about the first row in the recordset using the *rst1* object reference. The first set of output lines, shown in Figure 2-2, presents the output from the procedure's first part. The recordset opens with the default forward-only cursor. While the code shows how to decipher a cursor type, be aware that you cannot override the default setting when working with a URL as an *ActiveConnection*. (I left in the deciphering code because I thought some readers might enjoy examining the approach.) Notice in Figure 2-2 that the recordset for the URL contains 20 fields. The screen shot shows the name of the first field as well as its value, which happens to be the file or folder name in the Web site's root folder.

```
Sub OpenRecordWithRecordsetSource()
Dim rec1 As ADODB.Record
Dim rst1 As ADODB.Recordset
Dim strURL As String
Dim enm1 As Integer
Dim strenm1 As String

'Instantiate recordset and record
Set rst1 = New ADODB.Recordset
Set rec1 = New ADODB.Record

'Open recordset based on folders and files in
'the PMA11 Web site on the CabSony1 Web server
strURL = "URL=http://CabSony1/PMA11"
rst1.Open "", strURL, , , adCmdTableDirect

'Print CursorTypeEnum for the recordset, number of
'fields in recordset, along with name and value of first field
'on the recordset's first row
enm1 = rst1.CursorType
strenm1 = Choose(enm1 + 1, "adOpenForwardOnly", _
    "adOpenKeyset", "adOpenDynamic", "adOpenStatic")
Debug.Print "Selected data for recordset and its first row"
Debug.Print "CursorTypeEnum name is: " & strenm1
Debug.Print "Number of fields in recordset is: " & _
    rst1.Fields.Count
Debug.Print "Name for first field is: " & _
    rst1.Fields(0).Name
Debug.Print "Value for first field is: " & _
    rst1(0).Value & vbCrLf

'Open record based on recordset's current row, and
'print the number of fields in record, along with the
'name and value of the first field in the record
rec1.Open rst1
Debug.Print "Selected data for record based on " & _
    "recordset's first row"
Debug.Print "Number of fields in records is: " & _
    rec1.Fields.Count
Debug.Print "Name for first field is: " & _
    rec1.Fields(0).Name
Debug.Print "Value for first field is: " & _
    rec1(0)
Debug.Print rec1(0) & _
    IIf(rec1("RESOURCE_ISCOLLECTION"), _
    " is a folder.", " is not a folder.")
```

(continued)

```
'Move to the recordset's next row; then close the record
'based on the first row and reopen it for the second row
rst1.MoveNext
rec1.Close
rec1.Open rst1
'Print the value and
'folder status of the first field in the second record
Debug.Print vbCrLf & "Selected data for record based on " & _
    "recordset's second row"
Debug.Print "The first field's value for"
Debug.Print "the recordset's second row: " & rst1(0)
Debug.Print rec1(0) & _
    IIf(rec1("RESOURCE_ISCOLLECTION"), _
    " is a folder.", " is not a folder.")

'Clean up objects
rst1.Close
rec1.Close
Set rst1 = Nothing
Set rec1 = Nothing

End Sub
```

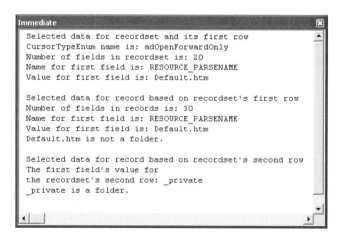

```
Immediate                                                    ☒
    Selected data for recordset and its first row             ▲
    CursorTypeEnum name is: adOpenForwardOnly
    Number of fields in recordset is: 20
    Name for first field is: RESOURCE_PARSENAME
    Value for first field is: Default.htm

    Selected data for record based on recordset's first row
    Number of fields in records is: 30
    Name for first field is: RESOURCE_PARSENAME
    Value for first field is: Default.htm
    Default.htm is not a folder.

    Selected data for record based on recordset's second row
    The first field's value for
    the recordset's second row: _private
    _private is a folder.                                      ▼
◄                                                            ►
```

Figure 2-2   Representative output from running the *OpenRecordWith-RecordsetSource* procedure.

To open a record based on the current row of a recordset, just designate the recordset object reference as the *Source* argument for the record. The first line in the second section of code illustrates how simple this syntax is. You should always move the recordset's current row to the row that you want to serve as the source for the record. After opening a record based on the first record, the procedure prints selected information for the row.

The second block of output shown in Figure 2-2 illustrates the output from the procedure's second part. Since the source for the first and second blocks of code is the same, it is not surprising that the field names and values are identical in both blocks. The output does confirm that there are more fields for the source of a record than for a recordset. In addition, the code for the second part of the procedure demonstrates how to detect whether a row item is a file or a folder. If the *RESOURCE_ISCOLLECTION* field is *True*, the source for the record or the recordset's current row is a folder. Otherwise, the source is a file.

The next block of code in the *OpenRecordWithRecordsetSource* procedure defines the third part of the procedure. This block starts by invoking the *Move-Next* method for *rst1*, which advances the recordset to its second row. You must always position a recordset's current row to the one that you want to serve as the source for a record. The sample then closes the record object, *rec1*, in order to reopen it based on the newly positioned row in the recordset. The third block of output lines seen in Figure 2-2 corresponds to the *Debug.Print* statements that detail information for the record based on the recordset's second row.

I included the preceding code sample as a tutorial on the syntax for extracting resources about the files and folders within a URL. In practice, this is not a procedure that you are likely to write. However, you might want to run a variation of the two procedures shown in the next code sample because they generate a standard report about the files and folders at a URL. The first procedure, *CallListSiteFilesAndFolders*, offers an easy way to print the report for either of two URLs. This procedure presents a message box that asks if a user wants to process the root directory. Depending on the answer, the procedure prepares a recordset via the *GetChildren* method. The recordset can contain information about the files and folders in the http://*CabSony1/* URL or the http://*CabSony1/PMA11* URL. A second procedure, *ListSiteFilesAndFolders*, accepts the recordset generated in the first procedure and prepares a report for the Immediate window with the file names, paths, whether a folder is a root directory of another Web site, and whether the directory entry is a file or a folder.

Figure 2-3 shows the reports for both URLs, one after the other. The first line of each report details the URL name and date of printing. The report prints this information from the first procedure in the code sample. The remaining lines in each report appear from the code sample's second procedure, *ListSite-FilesAndFolders*. For each of the two possible sources, the report prints four columns, which correspond to the fields *RESOURCE_PARSENAME*, *RESOURCE_ABSOLUTEPARSENAME*, *RESOURCE_ISROOT*, and *RESOURCE_IS COLLECTION* in the *rst1* recordset. The parse name and absolute parse name columns return relative and absolute URL information for each entry in a folder. The *RESOURCE_ISROOT* field returns a value of *True* whenever the folder on its row is the root directory of a Web site. For example, notice that the PMA11 row in the second report has a value of *True*. The PMA11 folder is the root directory for the files and folder listing in the first report. The *RESOURCE_ISCOLLECTION* column also returns a *Boolean* value that is *True* whenever the item for a row in the recordset is a folder.

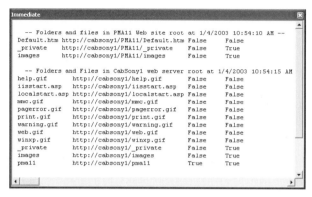

Figure 2-3   Representative output from running the *CallListSiteFiles-AndFolders* and *ListSiteFilesAndFolders* procedures.

```
Sub CallListSiteFilesAndFolders()
Dim strURL As String
Dim rec1 As ADODB.Record
Dim rst1 As ADODB.Recordset
Dim str1 As String

'Instantiate Record and Recordset objects
Set rec1 = New ADODB.Record
Set rst1 = New ADODB.Recordset

'Prompt for print for printing files and
'folders from root or other directory
If MsgBox("Do root directory?", vbYesNo, _
    "Web directory prompt") = vbYes Then
    strURL = "URL=http://CabSony1/"
    Debug.Print vbCrLf & "  -- Folders and Files in " & _
        "CabSony1 web server root at " & Now() & " --"
Else
    strURL = "URL=http://CabSony1/PMA11"
    Debug.Print vbCrLf & "  -- Folders and files in " & _
        "PMA11 Web site root at " & Now() & " --"
End If

'Get recordset with files and folders
'from the target directory
rec1.Open "", strURL, adModeRead, _
    adOpenIfExists Or adCreateCollection
```

```vb
Set rst1 = rec1.GetChildren

'Print results
ListSiteFilesAndFolders rst1

'Assignment to recover from implicit
'connection assignment to non-root directory
str1 = rec1.ActiveConnection.ConnectionString

'Clean up objects
rst1.Close
rec1.Close
Set rst1 = Nothing
Set rec1 = Nothing

End Sub

Sub ListSiteFilesAndFolders(rst1 As ADODB.Recordset)
Dim int1 As Integer
Dim int2 As Integer

'Find length of longest RESOURCE_PARSENAME field value
int1 = FindTheLongest(rst1, "RESOURCE_PARSENAME") + 1
rst1.MoveFirst
int2 = FindTheLongest(rst1, "RESOURCE_ABSOLUTEPARSENAME") + 1

'Move to beginning of recordset, and print for each row in the
'recordset RESOURCE_PARSENAME and RESOURCE_ABSOLUTEPARSENAME
'fields, along with Boolean values indicating whether the row
'item is a root or a collection (folder)
rst1.MoveFirst
Do Until rst1.EOF
    Debug.Print rst1("RESOURCE_PARSENAME") & _
        String(int1 - Len(rst1("RESOURCE_PARSENAME")), " ") & _
        rst1("RESOURCE_ABSOLUTEPARSENAME") & _
        String(int2 - _
            Len(rst1("RESOURCE_ABSOLUTEPARSENAME")), " ") & _
        rst1("RESOURCE_ISROOT"), rst1("RESOURCE_ISCOLLECTION")
    rst1.MoveNext
Loop

End Sub

Function FindTheLongest(rst1 As ADODB.Recordset, _
    FieldIndex As String) As Integer
Dim Length As Integer
```

(continued)

```
'Loop to return longest string in a field.
Do Until rst1.EOF
    Length = Len(rst1.Fields(FieldIndex))
    If Length > FindTheLongest Then
        FindTheLongest = Length
    End If
    rst1.MoveNext
Loop

End Function
```

The second procedure accepts the recordset passed to it by the first procedure. After computing the length of the report's first two columns, the procedure prints the rows of the report with the help of a *Do* loop.

With one minor exception, this code sample covers techniques presented earlier in this section or previously in the book. The exception is the assignment statement for the *str1* variable in the *CallListSiteFilesAndFolders* procedure. The expression to the right of the assignment references the *ActiveConnection* property of the *Record* object used to return the files and folders in a directory. By exposing the connection for the *Record* object in the procedure, the application can release a subdirectory of the root directory. Without this assignment, an attempt to print a report for the root directory fails if it occurs after a report for the subdirectory, PMA11.

Reading Text Files with Streams

This section introduces you to techniques for working with *Stream* objects and text files at a URL. Hypertext Markup Language (HTML) files and files with Active Server Pages (ASP) scripting are text files. You therefore can print them programmatically with a text *Stream* object. You can also selectively read the content of a text file with a *Stream* object. Invoke the *ReadText* method to return the characters in the stream. Because you can base streams on records, streams are a natural tool to use for ADO programming. And because streams can process binary files, you can also use them to manipulate files with graphic formats into and out of databases.

Retrieving Data from Web Files

The following procedure, *ShowStreamForRecord*, illustrates just how easy it is to print the contents of a file that you have in a record. After pointing a record at a file using a URL and instantiating a stream, the procedure sets a couple of stream properties before opening the stream on the record. The *Charset* property assignment is essential for this task. The *Type* property assignment is not strictly necessary here because it assigns the default value. Invoking the stream's *Open* method copies the text for the file to which the record points from disk to memory. The procedure concludes by copying the stream's content to a string variable that it prints.

```
Sub ShowStreamForRecord()
Dim rec1 As ADODB.Record
Dim stm1 As ADODB.Stream
Dim str1 As String

'Instantiate Record and Stream objects
Set rec1 = New ADODB.Record
Set stm1 = New ADODB.Stream

'Open a record for an HTML file
rec1.Open "postinfo.html", "URL=http://CabSony1/"

'Set selected stream properties for printing with an
'ASCII character set, and open the stream on the file
'to which the record points
stm1.Type = adTypeText
stm1.Charset = "ascii"
stm1.Open rec1, adModeRead, adOpenStreamFromRecord

'Read all the lines from the stream to a string variable,
'and print the string variable
str1 = stm1.ReadText
Debug.Print str1

End Sub
```

The next sample uses two procedures to print the metatags of any text file at a Web folder. The first file, *CallPrintMetaTags*, assigns two strings. The first string points at the file for which you want print metatags. The second string indicates the Web folder's URL. This sample works for any text file in a Web folder.

The second file, *PrintMetaTags*, begins by instantiating a record that it opens to the designated file within the Web folder. While the preceding sample reads the whole file into a string variable at one time, this sample reads the text file one line at a time while looking for metatags on each line. It's common practice to embed these metatags between the <head> and </head> tags; the code relies on this style convention to sharpen the focus of its search. If you are using files that follow a different convention, change the code accordingly. In any event, the procedure stops reading lines from the stream after encountering an *EOS* property value. The *EOS* property for a stream is similar to the *EOF* property in a recordset. By extending the logic of this procedure, you can start to devise your own procedures for parsing .xml files.

```
Sub CallPrintMetaTags()
Dim str1 As String
Dim str2 As String

'Use str1 and str2 as the names for the file
'and URL, respectively
str1 = "Default.htm"
str2 = "URL=http://CabSony1/PMA11/"

'Pass arguments to subprocedure
PrintMetaTags str1, str2

End Sub

Sub PrintMetaTags(str1 As String, str2 As String)
Dim rec1 As ADODB.Record
Dim str3 As String
Dim stm1 As ADODB.Stream

'Open record based on current recordset row
Set rec1 = New ADODB.Record
rec1.Open str1, str2

'Instantiate stream, set properties for a reading text
'file, and open it on the file to which the
'record points
Set stm1 = New ADODB.Stream
stm1.Type = adTypeText
stm1.Charset = "ascii"
stm1.Open rec1, adModeRead, adOpenStreamFromRecord

'Print just metatag content
'Exit loop, even if there are no <head> tags
Do
    str3 = stm1.ReadText(adReadLine)
    If (InStr(str3, "</head>")) Then Exit Do
    If stm1.EOS = True Then Exit Do
    If (InStr(str3, "<meta")) Then
        Debug.Print str3
    End If
Loop

'Clean up objects
stm1.Close
```

```
rec1.Close
Set stm1 = Nothing
Set rec1 = Nothing

End Sub
```

Saving To and Recovering From Streams

The *Stream* object is especially convenient for working with all kinds of string data, and this object interoperates nicely with the recordset's *Save* method. Therefore, instead of using the *Save* method to persist a recordset to a file, you can pass it off to a *Stream* object. When you need to represent the contents of a recordset in memory and you wish to have easy access to the individual characters within a recordset, saving a recordset to a stream instead of a file is a natural choice. In addition, data retrieval is faster from a stream in memory than from a recordset or a file on disk.

The syntax of the *Save* method makes it easy to save a recordset to a stream in memory instead of to a file on a disk. When you save the file in XML format, the stream is a sequence of text characters. Therefore, you can parse its contents with the *ReadText* method. The XML generated by the *Save* method is relatively easy to read, but the XML file created by the method contains XML tags, attribute assignments, and schema information. This formatting distracts attention from the data in the file. See Figure 1-6 in Chapter 1, which shows the XML file generated by the *Save* method for a recordset based on the *Shippers* table in the Northwind database. The table contains just three rows of data, but the file is loaded with extra content. In addition, the column values appear in the figure in a different order than in the original table within the Northwind database. There is no formatting argument for the *Save* method that allows you to control the order in which columns appear.

The following procedure for *SaveToAndRecoverFromStream* illustrates the syntax for saving a recordset to a stream as a series of characters, recovering a subset of the characters, and displaying the results in a new column order. The code is purposefully verbose to make it easy to follow. The procedure has five code blocks after the declaration of its variables. The first two of these blocks open a recordset on the *Shippers* table in the Northwind database. The third block demonstrates the syntax for saving a recordset to a stream in memory (*stm1*) instead of to a file on a disk. By designating *adPersistXML* as a *Persist-Format* argument, the statement invoking the *Save* method creates *stm1* as a text *Stream* object. Therefore, the *ReadText* method is suitable for reading characters in the stream.

The format of *stm1* reflects the layout of Figure 1-6 in Chapter 1, except that the contents on one line can spread across multiple lines. For example, the lines beginning with <z:row span two lines in the stream, but only one line in the figure. As a consequence, the code for extracting characters must account for the physical arrangement of the characters on multiple lines as well as the formatting of the XML document saved to a file. You can navigate an XML document by its element tags and attribute assignments. The <z:row character sequence is a tag element denoting the beginning of a tag element containing a row of data. The actual column values for a row appear as attribute assignments, such as *CompanyName='Speedy Express'*.

The fourth code block in *SaveToAndRecoverFromStream* demonstrates one approach to extracting characters and displaying them as column values from the XML document saved as a stream to memory. The code implements four main tasks. First, an outer *Do* loop terminates processing after passing the end of the stream in the loop. Next, the code reads a line or resets two *Boolean* variables that help to track which line is being processed. Third, the code block detects if the line starts a row of data from the *Shippers* table. If yes, then the procedure continues reading and extracting values until done, when the code writes the results to the Immediate window with *ShipperID* as the first column value (instead of the last column value as in Figure 1-6).

```
Sub SaveToAndRecoverFromStream()
Dim stm1 As ADODB.Stream
Dim cnn1 As ADODB.Connection
Dim rst1 As ADODB.Recordset
Dim str1 As String
Dim int1 As Integer
Dim int2 As Integer
Dim bolAlmostDone As Boolean
Dim bolDone As Boolean
Dim strShipperID As String
Dim strCompanyName As String
Dim strPhone As String

'Create the connection.
Set cnn1 = New ADODB.Connection
cnn1.Open "Provider=Microsoft.Jet.OLEDB.4.0;" & _
    "Data Source=\\ccs1\c\Program Files\Microsoft Office\" & _
    "Office11\Samples\Northwind.mdb;"

'Open recordset on Shippers table in the copy of
'Northwind.mdb on a machine named ccs1.
Set rst1 = New ADODB.Recordset
rst1.Open "Shippers", cnn1, adOpenKeyset, _
    adLockOptimistic, adCmdTable

'Persist the recordset to a stream
```

```vb
Set stm1 = New ADODB.Stream
rst1.Save stm1, adPersistXML

'End outer loop when past last character in stream.
'Read a new line or reset to False both Boolean variables.
'If a line starts a row, read until done with row.
'When done, print ShipperID, CompanyName, and Phone.
Do Until stm1.EOS
    If bolAlmostDone = True And bolDone = True Then
        bolAlmostDone = False
        bolDone = False
    Else
        str1 = stm1.ReadText(adReadLine)
    End If
    If InStr(str1, "<z:row") Then
        Do
            If InStr(str1, "CompanyName='") > 0 Then
                int1 = InStr(str1, "CompanyName='") + Len("CompanyName='")
                int2 = InStr(int1, str1, "'")
                strCompanyName = Mid(str1, int1, int2 - int1)
            End If
            If InStr(str1, "Phone='") > 0 Then
                int1 = InStr(str1, "Phone='") + Len("Phone='")
                int2 = InStr(int1, str1, "'")
                strPhone = Mid(str1, int1, int2 - int1)
            End If
            If InStr(str1, "ShipperID='") > 0 Then
                int1 = InStr(str1, "ShipperID='") + Len("ShipperID='")
                int2 = InStr(int1, str1, "'")
                strShipperID = Mid(str1, int1, int2 - int1)
            End If
            str1 = stm1.ReadText(adReadLine)
            If bolAlmostDone = True Then bolDone = True
            If Right(str1, 2) = "/>" Then bolAlmostDone = True
        Loop Until bolAlmostDone And bolDone
        Debug.Print strShipperID, strCompanyName, strPhone
    End If
Loop

'Clean up objects
stm1.Close
rst1.Close
cnn1.Close
Set cnn1 = Nothing
Set rst1 = Nothing
Set stm1 = Nothing

End Sub
```

Figure 2-4 shows the Immediate window results generated by the *SaveToAndRecoverFromStream* procedure. Compare it to the display in Figure 1-6. As you can see, Figure 2-4 represents just the column values for the rows in the *Shippers* table much more compactly than the more verbose contents of Figure 1-6.

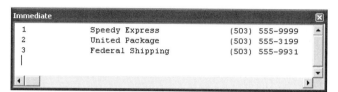

Figure 2-4   Output from running the *SaveToAndRecoverFromStream* procedure.

Summary

This is the second of two chapters that target ADO data access issues for Access developers. The techniques presented in this chapter expand and complement those presented in Chapter 1 by examining *Command* objects and how to use them with *Parameter* objects to support user interaction at run time. Next, you were presented a set of techniques for managing inserts, updates, and deletes based on SQL statements and *Command* objects. Chapter 1 described and demonstrated how to insert, update, and delete table and query rows from a *Recordset* object. Each approach has merit. Using a *Recordset* object has the merit of not requiring any knowledge of the SQL language for a database. The approach presented in this chapter requires a knowledge of the SQL language for a database, but it can generate faster results—especially when working with record sources that have many rows. While Chapter 1 initiated a discussion of recordsets, this chapter revisits the *Recordset* object to examine how it interoperates with the *Record* object. You also gain exposure to *Stream* objects, which were not covered at all in the earlier chapter.

3

The ADOX Library and Tables

Much of Chapter 1 and Chapter 2 focused on a single model of ActiveX Data Objects (ADO): the ADODB model for data access. This chapter examines another of the three ADO models: the ADOX library. This chapter delivers a quick overview of the ADOX library and then provides a diverse series of samples, many of which demonstrate how to program table components, such as columns, keys, and indexes. The samples will lay a firm foundation for your understanding of how to use the ADOX model for table design and table-related schema management, including the enumeration, deletion, and counting of tables and table components in a database. In Chapter 4, we'll explore using the ADOX model with query design and management, while later in Chapter 10 we'll look at ADOX database security features.

The main objective of this chapter is to equip you with the skills needed to start designing tables with the ADOX object model for Jet databases. This chapter assumes you have a working knowledge of table design elements, such as primary and foreign keys. However, the chapter assumes only a novice or intermediate level of experience with the ADOX library, as will be the case for most Microsoft Access developers switching from Access 97 and earlier versions to Access 2003. Even if you have some exposure to ADOX programmatic table design, this chapter will reinforce your existing ADOX skills and prepare you for more advanced programmatic table design. The chapter concludes with a series of samples that illustrate how to populate tables with data after creating them with the ADOX model. The samples focus primarily on gathering data from sources outside the current Access project, including text files.

Overview of the ADOX Model

The ADOX library supports schema and security tasks. You can use this library to manage objects and thereby modify the architecture of your application's design. With the exception of the *Catalog* object, all objects in the ADOX library have matching collections. The catalog is the container of the elements within an Access database file. For example, within a Jet database there is a *Tables* collection of *Table* objects. You use ADOX collections to add and organize new objects in a catalog. Selected objects—such as a table, an index, a key, and a column—have a *Properties* collection. You use these *Properties* collections to manage the behavior of the objects within an application. You manage the *Users* and *Groups* collections to control permissions for other ADOX objects, such as tables, views, and procedures. Figure 3-1 shows an overview of the ADOX library.

> **Note**   You must impose a logon requirement before your application can list the members of the *Users* and *Groups* collections. Any attempt to process the members of these collections without logging on can generate a run-time error. You can impose a logon requirement by setting a password for the Admin user.

The ADOX library is an extension of the ADODB library. The Jet ADO provider fully supports ADOX. You can use the two libraries together to build applications. For example, you can build *Command* objects with the ADODB library and then save them as procedures with the ADOX library. The ADOX library enables you to build tables in ADOX programmatically, as well as to search for tables and their elements in a database. For example, you can determine whether a table with a particular name exists in a database, and you can examine the table's columns to discover their names, data types, and membership in keys and indexes. If a table does not exist, you can add it to the database and populate it with values. Alternatively, you can rename or delete an existing table from a database and replace it with a new one. The ability of the ADOX library to define new data structures and modify existing ones makes it a viable alternative to the SQL Data Definition Language.

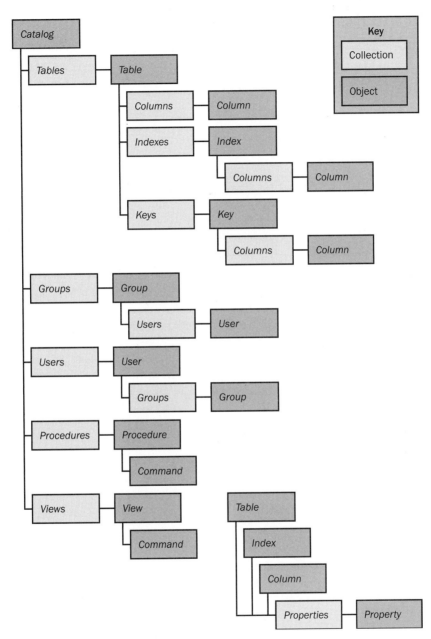

Figure 3-1   The ADOX object library.

The *Catalog* Object

The *Catalog* object is the highest-level container in the ADOX library. Its members define the schema and security model for a database. Its *ActiveConnection* property defines the connection to which the catalog belongs. The *Catalog* object is the database's container for tables, views, procedures, users, and groups within a connection or database. A *Catalog* object does not require a name, because there will be only one such object per database. Nevertheless, your application can have multiple catalogs open concurrently, with each pointing to a different database. Use the *Catalog* object's *Create* method to open a new database and access its catalog.

You need a *Connection* object for the catalog so that ADO knows which catalog to make available. You assign the Connection object to the catalog by setting its *ActiveConnection* property. Once ADO knows which database to reference with a catalog, you have programmatic access to the contents of the catalog. You control access using database and user-level security techniques. While you can reference a table's contents with an ADODB library reference, you must use an ADOX reference to loop through the *Columns* collection of a table. Only the ADOX library has *Tables* and *Columns* collections.

You can use the *Catalog* object to enumerate the members of any of the collections within it. This chapter will demonstrate techniques for enumerating the members of the *Tables* collection. In addition, you'll learn how to loop through the elements of tables, such as columns, keys, and indexes.

The *Table* Object

The *Table* object is a member of the *Tables* collection, which is a member of the *Catalog* object. Each *Table* object has a *Name* property and a *Type* property. A *Table* object can be a standard table within the current database or a linked table based on ODBC and non-ODBC data sources. A *Table* object can even be a view. The *Type* property values also include two system table types: Jet system tables and the Access system tables. Table 3-1 shows these property values.

Table 3-1   ADOX Type Values for the *Table* Object

Type Value	Description
ACCESS TABLE	An Access system table
LINK	A linked table from a non-ODBC data source
PASS-THROUGH	A linked table through an ODBC data source
SYSTEM TABLE	A Jet system table
TABLE	A table developed by or for your application
VIEW	A virtual table from a nonparameterized query that returns rows

You also are likely to find the *ParentCatalog* property particularly useful. This property must be set if you plan to invoke the *AutoIncrement* property for a column. You need the *AutoIncrement* property to create *AutoNumber* data types programmatically with ADOX, but you cannot set the *AutoIncrement* property to *True* unless you first set the *ParentCatalog* property to point at the catalog for a column's parent. (A column's parent is simply the table to which the *Column* object belongs.)

In addition to the *Columns* collection, a *Table* object has a *Keys* collection and an *Indexes* collection. You probably will use the primary key and foreign key property settings frequently. There is also a unique key property for tables that can benefit from a candidate key. Members of the *Indexes* collection can speed up some tasks (such as sorting) and enable others (such as using the *Seek* method to find a subset or records in a recordset).

> **Note**   A candidate key is a subset of column values that uniquely identifies the rows in a table. When a table has more than one candidate key, a database designer can select any one of them to be the table's primary key.

The *Column* Object

A *Columns* collection can belong to tables, keys, and indexes. A *Column* object is roughly comparable to a *Field* object in the ADODB library. A column represents a set of data that refers to a specific characteristic of the entity represented by the table. The *Column* object has several properties:

- **Name**   This property is the name of the column.

- **Type**   This property indicates the data type of the column. All the data within a column is of the same type.

- **Attributes**   This property describes the two possible characteristics of a column: whether the column can contain Nulls and whether it has a fixed length.

- **DefinedSize**   This property designates the maximum size in number of characters for entries within the column.

- **Precision and NumericScale**   These properties are used exclusively for fields with a decimal data type. *Precision* represents the maximum total number of digits used to convey a value in the column. *NumericScale* designates how many digits to the right of the decimal point are available to express a value.

When a *Column* object is an index or a key, other properties are available too, such as *SortOrder* and *RelatedColumn*.

The *Index* Object

The *Index* object sets indexes for a table. It has five properties: *Name*, *IndexNulls*, *PrimaryKey*, *Unique*, and *Clustered*. With the exception of the *Name* property, all these properties will be read-only after you append the index. The *Name* property represents the name of the index. The *PrimaryKey*, *Unique*, and *Clustered* properties are *Boolean* and indicate, respectively, whether the index is a primary key, unique, or clustered. (An index is described as clustered when the physical order of rows on a storage device matches the indexed order of rows.)

> **Note**   Jet databases do not support the clustered property for an index. Therefore, the value of this property will always be *False* for any index in a Jet database.

The *IndexNulls* property can assume one of three different values. Setting this property to *adIndexNullsDisallow*, the default setting, causes the *Index* construction to fail if a *Null* exists in the column's index. Assigning the *adIndexNullsIgnore* constant to *IndexNulls* allows the construction of the index if a *Null* exists in the index but sets the Ignore Nulls box in the Indexes window to Yes. Using *adIndexNullsIgnoreAny* also constructs the index even when the index contains a *Null*, but it sets the Ignore Nulls box in the Indexes window to No. Finally, assigning *adIndexNullsAllow* permits the entry of *Null* key column values without consequence.

The *Key* Object

The *Key* object embodies the behavior of foreign keys in its properties. Of course, the *Name* property is the name of the key. The *RelatedTable* property designates the table to which a foreign key points. The *DeleteRule* and *UpdateRule* properties determine what happens when a primary key is deleted or updated. The *Type* property of the *Key* object represents the type of key and has three options: *adKeyForeign* for foreign keys, *adKeyPrimary* for primary keys, and *adKeyUnique* for unique keys.

Creating a New Database

The *Catalog* object is at the top of the ADOX object model. You can use this object to iterate through the members of its collections or to create a new database whose collections you subsequently populate. The two procedures in the following listing demonstrate the syntax for programmatically creating a new Access database. If an existing file has the same name as the target file for the new database, a run-time error occurs. The second procedure recovers from this failure by deleting the existing file and resuming. You can use the *FileSystemObject* object in the Microsoft Scripting Runtime library to perform a more sophisticated solution, such as renaming an existing file. The Persisting Quarterly Totals to a Text File section in Chapter 1 demonstrates use of the *FileSystemObject,* and the concluding sample in this chapter revisits the topic. After adding a reference to the Microsoft Scripting Runtime library, you can use the Object Browser to explore the methods of the *FileSystemObject.*

The initial procedure performs just two functions. First, it specifies the path and filename for the new Access database file. Second, it passes these as a single variable to the second procedure. The second procedure instantiates a new *Catalog* object and then uses the *Create* method to generate a new Access database file. The *Create* method takes a simple ADO connection string as an argument. The connection string consists of the designation of a data provider (for a Jet 4 database in this sample) and the string variable passed to the procedure with the path and filename for the new database. Because the ADOX model is a special ADO extension for Jet, you should use the ADOX model to create Access database files only.

```
Sub CallMakeAJetDB()
Dim str1 As String

'Specify path and filename for the new database
str1 = "C:\Access11Files\Chapter03\MyNewDB.mdb"
MakeAJetDB str1

End Sub

Sub MakeAJetDB(str1 As String)
On Error GoTo MakeAJetDB_Trap
Dim cat1 As ADOX.Catalog

'Instantiate catalog, and create a new
'database file based on it
Set cat1 = New ADOX.Catalog
cat1.create "Provider=Microsoft.Jet.OLEDB.4.0;" & _
    "Data Source=" & str1
```

(continued)

```
MakeAJetDB_Exit:
'Clean up objects
Set cat1 = Nothing
Exit Sub
MakeAJetDB_Trap:
If Err.Number = -2147217897 Then
'When the file already exists,
'kill the prior version
    Debug.Print str1
    Kill (str1)
    Resume
Else
    Debug.Print Err.Number, Err.Description
    MsgBox "View Immediate window for error diagnostics.", _
        vbInformation, "Programming Microsoft Access 2003"
End If

End Sub
```

Enumerating Tables

The *Tables* collection in the ADOX object model offers an easy route for enumerating tables in an Access database. Table 3-1 shows that the *Tables* collection contains several types of tables. You might prefer to filter out one or more of these table types during a typical enumeration task. Besides the ADOX library, you can also use *AccessObject* objects to enumerate tables. *AccessObject* object types correspond to major elements within an Access database file. The next section in this chapter concentrates on *AccessObject* objects for tables.

Listing All Table Types in a Catalog

The first code sample for enumerating tables lists all the tables within a catalog's *ActiveConnection* property setting. This setting is just a connection string that points at a data source through an ADO data provider. The sample consists of two procedures. The first procedure designates a data source argument for the connection string. The listing that appears here sets the string variable *str1* to the path and filename for the Northwind database. You can designate any Access database file that you prefer to use instead of the Northwind database. For example, this listing contains an alternate file named MyNewDB that is commented out. This file was generated in the preceding sample.

```
Sub CallListTablesRaw()
Dim str1 As String

'Run with either backup copy of Northwind or MyNewDB.mdb
str1 = "C:\Program Files\Microsoft Office\" & _
```

```
        "Office11\Samples\Northwind.mdb"
'str1 = "C:\Access11Files\Chapter03\MyNewDB.mdb"
ListTablesRaw str1

End Sub

Sub ListTablesRaw(str1)
Dim cat1 As ADOX.Catalog
Dim tbl1 As ADOX.Table
Dim str2 As String
Dim str3 As String
Dim mwd As Integer

'Instantiate a catalog, and point it to the target database.
Set cat1 = New ADOX.Catalog
cat1.ActiveConnection = "Provider=Microsoft.Jet.OLEDB.4.0;" & _
    "Data Source=" & str1

'Compute the length of the longest table name in the database.
'Assume minimum length of 5 characters.
mwd = 5
For Each tbl1 In cat1.Tables
    If  Len(tbl1.Name) > mwd Then mwd = Len(tbl1.Name)
Next tbl1
mwd = mwd + 1

'Print a row to the Immediate window containing the name
'and type of member in the catalog's Tables collection
For Each tbl1 In cat1.Tables
    str2 = tbl1.Name
    str3 = String(mwd - Len(str2), " ")
    Debug.Print str2 & str3 & tbl1.Type
Next tbl1

'Clean up objects
Set cat1 = Nothing

End Sub
```

After its declarations, the second procedure instantiates a *Catalog* object and sets its *ActiveConnection* property to the path and filename passed from the first procedure. Next, the second procedure passes through the members of the *Tables* collection to compute the longest table name. This permits the next block of code to space content evenly across the Immediate window for any table name in the catalog. Figure 3-2 shows the output to the Immediate window from the Northwind database. Notice the first column lists many more tables than you normally see in the Database window when you open the

Northwind database. The second column shows each table type. This enumeration lists all the table types in the Northwind database but not all possible table types. Review Table 3-1 for a complete list of the possible table types along with a brief description of each. Those tables with a *TABLE* type specification appear in the Database window by default. Recall from Table 3-1 that views are virtual tables. The term *virtual table* correctly conveys the notion that a view is not actually a table. Instead, it is a SQL statement that returns a rowset, which it can present in a datasheet—just like the rowset contained in a real table.

```
Immediate                                              ☒
Alphabetical List of Products VIEW                     ▲
Categories                    TABLE
Category Sales for 1997       VIEW
Current Product List          VIEW
Customers                     TABLE
Employees                     TABLE
Invoices                      VIEW
MSysAccessObjects             ACCESS TABLE
MSysACEs                      SYSTEM TABLE
MSysCmdbars                   ACCESS TABLE
MSysIMEXColumns               ACCESS TABLE
MSysIMEXSpecs                 ACCESS TABLE
MSysObjects                   SYSTEM TABLE
MSysQueries                   SYSTEM TABLE
MSysRelationships             SYSTEM TABLE
Order Details                 TABLE
Order Details Extended        VIEW
Order Subtotals               VIEW
Orders                        TABLE
Orders Qry                    VIEW
Product Sales for 1997        VIEW
Products                      TABLE
Products Above Average Price  VIEW
Products by Category          VIEW
Quarterly Orders              VIEW
Sales by Category             VIEW
Shippers                      TABLE
Suppliers                     TABLE
Ten Most Expensive Products   VIEW                      ▼
◄                                                   ► 
```

Figure 3-2   Output from the *CallListTablesRaw* and *ListTablesRaw* procedures for a clean backup copy of the Northwind database.

The output of MyNewDB might surprise you. Running *CallListTablesRaw* on MyNewDB generates output even before we populate the database file with any user-defined tables, such as those with a type of *TABLE*, *LINK*, or *PASS-THROUGH*. The listing of tables for the empty MyNewDB database consists of the *SYSTEM TABLE* type. This table category depends on system-generated activity, as opposed to end-user activity or developer activity.

Filtering Table Types Before Enumerating

The preceding sample includes some of the resources that table enumeration can deliver to an application. However, instead of having a broad array of every table type, you can specify the return of a small subset of the total tables by designating the return of just one table type. By implementing this capability, you can gather precise information about the tables in any Access database file on a local area network (LAN) or wide area network (WAN). The reduced number of items associated with a filtered subset makes for a better record source for a combo box or list box. User interfaces work best when they show users only the information that they need to view.

The next pair of procedures implements filtering to return just one type of table. The first procedure has three variables for a user to set. The first is a string variable that designates the path and filename for an Access database file. You must also assign a value to a second string variable that specifies a table type to return from the search target. This next listing sets this second string variable to the *TABLE* type. Recall that this type of table includes just tables in the local database created by or for users. The third variable has a *Boolean* data type. Setting the *Boolean* variable to *True* in the first procedure causes the second procedure to return a list of tables in the current Access database file. A *False Boolean* value points the catalog at the database specified by the first string, *str1*.

```
Sub CallListTablesTypeFilter()
Dim str1 As String
Dim str2 As String
Dim bol1 As Boolean

str1 = "C:\Program Files\Microsoft Office\" & _
    "Office11\Samples\Northwind.mdb"
str2 = "TABLE"
bol1 = False
ListTablesTypeFilter str1, str2, bol1

End Sub


Sub ListTablesTypeFilter(str1 As String, _
    str2 As String, bol1 As Boolean)
Dim cat1 As ADOX.Catalog
Dim tbl1 As ADOX.Table
Dim str3 As String
Dim str4 As String
Dim mwd As Integer

'Instantiate catalog, and connect to CurrentProject
'or another database.
Set cat1 = New ADOX.Catalog
If bol1 = True Then
    Set cat1.ActiveConnection = _
        CurrentProject.Connection
Else
    cat1.ActiveConnection = _
        "Provider=Microsoft.Jet.OLEDB.4.0;" & _
        "Data Source=" & str1
End If
```

(continued)

```
'Create reference to Tables collection for catalog,
'and determine longest table name in the catalog.
mwd = 5
For Each tbl1 In cat1.Tables
    If (tbl1.Type = str2) Then _
        If Len(tbl1.Name) > mwd Then mwd = Len(tbl1.Name)
Next tbl1
mwd = mwd + 1

'Print table names and their type.
For Each tbl1 In cat1.Tables
    If tbl1.Type = str2 Then
        str3 = tbl1.Name
        str4 = String(mwd - Len(str3), " ")
        Debug.Print str3 & str4 & tbl1.Type
    End If
Next tbl1

'Clean up objects.
Set cat1 = Nothing

End Sub
```

The second procedure in this sample employs the design of the previous sample, with one major exception. This exception relates to how the sample develops a setting for the *Catalog* object's *ActiveConnection* property. An *If...Else* statement assigns one of two data sources for the catalog's *ActiveConnection* property. The second procedure chooses a path from the *If...Else* statement based on the *Boolean* value passed to it from the first procedure. By using a *Select...Case* statement, the second procedure could easily enable the selection of any of a wide set of specified sources for the catalog's *ActiveConnection* property.

Printing Data for the Table Details View

The Details view in the Access Database window returns more than just the name of a table and its type. It also returns two other particularly useful bits of information, the table's date of creation and its last modification date. Because the *Table* object exposes *DateCreated* and *DateModified* properties, generating a display like the one in the Database window's Details view is relatively straightforward—just make the width of the *Description* column zero after clicking the Details control on the Database window.

To keep the design of the next code listing simple, the first procedure passes just one argument to the second procedure. This argument is a string parameter that designates the filename and path for the target database file. The argument designates the Northwind_backup.mdb file. In my office, I use the Northwind_backup.mdb file when I want to work with an unedited version of the Northwind database. Recall that I initially referred to the Northwind_backup.mdb file in the "Connecting to Jet Databases" section of Chapter 1. The second procedure has hard-coded filters that return only user-defined tables in the target database. Because this sample generates four columns of output, it prints a row of headers that clarify what each column contains for the members of the tables collection.

```
Sub CallTablesDetail()
Dim str1 As String

str1 = "C:\Program Files\Microsoft Office\" & _
    "Office11\Samples\Northwind_backup.mdb"
TablesDetail str1

End Sub

Sub TablesDetail(str1 As String)
Dim cat1 As ADOX.Catalog
Dim tbl1 As Table
Dim mwd As Byte

'Instantiate a catalog, and point it at the target database.
Set cat1 = New ADOX.Catalog
cat1.ActiveConnection = "Provider=Microsoft.Jet.OLEDB.4.0;" & _
    "Data Source=" & str1

'Compute the length of the longest table name in the database.
'Minimum length of 10 provides for the length of the column header.
mwd = 10
For Each tbl1 In cat1.Tables
    If tbl1.Type = "TABLE" Then _
        If Len(tbl1.Name) > mwd Then mwd = Len(tbl1.Name)
Next tbl1
mwd = mwd + 1

'Print a row of column headers to the Immediate window before
'printing the name, date modified, date created, and type of members
'in the catalog's Tables collection.
Debug.Print "Table Name" & String(mwd - Len("Table Name"), " ") & _
    "Date Modified" & String(22 - Len("Date Modified"), " ") & _
```

(continued)

```
        "Date Created" & String(22 - Len("Date Created"), " ") & "Type"
For Each tbl1 In cat1.Tables
    If tbl1.Type = "TABLE" Then _
        Debug.Print tbl1.Name & String(mwd - Len(tbl1.Name), " ") & _
        tbl1.DateModified & _
        String(22 - Len(tbl1.DateModified), " ") & _
        tbl1.DateCreated & String(22 - Len(tbl1.DateCreated), " ") & _
        tbl1.Type
Next tbl1

'Clean up objects.
Set cat1 = Nothing

End Sub
```

Figure 3-3 shows the Immediate window output from the preceding sample positioned above the Details view from the Database window for the Northwind_backup.mdb Access database file. Notice that the information about Modified and Created dates is the same in both windows. In addition, both listings of tables contain the same table names in the same order.

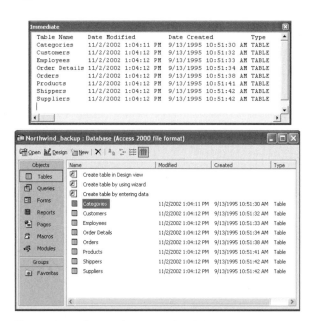

Figure 3-3 Output from the *CallTablesDetail* and *TablesDetail* procedures contrasted with the Details view from the Database window for the same target database.

Using the *AllTables* Collection

The *AllTables* collection can enumerate tables in a style similar to that of the *Tables* collection in the ADOX library. Unlike the *Tables* collection, the *AllTables* collection does not require the creation of a special reference to the ADOX library. This is because the *AllTables* collection is a part of the Microsoft Access 2003 Object Library. Therefore, when you start Access, the *AllTables* collection is available automatically. Access refers to the members of the *AllTables* collection as *AccessObject* objects.

The Access library contains multiple *Allxxx* collections, including *AllTables*, *AllForms*, *AllQueries*, and *AllReports*. The *AccessObject* can refer to a member of any of these collections. You can use the *Type* property to distinguish among the members of these different collections. An *AccessObject* object has the same *Name* property setting as the database object to which it refers. For example, the *AccessObject* object named *Categories* corresponds to the *Categories* table in the Northwind database. You can use an *AccessObject* object to enumerate forms and reports even when they are closed. In addition, you can use an *AccessObject* object to determine whether the database object corresponding to that *AccessObject* object is open.

The similarities between the *Allxxx* collection members and the ADOX collection members should not obscure the fundamental distinctions among them. For example, the *Type* property for an ADOX *Tables* collection member denotes a type of table, such as local or linked. The *Type* property for an *AllTables* collection member identifies a type of *AccessObject* object, such as an object pointing at a table (rather than an object pointing at a form, for example). Therefore, the *AllTables* collection has no built-in feature for filtering tables by their type. In addition, the *AllTables* collection automatically excludes views, while the *Tables* collection includes them. (Recall that a view is a special type of stored query.) Even more critical is the fact that *Allxxx* collections exclusively apply to the current project or a project linked to the current project via a reference. However, the collections in the ADOX library can refer to any Access database file.

Printing Table Details with the *AllTables* Collection

The next sample enumerates the tables in the current project via the *AllTables* collection. Notice that the *AllTables* collection belongs to the *CurrentData* object in the Access *Application* object. The *atc1* variable points to this collection. The program requires an *AccessObject* object to enumerate the members of the collection. The sample references the *AccessObject* object with the *atb1* variable. Since *AccessObject* objects have *DateModified* and *DateCreated* properties, you can create a report similar to the one made for the Details view of tables in an Access Database window. The following listing shows the code to print the name, date last modified, date created, and type of *AccessObject* object for the members of the *AllTables* collection in the *CurrentData* object:

```
Sub TablesDetailFromAllTables()
Dim atb1 As Access.AccessObject
Dim atc1 As Object
Dim mwd As Integer

'Create object reference to AllTables
'in CurrentProject
Set atc1 = Application.CurrentData.AllTables

'Determine name of longest table
mwd = 10
For Each atb1 In atc1
    If Len(atb1.Name) > mwd Then mwd = Len(atb1.Name)
Next atb1
mwd = mwd + 1

'Print header for table detail followed by
'a row for each table
Debug.Print "Table Name" & _
    String(mwd - Len("Table Name"), " ") & _
    "Date Modified" & String(24 - Len("Date Modified"), " ") & _
    "Date Created" & String(28 - Len("Date Created"), " ") & "Type"
For Each atb1 In atc1
    Debug.Print atb1.Name & _
        String(mwd - Len(atb1.Name), " ") & _
        atb1.DateModified, atb1.DateCreated, _
        IIf(atb1.Type = acTable, "Table", "Error")
Next atb1

End Sub
```

The members of the *AllTables* collection include local tables as well as linked tables based on ISAM (indexed sequential access method) and ODBC data sources. In addition, the *AllTables* members include system tables. Because the *AllTables* collection has no *Type* property that distinguishes among these different types of tables, there is no easy way to enumerate the tables of just one type. The output from the preceding code sample appears in Figure 3-4. By comparing this output with the output in Figure 3-2, you can see that the tables in Figure 3-4 include the system, Access, and other kinds of tables.

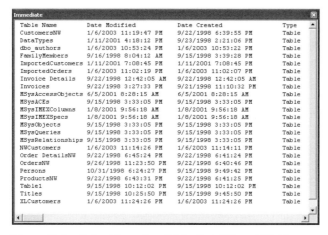

Figure 3-4   Output from the *TablesDetailFromAllTables* procedure. Contrast with the output in Figure 3-2 to appreciate the differences between the *AllTables* collection and the *Tables* collection.

Detecting When Tables Are Open

One of the main benefits of *AccessObject* objects is their ability to determine whether a matching database object with the same name is open or closed. The following sample uses the *atb1* variable that points to an *AccessObject* object to tell whether a table is open (or loaded). If the table is open, the procedure prints the table's name before closing it without saving any changes. The sample repeats this process for each member in the *AllTables* collection.

```
Sub PrintAndCloseOpenTables()
Dim atb1 As Access.AccessObject
Dim atc1 As Object

'Create object reference to AllTables
'in CurrentProject
Set atc1 = Application.CurrentData.AllTables

'Loop through the members of the AllTables collection
Debug.Print "The following tables are open. " & _
    "I will close them without saving changes for you."
For Each atb1 In atc1
    If atb1.IsLoaded = True Then
        Debug.Print atb1.Name
        DoCmd.Close acTable, atb1.Name, acSaveNo
    End If
Next atb1

End Sub
```

Populating Tables with Data

The major reason for creating tables is to populate them with data. One obvious way to satisfy this objective is to open a recordset on a table and then invoke the *AddNew* method for the recordset. Another approach for adding data to a table is to use SQL statements, such as *INSERT INTO*. Other attractive techniques also exist, but they rely on stored queries, which Chapter 4 examines.

This section provides an overview of the resources available for adding data to tables. The initial sample contrasts populating a table with data from a SQL statement and copying data from one table to another via recordset objects. Once you have data in a recordset, transferring it to another recordset is straightforward. Therefore, you can benefit from revisiting the discussion of recordsets in Chapter 1, particularly the review of the recordset *Open* method.

In this section, we'll examine creating read/write links with non-Access data sources, such as Microsoft Excel workbooks and Microsoft SQL Server databases. You can manage links programmatically either through an ADO *Connection* object or by creating a linked table in a Database window with the *DoCmd* object. With either approach, you generally can create read/write or read-only links. However, links to text files through an ISAM driver are always read-only.

Inserting vs. Copying

The first listing in this section contrasts two approaches to populating a table with data. The sample creates fresh copies of the *FamilyMembers* and *FamilyMembers2* tables in the MyNewDB database. Then, it adds records to one table and copies those records to the other table. The code sample reinforces techniques covered earlier in the chapter by applying them to the chores for this application.

The sample consists of two procedures. The first procedure designates three parameters and passes them to the second procedure, which performs the main objectives of the sample. The three parameters designate the path and filename of an Access database file and the names of the two tables within the database that the application uses.

The second procedure enters some data into the *FamilyMembers2* table with an *INSERT INTO* statement. You probably won't populate many databases this way, but the approach does work for small record sources, such as the one in this sample. Next, the sample illustrates the syntax for copying records from one record source (namely, the *FamilyMembers2* table) to another record container (in this instance, the *FamilyMembers* table). This part of the application is both easy to understand and easy to apply. It is also very flexible because you can readily filter a recordset to contain a subset of the original recordset's rows and columns before copying it to a second record container.

> **Note**   SQL statements are widely regarded as a fast way to process record sources because you work with the record source as a whole instead of just its individual records. On the other hand, looping techniques for records with ADO recordsets are easy to understand and grasp. As long as your record sources are not too large (thousands of records as opposed to hundreds of thousands of records or more), you can achieve acceptable performance with ADO looping methods.

The second procedure starts by calling the *DeleteATable* procedure to remove the *FamilyMembers2* table from the MyNewDB database. This can generate an error if the table is not already there, but the application ignores the error with an *On Error* statement that resumes with the next line of code. Next, the procedure creates a fresh copy of the *FamilyMembers2* table. The procedure then repeats this entire process to create a fresh copy of the *FamilyMembers* table as well. After creating the tables, the procedure moves on to populate them with data. First, it runs a series of *INSERT INTO* statements to add records to the *FamilyMembers2* table. Then, it creates two recordsets—one pointed at the *FamilyMembers2* table and the other pointed at the *FamilyMembers* table. With a *Do* loop, the procedure iterates through each of the rows in the *FamilyMembers2* table. For each row in the *FamilyMembers2* table it invokes the *AddNew* method to add a new row to the *FamilyMembers* table. Nested within the *Do* loop is a *For…Each* loop that passes through each field of the *FamilyMembers2* recordset, copying column values from one recordset to the other. After completing the *For…Each* loop, the procedure invokes the *Update* method to transfer the copied values to the *FamilyMembers* table.

```
Sub CallTwoWaysToPopulateTables()
Dim str1 As String
Dim str2 As String
Dim str3 As String

'Assign strings to pass arguments
str1 = "C:\Access11Files\Chapter03\MyNewDB.mdb"
str2 = "FamilyMembers2"
str3 = "FamilyMembers"

'Pass arguments
```
(continued)

```
    TwoWaysToPopulateTables str1, str2, str3

End Sub

Sub TwoWaysToPopulateTables(str1 As String, str2 As String, _
    str3 As String)
Dim cmd1 As ADODB.Command
Dim rst1 As ADODB.Recordset
Dim rst2 As ADODB.Recordset
Dim fld1 As ADODB.Field

'Delete source table (str2), and re-create it
'to make sure you start with a fresh table.
On Error Resume Next
DeleteATable str1, str2
On Error GoTo 0
MakeFamilyMembers2TableInMyNewDB

'Delete destination table (str3), and re-create it
'to make sure you start with a fresh table; placed
'early in the procedure on purpose to allow time
'for automatic refresh to work because Refresh method used
'later in the procedure is not fast enough.
On Error Resume Next
DeleteATable str1, str3
On Error GoTo 0
MakeFamilyMembersTableInMyNewDB

'Add an index for the primary key on FamID.

AddPK

'Populate FamilyMembers2 table with command
'object based on a SQL statement.
Set cmd1 = New ADODB.Command
With cmd1
    .ActiveConnection = "Provider=Microsoft.Jet.OLEDB.4.0;" & _
        "Data Source=" & str1

    .CommandText = "INSERT INTO " & str2 & _
        "(Fname, Lname, Relation) VALUES ('Rick','Dobson','me')"
    .CommandType = adCmdText
    .Execute
    .CommandText = "INSERT INTO " & str2 & _
        "(Fname, Lname, Relation) VALUES ('Virginia','Dobson','wife')"

    .Execute
    .CommandText = "INSERT INTO " & str2 & _
        "(Fname, Lname, Relation) VALUES ('Glen','Hill','son')"
```

```
        .Execute
        .CommandText = "INSERT INTO " & str2 & _
            "(Fname, Lname, Relation) VALUES ('Tony','Hill','son')"

        .Execute
        .CommandText = "INSERT INTO " & str2 & _
            "(Fname, Lname, Relation) VALUES " & _
            "('Charles','Hinkle','father-in-law')"

        .Execute
End With

'Open recordsets pointed at populated FamilyMembers2 table
'and unpopulated FamilyMembers table.
Set rst1 = New ADODB.Recordset
Set rst2 = New ADODB.Recordset
rst1.Open "FamilyMembers2", cmd1.ActiveConnection
rst2.Open "FamilyMembers", cmd1.ActiveConnection, _
    adOpenKeyset, adLockOptimistic, adCmdTable

'Use ADO techniques to populate one table
'based on the values in another.
With rst2
    Do Until rst1.EOF
        .AddNew
            For Each fld1 In rst1.Fields
                .Fields(fld1.Name) = fld1.Value
            Next fld1
        .Update
    rst1.MoveNext
    Loop

End With

'Clean up objects.
Set cmd1 = Nothing
rst1.Close
rst2.Close
Set rst1 = Nothing
Set rst2 = Nothing

End Sub
```

Linking via the *Connection* Object

You can link a database through the ADO *Connection* object and then select a specific record source within the database to populate a table with data. One key advantage of using a *Connection* object as opposed to a classic Access linked table is that the object does not appear in the Database window. This helps to maintain the security and integrity of your database. By using the *Connection* object, you can expose a record source in any mode that your *Connection* object and *Recordset* object settings permit. For example, by using a keyset cursor with a connection to a remote database, you can enable reading and writing to a record source within a database.

The following listing shows how to apply these concepts to an Excel spreadsheet file. The approach demonstrated in the sample uses a connection string to designate an ISAM driver. The inclusion of the Excel 8.0 property specifies the driver for Excel 97 and later workbook files. The source argument for the recordset *Open* method points to a range within the worksheet. In Excel, point to Name on the Insert menu and choose Define to create and update custom ranges that meet your application requirements.

Notice that the *Open* method in the following listing uses cursor settings that make the spreadsheet available for editing. In fact, the code sample appends *xxxx* to the first column in the first row. The procedure also prints to the Immediate window the first two columns of each row in the Customers range within the Customers.xls workbook file.

```
Sub OpenAndWriteToXLDataSource()
Dim cnn1 As New ADODB.Connection
Dim rst1 As Recordset
Dim bol1 As Boolean

'Open and set recordset
cnn1.Open "Provider=Microsoft.Jet.OLEDB.4.0;" & _
    "Data Source=C:\Access11Files\Chapter03\Customers.xls;" & _
    "Extended Properties=Excel 8.0;"
Set rst1 = New ADODB.Recordset
rst1.CursorType = adOpenKeyset
rst1.LockType = adLockOptimistic
rst1.Open "Customers", cnn1, , , adCmdTable

'Open recordset, and print a test record.
Do Until rst1.EOF
    If bol1 = False Then
        rst1(0) = rst1(0) & "xxxx"
        bol1 = True
    End If
    Debug.Print rst1.Fields(0).Value, rst1.Fields(1).Value
    rst1.MoveNext
Loop

'Clean up objects.
```

```
rst1.Close
Set rst1 = Nothing
cnn1.Close
Set cnn1 = Nothing

End Sub
```

> **Note**   The Chapter03.mdb file includes a procedure named *Open-AndRestoreXLDataSource* that removes the trailing *xs* added by the *OpenAndWriteToXLDataSource* procedure.

The next listing shows the same technique, but this time the target data source is a table in a SQL Server database. Because the sample uses the MSDASQL provider, you can use the same basic code with any ODBC data source. The sample references the *Authors* table in the pubs database. The sample uses a DSN (data source name) to abbreviate the connection string for the data source. Abbreviating the connection string using a DSN requires that you previously define a DSN on the workstation with the correct connection string details. One advantage of using a DSN for small and mid-sized organizations is that you can use the ODBC Administrator interface to define the connection string graphically. Some large businesses write custom procedures to automate the installation of DSNs on workstations throughout an organization. Therefore, DSNs are appropriate for solutions in large and small organizations.

Notice the similarity of the following listing's design with that of the preceding one. This similarity occurs despite the fact that one listing references a spreadsheet and the other references a SQL Server database. That's a big advantage of using the ADO approach. This similarity also positions Access as a development environment for analyzing data from heterogeneous data sources.

```
Sub OpenAndWriteToODBCDataSource()
Dim cnn1 As New ADODB.Connection
Dim rst1 As ADODB.Recordset
Dim bol1 As Boolean

'Open ODBC sources with MSDASQL provider and DSN reference.
cnn1.Open "Provider=MSDASQL;DSN=Pubs;"
Set rst1 = New ADODB.Recordset
rst1.CursorType = adOpenKeyset
rst1.LockType = adLockOptimistic
rst1.Open "authors", cnn1, , , adCmdTable
```

(continued)

```
'Open recordset and print a test record.
Do Until rst1.EOF
    If bol1 = False Then
        rst1(1) = rst1(1) & "xxxx"
        bol1 = True
    End If
    Debug.Print rst1.Fields(0).Value, _
        rst1.Fields(2), rst1.Fields(1).Value
    rst1.MoveNext
Loop

'Clean up objects.
rst1.Close
Set rst1 = Nothing
cnn1.Close
Set cnn1 = Nothing

End Sub
```

I restored the *Authors* table from the *Pubs* database with a procedure named *OpenAndRestoreODBCDataSource*. Just as the program for copying the *x*s to a data source had the same structure whether it was an XL file or an ODBC data source, so it is that the program to remove trailing *x*s also has the same structure for both sources. The sole distinction is to specify the connection string properly. You will need to update the connection string and the DSN so that they point at the proper data source. The connection string for the restore program for the sample appears below. Update the *Server* argument so that it points at a server in your environment instead of the CabSony1 server that I used for this book.

```
cnn1.Open "Provider=MSDASQL;DRIVER=SQL Server;" & _
    "SERVER=CabSony1;DATABASE=Pubs;uid=sa;pwd=password;"
```

Linking Using the *DoCmd* Method

You can link or import data sources with the *DoCmd* method. Since many developers and users are familiar with linked tables, this approach will appeal to those who prefer traditional techniques. The next listing includes three procedures. The first one links to a spreadsheet range. The second procedure links to an ODBC data source, and the third creates a linked table that points to a table in another Access database file. If you are an experienced Access developer, chances are you have applied these methods in the past. They appear here as a reminder that a venerable object, such as *DoCmd*, can still serve some important and valuable purposes. If you are just beginning to program Access, you might find extensions to these samples an especially easy way to link data from data sources outside the current Access database file. Access Help provides full explanations of all the arguments. The code presented here complements those explanations with easy-to-follow examples of the commands in action.

> **Note**   If you already have a linked table in your database by the name that the *TransferSpreadsheet* or *TransferDatabase* method specifies, the method will create a linked table with a new name. The new name consists of the table name specified by the method argument followed by a number. So, if your method attempts to create a linked table named *dboAuthors* when a linked table with that name already exists, the method creates a linked table with the name *dboAuthors1*.

```
Sub linkXLCustomers()
Dim rst1 As ADODB.Recordset
Dim bol1 As Boolean

'Use DoCmd to programmatically make the link.
DoCmd.TransferSpreadsheet acLink, acSpreadsheetTypeExcel97, _
    "XLCustomers", "C:\Access11Files\Chapter03\Customers.xls", _
    True, "Customers"

'Open and set recordset
Set rst1 = New ADODB.Recordset
rst1.ActiveConnection = CurrentProject.Connection
rst1.CursorType = adOpenKeyset
rst1.LockType = adLockOptimistic
rst1.Open "XLCustomers", , , , adCmdTable

'Open recordset, and print a test record.
Do Until rst1.EOF
    Debug.Print rst1.Fields(0).Value, rst1.Fields(2)
    rst1.MoveNext
Loop
'Clean up objects.
rst1.Close
set rst1 = Nothing

End Sub
```

(continued)

```
Sub linkODBCAuthors()
Dim rst1 As ADODB.Recordset

'Use DoCmd to programmatically make the link.
DoCmd.TransferDatabase acLink, "ODBC Database", _
    "ODBC;DSN=Pubs;", _
    acTable, "Authors", "dboAuthors"

'Open and set recordset
Set rst1 = New ADODB.Recordset
rst1.ActiveConnection = CurrentProject.Connection
rst1.CursorType = adOpenKeyset
rst1.LockType = adLockOptimistic
rst1.Open "dboAuthors", , , , adCmdTable

'Open recordset, and print a test record.
Do Until rst1.EOF
    Debug.Print rst1.Fields(0).Value, rst1.Fields(2)
    rst1.MoveNext
Loop

'Clean up objects.
rst1.Close
set rst1 = Nothing

End Sub

Sub linkNWCustomers()
Dim rst1 As ADODB.Recordset

'Use DAO to programmatically make the link.
DoCmd.TransferDatabase acLink, "Microsoft Access", _
    "C:\Program Files\Microsoft Office\" & _
 "Office11\Samples\Northwind.mdb", _
    acTable, "Customers", "NWCustomers"

'Open and set recordset
Set rst1 = New ADODB.Recordset
rst1.ActiveConnection = CurrentProject.Connection
rst1.CursorType = adOpenKeyset
rst1.LockType = adLockOptimistic
rst1.Open "NWCustomers", , , , adCmdTable

'Open recordset, and print a test record.
Do Until rst1.EOF
    Debug.Print rst1.Fields(0).Value, rst1.Fields(2)
    rst1.MoveNext
```

```
Loop

'Clean up objects.
rst1.Close
Set rst1 = Nothing

End Sub
```

If you plan to work with linked tables programmatically, you need a way to track and manage the linked tables. Before we examine how to do this, recall that Access can represent linked tables in two ways. Linked tables pointing at ISAM data sources, such as an Excel workbook file or another Access database file, have a table *Type* property of *LINK*. Linked tables pointing at ODBC data sources, such as a SQL Server database, have a table *Type* property of *PASS-THROUGH*. To denote the set of all linked tables, you must specify tables with both *Type* properties.

The following listing can print the names of all linked tables in the Immediate window for any Access database that you specify. The listing specifically refers to the current project's connection, but this is just for convenience (you denote the Access database file in the first procedure). The application passes the database file path and filename to the second procedure, which creates a catalog that points at the database. Then, the procedure loops through the catalog's *Tables* collection, filtering for linked tables that are user defined. When the procedure finds a user-defined linked table of type *LINK* or *PASS-THROUGH*, it prints the table name and type to the Immediate window.

```
Sub CallListLinkedTables()
Dim str1 As String

str1 = CurrentProject.Connection.ConnectionString
ListLinkedTables str1

End Sub

Sub ListLinkedTables(str1 As String)
Dim cat1 As adox.Catalog
Dim tbl1 As adox.Table
Dim str2 As String
Dim mwd As Integer

'Point catalog at target database file.
Set cat1 = New adox.Catalog
cat1.ActiveConnection = "Provider=Microsoft.Jet.OLEDB.4.0;" & _
    "Data Source=" & str1
```

(continued)

```
'Find length of longest table name.
mwd = 1
For Each tbl1 In cat1.Tables
    If (tbl1.Type = "LINK" Or tbl1.Type = "PASS-THROUGH") _
        Then If mwd < Len(tbl1.Name) Then mwd = Len(tbl1.Name)
Next tbl1
mwd = mwd + 1

'Print linked table names.
For Each tbl1 In cat1.Tables
    If (tbl1.Type = "LINK" Or tbl1.Type = "PASS-THROUGH") _
        And Left(tbl1.Name, 4) <> "~TMP" Then
        str2 = String(mwd - Len(tbl1.Name), " ")
        Debug.Print tbl1.Name & str2 & tbl1.Type
    End If
Next tbl1

'Clean up objects.
Set cat1 = Nothing

End Sub
```

A variation of the procedure just shown deletes all linked tables from a designated database. This variation merits special attention because you cannot use a *For…Each* loop to pass through the members of the *Tables* collection if you are going to delete a table within the loop. This is because the *Delete* method forces a reindexing of the objects in a collection each time that you invoke it. This reindexing causes the *Delete* method to miss some items that you meant to delete.

The solution to this problem is to use a *For…Next* loop that steps from the last to the first item in a collection. This approach ensures that the *Delete* method operates on each qualified member of a collection. The following listing illustrates the syntax for this approach:

```
Sub CallDeleteLinkedTables()
Dim str1 As String

str1 = CurrentProject.Connection.ConnectionString
DeleteLinkedTables str1

End Sub

Sub DeleteLinkedTables(str1 As String)
Dim cat1 As ADOX.Catalog
Dim tbl1 As ADOX.Table
Dim int1 As Integer
```

```
'Point catalog at target database file
Set cat1 = New ADOX.Catalog
cat1.ActiveConnection = "Provider=Microsoft.Jet.OLEDB.4.0;" & _
    "Data Source=" & str1

'Loop through ISAM and ODBC linked tables
'to delete all linked tables.
For int1 = cat1.Tables.Count - 1 To 0 Step -1
    Set tbl1 = cat1.Tables(int1)
    If (tbl1.Type = "LINK" Or tbl1.Type = "PASS-THROUGH") _
        And Left(tbl1.Name, 4) <> "~TMP" Then
        cat1.Tables.Delete tbl1.Name
    End If
Next int1

'Refresh Database window to show deleted
'table links.
Application.RefreshDatabaseWindow

'Clean up objects.
Set cat1 = Nothing

End Sub
```

Importing Data from Text Files

One common need that arises when populating a database is to import delimited text data into an Access database. This need is especially common when you are working with legacy mainframe applications or UNIX applications. Developers can use the *TransferText* method of the *DoCmd* object to assist with this task. Because this is one of the method's most straightforward uses, you can designate just three arguments for it: the type of source (such as a delimited text file), the table name for the target within the Access database file, and the path and filename of the text file.

To demonstrate how this process works, you can export a table or two (such as the Northwind *Orders* table) from the Access database to create a suitable source for importing. Figure 3-8 shows the first several rows of the *Orders* table as a text file named Orders.txt. Notice the file has a typical comma delimited-format delimited with quotes around text fields. This is a common format for many text files. The whole file corresponding to the *Orders* table is also provided for you in the companion content for this book. The lines can wrap in Notepad view.

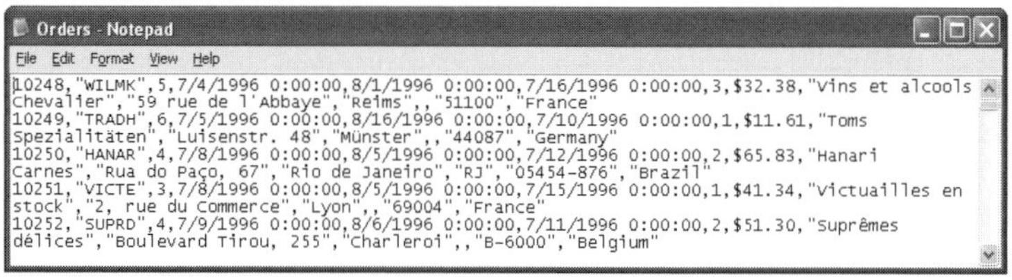

Figure 3-5   The first several rows of the Orders table from the Northwind database in a text file named Orders.txt and viewed in Notepad.

You can readily process text files in alternative formats to the one shown in Figure 3-8. When using these alternate formats, you might find a specification helpful for importing the data from the text file. One especially easy way to develop a specification is by pointing to Get External Data on the File menu in Excel and then choosing Link Tables. Then, select the Text Files file type. Select a file to link, then click the Link button. Click the Advanced button at the lower-left corner of the first Link Text Wizard page. Then, make selections, assign field names, and specify data types in the Link Specification dialog box. Click the Save As button to save your set of specifications with a name that lets you reuse it by designating this name as the second argument in the *TransferText* method. For a well-formed text file, the use of a specification is optional.

Note   The *TransferText* method has arguments that appear to enable the linking and importing of text data. However, you should understand that the text ISAM driver does not permit you to update the text source for a linked file from Access.

The following listing shows the syntax for basic use of the *TransferText* method. Notice that this sample specifies just three arguments. You can designate input and output formats for data other than *acLinkDelim*. That intrinsic constant denotes the input of a delimited text file. The second argument, a specification name, is blank. If you use a specification name, you enclose its name in double quotes. The third argument is the name of the table that contains the text file data. The fourth argument is the path and filename for the text file. An excerpt from this file appears in Figure 3-8.

The sample consists of three procedures. The first procedure manages the overall task and invokes the other two. Initially, the application deletes any previously existing version of the linked table that it will create for Orders.txt. A call to the *DeleteTable* procedure performs this task. Next, the first procedure invokes the *TransferText* method for the *DoCmd* object. The arguments for the method enable it to create a linked table named after the value in *str2*. The *RstForTxt* procedure handles this task and returns a *Recordset* object pointing at the linked table. The first procedure concludes by printing the first five rows from the returned recordset.

```
Sub ImportTxtToMyLinkedUneditedTable()
Dim str1 As String
Dim str2 As String
Dim rst1 As ADODB.Recordset
Dim int1 As Integer

'Assign values to string variables.
str1 = "C:\Access11Files\Chapter03\Orders.txt"
str2 = "MyLinkedTableUnedited"

'Remove previous version of table if it exists
DeleteTable str2

'Make a table and recordset based on imported data.
Set rst1 = RstForTxt(str1, str2)

'Print first five rows from recordset..
For int1 = 1 To 5
    Debug.Print rst1(0), rst1(1), rst1(2), rst1(3)
    rst1.MoveNext
Next int1

End Sub

Function RstForTxt(strInputPathFile As String, _
    strTableName As String) As ADODB.Recordset
Dim rst1 As ADODB.Recordset

'Import a delimited text file to the MyLinkedTable table.
DoCmd.TransferText _
    acLinkDelim, , _
    strTableName, _
    strInputPathFile

'Make a recordset based on imported data.
Set rst1 = New ADODB.Recordset
rst1.Open strTableName, CurrentProject.Connection, , , adCmdTable

'Return recordset for text file
Set RstForTxt = rst1
```

(continued)

```
End Function

Sub DeleteTable(strTableName As String)
Dim aot As AccessObject

'Loop for target table to delete
For Each aot In CurrentData.AllTables
    If aot.Name = strTableName Then _
        DoCmd.DeleteObject acTable, strTableName
Next aot

End Sub
```

By using the *FileSystemObject* to supplement the *TransferText* method, it is possible to edit a text file in a way that is not possible with the *TransferText* method alone. The *ReadAndEditTextFile* procedure demonstrates an approach to the task. This sample is from Module1 in the Chapter03.mdb file. The VBA project for the Access project has a reference to the Microsoft Scripting Runtime library. This reference is necessary for the syntax applied by the sample.

> **Note**   A VBA project in an Access database file refers to any VBA code in standalone modules, class modules, and modules behind forms and reports.

The declaration area at the top of the procedure creates a new instance (*fso*) of the *FileSystemObject*. In turn, the *OpenTextFile* and *CreateTextFile* methods for the instance create read and write versions of *TextStream* objects. Recall from Chapter 2 that a text stream is an in-memory stream of bytes representing text characters. You can read and write to text stream objects by a character, a line, or a whole stream at a time. The *f_txt* text stream contains the characters in the original text file (Orders.txt). The procedure loops through the first five lines in *f_txt* and converts all instances of 1996 to 2000 with the VBA *Replace* function. After converting the values on each of the first five lines, the procedure writes the new converted lines to the *nuf_txt* stream object, which passes the data to Orderswritten.txt because of the *CreateTextFile* method used to instantiate the text stream. After completing the editing, the procedure closes the files and stream objects.

Next, the procedure generates a linked table named *MyLinkedTable-Unedited*. In fact, the procedure generates this linked table twice—once for the initial text file (Orders.txt) and a second time for the edited text file (Orderswritten.txt). Each time the sample generates the linked table, it prints the first five rows to the Immediate window. In essence, the sample edits a text file and shows the changes in an Access module. The sample concludes with the linked table (*MyLinkedTableUnedited*) reflecting the edited values. This result is not possible with the *TransferText* method alone because the ISAM driver that the method uses does not enable editing a text file. By reading the data as a text stream, the sample is able to accomplish what the *TransferText* method cannot accomplish by itself. However, the sample still takes advantage of the *Transfer-Text* method for readily creating a linked table based on a text file.

```
Sub ReadAndEditATextFile()
Dim str1 As String
Dim f_txt As TextStream
Dim nuf_txt As TextStream
Dim fso As New FileSystemObject
Dim rst1 As ADODB.Recordset
Dim str2 As String
Dim str3 As String
Dim int1 As Integer

'Assign the path to the initial text file.
str1 = "C:\Access11Files\Chapter03\Orders.txt"

'Instantiate two TextStream objects:
'one for reading and one for writing.
Set f_txt = fso.OpenTextFile(str1, ForReading)
Set nuf_txt = fso.CreateTextFile(Left(str1, Len(str1) - 4) & "written.txt")

'Edit the first five rows and write out the edited lines.
For int1 = 1 To 5
    str2 = f_txt.ReadLine
    str3 = Replace(str2, "1996", "2000")
    nuf_txt.WriteLine (str3)
Next int1

'Clean up the references to the files.
f_txt.Close
nuf_txt.Close
Set f_txt = Nothing
Set nuf_txt = Nothing
Set fso = Nothing

'Use str2 to name the linked table.
str2 = "MyLinkedTableUnedited"

'Remove previous version of table if it exists
'before creating a new version of the linked table.
DeleteTable str2
```

(continued)

```
Set rst1 = RstForTxt(str1, str2)

'Print first five rows from the recordset based
'on the table.
Debug.Print "Initial, Unedited Values"
For int1 = 1 To 5
    Debug.Print rst1(0), rst1(1), rst1(2), rst1(3)
    rst1.MoveNext
Next int1

'Remove previously created version of the linked table.
DeleteTable str2

'Specify the edited file, Orderswritten.txt, as the
'source for the new linked table and recordset.
str1 = "C:\Access11Files\Chapter03\Orderswritten.txt"
Set rst1 = RstForTxt(str1, str2)

'Print first five rows from recordset.
Debug.Print String(2, vbCrLf) & "Edited Values"
For int1 = 1 To 5
    Debug.Print rst1(0), rst1(1), rst1(2), rst1(3)
    rst1.MoveNext
Next int1

End Sub
```

Summary

This chapter has a main objective and a supporting objective. The main objective is to acquaint you with the ADOX object model. The supporting objective demonstrates how to populate tables with values from values outside of the current Access project. A major reason for creating tables is to populate them with values. These values often are from sources other than the current Access project. In particular, the code samples illustrate how to add values to Access tables in the current project from an Excel workbook, another Access database, an ODBC source, and a text file. In each case, the samples enable your solutions to update the data in Access and to modify the original source as well.

4

Jet SQL, the ADOX Library, and Queries

Tables are the basic building blocks of databases, but queries are where much of the literal and figurative action occurs. Developers use queries to extract information from tables. These queries often serve as the record sources for forms, reports, and Web pages. Therefore, database users typically view database tables filtered through queries.

In addition to this support for forms, reports, and Web pages, queries and languages for expressing them (ADOX and Jet SQL) support three literal kinds of action. First, you can use parameter queries to enable run-time user interaction with an application. Second, you can use queries to insert, delete, and update the records in a record source. Third, you can use Jet SQL, the language for expressing queries for the Jet database engine, to create tables and other database objects. Using Jet SQL to create database objects is an alternative to performing data definition tasks with the ADOX library.

This chapter contains four major sections. The first section examines the most common Jet SQL formulations for returning records from tables. Learning Jet SQL liberates you from depending on the Microsoft Access Query Designer to develop queries, thus allowing you to create solutions faster. Mastering Jet SQL will help you expand the roles that recordsets play in your applications and allow you to secure your applications by not putting all your objects in the Database window.

The second section, "Managing Row-Returning Queries with ADOX," shows you how to create new queries programmatically by adding members to the *Views* and *Procedures* collections. This section also demonstrates how to add or modify database queries with your workstation temporarily disconnected from the database.

"Creating and Running Action Queries with ADOX" takes a close look at the design and use of parameter queries. This final section of the chapter pays special attention to using parameters for inserting, deleting, and updating records from a record source. It also discusses the use of Jet SQL for table definition tasks. By learning how to perform data definition with Jet SQL, you can take advantage of features not supported by the ADOX library or Access user interface, such as controlling the step size and seed value for *AutoNumber* columns.

Jet SQL Syntax for Select Queries

When using ADO, you frequently will want to code a SQL statement when setting properties or calling methods for connections, recordsets, and commands. Therefore, to fully exploit the potential of these ADO and Access objects, you need some knowledge of SQL. This section details the use of Jet SQL for select queries. Because applications frequently rely on select queries to provide record sources for forms, reports, and Web pages, learning the syntax of these queries can be very helpful.

> **Note**   It is common in Access to create queries graphically with the help of the Query Designer. You can then copy the SQL view of a query and paste it into your code. While this technique works, it makes your code-based application development dependent on a graphical tool. If you learn a few basic SQL design principles, however, you will be able to manually code most or all of your queries without the help of the Query Designer.

This section systematically examines nearly all the Jet SQL clauses that assist in returning rows from record sources. By mastering the samples in this section, you will gain two benefits. First, you'll learn to rapidly design the types of select queries that you're most likely to use. Second, you'll gain the confidence needed to easily understand select queries that are not explicitly covered in this section.

Basic Select Queries

Perhaps the best place to start learning SQL is with the most basic statement, which returns all the columns from all the rows of a record source. This record source can be a table, another query, or a combination of two or more tables and queries. In its most basic format, the source for a select query is a table. The statement's general form is:

```
SELECT * FROM <table-name>
```

Traditionally, SQL developers express keywords in uppercase, such as *SELECT* and *FROM*, but Jet SQL and many other SQL dialects do not require you to use uppercase for keywords. The asterisk (*) is a shortcut that denotes all the fields in a record source. The <table-name> placeholder appearing directly after the *FROM* keyword denotes the record source for the query.

While select queries have uses in several ADO contexts, one of their most typical uses is as the source argument for a recordset. This is because select queries return a virtual table that *Recordset* objects are especially equipped to process. For example, recordsets have navigation methods and collections for passing through the data values in the virtual table returned by a select query.

This chapter's first code sample, which follows, demonstrates the most basic SQL select query. It returns all the columns from all the rows of the *Orders* table in the Northwind database. The first procedure, *SelectAllFields*, assigns values to as many as two string variables. The application requires a first string of *strSQL*. This variable contains a Jet SQL statement that can generate a recordset. The second string, *strSrc*, is optional. This second string points at the connection string for a Jet data source. The first procedure concludes by invoking *PreviewRecordsetSource*, the second procedure. The code sample shows only the designation of the required argument. This syntax passes an empty string ("") as the value of the optional second argument, *strSrc*. By removing the comment markers from the assignment statement for *strSrc* at the top of the procedure and inserting the path to the database file you want to use, you can ready *strSrc* for passing to *PreviewRecordsetSource*. Then, when you invoke the second procedure, insert a comma after *strSQL* and type *strSrc*.

> **Note**   The *PreviewRecordsetSource* procedure demonstrates the syntax for specifying an optional argument. The *Optional* keyword must follow any required arguments for a procedure. All arguments after the *Optional* keyword are optional. Therefore, if you have more than one optional argument, the *Optional* keyword only needs to appear before the first one.

The basic design of this first sample will be the standard format I'll use to demonstrate all select query samples in this section of the chapter. In fact, all the subsequent code samples in this section reuse the *PreviewRecordsetSource* procedure, which enumerates all the columns for the first 10 rows of the result set returned by the SQL statement. It organizes and labels the results by record. As we move on to more complex select queries, this procedure will help you understand the effects of alternate SQL syntax formulations. In addition, you can use the second procedure to explore your own design changes to the samples in this chapter.

```
Sub SelectAllFields()
Dim strSrc As String
Dim strSQL As String

'Remove comment markers to test optional source
'strSrc = "Provider=Microsoft.Jet.OLEDB.4.0;" & _
'    "Data Source=C:\Program Files\Microsoft Office\" & _
'    "Office11\Samples\Northwind_backup.mdb"

'Query, selecting all fields from the Orders table
strSQL = "SELECT * FROM Orders"

'Pass arguments to PreviewRecordsetSource, including
'strSQL, and, optionally, strSrc.
PreviewRecordsetSource strSQL

End Sub

Sub PreviewRecordsetSource(strSQL As String, _
    Optional strSrc As String)
Dim rst1 As ADODB.Recordset
Dim fld1 As Field
Dim int1 As Integer

'Assign a default data source if none is designated.
If strSrc = "" Then
    strSrc = "Provider=Microsoft.Jet.OLEDB.4.0;" & _
        "Data Source=C:\Program Files\Microsoft " & _
        "Office\Office11\Samples\Northwind.mdb"
End If

'Open recordset on passed SQL string (strSQL)
'from the designated data source (strSrc)
Set rst1 = New ADODB.Recordset
rst1.ActiveConnection = strSrc
rst1.Open strSQL

'Loop through first 10 records,
'and print all non-OLE object fields to the
'Immediate window.
int1 = 1
Do Until rst1.EOF
    Debug.Print "Output for record: " & int1
    For Each fld1 In rst1.Fields
        If Not (fld1.Type = adLongVarBinary) Then _
```

```
            Debug.Print String(5, " ") & _
                fld1.Name & " = " & fld1.Value
    Next fld1
    rst1.MoveNext
    If int1 >= 10 Then
        Exit Do
    Else
        int1 = int1 + 1
        Debug.Print
    End If
Loop

'Clean up objects.
rst1.Close
Set rst1 = Nothing

End Sub
```

Figure 4-1 presents an excerpt from the output generated by running this code sample. This screen shot of the Immediate window shows the output from the last two records. The Northwind database contains 830 records in its *Orders* table, but the second procedure limits the rows processed to the first 10 rows. However, the procedure does print values for all the columns available on each row. Each row's output starts with a header label. Then, the procedure shows each column's name and value separated by an equal sign (=).

Figure 4-1   Output from the *SelectAllFields* procedure used with the *PreviewRecordsetSource* procedure.

Selecting Fields from Every Record

Instead of displaying all fields from a record source, a select query can return a subset of the columns. To achieve this, you list individual field names within the *SELECT* statement in the order that you want them to appear. The following sample prints values from just two columns in the *Products* table to the Immediate window:

```
Sub SelectSomeFields()
Dim strSrc As String
Dim strSQL As String

'Query returning selected fields from the Products table
strSQL = "SELECT ProductName, Discontinued FROM Products"

PreviewRecordsetSource strSQL

End Sub
```

In general, you should return only the subset of columns that your application needs. This improves performance. If your application needs all the columns in a record source, you can list them in the *SELECT* statement. However, using the asterisk wildcard symbol (*) to indicate that you want all the columns eliminates the need to update your code if a column is added, deleted, or renamed in the table.

Selecting Fields from Some Records

Many applications require a subset of both the columns and rows from an original record source. When you need to filter the rows, add a *WHERE* clause to your select query. This clause should have at least one character, such as a blank space or carriage return, between its start and the *FROM* keyword argument. The *WHERE* clause arguments correspond to the Criteria row of the Query Designer. The following code sample returns rows that represent all currently active inventory items in the *Products* table. The *WHERE* clause excludes selected rows based on their *Discontinued* column values. Whenever the expression in the *WHERE* clause is true, the corresponding row from the original source appears in the result set. This code sample differs from the preceding one, which showed products regardless of whether they were still being sold.

```
Sub SelectSomeFieldsAndRows()
Dim strSrc As String
Dim strSQL As String
Dim bol1 as Boolean

'Query demonstrates use of Boolean variable in WHERE clause
'to return a list of discontinued  products.
```

```
bol1 = False
strSQL = "SELECT ProductName, Discontinued  FROM Products " & _
    "WHERE Discontinued  = " & bol1

PreviewRecordsetSource  strSQL

End Sub
```

WHERE clause arguments frequently have the form *<columnname> <operator> <expression>*, such as *Discontinued = False*. You can also write compound expressions by using the *AND* and *OR* operators. In addition, you can use parentheses to designate the order in which operators compute. Enclose terms and operators in parentheses when you want the operator between them to compute before adjacent operators.

Your expressions for *WHERE* clauses can draw on the full extent of SQL. For example, you can use the *IN* keyword as an operator. Using the *IN* keyword enables you to easily specify values for any column that qualify a record for inclusion in a select query's result set. The following sample shows only customers from the United Kingdom and the United States:

```
Sub SelectWithInClause()
Dim strSrc As String
Dim strSQL As String

'Query demonstrates use of IN keyword to return customers
'from UK and USA
strSQL = "SELECT CompanyName, ContactName, Country FROM Customers " & _
    "WHERE Country IN ('UK', 'USA')"

PreviewRecordsetSource  strSQL

End Sub
```

Writing Criteria Expressions with Wildcards

Wildcard symbols in expressions expand the flexibility with which you can designate rows for inclusion in a select query's result set. However, some traditional wildcard symbols used with the Query Designer need modification before you can use them in SQL *WHERE* clauses with ADO. This can be confusing because it means you cannot simply cut and paste code from the Query Designer's SQL windows into the source argument for a recordset's *Open* method; before the copied code can run, you must translate wildcard symbols for use with ADO. Table 4-1 compares traditional Access wildcard parameters with those suitable for use in SQL *WHERE* clauses with ADO.

Table 4-1 Correspondence of Access and ADO Wildcard Symbols

Access Wildcard	Wildcard Symbol for SQL	Symbol
Expressions in ADO	Meaning	
*	%	Zero or more characters
?	_	Any single character
!	!	Not (used in conjunction with a list or range of characters in brackets); note that this is not compliant with SQL Server

You can use the percent symbol (%) at either the beginning or the end of an expression for a LIKE argument. You can also use % in combination with the other symbols shown in Table 4-1. The pattern-matching code samples, which appear after the % and underscore (_) samples in this section, show how to use the exclamation point (!) and % symbols together. One of the most common uses of the % symbol is for extracting all records with a particular prefix. The following sample shows the syntax for extracting all customers from countries beginning with the letter *U*. In the Access Northwind database, this code would return only customers from the United Kingdom and the United States—the same results you just saw in the *IN* keyword sample. However, adding the % symbol might return more results, depending on the table's contents. If the source table included customers from Uruguay, the *LIKE 'U%'* expression would include these customers in its result set, but the *IN ('UK', 'USA')* expression would not.

```
Sub SelectWithMultiCharacterWildcard()
Dim strSrc As String
Dim strSQL As String

'Use % instead of * with multicharacter wildcard searches.
'Query returns customers from any country beginning with U.
strSQL = "SELECT CompanyName, ContactName, Country FROM Customers " & _
    "WHERE Country LIKE 'U%'"

PreviewRecordsetSource strSQL

End Sub
```

The next sample shows the use of the _ wildcard symbol. This symbol matches any single character in a string. You use the _ symbol to develop more restrictive criteria than the % symbol allows. In this sample, the *TRA_H* argument for the *LIKE* operator extracts records with *CustomerID* column values of TRADH and TRAIH. Any customer record will match the expression, as long as the first three characters for *CustomerID* are TRA and the fifth character is H.

```
Sub SelectWithSingleCharacterWildcard()
Dim strSrc As String
Dim strSQL As String

'Use _ instead of ? with single-character wildcard searches.
'Query returns any customer starting with TRA and ending
'with H (CustomerID is always 5 characters long).
strSQL = "SELECT CustomerID, CompanyName, ContactName, " & _
    "Country FROM Customers " & _
    "WHERE CustomerID LIKE 'TRA_H'"

PreviewRecordsetSource   strSQL

End Sub
```

You can use the wildcard symbols with [ ] delimiters to denote lists and ranges of characters that satisfy a criterion. The expression *[ACEH-M]* indicates a match with the letters A, C, E, or any letter from H through M. The expression *A[A-M]%* in the following sample specifies a *CustomerID* field value with A as its first character and any letter from A through M as its second character, with no restrictions on the remaining *CustomerID* characters. For the *Customers* table, this criterion expression returns a single record whose *CustomerID* field value is ALFKI.

```
Sub SelectWithPatternMatch()
Dim strSrc As String
Dim strSQL As String

'Use traditional [begin-end] syntax for pattern matches.
'Query returns customer IDs beginning with A and containing
'any of the first 13 letters of the alphabet in their
'second character.
strSQL = "SELECT CustomerID, CompanyName, ContactName, " & _
    "Country FROM Customers " & _
    "WHERE CustomerID LIKE 'A[A-M]%'"

PreviewRecordsetSource   strSQL

End Sub
```

The next two samples reinforce the use of [ ] delimiters in *LIKE* arguments while introducing the ! symbol. When used within brackets, the ! symbol serves as a *NOT* operator. The first of these two samples has an argument of *A[N-Z]%*. This argument specifies all records with a customer ID that begins with A and is followed by any letter from N through Z. The expression places no restrictions on the remaining customer ID characters. For the *Customers* table in the Northwind database, this criterion expression returns records with customer ID values of ANATR, ANTON, and AROUT.

The second sample places a ! symbol in front of the range N through Z for the second character. Here, the ! symbol specifies that this character cannot fall in the range of N through Z; in other words, the letters A through M—as well as numbers, punctuation characters, and so forth—satisfy the criterion. This second sample returns a record with a *CustomerID* value of ALFKI. Because of a constraint (or validation rule) for the *CustomerID* field in the *Customers* table, only letters are legitimate characters for *CustomerID* field values.

```
Sub SelectWithPatternMatch2()
Dim strSrc As String
Dim strSQL As String

'Query returns CustomerIDs beginning with A and any of the
'last thirteen letters of the alphabet in their second character
strSQL = "SELECT CustomerID, CompanyName, ContactName, " & _
    "Country FROM Customers " & _
    "WHERE CustomerID LIKE 'A[N-Z]%'"

PreviewRecordsetSource strSQL

End Sub

Sub SelectWithPatternMatch3()
Dim strSrc As String
Dim strSQL As String

'Query returns CustomerIDs beginning with A and not any of the
'last thirteen letters of the alphabet in their second character
strSQL = "SELECT CustomerID, CompanyName, ContactName, " & _
    "Country FROM Customers " & _
    "WHERE CustomerID LIKE 'A[!N-Z]%'"

PreviewRecordsetSource strSQL

End Sub
```

Using SQL Server–Compatible Syntax Switches

As noted in the previous discussion, traditional Access wildcard symbols differ from the wildcard symbols in ADO SQL expressions. An alternate set of Access wildcard symbols is available, however. The traditional symbols are the default symbols in the Query Designer, but the setting can be changed from the wildcard symbols in the first column of Table 4-1 to those in the second column. To change the default setting in Access, choose Options on the Tools menu. Then, select the Tables/Queries tab in the Options dialog box. The first check box in the SQL Server Compatible Syntax (ANSI 92) area on the Tables/Queries tab permits you to invoke the alternate set of wildcard symbols for the current database. An additional check box lets you select the alternate set of wildcard symbols as the default when creating a new database. However, you cannot affect the wildcard setting for other existing databases. Also, changing the wildcard setting can break existing query expressions that use the traditional wildcard symbols in the current database.

The Help display for these controls says they ensure SQL Server compatibility. This is true for the * and ? wildcard symbols. However, when working with a Jet database, the traditional ! symbol applies rather than the caret symbol (∧) that SQL Server uses. For example, the following SQL statement returns one record with a *CustomerID* value of ALFKI when run from a Query Designer SQL window against the Access Northwind database. The same statement run from the SQL Server Query Analyzer against the SQL Server Northwind database returns three records with *CustomerID* field values of ANATR, ANTON, and AROUT because SQL Server interprets an ! as a regular character in the character list instead of as a wildcard.

```
SELECT CustomerID, CompanyName, ContactName, Country
FROM Customers
WHERE CustomerID LIKE 'A[!N-Z]%'
```

By changing the ! to a ∧ in the SQL Server Query Analyzer (as shown in the following code), you can return a single record whose *CustomerID* is ALFKI. However, this same expression returns three rows with *CustomerID* values of ANATR, ANTON, and AROUT when run from the Query Designer SQL window against the Access Northwind database. That's because Access interprets the ∧ character as a regular character instead of as a wildcard.

```
SELECT CustomerID, CompanyName, ContactName, Country
FROM Customers
WHERE CustomerID LIKE 'A[^N-Z]%'
```

Selecting with the *DISTINCT* Keyword

When working with imported data from legacy systems, you will commonly encounter situations where values in fields are repeated. Many applications working with this kind of data will nevertheless require a list of unique column values in a result set. For example, when working with a combo box, you do not want the items in the drop-down box to be repeated, even if they are repeated in the original record source.

The *Order Details* table in the Northwind database repeats values in an important field named *OrderID*. This field occurs once for each line item within an order. The Northwind database contains a separate *Orders* table that has *OrderID* as its primary key; however, legacy databases do not always offer this convenience. Even if the legacy database you're using does have this feature, a copy of it might not be available when you need it.

The next two procedures provide a listing of *OrderID* field values from the *Order Details* table. The procedure named *SelectNotDistinctOrderDetails* defines a basic select query against the *Order Details* table with *OrderID* as the sole field returned. The first 10 rows from this query—see the list on the left in Figure 4-2—repeats *OrderID* whenever an order has more than one line item. For example, in the first three rows *OrderID* is equal to 10248. The *SelectDistinct-OrderDetails* procedure adds the *DISTINCT* keyword to the basic select query syntax. The addition of the *DISTINCT* keyword eliminates duplicates in the result set from the query. The list on the right in Figure 4-2 shows each *OrderID* on just one row. In the following code, note the brackets around *Order Details*. These are necessary because the table name contains an internal blank character.

```
Sub SelectNotDistinctOrderDetails()
Dim strSrc As String
Dim strSQL As String

'Query returns order IDs from line items even if they repeat
strSQL = "SELECT OrderID FROM [Order Details] "

PreviewRecordsetSource  strSQL

End Sub

Sub SelectDistinctOrderDetails()
Dim strSrc As String
Dim strSQL As String

'Query returns unique order IDs from table of order line
```

```
'items (Order Details)
strSQL = "SELECT DISTINCT OrderID FROM [Order Details] "

PreviewRecordsetSource  strSQL

End Sub
```

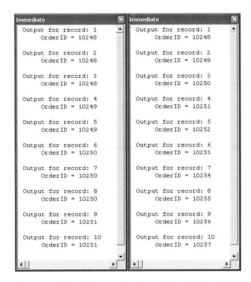

Figure 4-2   The output on the left comes from the *SelectNotDistinct-OrderDetails* procedure. The output on the right without repeated values is produced by the *SelectDistinctOrderDetails* procedure.

The *DISTINCT* keyword is a predicate for a *SELECT* statement in SQL. As you can see, it modifies the behavior of the *SELECT* keyword. Jet SQL supports other predicates that you might find useful, including *TOP*, *DISTINCTROW*, and *ALL*. Access Help for Jet SQL contains discussions and samples of these predicate terms. Table 4-2 lists the *SELECT* keyword predicates and brief descriptions of their behavior.

Table 4-2   Jet SQL SELECT Keyword Predicates

Predicate	Behavior
ALL	Directs *SELECT* to return all the rows in a result set without any filtering. This is the default *SELECT* behavior.
DISTINCT	Corresponds to the *Unique Values* property of an Access query. *DISTINCT* filters out rows from the final result set that have duplicate field values. You cannot update result set rows directly through the query.

(continued)

Table 4-2 **Jet SQL SELECT Keyword Predicates** *(continued)*

Predicate	Behavior
DISTINCTROW	Corresponds to the *Unique Records* property of an Access query. In most cases, you'll find the *DISTINCT* predicate more suitable for removing duplicates. *DISTINCTROW* is most useful for joins between record sources where the *SELECT* field list does not include at least one column from each table. You can update result set rows directly through the query. (Joins are discussed later in this chapter.)
TOP n [Percent]	Returns the top *n* records or *n* percent of records only, where *n* is an integer value.

Selecting and Ordering with Calculated Fields

A calculated field is a field that your SQL code computes for each row in a record source. The calculation can be for string, date, integer, currency, or floating-point values. A calculated field unites two or more independent column values into a new column within the virtual table that a *SELECT* statement defines.

Use the *ORDER BY* clause in a *SELECT* statement to override the default order of rows in a result set. The *ORDER BY* clause should be the last clause in a select query's SQL statement. The arguments within an *ORDER BY* clause specify on which fields to sort rows in the result set. When you have more than one field on which to sort records, separate them by commas. When you have multiple sort fields, records are sorted according to the order of the field names in the *ORDER BY* clause. The default sort order for individual fields in an *ORDER BY* clause is ascending. You can explicitly specify to sort records in an ascending order by following the column name with a space and the keyword *ASC*. If you want rows to appear in descending order, use the keyword *DESC*.

If you do not designate an *ORDER BY* clause, Jet arranges rows in the order of the primary key. When a select query joins two or more tables, Jet's default order is determined by the primary key of the table that participates on the one-side of a one-to-many relationship at the top-level join in the record source. If no primary key exists, Jet arranges the records in the order of entry.

SQL does not require any special correspondence between the *ORDER BY* clause and calculated fields. However, using calculated fields when ordering the rows of a virtual table can lead to several special issues, which I'll discuss here.

The next sample demonstrates the syntax for combining two columns with string values into a calculated column. The input columns are *FirstName* and *LastName*; they originate from the *Employees* table in the Northwind database. The expression for the calculated field creates a new column by combining the *FirstName* and *LastName* columns with a blank space between them.

```
Sub SelectWithCalculatedField()
Dim strSrc As String
Dim strSQL As String

'A calculated field (Full name) based on text columns
strSQL = "SELECT FirstName & ' ' & LastName AS [Full name], " & _
    "City FROM Employees"

PreviewRecordsetSource  strSQL

End Sub
```

Although the *EmployeeID* field does not appear in the SQL statement in the *SelectWithCalculatedField* procedure, the records appear sorted according to the value of this field because *EmployeeID* is the primary key for the *Employees* table. You can override this default order by appending an *ORDER BY* clause to the SQL statement. You can force a sort on any original field or on a field calculated from within the SQL statement. The following sample sorts the result set. The result set from the next SQL statement shows the calculated *Full name* field sorted by the *LastName* column from the *Employees* table.

```
Sub SelectWithCalculatedFieldAndOrderLastNames()
Dim strSrc As String
Dim strSQL As String

'A calculated field (Full name) based on text columns
'with a sort on an original text column (LastName)
strSQL = "SELECT FirstName & ' ' & LastName AS [Full name], " & _
    "City FROM Employees ORDER BY LastName"

PreviewRecordsetSource  strSQL

End Sub
```

The next sample includes a SQL statement that returns all rows from the *Orders* table with an *OrderDate* field value less than or equal to the last day in 1997. The *ORDER BY* clause sorts the rows, using the most recent date as the first record. This SQL statement shows the syntax for including a date as a criterion. Notice that the date appears within two pound signs (#). Recall that Access represents dates as floating numbers internally. The larger the number's value, the more recent the date. Therefore, you use DESC to sort records with the most recent date appearing first.

```
Sub SelectForDateCriterionAndDescendingOrder()
Dim strSrc As String
Dim strSQL As String
Dim strDate As String
```

(continued)

```
strDate = "#12/31/97#"

'Query returns orders through end of 1997 sorted
'with most recent dates first
strSQL = "SELECT OrderID, OrderDate FROM Orders " & _
    "WHERE OrderDate <= " & strDate & _
    " ORDER BY OrderDate DESC"

PreviewRecordsetSource  strSQL

End Sub
```

The two samples you just saw illustrate how to use the *ORDER BY* clause with columns that already exist in a record source. However, the syntax changes slightly if you use the *ORDER BY* clause with a calculated field. In such an instance, you cannot use the name of the calculated field; instead your SQL statement must restate the expression for the calculated field in the *ORDER BY* field list. The following sample sorts its rows by a calculated field named *Total Revenue*, which is the product of the *UnitPrice* and *Quantity* columns multiplied by 1 minus the value of the *Discount* column. Notice that the *ORDER BY* clause repeats the full expression for the calculated *Total Revenue* field rather than using just the field name, as in the two samples we just looked at. The SQL statement in the next sample uses the *FORMATCURRENCY* function to apply a currency format to a calculated field. Notice that you can designate the number of places that appear after the decimal point. The sample shows *Total Revenue* to the nearest penny for line items in the *Order Details* table.

> **Note**   *Total Revenue* has a data type of *Single* because it relies on a product including *Discount*, which has a data type of *Single*. Multiplying any value by a data type of *Single* creates another value with a data type of *Single* unless Access must promote the data type to a data type of *Double* to represent the outcome correctly.

```
Sub SelectDescendingOnACalculatedField()
Dim strSrc As String
Dim strSQL As String

'Query returns order line items with formatted, calculated
'field (Total Revenue) and sorts in descending order on the
'same field
strSQL = "SELECT OrderID, " & _
    "FORMATCURRENCY(UnitPrice*Quantity*(1-Discount),2) " & _
```

```
        "AS [Total Revenue] FROM [Order Details] " & _
        "ORDER BY UnitPrice*Quantity*(1-Discount) DESC"

    PreviewRecordsetSource  strSQL

End Sub
```

Using Aggregates with *GROUP BY* and *HAVING* Clauses

An aggregated field is a calculated field that computes a result across multiple rows instead of within a single row. In addition, an aggregated field relies on SQL aggregate functions. The obvious SQL functions are *SUM*, *AVG*, and *COUNT*. The other SQL functions an aggregated field might use include those for computing standard deviation and variance, finding minimum or maximum values, and returning the first or last row in a result set.

You will frequently invoke an aggregate function in a SQL statement that includes a *GROUP BY* clause. The *GROUP BY* clause collapses multiple records with the same field values into a single row within the result set. If you specify an aggregate function for a column in the collapsed rows, that function reflects the aggregated field value for the rows that are collapsed. If you use an aggregate function without a *GROUP BY* clause, the function computes its aggregated results across all the records in the recordset; that is, all the records denoted by the arguments of the *FROM* clause.

The following sample demonstrates the use of the *SUM*, *AVG*, and *COUNT* functions to compute aggregated results across all the records in the *Order Details* table. The SQL statement returns a single row with three fields labeled *Total Revenue*, *Total Order Line Items*, and *Avg Revenue/Item*. The *SUM* function aggregates the extended price, *UnitPrice*Quantity*(1-Discount)*, across all line items to generate *Total Revenue*. The *Total Order Line Items* column value reflects the number of line item rows in the *Order Details* table through the application of the *Count* function to *OrderID*. The *Avg Revenue/Item* column value is the average extended price for all line items—again across every row in the *Order Details* table. This last column demonstrates the use of the *AVG* aggregate function.

```
Sub SelectWithAggregatedFunctions()
Dim strSrc As String
Dim strSQL As String

'Selected aggregate function results
strSQL = "SELECT " & _
    "FORMATCURRENCY(SUM(UnitPrice*Quantity*(1-Discount)),2) " & _
    "AS [Total Revenue], " & _
    "COUNT(OrderID) AS [Total Order Line Items], " & _
```

(continued)

```
"FORMATCURRENCY(AVG(UnitPrice*Quantity*(1-Discount)),2) " & _
"AS [Avg Revenue/Item] " & _
"FROM [Order Details]"

PreviewRecordsetSource strSQL

End Sub
```

Many applications require aggregated results across subsets of the records in a record source instead of across the whole recordset. Adding a *GROUP BY* clause to a SQL statement with an aggregate function satisfies this need. You can invoke the *GROUP BY* clause with one or more fields in its list, just as you can with the *ORDER BY* clause. If you have more than one field in the list for a *GROUP BY* clause, the records will group in a nested fashion (the second field nesting within the first field, the third field nesting within the second, and so forth).

The following sample computes the units in stock from the *Products* table of the Northwind database for product groupings defined by whether they have been discontinued and by their category. Figure 4-3 presents an excerpt from the sample's output. The first five records in the result set all represent discontinued products. All the remaining records in the result set (of which the excerpt shows three) denote current products. This ordering of records occurs because the *Discontinued* column appears before *CategoryID* in the *GROUP BY* list. Notice also that the output does not contain output for discontinued items with *CategoryID* values of 3 and 4. This is because the *Products* table has no rows with discontinued products for these categories. Finally, observe that the second record's output has no units in stock. This record appears in the result set because there is a discontinued product with a value of 0 representing the units in stock. The alias for the *UnitsInStock* column provides for a nicer label in the output.

```
Sub SelectGroupBy()
Dim strSrc As String
Dim strSQL As String

'Query returns sum of units in stock by category,
'regardless of whether the product is discontinued
strSQL = "SELECT Discontinued , CategoryID, SUM(UnitsInStock) " & _
    "AS [Units In Stock]" & _
    "FROM Products " & _
    "GROUP BY Discontinued , CategoryID"

PreviewRecordsetSource strSQL

End Sub
```

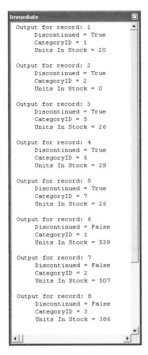

Figure 4-3   Output of the *SelectGroupBy* procedure demonstrates the effect of a *GROUP BY* clause on the result set from a select query's SQL statement.

By adding a *HAVING* clause to a SQL statement with a *GROUP BY* clause, you can filter the result set from the SQL statement. The *HAVING* clause operates like a *WHERE* clause, except that the *HAVING* clause filters results from a *GROUP BY* clause. For example, the *SelectGroupByWithHaving* procedure shown next returns only four records. These four records denote products that are discontinued, because the expression in the *HAVING* clause filters for just these records from the *GROUP BY* clause. In addition, the result set excludes the row containing a value of 0 for units in stock. The second term in the *HAVING* clause filters such records from the result set.

```
Sub SelectGroupByWithHaving()
Dim strSrc As String
Dim strSQL As String

'Query returns sum of units in stock by category
'for discontinued  products only
strSQL = "SELECT Discontinued , CategoryID, SUM(UnitsInStock) " & _
    "AS [Units In Stock]" & _
    "FROM Products " & _
```

(continued)

```
        "GROUP BY Discontinued , CategoryID " & _
        "HAVING Discontinued =True and SUM(UnitsInStock)>0"

    PreviewRecordsetSource  strSQL

    End Sub
```

Selecting with Inner Joins

One of the most powerful features of select queries is their ability to combine two or more tables into one virtual table. An inner join offers one way to accomplish this. This technique permits only the merger of two tables. But you can join two merged tables with a third record source, and you can merge that result with yet another, and so on. These nested inner joins can occur in a single *SELECT* statement. The result set from the select query can include fields from any record sources that it merges.

You can join two record sources on any field or fields with the same data type (other than *Memo* or *OLEObject* data types). Designate the tables to join as arguments of the *FROM* keyword in a select query. Separate the table names with the *INNER JOIN* keywords. Follow the second record source with the *ON* keyword, which signals the subsequent identification of the fields on which to join the record sources. Typically, you merge record sources when the corresponding fields from each record source are equal (called an equijoin), but you can use any equality operator, including <, >, <=, >=, and <>.

The following code sample, the *SelectInnerJoin* procedure, demonstrates the syntax for an inner join between the *Categories* and *Products* tables in the Northwind database. The SQL statement merges the two record sources with an equijoin of the *CategoryID* field in each table. The *SELECT* statement has a field list that extracts the *CategoryName* column from the *Categories* table and the *ProductName* and *Discontinued* columns from the *Products* table. Notice that table names serve as prefixes to field names. Using table names as prefixes is optional, unless two or more tables in the SQL statement contain fields with the same name.

```
Sub SelectInnerJoin()
Dim strSrc As String
Dim strSQL As String

'Query returns products with their category names
strSQL = "SELECT Categories.CategoryName, Products.ProductName, " & _
    "Products.Discontinued  " & _
    "FROM Categories INNER JOIN Products " & _
    "ON Categories.CategoryID = Products.CategoryID"
```

```
PreviewRecordsetSource  strSQL

End Sub
```

The *SelectInnerJoinWithAliases* procedure performs an identical join to the sample you just saw. However, it uses aliases to designate record sources. The letter *c* represents the *Categories* table name, and the letter *p* denotes the *Products* table. The syntax shows how you define the table aliases as arguments for the *FROM* keyword. You can use the aliases in place of record source names both in the *SELECT* statement field list and as prefixes for the fields listed as *ON* keyword arguments for merging the two record sources. The following code sample illustrates this concept:

```
Sub SelectInnerJoinWithAliases()
Dim strSrc As String
Dim strSQL As String

'Query returns products with their category names
strSQL = "SELECT c.CategoryName, p.ProductName, " & _
    "p.Discontinued  " & _
    "FROM Categories c INNER JOIN Products p " & _
    "ON c.CategoryID = p.CategoryID"

PreviewRecordsetSource  strSQL

End Sub
```

The final inner join sample we'll look at demonstrates the integration of several design elements of select queries. This next sample shows the syntax for joining three tables in a single *SELECT* statement. The first join is between the *Customers* and *Orders* tables. The merge occurs on the *CustomerID* field in both tables. The result set from that merger joins with the *Order Details* table on the *OrderID* field. This field exists in the merger of the *Customers* and *Orders* tables as well as in the *Order Details* table.

The SQL statement for this final inner join sample groups records by the *CompanyName* field in the *Customers* table, and it computes the revenue for each customer. The code uses a *SUM* function to aggregate revenue. The *GROUP BY* clause causes *SUM* to aggregate revenue by customer, or more specifically, by the *CompanyName* field. Nesting the *SUM* function within a *FORMATCURRENCY* function makes the aggregated revenue easy to read. The SQL statement's closing *ORDER BY* clause arranges the records so that the company with the largest revenue appears first.

```
Sub SelectThreeTableJoin()
Dim strSrc As String
Dim strSQL As String
```

(continued)

```
'Compute revenue from each customer and return orders by revenue
strSQL = "SELECT c.CompanyName, " & _
    "FORMATCURRENCY(" & _
    "SUM(od.[UnitPrice]*od.[Quantity]*(1-od.[Discount])),2) " & _
    "AS Revenue " & _
    "FROM (Customers c " & _
    "INNER JOIN Orders o ON c.CustomerID = o.CustomerID) " & _
    "INNER JOIN [Order Details] od " & _
    "ON o.OrderID = od.OrderID " & _
    "GROUP BY c.CompanyName " & _
    "ORDER BY " & _
    "SUM(od.[UnitPrice]*od.[Quantity]*(1-od.[Discount])) DESC"

PreviewRecordsetSource  strSQL

End Sub
```

Selecting with Outer Joins and Self Joins

Inner joins merge records from two tables when the records satisfy join criteria, such as having equal values for a designated field. Access permits other kinds of joins as well. For example, you can force all the records from one table into a result set regardless of whether they satisfy a matching criterion. This is called an outer join. You can also merge the records of a table with themselves; SQL calls this a self join. This type of join can be useful when you have two fields in the same table that denote related concepts with the same data type.

> **Note**   A type of join not explicitly considered in this book is the cross join. This type of join, which has limited practical applications, merges all the rows in one record source, such as a table, with all the rows in another record source.

Right Outer Joins

As we've discussed, a join takes place between two record sources. SQL designates these sources as left and right sources depending on their order in the *FROM* argument list. The first record source is the left source, and the second record source is the right. A right outer join forces all records from the second source into the result set even when no match for them exists in the left source. Entries from the left source can enter the result set only when they satisfy a matching criterion with a record from the right source.

Figure 4-4 contrasts three join types: equijoins, left outer joins, and right outer joins. All three joins in the table join the same left and right tables. The left and right tables have two records with matching join field values: A and B. The left table has a join field value, C, that does not match any join field value in the right table. Similarly, the right table has a join field value, D, that does not match any join field value in the left table. The equijoin generates a result set with just two records having join field values of A and B. The left outer join includes three records in the result set whose join field values are A, B, and C. The right outer join also includes three records in its result set, but the join field values for this result are A, B, and D.

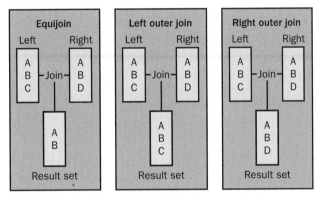

Figure 4-4   A schematic contrasting equijoins, left outer joins, and right outer joins.

In the *SelectRightOuterJoin* procedure below, the SQL statement for a right outer join appears as the assignment for the *strSQL* string. The keywords *RIGHT OUTER JOIN* denote the type of join. Because the *Products* table appears to the right of the keywords, it is the right record source. Therefore, the join unconditionally selects each record from the *Products* table for inclusion in the query's result set. Rows from the *Categories* table enter the select query's result set only when they match join criteria specified by the *ON* keyword. In addition, a *WHERE* clause further filters the result set. The argument for the *WHERE* clause specifies that records must have a Null *CategoryID* value in the *Products* table.

To ensure that there is at least one record from the *Products* table that doesn't have a matching *CategoryID* value in the *Categories* table, the *SelectRightOuterJoin* procedure adds a record to the *Products* table by specifying just its *ProductName*. The procedure uses the recordset *AddNew* method to accomplish the task. If you work with a freshly installed version of the Northwind database, *SelectRightOuterJoin* returns just the newly added record when it invokes the *PreviewRecordsetSource* procedure. After printing the newly added record to the Immediate window with the *PreviewRecordsetSource* procedure, the sample restores the *Products* table by deleting the newly added record.

```
Sub SelectRightOuterJoin()
Dim rst1 As ADODB.Recordset
Dim strSrc As String
Dim strSQL As String

'Create strings for connection (strSrc) and right outer join (strSQL).
'Inclusion of OUTER in RIGHT OUTER JOIN is optional.
'Query returns data on Products rows with a Null CategoryID.
strSrc = "Provider=Microsoft.Jet.OLEDB.4.0;" & _
    "Data Source=C:\Program Files\Microsoft Office\" & _
    "Office11\Samples\Northwind.mdb"

strSQL = "SELECT c.CategoryName, p.ProductName, " & _
    "p.Discontinued  " & _
    "FROM Categories c RIGHT OUTER JOIN Products p " & _
    "ON c.CategoryID = p.CategoryID " & _
    "WHERE IsNull(p.CategoryID)"

'Open recordset on Products table in the connection
'that permits adding a record to the recordset
Set rst1 = New ADODB.Recordset
rst1.ActiveConnection = strSrc
rst1.Open "Products", , adOpenKeyset, adLockOptimistic, adCmdTable

'Add a record with a ProductName of foo, but no CategoryID value.
'Close recordset and set to Nothing to flush the change through.
rst1.AddNew
    rst1("ProductName") = "foo"
rst1.Update
rst1.Close
Set rst1 = Nothing

'Preview right outer join with newly added record.
PreviewRecordsetSource  strSQL

'Reopen the rst1 recordset to find a record
'with a ProductName of foo and delete it.
Set rst1 = New ADODB.Recordset
rst1.ActiveConnection = strSrc
rst1.Open "Products", , adOpenKeyset, adLockOptimistic, adCmdTable
rst1.Find "ProductName = 'foo'"
rst1.Delete

'Clean up objects.
```

```
rst1.Close
Set rst1 = Nothing

End Sub
```

Self Joins

The classic self join sample from the Northwind database finds the managers from the *Employees* table. This table uses two separate columns to represent two related concepts. First, each employee has a unique *EmployeeID* value; this is the table's primary key. Second, all employees except one have a *ReportsTo* column value. This value denotes the *EmployeeID* for an employee's immediate manager. The top-level manager, Andrew Fuller, does not have a value in the *ReportsTo* column because he does not report to another employee in the table.

A handy SQL trick when joining a table with itself is to assign the table two different aliases. The *SelectSelfJoinForManagers* procedure shown next demonstrates the syntax for this. The two aliases for the *Employees* table are *eMgr* and *eInfo*. The procedure's logic uses *eMgr* to refer to managers found in any employee's *ReportsTo* column and *eInfo* to refer to the information for each manager. The arguments for the *ON* keyword specify the joining of these two tables. The sample seeks to generate a list of managers, so it prefixes the *EmployeeID*, *FirstName*, and *LastName* fields in the *Select* field list with *eInfo* because each manager's ID and name are contained in *eInfo*. (If the sample used the ID and name from *eMgr*, it would print the information for the employee who reports to that manager.) And because managers can have more than one direct report, we eliminate identical rows using the *DISTINCT* predicate.

```
Sub SelectSelfJoinForManagers()
Dim strSrc As String
Dim strSQL As String

'Select employees whose EmployeeID is in the ReportsTo column
strSQL = "SELECT DISTINCT eInfo.EmployeeID, eInfo.FirstName, " & _
    "eInfo.LastName " & _
    "FROM Employees AS eMgr INNER JOIN Employees AS eInfo " & _
    "ON eMgr.ReportsTo = eInfo.EmployeeID"

PreviewRecordsetSource  strSQL

End Sub
```

The next sample lists orders placed during 1998 that shipped after the required date. The *Orders* table contains *ShippedDate* and *RequiredDate* columns, making it possible to perform the task with a self join. The *o1* alias refers to the columns associated with the *ShippedDate*; the *o2* alias designates columns associated with the *RequiredDate*.

The arguments for the *ON* keyword include two join criteria. First, the *OrderID* column value must match between the two aliases. Second, the *ShippedDate* column value must be greater than (temporally later than) the *RequiredDate* column value.

The SELECT field list in this instance can use either alias for its prefixes. In addition, you don't need a *DISTINCT* predicate because the *OrderID* requirement in the ON argument removes duplicates. Let's take a look at the code now:

```
Sub SelectSelfJoinForMissed1998Dates()
Dim strSrc As String
Dim strSQL As String

'Select orders with matching OrderIDs where the ShippedDate
'is later than the RequiredDate in 1998
strSQL = "SELECT o1.OrderID, o1.ShippedDate, " & _
    "o2.RequiredDate " & _
    "FROM Orders AS o1 " & _
    "INNER JOIN Orders AS o2 " & _
    "ON (o1.OrderID = o2.OrderID) " & _
    "AND (o1.ShippedDate > o2.RequiredDate)" & _
    "WHERE Year(o1.OrderDate) = 1998"

PreviewRecordsetSource  strSQL

End Sub
```

Selecting with Subqueries

A subquery is a *SELECT* statement that is nested within another *SELECT* statement. The nested query is sometimes called an inner query, and the query that surrounds the inner query is sometimes called an outer query. There are two types of subqueries. First, you can express the subquery so that the inner query computes just once for the outer query. SQL terminology uses the term *subquery* for this scenario. Second, you can write a subquery that computes the inner query for each row in the outer query's result set. SQL terminology refers to this second scenario as a *correlated subquery*.

Often, you can also express a basic subquery either as an inner join or a self join. These alternative formulations can sometimes lead to faster performance. Explore them when you are working with a record source large enough that performance matters substantially.

Expressing a select query with a subquery can be a more natural approach than creating a join to obtain a result set. The following sample shows a query of the Northwind *Employees* table that returns all employees who are managers. The query returns the *EmployeeID*, *FirstName*, and *LastName* column values for any employee whose *EmployeeID* field value is in the *ReportsTo* column. The inner query computes just once for the outer query in this sample. If you are like me, the subquery formulation will be a more natural approach to finding managers in the table than the *SelectSelfJoinForManagers* sample query given earlier, which demonstrated a self join. Unless performance issues are substantial, deciding whether to use a subquery or a join might simply be a matter of personal preference.

```
Sub SelectSubQuery()
Dim strSrc As String
Dim strSQL As String

'Select employees with another employee reporting to them
strSQL = "SELECT DISTINCT EmployeeID, " & _
    "FirstName, LastName " & _
    "FROM Employees " & _
    "WHERE EmployeeID IN (SELECT ReportsTo FROM Employees)"

PreviewRecordsetSource  strSQL

End Sub
```

This next code sample demonstrates the use of a correlated subquery to find the *OrderID* with the largest extended price for each *ProductID*. The outer query specifies the return of *OrderID*, *ProductID*, and the following calculated field for computing extended price: *UnitPrice*Quantity*(1-Discount)*. The query displays extended price with a currency format. For each row, the outer query looks in the inner query to see whether there is a match for its calculated field value. The inner query computes the maximum extended price for a *ProductID* in the *Order Details* table for rows in which the inner query's *ProductID* (*odsub.ProductID*) matches the outer query's *ProductID* (*od.ProductID*). The *WHERE* clause for the inner query causes the code to recompute each row of the outer query.

```
Sub SelectCorrelatedSubQuery()
Dim strSrc As String
Dim strSQL As String

'Find OrderIDs with the maximum price for a ProductID
strSQL = "SELECT od.OrderID, od.ProductID, " & _
    "FORMATCURRENCY(od.UnitPrice*od.Quantity*od.Quantity" & _
    "*(1-od.Discount), 2) AS Price " & _
    "FROM [Order Details] od " & _
    "WHERE od.UnitPrice*od.Quantity*(1-od.Discount) IN " & _
    "(SELECT " & _
    "MAX(odsub.UnitPrice*odsub.Quantity*(1-odsub.Discount)) " & _
    "FROM [Order Details] odsub " & _
    "WHERE od.ProductID = odsub.ProductID)"
```

(continued)

```
PreviewRecordsetSource strSQL

End Sub
```

Selecting with Unions

All the ways to merge record sources we've discussed so far focused on joining two or more sources on one or more common fields. Think of this as a side-by-side linking of record sources. A union query, on the other hand, merges record sources in a very different way. It stacks one record source on top of another. Fields from different record sources participating in a union query must have matching data types for at least those fields involved in the query. If the data types or the data itself among record sources that you want to combine with a union query do not exactly correspond, you might be able to compute calculated fields that are compatible between record sources. For example, the *Customers* table has a *ContactName* column that contains first and last names. The *Employees* table has two separate columns for first and last names. By creating a calculated field to concatenate the *FirstName* and *LastName* columns in the *Employees* table within the union query, you can merge the *Employees* table with the *Customers* table.

The syntax for a union query reflects the design of the record sources that it merges. A union query merges multiple record sources, and it builds its syntax much like a multidecker sandwich. *SELECT* statements layer between *UNION* keywords. Each *SELECT* statement points at one of the record sources for the union query to merge. The field list for the *SELECT* statements must have matching data types.

The *SelectThreeTableUnion* procedure merges three record sources from the Northwind database: the *Customers*, *Suppliers*, and *Employees* tables. The field list for the *SELECT* statements of the *Customers* and *Suppliers* tables each include *CompanyName*, *ContactName*, and *Phone* from their record sources. The *SELECT* statement for the *Employees* table differs from the *Customers* and *Suppliers* tables in several respects. First, it uses a string constant, "*Northwind*", for the *CompanyName* field. Second, it creates a calculated field, called *ContactName*, to match a column from the other two tables. The calculated field combines the *FirstName* and *LastName* column values from the *Employees* table. Third, it uses *HomePhone* as the field to match *Phone* in the preceding *SELECT* statements. Let's take a look at the syntax now:

```
Sub SelectThreeTableUnion()
Dim strSrc As String
Dim strSQL As String

'Concatenate Supplier contact info after employees contact info.
```

```
'Sorts by default on first column.
strSQL = "SELECT CompanyName, ContactName, Phone " & _
    "FROM Customers " & _
    "UNION " & _
    "SELECT CompanyName, ContactName, Phone " & _
    "FROM Suppliers " & _
    "UNION " & _
    "SELECT 'Northwind', " & _
    "FirstName & ' ' & LastName AS ContactName, HomePhone " & _
    "FROM EMPLOYEES"

PreviewRecordsetSource  strSQL

End Sub
```

This procedure offers one considerable advantage over working with the three tables independently. It provides a common interface for all the contact information for customers, suppliers, and employees. But the procedure has at least two weaknesses. First, it does not specify the source for a contact. Second, it sorts records by default order according to the first column. However, your application might require a different sort (for example, sorting by *ContactName* values instead of *CompanyName* values). The *SelectSortedUnion* procedure shows how easy it is to adapt the union query to meet these requirements:

```
Sub SelectSortedUnion()
Dim strSrc As String
Dim strSQL As String

'A single ORDER BY clause for the last SELECT can
'apply to all preceding SELECT statements in the UNION.
'You can add columns (like Source in this example) inside
'UNION queries.
strSQL = "SELECT CompanyName, ContactName, Phone, " & _
    "'Customers' AS Source " & _
    "FROM Customers " & _
    "UNION " & _
    "SELECT CompanyName, ContactName, Phone, " & _
    "'Suppliers' AS Source " & _
    "FROM Suppliers " & _
    "UNION " & _
    "SELECT 'Northwind' AS CompanyName, " & _
    "FirstName & ' ' & LastName AS ContactName, HomePhone, " & _
    "'Employees' AS Source " & _
    "FROM EMPLOYEES " & _
    "ORDER BY ContactName"

PreviewRecordsetSource  strSQL

End Sub
```

Figure 4-5 shows an excerpt from the *SelectSortedUnion* procedure's output. Notice that the output contains four fields for each record; one of these denotes the source for a record. The first five records come from the *Customers* table, but the sixth record comes from the *Employees* table. Also, the records sort according to *ContactName*—not *CompanyName*, which is the default. The sort order reflects the *ORDER BY* clause at the end of the *SelectSortedUnion* procedure.

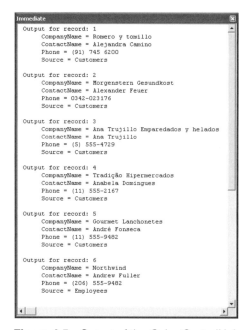

```
Immediate                                              ☒
Output for record: 1
     CompanyName = Romero y tomillo
     ContactName = Alejandra Camino
     Phone = (91) 745 6200
     Source = Customers

Output for record: 2
     CompanyName = Morgenstern Gesundkost
     ContactName = Alexander Feuer
     Phone = 0342-023176
     Source = Customers

Output for record: 3
     CompanyName = Ana Trujillo Emparedados y helados
     ContactName = Ana Trujillo
     Phone = (5) 555-4729
     Source = Customers

Output for record: 4
     CompanyName = Tradição Hipermercados
     ContactName = Anabela Domingues
     Phone = (11) 555-2167
     Source = Customers

Output for record: 5
     CompanyName = Gourmet Lanchonetes
     ContactName = André Fonseca
     Phone = (11) 555-9482
     Source = Customers

Output for record: 6
     CompanyName = Northwind
     ContactName = Andrew Fuller
     Phone = (206) 555-9482
     Source = Employees
```

Figure 4-5   Output of the *SelectSortedUnion* procedure.

Managing Row-Returning Queries with ADOX

Saving, updating, and deleting queries that return rows are some of the most common programmatic database design changes you'll want to implement. Chapter 1 and Chapter 2 examined techniques for running row-returning queries. Earlier in this chapter, the section "Jet SQL Syntax for Select Queries" presented Jet SQL rules for expressing row-returning queries. In this section we'll focus on techniques for programmatically building and managing query objects that return rows. In particular, you'll learn how to use an ADOX *View* object to add or remove a query from a database. Next, we'll discuss designing and running a query that accepts parameters. Parameters are especially important because they permit run-time control over the rows that a query returns. The samples illustrating this topic will increase your understanding of how to use parameters with the ADOX and ADODB libraries. The closing samples in this section demonstrate techniques for adding queries to a database's schema even when you are disconnected from it. This code outlines a process for persisting a database design to disk, modifying the design while you are disconnected from the database, and then updating the original database with the queries you added or changed while disconnected.

Adding and Removing Queries

Adding a query to a database programmatically is a simple process. You start by defining a new view. This merely involves instantiating an ADOX *View* object and assigning its properties. *Command* is among the most important of these properties. To set the view's *Command* property, you can create a local command, assign its properties, and then assign the local command to the view's *Command* property. Creating a local *Command* object enables you to set its *CommandText* property, through which you specify the Jet SQL that defines the query. To finish adding the query to a database, you append the command to the *Views* collection of the catalog for the target database file.

> **Note**   After you append a view to the *Views* collection of a catalog to create a stored query for the current database, the view will not appear in the database file's Database window—although you can enumerate it programmatically. When you append a view (or a procedure) to another database file, the view will be visible in the Database window of the other file—after the window refreshes.

The next sample details the process of adding a view to a database as a stored query. In the first procedure, *CallAddAView*, the sample defines three string variables. The first variable is the path and filename for the Access database file to which you will add a query. The second variable, *strSQL*, is the Jet SQL statement for the query. The third variable, *strQry*, designates a name for the new query.

The *AddAView* procedure contains just three essential steps. First, it instantiates a catalog and points it at the database filename passed to it from *CallAddAView*. Second, it instantiates a command. The command does not require an *ActiveConnection* property setting because we're just using it as a container for a Jet SQL statement represented as a string. The command's *CommandText* property holds the Jet SQL expression for the query. The third step for adding a view to a database's schema as a query is to append the view to the catalog. To do so, you invoke the *Append* method for the catalog's *Views* collection. The

Append method requires two arguments: a string to name the query and a *Command* object that defines the query. If you repeatedly work with a catalog's schema, you might encounter a situation in which you attempt to save a view using a name that already exists. This will generate a run-time error. The following sample addresses this issue by using an error trap that calls the *RemoveAView* procedure, which removes a targeted query from a database. I will discuss this procedure momentarily, after we examine the logic for adding a view. Once the error trap removes the prior version of the query, the *AddAView* procedure resumes the attempt to save the local *Command* object to the database as a query.

```
Sub CallAddAView()
Dim strSrc As String
Dim strSQL As String
Dim strQry As String

'Set strSrc to the path and filename of the database in which
'you want to create a view, strSQL to the SQL string, and strQry
'to the name of the view that you want to add.
strSrc = "C:\Program Files\Microsoft Office\" & _
    "Office11\Samples\Northwind.mdb"
strSQL = "SELECT * FROM Orders"
strQry = "AllOrders"

'Pass arguments to AddAView.
AddAView strSrc, strSQL, strQry

End Sub

Sub AddAView(strSrc As String, strSQL As String, _
    strQry As String)
On Error GoTo AddAView_Trap
Dim cat1 As ADOX.Catalog
Dim cmd1 As ADODB.Command

'Instantiate a catalog for the Access data
'source named in strSrc.
Set cat1 = New ADOX.Catalog
cat1.ActiveConnection = _
    "Provider=Microsoft.Jet.OLEDB.4.0;" & _
    "Data Source=" & strSrc

'Instantiate a command with the SQL statement
'in strSQL.
Set cmd1 = New ADODB.Command
cmd1.CommandText = strSQL
```

```
'Append the view with the name in strQry and the
'CommandText in cmd1.
cat1.Views.Append strQry, cmd1

'Clean up objects.
AddAView_Exit:
Set cmd1 = Nothing
Set cat1 = Nothing
Exit Sub

AddAView_Trap:
If Err.Number = -2147217816 Then
'If view already exists, remove old version and resume.
    RemoveAView strSrc, strQry
    Resume
Else
'Otherwise, print error message and exit gracefully.
    Debug.Print Err.Number, Err.Description
End If

End Sub
```

As you work with a database's design, you will encounter situations in which you need to remove database objects. The preceding sample's error trap shows one scenario in which this need might arise. Normal database maintenance requires you to remove obsolete queries from a database file periodically. Databases load faster and are easier to manage when they contain just the objects that are necessary for an application. To remove a query from a database programmatically, you invoke the *Delete* method. The following sample demonstrates how to perform this process for a view, but the technique is the same for a procedure. You simply invoke the *Delete* method for the *Views* (or *Procedures*) collection of a catalog pointing at the appropriate database. This next sample contains two procedures. The first assigns one string for the path and filename for the Access database file with the obsolete query and a second string for the name of the query to remove.

The second procedure starts by instantiating a catalog and pointing it at the database with the query to remove. If the specified query is not found in the database, a run-time error occurs when the procedure invokes the *Delete* method for the *Views* collection. Instead of implementing a labeled error trap to catch these mistakes, the sample implements an in-line error trap. The code first clears the *Err* object to make sure no entries from prior errors exist. Then, it instructs the VBA processor to respond to an error by resuming at the line after the line that generated the error. When it invokes the *Delete* method for the *Views* collection, if all goes well, the method completes successfully, and the

Err object retains its 0 value. The program then exits with a confirmation message and clears the catalog from memory. If the *Delete* method does not execute successfully, Access updates the *Err* object with the number for the error and the procedure issues a message that the deletion failed.

The *RemoveAView* design is convenient because it provides interactive user feedback through a message box. However, when you want a procedure to run automatically without user interaction, this feedback can actually stall a process. You can handle this issue in any of a number of ways, including by making the feedback available only when a calling procedure explicitly requests it. Here's the syntax for the *CallRemoveAView* and *RemoveAView* procedures:

```
Sub CallRemoveAView()
Dim strSrc As String
Dim strQry As String

'Set strSrc to the path and filename of the database in which
'you want to delete a view and strQry to the name of the view
'that you want to remove.
strSrc = "C:\Access11Files\Samples\Northwind.mdb"
strQry = "AllOrders"

'Pass arguments to RemoveAView.
RemoveAView strSrc, strQry

End Sub

Sub RemoveAView(strSrc As String, strQry As String)
Dim cat1 As ADOX.Catalog
Dim vew1 As ADOX.View
Dim cmd1 As ADODB.Command

'Instantiate a catalog for the Access data
'source named in strSrc.
Set cat1 = New ADOX.Catalog
cat1.ActiveConnection = _
    "Provider=Microsoft.Jet.OLEDB.4.0;" & _
    "Data Source=" & strSrc

'Remove the view named in strQry, and report
'success or failure of attempt in a message box
Err.Clear
On Error Resume Next
cat1.Views.Delete cat1.Views(strQry).Name
If Err <> 0 Then
```

```
        MsgBox "Deletion of view failed.", vbCritical, _
        "Programming Microsoft Access Version 2003"
        Exit Sub
    Else
        MsgBox "Deletion of view succeeded.", vbInformation, _
            "Programming Microsoft Access Version 2003"
    End If
    Set cat1 = Nothing

    End Sub
```

Creating and Using Parameter Queries

With parameters, you can allow users to vary the result set of a query at run time. You add parameter queries through the *Procedures* collection instead of through the *Views* collection. ADOX lets you save a parameter query with or without a *PARAMETERS* declaration. However, keep in mind that the parameter query statement itself is a Jet SQL statement—not an ADOX statement. Omitting the *PARAMETERS* declaration can prevent you from correctly enumerating the members of a query's *Parameters* collection. On the other hand, failing to specify a *PARAMETERS* declaration does *not* stop your application from running the query and supplying parameter values at run time.

The *SelectInClauseParameters* sample demonstrates how to add a parameter query named *TwoParametersIn* to the Northwind database file. The sample starts by defining two strings: *strSrc* for the connection string to the database file, and *strSQL* for the Jet SQL statement defining the parameter query. The procedure actually includes two versions of the Jet SQL statement for the parameter query; the uncommented version does not have a *PARAMETERS* declaration, but the commented version does. Either version will enable you to save the parameter query and run it successfully. If you want to, you can use the version that doesn't contain the *PARAMETERS* declaration and then use ADOX to add a *Parameters* collection to the *Command* object for the query before saving it. This achieves nearly the same result as including a *PARAMETERS* declaration in the Jet SQL statement for the command. The only difference between adding a *Parameters* collection before saving a parameter query and saving the query without the collection is the effect it has on your ability to enumerate the parameters. Refer back to the *EnumerateCommandTextAndParameters* procedure we examined earlier in this chapter to see how to enumerate the *Parameters* collection members.

> **Note** Developers who are more familiar with Access data type names than they are with ADO names might find declaring parameter variables with the *PARAMETERS* keyword inside the query preferable to adding parameters outside the Jet SQL statement. Using the *PARAMETERS* keyword requires the use of Access data type designations.

After defining the strings for the database and the Jet SQL statement, the *SelectInClauseParameters* procedure instantiates a command and assigns properties to it. Just as with adding a command to the *Views* collection, you do not need to assign the *ActiveConnection* property for a command you append to the *Procedures* collection; this is because the *Catalog* object contains the connection information. Simply set the *Name* and *CommandText* properties for the command. Then, instantiate a catalog that points at the database to which you want to add the procedure as a stored query. Conclude the task by invoking the *Append* method for the catalog's *Procedures* collection. A simple error trap recovers from cases in which a user attempts to append a procedure with the same name as a query that already exists in the database. The error trap in this routine works just like the one in the AddAView procedure. Here's the code:

```
Sub SelectInClauseParameters()
On Error GoTo InParameters_Trap
Dim strSrc As String
Dim strSQL As String
Dim cmd1 As ADODB.Command
Dim cat1 As ADOX.Catalog
Dim prm1 As ADODB.Parameter
Dim prm2 As ADODB.Parameter

'Assign strSrc value for connection string to database
'that will gain the new procedure
strSrc = "Provider=Microsoft.Jet.OLEDB.4.0;" & _
    "Data Source= C:\Program Files\Microsoft Office\" & _
    "Office11\Samples\Northwind.mdb"

'Query demonstrates use of IN keyword to return customers
'matching two parameters (Country1 and Country2).
'Use of a PARAMETERS declaration is optional (see commented strSQL).
strSQL = "SELECT CompanyName, ContactName, Country FROM Customers " & _
    "WHERE Country IN (Country1, Country2)"
'strSQL = "PARAMETERS " & _
'    Country1 Text ( 255 ), Country2 Text ( 255 ); " & _
'    "SELECT CompanyName, ContactName, Country FROM Customers " & _
```

```
'      "WHERE Country IN (Country1, Country2)"

'Instantiate a command based on the parameter query.
Set cmd1 = New ADODB.Command
cmd1.Name = "TwoParametersIn"
cmd1.CommandText = strSQL

'Instantiate a catalog, and append command to the
'catalog as a procedure
Set cat1 = New ADOX.Catalog
cat1.ActiveConnection = strSrc
cat1.Procedures.Append cmd1.Name, cmd1

InParameters_Exit:
Set cmd1 = Nothing
Set cat1 = Nothing
Exit Sub

InParameters_Trap:
If Err.Number = -2147217816 Then
'If procedure exists, delete it.
    cat1.Procedures.Delete cmd1.Name
    Resume
Else
    Debug.Print Err.Number, Err.Description
    MsgBox "Program aborted for unanticipated reasons.", _
        vbCritical, "Programming Microsoft Access Version 2003"
End If

End Sub
```

Once a parameter query has been added to a database, running it differs only slightly from running a *Command* object with parameters in the *CommandText* property's SQL string. (See "Creating a Recordset with a Parameter Query" in Chapter 2 for a sample that demonstrates how to run a *Command* object with parameters.) The following procedure, *RunTwoParametersIn*, illustrates how to run a parameter query that has been added to a database. It runs the parameter query added in the preceding code sample.

The *RunTwoParametersIn* procedure has three sections. First, it instantiates a catalog and points it at the database with the stored parameter query. Second, it assigns a reference to the *Command* property of the stored query, *TwoParametersIn*, to a local variable. Then, it assigns parameter values for the *Country1* and *Country2* parameters. Before executing the command, the VBA procedure must append the parameters to the *Command* object. In the third part, the procedure executes the query and saves a reference to the resulting recordset, and then prints the first 10 records.

```
Sub RunTwoParametersIn()
Dim cat1 As ADOX.Catalog
Dim cmd1 As ADODB.Command
Dim rst1 As ADODB.Recordset
Dim prm1 As ADODB.Parameter
Dim prm2 As ADODB.Parameter
Dim int1 As Integer
Dim fld1 As ADODB.Field

'Instantiate catalog for Northwind database
Set cat1 = New ADOX.Catalog
cat1.ActiveConnection = "Provider=Microsoft.Jet.OLEDB.4.0;" & _
    "Data Source= C:\Program Files\Microsoft Office\" & _
    "Office11\Samples\Northwind.mdb"

'Assign a reference to TwoParametersIn Command property
Set cmd1 = cat1.Procedures("TwoParametersIn").Command

'Create parameters, and assign values for them.
'Append parameters to command.
Set prm1 = cmd1.CreateParameter("Country1", adVarWChar, _
    adParamInput, 255, "UK")
Set prm2 = cmd1.CreateParameter("Country2", adVarWChar, _
    adParamInput, 255, "USA")
cmd1.Parameters.Append prm1
cmd1.Parameters.Append prm2

'Execute and save reference to resulting recordset.
'Print first 10 records to Immediate window.
Set rst1 = cmd1.Execute
int1 = 1
Do Until rst1.EOF
    Debug.Print "Output for record: " & int1
    For Each fld1 In rst1.Fields
        If Not (fld1.Type = adLongVarBinary) Then _
            Debug.Print String(5, " ") & _
            fld1.Name & " = " & fld1.Value
    Next fld1
    rst1.MoveNext
    If int1 >= 10 Then
        Exit Do
    Else
        int1 = int1 + 1
        Debug.Print
    End If
Loop
```

```
'Clean up objects.
Set cat1 = Nothing
rst1.Close
Set rst1 = Nothing
Set cmd1 = Nothing

End Sub
```

You have to invoke the stored query with a *Command* object because recordsets do not support parameters. Also note that the stored query includes parameters, but you have to set specific values for those parameters. You can use the *CreateParameter* method to do this. In addition, when you execute the command, you need to save a reference to the resulting recordset so that you can use the result set after running the stored query. *Command* objects do not offer the same properties and methods for working with result sets that record-sets do.

Creating and Running Action Queries with ADOX

Inserting, deleting, and updating records in a record source are classic database tasks. From its inception, Access offered special queries to facilitate these tasks; these queries are known as action queries. Although you can specify these tasks with SQL text each time you perform them, the operations perform faster when you run them from a stored query. This is because Jet already has the SQL statement compiled when it runs a stored query; Jet doesn't have to com-pile the statement each time as it would if you passed it a SQL string.

Stored action queries are most versatile when you design them with parameters. The parameters allow users to reuse stored action queries in more circumstances. For example, you can re-use the same insert parameter query to add many different records to a database. This, in turn, reduces the number of queries in a database file, which can help your custom applications load faster.

This section discusses different ways to use parameters with stored action queries. It shows you the Jet SQL statements for adding, deleting, and updating records and demonstrates how to use parameters with those statements. It cov-ers how to save the action queries and how to assign parameters when you are ready to run those queries.

An Insert Parameter Query

The key to saving an insert action query with one or more parameters is to understand the structure of the *INSERT INTO* statement in SQL. After the *INSERT INTO* keywords, designate the name of the table to which you will add a record. Follow the table name with a list in parentheses of field names. The field names denote those fields for which your statement specifies values. Although using the list is optional when you specify values for all fields in the order in which the fields exist in the record source, it is good practice to use the list in all instances. Follow the list of field names with the *VALUES* keyword. This keyword signals the beginning of a list in parentheses of values that matches the order of the field name list. When creating a parameter query to let users enter the values to insert at run time, specify parameter names instead of actual values. After designing the Jet SQL statement for an action query, save it by assigning the statement to a *Command* object and appending the command to the *Procedures* collection of a database's catalog.

> **Note** Jet SQL supports copying a group of records from one table to another. This approach follows the format for a typical append query with the Query Designer. You can use the Query Designer's SQL View for any typical append query to review the Jet SQL syntax for that design.

The following procedure, *ParamQInsertsShippers*, demonstrates the syntax for saving an insert action query. The stored query inserts one new record into the *Shippers* table in the Northwind database. The procedure begins by assigning the connection string to a string variable, *strSrc*. Then, it assigns the SQL statement with the parameters to a second string variable, *strSQL*. Next, the procedure instantiates a command and assigns the *strSQL* string to its *CommandText* property. It names the command *InsertAShipper*. Finally, the sample instantiates a catalog and assigns the *strSrc* string to its *ActiveConnection* property.

Instead of using a labeled error trap to recover from an attempt to save over an existing procedure in the catalog, the sample uses an in-line trap design. (The *RemoveAView* procedure, which we examined earlier in this chapter, uses a similar approach to recover from an attempt to delete a view that's not in a catalog.)

```
Sub ParamQInsertsShippers()
Dim strSrc As String
Dim strSQL As String
Dim cmd1 As ADODB.Command
Dim cat1 As ADOX.Catalog

'Assign strSrc value for connection string to database
```

```
'that will gain the new procedure
strSrc = "Provider=Microsoft.Jet.OLEDB.4.0;" & _
    "Data Source= C:\Program Files\Microsoft Office\" & _
    "Office11\Samples\Northwind.mdb"

'Instantiate a command based on a parameter query.
strSQL = "INSERT INTO Shippers (CompanyName, Phone) " & _
    "VALUES (CNameIn, PhoneIn)"
Set cmd1 = New ADODB.Command
cmd1.Name = "InsertAShipper"
cmd1.CommandText = strSQL

'Instantiate a catalog, and point it at the command's
'database connection.
Set cat1 = New ADOX.Catalog
cat1.ActiveConnection = strSrc

'Create a new procedure that appears in the
'Database window as a new query; embed process in
'an error trap that relies on the Err object
'to check for an already existing query
Err.Clear
On Error Resume Next
cat1.Procedures.Append cmd1.Name, cmd1
If Err.Number = -2147217816 Then
    cat1.Procedures.Delete cmd1.Name
    cat1.Procedures.Append cmd1.Name, cmd1
ElseIf Err.Number <> 0 Then
    Debug.Print Err.Number, Err.Description
    MsgBox "Error; see Immediate window diagnostics.", _
        vbCritical, "Programming Microsoft Access Version 2003"
    Exit Sub
End If

'Clean up objects.
    Set cmd1 = Nothing
    Set cat1 = Nothing

End Sub
```

Although this sample saves a parameter query, it does not run the query. Therefore, you still need to invoke the parameter query to add a record to the *Shippers* table. To do so, you must run the *Execute* method using a local reference to the stored action query's command. The following procedure illustrates how to run a stored parameter query for inserting new records into the *Shippers* table. The procedure starts by instantiating a catalog for the Northwind database. Next, it creates a reference named *cmd1* to the *Command* property for the *InsertAShipper* query. Then, the sample invokes the *CreateParameter* method a couple of times to create parameters for the *cmd1* object. The *CreateParameter* method adds a new parameter, but assigning a value to the parameter with this method is optional. This sample sets the parameter values directly using a couple of *InputBox* function statements. After a user responds to the InputBox dialog boxes, the procedure appends the parameters to the *Parameters* collection for the *cmd1* object. Finally, the procedure executes the *cmd1* object's command.

```
Sub RunParamQInsertsShippers()
Dim cat1 As ADOX.Catalog
Dim cmd1 As ADODB.Command
Dim prm1 As ADODB.Parameter
Dim prm2 As ADODB.Parameter

'Instantiate catalog for Northwind database.
Set cat1 = New ADOX.Catalog
cat1.ActiveConnection = "Provider=Microsoft.Jet.OLEDB.4.0;" & _
    "Data Source= C:\Program Files\Microsoft Office\" & _
    "Office11\Samples\Northwind.mdb"

'Assign a reference to the InsertAShipper query's
'Command property.
Set cmd1 = cat1.Procedures("InsertAShipper").Command

'Create parameters and assign values for them.
'Append parameters to command.
Set prm1 = cmd1.CreateParameter("CnameIn", adVarWChar, _
    adParamInput, 40)
Set prm2 = cmd1.CreateParameter("Phone", adVarWChar, _
    adParamInput, 24)

prm1.Value = Left(InputBox("Company Name: "), 40)
prm2.Value = Left(InputBox("Phone: "), 24)
cmd1.Parameters.Append prm1
cmd1.Parameters.Append prm2

'Run the insert action query.
cmd1.Execute

'Clean up objects.
Set cmd1 = Nothing
Set cat1 = Nothing

End Sub
```

You do not have to repeat all the setup steps to run a stored action query each time you add a new record. If an application adds more than one new record at a time, you can just change the parameter value assignments—don't append the parameters a second time—and re-execute the *cmd1* object.

A Delete Parameter Query

The sample for adding an insert action query that you just saw is easy to follow, but you might want a more general model for saving action queries or any type of query that can be a member of the *Procedures* collection in the ADOX object library. The next sample you'll see for saving a delete action query provides a more general design. While the upcoming sample is suitable for the delete action query that it presents, you can readily adapt the code for use with any action query, including the *InsertAShipper* action query you saw in the previous code sample. Of course, even if you have a general routine for saving an action query with parameters, you still need a specific VBA procedure to invoke the action query that passes the query the appropriate parameters.

Together, the next two procedures create a delete action query. The first procedure, *CallAddParamQuery*, assigns three string constants—one for the database in which to store the action query, another for the SQL statement defining the action query, and a third with the name of the action query. By changing the SQL string, this sample could create an insert or update action query just as easily as it creates a delete action query. The *WHERE* clause in the SQL statement for *strSQL* contains a parameter named *CNameOut*. When your application invokes the query, Access will delete all records from the *Shippers* table for the shipper indicated by the *CNameOut* parameter. Here's the *CallAddParamQuery* procedure:

```
Sub CallAddParamQuery()
Dim strSrc As String
Dim strSQL As String
Dim strQry As String

'Assign strSrc for connection to database
'that will gain the new query
strSrc = "Provider=Microsoft.Jet.OLEDB.4.0;" & _
    "Data Source= C:\Program Files\Microsoft Office\" & _
    "Office11\Samples\Northwind.mdb"
'Assign the SQL statement
strSQL = "DELETE * FROM Shippers " & _
    "WHERE CompanyName = CNameOut"
strQry = "RemoveAShipper"

'Pass arguments.
AddParamQuery strSrc, strSQL, strQry

End Sub
```

The actual process of adding the query to a database file takes place in the second procedure. The steps for performing this task should be familiar by now. Their presentation here illustrates two points: how to use the steps with an action query, and how to make the steps more general so that they are suitable for saving any query that belongs to the *Procedures* collection. Here's the *AddParamQuery* procedure:

```
Sub AddParamQuery(strSrc As String, _
    strSQL As String, strQry As String)
Dim cmd1 As ADODB.Command
Dim cat1 As ADOX.Catalog

'Instantiate a command based on the parameter query.
Set cmd1 = New ADODB.Command
cmd1.Name = strQry
cmd1.CommandText = strSQL

'Instantiate a catalog, and point it at the command's
'database connection.
Set cat1 = New ADOX.Catalog
cat1.ActiveConnection = strSrc

'Create a new procedure that appears in the
'Database window as a new query; embed process in
'an error trap that relies on the Err object
'to check for an already existing query

Err.Clear
On Error Resume Next
cat1.Procedures.Append cmd1.Name, cmd1
If Err.Number = -2147217816 Then
    cat1.Procedures.Delete cmd1.Name
    Err.Clear
    cat1.Procedures.Append cmd1.Name, cmd1
ElseIf Err.Number <> 0 Then
    Debug.Print Err.Number, Err.Description
    MsgBox "Error; see Immediate window diagnostics.", _
        vbCritical, "Programming Microsoft Access Version 2003"
    Exit Sub
End If

'Clean up objects.
Set cmd1 = Nothing
Set cat1 = Nothing

End Sub
```

Once you save the action query to delete records, you still need a routine to set the parameters and invoke the query. The *RunRemoveShippers* procedure that appears next provides that model. The overall process is straightforward. First, create a catalog that points at the database file with the action query. Second, create a reference to the action query's *Command* property. Third, create a parameter for the query, assign it a value, and append the parameter to the *Parameters* collection for the *Command* object. Finally, execute the local reference to the command.

Designating the parameter value is the only part of the process for running the *RemoveAShipper* query that isn't generic. You should prompt for a value that is appropriate for the specific parameter query with which you are working. In this case, the sample uses an *InputBox* function to prompt for a company name to use as the *CNameOut* parameter:

```
Sub RunRemoveShippers()
Dim cat1 As ADOX.Catalog
Dim cmd1 As ADODB.Command
Dim prm1 As ADODB.Parameter

'Instantiate catalog for Northwind database.
Set cat1 = New ADOX.Catalog
cat1.ActiveConnection = "Provider=Microsoft.Jet.OLEDB.4.0;" & _
    "Data Source= C:\Program Files\Microsoft Office\" & _
    "Office11\Samples\Northwind.mdb"

'Assign reference to the RemoveAShipper query's
'Command property.
Set cmd1 = cat1.Procedures("RemoveAShipper").Command

'Create parameter, and assign value for it.
'Append parameter to command.
Set prm1 = cmd1.CreateParameter("CNameOut", adVarWChar, _
    adParamInput, 40)

prm1.Value = Left(InputBox("Company Name: "), 40)
cmd1.Parameters.Append prm1

'Run the delete action query.
cmd1.Execute

'Clean up objects.
Set cmd1 = Nothing
Set cat1 = Nothing

End Sub
```

An Update Parameter Query

The *UPDATE* statement in SQL lets you change an old field value to a new one. By using parameters, you can let users designate the old and new values at run time. An *UPDATE* statement contains three clauses. In the first clause, the *UPDATE* keyword designates a record source for updating. The *SET* keyword, the second clause in an *UPDATE* statement, assigns a new value for a field name. Without the optional third clause, the *UPDATE* statement transforms the field value for each row within a record source to the new value designated by the *SET* clause. If your update includes an optional *WHERE* clause, it can restrict which rows change to the new value. This *WHERE* clause can take any expression appropriate for a *WHERE* clause in a normal *SELECT* statement.

The following sample creates an update action query in the Northwind database. Notice that the sample calls the *AddParamQuery* procedure from the previous section. This reuse of the AddParamQuery procedure demonstrates its versatility with another type of parameter action query.

The Jet SQL statement for the update action query is saved in the *strSQL* string variable. The statement has two parameters for the *CompanyName* field in the *Shippers* table of the Northwind database. The *CNameNew* parameter specifies the new name that you want to set in the *CompanyName* field. The *CNameOld* parameter signifies which records in the *Shippers* table to transform to the new value. Only rows with a *CompanyName* field equal to the value of the *CNameOld* parameter get their *CompanyName* field transformed to the value of the *CNameNew* parameter.

```
Sub CreateParamQForUpdating()
Dim strSrc As String
Dim strSQL As String
Dim strQry As String

'Assign strSrc value for connection to database
'that will gain the new query.
strSrc = "Provider=Microsoft.Jet.OLEDB.4.0;" & _
    "Data Source= C:\Program Files\Microsoft Office\" & _
    "Office11\Samples\Northwind.mdb"
'Assign SQL statement.
strSQL = "UPDATE Shippers SET CompanyName = CNameNew " & _
    "WHERE CompanyName = CNameOld"
strQry = "UpdateOldToNewShipper"

'Pass arguments.
AddParamQuery strSrc, strSQL, strQry

End Sub
```

After running *CreateParamQForUpdating*, you will have an update action query in the Northwind database. The next pair of procedures allows you to see the behavior of the update action query. The *AddFooRecord* procedure adds a record to the *Shippers* table with a *CompanyName* of *foo*. You should run the procedure and then open the Northwind database to verify the addition of the new record before running the second procedure. The second procedure, *RunUpdateFooToBoo*, transforms any *CompanyName* with a value of foo to boo. After running the second procedure, you will see a new company named boo in the *Shippers* table.

The *RunUpdateFooToBoo* procedure applies standard techniques for running a parameter query. First, it creates a catalog that points at the database file containing the parameter query. Second, it creates a reference to the parameter query's *Command* property. Third, it creates parameters for the command that correspond to those for the stored parameter query. This involves assigning values to the parameters and appending them to the *Command* object. Finally, it executes the local *Command* object.

```
Sub AddFooRecord()
Dim cmd1 As ADODB.Command
Dim strSrc As String
Dim strSQL As String

strSrc = "Provider=Microsoft.Jet.OLEDB.4.0;" & _
    "Data Source= C:\Program Files\Microsoft Office\" & _
    "Office11\Samples\Northwind.mdb"
strSQL = "INSERT INTO Shippers (CompanyName) " & _
    "Values ('foo')"

Set cmd1 = New ADODB.Command
cmd1.ActiveConnection = strSrc
cmd1.CommandText = strSQL
cmd1.Execute

End Sub

Sub RunUpdateFooToBoo()
Dim strSrc As String
Dim strSQL As String
Dim cat1 As ADOX.Catalog
Dim cmd1 As ADODB.Command
Dim prm1 As ADODB.Parameter
Dim prm2 As ADODB.Parameter

'Assign strSrc value for connection string to database
'that contains the query you want to run.
```

(continued)

```
strSrc = "Provider=Microsoft.Jet.OLEDB.4.0;" & _
    "Data Source= C:\Program Files\Microsoft Office\" & _
    "Office11\Samples\Northwind.mdb"

'Instantiate catalog for Northwind database.
Set cat1 = New ADOX.Catalog
cat1.ActiveConnection = strSrc

'Assign reference to UpdateOldToNewShipper query's
'Command property.
Set cmd1 = cat1.Procedures("UpdateOldToNewShipper").Command

'Create parameters, and assign values for them.
'Append parameters to command.
Set prm1 = cmd1.CreateParameter("CnameNew", adVarWChar, _
    adParamInput, 40, "boo")
Set prm2 = cmd1.CreateParameter("CnameOld", adVarWChar, _
    adParamInput, 40, "foo")
cmd1.Parameters.Append prm1
cmd1.Parameters.Append prm2
cmd1.Execute

End Sub
```

Introduction to Jet SQL's DDL

In addition to row-returning queries and action queries, Jet SQL also supports a data definition language (DDL). Developers can use this language to create database objects, such as tables and queries. Because DDL and ADOX both let you create database objects, you can use them interchangeably in many circumstances. DDL offers a series of statements for creating and modifying objects. For example, you use the *CREATE TABLE* statement to make a new table; you run an *ALTER TABLE* statement to modify an existing table; and you run a *DROP TABLE* statement to delete a table. Because DDL is not a hierarchical model and is not VBA-based, Access developers might prefer ADOX. Nevertheless, Jet SQL's DDL has a very intimate relationship with Jet databases, and you will find that learning its syntax yields many advantages, such as improved performance.

Creating a Table with Custom *AutoNumber* Settings

One advantage of using Jet SQL to create tables is that your application does not require a reference to the ADOX library. This is because you can run Jet SQL statements from *Command* objects. Recall that *Command* objects are members of the ADODB library. Because applications require the ADODB library for basic data access functions and Access creates a default reference to the library, the ADODB library is likely to be available without you having to perform any special measures, such as creating a reference.

The syntax for creating a table requires the *CREATE TABLE* keywords, followed by a table name. For example, to create a table named *Contacts*, specify a *CommandText* property equal to "*CREATE TABLE Contacts*". This statement creates an empty table with no columns. The table name will appear in the Database window, but there will be nothing for the Datasheet view to show—not even an empty row.

You need to add one or more columns in the *CREATE TABLE* statement. Column specifications appear in parentheses after the table name in this statement. Within parentheses after the table name, you separate column specifications with commas. At a minimum, you must designate a column name and data type for each column. You are likely to reference the *INTEGER* and the *CHAR* data types. An *INTEGER* data type can have an *IDENTITY* setting. This enables the column to behave as though it contained *AutoNumber* field values. However, you have more control over *AutoNumber* field values through the Jet SQL *IDENTITY* setting than through the Access user interface because you can specify start and step values. Column specifications can also include constraints that restrict the column values. For example, you can include the *PRIMARY KEY* keywords after the data type for a column to indicate that the column is a primary key for a table.

The following code sample illustrates a very basic task: creating a table named *Contacts*. The table has two columns, one named *ContactID* and the other named *ContactName*. The *ContactID* column has an *INTEGER* data type with an *IDENTITY* setting. Recall that these settings correspond to an *AutoNumber* data type setting. As is typical for columns with *AutoNumber* data types, the *ContactID* column is a primary key. The *ContactName* field has a *CHAR* data type with a maximum size of 50 characters.

This sample does considerably more than just create the *Contacts* table; it also adds data and prints the table. Creating the table requires just two steps. First, you need to specify a connection. You can accomplish this by instantiating a *Connection* object and then opening the object so that it points at a database file. Second, you need to instantiate a *Command* object, set its properties, and then execute the command. Because the *Command* object includes an *Active-Connection* property, you can omit the first step if you set the command's *ActiveConnection* property directly. The *CommandText* property accepts the

SQL statement. This statement implements the table design described in the preceding paragraph.

```
Sub SetStartAndStep()
On Error GoTo StartAndStep_Trap
Dim cnn1 As ADODB.Connection
Dim cmd1 As ADODB.Command
Dim strSrc As String
Dim strSQL As String
Dim strTemp As String

'Instantiate a connection, and point it at a database.
Set cnn1 = New ADODB.Connection
strSrc = "Provider=Microsoft.Jet.OLEDB.4.0; " & _
    "Data Source= C:\Program Files\Microsoft Office\" & _
    "Office11\Samples\Northwind.mdb"

cnn1.Open strSrc

'Instantiate a command for adding a database object
'and adding data to the database.
Set cmd1 = New ADODB.Command
With cmd1
    .ActiveConnection = cnn1
'First create a table with two columns.
'Assign IDENTITY setting to PRIMARY KEY column.
'Set its start value (2) and its step value (4).
    .CommandType = adCmdText
    .CommandText = "CREATE TABLE Contacts (ContactID INTEGER " & _
        "IDENTITY(2,4) PRIMARY KEY, ContactName CHAR(50))"
    .Execute

'After creating the table with the autoincrement/identity
'column, you should add data.
    .CommandText = "INSERT INTO Contacts(ContactName) " & _
        "Values ('Kevin Charney')"
    .CommandType = adCmdText
    .Execute
    .CommandText = "INSERT INTO Contacts(ContactName) " & _
        "Values ('Doug Fink')"
    .CommandType = adCmdText
    .Execute
    .CommandText = "INSERT INTO Contacts(ContactName) " & _
        "Values ('Neil Yoder')"
    .CommandType = adCmdText
    .Execute
End With
```

```
'Close connection to flush changes through
cnn1.Close
Set cnn1 = Nothing

'Echo Contacts table to Immediate window using
'query selecting all fields from the Orders table.
strSQL = "SELECT * FROM Contacts"
PreviewRecordsetSource  strSQL

StartAndStep_Exit:
Set cmd1 = Nothing
Exit Sub

StartAndStep_Trap:
If Err.Number = -2147217900 Then
'If table exists, drop it
'before resuming.
    strTemp = cmd1.CommandText
    cmd1.CommandText = "DROP TABLE Contacts"
    cmd1.Execute
    cmd1.CommandText = strTemp
    Resume
Else
    Debug.Print Err.Number, Err.Description
    MsgBox "Error; see Immediate window diagnostics.", _
        vbCritical, "Programming Microsoft Access Version 2003"
End If

End Sub
```

This sample also implements an error trap for trying to create the *Contacts* table if it already exists in a database. In this case, the procedure saves the *CommandText* setting in a string variable, *strTemp*. Then, it executes a command to drop the old version of the *Contacts* table from the database. Finally, the trap copies the *strTemp* string back to the *CommandText* property and resumes at the point that generated the error.

After the first *Execute* method creates the table, the procedure adds three contacts to the table using the *INSERT INTO* keywords so that we can observe the behavior of the *AutoNumber* data type in the *ContactID* column. Notice from the Jet SQL statement for the table that the *AutoNumber* values have a start value of 2 and a step value of 4. Therefore, the *ContactID* column values should be 2, 6, and 10. This behavior is not possible with the Access user interface, which always has start and step values of 1. After populating the table with records, the procedure prints the records to the Immediate window to confirm the results.

Changing *AutoNumber* Settings

One especially cool feature of Jet SQL is its ability to reset *AutoNumber* columns, such as *ContactID*, on the fly. You can reset both the start and the step values. To perform this task, alter the column settings for the *AutoNumber* column. You can do this by embedding an *ALTER COLUMN* statement within an *ALTER TABLE* statement. After the *ALTER COLUMN* statement, designate the column name. Follow that with the *IDENTITY* keyword, adding the start and step values in parentheses. You can execute the *ALTER TABLE* statement with its nested *ALTER COLUMN* statement from either a *Command* or a *Connection* object.

The next sample demonstrates the syntax for altering an *AutoNumber* column on the fly. It starts by instantiating a connection and pointing it at the database with the *AutoNumber* column to update. Next, it sets new start and step values for the *AutoNumber* column and passes these values, the database connection, and the *AutoNumber* column name to the *ResetCounter* procedure. *ResetCounter* constructs a string with the proper syntax for the *ALTER TABLE* statement and executes the statement using the *Execute* method for the connection. When *ResetCounter* returns control to the procedure that called it, the sample inserts three more records into the *Contacts* table. Then, the code prints the contents of a recordset based on the *Contacts* table to the Immediate window. This output starts with three records that use the initial start and step values of 2 and 4. Then, the output shows three additional records with start and step values of 100 and 10. See Figure 4-6 for the display of the records in the Immediate window. Note that the start and step values you specify should not cause duplicate indexes; otherwise, the new records you add will be rejected.

```
Sub CallAndDemoResetCounter()
Dim cnn1 As ADODB.Connection
Dim cmd1 As ADODB.Command
Dim int1 As Integer
Dim int2 As Integer
Dim str1 As String

'Instantiate a connection and point it at a database.
Set cnn1 = New ADODB.Connection
cnn1.Open "Provider=Microsoft.Jet.OLEDB.4.0; " & _
    "Data Source=C:\Program Files\Microsoft Office\" & _
    "Office11\Samples\Northwind.mdb"

'Reset AutoNumber start (int1) and step (int2) values; then
'pass these along with table name and database connection to
'the procedure to reset the counter for a table.
int1 = 100
int2 = 10
str1 = "Contacts"
```

```
ResetCounter int1, int2, cnn1, str1

'Add data with new start and step settings.
Set cmd1 = New ADODB.Command
With cmd1
    .ActiveConnection = cnn1

    .CommandText = "INSERT INTO Contacts(ContactName) " & _
        "Values ('Tony Hill')"
    .CommandType = adCmdText
    .Execute
    .CommandText = "INSERT INTO Contacts(ContactName) " & _
        "Values ('Virginia Dobson')"
    .CommandType = adCmdText
    .Execute
    .CommandText = "INSERT INTO Contacts(ContactName) " & _
        "Values ('Dee Simmons')"
    .CommandType = adCmdText
    .Execute
End With

'Close connection to flush changes through
cnn1.Close
Set cnn1 = Nothing

'Echo Contacts table to Immediate window.
 str1 = "SELECT * FROM Contacts"
PreviewRecordsetSource  str1

'Clean up objects.
Set cmd1 = Nothing

End Sub

Sub ResetCounter(int1 As Integer, _
    int2 As Integer, cnn1 As ADODB.Connection, _
    str1 As String)
Dim str2 As String

'Revise start and step autoincrement values
'according to int1 and int2 settings/
str2 = "ALTER TABLE " & str1 & vbCrLf & _
    "ALTER COLUMN ContactID IDENTITY (" & _
    int1 & ", " & int2 & ")"

cnn1.Execute str2

End Sub
```

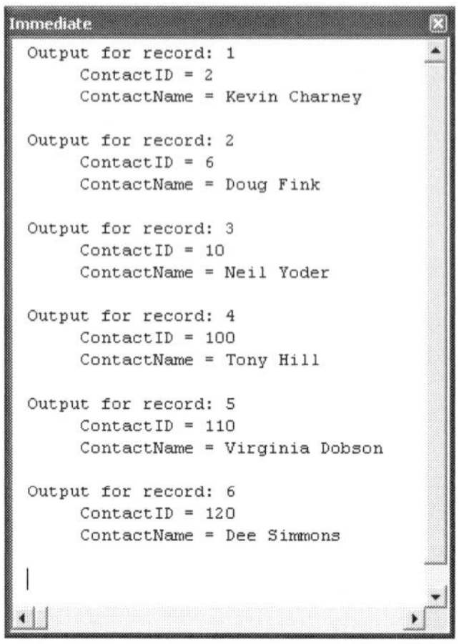

Figure 4-6 Output from the *CallAndDemoResetCounter* procedure that confirms programmatic changes to start and step *AutoNumber* values.

Creating Check Constraints for Columns

Column check constraints enable the designation of a range of legitimate values for a column through an expression. The Access user interface (and the Data Access Objects [DAO] model) allows you to set these constraints through the validation rule property. The ADOX library exposes a validation rule property as well, but this property is buried in the provider-specific properties for *Column* objects. ADO developers using Jet SQL's DDL can take advantage of the *CHECK* keyword when creating or altering a table. The *CHECK* keyword enables you to write an expression that restricts the range of legitimate values for a field. Although the expression constrains the values in a column and acts like a normal validation rule, it does not appear within the Access user interface.

> **Note** In ADOX, the syntax for adding provider-specific properties has a somewhat different appearance than that of standard property settings. Here's how you might create a validity rule and its corresponding text in ADOX:
>
> ```
> col.Properties("Jet OLEDB:Column Validation Rule").Value = "> Date()" _
>     col.Properties("Jet OLEDB:Column Validation Text").Value = _
>     "Must be greater than today."
> ```

The next sample shows the syntax for creating a column check constraint with the *CHECK* keyword and demonstrates the constraint's behavior. In the first *CommandText* string, notice the *CHECK* keyword at the end of the table definition. A comma separates it from the last column definition, which denotes the *EAddress* column. This column contains e-mail addresses, and the column values should therefore include the at sign (@). The *CHECK* keyword and expression causes Access to use this rule to verify the value for the *EAddress* column before accepting a row into the table. A failure of the rule generates a run-time error with a number of –2147467259. An error trap toward the end of the procedure replaces the default error message with a more specific one that might be easier for users to understand. The attempt to enter the third record for Neil Yoder triggers the error, because his e-mail address contains a # rather than an @. In addition to printing the message, the table rejects the record for Neil Yoder.

```
Sub CheckEAddress()
On Error GoTo StartAndStep_Trap
Dim cnn1 As ADODB.Connection
Dim cmd1 As ADODB.Command
Dim strTemp As String
Dim strSQL As String

'Instantiate a connection, and point it at a database.
Set cnn1 = New ADODB.Connection
cnn1.Open "Provider=Microsoft.Jet.OLEDB.4.0; " & _
    "Data Source=C:\Program Files\Microsoft Office\" & _
    "Office11\Samples\Northwind.mdb"

'Instantiate a command for adding a database object
'and adding data to the database.
Set cmd1 = New ADODB.Command
With cmd1
    .ActiveConnection = cnn1
'Same table as in SetStartAndStep, except this table has an
'EAddress field with a check constraint for @ in the field value.
    .CommandType = adCmdText
    .CommandText = "CREATE TABLE Contacts (ContactID " & _
        "IDENTITY(2,4) PRIMARY KEY, ContactName CHAR(50), " & _
        "EAddress CHAR, CHECK(Instr(EAddress, '@')))"
    .Execute
    .CommandText = "INSERT INTO Contacts(ContactName, EAddress) " & _
        "Values ('Kevin Charney', 'kcharney@cab.com')"
    .CommandType = adCmdText
    .Execute
    .CommandText = "INSERT INTO Contacts(ContactName, EAddress) " & _
        "Values ('Doug Fink','dfink@cab.com')"
    .CommandType = adCmdText
    .Execute
'The e-mail address for Neil Yoder does not contain @.
'Therefore, its input forces an error from the CHECK clause.
    .CommandText = "INSERT INTO Contacts(ContactName, EAddress) " & _
        "Values ('Neil Yoder','nyoder#cab.com')"
```

(continued)

```
          .CommandType = adCmdText
          .Execute
     End With

     StartAndStep_Exit:
     Set cmd1 = Nothing
     Exit Sub

     StartAndStep_Trap:
     Debug.Print Err.Number, Err.Description
     If Err.Number = -2147217900 Then
     'If table exists, drop it
     'before resuming
          strTemp = cmd1.CommandText
          cmd1.CommandText = " DROP TABLE Contacts"
          cmd1.Execute
          cmd1.CommandText = strTemp
          Resume
     ElseIf Err.Number = -2147467259 Then
          MsgBox "An e-mail address failed to contain @.", _
               vbCritical, "Programming Microsoft Access Version 2003"
     Else
          Debug.Print Err.Number, Err.Description
          MsgBox "Unanticipated error.  See details in Immediate window.", _
               vbCritical, "Programming Microsoft Access Version 2003"
     End If

     End Sub
```

Summary

This chapter is about managing the operation of Jet SQL inside Access applications. The chapter begins with an introduction to the basics of Jet SQL for several common data access tasks. Next, the chapter introduces ADOX views and procedures collections. Both views and procedures contain Jet SQL statements. Two subsequent sections drill deeper on views and procedures; the first investigates row-returning queries and the second demonstrates how to create and run action queries with parameters for inserting, updating, and deleting rows through record sources such as tables and queries. The chapter concludes with a section that demonstrates selected data definition language (DDL) capabilities of Jet SQL, in particular how to create a table and modify the seed and step values for an *AutoNumber* field.

5

Forms, Controls, and Data

Applications use forms, along with reports, to present data. Forms are also a means of accepting and responding to user input. Because database application users interact with an application almost entirely through forms, form design and behavior are very important. This chapter discusses how to use Microsoft Access forms with data and offers a general introduction to working with forms and their controls. You also learn about the more general roles that forms perform, including forms as timers.

The first samples in this chapter illustrate techniques for developing and presenting application splash screens and switchboard forms. In the process, you'll get an introduction to the form's *Timer* event and to ways of using hyperlinks to invoke Visual Basic for Applications (VBA) procedures. The *Timer* event is particularly useful when you need to execute an action at regular intervals. For example, this chapter includes a sample that illustrates how to publish a datasheet to a Web site at 30-second intervals with the help of a form's *Timer* event.

Next, the focus shifts to using forms with data. A progression of examples and samples demonstrate techniques building simple bound forms and linking them to programmatically controlled record sources. Particular attention is paid to how to use ADO recordsets as record sources for forms. After an introduction to using forms with record sources, the chapter switches its focus to main/subform design and data management issues. The presentation of this topic focuses on the parent-child relationship in the data behind the form. You'll learn about the relationships between main/subforms and subdatasheets for tables. The code samples demonstrate how to reference and manipulate the controls in subforms, a subform control on a subform, and how to display an aggregation of subform control values on a main form. Two additional collections of samples round out the treatment of data via forms. One of these sample collections demonstrates conditionally formatting the display of data values on forms. The other collection dwells on techniques for looking up and displaying data via Access forms. A pair of samples illustrates how to support user interactivity via a parameter query and an ADO *Command* object.

The chapter concludes with a section that demonstrates techniques for enumerating and managing the status of forms in applications, including working with the forms in another Access database file.

Developing solutions with forms is integral to most Access solutions. Therefore, do not expect to find every possible technique for using forms with Access in this chapter. The presentation of reports in the next chapter offers additional information that can help you build Access solutions with forms. Chapter 12 includes more samples of using forms with Access projects, but some of those samples bear on the use of forms with Access database files—just as many of the samples in this chapter apply to Access projects.

Note   This book assumes you have some knowledge of VBA, but for more information, see *www.programmingmsaccess.com/ForA2002 /Ch01A2002.htm*. In addition, if you want to learn more about programming classes with VBA, see *www.programmingmsaccess.com /ForA2002/Ch09A2002.htm*.

Using the Form *Timer* Event

The *Timer* event lets you set an event to fire at the end of an interval. In your *Timer* event procedure, you can cause anything to happen that you can program using VBA. The samples in this section introduce you to forms with three applications for this exceedingly useful event. The first is a splash form that demonstrates an application that needs to run the *Timer* event just once. The second sample highlights how to use the *Timer* event to refresh a form automatically. This second application repeatedly runs the *Timer* event, and it reconnects a computer screen with a record source so that the screen always shows the most recent data in the source. The third sample applies the same kind of approach to publishing a table from an Access database to a page at a Web site. By repeatedly publishing the page at regular intervals, the application assures that visitors will obtain recent data. It is interesting that you can accomplish this goal with just a few lines of VBA code—no knowledge of HTML or Active Server Pages (ASP) is required.

Splash Screen Forms

One easy way to get started with forms is by creating a splash screen. A splash screen is a form that appears before another, more interactive form appears. Splash screens often state what an application does or who created it. You can easily control how long this form stays visible using the *Timer* event. Figure 5-1 shows a sample splash screen from the Chapter05.mdb file, which you can adapt to your own purposes. The Chapter05.mdb file is available with the companion content for this book.

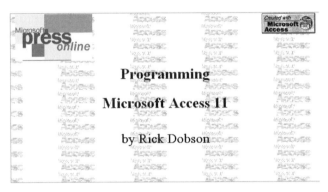

Figure 5-1   A sample splash screen.

Creating a Splash Screen

You can start by creating a tiled background. You do so by setting two form properties while the form is open in Design view. First, you set the form's *Picture* property (on the Format tab of the property sheet) to the path and filename for the image. You can use a bitmap in .eps, .ico, .dib, .wmf, or .emf format, as well as other graphic file formats. Access can also use any graphic file formats for which you have filters installed. Images that contain gray or other muted colors work best for backgrounds because they make your foreground images and text look more prominent. Second, you change the form's *PictureTiling* property to Yes (the default is No).

> **Note**   Access 2003 embeds images in a database by default. This means that the database file grows to accommodate any images that you add to an application. You can choose Linked instead of Embedded as the *PictureType* property to allow Access to utilize a graphic file outside the database file. If you take this approach, then you must coordinate the location of graphic image files with the database files

(continued)

> through the form's *Picture* property. If you move or alter the graphic image files, the form will not appear as initially designed. The splash screen in Figure 5-1 contains three graphic image files embedded in the database, but these files are also available in the sample materials for this chapter so that you can test the Linked setting for the form's *Picture* property.

Next, you can add a foreground image by choosing Picture from the Insert menu. You can also add an Image control to the form. Either method opens the Insert Picture dialog box, where you can select an image to add. Clicking OK automatically sets the image's *Picture* property. Access lets you programmatically set the *Picture* property with VBA so that you can construct the look of a form dynamically in response to user input (such as a text box entry) or environmental factors (such as a user's security ID). You can position and size the image and use the special effects created by various *SizeMode* property settings. The property accepts three values: Clip, Stretch, and Zoom.

As you build this sample, there are at least six other form properties that you will want to change from their default settings. Three of these are the *Record Selectors*, *Navigation Buttons*, and *Dividing Lines* properties. By default, these properties are set to Yes, which generally works well for forms that permit users to display and edit data for a form bound to a record source. However, a splash form does not show data. Therefore, changing the three properties from their default setting of Yes to No creates a more attractive form by removing unnecessary design elements. Two additional properties, *Scroll Bars* and *Border Style*, affect the look of the form. Change the *Scroll Bars* setting to Neither, and the *Border Style* setting to None. You can use drop-down controls on the Format tab of the form's property sheet to adjust five of the six property settings. When you close the form to commit your design changes, assign the name *frmSplashTimer* (or whatever name you prefer) to the form. This sets the form's *Name* property, which you can reference programmatically or through the Rename command on the shortcut menu when you right-click the form in the Database window.

You complete the splash screen by adding one or more Label controls. You can use VBA to set properties for the Label controls at run time. This lets you dynamically format a splash screen's text. You can set a splash screen to open automatically by choosing Startup from the Tools menu and selecting the splash screen's form name in the Display Form/Page drop-down list in the Startup dialog box. You can also hide the Database window when an application opens by deselecting the Display Database Window check box in the Startup dialog box. Click OK to save your choices.

Controlling Display Duration

The following pair of event procedures displays a splash screen for 10 seconds. (To get to the VBA behind a form in Design view, right-click on the form, choose Build Event from the shortcut menu, and then select Code Builder in the Choose Builder dialog box and click OK.) The *Form_Open* event procedure sets the form's *TimerInterval* property value to 10,000. (This value is equal to 10 seconds; the *TimerInterval* property is in milliseconds.) Notice that the *Form_Open* event procedure uses the *Me* keyword to denote the form. You could replace the first instance of *"frmSplashTimer"* with *Me.Name* in the *Form_Timer* event procedure; the *Me* naming convention is more robust because it lets you change a form's name without revising the code. Replacing the second instance of *"frmSplashTimer"* is also possible, but you must use a slightly different technique because the form to which *Me* refers is closed when the procedure reaches the second instance.

Because of the settings made in the Startup dialog box, Access opens the form when the database is opened. As the form opens, Access fires the *Open* event, which causes the *Form_Open* procedure to run. The *Form_Open* procedure sets a timer interval that causes Access to fire the *Timer* event when the interval expires. When the *Timer* event fires, Access calls the *Form_Timer* event procedure.

```
Private Sub Form_Open(Cancel As Integer)

'When form opens, wait 10 seconds before
'firing the Timer event
Me.TimerInterval = 10000

End Sub

Private Sub Form_Timer()
#Const OpenDBWindow = True

'When the timer event happens, close the form and
'then expose the Database window or
'a switchboard form
DoCmd.Close acForm, "frmSplashTimer"

#If OpenDBWindow = True Then
    DoCmd.SelectObject acForm, "frmSplashTimer", _
        True
#Else
    DoCmd.OpenForm "frmHyperlinkSwitchboard"
#End If

End Sub
```

The *Form_Timer* event procedure closes the form and opens either the Database window or a sample switchboard form. A conditional compilation constant and an *#If...Then...#Else* statement control which option the procedure selects. Use the *OpenForm* method of the *DoCmd* object to open a form. This method can take several arguments. However, if you simply want to show a form, just name the form using a string variable or string constant. Exposing a hidden Database window is a less obvious process. To accomplish this, you can select an object from the Database window and elect to show the selected object in the Database window. The *DoCmd* object's *SelectObject* method can accomplish this. This method takes three arguments for this purpose, listed here with the values used in our sample:

- **ObjectType**   The intrinsic constant *acForm* denotes a form object.

- **ObjectName**   Using the name of the splash form, *frmSplashTimer*, ensures that the object exists in the database.

- **InDatabaseWindow**   Using *True* causes Access to select the object in the Database window.

Automatically Requerying Forms

While the splash screen application for the *Timer* event is interesting, it falls more in the category of "look and feel" rather than data delivery. However, automatically refreshing a form or report at intervals can ensure a timely display even with inexperienced operators. Because the *Timer* event recurs at regular intervals—namely, the interval specified by the *TimerInterval* property—you can force a form or report to requery the data source at the end of each interval. The *TimerInterval* property can assume values from 0 milliseconds through 2,147,483,647 milliseconds (nearly 25 days). Because computers with sufficient power to run Access are inexpensive, organizations can afford to deploy them in many situations that demand constantly fresh data—for example, manufacturing and health applications.

Figure 5-2 shows two forms based on the *Shippers* table from the Northwind database. The table in the bottom window shows the addition of a new record (highlighted). The two forms at the top are the same, except that one has a *Timer* event procedure that requeries the data behind the form every 10 seconds. Therefore, that form reflects the new record count of 4. Because the form on the left has no *Timer* event, it reflects the original record count of 3.

The code behind the form on the right appears next. Again, the sample uses two procedures. The *Open* event procedure, shown first, sets the requery interval to 10 seconds. Neither of the two event procedures in this sample close or change the display. Therefore, the *Timer* event will continue to recur at 10-second intervals until a user closes the form.

Figure 5-2   Two forms that reveal the ability of the *Timer* event to requery the record source behind a form to show the most recent data automatically.

The second procedure is a *Timer* event procedure. It controls the action that occurs when the timer goes off every 10 seconds, which in this case is to requery the form's record source. This requerying allows the form on the right to reflect without manual intervention data changed from other workstations. The procedure starts by saving the primary key for the current record in *int1*. Then, it turns off screen refreshing by invoking the *DoCmd* object's *Echo* method with a setting of *False*. After that, the procedure requeries the data source. The requery captures new additions or updates and clears away deletions from other workstations, and it moves the current record position back to the first record in the source behind the form. Using the *FindRecord* method for the *DoCmd* object with the saved primary key value from before the requery allows the application to restore the initial position. (If the record being viewed was deleted, the current position reverts to the top of the data source.) Setting the focus to the *ShipperID* field before invoking the *FindRecord* method allows the method to run without a special argument setting that tells the method to search only the current column.

When using the *Echo* method, be sure to restore screen updates if you turn them off. (To turn screen updates off, use a value of *False* with the *Echo* method.) You can restore screen updates by running the *Echo* method with a value of *True*. If you fail to restore screen updates, your application's users will not be able to view any changes to the screen.

```
Private Sub Form_Open(Cancel As Integer)

'When form opens, wait 10 seconds before
'firing the Timer event
Me.TimerInterval = 10000

End Sub
```

(continued)

```
Private Sub Form_Timer()
Dim int1 As Long

'Save value of primary key before requerying
int1 = Me.ShipperID

'Turn off echo and requery
DoCmd.Echo False
Me.Requery

'Move focus to primary key field and move to
'record in field that was current before requerying;
'turn echo back on
Me.ShipperID.SetFocus
DoCmd.FindRecord int1
DoCmd.Echo True

End Sub
```

Automatically Publishing a Datasheet to a Web Site

Web applications are a convenient way to present information such as the contents of an Access database. A browser is all a client needs to view content at a Web site. Making a Web page dynamic so that it shows the most recent information can involve programming ASP, however. With ASP, developers can build live connections to their databases and guarantee fresh data, but this approach demands skills that are unfamiliar to many Access developers. The *OutputTo* method for the *DoCmd* object in combination with an Access form's *Timer* event offers more familiar tools for generating dynamic Web content based on an Access database.

The *frmPublishShippersTable* form in the Chapter05.mdb file illustrates an approach to this task, as well as some general form design issues. Figure 5-3 presents the form in both Design view (top) and Form view (bottom). Notice that in the Design view the form contains a single label control with a *Caption* property setting of Anything. In addition, the label control is small and poorly positioned on the page. In Form view, the label grows to accommodate a label that describes the purpose of the form. Since the Design view shows the form and control settings at design time, a program must perform the transformation in the form's appearance at run time. By programmatically assigning values to the label control as well as to other aspects of the form, you create a VBA script that is easy to read and edit. While you lose the convenience of graphical form design, you gain the ability to easily modify a design by modifying a program. Even more importantly, you can copy the code for a control or other aspect of a form's design to another form in the current application or even to another application.

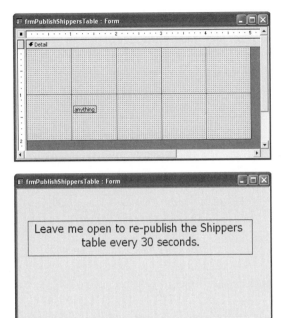

Figure 5-3   The *frmPublishShippersTable* form in Design view (top) and Form view (bottom).

The code behind *frmPublishShjppersTable* consists of two event procedures. The *Form_Load* event procedure performs two primary tasks. First, it assigns a value of 30 seconds to the form's *TimerInterval* property. Next, the *Form_Load* event procedure formats the form and its label control. You can perform these assignments using the form's graphical design interface. However, if you have ever found yourself furiously searching through a property sheet to find the property that you want to manipulate, this approach might be worth the effort.

Every 30 seconds, the *Form_Timer* event procedure runs. This procedure uses the *OutputTo* method for the *DoCmd* object to post the *Shippers* table to the pma11 Web site on the local Web server. The table's contents at the Web site exist in a file named ShippersTable.htm. If the file exists at the Web site already, the *OutputTo* method copies over it. Users can open this page in any standard browser that can read plain HTML. The content of the Web page will be no more than 30 seconds behind any actual updates to the *Shippers* table in the Northwind database file. This approach demonstrates a fast and easy way to publish dynamic content to a Web site that takes advantage of the *Timer* event for an Access form. You also can use the *OutputTo* method to post the data values of other Access objects, such as queries, forms, and reports.

> **Note** The pma11 Web site was introduced in the "Printing Web Folder Contents" section of Chapter 2. Chapter 14 demonstrates how to create a Web site like pma11 with FrontPage 2003.

```
Private Sub Form_Load()
Const conTextAlignCenter = 2
Const conScrollBarsNeither = 0

'Set timer interval to 30 seconds
Me.TimerInterval = 30000

'Format form
Me.RecordSelectors = False
Me.NavigationButtons = False
Me.DividingLines = False
Me.ScrollBars = conScrollBarsNeither

'Format label control
'The Caption property takes a string expression;
'all other property settings are in twips,
'except for FontSize, which is in points
Me.Label0.Caption = _
    "Leave me open to re-publish the Shippers table every" & _
    CStr(CLng(Me.TimerInterval) / 1000) & " seconds."
Me.Label0.Top = Me.InsideHeight * 0.25
Me.Label0.Left = 360
Me.Label0.Width = Me.Width
Me.Label0.Height = 1080
Me.Label0.TextAlign = conTextAlignCenter
Me.Label0.FontSize = 18

End Sub

Private Sub Form_Timer()

'Publish the Shippers table
DoCmd.OutputTo acOutputTable, "Shippers", acFormatHTML, _
    "C:\inetpub\wwwroot\pma11\ShippersTable.htm", False

'Print time table was published
Debug.Print "Refreshed ShippersTable.htm at "; Now()

End Sub
```

Switchboard Forms

Switchboard forms are a common way to facilitate navigation among other forms in an application. Switchboard forms typically contain several command buttons that users can click to open another form. This section offers three approaches for implementing switchboard forms: using hyperlinks without any associated code, invoking function procedures in a standalone code module from hyperlinks on a form, and using VBA procedures in a module behind a form.

Navigating with Hyperlinks

Hyperlink navigation is particularly easy to construct because you do not have to write any code (although you can manage hyperlinks with VBA). Hyperlinks can act as shortcuts to database objects in an application, documents on your hard drive, files on a network, or Web pages on the Internet or an intranet. Access lets you assign hyperlinks to labels, buttons, and images.

You can set and edit hyperlink properties from a form's Design view or programmatically using VBA. Using the manual procedures for setting and editing hyperlinks is easier and can yield faster-loading forms because forms with hyperlinks created in Design view do not require a module containing VBA code. To deliver this benefit, a form must have its *HasModule* property set to No.

> **Note**   The Hyperlink data type lets an Access application launch hyperlinks from table or query fields. While hyperlink fields are in many ways like the hyperlink properties, you use them differently. See Chapter 14 for coverage of using hyperlinks for Web development.

Figure 5-4 shows four forms that demonstrate the operation of a simple navigation system. The main switchboard form on the left transfers focus to one of the other three forms when the user clicks a hyperlink. Once another form has the focus, the user can return the focus to the switchboard form by clicking the hyperlink to it.

You can easily introduce more than two tiers into a navigation system. Typically, each child form can return focus to its parent form. Main forms often include a way to exit the application or exit Access.

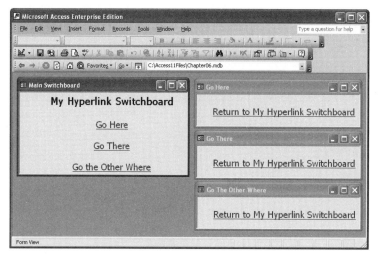

Figure 5-4 A simple hyperlink form navigation system.

To create a hyperlink using the Label control, follow these steps:

1. Click the Build button (...) next to the *HyperlinkAddress* property or the *HyperlinkSubAddress* property on the label's property sheet.

2. In the Insert Hyperlink dialog box, select the type of object to link to from the Link To list on the left edge of the dialog box.

3. Enter the appropriate information for the type of object you selected.

4. Click OK.

> **Note** By default, unfollowed hyperlinks in an Access session are blue and followed hyperlinks are violet. You can change these colors by choosing Options from the Tools menu, clicking on the General tab, and then clicking Web Options. Use the two list boxes in the Web Options dialog box to set the colors. The Web Options dialog box also offers a check box that lets you set whether hyperlinks are underlined. Any settings that you make in the Web Options dialog box will affect new hyperlinks that you create but not previously created hyperlinks.

Figure 5-5 shows the Insert Hyperlink dialog box for the label on the *frmGoHere* form in this chapter's sample database. The hyperlink simply transfers focus back to the switchboard form.

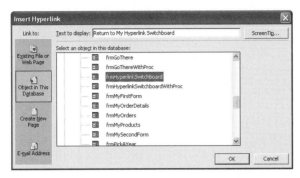

Figure 5-5   The Insert Hyperlink dialog box for the label on the *frmGoHere* form.

Navigating with Code Behind Form

Another common way to manage switchboard navigation is with VBA code from *Click* events for command buttons. Because you can mix navigation functions with other events, such as the closing of a form, this approach offers richer exposure to Access functionality than hyperlink-based navigation without calls to function procedures.

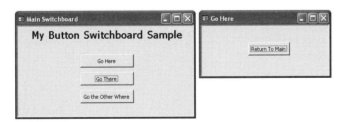

Figure 5-6   These forms use code behind button *Click* events to perform navigation.

An event procedure also gives you greater control over multiple database objects. Hyperlink-based navigation merely transfers focus to another object, such as a form.

Figure 5-6 shows a pair of forms that use the VBA approach to navigation. This sample relies on command button *Click* events. When the user clicks one of the switchboard buttons, the code for the button's *Click* event opens the target form and closes the main switchboard. Clicking the Return To Main button on the target form closes the form and opens the main switchboard form. (The sample uses command buttons, but you can use any other type of control that lets a user generate events.)

The following pair of event procedures shows the code for the *Click* events of the two buttons in Figure 5-6. The first procedure switches control from the main switchboard form to the second form. It also closes the main form. The second procedure transfers control back to the main switchboard and then closes the second form. I used the Command Button Wizard to create a first draft of each procedure; I then added a line of code to each procedure to close the appropriate form.

```
Private Sub cmdGoHere_Click()
On Error GoTo Err_cmdGoHere_Click

Dim strDocName As String

strDocName = "frmButtonGoHere"
DoCmd.OpenForm strDocName
DoCmd.Close acForm, "frmButtonSwitchboard"

Exit_cmdGoHere_Click:
Exit Sub

Err_cmdGoHere_Click:
MsgBox Err.Description
Resume Exit_cmdGoHere_Click

End Sub

Private Sub cmdReturnToMain_Click()
On Error GoTo Err_cmdReturnToMain_Click

Dim strDocName As String
Dim strLinkCriteria As String

strDocName = "frmButtonSwitchboard"
DoCmd.OpenForm strDocName
 DoCmd.Close acForm, "frmButtonGoHere", acSaveNo

Exit_cmdReturnToMain_Click:
Exit Sub
```

```
Err_cmdReturnToMain_Click:
MsgBox Err.Description
Resume Exit_cmdReturnToMain_Click

End Sub
```

Running Procedures from Hyperlinks

A drawback of the navigation system we just examined is that the form stays open after the hyperlink transfers the focus from the current form to another location. Recall that one key advantage of a hyperlink navigation system is that your forms do not require modules behind them. This absence robs your application of the traditional place where code resides to close forms automatically.

You can still automatically remove forms from the screen when using hyperlink navigation. The trick is to use a function procedure in a standalone module or a macro. (You cannot use a subprocedure.) Many different hyperlinks can call the same function procedure. The argument that the link passes to the function procedure tells the procedure which form to close. You can invoke the function procedure from the On Click event setting of a hyperlink's label control. The event procedure fires before the hyperlink action transfers the focus.

Figure 5-7 shows a label control selected with a hyperlink setting. The property sheet below the form shows the expression for invoking the *CloseNamedForm* function procedure from the *Click* event of the hyperlink. Notice that the name of a form appears as an argument in the function procedure call. This design lets multiple hyperlinks from different forms use the same function procedure. The following code demonstrates that it takes just one function procedure to close all the forms in a hyperlink navigation system, such as the system shown in Figure 5-4:

```
Function CloseNamedForm(frmName)

'Closes the form whose name is passed
'to it
DoCmd.Close acForm, frmName

End Function
```

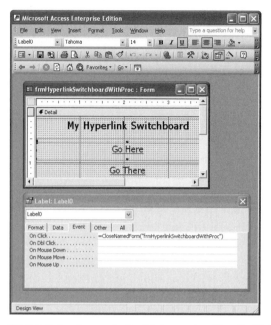

Figure 5-7   A sample On Click event setting that lets a hyperlink execute a function procedure even though the form on which the hyperlink resides has no module behind it.

Linking Forms to a Single Record Source

Access has always let you bind forms to data simply and easily. This is one major reason why it is a rapid application development environment. In this section, we'll look at several ways to bind forms to data. I'll start with creating a simple bound form and then move on to dynamically assigning ADO recordsets and SQL statements as form sources. Next, I'll show you how to use an ADO recordset assignment to update form data. And finally, I'll cover using an ADO recordset to insert data via a form.

Creating a Simple Bound Form

To bind a form to data, you can use the AutoForm Wizard. Select a table or query in the database window and click the New Object: AutoForm button on the Database toolbar. The wizard opens a new form that binds directly to the selected data source. Figure 5-8 shows a sample form based on the *Order Details* table, which is a linked table in this chapter's sample database that points to the table of the same name in the Northwind database. You can use this form for browsing, editing, adding, and deleting records in the *Order Details* table. The form is available in the Chapter05.mdb file as *frmOrderDetailsAutoForm*.

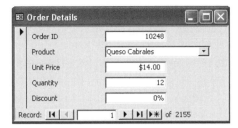

Figure 5-8   A form based on a single record source (the *Order Details*
table) created by the AutoForm Wizard.

Because the data source for the form's *Product* field is a lookup field in
the underlying *Order Details* table, the *Product* field automatically appears as a
combo box that displays product names instead of the underlying *ProductID*
values. All of this functionality is provided automatically by the wizard.

If the table or query that you select as the record source for a form has a
one-to-many relationship with another record source, Access 2003 automatically creates a main/subform. If your application calls for a sole main form
bound to a table or query, you can open the form in Design view and remove
the subform control. The section "Processing Main/Subforms" in this chapter
takes a closer look at subform controls.

Dynamically Assigning Record Sources to Forms

The ease of applying the AutoForm Wizard and the flexibility of its forms are
two of the reasons Access is such a popular database development package.
Another reason for Access's popularity is that you can readily adapt forms created by the AutoForm Wizard to any custom data source created on the fly.

Access offers two complementary techniques for adapting a wizard-generated form for use with a dynamically assigned source. First, you can set the form's
Recordset property. (Access 2000 was the first version to enable developers to
assign the *Recordset* property of its forms.) Because this book emphasizes
ActiveX Data Objects (ADO), I will explain how to use an ADO recordset to create a record source behind a form. However, you can also use a traditional Data
Access Objects (DAO) recordset to do this. Second, you can also use a SQL statement, which is a traditional way to dynamically specify a form's record source.

Assigning an ADO Recordset as the Source

After creating a bound form with the AutoForm Wizard, you can use the form
for dynamic record source assignment. Dynamically assigning record sources to
forms greatly increases their flexibility. Taking advantage of this capability
allows you to reduce the size of a database behind a form or take advantage of
a record source that is already open, thus improving the form's load time.

There are two techniques for converting a form created by the AutoForm Wizard to one that is suitable for dynamic record source assignment. First, you can clear the *RecordSource* property setting from the form's property sheet. (When you view such a form without first dynamically assigning a record source to it, its text boxes initially open with the message "#Name?.) Second, you can leave the *Record Source* setting created by the AutoForm Wizard. This approach uses the AutoForm *RecordSource* property setting as a default record source. When your application programmatically assigns a record source, it overrides the default setting.

Each of the two approaches has its advantages. Leaving the form's settings undisturbed avoids a form opening with #Name? in its text boxes when no dynamic record source assignment exists. If your application does not logically have a default record source for a form, clearing the *Record Source* setting ensures that the form will never display data unless the application specifically assigns it to the form. The samples in this section use a wizard-generated form that has its *Record Source* setting cleared. The form is otherwise identical to the one shown in Figure 5-8. When you dynamically assign a record source to a form, the source lasts as long as the form is open. If a user opens the form without using the application, the form will not have a dynamic record source assignment, even if it was previously opened through the application.

By dynamically assigning a record source to a form, you can use the same form for different needs within a single application. For example, a single form can show sales for different employees, customers, date ranges, departments, and products. Your application simply needs to create a recordset with the proper SQL statement for the *Open* method of an ADO recordset. Then, just assign the ADO recordset to the form's *Recordset* property, and your application can display that data in the form. This assignment is only possible programmatically.

When you assign an ADO recordset with the default *CursorLocation* property setting, you create a read-only form. The form supports browsing, but users cannot add, update, or delete records through it. It doesn't matter if your application specifies a keyset cursor. Your application is still read-only with the default *CursorLocation* property setting. To enable read/write access, you must explicitly assign the *adUseClient* intrinsic constant to the *CursorLocation* property setting of a recordset for a form. The next sample we'll examine shows the syntax and behavior of a form based on the default *CursorLocation* property setting.

> **Note** If you assign an ADO recordset based on a single table to a form in an Access project (as opposed to an Access database file), your form will be read/write by default. Chapter 12 extends this chapter's coverage of forms and explores topics that pertain particularly to the use of forms in Access projects (.adp files).

The following code sample demonstrates the syntax for dynamically assigning a recordset to a form. After assigning the form's *Recordset* property, the code browses the form and attempts to update a field value through the form. Because the form uses the default *CursorLocation* property, the attempt to revise a field value generates a run-time error that the procedure traps.

The procedure begins by instantiating a *Connection* object, *cnn1*, and pointing it at the Northwind database. Next, the procedure instantiates a record-set, *rst1*. The form's *CursorType* and *LockType* properties permit updating. (But the sample demonstrates that these settings are not sufficient to enable updating.) Then, the procedure uses *cnn1* to open the *rst1* recordset based on an inner join of the *Orders* and *Order Details* tables. The recordset returns the five fields from the *Order Details* tables for all records whose *OrderDate* field value is in 1998.

After creating the recordset for the form, the focus shifts to the form. The code uses the *DoCmd* object's *OpenForm* method to open a form named *frmSimpleUnboundForm*. This form has the same layout as the one in Figure 5-8. In addition, this form has no *RecordSource* property setting. The line after the *OpenForm* method dynamically assigns the *rst1* recordset to the form's *Recordset* property.

After executing the line that makes the *Recordset* property assignment, you have a form with a recordset that is open in Access. If you place a breakpoint at the next line, you can click the View Microsoft Access control on the Standard toolbar in the Visual Basic Editor (VBE) window and see the open form.

The procedure goes on to use the form programmatically. First, it invokes the *DoCmd* object's *GoToRecord* method with an argument of *acNext* to move from the first to the second record. Then, the procedure returns to the initial record in the record source behind the form. This confirms the ability to browse using the form. Next, the procedure modifies the value in the Quantity text box control on the form and attempts to revise the database through the form's *Refresh* method. Because the form is read-only, invoking the *Refresh* method generates a run-time error that the program traps. After presenting a message box about the form's read-only status, the code exits the procedure by passing control to *BindRst_Exit*. Let's take a look at the syntax now.

```
Sub BindRstToSimpleUnboundFormRO()
On Error GoTo BindRst_Trap
Dim cnn1 As ADODB.Connection
Dim rst1 As Recordset
Dim str1 As String

'Create the connection
Set cnn1 = New ADODB.Connection
cnn1.Open "Provider=Microsoft.Jet.OLEDB.4.0;" & _
"Data Source=C:\Program Files\Microsoft Office\" & _
    "Office11\Samples\Northwind.mdb;"
```

(continued)

```
'Create recordset reference and set its properties
Set rst1 = New ADODB.Recordset
rst1.CursorType = adOpenKeyset
rst1.LockType = adLockOptimistic

'Open recordset based on orders in 1998 for
'frmSimpleUnboundForm
rst1.Open "SELECT od.OrderID, od.ProductID, od.UnitPrice, " & _
    "od.Quantity, od.Discount " & _
    "FROM [Order Details] AS od " & _
    "INNER JOIN Orders AS o " & _
    "ON od.OrderID = o.OrderID " & _
    "WHERE Year(o.OrderDate) = 1998", cnn1

'Assign ADO recordset to Recordset property of
'Forms("frmSimpleUnboundForm")
str1 = "frmSimpleUnboundForm"
DoCmd.OpenForm str1
Set Application.Forms(str1).Recordset = rst1

'Browse the form by moving to the next record
'and then back again
DoCmd.GoToRecord , , acNext
DoCmd.GoToRecord , , acPrevious

'Attempt to modify a field in the form
Forms(str1).Quantity = 2000
Forms(str1).Refresh

BindRst_Exit:
rst1.Close
cnn1.Close
Set rst1 = Nothing
Set cnn1 = Nothing
DoCmd.Close acForm, str1
Exit Sub

BindRst_Trap:
If Err.Number = -2147352567 Then
    MsgBox "The form is open in read-only mode. ", _
        vbCritical, "Programming Microsoft Access 2003"
    Resume BindRst_Exit
Else
    Debug.Print Err.Number, Err.Description
    MsgBox "Program aborted for unanticipated reasons.", _
        vbCritical, "Programming Microsoft Access 2003"
End If

End Sub
```

Assigning a SQL Statement as the Source

You can use VBA to assign a SQL string as a record source for a form through its *RecordSource* property. The form's *RecordSource* property corresponds to the Record Source setting in the form's property sheet. Therefore, you can set the *RecordSource* property programmatically or manually. When you set the property programmatically, it overrides any manual setting. When you make the assignment via VBA as described, the setting lasts only until you close the form.

> **Note**   VBA allows you to set a form's *RecordSource* property in Design view. When you do this, the assignment persists beyond the current form session. You cannot assign an ADO recordset to a form in Design view. Any setting to a form's *Recordset* property will always be transient.

Using a SQL string requires that you get the SQL syntax right for the database server that you are using. This approach does not allow you to take advantage of saved queries in other Access database files or of stored procedures in Microsoft SQL Server and other client/server databases. However, using the *Recordset* property to assign the record source for a form does. When you use a SQL string to designate a record source for a form, the database server must always compile the SQL string. When you set a form's *Recordset* property to an ADO recordset, you automatically gain access to the result set from a previously compiled SQL string—namely, the SQL statement corresponding to the *Source* property for the recordset.

The following sample demonstrates the syntax for assigning a SQL string to a form. It uses the same SQL string from the preceding sample. After assigning a SQL string to the form's *RecordSource* property, the sample reopens the form in Form view and browses the record source through the form. In addition, it updates the record source via the form, and closes the form without saving the assignment of the SQL string to the form. The remainder of the sample confirms the modification of the record source using an ADO recordset. Then, it restores the updated field value to its original value.

This sample starts by immediately opening the form with the *DoCmd* object's *OpenForm* method. This method opens a form in Normal view unless you use an intrinsic constant to specify a different view. For example, to open a form in Design view, you use this syntax:

```
DoCmd.OpenForm "frmSimpleUnboundForm", acDesign
```

Using Design view enables an application to persist changes to the *RecordSource* property beyond the current form session.

The sample's next statement shows the syntax for assigning a SQL string to a form's *RecordSource* property. This approach requires just two lines of code to open a form with a dynamically assigned record source.

After assigning the record source using a SQL string, you can browse records and add, update, and delete them through the form. The following two lines of code demonstrate browsing by moving forward and backward one record. Next, the sample revises the value in the Quantity text box to 2000 for the form's first record and invokes the form's *Refresh* method. This does not generate an error because the form's record source is set to a SQL string. Before updating the value in the Quantity text box, the sample saves the original Quantity value as well as the values in the *OrderID* and *ProductID* text boxes. These values are necessary for restoring the first record to its original state.

> **Note**   When Access generates the source for a form from an assignment to the *RecordSource* property setting at design time or at run time, the corresponding recordset for the form is a DAO (as opposed to an ADO) recordset. This feature automatically enables the updating of record field values.

The remainder of the sample uses ADO to confirm that an updated *Quantity* value exists and restores the initial value. First, the sample instantiates a connection and points it at the Northwind database. Next, it instantiates *rst1*, a recordset that is suitable for seeking the updated record. The recordset explicitly sets its *Index* property to the index named *PrimaryKey* for the *Order Details* table. This index has two fields: *OrderID* and *ProductID*. The code explicitly sets *CursorLocation* to *adUseServer* for the *Seek* method. In addition, the recordset's *Open* method specifies *adCmdTableDirection* for its *Options* argument. After taking these steps, the procedure invokes the *Seek* method for *rst1* with the *OrderID* and *ProductID* values previously saved in the *int2* and *int3* variables.

Once the procedure finds the altered record, it prints the current record to the Immediate window. The fourth recordset field will be 2000. This is the record's *Quantity* field. Next, the procedure updates the altered *Quantity* field by assigning to it the saved original value (*int1*). This restores the field to the value it had before the sample updated the field through the form. After restoring the value, the procedure again prints the record to the Immediate window. The fourth field now shows its initial value of 20.

```
Sub BindSQLToSimpleUnboundForm()
Dim int1 As Integer
Dim int2 As Long
Dim int3 As Long
Dim cnn1 As ADODB.Connection
Dim rst1 As Recordset
Dim str1 As String

'Assign SQL to Recordsource property of
'Forms("frmSimpleUnboundForm").
'Form must be closed before running this routine.
DoCmd.OpenForm "frmSimpleUnboundForm"
Forms("frmSimpleUnboundForm").RecordSource = _
    "SELECT od.OrderID, od.ProductID, " & _
    "od.UnitPrice, od.Quantity, od.Discount " & _
    "FROM [Order Details] AS od " & _
    "INNER JOIN Orders AS o " & _
    "ON od.OrderID = o.OrderID " & _
    "WHERE Year(o.OrderDate) = 1998"

'Browse the form by moving to the next record
'and then back again
DoCmd.OpenForm "frmSimpleUnboundForm", acNormal
DoCmd.GoToRecord , , acNext
DoCmd.GoToRecord , , acPrevious

'Save original Quantity field value along with primary
'key values (OrderID and ProductID) before updating
'the Quantity field through the form.
'Close form when done.
int1 = Forms("frmSimpleUnboundForm").Quantity
int2 = Forms("frmSimpleUnboundForm").OrderID
int3 = Forms("frmSimpleUnboundForm").ProductID
Forms("frmSimpleUnboundForm").Quantity = 2000
Forms("frmSimpleUnboundForm").Refresh
DoCmd.Close acForm, "frmSimpleUnboundForm"

'Create the connection
Set cnn1 = New ADODB.Connection
cnn1.Open "Provider=Microsoft.Jet.OLEDB.4.0;" & _
"Data Source=C:\Program Files\Microsoft Office\" & _
    "Office11\Samples\Northwind.mdb;"
'Set cnn1 = CurrentProject.Connection

'Create recordset reference and set its properties
Set rst1 = New ADODB.Recordset
With rst1
    .Index = "PrimaryKey"
    .CursorType = adOpenKeyset
    .LockType = adLockOptimistic
    .CursorLocation = adUseServer
```

(continued)

```
        .Open "Order Details", cnn1, , , adCmdTableDirect
        .Seek Array(int2, int3)
    End With

    'Print record with revised Quantity field
    Debug.Print rst1(0), rst1(1), rst1(2), rst1(3), rst1(4)

    'Restore Quantity field value and print again
    rst1(3) = int1
    rst1.Update
    Debug.Print rst1(0), rst1(1), rst1(2), rst1(3), rst1(4)

    'Clean up objects
    rst1.Close
    cnn1.Close
    Set rst1 = Nothing
    Set cnn1 = Nothing

End Sub
```

The Chapter05.mdb file contains a sample, *BindRstToSimpleUnboundForm-RO2RW*, that demonstrates how to extract the *Source* property from an ADO recordset and assign it to a form's *RecordSource* property at run time. This approach allows you to convert an ADO recordset to a DAO recordset through Access and thus make the record source for the form read/write. Since the next two sections demonstrate more direct approaches to updating from an ADO recordset source for a form, the procedure's listing does not appear in the book.

Updating Form Data with an ADO Recordset Assignment

As demonstrated, you can routinely update form data when you use a SQL string to designate the form's record source. When you assign an ADO recordset to a form's *Recordset* property with the default *CursorLocation* setting (adUseServer), users cannot update the data with the form. For some applications, the easy availability of read-only forms is an advantage. You can make forms read-only when you assign their record source with a SQL string, but this requires additional property settings. (For example, see the form's *AllowEdits*, *AllowDeletions*, *AllowAdditions*, and *DataEntry* property descriptions in Access Help.)

If you want to use ADO to create forms that permit users to edit data, you simply need to set the source recordset's *CursorLocation* property to *adUseClient*. Making this simple adjustment before assigning a recordset to a form will allow users to update the data in a form based on a single table. The next sample demonstrates this feature.

While the sample for this section contains only one new line for assigning the *CursorLocation* property, the listing is complete because this sample incorporates a mixture of code from the two preceding samples. The sample begins by creating a connection to the Northwind database. Then, it instantiates a recordset that uses the connection. However, before opening the recordset for the SQL string (the same one used in the preceding two samples), the code sets the *CursorLocation* property to *adUseClient*. This simple step makes the form's control values updateable.

The remainder of the sample assigns the recordset to a form's *Recordset* property and updates the Quantity text box value for the first record to 2000. After closing the form, the sample prints the updated record to the Immediate window before restoring the *Quantity* field in the recordset to its original value. Finally, the code prints the record again after restoring the field's value.

```
Sub BindRstToSimpleUnboundFormRWUpdate()
Dim cnn1 As ADODB.Connection
Dim rst1 As Recordset
Dim int1 As Integer
Dim str1 As String

'Create the connection
Set cnn1 = New ADODB.Connection
cnn1.Open "Provider=Microsoft.Jet.OLEDB.4.0;" & _
"Data Source=C:\Program Files\Microsoft Office\" & _
    "Office11\Samples\Northwind.mdb;"

'Create recordset reference and set its properties
'to permit read/write access to recordset
Set rst1 = New ADODB.Recordset
rst1.CursorType = adOpenKeyset
rst1.LockType = adLockOptimistic
rst1.CursorLocation = adUseClient

'Open recordset based on orders in 1998 for
'frmSimpleUnboundForm
rst1.Open "SELECT od.OrderID, od.ProductID, od.UnitPrice, " & _
    "od.Quantity, od.Discount " & _
    "FROM [Order Details] AS od " & _
    "INNER JOIN Orders AS o " & _
    "ON od.OrderID = o.OrderID " & _
    "WHERE Year(o.OrderDate) = 1998", cnn1

'Assign ADO recordset to Recordset property of
'Forms("frmSimpleUnboundForm")
str1 = "frmSimpleUnboundForm"
DoCmd.OpenForm str1
Set Application.Forms(str1).Recordset = rst1
```

(continued)

```
'Modify Quantity field through the form, but
'save the original value first
int1 = Forms(str1).Quantity
Forms(str1).Quantity = 2000
Forms(str1).Refresh
DoCmd.Close acForm, str1

'Print record with revised Quantity field
Debug.Print rst1(0), rst1(1), rst1(2), rst1(3), rst1(4)

'Restore Quantity field value and print again
rst1(3) = int1
rst1.Update
Debug.Print rst1(0), rst1(1), rst1(2), rst1(3), rst1(4)

'Clean up objects
rst1.Close
cnn1.Close
Set rst1 = Nothing
Set cnn1 = Nothing

End Sub
```

Inserting Data Using a Form Based on an ADO Recordset

The *CursorLocation* setting that you assign to a form's *Recordset* property can determine whether the form is read-only or updateable. The same setting also determines whether users can insert new records with a form. The process of setting up a form so that users can read from it and write to it is the same whether you update existing values or add new ones programmatically. However, the process of actually inserting or deleting a record is different than that of updating a record.

The next sample sets up a form for read/write access and demonstrates how to insert and delete a record through the form. Even though users might manually perform some of these steps, it's important to know how to add a record programmatically through a form.

After creating the *rst1* recordset for the form, the sample opens the form the same way the preceding sample opened a form. However, the code next assigns the open form, *frmSimpleUnboundForm*, to the *frm1* object reference.

The code uses this reference as a pointer to the open form. For example, the line after the form reference assignment sets the *rst1* recordset to the *Recordset* property of *frm1*. Then, the procedure saves the *OrderID* field value for the first record to the *int1* variable.

The procedure launches the process of adding a new record by invoking the *DoCmd* object's *GoToRecord* command with an *acNewRec* argument. This displays a blank form and prepares Access to insert a new record. Inserting a new record is a two-step process. First, the code assigns values to the form fields. The sample adds a new line item for the order using the first *OrderID* in the *rst1* recordset, which is the value in *int1*. As the procedure adds a new record, it saves the *ProductID* for the new record. (The sample will use these saved values to remove the new records later.) Then, the sample invokes the form's *Requery* method to insert the form's control values into the recordset behind the form. After inserting the record, the procedure closes the form.

> **Note**   After invoking the *GoToRecord* method with the *acNewRec* argument, you do not have to use the *Requery* method to enter a new record. Closing the record without invoking the *Requery* method, or invoking the *Refresh* method instead of the *Requery* method, will also add a new record.

The remainder of the sample finds the newly added record and removes it from the recordset. The code uses the *Seek* method to search for all records matching the *OrderID* to which the form added a record. Then, the code loops through the line items for the *OrderID* until it discovers the one with a *ProductID* equal to the *ProductID* on the new line item. When the sample discovers the line item with a *ProductID* that matches the newly added record, it deletes the record and exits the loop.

```
Sub BindRstToSimpleUnboundFormRWInsert()
Dim cnn1 As ADODB.Connection
Dim rst1 As Recordset
Dim frm1 As Form
Dim int1 As Long
Dim int2 As Long
Dim str1 As String

'Create the connection
Set cnn1 = New ADODB.Connection
cnn1.Open "Provider=Microsoft.Jet.OLEDB.4.0;" & _
    "Data Source=C:\Program Files\Microsoft Office\" & _
    "Office11\Samples\Northwind.mdb;"

'Create recordset reference and set its properties
'to permit read/write access to recordset
Set rst1 = New ADODB.Recordset
rst1.CursorType = adOpenKeyset
rst1.LockType = adLockOptimistic
```

(continued)

```
rst1.CursorLocation = adUseClient

'Open recordset based on orders in 1998 for
'frmSimpleUnboundForm
rst1.Open "SELECT od.OrderID, od.ProductID, od.UnitPrice, " & _
    "od.Quantity, od.Discount " & _
    "FROM [Order Details] AS od " & _
    "INNER JOIN Orders AS o " & _
    "ON od.OrderID = o.OrderID " & _
    "WHERE Year(o.OrderDate) = 1998", cnn1

'Assign ADO recordset to Recordset property of
'Forms("frmSimpleUnboundForm")
str1 = "frmSimpleUnboundForm"
DoCmd.OpenForm str1
Set frm1 = Forms(str1)
Set frm1.Recordset = rst1

'Add a new record through the form for the current OrderID
int1 = frm1.OrderID
DoCmd.GoToRecord , , acNewRec
With frm1
    .OrderID = int1
    .ProductID = 1
    int2 = .ProductID
    .Quantity = 1
    .UnitPrice = 1
    .Discount = 0
    .Requery
End With
DoCmd.Close acForm, frm1.Name

'Create recordset reference and set its properties so
'you can seek the records for the OrderID to which you
'added a record
Set rst1 = New ADODB.Recordset
With rst1
    .Index = "OrderID"
    .CursorType = adOpenKeyset
    .LockType = adLockOptimistic
    .Open "Order Details", cnn1, , , adCmdTableDirect
    .Seek int1
End With

'Loop through line items for OrderID to which you
'previously added a record; delete the record
'when you find it
Do Until rst1(0) <> int1
    If rst1(1) = int2 Then
```

```
'Delete the record because we do not want to change
'the Northwind database, but only show that we can
        rst1.Delete
        Exit Do
    End If
    rst1.MoveNext
Loop

'Clean up objects
rst1.Close
cnn1.Close
Set rst1 = Nothing
Set cnn1 = Nothing

End Sub
```

Processing Main/Subforms

A main/subform allows you to display a parent-child relationship between two record sources on a single form. The feature that makes the main/subform especially powerful is the way it links its two parts: the main form and the subform. The main/subform restricts the entries on the subform to just those records that match the current record on the main form.

Any pair of tables in a one-to-many relationship is a candidate for display via a main/subform. In relational database terms, the table on the one side of the relationship is the parent, and the table on the many side is the child. Access relies on the matching field values between the parent and child record sources to display just the child records that correspond to the current parent record.

The Access user interface offers at least two ways to create main/subforms. First, the AutoForm Wizard can automatically create a main/subform for any table that has a one-to-many relationship with another table. With this approach, you do not need a standalone form for the child record source. Access displays the Datasheet view of the child record source within the main form for the parent record source. Second, you can create separate forms for the child and parent record sources and then drag the form for the child record source from the Database window into the Design view of the form for the parent record source. As long as the parent and child record sources have a relationship defined in the Relationship window (or a subdatasheet relationship, which we'll discuss in a moment), Access will automatically match the child records to the parent records with related tables or tables with subdatasheet specifications. Otherwise, Access pops up a dialog box that prompts you for the matching fields in the parent and child record sources.

Subdatasheets

Subdatasheets provide a way to display parent-child relationships from a table's Datasheet view, regardless of whether a one-to-many relationship exists between record sources. Main/subforms interact with and build on Access subdatasheet technology. Figure 5-9 shows subdatasheets for the *Order Details* table within the *Orders* table. The screen shot expands the subdatasheets for orders 10248 and 10249. The other orders have their subdatasheet collapsed. Clicking the plus sign (+) next to an *OrderID* field with a collapsed subdatasheet expands the subdatasheet. To close an expanded subdatasheet, just click the minus sign (-) next to an *OrderID* field value.

> **Note**   You can use the Format-Subdatasheet menu from the Datasheet view of a parent record source to manage the default display of subdatasheets. By default, Access collapses all subdatasheets. You can expand all subdatasheets by choosing Format-Subdatasheet-Expand All. You can restore the default display rule for subdatasheets by choosing Format-Subdatasheet-Collapse All.

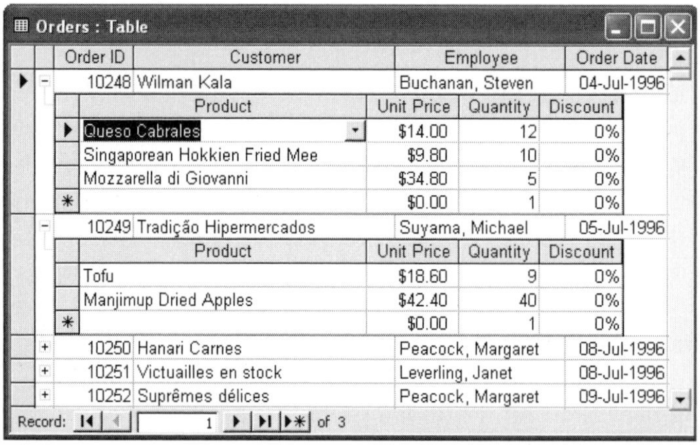

Figure 5-9   Subdatasheets for the *Order Details* table within the *Orders* table.

Access automatically builds subdatasheets for tables that share relationships in the Relationships window. If no prespecified relationship exists between two record sources, you can still create a subdatasheet for a child record source within its parent. Simply open the parent record source in Datasheet view and choose Insert-Subdatasheet from the menu. Then, choose the table or query from the current database that you want as a child record source. If the child record source has one or more fields with names that match those in the parent source, Access automatically suggests matching the two record sources on these fields. If no fields in the parent and child record sources have the same names, you can use the combo boxes at the bottom of the Insert Subdatasheet dialog box to specify the fields for matching child records to parent records. Use a semicolon delimiter to separate fields when the record sources contain more than one matching field.

> **Note**   You can delete a subdatasheet by choosing the Format-Sub-datasheet-Remove command from the Datasheet view menu for the parent record source. This does not delete the child resource—just its subdatasheet relationship to the parent record source. Although Access inherits subdatasheets for linked tables, you cannot remove a subdatasheet from a linked table in the source database. Instead, open the Access database file with the local table and remove the sub-datasheet from there.

Creating Main/Subforms

When specifying record sources for main/subforms, you will often want to designate queries as record sources. This makes it easy to select columns and join tables to provide main or subform fields. After deciding on your sources for the forms, you can build the query graphically or programmatically. (See Chapter 4 for code samples that illustrate how to programmatically add queries to a database.)

My subform sample has two levels of subforms. The main form has a subform that, in turn, has a subform of its own. The sample relies on three SQL statements. The outer query has the name *MyOrders*; this query is the record source for the main form. The query nested within *MyOrders* has the name *MyOrderDetails*; this query is the record source for the subform on the main form. The lowest-level query is *MyProducts*; this is the record source for the subform of the subform on the main form. The SQL statement for the main form (*frmMyOrders*) follows.

```
SELECT Orders.OrderID, Orders.CustomerID, Orders.EmployeeID,
    Orders.OrderDate, Orders.RequiredDate, Orders.ShippedDate,
    Orders.ShipVia, Orders.Freight, Orders.ShipName,
    Orders.ShipAddress, Orders.ShipCity, Orders.ShipRegion,
    Orders.ShipPostalCode, Orders.ShipCountry
    FROM Orders
```

The SQL statement for the subform (*frmMyOrderDetails*) of the main form follows:

```
SELECT [Order Details].OrderID, [Order Details].ProductID,
    [Order Details].UnitPrice, [Order Details].Quantity,
    [Order Details].Discount
    FROM [Order Details]
```

The following is the SQL statement for the subform to the subform (*frmMyProducts*):

```
SELECT Products.ProductID, Products.UnitsInStock,
    Suppliers.CompanyName, Suppliers.ContactName,
    Suppliers.Phone
    FROM Suppliers INNER JOIN Products
    ON Suppliers.SupplierID = Products.SupplierID
```

These queries inherit the relationships between data sources in the Northwind database. Therefore, as you create the forms with the AutoForm Wizard, the wizard automatically builds in the subforms. Because these automatically generated subforms do not depend on any custom record source specifications in custom queries, you can delete the subform controls within forms in order to add subforms with custom *RecordSource* property values.

After preparing the individual main and subforms, you can start combining them. First, open *frmMyOrderDetails* in Design view and drag *frmMyProducts* from the Database window. After saving and closing the new *frmOrderDetails* form, open the *frmMyOrders* form in Design view. Then, drag the modified *frmOrderDetails* form from the Database window.

After completing the nesting layout issues, you still have a couple more matters to address. First, you change the *DefaultView* property setting for the *frmMyProducts* and *frmMyOrderDetails* forms to Datasheet view. This *DefaultView* adjustment enables the subforms to appear automatically as datasheets. Second, you assign appropriate Link Child Fields and Link Master Fields property settings for the subform control in the main form and the subform control in the subform of the main form. You can do this by opening the subform control's property sheet to the appropriate tab. Select the Data tab of the subform control's property sheet to display boxes for setting the Link Child Fields and Link Master Fields properties. Clicking the Build button to the right of either property displays a dialog box that helps you select fields from the record sources for the main and subforms.

In the example, you click the *MyProducts* subform control in the *MyOrderDetails* subform. Then, you designate the *ProductID* for the Link Child Fields and Link Master Fields settings. Next, you click the *MyOrderDetails* subform control on the *frmMyOrders* form and specify *OrderID* for matching the subform records with its main form.

Figure 5-10 shows the sample form containing a subform within a subform. The main form provides details from the *MyOrders* record source. Its subform shows details from the *MyOrderDetails* record source. Notice that all the records on the subform have an OrderID value that matches the one on the main form. Finally, the subdatasheet within the subform displays data from the *MyProducts* record source. Again, the *ProductID* value on the subdatasheet corresponds to the subform *Product* field. However, recall that the *ProductID* field in the original Northwind *Order Details* table is a lookup field that shows the *Product* name instead of the *ProductID* value, and the *ProductID* field has a caption that shows *Product* instead of *ProductID* for a control based on the field.

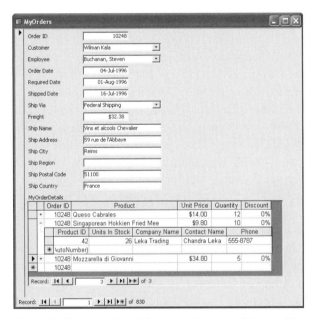

Figure 5-10   A main/subform that has a subform within a subform that appears as a subdatasheet.

Programmatically Referencing Main and Subform Controls

When programmatically referencing subform controls, you need to keep a couple of issues in mind. First, the subform is a control on the main form. This means you cannot refer to the subform controls directly. Instead, you must reference the *Form* property of the subform control. Then, you can reference the subform controls in the standard way. (VBA code can process the controls on forms. The introduction to this chapter concludes with a URL reference containing code samples that demonstrate basic VBA techniques for working with forms.) Second, when dealing with subforms with multiple levels of nesting, you can selectively choose to deal with only the levels your application requires. Therefore, if you have a set of forms with three levels (main form, subform within main, and subform within subform on main form), you can deal with just the top two levels if that's all your application requires.

The following sample demonstrates the syntax for processing the main/ subform shown in Figure 5-10. Although the form includes two levels of subforms, this sample processes just the main form and its subform. (The *Syntax-ForSubForms* procedure to follow deals with the three levels of forms simultaneously.) The sample begins by demonstrating a couple of syntax conventions for referencing subform control values. Next, it contrasts conventions that expose the record sources of the main form and the subform. Then, the code illustrates how to count the total number of controls on the main and subforms. The sample concludes by enumerating the first 10 records on the main form and printing the subform records for each.

The procedure in this code sample starts by opening the *frmMyOrders* form, the main form in the example. After opening this form so that it becomes a member of the *Forms* collection, the sample sets a form object reference, *frm1*, to the *frmMyOrders* form. Then, it sets a control reference, *ctl1*, to the main form's subform control. This control has the name MyOrderDetails—the same name as the record source behind the subform. The next two lines of code demonstrate two different programming styles for referencing the OrderID text box control on the subform. The style that explicitly invokes the *Form* property of the subform control is very robust; you will often need to reference subform objects and properties with this syntax. In addition, the syntax makes it clear that the subform is a control on the main form that has a *Form* property.

The next two blocks of code demonstrate the similarity between referencing properties and collections for the main and subforms. The *RecordSource* property represents a SQL string or an object name representing the data behind the form. Because queries exist for both the main and subforms, the references to their record sources return the query names. Notice that *ctl1.Form* represents a form (the subform) in the same way that *frm1* represents the main form. A form's *Controls* collection contains all the controls on a form. In addition to text boxes and combo boxes, controls can include labels, lines, and subform controls. The *Count* property of the *Controls* collections of the main and subforms returns the count of all the controls—not just those that display data.

Perhaps the most interesting segment of the sample is the portion that contains three nested loops. The outer loop passes through the first 10 records on the main form. The middle loop iterates through the subform records for the current main form record. The inner loop searches the subform controls for either Text Box or Combo Box controls. When the inner loop finds either type of control, the sample prints a short message stating the name of the control and its current value.

The syntax in these three loops reinforces some familiar concepts and introduces some new ones. Notice that the *Form* property of the subform control has a hierarchically nested *Recordset* object. The procedure uses the *RecordCount* property of this object to loop as many times as there are subform records for the current main form record. The procedure also invokes the *MoveNext* method of the subform's *Recordset* object to navigate from the first subform record through the last. Within a subform record, the procedure iterates through the *Controls* collection of the subform. The *TypeOf* function ascertains whether the current control is either a text box or a combo box. Let's take a look at the syntax:

```
Sub SyntaxForSubForms()
Dim frm1 As Form
Dim ctl1 As Control
Dim ctl2 As Control
Dim int1 As Integer
Dim int2 As Integer

'Open a main/subform
DoCmd.OpenForm "frmMyOrders"

'Assign pointers for main form and sub
'form control; MyOrderDetails is the name of the
'subform control on the frmMyOrders main form
Set frm1 = Forms("frmMyOrders")
Set ctl1 = frm1.MyOrderDetails

'Two different ways to print the OrderID control value
'on the subform
Debug.Print ctl1!OrderID
Debug.Print ctl1.Form.Controls("OrderID")
Debug.Print

'Print the record source settings for the main form
'and the subform
Debug.Print frm1.RecordSource
Debug.Print ctl1.Form.RecordSource
Debug.Print

'Print the number of controls on the main and subforms
Debug.Print frm1.Controls.Count & _
    " controls are on the main form."
Debug.Print ctl1.Form.Controls.Count & _
    " controls are on the subform."
```

(continued)

```
Debug.Print

'Move to the form's first record, and loop through the
'next 10 main form records and the subform records
'corresponding to each main record; within each subform
'record, loop through the controls on the subform
DoCmd.GoToRecord , , acFirst
For int1 = 1 To 10
    Debug.Print vbCrLf & "Data for record " & int1 & "."
    For int2 = 0 To ctl1.Form.Recordset.RecordCount - 1
        For Each ctl2 In ctl1.Form.Controls
            If TypeOf ctl2 Is TextBox Then
                Debug.Print String(5, " ") & ctl2.Name & _
                " is a text box that equals " & _
                ctl2.Value & "."
            ElseIf TypeOf ctl2 Is ComboBox Then
                Debug.Print String(5, " ") & ctl2.Name & _
                " is a combo box that equals " & _
                ctl2.Value & "."
            End If
        Next ctl2
        ctl1.Form.Recordset.MoveNext
        Debug.Print String(5, "-")
    Next int2
    DoCmd.GoToRecord , , acNext
Next int1
DoCmd.Close acForm, "frmMyOrders"

'Clean up objects
Set ctl1 = Nothing
Set frm1 = Nothing

End Sub
```

Programming a Subform's Subdatasheet Controls

This next sample builds on the previous one by adding another form level. Happily, adding another level of subform does not substantially change how you programmatically access controls. This section demonstrates how to access the subdatasheet of a subform on a main form. You still have to refer to the *Form* property of the subform control on the main form. In addition, you need to use this same referencing scheme for the subform control on the subform. This second reference provides a path to subdatasheet values.

There is another critical trick for accessing the control values in a subdatasheet for a subform: the subdatasheet must be open. You do this by setting the main form's subform *SubdatasheetExpanded* property to *True*. Without this step, references to subdatasheet control values can generate a run-time error.

The sample checks to see if the *SubdatasheetExpanded* property is *False*. If it is, then the code sets the property to *True* and invokes the *DoEvents* function. The execution of the function allows the operating system to respond to the new setting for the *SubdatasheetExpanded* property.

In this sample, at the subdatasheet level the code merely prints the values of the subdatasheet row. The subdatasheet row specifies the additional detail, such as on-hand inventory or supplier name and contact information for the product in an individual line item of an order. See Figure 5-10 for a sample of the data that is available in the subdatasheet.

The code sample begins by opening the *frmMyOrders* form and creating three object references, which simplify the expressions throughout the procedure. The first object reference, *frm1*, points at the main form. The second reference, *ctl1*, points at the subform control on the main form, and the third reference, *ctl3*, points at the subdatasheet on the subform.

The next two blocks of code print the *RecordSource* property settings for the main form, its subform, and the subdatasheet on the subform. Notice that the code sets the *SubdatasheetExpanded* property to *True* before attempting to reference the subdatasheet. Next, the procedure illustrates the syntax for counting the controls on the main form and the two subforms nested successively below it.

The next block repeats the code for enumerating the subform control values for each record on the main form. In addition, this sample accesses the control values on the subdatasheet. This provides the additional product detail described a moment ago.

The loop for the subform nested within a subform is less complicated than the loop for a subform on the main form. There are several reasons for this. Only one subdatasheet row exists per subform record. All the controls with data on the nested subform are text boxes. The program follows:

```
Sub SyntaxForSubDatasheetOnSubForm()
Dim frm1 As Form
Dim ctl1 As Control
Dim ctl2 As Control
Dim ctl3 As Control
Dim ctl4 As Control
Dim int1 As Integer
Dim int2 As Integer

'Open a main/subform
DoCmd.OpenForm "frmMyOrders"

'Assign pointers for main form and sub
'form control
Set frm1 = Forms("frmMyOrders")
```

(continued)

```
Set ctl1 = frm1.MyOrderDetails
Set ctl3 = ctl1.Form.MyProducts

'Print the record source settings for
'the main form, the subform, and the
'expanded subdatasheet of the subform
Debug.Print frm1.RecordSource
Debug.Print ctl1.Form.RecordSource
If ctl1.Form.SubdatasheetExpanded = False Then
    ctl1.Form.SubdatasheetExpanded = True
    DoEvents
End If
Debug.Print ctl3.Form.RecordSource

Debug.Print

'Print the number of controls on the main and subforms
Debug.Print frm1.Controls.Count & _
    " controls are on the main form."
Debug.Print ctl1.Form.Controls.Count & _
    " controls are on the subform."
Debug.Print ctl3.Form.Controls.Count & _
    " controls are on the subdatasheet."

'Move to the form's first record, and loop through the
'next 5 main form records and the subform records
'corresponding to each main record; within each subform
'record, loop through the controls on the subform
DoCmd.GoToRecord , , acFirst
For int1 = 1 To 5
    Debug.Print vbCrLf & "Data for record " & int1 & "."
    For int2 = 0 To ctl1.Form.Recordset.RecordCount - 1
        For Each ctl2 In ctl1.Form.Controls
            If TypeOf ctl2 Is TextBox Then
                Debug.Print String(5, " ") & ctl2.Name & _
                " is a text box that equals " & _
                ctl2.Value & "."
            ElseIf TypeOf ctl2 Is ComboBox Then
                Debug.Print String(5, " ") & ctl2.Name & _
                " is a combo box that equals " & _
                ctl2.Value & "."
            End If
        Next ctl2
'Loop through the controls on the subdatasheet
'returning just text boxes and their values
        For Each ctl4 In ctl3.Form.Controls
            If TypeOf ctl4 Is TextBox Then
                Debug.Print String(10, " ") & ctl4.Name & _
```

```
                          " is a text box that equals " & _
                          ctl4.Value & "."
                End If
            Next ctl4
            ctl1.Form.Recordset.MoveNext
            Debug.Print String(5, "-")
        Next int2
        DoCmd.GoToRecord , , acNext
    Next int1
    DoCmd.Close acForm, "frmMyOrders"

    'Clean up objects
    Set ctl1 = Nothing
    Set ctl3 = Nothing
    Set frm1 = Nothing

End Sub
```

Figure 5-11 shows an excerpt from the output of this program. Notice that the output starts by listing the query names for the forms. Next, it reports a count of the controls on each form. The last information from the Immediate window displays the subform record values along with the subdatasheet values for that subform record indented to the right. The sample shows the data for two order line items that correspond to the first record in the *Orders* table.

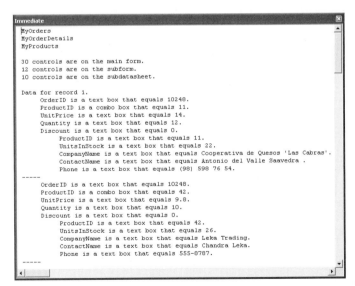

Figure 5-11   An excerpt of output from the *SyntaxForSubDataSheetOn-SubForm* procedure.

Programmatically Inserting Data into a Subform Record

With a good grasp of the syntax for working with controls on subforms and inserting records into forms, you can readily insert records into subforms based on ADO recordsets. The code sample in this section demonstrates one way to do this.

The sample's first task is to create a recordset for the main form. The SQL string for the *rst1* recordset extracts records from the *Orders* table if their *Order-Date* field value is in 1998.

I continue using the *frmMyOrders* main/subform. The sample opens this form and assigns the *rst1* recordset to the form's *Recordset* property. The sample assigns *adUseClient* to the recordset's *CursorLocation* property to facilitate data entry via the form. The block of code opening the sample also includes an object reference assignment for *ctl1*, which represents the subform control on *frmMyOrders*, namely the *frmMyOrderDetails* subform.

Before creating a new record, the sample saves the *OrderID* value for the main form. This *OrderID* value is the first order in 1998. (The *OrderID* value happens to be 10808.) The sample saves this value in *int1*. Then, the procedure invokes the *DoCmd* object's *GoToRecord* method with an *acNewRec* argument. This creates a blank form for data entry. Next, the sample populates the controls in the subform inside a loop. Notice that the sample saves the *ProductID* field value in *int2*. After passing through all the subform controls, the procedure closes the form. This action commits the new record to the form's record source.

The remainder of the sample removes the newly added record. This sample merely serves to demonstrate adding a record through the form—we do not actually want to change the standard Northwind table. The procedure invokes the *Seek* method to find those records from the *Order Details* table that match the value in *int1* (10808). It loops through these records to locate the one with the *ProductID* value for the newly added record. When the code finds the newly added record, it invokes the *Delete* method to remove the record.

```
Sub BindRstToSimpleMainSubFormRWInsert()
Dim cnn1 As ADODB.Connection
Dim rst1 As ADODB.Recordset
Dim frm1 As Form
Dim ctl1 As Control
Dim ctl2 As Control
Dim int1 As Long
Dim int2 As Long

'Create the connection
Set cnn1 = New ADODB.Connection
cnn1.Open "Provider=Microsoft.Jet.OLEDB.4.0;" & _
    "Data Source=C:\Program Files\Microsoft Office\" & _
    "Office11\Samples\Northwind.mdb;"
```

```
'Create recordset reference and set its properties
'to permit read/write access to recordset
Set rst1 = New ADODB.Recordset
rst1.CursorType = adOpenKeyset
rst1.LockType = adLockOptimistic
rst1.CursorLocation = adUseClient

'Open recordset based on orders in 1998 for
'frmSimpleUnboundForm
rst1.Open "SELECT * FROM Orders o " & _
    "WHERE Year(o.OrderDate) = 1998", cnn1

'Open a main/subform, assign pointers for main
'form and subform control, and assign recordset
'to the main form's Recordset property
DoCmd.OpenForm "frmMyOrders"
Set frm1 = Forms("frmMyOrders")
Set ctl1 = frm1.MyOrderDetails
Set frm1.Recordset = rst1

'Add a new record through the subform to the current OrderID
'value on the main form
int1 = frm1.OrderID
DoCmd.GoToRecord , , acNewRec
For Each ctl2 In ctl1.Form.Controls
    If TypeOf ctl2 Is TextBox Or TypeOf ctl2 Is ComboBox Then
        Select Case ctl2.Name
            Case "OrderID"
                ctl2.Value = int1
            Case "ProductID"
                ctl2.Value = 1
                int2 = ctl2.Value
            Case "Quantity"
                ctl2.Value = 1
            Case "UnitPrice"
                ctl2.Value = 1
            Case "Discount"
                ctl2.Value = 0
            Case Else
                MsgBox "Error on Insert."
                Exit Sub
        End Select
    End If
Next ctl2
DoCmd.Close acForm, frm1.Name

'Create recordset reference and set its properties so that
'you can seek the records for the OrderID to which you
'added a record
Set rst1 = New ADODB.Recordset
```

(continued)

```
rst1.Index = "OrderID"
rst1.CursorType = adOpenKeyset
rst1.LockType = adLockOptimistic
rst1.Open "Order Details", cnn1, , , adCmdTableDirect
rst1.Seek int1

'Loop through line items for OrderID to which you
'previously added a record; delete the record
'when you find it
Do Until rst1(0) <> int1
    If rst1(1) = int2 Then
'Delete the record because we do not want to change
'the Northwind database, but only show that we can
        rst1.Delete
        Exit Do
    End If
    rst1.MoveNext
Loop

'Clean up objects
rst1.Close
cnn1.Close
Set frm1 = Nothing
Set rst1 = Nothing
Set cnn1 = Nothing

End Sub
```

Summing Subform Control Values on a Main Form

A typical application requirement is the display of some aggregate of subform control values on a main form. For example, many applications might include a form like *frmMyOrders* and require a total extended price on the main form. This aggregate value derives from the extended price of the individual line items for an order, which are based on values in the subform—namely, the product of *Quantity* and *UnitPrice* times one minus *Discount*. The sample in this section demonstrates how to display total extended price on a variation of *frmMyOrders*.

I began constructing the sample by copying *frmMyOrders* and *frmMy-OrderDetails* to new forms named *frmMyOrdersSubtotal* and *frmMyOrder-DetailsSubtotal*. Next, in Design view I added a text box and its matching label to *frmMyOrdersSubtotal*. Then, I added a pair of event procedures to the code behind *frmMyOrdersSubtotal*. The main event procedure for *frmMyOrdersSubtotal* was *Form_Current*. This event fires whenever a new record becomes current. The *Current* event also fires when your application requeries or refreshes a form.

The code inside the *Form_Current* event procedure iterates through the records in the subform that match the current record in the main form. The *ctl1* variable points at the *subform* control on the main form, *frmMyOrdersSubtotal*.

Although the name of the subform is *frmMyOrderDetailsSubtotal*, the subform control still has the name *MyOrderDetails* because the subform is a copy of *frmMyOrderDetails*. For each record in the subform, the procedure computes the extended price. The procedure uses the Form property of the subform control to access the Quantity, UnitPrice, and Discount control values for each record. The *For…Next* loop that passes through the subform records also aggregates the extended price across the records. After exiting the loop, the procedure assigns the aggregated value to a Text Box control (*txtTotalExtendedPrice*) on the main form.

A *Form_Load* event procedure participates in the solution. This procedure formats the value in the text box on the main form so that it shows its value right aligned. Text Box controls left align their contents by default. An assignment to the *TextAlign* property for the *txtTotalExtendedPrice* control achieves this result. It is necessary to make this assignment just once when the form opens. Both event procedures appear next.

```
Private Sub Form_Open(Cancel As Integer)
Const conRightAlign = 3

'Right-align value in text box
Me.txtTotalExtendedPrice.TextAlign = conRightAlign

End Sub

Private Sub Form_Current()
Dim ctl1 As Control
Dim ctl2 As Control
Dim dbl1 As Double

'Assign a pointer for the subform control
Set ctl1 = Me.MyOrderDetails

'Iterate through the records on the subform to
'accumulate the total extended price
For int2 = 0 To ctl1.Form.Recordset.RecordCount - 1

    dbl1 = dbl1 + _
        (ctl1.Form.Controls("Quantity").Value * _
        ctl1.Form.Controls("UnitPrice") * _
        (1 - ctl1.Form.Controls("Discount")))

    ctl1.Form.Recordset.MoveNext

Next int2

'Display the total in a text box on the main form
Me.txtTotalExtendedPrice = Format(dbl1, "Currency")

End Sub
```

Figure 5-12 presents *frmMyOrdersSubtotal* with its text box showing the sum of the extended price for the line items corresponding to *OrderID* 10248. Navigating through the main form records updates the *txtTotalExtendedPrice* control value to match the line items in the subform. The update appears to happen instantaneously because the loop in the *Form_Current* event procedure just has to pass through the line items matching the *OrderID* control value on the main form.

Figure 5-12 The *frmMyOrdersSubtotal* form presents the total extended price for the line items appearing on its subform.

Formatting Controls on Main and Subforms

Formatting form controls—especially dynamically—is always an interesting topic. Often you will want to contrast some control values with other values. This section details three approaches to this. The first approach relies on manually creating conditional formats, which you can use to format controls dynamically without writing programs. Even experienced coders might find it desirable to try a formatting look without writing any programs. Second, you can programmatically set conditional formats using the *FormatConditions* collection and *FormatCondition* objects. The third approach—using event procedures and control properties—was the only way to achieve conditional formatting for controls before conditional formats were introduced in Access 2000. This approach might be more code intensive than working with conditional formats manually or programmatically, but it offers more flexibility.

Conditional Formatting

Access 2003 lets you conditionally format the data displayed by a Text Box or Combo Box control without programming. You can selectively apply formatting to form controls for both bound and calculated fields.

Figure 5-13 shows three instances of the same form. I used conditional formatting to control the appearance of the *Discount* and *Extended Price* fields. The *Discount* field in the top form is disabled. The middle form highlights the value in the *Extended Price* field using bold and italic formatting. The bottom form enables the *Discount* field and highlights the value in the *Extended Price* field.

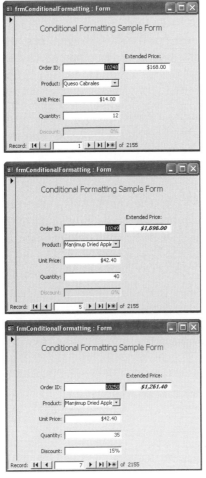

Figure 5-13   Conditional formatting controls the appearance of the *Extended Price* and *Discount* fields on this form.

The *Extended Price* field is calculated; it does not derive its value directly from an underlying table. The expression [UnitPrice]*[Quantity]*(1-[Discount]) in the text box's *ControlSource* property setting computes the value when the user moves to a new record or updates the *UnitPrice*, *Quantity*, or *Discount* field of the current record. (The terms in brackets reference controls, not field names for the underlying data source.)

> **Note** Novice programmers sometimes give fields and controls the same name. This practice can be confusing and can lead to errors. (The AutoForm Wizard and the Northwind sample are also guilty of this practice.) Consider adding prefixes to control names to distinguish them from their underlying field names. For example, txtUnitPrice is a good name for a Text Box control that is bound to a field named *UnitPrice*.

To apply conditional formatting to a control, select the control and choose Conditional Formatting from the Format menu to open the Conditional Formatting dialog box, shown in Figure 5-14. Every control with conditional formatting has at least two formats—a default format and one special format when a specified condition is *True*. The Conditional Formatting dialog box permits up to three conditional formats for a control. The dialog box offers six formatting controls to help you specify each conditional format. These permit you to manage the application of boldface, italics, underlining, background color, and foreground color, as well as whether a control is enabled.

You can format based on a control's field value, its expression value, or whether it has the focus. When you work with the field value for a control, you can select from a list of operators, such as equal to (=), greater than (>), and less than (<). The condition for the *Discount* field in Figure 5-14 is that the *Field* value is equal to 0. The formatting option for this condition disables the control when the discount is 0.

Figure 5-14 The Conditional Formatting dialog box.

If you apply conditional formatting to a calculated field, such as *Extended Price*, you must write an expression using standard VBA operators. The condition for the *Extended Price* field is that the expression is `txtExtended-Price.value>500`. (The name of the control that displays the calculated value is *txtExtendedPrice*.) When the field is greater than 500, bold and italic formatting highlight the text box contents.

You can easily apply another condition and special format to a control by clicking the Add button in the Conditional Formatting dialog box and specifying the new condition and its formatting information.

Programming Conditional Formats

As desirable as conditional formats are for eliminating or minimizing the programming of special formats for form controls, there are legitimate reasons for programming conditional formats. The Conditional Formatting dialog box restricts you to three formats (plus a default format) per control. If your application requires more diversity, you can dynamically manage conditional formats through their programmatic interface. In addition, if you want to apply a set of formats to several forms in the same or different applications, having the conditional formats programmatically defined simplifies applying the identical set of formats to different forms.

Each text box and combo box on a form has a *FormatConditions* collection containing *FormatCondition* objects. Even with the programmatic interface, each control is limited to three special conditions at any one time. However, you can program these conditions to have different values under different circumstances, thus multiplying the number of formats that you can manage programmatically. Because *FormatCondition* objects do not have name properties, you must reference them by their index numbers or property settings. For example, the *Type* property indicates that you apply the *FormatCondition* object via an expression or field value, or depending on whether a control has focus. Other properties let you set the expression values that determine whether to impose a format and its features, such as boldface, italics, and color. These property settings both define and identify the *FormatCondition* object.

The conditional-format programming sample that follows demonstrates several features of programmatically managing forms. The code begins by reinforcing your understanding of the process for dynamically assigning a recordset to the main form of a main/subform. After opening the form with an assigned recordset, the code prompts the user for the type of bolding on the form. Users can choose to bold all values for the *OrderID* control on the main form or any *Discount* control value greater than 14 percent on the subform, or they can select no boldface option at all. An *If...ElseIf* statement processes the user's reply to a message box to determine which path to pursue.

If a user chooses to bold all *OrderID* control values, the procedure uses the *DoCmd* object's *GoToRecord* method to navigate to the last record. After this, it saves the *OrderID* value for that record. After moving back to the first record, the code creates an expression with the *Add* method for a *FormatCondition* object that is *True* for any *OrderID* value less than or equal to that of the last record.

If the user chooses to apply a bold font to any *Discount* control value greater than .14 (14 percent), the procedure creates an object reference pointing to the *Discount* control on the subform. Then, the procedure invokes the *Add* method for the *FormatConditions* collection of the object reference. The syntax creates an expression that is *True* for any *Discount* control with a value greater than 14 percent. If the user chooses either Yes or No at the message box prompt, the code assigns a bold font to the *FormatCondition* object, *frc1*. The expression and the control for the *FormatCondition* object determine when to apply a bold font and which control to apply it to. If the user chooses Cancel in reply to the message box prompt, the program bypasses the creation of a *FormatCondition* object and the assignment of a format property for it.

```
Sub CreateConditionalFormat()
Dim cnn1 As ADODB.Connection
Dim rst1 As ADODB.Recordset
Dim frm1 As Form
Dim ctl1 As Control
Dim ctl2 As Control
Dim frc1 As FormatCondition
Dim int1 As Integer
Dim int2 As Integer
Dim str1 As String

'Create the connection
Set cnn1 = New ADODB.Connection
cnn1.Open "Provider=Microsoft.Jet.OLEDB.4.0;" & _
    "Data Source=C:\Program Files\Microsoft Office\" & _
    "Office11\Samples\Northwind.mdb;"

'Create recordset reference and set its properties
'to permit read/write access to recordset
Set rst1 = New ADODB.Recordset
rst1.CursorType = adOpenKeyset
rst1.LockType = adLockOptimistic
rst1.CursorLocation = adUseClient

'Open recordset based on orders in 1998 for
'frmSimpleUnboundForm
```

```
rst1.Open "SELECT * FROM Orders o " & _
    "WHERE Year(o.OrderDate) = 1998", cnn1

'Open a main/subform, assign pointers for main
'form and subform control, and assign recordset
'to the main form's Recordset property
str1 = "frmMyOrders"
DoCmd.OpenForm str1
Set frm1 = Forms(str1)
Set ctl1 = frm1.[MyOrderDetails]
ctl1.Form.SubdatasheetExpanded = False
Set frm1.Recordset = rst1

'Depending on user input, add a format condition
'to a main form control or a subform control
int1 = MsgBox("Do you want to bold OrderID " & _
    "values on the Main form? (choosing 'No' bolds Discounts " & _
    "on the subform greater than 14%.)", vbYesNoCancel, _
    "Programming Microsoft Access Version 2003")
If int1 = vbYes Then
    DoCmd.GoToRecord , , acLast
    int2 = frm1.Controls("OrderID")
    DoCmd.GoToRecord , , acFirst
    Set frc1 = frm1.Controls("OrderID"). _
        FormatConditions.Add(acFieldValue, _
            acLessThanOrEqual, int2)
ElseIf int1 = vbNo Then
    Set ctl2 = ctl1.Form.Controls("Discount")
    Set frc1 = ctl2.FormatConditions. _
        Add(acFieldValue, acGreaterThan, 0.14)
Else
    GoTo ConditionalFormatSample_Exit
End If

'Set a format condition to bold a control value
With frc1
    .FontBold = True
End With

'Clean up objects
ConditionalFormatSample_Exit:
Set ctl2 = Nothing
Set ctl1 = Nothing
DoCmd.Close acForm, frm1.Name
Set frm1 = Nothing
rst1.Close
Set rst1 = Nothing
Set cnn1 = Nothing

End Sub
```

This sample offers an attractive template for dynamically applying conditional formats to controls on main forms and subforms. The sample does not persist conditional formats to a *Form* object. Therefore, if a user opens a form outside the application code for dynamically assigning the conditional formats, the form controls will not appear with the formats. You can programmatically persist conditional formats to a form object, however. The next sample demonstrates the syntax for doing this to both main and subforms.

There are two tricks for persisting conditional formats. The first one requires you to use the *Save* method of the *DoCmd* object to save the form after creating the conditional format. The *acSaveYes* argument for the *DoCmd* object's *Close* method does not persist conditional formats to *Form* objects when it closes them. The second trick is to not persist conditional formats for subform controls through the *Form* property of a subform control on a main form. Instead, you must close the main form and open the subform so that you can apply conditional formats to it as a standalone form. Then, you can close the subform and restore the main form. This convention is a departure from many of the subform samples discussed so far. In fact, the preceding sample demonstrates that you can create a conditional format for a control on a subform through the *Form* property of a subform control. However, you cannot save a conditional format created this way.

The next sample shows how to save conditional formats for controls on main forms and subforms. Because the subforms in this code sample operate differently than in many of the preceding examples, this sample includes a conditional compilation with an original value of *True* for the *SubFormFix* compilation constant. This setting causes the code to save successfully conditional formats for subform controls. Setting the constant to *False* follows the traditional route for processing subform controls, and it does not persist a conditional format created for a subform control.

The sample to follow starts by opening the *frmMyOrders* form and setting references to the main form and subform control on the main form. The code also saves the *SubdatasheetExpanded* property setting so that it can restore the setting later, if necessary. Next, the sample presents a message box prompt as in the preceding sample. If the user chooses to set a conditional format for the *OrderID* control on the main form, the program logic proceeds as in the earlier sample until it reaches the code block with the label `'Save conditional formats`. The code block contains two lines. One invokes the *DoCmd* object's *Save* method with the form name as an argument. This action persists the conditional format created for the *OrderID* control. If you set the *SubFormFix* compilation constant to a value of *False*, the sample attempts to save a conditional format for a subform control after creating it the same way as in the preceding sample. However, the action fails silently for the subform control.

When the *SubFormFix* compilation is *True*, the sample adopts special measures to create and save the conditional format for the subform control. Examine the *#Else* path to see the code for creating and saving a conditional format for a subform. This code segment starts by closing the main form, *frm-MyOrders*. Then, it opens the subform, *frmMyOrderDetails*, as a standalone form. Next, it creates a *FormatCondition* object for the Discount control on the form and assigns a bold formatting property setting to the *FormatCondition* object. The task of persisting the conditional form requires you to save and close the form. For your convenience, this sample restores the main form before exiting the procedure. It even reinstates the status of the *Subdatasheet-Expanded* property.

```
Sub PersistAConditionalFormat()
Dim cnn1 As ADODB.Connection
Dim rst1 As ADODB.Recordset
Dim frm1 As Form
Dim ctl1 As Control
Dim ctl2 As Control
Dim frc1 As FormatCondition
Dim int1 As Integer
Dim bol1 As Boolean
#Const SubFormFix = True

'Open a main/subform, assign pointers for main
'form and subform control, and save
'SubdatasheetExpanded setting
DoCmd.OpenForm "frmMyOrders"
Set frm1 = Forms("frmMyOrders")
Set ctl1 = frm1.MyOrderDetails
bol1 = ctl1.Form.SubdatasheetExpanded

'Depending on user input, add a format condition
'to a main form control or a subform control
int1 = MsgBox("Do you want to bold OrderID " & _
    "10248 on the Main form? (choosing 'No' bolds Discounts " & _
    "on the subform greater than 14%.)", vbYesNoCancel, _
    "Programming Microsoft Access Version 2003")
If int1 = vbYes Then
    Set frc1 = frm1.Controls("OrderID"). _
        FormatConditions.Add(acFieldValue, acEqual, 10248)
ElseIf int1 = vbNo Then
    #If SubFormFix = False Then
        Set ctl2 = ctl1.Form.Controls("Discount")
        Set frc1 = ctl2.FormatConditions. _
            Add(acFieldValue, acGreaterThan, 0.14)
    #Else
'Close the main/subform so that you can open the
'subform as a standalone form
```

(continued)

```
        DoCmd.Close acForm, "frmMyOrders"
'Open subform, apply conditional format, and save it
        DoCmd.OpenForm "frmMyOrderDetails"
        Set frc1 = Forms("frmMyOrderDetails"). _
            Controls("Discount").FormatConditions. _
            Add(acFieldValue, acGreaterThan, 0.14)
        With frc1
            .FontBold = True
        End With
        'Forms("frmMyOrderDetails").SubdatasheetExpanded = True
        'Forms("frmMyOrderDetails").SubdatasheetExpanded = False
        DoCmd.Save acForm, "frmMyOrderDetails"
        DoCmd.Close acForm, "frmMyOrderDetails"
'Reopen main/subform
        DoCmd.OpenForm "frmMyOrders"
        Set frm1 = Forms("frmMyOrders")
        Set ctl1 = frm1.MyOrderDetails
        ctl1.Form.SubdatasheetExpanded = bol1
        Exit Sub
    #End If
Else
    GoTo ConditionalFormatSample_Exit
End If

'Set a format condition to bold a control value
With frc1
    .FontBold = True
End With

'Save conditional formats
DoCmd.Save acForm, "frmMyOrders"
DoCmd.Close acForm, "frmMyOrders"

'Clean up objects
ConditionalFormatSample_Exit:
Set ctl2 = Nothing
Set ctl1 = Nothing
Set frm1 = Nothing

End Sub
```

Selecting the option to format the *OrderID* field on the main form causes *frmMyOrders* to close. Users can view the result of the formatting by manually re-opening the main form. If you choose to persist a format for the *Discount* field on the *frmMyOrderDetails* subform, the main form remains open and shows the bold format for all *Discount* field values greater than .14. However, closing and then re-opening the form causes the *Discount* field to flicker so that its values are difficult to read.

The *frmPersistedFormatManager* form offers workarounds to the issue associated with persisting a format to subform fields, such as *Discount*. The form contains four buttons named Command0 through Command3 from top to bottom. The *Click* event procedure for the first button invokes the *PersistACon-ditionalFormat* procedure and closes the form. This step requires a user to open the *frmMyOrders* form to see any selected formatting. The second button converts the *DefaultView* property for the *frmMyOrderDetails* form from Datasheet to SingleForm. This suppresses the flickering of the *Discount* field and shows the formatting. The third button assigns Datasheet as the *Default-View* property of *frmMyOrderDetails* before opening *frmMyOrders*, the main form. In order to suppress the flickering for the *Discount* field, the *Click* event procedure for the third button expands and then collapses the subform. The latter step suppresses flickering for the *Discount* field. Even with these options for suppressing flickering, there is still a flickering problem. If a user opens *frmMy-Orders* outside of the *frmPersistedManager*, the *Discount* field will still flicker. This is because of the conditional format assigned to the *Discount* field by the *PersistAConditionalFormat* procedure. Therefore, the fourth button on *frmPer-sistedFormatManager* removes the conditional format for the *Discount* field. This enables a user to open *frmMyOrders* without viewing flickering for the *Discount* field (although it also fails to highlight *Discount* values greater than .14).

The code for the four *Click* event procedures behind *frmPersistedFormat-Manager* appears below. Three global declarations precede the procedure listings. At least two procedures use each of the global declarations.

```
Const conSingleForm = 0
Const conDatasheet = 2
Dim str1 As String

Private Sub Command0_Click()

'Run PersistAConditionalFormat procedure
PersistAConditionalFormat
DoCmd.Close acForm, "frmMyOrders"

End Sub

Private Sub Command1_Click()

'Make SingleForm DefaultView property for frmMyOrderDetails
str1 = "frmMyOrderDetails"
DoCmd.OpenForm str1, acDesign
Forms(str1).DefaultView = conSingleForm
DoCmd.Save acForm, str1
```

(continued)

```
DoCmd.Close acForm, str1

'Open frmMyOrders
DoCmd.OpenForm "frmMyOrders"

End Sub

Private Sub Command2_Click()

'Make Datasheet DefaultView property for frmMyOrderDetails
str1 = "frmMyOrderDetails"
DoCmd.OpenForm str1, acDesign
Forms(str1).DefaultView = conDatasheet
DoCmd.Save acForm, str1
DoCmd.Close acForm, str1

'Open frmMyOrders
DoCmd.OpenForm "frmMyOrders"

'Manipulate subdatasheet to fix appearance of the
'formatted control
Forms("frmMyOrders").MyOrderDetails.Form.SubdatasheetExpanded _
    = True
Forms("frmMyOrders").MyOrderDetails.Form.SubdatasheetExpanded _
    = False

End Sub

Private Sub Command3_Click()

'Remove format
str1 = "frmMyOrderDetails"
DoCmd.OpenForm str1, acDesign
Forms(str1).Controls("Discount").FormatConditions.Delete
DoCmd.Save acForm, str1
DoCmd.Close acForm, str1

End Sub
```

Formatting with Conditional Formats and Event Procedures

Before the introduction of conditional formats, the most popular way to assign formats to form controls was with event procedures for form events. Event procedures can test conditions for imposing a format on a control. The next example of formatting form controls mixes both conditional formats and event procedures to control the display of content on a main/subform.

The sample form we'll discuss appears in Figure 5-15. It shows a main/subform for the *Orders* and *Order Details* tables. These two tables are linked in the Chapter05.mdb sample file that points back to the Northwind database. The main form's name is *frmConditionalMainSub*, and the subform's name is *frmConditionalOD*. The figure shows that the *OrderID* control is disabled on the main form. In addition, the *OrderID* and *ProductID* controls on the subform are disabled. Recall that the *ProductID* control relies on a lookup field that automatically shows the ProductName from the *Products* table instead of the matching *ProductID* value in the *Order Details* table. Event procedures disable the main form and subform controls. In addition, the *Discount* control on the subform has three conditional formats. Values less than 5 percent appear in a green font, and values greater than 15 percent appear in red. *Discount* control values ranging from 5 to 15 percent appear in a shade of orange when the monitor is set to Highest (32 bit) Color quality.

Figure 5-15   Conditional formatting controls the appearance of the *Discount* control values on this form, and event procedures conditionally disable the *OrderID* control on the main form and the *OrderID* and *ProductID* controls on the subform.

Figure 5-16 presents the Conditional Formatting dialog box for the *Discount* control in the subform. Its top, middle, and bottom expressions set green, orange, and red fonts, respectively. I opened the dialog box by selecting the *Discount* control on the subform in Design view and choosing Format, Conditional Formatting.

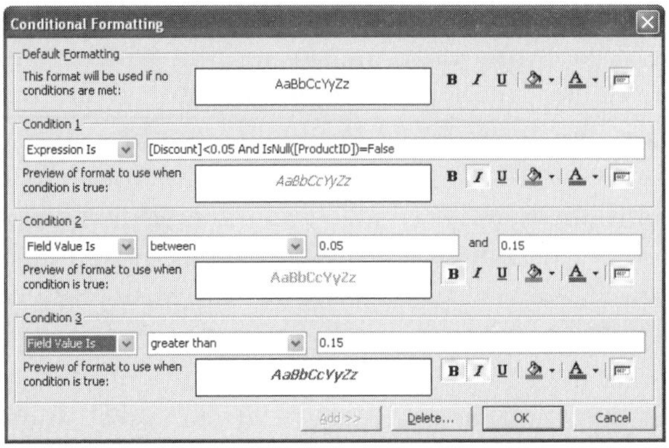

Figure 5-16 The expressions for the *Discount* control values in Figure 5-13.

The event procedures for the main and subforms rely on the *Current* event. Recall that this form event occurs when the focus moves to a record, making it the current one, or when a user requeries or refreshes a form so that the values of the form's controls might change. The *Current* event actually occurs before the record gains focus or the refresh or requery operation takes place. This event allows your program to test the control values before they are displayed. The sample's event procedures set the *Enabled* property of the controls. A compilation constant at the beginning of both event procedures simplifies turning off the effects of the procedures.

In the sample's main form, the *Form_Current* event procedure sets the *OrderID* control's *Enabled* property to a *Boolean* value. Setting a control's *Enabled* property to *False* protects its value from change. The *OrderID* field is the primary key for the record source behind the main form. While you might want to protect the value in this field for existing records, you will definitely want the control enabled if you have to enter values into it to complete a new record. When the control is *Null* (for example, when a user creates a new record), the *Form_Current* event procedure sets the control's *Enabled* property to *True*. This enabled setting is necessary so that Access can assign a new *AutoNumber* to the control. (A user can't edit the *AutoNumber* field, even if it is enabled.) The procedure moves the focus to the *CustomerID* control so that the user can start entering data with that control.

```
Private Sub Form_Current()
#Const EnableOnOff = True

#If EnableOnOff = True Then
'If cell is not Null, protect the
'primary key of the previously entered record;
'otherwise, enable the OrderID text box
    If IsNull(Me.OrderID) = False Then
```

```
            Me.OrderID.Enabled = False
        Else
            Me.OrderID.Enabled = True
            Me.CustomerID.SetFocus
        End If
#End If

End Sub
```

The next *Form_Current* event procedure is for the subform. Notice that in the event procedures for both the main and subform, you can use the simple *Me* notation to reference controls on a form. You can create or edit the *Current* event procedure for a subform in the usual way. First, select the subform. Do this by clicking the top-left box of the subform control on the main form. Then, open its property sheet in Design view and click the Build button next to the On Current event setting. This will open the shell for a new or an existing *Form_Current* event procedure.

The *Form_Current* event procedure for the subform disables the *OrderID* and *ProductID* controls by setting their *Enabled* property to *False* if the *OrderID* control and the *ProductID* control are both populated. In this case, the event procedure sets the focus to *Quantity*, the first control after *ProductID* on the subform. When you move to a blank main form record to enter a new order and select a customer, Access automatically enters a value into the *OrderID* control on the main form and current row of the subform. However, *ProductID* value for the current row on the subform contains a *Null*, and the procedure enables the *ProductID* controls. In addition, it sets the focus to the *ProductID* control. This is perfectly reasonable here because the user needs to input values to the *ProductID* control to complete the record so that Access will enter it into the record source for the subform. Here's the subform's event procedure:

```
Private Sub Form_Current()
#Const EnableOnOff = True

#If EnableOnOff = True Then
'If primary key is not Null, protect the
'primary key of the previously entered record;
'otherwise, enable the ProductID text box
    If IsNull(Me.OrderID) = False And _
        IsNull(Me.ProductID) = False Then
        Me.Quantity.SetFocus
        Me.OrderID.Enabled = False
        Me.ProductID.Enabled = False
    Else
        Me.ProductID.Enabled = True
        Me.ProductID.SetFocus
    End If
#End If

End Sub
```

Looking Up and Displaying Data

A lookup form is similar to a parameter query with a custom front end; the form simply collects input that drives a query. When you use forms and VBA, you can be flexible about gathering input as well as the type of information you can return to users.

Creating a Lookup Form

The easiest way to implement a form that looks up information is to have the user type the lookup information in a text box and click a button to start the search. The text box should be unbound because it doesn't enter information into the database; it simply gathers search information from the user. A query uses the value specified in the text box to find the matching information.

Figure 5-17 shows a form that opens the *qprHistoryfromTextBox* query when the user types a customer ID in the text box and clicks Look It Up. The query finds the total quantity ordered of each product bought by that customer.

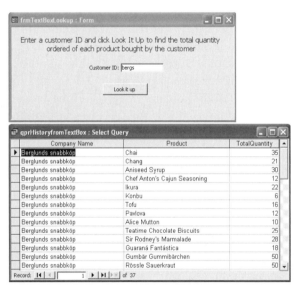

Figure 5-17   A form that performs a simple lookup operation.

The SQL statement for the *qprHistoryfromTextBox* query follows. Notice that the syntax specifies a parameter query. The parameter value is provided by the text box, *txtCustomerID*, on the *frmTextBoxLookup* form. This form appears at the top of Figure 5-17. If the *frmTextBoxLookup* form is closed when a user attempts to open the query, Access automatically prompts for a parameter to denote the value that the text box normally supplies. The query joins three tables to compute the quantity of each product ordered by the customer whose customer ID is in the *txtCustomerID* text box.

```
SELECT Customers.CompanyName, [Order Details].ProductID,
Sum([Order Details].Quantity) AS TotalQuantity
FROM (Customers INNER JOIN Orders
ON Customers.CustomerID = Orders.CustomerID)
INNER JOIN [Order Details]
ON Orders.OrderID = [Order Details].OrderID
WHERE Customers.CustomerID=Forms.frmTextBoxLookup.txtCustomerID
GROUP BY Customers.CompanyName, [Order Details].ProductID
```

The final element is a short VBA event procedure that fires when the user clicks the form's command button. The procedure has a single line that opens the query *qprHistoryfromTextBox*:

```
Private Sub cmdLookup_Click()
    DoCmd.OpenQuery "qprHistoryfromTextBox"
End Sub
```

Using a Combo Box for User Input

The form, *frmComboLookupSQL*, shown in Figure 5-18 has a better design than the one in Figure 5-17, provided that your list of customers isn't too long. Instead of forcing the user to enter a correct *CustomerID* field value, this form lets the user select the customer's name from a combo box. A procedure for the combo box's *AfterUpdate* event opens the *qprHistoryfromComboBox* query that uses the customer selected by the user, so the command button is unnecessary.

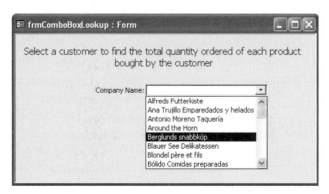

Figure 5-18   A Combo Box lookup form.

> **Note**   Combo Box lookup forms can become prohibitively slow as the number of lookup items becomes large. In this situation, you have at least two choices. First, you can revert to the text box lookup form (see Figure 5-17). Second, you can create a tiered system in which users make choices that restrict the range of items a combo box will make available. Essentially, you can split the list for one combo box across two or more other combo boxes. See "Programming Conditional Combo Boxes" in Chapter 12 for a sample implementing this approach.

To populate the combo box with the values for the application, follow these simple steps:

1. Set the control's *RowSourceType* property to Table/Query (the default).

2. Set the control's *RowSource* property to a SQL string that returns the fields you want. (The SQL string for the sample is "*SELECT CustomerID, CompanyName FROM Customers*".)

3. Set the control's *ColumnCount* property to 2.

4. Specify the column widths, separated by a semicolon. (The first value should always be 0.)

If you prefer, the Combo Box Wizard can create the control for you. Simply click the Control Wizards button on the Toolbox, and then add the combo box to the form.

Your goal is to populate the combo box with two columns. The first column contains the customer IDs, and its width is 0. The second column contains customer names, and its width is appropriate for displaying these names. When the user opens the combo box, he or she sees the customer names. However, when the user makes a selection, the combo box assumes the value of the *CustomerID* corresponding to the selected customer. You need to understand this distinction because the query must use the *CustomerID* value and not the customer name as a criterion value. The following SQL statement for the *qprHistoryFromComboBox* query reinforces this point. Notice that the *WHERE* clause sets the *cboLookup* control on the *frmComboBoxLookup* form to *CustomerID*—not *CompanyName*.

```
SELECT Customers.CompanyName, [Order Details].ProductID,
Sum([Order Details].Quantity) AS TotalQuantity
FROM (Customers INNER JOIN Orders
ON Customers.CustomerID = Orders.CustomerID)
INNER JOIN [Order Details]
ON Orders.OrderID = [Order Details].OrderID
WHERE Customers.CustomerID=Forms.frmComboBoxLookup.cboLookup
GROUP BY Customers.CompanyName, [Order Details].ProductID
```

Displaying Results in a Message Box

The preceding samples in this section suffer from two weaknesses. First, they pass values to and expose values from queries in Datasheet view. This means that users can inadvertently damage the query's design. Second, a user can modify the data underlying a query.

The sample lookup form at the top of Figure 5-19 remedies both of these deficiencies by using VBA and ADO. The input form has the same look and feel as the form in Figure 5-18. While the result sets of the queries opened by both forms are identical, they are displayed in different ways. The sample in Figure 5-19 displays its result set in message boxes rather than in a query window in Datasheet view. (The sample uses as many message boxes as necessary to display its result set.) This protects the underlying data from inadvertent damage by a user.

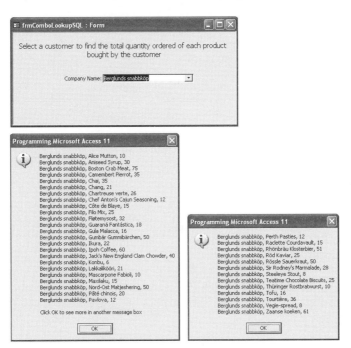

Figure 5-19   The form at the top displays its result set in message boxes so that users can view the result set but not alter its underlying data.

The following procedure fires on the *AfterUpdate* event of the combo box in Figure 5-19. It executes a command based on a query to develop a result set. It then assigns the result set from the command to a recordset and displays the recordset using one or more message boxes.

```
Private Sub cboLookup_AfterUpdate()
Dim ctl1 As Control
Dim cmd1 As Command
Dim rst1 As Recordset
Dim str1 As String

'Set reference to combo box control
Set ctl1 = Me.Controls("cboLookup")
'Create and define command.
'Use combo box value in SQL string for command.
    Set cmd1 = New ADODB.Command
    With cmd1
        .ActiveConnection = CurrentProject.Connection
        .CommandText = "SELECT Customers.CompanyName, " & _
            "Products.ProductName, " & _
            "SUM([Order Details].Quantity) AS TotalQuantity " & _
            "FROM Products INNER JOIN ((Customers INNER JOIN Orders " & _
            "ON Customers.CustomerID = Orders.CustomerID) " & _
            "INNER JOIN [Order Details] ON " & _
            "Orders.OrderID = [Order Details].OrderID) " & _
            "ON Products.ProductID = [Order Details].ProductID " & _
            "WHERE Customers.CustomerID = '" & ctl1.Value & "'" & _
            "GROUP BY Customers.CompanyName, Products.ProductName;"
        .CommandType = adCmdText
        .Execute
    End With

'Create recordset based on result set from SQL string
    Set rst1 = New ADODB.Recordset
    rst1.Open cmd1, , adOpenKeyset, adLockOptimistic

'Loop through result set to display in message box(es)
'in blocks of 925 characters or less
    Do Until rst1.EOF
        str1 = str1 & rst1.Fields(0) & ", " & _
            rst1.Fields(1) & ", " & rst1.Fields(2)
        str1 = str1 & vbCrLf
        If Len(str1) > 925 Then
            str1 = str1 & vbCrLf & "Click OK to see more " & _
                "in another message box"
            MsgBox str1, vbInformation, _
                "Programming Microsoft Access 2003"
            str1 = ""
        End If
```

```
        rst1.MoveNext
Loop
MsgBox str1, vbInformation, _
    "Programming Microsoft Access 2003"
```

End Sub

I could not use the SQL code from a query window in Design view in this procedure because the SQL string for a *Command* object does not support lookup fields. Therefore, I added the *Products* table to the query design so that I could report each product's name in the result set instead of just a product ID from the *Order Details* table. Adding this extra table further complicated the join logic for the query. (See Chapter 4 for an introduction to the SQL statement syntax.)

A *Do* loop steps through the recordset sequentially and writes its contents to a string. At the end of each record, the loop inserts a carriage return and a linefeed. If the string length exceeds 925 characters, the procedure inserts a blank line and an instruction to view the continuation of the sales history for the customer in the next message box. A message box can hold just over 1000 characters. (The *testmsgbox* procedure in this chapter's sample database helps you determine the maximum number of characters that a message box can hold; note that each of the top 19 lines in this test routine's output contains two non-printing characters.) Limiting additions to the current message box to 925 characters allows the message box to be filled without truncating any characters.

Dynamically Displaying Information

You can display data, such as a record, in a form, and you can even design a form so that users can view the record but not edit it. Figure 5-20 shows a pair of forms that work together to let the user view a customer's record. The user selects a customer in the *frmCustomerLookup* form and clicks the Show Customer In Form button to open the Customers form, which displays the customer's record. (The *Allow Edits*, *Allow Deletions*, and *Allow Additions* properties of the *Customers* form are set to No, which prevents the user from changing the data.) The user can then click the Return To Customer Lookup Form button to transfer control back to the initial lookup form. The user can also launch another lookup or exit the application from this form.

The following elegant and simple event procedure is the code behind the command button with the Show Customer In Form caption:

```
Private Sub cmdShowCustomer_Click()
On Error GoTo ShowCustomerTrap
Dim str1 As String
Dim str2 As String
```

(continued)

```
str1 = Me.cboCompanyName.Value
DoCmd.OpenForm "frmCustomers", acNormal, , _
    "CustomerID = '" & str1 & "'"

ShowCustomerTrapExit:
Exit Sub

ShowCustomerTrap:
If Err.Number = 94 Then
    MsgBox "Select a customer in the combo box " & _
        "before attempting to open the Customer form.", _
        vbExclamation, "Programming Microsoft 2003"
Else
    str2 = "Error number: " & Err.Number & "caused " & _
        "failure.  Its description is:" & vbCrLf & _
        Err.Description
    MsgBox str2, vbExclamation, _
        "Programming Microsoft Access 2003"
End If
Resume ShowCustomerTrapExit

End Sub
```

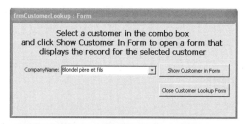

Figure 5-20   These forms let the user select and view a customer's record.

User Interactivity Based on Parameter Queries and ADO

The dynamic output generated to this point relies on SQL string expressions with variables. The variable values change the value returned by the SQL string. However, parameter queries are another common and powerful approach to obtaining dynamic output from Access. This section illustrates a couple of approaches to processing Access parameter queries with ADO.

Both approaches use the same parameter query, which is not a stored query in Access. By leaving the parameter query unstored, the sample demonstrates how to secure a query from anyone who can list or view the queries in a database file. A function procedure, *LookupOrders*, in a standard module evaluates the parameter query and returns an ADO recordset with rows based on the parameter value passed to the function procedure. The sample has the procedure in the sole standard module within the Chapter05.mdb file. By using a procedure in a standard module, multiple forms can re-use the same code.

The following listing shows the logic behind the function procedure that takes a parameter value and returns an ADO *Recordset* object. The procedure's parameter is a *CustomerID* value, such as one from the *Customers* table in the Northwind database. The result set from the parameter query is a set of rows listing order information for the customer specified by the parameter value. The columns in the rowset include *CustomerID*, *OrderID*, and *OrderDate*. The SQL string for the parameter is the *CommandText* property value for an ADO *Command* object. The procedure applies the *CreateParameter* method, initially discussed in Chapter 2, to instantiate a parameter for the *Command* object that will allow a specification of the parameter by the *CommandText* property.

```
Function LookupOrders(str1 As String) _
    As ADODB.Recordset

Dim cmd1 As New ADODB.Command
Dim prm1 As ADODB.Parameter

'Specify a parameter query cut and paste from the
'SQL view window
cmd1.ActiveConnection = CurrentProject.Connection
cmd1.CommandText = "PARAMETERS [Which customer?] Text(5); " & _
    "SELECT Customers.CustomerID, " & _
    "Orders.OrderDate, Orders.OrderID " & _
    "FROM Customers INNER JOIN Orders " & _
    "ON Customers.CustomerID = Orders.CustomerID " & _
    "WHERE (((Customers.CustomerID) = [Which customer?]))"

'Assign the value in the Text0 control to the
'parameter for cmd1
Set prm1 = cmd1.CreateParameter("[Which customer?]", _
```

(continued)

```
    adVarWChar, adParamInput, 5)
cmd1.Parameters.Append prm1
prm1.Value = str1

'Execute cmd1 and return the result set
Set LookupOrders = cmd1.Execute

End Function
```

Displaying Returned Rows via a Message Box

The form that displays the result set from the parameter query in a message box has three controls—text box, its matching label, and a command button (see Figure 5-21). A user inputs a *CustomerID* code into the text box and clicks the command button. The click starts the presentation of one or more message boxes that display the orders for the customer corresponding to the *CustomerID* in the message box.

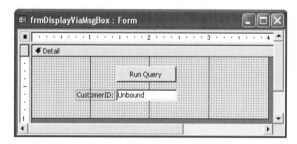

Figure 5-21 A form to display customer orders in one or more message boxes.

The code behind the form consists of two event procedures. The *Form_Load* event procedure formats the form by adding a caption and removing the record selector, dividing lines, and navigation buttons. The text specifying the *Caption* property appears in the form's border when the form is open in Form view (Figure 5-21 shows the form in Design view). The *Click* event procedure for the command button, *cmdRunQuery*, starts by invoking the *LookupOrders* function procedure described previously. The return from the function procedure is a recordset that the procedure displays in one or more text boxes. Within a *Do* loop, the procedure displays orders in blocks of 10 each. The procedure presents any orders not displayed within the loop immediately after exiting the loop. This can occur when the last block of orders contains fewer than 10 orders.

```
Private Sub Form_Load()

    Me.Caption = "Show orders for CustomerID in a message box"
```

```
        Me.RecordSelectors = False
        Me.DividingLines = False
        Me.NavigationButtons = False

End Sub

Private Sub cmdRunQuery_Click()

Dim rst1 As ADODB.Recordset
Dim str1 As String
Dim int1 As Integer

'Invoke parameter query through function
'procedure
Set rst1 = LookupOrders(Text0.Value)

'Loop through the result set from the parameter
'query and form a string for display; display
'ten rows at a time
int1 = 0
Do Until rst1.EOF

    str1 = str1 & rst1("CustomerID") & ", " & _
        rst1("OrderDate") & ", " & rst1("OrderID") & _
        vbCr
    rst1.MoveNext

    int1 = int1 + 1
    If int1 = 10 Then
        MsgBox str1, vbInformation, _
            " Programming Microsoft Access 2003"
        int1 = 0
        str1 = ""
    End If

Loop

'Display any odd lot of rows in the result set
If int1 > 1 Then
    MsgBox str1, vbInformation, _
        "Programming Microsoft Access 2003"
End If

End Sub
```

Displaying Returned Rows Via a List Box

The form to display orders in a list box appears in Figure 5-22. The Combo Box control has the name *cboCustomers*. This control displays a list of customer names and stores the *CustomerID* of any customer a user selects. After the user makes a selection, the List Box control, *lstOrders*, displays the orders for the customer selected in the combo box. The default vertical scrollbar for the list box permits users to navigate to an order not showing in the control's window.

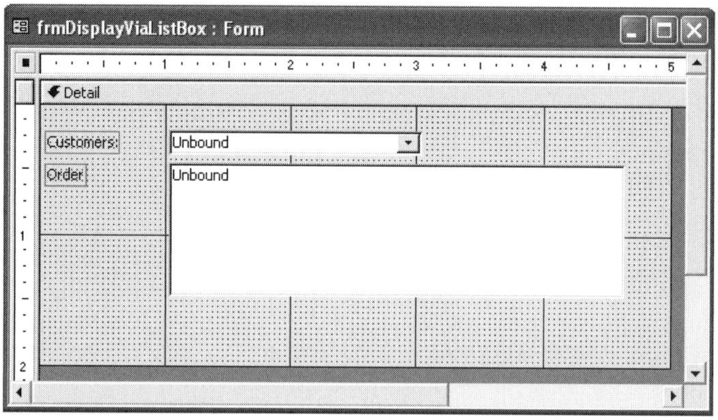

Figure 5-22   A form to display customer orders in the List Box control.

Two event procedures behind the form in Figure 5-22 enable the functionality described for the form, as well as format the layout of the form. The *Form_Load* event procedure populates *cboCustomers* with *CustomerID* and *CustomerName* column values from the *Customers* table. The load event procedure also specifies a Value List as the *RowSourceType* property for *lstOrders*. This setting enables the code to populate the *lstOrders* control with the values from the recordset returned by the *LookupOrders* procedure, instead of relying on an Access object such as a stored query. The *Form_Load* procedure closes by formatting the form. For example, it assigns a *Caption* property to the form declaring that the procedure displays orders in a list box.

The *cboCustomers_AfterUpdate* event procedure populates *lstOrders* with the orders for the customer selected in *cboCustomers*. The event procedure performs three tasks. First, it invokes the *LookupOrders* procedure to return a recordset with the orders for the customer selected in *cboCustomers*. Next, the procedure clears any prior contents for the *RowSource* property of the *lstOrders* List Box control. This prepares *lstOrders* to show just orders for the last selected customer from *cboCustomers*. Finally, the procedure iterates through the rows of the *rst1* recordset and adds them one at a time to *lstOrders*. The *AddItem* method for List Box controls facilitates this objective. In order for this process to work, it is also necessary for the control's *RowSourceType* property to equal Value List. Here's the listing for the code behind the form in Figure 5-22.

```
Private Sub Form_Load()
```

```
'Initialize cboCustomers control
With cboCustomers
    .RowSource = "SELECT CustomerID, " & _
        "CompanyName FROM Customers"
    .BoundColumn = 1
    .ColumnCount = 2
    .ColumnWidths = "0 in; 1.75 in"
    .Width = 2880
End With

'Assign Value List as RowSourceType property
'for lstOrders
lstOrders.RowSourceType = "Value List"

'Format form
Me.Caption = "Show orders for customer in a list box"
Me.RecordSelectors = False
Me.DividingLines = False
Me.NavigationButtons = False

End Sub

Private Sub cboCustomers_AfterUpdate()
Dim rst1 As ADODB.Recordset

'Open recordset based on selection for
'cboCustomers
Set rst1 = LookupOrders(cboCustomers.Value)

'Clear prior RowSource property setting
'for lstOrders
lstOrders.RowSource = ""

'Loop through the result set from the parameter
'query and form a string for display in listbox
'control
Do Until rst1.EOF
    str1 = rst1("CustomerID") & ";" & _
        rst1("OrderDate") & ";" & rst1("OrderID")
    lstOrders.AddItem str1
    rst1.MoveNext
Loop

End Sub
```

Charting a Subset of Data

The Microsoft Graph 2000 *Chart* object makes it easy to create professional-looking charts. (The *Chart* object is a mature Access development feature available since the first version of Access.) The object, which sits in an OLE Unbound Object Frame control on a form, can be bound to Access tables and queries, and you can choose from a wide selection of graph types and formatting options. (Double-click the object on a form in Design view to expose the custom menu for the object. When you finish using the Chart object's custom menu, click on the form outside the object to restore the normal Access form Design menu.)

You can add a Chart object manually, but using the Chart Wizard is easier. Simply follow these steps:

1. Click the Forms object in the Database window and then click New.

2. In the New Form dialog box, select Chart Wizard and the table or query on which your chart will be based, and then click OK.

3. On the first page of the Chart Wizard, select the fields that will be on your chart datasheet and then click Next.

4. Select the chart type and click Next.

5. Drag and drop the desired field buttons to the chart and click Next.

6. Select the Modify The Design Of The Form Or The Chart option and click Finish.

You can add aggregation and formatting functions by modifying the SQL statement in the *RowSource* property for the unbound object control containing the *Chart* object. (The wizard creates a SQL statement for you.)

Figure 5-23 shows two forms that let the user chart sales for a selected month. The top form lets the user select any year in the Orders table. The combo box's AfterUpdate event opens the bottom form, which uses the Microsoft Graph 2000 Chart object to display total sales quantity by month for the specified year. In Figure 5-23, the chart is based on a query that retrieves all orders from the specified year. The query translates each order date to the first of its month. (The underlying data remains unchanged.) This makes it simple to aggregate sales quantity by month, which in turn makes it easy to chart sales quantity by month. (The Chart Wizard automatically sums sales quantity by month for a record source such as this.)

The following three event procedures control the interaction between the two forms. The *cboPickAYear_AfterUpdate* procedure loads the charting form and minimizes the form in which the user selects a year. (You must minimize instead of close this form because the query for the chart determines what year the user selected using the combo box on the first form.)

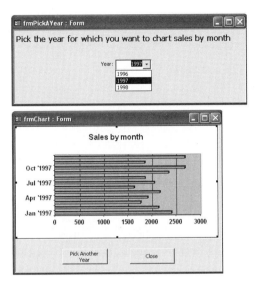

Figure 5-23   These forms let the user see monthly sales data for a selected year.

Manipulating Forms with VBA

This section describes some techniques for automating the use of forms. In particular, it illustrates how to enumerate forms and controls, techniques for programmatically hiding and showing forms, and methods for listing the forms in another project.

Enumerating Forms and Controls

The *AllForms* collection, which belongs to the *CurrentProject* object, contains an item for each form in a project. An application can enumerate the *AccessObject* objects in the *AllForms* collection to find all the forms in a project. The *AccessObject* object's *Name* and *IsLoaded* properties are particularly convenient: the *Name* property represents the name of each form in a project, and the *IsLoaded* property indicates whether the form is open. If you need to know whether a form with a certain name is in a project, manipulating the *AllForms* collection is the way to do it—whether or not the form is open.

The following procedure uses the *Count* property of the *AllForms* collection to determine how many forms are in the current project. Then, it prints the name and loaded status of each form in the project. (The *AllForms* collection is indexed beginning with 0; therefore, the *For* loop runs from 0 to one less than the total number of forms in the project.)

```
Sub ListAllForms()
Dim int1 As Integer

'Print the number of forms in the project
Debug.Print CurrentProject.AllForms.Count
Debug.Print

'Enumerate each form in the project
For int1 = 0 To CurrentProject.AllForms.Count - 1
    Debug.Print CurrentProject.AllForms.Item(int1).Name
    Debug.Print CurrentProject.AllForms.Item(int1).IsLoaded
    Debug.Print
Next int1

End Sub
```

The *Forms* collection contains the set of all open forms in a project, and the *Controls* collection of the Form object contains the set of controls on a form. Your applications can use these collections to find a specific form and an individual control on that form.

The following procedure enumerates all open forms in a project. For each open form, the procedure lists the form's controls by name and type. The *Control* object's *ControlType* property indicates the type of control. You can use the *TypeOf* keyword in a similar way.

```
Sub ListControlsOnOpenForms()
Dim frm1 As Form, ctl1 As Control

'Enumerate all open forms
For Each frm1 In Forms
    Debug.Print frm1.Name

'Enumerate each control on a specific open form
    For Each ctl1 In frm1.Controls
        Debug.Print "      " & ctl1.Name & ", " & _
            IIf(ctl1.ControlType = acLabel, "label", "not label")
    Next ctl1
Next frm1

End Sub
```

Notice that the procedure decodes the value of the *ControlType* property. When this value is the intrinsic constant *acLabel*, the control is a label. In a practical decoding exercise, you are more likely to use a *Select Case* statement than the *Immediate If (IIf)* function in the preceding sample. The *Immediate If* function, however, works adequately for decoding a single value. You can view the complete list of *ControlType* intrinsic constants in the Object Browser, as shown in Figure 5-24. From this window, you can get additional help about any form's control type.

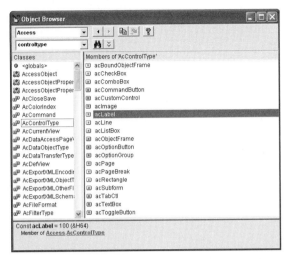

Figure 5-24   The complete list of Access form control types from the Object Browser.

Hiding and Showing Forms

You can use *VBA* and the *AllForms* collection along with some other objects to make forms invisible in the Database window. If you also make the form invisible in your application, the user might think that you removed the form. Hidden forms can still expose values for use by the other objects in an application.

The following pair of procedures hide and unhide an Access form:

```
Sub HideAForm(frmName As String)

'Close form if it is open so that it can be hidden
If CurrentProject.AllForms(frmName).IsLoaded = True Then
    DoCmd.Close acForm, frmName
End If

'Set form's Hidden property and do not show hidden
'objects in Database window
Application.SetHiddenAttribute acForm, frmName, True
Application.SetOption "Show Hidden Objects", False
End Sub


Sub UnhideAForm(frmName As String)

'If form is hidden, set form's hidden property to False
'and open form
If Application.GetHiddenAttribute(acForm, frmName) = True Then
    Application.SetHiddenAttribute acForm, frmName, False
    DoCmd.OpenForm frmName
End If

End Sub
```

The *SetHiddenAttribute* method sets or clears the *Hidden* attribute from the Database window for database objects, such as forms, reports, and queries. This method takes two arguments, an *AccessObject* object and a *Boolean* argument that indicates whether the object is to be hidden. Calling this method with an object and the value *True* is the same as setting the object's *Hidden* property in the Database window.

By itself, *SetHiddenAttribute* just grays the object; users can still select and use it. To make hidden objects invisible to the user, choose Options from the Tools menu, click Hidden Objects, and then click OK.

Before invoking *SetHiddenAttribute*, you should check the *AccessObject* object's *IsLoaded* property. If the object is loaded, you should close it before attempting to invoke *SetHiddenAttribute*; calling the method with an open object generates an error.

Enumerating Forms in Another Project

VBA does not restrict you to working with database objects in the current project. For example, you can test for the existence of forms in another instance of an Access application. One essential step in this process is to compare the Name property of AllForms members to the name of the target form. There is also a new trick to learn: You open a new instance of an Access Application with the target database in it, and then you use the *CurrentProject* object of that instance as the source for an *AllForms* collection. This subtle refinement lets you process database objects in another database file—namely, the one at which the Access Application instance points.

The following two procedures implement this technique with VBA. *FormToLookFor* sets the database path to the other database file and gathers the name of the target form. The second procedure, *FormExistsInDB*, searches for a target form. You call the second procedure from the first one.

```
Sub FormToLookFor()
Dim str1 As String
Dim str2 As String

'Search for forms in the Northwind database
str1 = "C:\Program Files\Microsoft Office\" & _
    "Office11\Samples\Northwind_backup.mdb"
'Get the name of the form to search for from the user.
str2 = InputBox("Enter name of form to search for: ", _
    "Programming Microsoft Access 2003")
```

```
'Call FormExistsInDB to check whether the form exists
FormExistsInDB str1, str2
End Sub

Sub FormExistsInDB(str1 As String, str2 As String)
Dim appAccess As Access.Application, int1 As Integer

'Return reference to Microsoft Access application
Set appAccess = New Access.Application

'Open a database in the other application
appAccess.OpenCurrentDatabase str1

'Check whether the form exists
For int1 = 0 To (appAccess.CurrentProject.AllForms.Count - 1)
    If (appAccess.CurrentProject.AllForms.Item(int1).Name = _
        str2) Then
        MsgBox "Form " & str2 & " exists in the " _
            & str1 & " database.", _
            vbInformation, "Programming Microsoft Access 2003"
        GoTo FormExistsExit
    End If
Next int1

'Report that form does not exist
MsgBox "Form " & str2 & " does not exist in the " _
    & str1 & " database."

'Close other Access application
FormExistsExit:
appAccess.Quit
Set appAccess = Nothing

End Sub
```

The first procedure sets *str1* equal to the path for the Northwind database. An *InputBox* function prompts the user to input the name of the form to search for, and then the first procedure calls the second procedure.

The second procedure sets and opens a reference for the new instance of the Access application, and then enters a loop that checks whether any of the forms in the new database match the target form name. The procedure reports whether it found the target form and frees its resources before returning.

Summary

This chapter is about creating custom solutions with forms. The emphasis is on programming, as opposed to how to use the many excellent built-in wizards and graphical design features for forms in Access. For example, this chapter repeatedly shows you how to set form and control property values programmatically at run time, although you can also set these properties manually at design time. Managing properties at run time is inherently more flexible because your applications can adapt to users and environmental conditions at startup and over the course of an application. Reviewing a VBA script that changes the default settings is a faster way to detect design changes than hunting through property sheet tabs.

Another major focus in this chapter is how to programmatically populate the *RecordSource* and *Recordset* properties of forms. This emphasis equips you with the skills needed to re-use your forms with different data sources. Two samples in the chapter illustrate how to work with parameter queries and ADO objects to support user interactivity via Access forms. Other samples demonstrate how to use familiar Access database objects and Jet SQL string expressions for the same objective. By using the principles and adapting the samples covered in this chapter, you can reduce the number of forms necessary for applications and create solutions that are more efficient to maintain.

The chapter's final major focus is the programmatic manipulation of form objects in an application. The chapter's concluding sections explain how to enumerate and manipulate the forms in an application whether or not they are open. You learn how to perform these tasks for other Access databases besides the current one. You also find out about the impact of changes to property settings in Form versus Design view. The chapter's concluding samples highlight techniques for instantiating and tracking multiple instances of the same form in an application.

6

Reports, Controls, and Data

Your understanding of forms gained from the previous chapter will serve you well as you consider how to use reports in your applications. Although reports do not support interactive controls like forms do, you can populate reports with controls that display data, such as text boxes and check boxes. Reports can contain bound and unbound graphic images and ActiveX controls for special displays, such as charts. The charting capability for reports in Microsoft Access 2003 is similar to that of forms. You can design main reports with subreport controls, just as main forms can contain subform controls.

Access reports are sometimes the only contact a user has with a database. As a developer, you will likely encounter well-defined opinions from clients about what reports should convey and how they should arrange and summarize data. This chapter aims to qualify you to respond creatively and rapidly to user-generated report specifications.

The chapter begins with an introduction to techniques for building reports manually, but it later provides a demonstration of creating reports programmatically. Using one of the many Access report wizards is often a great first step to developing a custom report. Instead of building a default layout, you can spend your time customizing a wizard-generated report. This effort can include customizing the record source as well as making the report's content or formatting responsive to run-time specifications. If you're going to create new reports programmatically, or edit existing reports, you need a solid understanding of the Access report architecture and its Design-view environment. The summary of manually created reports covers these topics.

This chapter also addresses programmatic issues. It starts out by covering approaches for creating and deploying snapshots of Access reports. The chapter ends with an examination of methods for making existing reports dynamic through programming.

Report Architecture and Creation Strategies

Access is a popular reporting engine because Access reports are easy to create and update. You can easily deploy them to non-Access users using the Snapshot format (this feature is covered later in the chapter). Because it's so easy to link Access to record sources from other databases, Access development commonly features report generation for ODBC and other legacy data sources as well as traditional Access databases.

Report Sections

One feature that makes Access such a popular database-reporting engine is its banded report sections. The standard default report design includes three sections: the Detail, Page Header, and Page Footer sections. The Detail section is bordered above and below, respectively, by the Page Header and Page Footer sections. The Page Header and Page Footer sections each appear once per page within a report. The Detail section repeats once for each record in a report's record source. In a simple tabular report, the Detail section is likely to repeat multiple times per page.

When you create a new report, Access relies on the current report template to determine the types of sections in the report, as well as the dimensions and other default property settings. When first installed, Access uses its Normal report template. However, you can import any other report in the current or another Access database file or Access project to use as the default template. Recall that an Access project is the client application of a Microsoft Access and SQL Server client/server solution (this concept is covered in more detail in Chapter 11). Choose Options on the Tools menu in the database window and select the Forms/Reports tab to expose the text box to specify a report template other than Normal. Changes to the Report Template text box on the Options dialog box will affect all future reports. Previously created reports retain the design specified in the Report Template text box when they were created unless you explicitly alter their design.

> **Note**   The Options command on the Tools menu in the database window displays the controls for setting the form template and the report template. You can use the Form Template text box just as you would use the Report Template text box to control the default design of a form.

The View menu in the report design window offers two commands for adding and removing sections within the report when it is open in Design view. These menu commands let you add or remove a pair of header/footer sections for the page or for the entire report. The menu items have toggle controls, but they do not simply toggle the visibility of a section; once you remove a section, you cannot use the menu to restore the section's content. Even if you do restore a section, its former content will be lost. The Page Header/Footer command on the View menu adds or removes the Page Header and Page Footer sections. The Report Header/Footer command adds or removes the Report Header and Report Footer sections. The Report Header and Report Footer sections appear once in each report—at the beginning and at the end, respectively. You can manually resize any section in a report by dragging its bottom edge up or down or dragging its right edge away from or toward its left edge. When you drag a section's right edge, you modify the size of all the report's sections—not just the one you are manipulating.

You can create custom header and footer report sections for groups that you create with the Sorting And Grouping command on the View menu in the report design window. The custom header sections are often convenient for providing information at the beginning of a group, while custom footer sections make a good location for unbound report controls that display subtotals for the records in a group.

Creating Reports

You can create reports both manually and programmatically. The AutoReport Wizard works the same way as the AutoForm Wizard—both wizards are available as selections from the New Object tool on the Database toolbar. Select any row-returning record source in the Database window. Then, just click the New Object: AutoReport button on the Database toolbar. Although the AutoReport Wizard functions identically to the AutoForm Wizard, you might find the resulting layout unappealing as a starting point for programmatic customization. The default columnar layout without a delimiter between records makes it hard to discern where one record ends and another begins.

The New Report dialog box offers additional report wizards, such as the AutoReport: Tabular Wizard. You can open the dialog box by selecting Reports in the Objects bar on the Database window and clicking the New button on the Database window. The AutoReport: Tabular Wizard provides a more typical layout for database reports than the columnar layout generated by the Auto-Report Wizard on the Database toolbar. Before clicking OK on the New Report dialog box to invoke the AutoReport: Tabular Wizard, you must use a drop-down control on the dialog box to specify a record source, such as a query, for the report. This wizard displays each record as a separate row in the Detail section. The wizard utilizes the Page Header section to display labels for the columns that appear on each page. If there are too many columns to fit on one page, the wizard positions the columns for a single record across two or more pages.

The Report Wizard provides a richer graphical interface than the Auto-Report: Tabular Wizard for designing single-column and multicolumn reports. For example, you do not need to specify a record source before clicking OK to launch this wizard from the New Report dialog box, because the wizard allows you to specify a record source from its own pages. The Report Wizard is especially convenient for designing reports that generate grand totals and subtotals for numeric fields. You can also use this wizard to create groups and specify sort orders for the rows of a report. A report's sort settings override any SQL instructions that specify the sort order for the report's record source.

Other specialized wizards you can use to create reports include the Label Wizard and the Chart Wizard.

The New Report dialog box also lets you enter Design view to create a new report. This affords more flexibility than the wizards do, but it requires a more advanced understanding of Access report design as well as a mastery of the Design view menu for reports. If you plan to program reports, you should familiarize yourself with this view. You can also enter Design view for an existing report, such as a report created with a wizard or one that was previously created manually and requires editing. To open an existing report in Design view, select its name in the Database window. Then, click the Design control on the Database window.

Finally, you can programmatically create reports, which provides substantial flexibility and permits you to make report design responsive and interactive. You can also programmatically manipulate existing reports to edit them permanently or to dynamically update them in response to user input or data values.

Creating Reports Programmatically

Because Access has such a powerful user interface for designing and manipulating reports, you probably will not find it convenient to create reports programmatically. However, if your application requires you to create a wizard that allows users to design custom reports, this section shows you how to get started. In addition, if you ever need to modify the controls on a large number of existing reports, this section provides you with useful background on the subject. Later sections in the chapter provide additional sample code that demonstrates how to manipulate existing reports programmatically.

Laying out a basic tabular report is a relatively simple task that requires just two methods: *CreateReport* and *CreateReportControl*. The Access *Application* object's *CreateReport* method creates a *Report* object. After you create a report, you need to assign a record source to it and populate the report with controls that display the contents of the record source. The Access *Application* object's *CreateReportControl* method adds controls to a report.

Creating and Saving an Unnamed Empty Report

Invoking the *CreateReport* method by itself creates an empty report. This method belongs to the *Application* object, which is the top level Access object. As a consequence, you can specify the *CreateReport* method without designating its object, which is the *Application* object. Unless you change the Report template setting, the *CreateReport* method generates an empty report with three sections: a Page Header, a Detail section, and a Page Footer. When you create a report with this method, that report will not exist in any Access database file or Access project. Access automatically assigns the report a name, such as *Report1*. If the application's file already has a report named *Report1*, Access names the report *Report2*, and so on.

The first programming sample in this section illustrates the syntax for creating an empty report with the default name. If you execute this procedure twice in a file that has no existing reports named *Reportx* (where *x* is a number), the procedure creates two reports: *Report1* and *Report2*. You can open either report in Design view and verify its empty status.

```
Sub CreateDefaultNamedReport()
Dim rpt1 As Report

'Create and save an empty report
'with a default name
Set rpt1 = CreateReport
DoCmd.Close , , acSaveYes

End Sub
```

Creating and Saving a Report with a Custom Name

The preceding sample generates reports named *Report1*, *Report2*, and so on with the *CreateReport* method because the method does not provide a means to name a report. Furthermore, the *DoCmd* object's *Close* method does not let you close a report and give it a custom name if the report does not already exist. The *acSaveYes* argument for the *DoCmd* object's *Close* method applies only to existing objects. In essence, this method lets you save over an existing object rather than save an object for the first time.

The *DoCmd* object's *Save* method can save a new object with a custom name. However, this method does not replace an existing object with a new object. Therefore, the trick to saving reports with a custom name is to use a two-step process. First, if the report already exists, you need to delete it. Once you have removed any prior versions of a report that have the custom name you want to use, you can perform the second step: using the *DoCmd* object's *Save* method to save the report. As long as you delete any prior versions of the report before invoking this method, it will always work correctly.

The following sample illustrates saving an empty report with a custom name. It relies on three procedures. The first procedure, *CallCreateCustom-NamedReport*, performs two tasks.

■ It assigns a value to a string variable, which is the custom name for the report.

■ It passes the string argument to the *CreateCustomNamedReport* procedure.

After creating a new report, the second procedure conditionally deletes any existing report that has the custom name passed to it. The code calls the *DoesReportExist* function procedure to assess this. If a report with the custom name already exists, the *DoesReportExist* procedure returns a *Boolean* value of *True*. When the function returns a value of *True*, the *CreateCustomNamed-Report* procedure invokes the *DeleteObject* method of the *DoCmd* object for the prior version of the report. After ensuring the deletion of the report's prior version, the procedure can invoke the *DoCmd* object's *Save* method without the risk of generating a run-time error by saving over an object that already exists.

The *DoesReportExist* function procedure passes through all the members of the *AllReports* collection for the *CurrentProject* object. Recall from Chapter 3 that members of the Access *Allxxx* collections are *AccessObject* objects. (Later in this chapter, the section "Manipulating Reports and Report Controls" deals more fully with the *AllReports* collection.) The syntax in the *DoesReportExist* function procedure is appropriate for either an Access database file or an Access project.

> **Note**   The *AllReports* collection contains the names of all reports, regardless of whether they are open or closed. The *Reports* collection is not useful for detecting whether a report already exists because this collection contains only open reports.

```
Sub CallCreateCustomNamedReport()
Dim str1 As String

str1 = "rpt1"
CreateCustomNamedReport str1

End Sub

Sub CreateCustomNamedReport(str1 As String)
Dim rpt1 As Access.Report

'Create a report
Set rpt1 = CreateReport

'If the name for your new report already exists,
'delete the old version before saving the new version
If DoesReportExist(str1) Then
    DoCmd.DeleteObject acReport, str1
End If
DoCmd.Save , str1
DoCmd.Close

End Sub

Function DoesReportExist(str1 As String) As Boolean
Dim aro As AccessObject

'Search the members of the AllReports collection
'for a report with the name in str1; return True
'if report exists and False otherwise
For Each aro In CurrentProject.AllReports
    If aro.Name = str1 Then
        DoesReportExist = True
        Exit Function
    End If
Next aro

End Function
```

Programmatically Creating a Report with Controls

As you can see, adding a custom report is not very complicated; the syntax for calling the *CreateReport* method is straightforward. Access Help documents two arguments for this method, but you do not need either of them unless you are using a nonstandard report template.

To add controls to a report created with the *CreateReport* method, you need to invoke the *Application* object's *CreateControlReport* method. The *Create-ControlReport* method can take as many as nine arguments, but Access requires only two. You will usually need to specify a handful of arguments. Just like the *CreateReport* method, the *CreateControlReport* method returns an object—in this case, a control for a report.

The required arguments for the *CreateReportControl* method include the report name that will contain the control and the type of control to be added. You can specify the control type with an intrinsic constant—for example, specify *acTextBox* for a text box control. Listing the members of the *AcControlType* in the Object Browser presents all the intrinsic constants for control types; reports and forms share the same control types. Although specifying a report section for the control is not mandatory (the Detail section is the default), you will normally specify the destination section for the report control. Any bound control, such as a text box, will require a *ColumnName* argument. This argument is equivalent to the *ControlSource* property for the control. Your *Column-Name* argument indicates the name of a column from the report's *RecordSource* property setting.

You often have to designate the position and size of controls. Parameters for these control properties can be set either in the *CreateReportControl* argument list or with separate property assignments. Both the method arguments and object properties use the same names to refer to these control settings. The *Top* and *Left* arguments indicate the offset of the control from the top-left corner of the report section in which the control resides. The *Width* and *Height* arguments denote a control's size. When designating the *Top*, *Left*, *Width*, or *Height* arguments in Microsoft Visual Basic for Applications (VBA), you should specify units in twips. (Recall that 1,440 twips equals 1 inch.)

A *Height* setting is necessary when working with label controls that serve as column headings in tabular report layouts. You can make this setting with an argument when you call the *CreateReportControl* method or by using a separate assignment statement.

The following code sample creates a report based on the *Customers* table in the Northwind database. The report shows four columns in a format that provides a basic telephone directory of customer contacts. Figure 6-1 shows an excerpt from the report's layout. Notice that the report's design distinguishes the column headers from the data rows by assigning them a bold font.

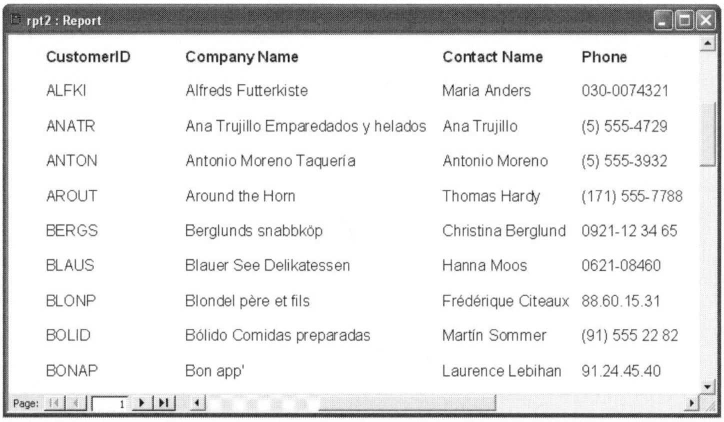

rpt2 : Report

CustomerID	Company Name	Contact Name	Phone
ALFKI	Alfreds Futterkiste	Maria Anders	030-0074321
ANATR	Ana Trujillo Emparedados y helados	Ana Trujillo	(5) 555-4729
ANTON	Antonio Moreno Taquería	Antonio Moreno	(5) 555-3932
AROUT	Around the Horn	Thomas Hardy	(171) 555-7788
BERGS	Berglunds snabbköp	Christina Berglund	0921-12 34 65
BLAUS	Blauer See Delikatessen	Hanna Moos	0621-08460
BLONP	Blondel père et fils	Frédérique Citeaux	88.60.15.31
BOLID	Bólido Comidas preparadas	Martín Sommer	(91) 555 22 82
BONAP	Bon app'	Laurence Lebihan	91.24.45.40

Figure 6-1 A report created programmatically based on the *CreateReport* and *CreateReportControl* methods.

The code for the report in Figure 6-1 has several sections. It begins by creating a report with the *CreateReport* method. Then, it assigns a SQL string to the *RecordSource* property of the report. Without this assignment, you would have to specify the record source for a report at run time before the report opens. Immediately after the record source assignment, the procedure specifies the height of the Details section as about a quarter of an inch. This height is needed to control the spacing between rows in the table. As with other size assignments for controls through VBA, the units are twips. Next, the procedure adds the controls for the four columns. After adding controls to display and label data, the procedure saves the report with a custom name (*rpt2*). This name appears in Figure 6-1 in the title bar. The closing segment of the procedure invokes the *DoesReportExist* function described earlier in the section.

Four blocks of code successively add each column to the report. A comment that mentions the data for the column precedes each block. Within each block, the *CreateReportControl* adds two controls—a text box and a label.

The *CreateReportControl* method for the text box in the first column has four arguments. These specify the report name, the type of control, the report section for the control, and the column name from the report's record source. This last argument sets the *ControlSource* property for the text box. The *CreateReportControl* method does not have an argument for naming the control, so the procedure assigns a string to the control's *Name* property immediately after the invocation of the *CreateReportControl* method. The second invocation of the *CreateReportControl* method for the *CustomerID* column creates the column header. The arguments for this control designate a label control type that resides in the report's Page Header section. In addition to assigning a name to the control, the property assignments for the label control specify *Caption*, *Width*, and *Height* properties. You must always set these label control properties. The code block closes by assigning a bold font setting to the label.

The blocks of code that create controls for the report's second through fourth columns follow the example of the first column—with one exception. The first block positions its label and text box controls flush with the report's left edge (which is the current printer's left margin setting). The second through fourth columns offset the left edge of their controls by the left edge of the text box for the preceding column plus the width of that text box plus 50 twips. The *wid1* memory variable is used to calculate this spacing by adding the prior column's *Width* setting to the prior *Left* setting. The sixth argument for the *CreateReportControl* method adds 50 as an additional offset to *wid1* when specifying the left edge of controls in the second through the fourth columns.

Note   Access 2002 introduced a new *Printer* object that is included in Access 2003. *Printer* objects are members of the *Printers* collection. Use members of this collection when you want to designate one printer from a choice of multiple printers to which an application can connect. With the *Printer* object, you can control settings such as the left margin, the number of copies, and the paper bin. See Access Help, Printer Object for more detailed information, including code samples.

There is one additional setting you can use when adding the controls for the columns. By default, the control width for text boxes is 1 inch (1,440 twips). This setting is appropriate for all columns in the report, except for the second column, which needs a width of 2,700 twips to accommodate longer customer names.

```
Sub CreateAReportWithASource()
On Error GoTo ReportSource_Trap
Dim rpt As Report
Dim txt1 As Access.TextBox
Dim lbl1 As Access.Label
Dim str1 As String
Dim wid1 As Integer

'Create a report with a RecordSource assignment
Set rpt1 = CreateReport
rpt1.RecordSource = "SELECT * FROM Customers"
rpt1.Section("Detail").Height = 365
```

```
'Add page column label and text box for CustomerID
Set txt1 = CreateReportControl(rpt1.Name, acTextBox, _
    acDetail, , "CustomerID")
txt1.Name = "txtCustomerID"
Set lbl1 = CreateReportControl(rpt1.Name, acLabel, _
    acPageHeader)
lbl1.Name = "lblCustomerID"
lbl1.Caption = "CustomerID"
lbl1.Width = txt1.Width
lbl1.Height = txt1.Height
lbl1.FontBold = True

'Add page column label and text box for CompanyName.
'Set the width of this column at 2700 twips, which is
'different than the default setting of 1440 twips.
wid1 = txt1.Width
Set txt1 = CreateReportControl(rpt1.Name, acTextBox, _
    acDetail, , "CompanyName", wid1 + 50)
txt1.Name = "txtCompany"
txt1.Width = 2700
Set lbl1 = CreateReportControl(rpt1.Name, acLabel, _
    acPageHeader, , , wid1 + 50)
lbl1.Name = "lblCompanyName"
lbl1.Caption = "Company Name"
lbl1.Width = 2700
lbl1.Height = txt1.Height
lbl1.FontBold = True

'Add page column label and text box for ContactName
wid1 = txt1.Left + txt1.Width
Set txt1 = CreateReportControl(rpt1.Name, acTextBox, _
    acDetail, , "ContactName", wid1 + 50)
txt1.Name = "txtContactName"
Set lbl1 = CreateReportControl(rpt1.Name, acLabel, _
    acPageHeader, , , wid1 + 50)
lbl1.Name = "lblContactName"
lbl1.Caption = "Contact Name"
lbl1.Width = txt1.Width
lbl1.Height = txt1.Height
lbl1.FontBold = True

'Add page column label and text box for Phone
wid1 = txt1.Left + txt1.Width
Set txt1 = CreateReportControl(rpt1.Name, acTextBox, _
    acDetail, , "Phone", wid1 + 50)
txt1.Name = "txtPhone"
Set lbl1 = CreateReportControl(rpt1.Name, acLabel, _
    acPageHeader, , , wid1 + 50)
```

(continued)

```
lbl1.Name = "lblPhone"
lbl1.Caption = "Phone"
lbl1.Width = txt1.Width
lbl1.Height = txt1.Height
lbl1.FontBold = True

'If the name for your new report already exists,
'delete the old version before saving the new version
str1 = "rpt2"
If DoesReportExist(str1) Then
    DoCmd.DeleteObject acReport, str1
End If
DoCmd.Save , str1
DoCmd.Close

ReportSource_Exit:
'Clean up objects
Set rpt = Nothing
Exit Sub

ReportSource_Trap:
If Err.Number = 2008 Then
'If the str1 report is already open,
'close it so that the procedure can delete it
    DoCmd.Close acReport, str1
    Resume
Else
    Debug.Print Err.Number, Err.Description
    MsgBox "Program aborted for unanticipated reasons.", _
    vbCritical, "Programming Microsoft Access 2003"
End If

End Sub
```

Creating Reports with Wizards

Since this is a programming book, you might be wondering why there is any mention of report wizards. However, wizards are an integral part of Access. If you build solutions and fail to take advantage of wizards that can address your problems meaningfully, you might as well use another development environment instead. In addition, wizards can create report shells that are well suited for customization via programming. The best way to learn about the various features and capabilities of Access wizards is to experiment with them.

Report wizards are great for performing tasks that are awkward to execute programmatically. The first example in this section builds a basic telephone directory report like the one discussed in the preceding section (see Figure 6-1). However, the Report Wizard automatically performs a lot of formatting, even with the most basic choices. In addition, the Report Wizard makes it easy to choose many formatting options and build many other kinds of reports. The second and third examples we'll look at in this section illustrate the capabilities of more specialized report wizards.

The Chart Wizard creates charts in Access reports. This wizard's charting capabilities resemble those available in Microsoft Excel, except that you can tap the wizard's charting capabilities more easily than you can by programmatically automating Excel. The charting examples presented in this section highlight how you can readily manipulate a chart both manually and programmatically with Access.

The Label Wizard integrates a highly functional label generator with a full-featured database manager. Later in this section, you'll see how to build a mailing label application.

Creating a Customer Phone List with the Report Wizard

The Access user interface makes it easy to create a report like the one shown in Figure 6-1. Because that report requires a subset of the columns in the *Customers* table, you can either invoke the AutoReport Wizard with a custom query that selects just the columns for the report or you can invoke the Report Wizard and select just the four report columns from the *Customers* table. Recall that the AutoReport Wizard creates a columnar report instead of a tabular one, such as the report shown in Figure 6-1. However, you can generate the columnar report with a single click. An AutoReport Wizard exists for tabular reports, but you must start it through the New Reports dialog box. After selecting the wizard in the New Reports dialog box, you must designate a record source in the drop-down box below the box listing the report wizards. You create the report by clicking OK.

The Report Wizard can produce many kinds of reports, including one similar to the customer phone list. You launch the Report Wizard from the New Report dialog box by double-clicking its name. On the wizard's first page, use the Tables/Queries drop-down list to select a table or query as a record source for the report. Figure 6-2 shows the Report Wizard with three columns selected and one more column about to be selected for inclusion in the report. After adding the *Phone* column to the Selected Fields list, you can accept the defaults through the wizard's last dialog box. The default naming convention for the report is to use the name of the record source. If a report with that name already exists, the wizard adds a number to the end of the report name to differentiate it from the names of other existing reports. You can override the default report name on the wizard's last page. I assigned the name *rptWiz-Customers* to the report created with the help of the Report Wizard.

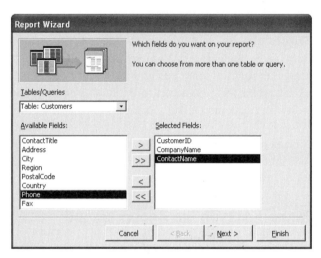

Figure 6-2 The first Report Wizard dialog box for creating the report shown in Figure 6-3.

Figure 6-3 shows an excerpt from the report generated by the Report Wizard. If you compare Figure 6-3 with Figure 6-1, you will see the contrast between programmatically and manually prepared reports. The wizard-generated report clearly looks better. For example, the wizard adds a report title, *rptWiz-Customers*. The wizard inserts the label displaying the title in the Report Header section so that it appears only on the report's first page. The column headers appear above a horizontal line that separates them from the data rows. You can't see it in this excerpt, but the wizard-generated report also includes a Page Footer section that marks each report page with the date the report prints, the current page number, and the total number of pages in the report. In addition, the Report Wizard offers many formatting and data layout options that this basic sample does not exploit.

The preceding example demonstrates the power of the Report Wizard in relation to a programmatic solution for creating a similar report. Although we could create the same report programmatically, doing so would substantially lengthen the code, which already exceeds several score of lines. When you simply need to crank out an ad hoc report or create a prototype for a collection of reports, using the Report Wizard can be an excellent choice.

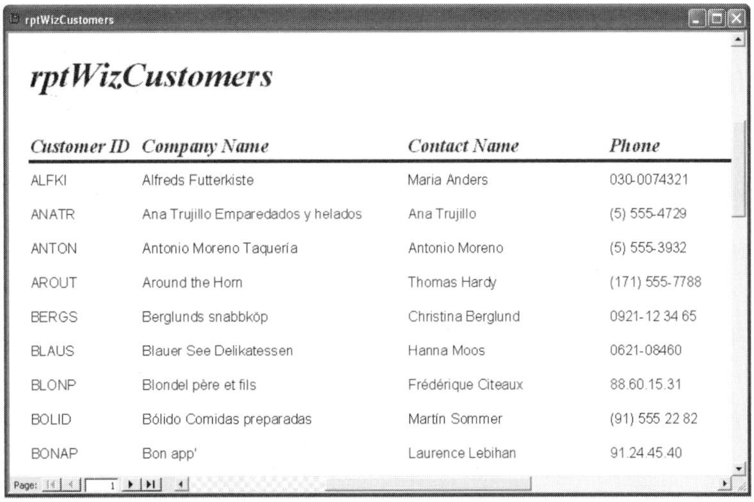
rptWizCustomers

rptWizCustomers

Customer ID	Company Name	Contact Name	Phone
ALFKI	Alfreds Futterkiste	Maria Anders	030-0074321
ANATR	Ana Trujillo Emparedados y helados	Ana Trujillo	(5) 555-4729
ANTON	Antonio Moreno Taquería	Antonio Moreno	(5) 555-3932
AROUT	Around the Horn	Thomas Hardy	(171) 555-7788
BERGS	Berglunds snabbköp	Christina Berglund	0921-12 34 65
BLAUS	Blauer See Delikatessen	Hanna Moos	0621-08460
BLONP	Blondel père et fils	Frédérique Citeaux	88.60.15.31
BOLID	Bólido Comidas preparadas	Martín Sommer	(91) 555 22 82
BONAP	Bon app'	Laurence Lebihan	91.24.45.40

Page: 1

Figure 6-3 A sample report generated by the Report Wizard in the style of the programmatically created report in Figure 6-1.

Using the Chart Wizard

Using the Chart Wizard is a little more complicated than using the Report Wizard. There are two reasons for this. First, the Chart Wizard adds an OLE object to the report. This OLE object actually charts the data. The Chart Wizard often aggregates data before charting it. Second, you frequently will find it useful to prepare a query for your charts so that you can merge data from two record sources or restrict the result set with a criterion.

To prepare a chart that shows sales (quantity) by month, you must prepare a query that contains both the *OrderDate* and *Quantity* fields. The following SQL statement does this. The statement joins the *Orders* and *Order Details* tables by their *OrderID* fields so that it can include the *OrderDate* and *Quantity* fields in a result set. Additionally, a *WHERE* clause restricts the output to orders made in 1997.

```
SELECT OrderDate, Quantity AS Sales
FROM Orders INNER JOIN [Order Details]
ON Orders.OrderID = [Order Details].OrderID
WHERE Year(OrderDate)=1997
```

After saving the query statement with a name such as *qryForChart*, you can launch the Chart Wizard from the New Report dialog box. To proceed to the first Chart Wizard page, you must designate the source of data for the chart. For example, select *qryForChart* from the drop-down list below the Wizard list. After clicking OK, move the *OrderDate* and *Sales* fields to the Fields For Chart box and click Next. Select a chart type, such as a 3-D Bar Chart. The wizard uses graphic images to denote the appearance of the various chart type options. (See Figure 6-4.) Click Next. To change the layout of your chart, you can move the fields around on the next wizard page. Simply click Next to bypass this page in the current sample.

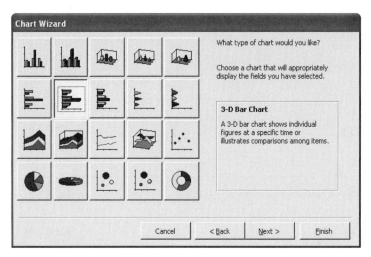

Figure 6-4   The Chart Wizard chart type page with a 3-D bar chart selected.

In the final Chart Wizard page, you can assign your chart a title, specify whether it will have a legend, and decide whether to view the chart or open it in Design view. The chart title is not the report name—it is merely a label that appears at the top of the chart. Select the No Don't Display A Legend option because we have just one field to plot against another. Choose to open the report with the chart displayed on it (instead of choosing to modify the report).

> **Note**   The appearance of the chart can depend on your Microsoft Data Access Component (MDAC) references. These references need to be present and valid in the database file with which you're working. If you attempt to generate a chart from an Access database file with missing MDAC references, the chart described in the example will not appear. This can be confusing since a database's MDAC references can be valid on one computer, but invalid on another computer. However, no matter what computer you use, the problem can be fixed by choosing valid MDAC references from the Visual Basic Editor (VBE) window. For a more extensive discussion of MDAC versions for Access developers see the "ADO Overview" section in Chapter 1.

Clicking Finish on the final Chart Wizard page generates our example's initial chart. After the chart appears, you can revert to Design view to edit its layout on the report. You can right-click on the chart in Design view and choose Chart Options to modify the chart itself.

When Access opens the chart in Design view, it presents you with three nested containers. The outer container is the report. The middle container is the Detail section of the report. This container holds an unbound OLE object, which is your interface to the Microsoft Graph 2000 Chart object. Actually, the *Class* property for the unbound OLE object indicates that it's a holdover from Access 97. The Class property setting is MSGraph.Chart.8. The *RowSource* property is an especially important property of the unbound OLE object. The setting for this property is a SQL statement that determines the record source for the chart. You can programmatically update this property to dynamically assign different record sources to a single chart. In addition, if the Chart Wizard fails to perform the aggregation that your application requires, you can enter a revised SQL string as the Row Source setting on the Properties dialog box for the unbound OLE object.

The kind of editing you are likely to perform includes removing unused report sections, resizing the chart so that it's bigger and easier to examine, and changing the page orientation if you're printing just one chart per page. Double-click the unbound OLE object to expose the Access menu's Chart menu command. For example, you can add a title for the horizontal axis by choosing Chart, Chart Options. Then, type the title you want for the horizontal axis into the Value (Z) Axis text box on the Titles tab in the Chart Options dialog box.

Figure 6-5 shows a completed chart for the SQL statement shown at the beginning of this section. The Chart Wizard has automatically aggregated the underlying data by month. You can verify or modify the chart's aggregation scheme by examining the unbound OLE object's Row Source property setting on its Properties dialog box. I added Unit Sales as the title for the horizontal axis using the technique described in the preceding paragraph. The chart's overall title, Sales Chart, came from a setting made on the last Chart Wizard page. After selecting the OLE object, you can double-click the chart's title to open a dialog box to modify the title's formatting. In fact, you can double-click on any chart element to update its formatting. The chart in Figure 6-5 is available in the *rpt-Chart* report for this chapter's sample file (Chapter06.mdb). Use it as a basis to experiment with custom formatting. The sample chart appears with gradient format effects. The chart area gradient runs in a direction counter to the gradient of the chart and axis titles.

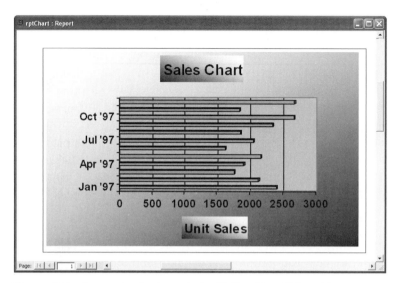

Figure 6-5 A sample chart created with the Chart Wizard for a query that selects the *OrderDate* and *Quantity* fields from the join of the *Orders* and *Order Details* tables in the Northwind database.

Using the Label Wizard

The Label Wizard is a great tool for creating reports that print batches of labels. The variety of label formats available is overwhelming. Standard label formats are available from 40 label manufacturers, and you can choose sheet or continuous-feed labels in either English or metric measurements. (The fact that selecting the right label format is one of the most difficult aspects of using the Label Wizard is a testimony to its flexibility.)

> **Note** The mailing label is one of the most commonly printed labels. If you use Avery labels or another brand with the same label format, choose product number 5260 for three-across laser labels. The Label Wizard example demonstrates how to automatically format a report for three-across laser mailing labels.

In addition, the Label Wizard offers tools to help you build and save your own label printing formats. This can be convenient if your application calls for printing to custom-sized labels or you want to develop a custom format for printing on a standard-sized label.

As with the Chart Wizard, you must specify a record source to start the Label Wizard from the New Report dialog box. For this example, you can choose the *Suppliers* table from the Northwind database; the sample database for this chapter links all the Northwind tables. In the first wizard page, select 5260 from the Product Number list and click Next. The next wizard page offers controls for altering the font and color of labels. For this example, click Next to bypass this page.

The next page is more critical since it allows you to pick and format fields from the record source for inclusion on the label. Figure 6-6 displays the design of a label just before adding the final field, *PostalCode*, to the label. You can insert carriage returns, punctuation marks, and blank spaces between the fields on a label.

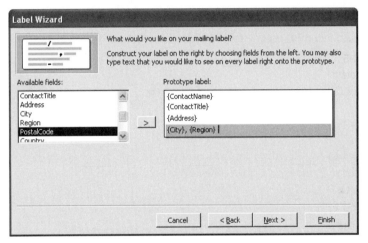

Figure 6-6   A wizard page depicting the layout of a mailing label just before adding the *PostalCode* field.

After you pick the fields to include on your label, the wizard offers you the opportunity to sort the order in which records appear as labels in the printed report. Sorting and bundling by ZIP code, or even subsets of a ZIP code, can sometimes help reduce mailing costs.

Finally, you can assign a name to the report. The default name is the word *Labels* followed by a space and the report's record source name. This name is how you will refer to the report in the Database window and programmatically in the *AllReports* and *Reports* collections.

Figure 6-7 displays an excerpt from the Labels Suppliers report. Notice that it automatically expands when a field, such as *Address*, extends beyond two lines. This feature is available because the wizard automatically selects Can

Grow for each text box control on the report. The Design view of the report shows just four text boxes. These controls also have their Can Shrink property set to Yes, which prevents blank rows from being printed on the labels when a field is empty. For example, if a record has a missing *Address* field value, Access prints the text box with the city, region, and postal code immediately after the text box with the company name.

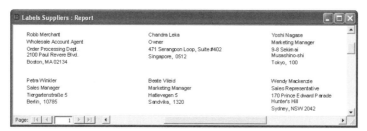

Figure 6-7   A sample report created by the Label Wizard for the *Suppliers* table.

After creating a report with the Label Wizard, you can reuse the report with new subsets of the original record source or with entirely new record sources. Alter the *RecordSource* property for the report programmatically or manually update the property on the report's Properties dialog box. Additionally, you can modify the contents of any text box by altering the *ControlSource* property for a text box control on the label report.

> **Note**   The Label Wizard in Access 2003 uses different label width, column width, and spacing assignments than in Access 2000—which is the last time the Label Wizard worked correctly for the Avery 5260 label. When you view the label report created in this example, Access 2003 displays a message stating that there is insufficient horizontal space on the page to display all the data in the report. To fix this, in Design view change all the label control Width settings to 2.1375 inches. Change the report's Width to 2.3375 inches. On the Margins tab of the Page Setup dialog box, change the Left margin to 0.3 inches. On the Columns tab of the Page Setup dialog box, change the Column Spacing to 0.4125 inches. These changes restore the Label Wizard settings from Access 2000 and print the labels without giving a warning about the horizontal space. Depending on your printer setup, you may need to specify slightly different values.

Creating Reports in Design View

Although this is a book about programming Access, let's review manual report design techniques for the same reasons we discussed report wizards. Access has an immensely powerful set of manual design techniques for reports. If you're a consultant building solutions for clients, many of your clients will expect you to deliver solutions that they can easily maintain and modify after your consulting engagement expires. Even if you manually design reports, there are many programmatic ways to make them dynamic after you create them. However, you will discover that crafting the basic layout of controls on a report is often best accomplished graphically.

This section explores three aspects of report functionality. First it examines techniques for expediting the manual layout of reports and their controls. Next, it moves on to discuss sorting and grouping techniques for the rows in a report's record source. Within this discussion, I'll cover the sorting and grouping of string data separately from the sorting and grouping of other kinds of data. The section concludes with a review of building reports that involve parent-child relationships. When I present this final topic, I'll drill down further into custom grouping and subreports. Here you'll learn how to use a chart just as you would a subreport.

Manually Laying Out a Customer Phone List Report

Although using the report wizards can expedite the preparation of specialized reports, you might find that they do not provide the flexibility you need for some custom reports. Even if you start with a wizard, it's probable that you will enter Design view to customize a report. Depending on your requirements, you might decide to build a report from scratch in Design view.

This section describes building the Customer Phone List report in Design view. The Design view for the finished report appears in Figure 6-8. You'll find the sample report, which is named *rptManCustomers*, in the sample database for this chapter. Notice that the report contains a Detail section sandwiched by the Page Header and Page Footer sections. The report populates all these sections with text box and label controls. A Report Header section contains a label control that displays the report's title. Since the Report Footer section has no controls, I dragged its bottom edge to make it flush with its top edge so that this section won't occupy any space on the report.

You can start to create a report similar to the one depicted in Figure 6-8 by using a blank report based on the default Report template. Unless you changed the Normal report template, the blank report will have a Detail section sandwiched between the Page Header and Page Footer sections. You create the blank report by double-clicking Design View in the New Report dialog box.

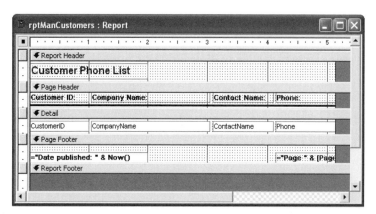

Figure 6-8   A Customer Phone List report prepared manually in Design view.

Immediately after opening the blank report, you should assign it a record source. Do this by opening the report's Properties dialog box. When you first open the report, it has the focus by default. However, if you've changed the focus to a particular section of the report, use the drop-down box at the top of the Properties dialog box to reselect the report. Then, select the Data tab on the Properties dialog box and click the drop-down arrow in the Record Source list. This opens a list of existing tables and queries in the current database. For this example, choose the *Customers* table as the report's record source. You can also enter a custom SQL string as the Record Source setting, or you can click the Build button to the right of the Record Source box. The Build button opens a graphical Query Designer that lets you create a custom record source for a report.

The next step is to add text box and label controls to the Detail and Page Header sections, respectively. If the Field List box isn't already open, open it by clicking the Field List button on the Report Design toolbar. When you initially drag a field from the list to the report's Detail section, that field appears with a label and a text box. Drag the *CustomerID* field from the Field List box to the report's Detail section. The label caption is the field name followed by a semicolon. To conform to our design goals, the caption needs to reside in the Page Header section. Therefore, you must select the label control, cut it from the Detail section, and paste it into the Page Header section. (To select a particular section, click the bar at the top of the section.) After you paste in the label control, it remains selected in the top-left corner of the Page Header section. Next, align the left edges of the label and text box controls. You can do this by holding down the Shift key and clicking the text box to select both the label and text box controls. Then, choose Format, Align, Left to align the left edges of the two controls. If you do not regularly design forms and reports manually, spend a moment exploring the Format menu, which offers commands in its Align and Size submenus for managing the arrangement and size of report controls—in fact, go ahead and re-size the Label control so that it is the same width as the Text Box control. Click anywhere in the Detail section (except on the text box control) to remove the focus from both controls. Then, click the text box again. Hold down the Ctrl key and click the up arrow until the text box is nearly flush with the top of the Detail section (see Figure 6-8 for the layout position).

When you initially drag a control to a report, Access binds together its label and text box. By cutting and pasting the label from the Detail section to the Page Header section, you unbind them. With the text box still selected, choose Format, Set Control Defaults. This step enables you to drag subsequent fields from the Field List box without an accompanying label control.

Next, drag *CompanyName* from the Field List box to the Detail section. Properly arrange its text box next to the *CustomerID* text box. From the Properties dialog box for *CompanyName*, select the Format tab. Then, enter **2** to specify the Width property of the control (in inches). Recall that the *CompanyName* text box must exceed the default length. You can drag the *ContactName* and *Phone* fields to the report without making any size adjustments. After adding all four fields to the Detail section and arranging their text boxes, drag the lower boundary of the Detail section so that it rests just below the lower edge of the text boxes.

You can now shift your attention to the Page Header section. We need four label controls in this section to act as column headers in the report. Select the label with the Customer ID caption and choose Edit, Duplicate. Arrange the new label so that its top edge aligns with that of the original label control and its left edge aligns with the left edge of the *CompanyName* text box. Then, select both labels and duplicate them. Arrange the new labels so that their top edges align with those of the other labels and their left edges match the two far right text boxes in the Detail section. Although it is not necessary to size label controls to match their corresponding text boxes, you might find it convenient. The Format, Size menu can help you accomplish this. Change the *Caption* property for the label controls so that the labels properly describe the text box controls for which they serve as column headers. Complete your work on the label controls by selecting all of them and choosing a *Font Weight* property of Semi-bold from the Format tab of their Properties dialog box.

After completing the labels in the Page Header section, add and format a line that extends below the labels. To do so, click the Toolbox control on the Report Design toolbar if the Toolbox is not already open. Then, select the Line control and drag it below the bottom edge of the label controls. With the line still having the focus, select the Format tab of its Properties dialog box and select 2 pt as the line's Border Width setting. Finally, complete your work on the Page Header section by dragging its lower edge until it's close to the line.

Shift the focus to the Page Footer section, and add a 2-inch-wide text box that's flush with the section's left edge. In the Control Source setting for the text box, enter the expression `="Date published: " & Now()`. This expression documents the date and time a report prints. Then, add a second text box to the Page Footer section, and align its right edge with that of the *Phone* text box. In the Control Source setting for the second text box, enter the expression `="Page " & [Page] & " of " & [Pages]`. This expression shows the current page number and the total number of pages in a report. Select both text boxes in the Page Footer section. Make sure both text boxes align at their bottom edges by choosing Format-Align-Bottom from the menu. Assign a Semi-bold *Font Weight* property setting to the controls. Conclude your work with the Page Footer section by dragging the right edge of the report so that it's flush with the page number's text box.

Finish the report by adding a label that contains the report title. To do so, choose View, Report Header/Footer. Then, drag the bottom edge of the Report Footer section until it's flush with the top edge. Select the Report Header section and insert a label control from the Toolbox. Type **Customer Phone List** inside the label control. Click outside the label control, and then click the control again to give it the focus. Assign a *Font Size* property of 12 points and a *Font Weight* property of Bold. Make the label flush with the left edge of the report, and assign it a Width property of 2 inches and a Height property of 0.25 inches. Conclude setting the report's layout by making the bottom edge of Report Header section slightly lower than the bottom edge of the label (see Figure 6-8).

Figure 6-9 displays two excerpts from this report. The top panel shows the report's title above the column headers on the first page. It also shows the first several rows of customer phone numbers. The bottom panel shows the Page Footer contents along with the last several rows of data on the first page. If you change the height of the Detail section from that displayed in the example, different rows will appear at the bottom of the page.

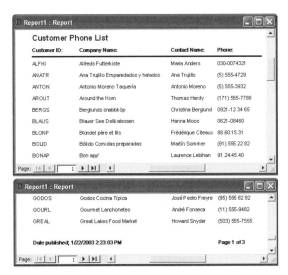

Figure 6-9   Two excerpts from a Customer Phone List report generated in Design view. The top panel shows the layout for the top of the first page; the bottom panel presents the layout for the bottom of the page.

Sorting and Grouping String Data

The report in Figure 6-9 sorts the customer phone list by the *CustomerID* field for the report's underlying record source. This is because *CustomerID* is the primary key for the *Customers* table. However, some uses for a customer phone list might be better served with rows sorted by the *ContactName* field. Using the View, Sorting And Grouping command on the Report Design menu, you can create custom sort orders that organize rows differently than a primary key for a table or an *ORDER BY* clause in a query statement.

The View, Sorting And Grouping command opens the Sorting And Grouping dialog box for a report. You can also open this dialog box by choosing the Sorting And Grouping button on the Report Design toolbar. The *Field/Expression* column in the dialog box allows you to select columns in the report's record source on which to sort rows. You can sort on multiple fields or expressions in the underlying record source. Access sorts at the highest level by the field or expression at the top of the column, and then it sorts by successive column entries in the dialog box. The dialog box's *Sort Order* column lets you choose to sort in ascending or descending order. The default order is ascending.

Figure 6-10 shows the Sorting And Grouping dialog box for the report design presented initially in Figure 6-8. The figure shows *ContactName* being selected as the sort column. For the moment, you can ignore the Group Properties settings in the lower portion of the dialog box.

Figure 6-11 shows the top of the first page from the sorted report. Not surprisingly, the records appear in ascending order based on the *ContactName* field. As you can see by comparing this figure with Figure 6-9, in which the rows are ordered by the customer ID, the sort settings in a report override any order settings in the underlying record source.

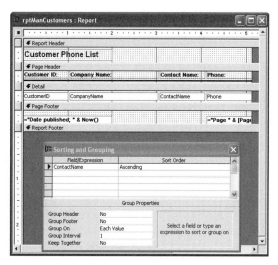

Figure 6-10   A setting in the Sorting And Grouping dialog box that alters the default order of the report.

rptManCustomers : Report			
Customer Phone List			
Customer ID:	**Company Name:**	**Contact Name:**	**Phone:**
ROMEY	Romero y tomillo	Alejandra Camino	(91) 745 6200
MORGK	Morgenstern Gesundkost	Alexander Feuer	0342-023176
ANATR	Ana Trujillo Emparedados y helados	Ana Trujillo	(5) 555-4729
TRADH	Tradição Hipermercados	Anabela Domingue	(11) 555-2167
GOURL	Gourmet Lanchonetes	André Fonseca	(11) 555-9482
EASTC	Eastern Connection	Ann Devon	(171) 555-0297

Figure 6-11   An excerpt from a report showing the customers phone list sorted in ascending order on the *ContactName* field for its record source.

As convenient as the preceding report is, it would be better if you could easily tell when a transition occurs from contacts whose first name begins with *A*, to contacts whose first name begins with *B*, and so on. Access reports offer two related features to accommodate this need. First, they allow you to group records on any field within the report's record source. When you group records on a field, Access automatically sorts them. However, your grouping and sorting criteria will often be different. Therefore, you'll need to set the sort criteria within the group criterion. Second, Access does not automatically separate or mark grouped records. However, you can specify places on a report that denote the beginning, the ending, or both the beginning and ending of a group.

Access calls the beginning and ending markers for groups Group Headers and Group Footers, respectively. These dividers introduce new sections within a report. Unlike the built-in report sections, you can elect to show just a Group Header or a Group Footer; you don't have to specify both.

Figure 6-12 shows a Sorting And Grouping dialog box for a modified Customer Phone List report that groups and sorts its records. The figure depicts the setting for grouping the records in the Group Properties area. The report groups records based on the first character in the *ContactName* field. By itself, this grouping criterion would not arrange a group's records in alphabetical order by *ContactName* field values. Instead, it would order the records within a group by their primary key value (*CustomerID*). However, because the Sorting And Grouping dialog box designates *ContactName* field values as a sort column in ascending order, the report shows the records in alphabetical order within each group. Since the Group Header setting is Yes, the report prints a divider at the start of each group. The report layout shown above the dialog box in Figure 6-12 shows an expression in the *ContactName* Header section. The expression retrieves the first letter of the *ContactName* field for the current record. Because this break occurs just once for each group, the expression causes the report to print the group's initial letter at the beginning of each group.

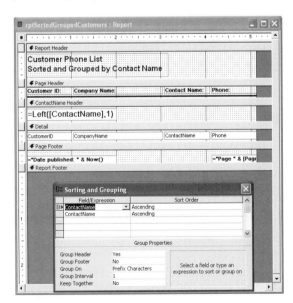

Figure 6-12   A report's Design view with its Sorting And Grouping dialog box that demonstrates how to group on the first letter of the *ContactName* field in the Customers table and sort the records within each group on the *ContactName* field values.

Figure 6-13 presents an excerpt from the report specified by the settings shown in Figure 6-12. Notice how easy it is to tell where a new group of contacts begins. Also, notice that the cost of improving the report was the time it took to add a single row in the Sorting And Grouping dialog box and an expression in the *ContactName* Header section. This ease of report formatting is one reason why Access is such a popular report generator for so many business applications.

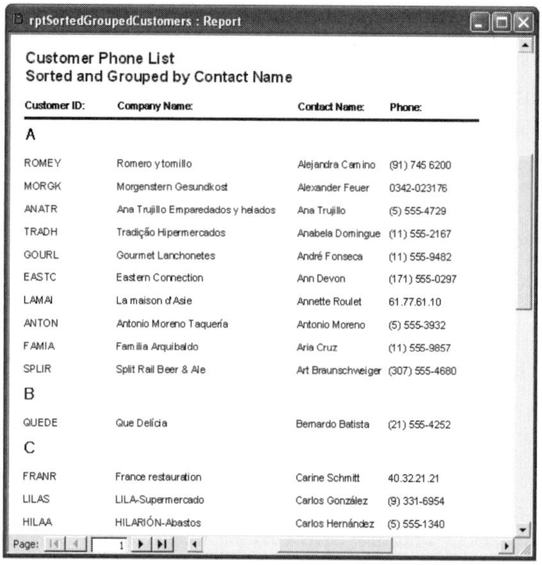

Figure 6-13   An excerpt from the report specified by the settings in Figure 6-12.

Sorting and Grouping by Date

Although sorting and grouping techniques are similar across data types, different data types can require slightly different settings. While the previous sample used the first character in a string, the three samples we'll discuss next illustrate the use of date/time data types for sorting and grouping. I will not provide step-by-step descriptions of how to lay out these sample reports because I already described these steps earlier in the section and these reports are available in this chapter's sample database file.

The following SQL statement is a query saved as *qryOrdersByMonth*. This query serves as the data source for the three sample reports that follow. The

SQL statement counts the number of order IDs by month. Notice that the statement nests the *Year* and *Month* functions and the value 1 as the day within a *DateSerial* function. By specifying the first day of the month regardless of the actual date contained in the underlying record, the *DateSerial* function generates a valid date that can be used to group records by month rather than by day.

```
SELECT DateSerial(Year([OrderDate]),Month([OrderDate]),1)
AS [Date], Count(OrderID) AS Orders
FROM Orders
GROUP BY DateSerial(Year([OrderDate]),Month([OrderDate]),1)
```

The left window in Figure 6-14 presents an excerpt from the first report that demonstrates the sorting of dates. This sample report mostly echoes the values from its *qryOrdersByMonth* record source. By presenting the query results in a report, you make it harder for users to accidentally manipulate the query's design. You can also apply formatting options that are not available in a query's Datasheet view. The right window in Figure 6-14 highlights some of these formatting options. Both the Report Header and Page Footer sections use a gray background. This sample accentuates the report's title by using large, white letters against the gray background. You can control color properties by clicking the Build button next to the appropriate property name on the control's or section's Properties dialog box. The Build button opens a Color dialog box that lets you pick from a set of predetermined colors as well as create your own colors.

Note   Not all date/time group functions work identically. Grouping by quarter aggregates all dates through the end of a quarter. This is true for all date/time serial values, right down to the days. However, grouping date/time serial values by hour lumps together all times extending through the middle of the hour. When the report's grouping feature does not aggregate the way you prefer, construct a new field that will lead to a more acceptable result for your application. For example, if you need times grouped through the end of the hour, add a new column to a report's record source that applies the *Hour* function to the date/time serial number values and group on the results from that function.

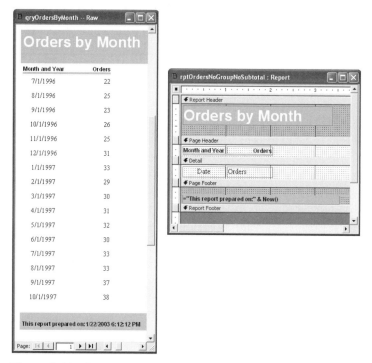

Figure 6-14 An excerpt from a report that displays the result set from the *qryOrdersByMonth* query.

The two text boxes in the report refer to the field names from the *qry-OrdersByMonth* result set. No special processing of the result set occurs for this sample's report. Since the *Orders* field has numeric values, its column is right-justified automatically without any special formatting. The *Orders* column heading has its *Text Align* property set to Right so that its caption is flush with the right edge of the control. The *Date* column and the label control for its column heading each have the *Text Align* property set to Center so that the dates are displayed in the middle of the column.

Showing data grouped in multiple ways is one function that cannot be easily performed with just a query. For example, it is difficult to show monthly data in a query while also presenting the data grouped by quarter. If you display a query using a report, the built-in Sorting And Grouping command on the Report Design menu radically simplifies this task: it features an option for grouping by quarter. Other date/time grouping options include the year, month, week, day, hour, and minute.

Figure 6-15 shows a sample report that groups the monthly data from the *qryOrdersByMonth* query by quarter. In the figure, the window on the left shows the layout of the report's data, and the window on the right displays the Report Design view along with its Sorting And Grouping dialog box. Notice the gap in the left window between the data for months within each quarter. Choosing *Qtr* for Group On and *Yes* for Group Footer in the Sorting And Grouping dialog box causes these gaps. You can see the Date Footer section in the report layout above the Sorting And Grouping dialog box. When you group data by a time period such as a quarter, the detailed data within a group does not automatically sort in ascending or descending order. The report in the left window illustrates this. To remedy the situation, add *Date* as a sort field below the *Date* as a grouping field. Leave the *Group On* setting at its default value of Each Value. If you want to sort in descending order, change the default *Sort Order* setting in the second column from Ascending to Descending.

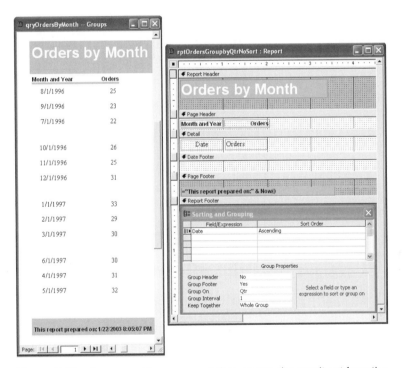

Figure 6-15   An excerpt from a report that groups the result set from the *qryOrdersByMonth* query by quarter.

Notice that the *Keep Together* property setting at the bottom of the Sorting And Grouping dialog box is Whole Group. This setting causes Access to keep together the three months of a quarter. If the group of months in a quarter would normally be split on the page, Access reformats the page so that the group of months in the quarter starts at the top of the next page.

Figure 6-16 presents the final example of a date-grouping report. This report does sort by month within a quarter. In addition, it calculates a subtotal of the monthly orders within a quarter. The expression in the Date Footer section shows that you can compute this result with a familiar aggregate function—namely, the *Sum* function. To help make the quarterly aggregate values stand out from the monthly order totals, the report applies a Bold *Font Weight* setting to the text box for the quarterly sum of orders. This text box differs from the two text boxes in the Detail section in that it's not bound to any particular columns in the report's record source. Instead, this text box depends on the expression within it.

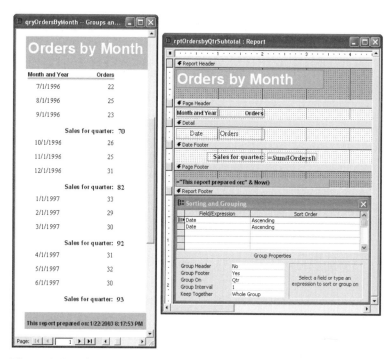

Figure 6-16   An excerpt from a report that groups and subtotals by quarter the result set from the *qryOrdersByMonth* query. Unlike the report shown in Figure 6-14, this report sorts the monthly totals by date within a quarter.

Hierarchical Reports with Groups, Subreports, and Charts

As a rule, subreports are less important to report design than subforms are to form design. This is because reports do not accommodate the input or updating of data—they merely reflect the contents of a record source in a format suitable for a printer. Nevertheless, subreports do play a role in report design. One major reason for using subreports and subforms is so that you can easily display data with hierarchical relationships, such as products within a category. This need is particularly evident when you want to include a graph that updates for each group within a report. In this kind of application, the chart serves a role similar to that of a subreport within the group.

Representing Parent-Child Relationships with Groups

Whenever possible, you should look for ways to design reports that show hierarchical data relationships with groups created via the Sorting And Grouping dialog box. This style of representing hierarchical relationships with reports is simpler than developing a main/subreport combination because you do not have to maintain the relationship between the two reports. To make this approach work, you may need to create a specific query to support the report's grouping requirements.

Figure 6-17 displays an excerpt from a report with a hierarchical relationship between customers and product sales. The report contains a group for each customer. The Group Header section indicates the parent data (customer) to which the following set of child data (product sales) belongs. The report's design presents the child data, in this case the number of orders and total extended price for each product, in the report's Detail section. The report's Group Footer section presents the parent data, in this case the total orders and extended price for an individual customer. This section even compares the data about the current customer with the data for all customers in the report by displaying the current customer's percent of the total orders and extended price in the entire report.

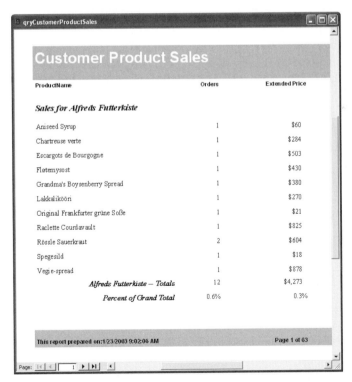

Figure 6-17   An excerpt from a single report that represents a hierarchical relationship between customers and product sales.

The main trick for representing parent-child relationships in a report is to specify the record source properly. The following SQL statement is the record source for the report just described. This statement appears in the sample database file for this chapter as *qryCustomerProductSales*. The three fields in the *SELECT* list are report fields. When you use an alias (such as *Orders* or *ExtPrice*) in a query for a calculated or an aggregated field, your Access report should refer to the result via the alias name.

```
SELECT cus.CompanyName, prd.ProductName,
Count(o.OrderID) AS Orders,
Sum(od.UnitPrice*[Quantity]*(1-[Discount])) AS ExtPrice
FROM Products AS prd INNER JOIN ((Customers AS cus
INNER JOIN Orders AS o ON cus.CustomerID = o.CustomerID)
INNER JOIN [Order Details] AS od ON o.OrderID = od.OrderID)
ON prd.ProductID = od.ProductID
GROUP BY cus.CustomerID, cus.CompanyName, prd.ProductName
```

Figure 6-18 shows the report in Design view; this report is available as *rptCustomerProductSales* in the Chapter06.mdb file. Notice that the Detail section uses aliases to refer back to the order count for a product (*Orders*) and the sum of the extended price (*ExtPrice*). When a field name appears within a function, you must delimit it with square brackets, such as *Sum([ExtPrice])*. Also, all expressions for the Control Source property of text boxes within a report must begin with an equal sign (=). If you forget this, Access will frequently insert a leading equal sign for you. The *CompanyName* Header section contains a text box with a string expression for labeling the sales of a customer.

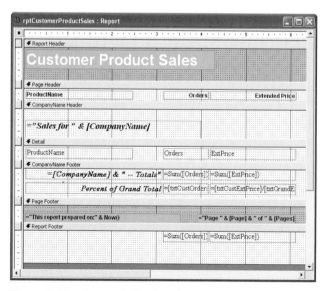

Figure 6-18   A report's Design view that displays a parent-child relationship between customers and their product sales rows based on the *qryCustomerProductSales* query.

The *Sum* function operates within the context of the section in which it resides. The *CompanyName* Footer section includes two *Sum* functions. These functions develop aggregates of product orders and the total extended price for that customer. The identical *Sum* functions in the Report Footer section generate the overall sum for all customers. The report names the two text boxes in the Report Footer section *txtGrandOrders* and *txtGrandExtPrice*. The corresponding two text boxes in the *CompanyName* Footer section are named *txtCustOrders* and *txtCustExtPrice*. The report uses these names to compute a customer's percentage of the grand total orders and extended price. Here are the Control Source expressions for the calculated percentages in the *CompanyName* Footer sections:

```
=[txtCustOrders]/[txtGrandOrders]
=[txtCustExtPrice]/[txtGrandExtPrice]
```

Representing Parent-Child Relationships with Main/Subreports

The next sample report deals with a parent-child relationship between categories in the Northwind *Categories* table and the total extended price for the category's products. The aggregated sales for individual products within a category represent the category's children. I used a SQL statement (shown next) that accumulates sales by product for shipments during 1997. This same statement serves as the record source for both the main report and subreport. The query includes *CategoryID*. This field is the primary key for the parent *Categories* table. When working with main/subreports, include the primary key for the parent table in the *SELECT* list. This example uses the primary key, *CategoryID*, to link the subreport to the main report. When you do this, you don't need to include a text box with the primary key on either the main report or the subreport. The following SQL statement is available as *qryProductSalesWithinCategory* in the Chapter06.mdb file:

```
SELECT cat.CategoryID, cat.CategoryName, prd.ProductName,
FormatCurrency(Sum(od.UnitPrice*[Quantity]*(1-[Discount])),2)
AS ProductSales
FROM (Categories AS cat INNER JOIN Products AS prd
ON cat.CategoryID = prd.CategoryID)
INNER JOIN (Orders AS o INNER JOIN [Order Details] AS od
ON o.OrderID = od.OrderID)
ON prd.ProductID = od.ProductID
WHERE o.ShippedDate Between #1/1/1997# And #12/31/1997#
GROUP BY cat.CategoryID, cat.CategoryName, prd.ProductName
```

Figure 6-19 displays an excerpt from the report for the first category, Beverages. The gray box below the statement about total sales within a category is the subreport. Everything else on the report is part of the main report. The individual rows within the subreport represent individual products within a category. As the main report enumerates different categories, it uses the subreport to show sales for just the products within that category. For example, all the products in the subreport shown in Figure 6-19 are beverages. In addition, the heading above the subreport includes the sum of sales for a category. This calculation changes for each category.

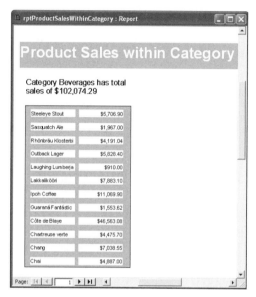

Figure 6-19 An excerpt from a main/subreport that represents a hierarchical relationship between categories and product sales.

Figure 6-20 shows the Design view for the main report (*rptProduct-SalesWithinCategory*) of the report we just discussed. Recall that the record source for the main report and subreport is *qryProductSalesWithinCategory*. The main report includes a CategoryName Header section. In fact, both of the main report's data-bound controls—the text box and the subreport—reside in the CategoryName Header section.

The subreport, *rptSubTableProductSales*, exists as a standalone report with just two fields in its Detail section. To construct the main/subreport, drag the subreport from the Database window into the Design view of the main report. Locate the control in the CategoryName Header section. You have the option to remove the label that the process assigns to the subreport control on the main report. If Access does not automatically prompt you to link fields between the main report and subreport, select the Data tab on the Properties dialog box for subreport control on the main report. Then, click the Build button to the right of either the Link Child Fields or Link Master Fields property setting box. This opens the Subreport Field Linker dialog box that lets you link fields from the record sources for the main report and subreport. The sample report uses the *CategoryID* field.

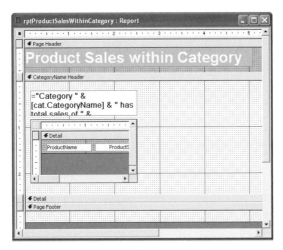

Figure 6-20   A report's Design view that displays a parent-child relation-ship between categories and their product sale rows based on the *qryProductSalesWithinCategory* query.

The control immediately above the subreport control on the main form is a text box. This text box contains an expression for its Control Source property setting. This expression references two fields from the report's record source:

```
="Category " & [cat.CategoryName] & "has total sales of " &
 FormatCurrency(Sum([ProductSales]),2)
```

Notice that the expression references the *CategoryName* field with the same prefix that appears in the SQL string for the report's form. You must use this prefix. In addition, the expression taps the *FormatCurrency* function for displaying the sum of the *ProductSales* field in currency format with two places after the decimal.

Graphing Child Data in a Main/Subreport Design

When you add a graph to a report, you can make it function like a subreport. In order to synchronize a chart's contents with a main report, make assignments to the Link Child Fields and Link Master Fields settings for the control containing the chart. You will need to add a new chart to a report rather than drag an existing chart report from the Database window. Use the Insert, Chart command in a report's Design view to launch the Chart Wizard. This adds a new chart to the report. The Chart Wizard includes pages for specifying the chart's record source and chart type as well as the fields for linking the chart to the main report. Despite your selections, the wizard might construct a record source that differs from your needs. If the chart does not display the data the way you want, respecify the *Record Source* property setting for the

Chart control. In the following example, I needed to respecify the *Record Source* property as the following:

```
SELECT ProductName, ProductSales FROM qryProductSalesWithinCategory
```

Figure 6-21 shows an excerpt from the report created by following the steps for adding a chart to the report shown in Figure 6-19. I had to edit the layout of the chart as well; in particular, I changed the font size for the horizontal and vertical axes to 7 point. In addition, I created more space for the chart on the report's pages by reducing the right margin setting in the File-Page Setup command to 0.25 inches. The other margins remained at their default setting of 1 inch.

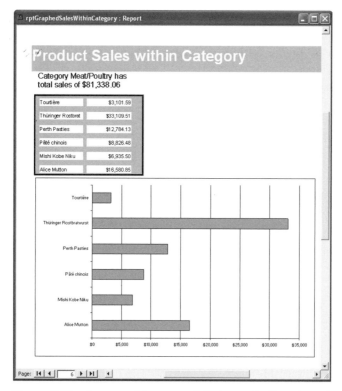

Figure 6-21   An excerpt from a main/subreport with a chart that depicts a hierarchical relationship between categories and product sales by plotting the product sales for each category immediately below the table showing product sales within a category.

Distributing Reports Using Snapshots

You can make Access reports available to others via the Internet and e-mail by using snapshot files. As such, snapshots allow a much wider audience for your reports, including users without Access and those not connected to your local area network (LAN). A workstation must have a Snapshot viewer to view a snapshot of an Access report. The viewer application, which ships with Access 2003 and is available as a free standalone application, includes an ActiveX control for use in Web browsers that support it, such as Internet Explorer 4 or later. Users can also view snapshots on remote computers without browsers capable of working with ActiveX controls. For example, a Netscape browser can download snapshot files over an HTTP connection. Netscape users can then use the standalone version of the Snapshot viewer with the saved file on their local hard disk.

> **Note**   The Web site *http://www.ProgrammingMSAccess.com* maintains an online tutorial on using and deploying Access snapshot solutions. The tutorial includes an overview of snapshots, step-by-step instructions for their use, and several samples that illustrate the performance of the Snapshot viewer in different contexts. If you use an older version of Access, or if you don't even use Access or Internet Explorer, you can still use Access snapshots. The tutorial explains how. The URL for downloading the free viewer is *http://www.microsoft.com/accessdev /prodinfo/snapshot.htm*.

Creating a Snapshot

You can create a snapshot for a report by selecting the report in the Database window and choosing File, Export. From the Save As Type drop-down list, select Snapshot Format. This enters the selected report name as the name of the snapshot file in the Export Report dialog box. (See Figure 6-22.) In the Save In drop-down list, designate a location for your snapshot file. Figure 6-22 shows the report you saw in Figure 6-5 being saved to a folder named pma11 that contains the intranet site for this book on my local computer. You will, of course, need to change this folder name for your computing environment. Clicking Export in the dialog box in Figure 6-22 opens a progress dialog box and, after the file has been saved, opens it in the Snapshot viewer. The file resides on the server and has an .snp extension.

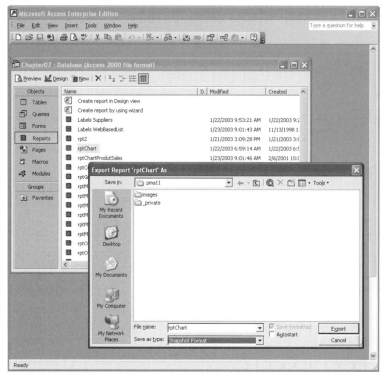

Figure 6-22 Creating a snapshot file manually.

You can also create a snapshot file for a folder on a LAN programmatically. The trick is to use the *OutputTo* method for the *DoCmd* object. When using *OutputTo* for this purpose, four arguments are required. You can list these arguments immediately after the command in the following order: *Object Type*, *Object Name*, *Output Format*, and *Output File*. The *Object Type* and *Output Format* arguments are always the same when generating a snapshot file. The *Object Type* must refer to a report; use the *acOutputReport* intrinsic constant to denote a report. Assign the string "*Snapshot Format*" to the *Output Format* argument. Use the remaining two arguments to specify the report name as well as the path and file name for your snapshot file.

The following pair of procedures illustrates the syntax for the *Output* method when saving a report as snapshot file. The sample saves *rptChart* as a snapshot in the pma11 intranet site on my local computer. The path to the Web site is C:\inetpub\wwwroot\pma11. The first procedure assigns the report name, as well as the path and file names for the snapshot, to string variables. If the file exists already, the procedure silently overwrites the prior version. The second procedure invokes the *OutputTo* method with the arguments passed to it and the two fixed arguments.

```
Sub CallCreateASnapShotReport()
Dim str1 As String
Dim str2 As String

'Assign string values for report name and
'path for saving snapshot (.snp) file
str1 = "rptChart"
str2 = "C:\inetpub\wwwroot\pmall\rptChart.snp"

'Call procedure for generating snapshot
CreateASnapShotReport str1, str2

End Sub

Sub CreateASnapShotReport(strReportName As String, _
    strSnapShotPathFile As String)

'Invoke OutputTo method with arguments for
'creating a snapshot on a LAN
DoCmd.OutputTo acOutputReport, _
    strReportName, _
    "SnapShot Format", _
    strSnapShotPathFile

End Sub
```

Viewing a Snapshot

A workstation running Internet Explorer 4 or later that has the Snapshot viewer installed can open the snapshot file. Figure 6-23 shows the report in Internet Explorer 6. The viewer appears to be inside the browser, but it actually takes control of the browser. Special navigator controls on a bar at the bottom of the ActiveX control enable navigation through the pages of a report. The same navigator bar also includes a button for printing. (This is because the control disables the native browser printing functionality.)

> **Note**   With its initial standard security setting, an Internet Explorer 6 browser prompts whether to open or save a snapshot file locally, because the snapshot file is an ActiveX control that can run a program. To view the report, users must choose to open or save the file.

Notice the close correspondence between the browser image in Figure 6-23 and the original report shown in Figure 6-5. This level of correspondence does not occur when you export to the HTML Documents format. In fact, the HTML Documents format cannot handle Access charts in reports. However, the Snapshot format accommodates both text and graphic content. In addition, exporting to HTML does not provide the built-in navigation functionality that the Snapshot viewer control offers.

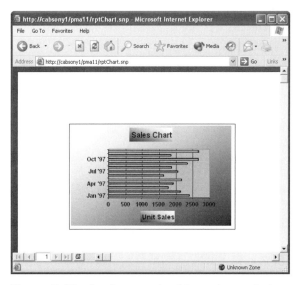

Figure 6-23 An Access chart-based report viewed from Internet Explorer 6.

The Snapshot viewer control lets you embed an Access report on a Web page along with other content. The following HTML excerpt shows the body of a Web page containing <h3> and <h4> tags before the object reference to the Snapshot viewer control. The full file is available with the support materials for this chapter. The text blocks preceding the control explain how to download the viewer if the report does not appear, and they offer a hyperlink to a site from which you can download the viewer. The instructions also explain how to view the report in Netscape Navigator. Of course you need to update the *SnapshotPath* parameter to the URL for the snapshot file that you want to show.

```
<body>
<H3>Snapshot Sample page</H3>
<H4>If you have an Internet Explorer 3 or later browser but
 cannot see the report below, download and install the
 <a href="http://www.microsoft.com/accessdev/prodinfo/snapdl.htm">
```

```
Microsoft Access Snapshot viewer</a>.
Then, refresh the page. Netscape Navigator users will not even see
the report container in their browsers, but they can open the report
outside their browser using the same Snapshot viewer just mentioned.
Netscape users can download the snapshot file from
a Web server through http protocol to their workstation.</H4>
<OBJECT ID="SnapshotViewer" WIDTH=640 HEIGHT=480
CLASSID="CLSID:F0E42D60-368C-11D0-AD81-00A0C90DC8D9">
    <PARAM NAME="_ExtentX" VALUE="16722">
    <PARAM NAME="_ExtentY" VALUE="11774">
    <PARAM NAME="_Version" VALUE="65536">
    <PARAM NAME="SnapshotPath"
    VALUE="http://cabsony1/pma11/rptChart.snp">
    <PARAM NAME="Zoom" VALUE="0">
    <PARAM NAME="AllowContextMenu" VALUE="-1">
    <PARAM NAME="ShowNavigationButtons" VALUE="-1">
</OBJECT>
</body>
```

Other Uses for Snapshots

Snapshot files based on Access reports have many other uses. For example, you can electronically mail a report as an attached snapshot file by right-clicking on the report in the Database window and choosing Send To and then Mail Recipient from the shortcut menu. Remember to include in your message a link to the download site for the Snapshot viewer if there is any possibility the client does not have the Snapshot viewer already installed.

You can also use the *DoCmd* object's *OutputTo* and *SendObject* methods to automate the conversion and copying of snapshot files to an intranet site or to e-mail recipients. The "Mailing Snapshots" section later in this chapter includes a code sample that can e-mail multiple files to one or more recipients. The "Creating a Snapshot" section presents the syntax and a code sample for using the *OutputTo* method to generate and save a snapshot file.

Making Reports Dynamic

Three report section events—*Format*, *Retreat*, and *Print*—can help you create dynamic formatting and content in a report. Other report events that can help you build smart reports include *Open*, *Close*, *No Data*, and *Page*. These events can also help you manage the application's behavior before, during, and after the opening of a report. You can use combinations of report events to create report formatting and special effects.

Use the *Open* event to programmatically set properties for reports and their controls. This is the first event that fires when a report is opened. When creating conditional formats for a specific instance of a report, use an *Open* event procedure to instantiate your *FormatCondition* objects and assign properties to them. If your application can have more than one report open at the same time, you can use the *Activate* and *Deactivate* events to monitor the flow of focus to and away from a report. Use the *Close* event to perform special actions just before a report closes, such as opening a form or presenting a message box.

You use the *NoData* event to detect a report that has no data in its record source. This event occurs after Access formats a report for printing. Your application can use this event to cancel a report that is about to print without any data. You can also program event procedures that prompt a user to enter data in the underlying record source or to select a different record source for the report.

Formatting Reports with the *Print* Event

The following sample formats a report using the *Print* event for various report sections. The *Print* event occurs after formatting for each section is complete but before the report actually prints. Each report section can have its own *Print* event procedure, and the event occurs each time Access works with that section to prepare the report. For example, the Report Header *Print* event occurs just once, unless a *Retreat* event forces Access to return to the Report Header section. The *Retreat* event enables Access to manage special report requirements, such as keeping a group together. In contrast to the Report Header section, the Detail section occurs at least once for each row in the record source for a report.

Figure 6-24 shows a report that uses the *Print* event for three sections to add red rectangles around the Report Header section and the Page Footer section. Note the different thicknesses of the rectangular borders. The Detail section displays an oval around all monthly order totals greater than or equal to 30.

Although the Report Header *Print* event occurs once per report and the Page Footer *Print* event occurs just once per page, the Detail section *Print* event occurs once for each row on a page. This means that for the page shown in Figure 6-24 the Detail section fires the *Print* event 16 times. With each event, your application can examine control values for the current record. Therefore, you can selectively display ovals around monthly order totals.

The code for the report in Figure 6-24 comprises the following three event procedures. Your applications can apply the *Line* method (as in the Report Header and Page Footer event procedures) to draw a rectangle around the report section. The first four arguments of the *Line* method have a data type of *Single* and are used to indicate two pairs of coordinates for the line. These four values specify the top, left, width, and height values for a rectangle in twips, which is the default metric for the *Line* method. The *ReportHeader_Print* procedure sets these parameters to the appropriate measurements for the Report Header section.

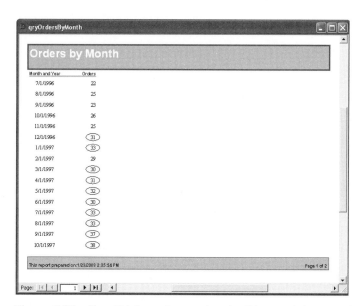

Figure 6-24   One *Print* event procedure for this report draws rectangles around the Report Header and Page Footer sections. Another *Print* event procedure selectively draws ovals around the monthly order totals.

Another argument of the *Line* method has a *Long* data type and designates the color of the rectangle's border. The sample uses the *RGB* function to designate a number that represents the color red in the *lngColor* variable. Just before invoking the *Line* method to draw the rectangle, the *ReportHeader_Print* procedure assigns a value to the report's *DrawWidth* property. This property always uses pixels. Therefore, the border around the Report Header section is 25 pixels. The *Line* method's closing argument, *B*, instructs the method to draw a rectangle or box using the two coordinates mentioned earlier as diagonally opposite endpoints.

```
Private Sub PageFooterSection_Print(Cancel As Integer, _
    PrintCount As Integer)
Dim sngTop As Single, sngLeft As Single
Dim sngWidth As Single, sngHeight As Single
Dim lngColor As Long
```

(continued)

```
    Const conPrinterFudge = 25

    'Set top, left, width, and height
    'conPrinterFudge accounts for printer-specific
    'variation of content placement near page edges
        sngTop = Me.ScaleTop
        sngLeft = Me.ScaleLeft
        sngWidth = Me.ScaleWidth - conPrinterFudge
        sngHeight = Me.ScaleHeight - conPrinterFudge
        'Set color
        lngColor = RGB(255, 0, 0)

    'Draw line as a box
        Me.Line (sngTop, sngLeft)-(sngWidth, sngHeight), lngColor, B

End Sub

Private Sub ReportHeader_Print(Cancel As Integer, PrintCount As Integer)
Dim sngTop As Single, sngLeft As Single
Dim sngWidth As Single, sngHeight As Single
Dim lngColor As Long

    'Set top, left, width, and height
        sngTop = Me.ScaleTop
        sngLeft = Me.ScaleLeft
        sngWidth = Me.ScaleWidth
        sngHeight = Me.ScaleHeight

    'Set color
        lngColor = RGB(255, 0, 0)

    'Draw line as a box
        Me.DrawWidth = 25
        Me.Line (sngTop, sngLeft)-(sngWidth, sngHeight), lngColor, B

End Sub

Private Sub Detail_Print(Cancel As Integer, PrintCount As Integer)
Dim sngHCtr As Single, sngVCtr As Single
Dim sngRadius As Single

    'Position and size circle
        sngHCtr = (Me.ScaleWidth / 2) - 3670
        sngVCtr = (Me.ScaleHeight / 2) - 20
        sngRadius = Me.ScaleHeight / 1.5

    'Conditionally draw circle; last argument sets aspect ratio
        If Me.CountOfOrderID.Value >= 30 Then
```

```
        Me.Circle (sngHCtr, sngVCtr), sngRadius, , , , 0.5
    End If

End Sub
```

The only differences between the *ReportHeader_Print* and *PageFooter_Print* procedures are the line setting the width of the rectangle's border and the offset factor to position the rectangle on a page. The Report Header section uses a width of 25 pixels, but the Page Footer section draws a rectangle with the default width of 1 pixel. This is the default value for the *DrawWidth* property. Both procedures draw a rectangle on a layer in front of the standard report layer. You can see that the red border from the *Line* method appears above the background shading for the report title. The *conPrinter-Fudge* constant is a printer-specific value in twips. Sometimes when you get near the edge of a page in an Access report, placement can depend on the printer. For the printer I used when testing the samples for this book, I needed an offset of 25 twips. A value of 0 caused the right and bottom lines of the rectangle for the Page Footer section to print off the page. You can determine the appropriate *conPrinterFudge* value for a specific printer through trial runs.

The Detail section's event procedure relies on the *Circle* method to draw an oval around the order totals for each row in that section. You must empirically determine horizontal and vertical centers as well as the radius of your circle. Use an aspect ratio argument in the *Circle* method to transform a circle to a long or narrow oval. Like the *Line* method, the *Circle* method draws its output on a layer in front of the standard report layer. Embedding the *Circle* method in an *If...Then* statement allows the procedure to draw the oval conditionally around some—but not all—*Orders* field values. The previous sample draws ovals around any orders greater than or equal to 30 in a month.

Formatting Report Controls with *FormatCondition* Objects

The application of the *Circle* method in the preceding sample illustrates a traditional technique for distinguishing values on a report. However, *FormatCondition* objects offer a newer approach that synchronizes with the Access user interface. Your clients are likely to request conditional formatting because Access users can readily implement such formats from the user interface.

The excerpt of a sample report shown in Figure 6-25 (*rptOrdersbyMonthConditionalFormat*) illustrates the use of *ConditionalFormat* objects with one other feature. Basically, the report prints monthly order totals in either of two colors. Each color corresponds to a *FormatCondition* object. The second feature makes the application of these contrasting colors dynamic. Just before the report opens, the application prompts the user for a cut-off value. Values below the cut-off criterion appear in red, otherwise they are green. By rerunning the report with different criterion values, users can change which values appear in red and which appear in green. As a reminder, the report documents the criterion a user entered in its Report Header section.

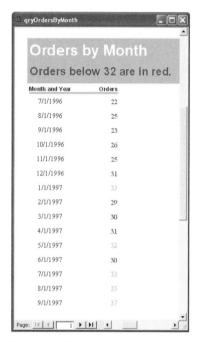

Figure 6-25 An excerpt from a report that uses *FormatCondition* objects to control the color of row values.

If you instantiate *FormatCondition* objects in a report's *Open* event, you need instantiate them only once. The *FormatCondition* objects remain in effect until the report closes. If a report already has conditional formats set through the Access user interface, the *FormatCondition* objects add to the existing objects. Because you can have only three *FormatCondition* objects at any time, you might need to manage the number of active *FormatCondition* objects. The *FormatConditions* collection offers a *Count* property that tells you the number of active conditional formats, and the *FormatCondition* object has a *Delete* method that enables you to remove a conditional format. See "Programming Conditional Formats" in Chapter 5 for more code samples containing *FormatCondition* objects.

The *Open* event procedure for the report excerpted in Figure 6-25 follows. An *InputBox* function prompts for a minimum sales target. Monthly order totals less than the minimum criterion that a user enters appear in red. The procedure assigns a caption value to document the criterion in effect for any printing or viewing of the report. Next, the procedure adds the first *FormatCondition* object, which applies to values greater than or equal to the criterion. Then, the focus shifts to the addition of the second *FormatCondition* object for values less than the criterion. Notice that the *RGB* function assigns the number for the color red to this *FormatCondition* object's *ForeColor* property.

After adding the *FormatCondition* objects through the *frc1* and *frc2* object references, the procedure can safely remove the object references from memory. Their purpose was to set the conditional formats for the *CountOfOrderID* control. The conditional formats remain in effect until the report closes.

```
Private Sub Report_Open(Cancel As Integer)
Dim frc1 As FormatCondition
Dim frc2 As FormatCondition
Dim int1 As Integer
Dim str1 As String

'Prompt for criterion value for color assignments, and
'update the lblTarget control caption
int1 = CInt(InputBox("What's the minimum sales target?", _
    "Programming Microsoft Access 2003", 30))
str1 = "Orders below " & int1 & " are in red."
Me.lblTarget.Caption = str1

'Condition for values greater than or equal to criterion;
'format is green
Set frc1 = Me.Controls("CountOfOrderID"). _
    FormatConditions. _
    Add(acFieldValue, acGreaterThanOrEqual, int1)
frc1.ForeColor = RGB(0, 255, 0)

'Condition for values less than criterion;
'format is bold, red
Set frc2 = Me.Controls("CountOfOrderID"). _
    FormatConditions. _
    Add(acFieldValue, acLessThan, int1)
frc2.FontBold = True
frc2.ForeColor = RGB(255, 0, 0)

'Clean up objects
Set frc1 = Nothing
Set frc2 = Nothing

End Sub
```

Summing Page Values

If your report requires totaling the entries on a report page, you must program these page sums using event procedures because Access offers no built-in way to do this. The sample we'll examine uses a text box with its Running Sum property set to Over All. This setting causes the text box to total its Control Source field over the whole report. Figure 6-26 shows the first and second pages of a report that contains an extra column for computing the running sum. The far-right column appears for tutorial purposes, but in practice, you'll set the Visible property for the control with the running sum to *False*. This sample gives you a way to show or hide this column through compiler constants and the report's *Open* event procedure. The second page of the report, which is shown in Figure 6-26, appears without the running sum column.

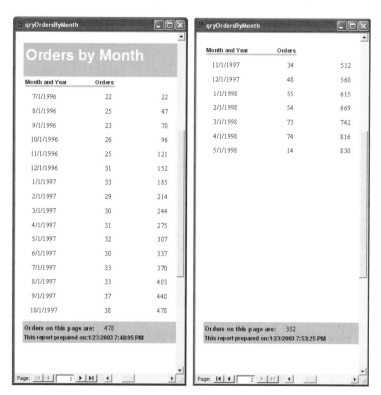

Figure 6-26 This report uses two event procedures and a text box to compute a page sum in its Page Footer section. A third event procedure lets the developer hide the text box that assists in computing the running sum.

You can compute page sums with as few as two event procedures (shown next). Public declarations make the variables conveniently available in either of the event procedures. The *PageFooterSection_Format* event procedure requires only two lines. First, it copies the value for the *pagesum* control with the running sum to *lngCurrentRSum*, a memory variable. Then, it sets another text box in the Page Footer section (*txtpagesum*) to the difference between *lngCurrent-*

RSum and *lngLastRSum*. The value of *lngLastRSum* is initially 0. After every page finishes formatting, a procedure firing with the report's *Page* event copies the current value of *lngCurrentRSum* into *lngLastRSum*. Therefore, the difference between *lngLastRSum* and *lngCurrentRSum* in the *Report_Page* event procedure is the page sum for the current page.

```
Public lngLastRSum As Long
Public lngCurrentRSum As Long
Public lngPageRSum As Long

Private Sub PageFooterSection_Format _
    (Cancel As Integer, FormatCount As Integer)
    lngCurrentRSum = Me.pagesum
    Me.txtpagesum = lngCurrentRSum - lngLastRSum
End Sub

Private Sub Report_Page()
    lngLastRSum = lngCurrentRSum
End Sub

Private Sub Report_Open(Cancel As Integer)
#Const ShowRunningSum = False

#If ShowRunningSum = True Then
    Me.pagesum.Visible = True
#Else
    Me.pagesum.Visible = False
#End If

End Sub
```

Notice that the *PageFooterSection_Format* event procedure in the sample computes and displays page sums by writing a value into a text box within the Page Footer section. *Print* event procedures do not allow this kind of manipulation because the *Print* event fires after the report is already formatted. The *Format* event fires as your application formats the report.

The *Open* event procedure lets you manage the visibility of the text box that assists with the computation of the running sum. The value of *ShowRunningSum*, a compiler constant, is set to *True* in the sample. Change this value setting to *False* to hide the *pagesum* text box. Regardless of whether the text box is visible, it will participate in the computation of the page sums.

Dynamically Updating Reports

In addition to revising the format of a report dynamically, you can devise solutions that let users dynamically specify the contents of a report. Use the *RecordSource* property of a report to set its records dynamically. Unlike Access forms, Access reports do not expose a *Recordset* property for Access database files. Therefore, you cannot dynamically assign an ADO recordset as the source for a report in these files. However, this section describes a workaround you can use.

> **Note** In contrast to Access database files, Access projects—which are used for SQL Server and MSDE (Microsoft SQL Server 2000 Desktop Engine) databases—do expose a *Recordset* property for their reports. Chapter 12 covers the use of reports in Access projects.

Programming the *RecordSource* Property

The *RecordSource* property takes a string value as a setting. Therefore, you can design a SQL string that specifies a record source for the report based on user input. This string can reference any local tables and queries, as well as any linked record sources from other databases. Your code can update the report's title to reflect the new content.

Figure 6-27 shows a form and a report. Users can manipulate the form to change the content for the report. The form includes a text box, an option group of five check boxes, and a command button. After entering a number in the text box and selecting a Price Comparison Operator, the user can click the command button to open the report shown on the right in Design view. Recall that this view is necessary to persist changes to the property settings for the form and its controls. The sample code in this case assigns a new *Record Source* property and updates the *Caption* property for the label that displays the report title. After programmatically updating the two report properties, the application opens the results in Preview mode to display the results of the new record source.

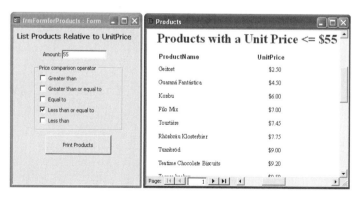

Figure 6-27 In the form on the left, users can designate a record source and a corresponding title for the report on the right.

The *cmdPrintThem_Click* event procedure (shown in the next code listing) for the command button in the form that appears in Figure 6-27 performs three tasks. First, it constructs a SQL string based on selections made in the form. Some default values are generated if the user doesn't set the controls before clicking the button. The procedure successively adds clauses to a starter statement that lists product name and unit price from the *Products* table. The procedure initially appends a *WHERE* clause to the core statement based on the selected check box and the quantity entered in the text box. After adding the *WHERE* clause, the procedure appends an *ORDER BY* clause that sorts the return set from the SQL string by unit price. If a user selects the greater than operator (>) or the greater than or equal to operator (>=), the procedure specifies a descending sort order. Otherwise, the return set sorts by unit price in the default ascending order.

The second component of the *cmdPrintThem_Click* procedure programmatically revises the record source setting and caption for a label on the report. After opening the report in Design view, the code executes a *With...End With* statement based on the report. To eliminate screen clutter, the second component invokes the *Echo* method with an argument of *False*. This suppresses screen updates until a subsequent statement invokes the *Echo* method with an argument of *True*. Inside the *With...End With* block, the procedure sets the report's *RecordSource* property to the SQL string computed from the first part of the procedure. Then, the procedure changes the caption for the label that displays the report's title. A string expression that draws on the option group value and the amount in the text box facilitates this task.

> **Note**   After making the changes in the second component, the procedure closes the report and saves the revisions. In some earlier versions of Access, it wasn't necessary to commit the changes in order to preview them. However, Access 2003 requires that you explicitly save the changes in Design view before you can view them in Preview mode.

The third component performs two functions. It opens the report in Preview mode so that users can see it. Then, the final command restores the *Echo* function, which displays the report. This technique of turning off and then restoring the *Echo* effect leads to crisp screen transitions.

```
Private Sub cmdPrintThem_Click()
Dim str1 As String, strOperator As String
Dim strWhere As String

'Set up SQL statement for report record source
```

(continued)

```
        str1 = "Select ProductName, UnitPrice " & _
            "from Products"
        If IsNull(optRule) Then optRule = 1
        If IsNull(txtAmount) Then txtAmount = 0
        strOperator = Choose(optRule, ">", ">=", "=", "<=", "<")
        strWhere = "Where UnitPrice" & strOperator & txtAmount
        str1 = str1 & " " & strWhere & " Order By UnitPrice"
        If optRule <= 2 Then
            str1 = str1 & " Desc"
        End If
'The commented Debug.Print statement is convenient for debugging
'your SQL statement; remove the comment when you change the
'SQL statement construction
'   Debug.Print str1

'Open report in Design view to set the report's record source
'and its label's caption
        DoCmd.Echo False
        DoCmd.OpenReport "rptProductsfromForm", acViewDesign
        With Reports("rptProductsfromForm")
            .RecordSource = str1
            .Controls("lblTitle").Caption = _
                "Products with a Unit Price " & strOperator & _
                " $" & txtAmount
        End With
        DoCmd.Close , , acSaveYes

'Now show the form to the user
        DoCmd.OpenReport "rptProductsfromForm", acViewPreview
        DoCmd.Echo True

End Sub
```

Using an ADO Recordset as the Report's Record Source

Recall that reports, unlike forms, do not expose a *Recordset* property within Access database files. Therefore, if you have an ADO recordset you're using for some other purpose, you cannot simply assign it to the *Recordset* property of a report. However, you can return the SQL statement for the data source of a recordset. Use the recordset's *Source* property to return its SQL statement. Then, you can assign the SQL statement that represents the source for the ADO recordset to the *RecordSource* property for a report. The connection from the report to the records does not actually pass through the recordset. However, an Access report can emulate the *Recordset* property for a form through this technique.

The next sample demonstrates how to use the records in an ADO recordset as the source for a report. By using an *InputBox* function, the sample lets a user dynamically select a subset of rows from the *Customers* table in the Northwind database as the source for a recordset. Next, the sample loops through the members of the *AllTables* collection to determine whether the Access database file contains a link to the data source for the recordset. If the database file already contains a link, the report can use the SQL statement that serves as the Source property for the recordset. If no link to the remote data source for the recordset exists, the procedure creates a link to the data source for the recordset's connection.

The sample procedure starts by instantiating and opening a connection to the Northwind database. Any database source will work, but you might have to change the method for linking the database. This sample demonstrates linking to an Access database file. (Chapter 1 includes a code sample for linking to any ODBC-compliant data source.) Next, the procedure prompts for the first letter of a customer ID. The *rst1* recordset uses this criterion value to select only those customer IDs with the specified first letter.

After opening the recordset, the procedure prepares to start using the excerpt from the *Customers* table as the source for a report of mailing labels. The Chapter06.mdb file contains the layout for the report saved in *rptMailingLabels*.

Before transferring the *Source* property from the recordset to the *RecordSource* property for the *rptMailingLabels* report, the procedure takes a couple of preliminary steps. First, the procedure lets the user know that it might take a while to compile the data for the report, and it temporarily turns off screen updating. Second, the procedure relies on the *IsLinked* function to search for a table named *Customers* in the current database. If the linked table does not exist, the procedure links to the *Customers* table in the Northwind database. Otherwise, the procedure uses the existing linked table. In any event, the procedure uses a *Boolean* memory variable (*bol1*) to note whether the linked table existed previously.

> **Note**   This sample assumes no conflicts exist between the names in the current database and those in the database to which you're connecting. You will typically control the names of the tables in the local database and sometimes even in the linked database.

At this point in the procedure, a link to the *Customers* table definitely exists in the Northwind database. Therefore, the sample assigns the recordset's *Source* property to the report's *RecordSource* property. After saving the change made in Design view to the report, the procedure opens the report in Preview mode and restores screen updating. This last step is necessary to view the report. As the procedure closes, it performs the usual object cleanup and checks whether it can remove the link to the *Customers* table in the Northwind database. If the link was added exclusively for the report, the procedure can delete the link; otherwise, it will not remove the link.

```
Sub ReportBasedOnADORecordset()
Dim cnn1 As ADODB.Connection
Dim rst1 As ADODB.Recordset
Dim str2 As String
Dim rpt1 As Access.Report
Dim bol1 As Boolean

'Open the Connection object
Set cnn1 = New ADODB.Connection
cnn1.Open "Provider=Microsoft.Jet.OLEDB.4.0;" & _
    "Data Source=C:\Program Files\Microsoft Office\" & _
 "Office11\Samples\Northwind.mdb;"

'Obtain a criterion for rst1 WHERE clause, and
'construct Select statement
str1 = InputBox("Enter the first letter for a CustomerID", _
    "Programming Microsoft Access 2003", "A")
str1 = "SELECT * FROM Customers WHERE Left(CustomerID,1) " & _
    "= '" & str1 & "'"

'Open the ADO Recordset object
Set rst1 = New ADODB.Recordset
rst1.ActiveConnection = cnn1
rst1.Open str1, , adOpenKeyset, adLockOptimistic, _
    adCmdText

'Link Customers if not in AllTables
MsgBox "Click OK to start compiling data for report.  " & _
    "Please be patient.", vbInformation, _
    "Programming Microsoft Access 2003"
DoCmd.Echo False
bol1 = IsLinked("Customers")
If bol1 = False Then
    DoCmd.TransferDatabase acLink, "Microsoft Access", _
        "C:\Program Files\Microsoft Office\" &_
        "Office11\Samples\Northwind.mbd" &_
        acTable, "Customers", "Customers", False
End If

'Assign Source property of ADO recordset to RecordSource
'property for the report, and save the report
```

```
str2 = "rptMailingLabels"
DoCmd.OpenReport str2, acViewDesign
Set rpt1 = Reports(str2)
rpt1.RecordSource = rst1.Source
DoCmd.Close , , acSaveYes

'Open report for viewing
DoCmd.OpenReport str2, acViewPreview
DoCmd.Echo True

'Clean up objects and links
rst1.Close
cnn1.Close
Set rst1 = Nothing
Set cnn1 = Nothing
If bol1 = False Then DoCmd.DeleteObject acTable, "Customers"

End Sub

Function IsLinked(str1 As String) As Boolean
Dim obj1 As Access.AccessObject

'Returns True if filename is in AllTables
For Each obj1 In CurrentData.AllTables
    If obj1.Name = str1 Then
        IsLinked = True
        Exit Function
    End If
Next obj1

End Function
```

> **Note**   Although it is not entirely relevant to the sample, I stuck the following *NoData* event procedure into the code for the *rptMailingLabels* report:
>
> ```
> Private Sub Report_NoData(Cancel As Integer)
>     MsgBox "No data for report. Report canceled."
>     Cancel = True
> End Sub
> ```
>
> This event procedure shows you the syntax to cancel a report when no data exists in the report's record source.

Manipulating Reports and Report Controls

In Chapter 5, you learned about the *AllForms* collection. Access also provides an *AllReports* collection as well as the *AllTables*, *AllQueries*, *AllMacros*, *AllViews*, *AllModules*, *AllStoredProcedures*, *AllDataAccessPages*, and *AllDataDiagrams* collections. A member of any of these collections is an *AccessObject* object. Microsoft first introduced *AccessObject* objects with Access 2000. You can refer to an *AllReports* member by one of three conventions:

```
AllReports (0)
AllReports ("name")
AllReports![name]
```

Enumerating Reports

Your code can enumerate *AccessObject* objects in any of the *Allxxx* collections to determine whether objects exist in a database connection. It does not matter whether the object is open or closed. When an *AccessObject* object is loaded or open, your application can work with corresponding collections that encompass all the open reports, forms, and other important objects in an Access database. For example, members of the *Reports* collection are individual reports that are open in an application. These open *Report* objects contain a richer set of properties than the more restricted set of objects in the *AllReports* collection. In addition, members of the *Reports* collection employ methods that the *AllReports* collection members do not make available. You can use the *Name* property in *AllReports* and *Reports* to identify a particular object in either collection. By using the *IsLoaded* property in the *AllReports* collection, you can verify whether you need to open a report before attempting to manipulate its properties and methods using the *Reports* collection.

The *ListAllReports* procedure that follows enumerates the members of the *AllReports* collection listing each report's name and loaded status. The *AllReports* collection belongs to either the *CurrentProject* or the *CodeProject*. *CurrentProject* and *CodeProject* are members of the *Application* object. You must reference one of these two members to expose the *AllReports* members. Therefore, the *ListAllReports* procedure starts by setting a reference to the *CurrentProject* member of the *Application* object. You need this reference to reach the members of the *AllReports* collection. Notice that the *For...Each* loop passes through each *AccessObject* object (*obj1*) in *AllReports*, but the path to *AllReports* starts with the reference to *Application.CurrentProject*.

```
Sub ListAllReports()
Dim obj1 As AccessObject, app1 As Object

'Create a reference to the current project instance
```

```
Set app1 = Application.CurrentProject

'List each report in the application, and
'describe as loaded or not
For Each obj1 In app1.AllReports
    If obj1.IsLoaded = True Then
        Debug.Print obj1.Name & " is loaded."
    Else
        Debug.Print obj1.Name & " is not loaded."
    End If
Next obj1

End Sub
```

The *AllReports* and *AllForms* collections are directly analogous to one another. You are not restricted to examining *AccessObject* members in the active project. The *ListAllFormsElsewhere* and *ListAllReportsElsewhere* procedures, which you'll see in a moment, show how to program both collections when they point at another project. Notice the similarity between the code that manipulates the two collections as well as between the procedure shown above, which works with the current project, and the two procedures shown below, which work with another project.

The *ListAllFormsElsewhere* procedure shown next prints the total number and the names of individual members in the *AllForms* collection for the Northwind database file from the Chapter06.mdb file. This procedure demonstrates how to enumerate *AccessObject* objects in the Northwind.mdb file.

```
Sub ListAllFormsElsewhere()
Dim appAccess1 As Access.Application
Dim obj1 As AccessObject

'Create a reference to another database file
Set appAccess1 = New Access.Application
appAccess1.OpenCurrentDatabase _
    "C:\Program Files\Microsoft Office\" & _
    "Office11\Samples\Northwind.mdb"

'Print the total number of forms in the database
Debug.Print appAccess1.CurrentProject.AllForms.Count
For Each obj1 In appAccess1.CurrentProject.AllForms
    Debug.Print obj1.Name
Next obj1

'Clean up objects
appAccess1.Quit
Set appAccess1 = Nothing

End Sub
```

The *ListAllReportsElsewhere* procedure shown next follows the same general design as the preceding one, although it deals with the *AllReports* collection instead of the *AllForms* collection. The layout is nearly identical except for the use of string variables to define the database name. This change is strictly for convenience and to make the code more generally applicable—nothing in Access or VBA mandates the use of a string variable instead of a string constant in the call to the *OpenCurrentDatabase* method.

```
Sub ListAllReportsElsewhere()
Dim obj1 As AccessObject
Dim strPath As String, strFile As String, strDBName As String

'Create a reference to another database file
Set appAccess1 = New Access.Application
strPath = "C:\Program Files\Microsoft Office\" & _
    "Office11\Samples\"
strFile = "Northwind.mdb"
strDBName = strPath & strFile
appAccess1.OpenCurrentDatabase strDBName

'Print the total number of reports in the database
Debug.Print appAccess1.CurrentProject.AllReports.Count
For Each obj1 In appAccess1.CurrentProject.AllReports
    Debug.Print obj1.Name
Next obj1

'Clean up objects
appAccess1.Quit
Set appAccess1 = Nothing

End Sub
```

Modifying Report Control Properties

Your application code can use the *AllReports* collection as a pathway to individual reports that are open and to their controls. Using this pathway, your application can read and modify the properties of these open reports and their controls. The *ControlsInReports* procedure (shown next) drills down from the *AllReports* collection members to the text box and label properties on individual reports that are open.

The *ControlsInReports* procedure starts with a *For...Each* loop that iterates through the members of the *AllReports* collection. If a member is open, as indicated by a value of *True* for its *IsLoaded* property, the code enters a nested *For...Each* loop to enumerate the controls on that report. You can use the *ControlType* property to determine a control's type. You need to know the control type because this determines the properties that the control exposes.

For example, a label control displays its *Caption* property, but a text box displays its *Text* or *Value* property. You can use the Object Browser in the VBE to view the intrinsic constants of other control types that you want to edit or examine. Forms and reports share the same set of control types. For the full set of control types from the Object Browser, see Figure 5-24 in Chapter 5.

> **Note**   For a *TextBox* control, the *Text* property returns or sets the formatted current value of a control. The *Value* property is the saved value of a *TextBox* control. These properties are often the same, but they can diverge. For example, when you change the *Text* property without committing the change, *Text* and *Value* properties can be different for a *TextBox* control.

This program contains an error trap in case the procedure loops to a report that's open in Design view. A report open in Design view has an *IsLoaded* property value of *True*. However, the display value of a text box is not available in Design view. Attempting to print or otherwise access this report generates an *Err* object with a *Number* property of 2186. The solution is to open the report in Preview mode. Then, when the procedure completes printing the text box values, the code restores the Design view for the report.

```
Sub ControlsInReports()
On Error GoTo ControlsInReports_Trap
Dim obj1 As AccessObject
Dim ctl1 As Control
Dim bol1 As Boolean

'Loop through the reports in the Access database file
'or Access project
For Each obj1 In CurrentProject.AllReports
    If obj1.IsLoaded = True Then
Start_Printing:
'If the report is open, loop through the report's
'controls and print property values for label and
'text box controls
        For Each ctl1 In Reports(obj1.Name).Controls
            If ctl1.ControlType = acLabel Then
                Debug.Print ctl1.Name, ctl1.Caption
            ElseIf ctl1.ControlType = acTextBox Then
                Debug.Print ctl1.Name, ctl1.Value
            Else
```

(continued)

```
                    Debug.Print ctl1.Name & " is not a" & _
                        " label or a text box."
                End If
            Next ctl1
    'Restore Design view if the procedure changed the view

            If bol1 = True Then
                DoCmd.OpenReport obj1.Name, acViewDesign
                bol1 = False
            End If
        End If
    Next obj1


    ControlsInReports_Exit:
    Exit Sub


    ControlsInReports_Trap:
    If Err.Number = 2186 Then
    'Open in Preview mode if Design view generates error
        DoCmd.OpenReport obj1.Name, acViewPreview
        bol1 = True
        Resume Start_Printing
    Else
        Debug.Print Err.Number, Err.Description
    End If

    End Sub
```

Mailing Snapshots

The next sample enumerates reports to determine whether they are marked for mailing as snapshot files. The sample relies on two procedures: *SendSnapshots* and *CheckMailItTag*. First, the *SendSnapshots* procedure enumerates the members of the *AllReports* collection. In order to check whether the report's *Tag* property is "mail it", the report must be open. The *Tag* property is not available through the *AllReports* collection—it is available only through the *Reports* collection. The *Send-Snapshots* procedure checks the *IsLoaded* status of each *AllReports* member. If the report is loaded, the procedure calls the *CheckMailItTag* procedure. If *IsLoaded* has a value of *False*, the procedure opens the report before calling the second procedure.

The sample does not call the *Echo* method with a *False* parameter, so a user can easily obtain feedback as the second procedure runs. This is particularly appropriate in cases where it takes a while to create and mail the snapshot file. By the way, in the collection of reports in the Chapter06.mdb file, only one report (*rptOrdersByMonth*) has a setting of "mail it" for its *Tag* property.

The *CheckMailItTag* procedure accepts the report name passed to it by *SendSnapshots*. *CheckMailItTag* uses this report name to create a reference to the *Reports* collection member with the same name. Then, *CheckMailItTag* checks the *Tag* property of the report to determine whether it equals "mail it". If it does, the procedure invokes the *DoCmd* object's *SendObject* method to create a snapshot file and send it to an e-mail address (in this case, virginia@cab-inc.net). You can replace the string constant for the address with any single address or series of addresses that your application requires. Be sure that the argument after the message body (*"Here is the report."*) remains *False*. If you use the default value of *True*, your procedure will halt with the message open and wait for the user to edit the message. Setting the value to *False* enables the procedure to loop through all the reports without any user intervention.

> **Note**   Make sure that Microsoft Outlook is open before invoking the *DoCmd.SendObject* command in the *CheckMailItTag* procedure. Otherwise, the *SendObject* method will try to launch Outlook and link to the Internet as if being launched for the first time. In any event, Outlook will likely query whether you want someone to send mail on your behalf. The "someone" in this case is the *CheckMailItTag* procedure. See Chapter 9 for samples that open Outlook and answer the query automatically.

```
Sub SendSnapshots()
Dim obj1 As AccessObject
Dim app1 As Object

'Create a reference to the current project instance
    Set app1 = Application.CurrentProject

'Enumerate each member in AllReports to verify if loaded.
'If not loaded, open before calling CheckMailItTag.
    For Each obj1 In app1.AllReports
        If obj1.IsLoaded = True Then
            CheckMailItTag obj1.Name
        Else
            DoCmd.OpenReport obj1.Name, acViewPreview
            CheckMailItTag obj1.Name
            DoCmd.Close acReport, obj1.Name, acSaveNo
        End If
    Next obj1
```

(continued)

```
End Sub

'Open Outlook before invoking this procedure
Sub CheckMailItTag(obj1name)
Dim rep1 As Report

'Set reference to Reports member corresponding
'to AllReports member
    Set rep1 = Reports(obj1name)

'If Tag property says "mail it",
'create a snapshot file and mail it
    If rep1.Tag = "mail it" Then
        DoCmd.SendObject acOutputReport, obj1name, _
        acFormatSNP, "virginia@cabinc.net", , , _
        "Snapshot Report", "Here is the report.", False
    End If

End Sub
```

Summary

This chapter aims to equip you to create static and dynamic reports by building on your knowledge of forms and their controls, report wizards, Access report architecture, and VBA collections, such as *Reports* and *AllReports*. Your applications can manage the controls on a report with the same set of properties for forms. In addition, this chapter demonstrates how to use a form as an interface for customizing the design of a report. This latter application type can create dynamic reports that adapt to user actions at run time.

While you can control the design of reports programmatically, just as with forms, with reports you are more likely to use the rich collection of built-in wizards for quickly creating the base version of a report. Then, if necessary, you can customize the report at design time or run time. It is also common to use Design view to manually construct Access reports. This process benefits from an understanding of Access report architecture, including the standard and custom report sections that you can create along with the sorting and grouping rules that you can specify for a report.

Although programming a report from scratch can be tedious, automatically modifying a manually created report via one or more procedures can be powerful and relatively easy. You can save and send reports as snapshot files with simple VBA procedures. In addition, you can readily customize the formatting of reports by showing values in different colors, and at run time you can even set which values receive which colors. Another typical programming application is to assign the record source for a report dynamically. Reusing the same report with different record sources can make your applications easier to manage by reducing the total number of reports. After you have a collection of reports in the current database file (or even another one), you can programmatically inventory and manage your reports through the *AllReports* and the *Reports* collections.

7

Designing and Using PivotTables and PivotCharts

This chapter explores the capabilities of PivotTables and PivotCharts in Microsoft Access 2003. PivotTables and PivotCharts initially gained popularity in Microsoft Excel, where they're used by financial and operational analysts to probe data that shapes strategic and tactical decision making. Access 2003 inherits its PivotTable and PivotChart functionality from the PivotTable list control and Chart control available through the Office 2003 Web Components. Chapter 14 revisits Office 2003 Web Components and drills down further into their capabilities. Access 95 was the first Access version to offer PivotTables. Since then, the capabilities and analytical speed of this feature have grown steadily. PivotCharts appeared for the first time in Access in the 2002 version.

Access 2003 offers Access developers the most advanced PivotTable and PivotChart capabilities, tightly integrated with the full range of Access features. The fact that tables, queries, forms, reports, views, and stored procedures in Access 2003 projects utilize PivotTable and PivotChart views is a testament to how integral PivotTables and PivotCharts have become. With Access 2003, developers can take advantage of the Microsoft Office 2003 Web Components (owc11.dll) object model to simplify constructing PivotTable and PivotChart objects programmatically.

Both PivotTables and PivotCharts enable you to display data in an interactive manner. End users are likely to find PivotTables and PivotCharts appealing because of their easy-to-use, interactive interface. And programmers can readily compute the data depicted in PivotTables and PivotCharts based on their clients' record sources. The usefulness of programmatically constructed PivotTables and PivotCharts might render obsolete some traditional data analysis tools, such as crosstab queries and charts based on older technology, such as the Microsoft Graph 2000 Chart ActiveX control. As the popularity of PivotTables and PivotCharts continues to grow among end users, the demand for programmers who can readily create and edit these display devices will increase as well. Read this chapter if you want to be one of those programmers.

Overview of PivotTables

A PivotTable summarizes and analyzes data in a datasheet. The datasheet for a PivotTable contains several sections known as drop areas into which you can deposit fields. A field can correspond to a column in a relational table from an Access database file or from a Microsoft SQL Server database. The PivotTable user interface (UI) and programmatic interface simplify computing statistics for the data in the detail drop area based on fieldsets in the row and column drop areas. (A fieldset is a collection of related fields.) PivotTables offer a generalized way to perform cross-tabulations of relational data. In addition, you can readily filter the data that appears in a PivotTable's datasheet.

The great thing about the widespread availability of PivotTables in Access is that programmers no longer have to transfer their output to Excel for their clients to view it in this format. PivotTables enable more end users to perform analyses with the data provided by programmers. Furthermore, the ease with which end users can manipulate data with a PivotTable increases the demand for the services of database programmers who understand how to create and manage PivotTables programmatically.

Just as you can with PivotTables, you can move PivotChart fields from one drop area to another. A PivotChart will automatically update as you move fields to and from its drop areas. You can also readily update the graph type of a PivotChart. Access 2003 offers 12 major graph types from which you can choose, including column, line, pie, and area charts. Each category of graph offers several subtypes of charts you can select from. Unlike the Microsoft Graph 2000 Chart ActiveX control, an Access PivotChart does not force you to work with an OLE DB object outside of Access.

Sample PivotTable

Figure 7-1 presents an excerpt from a sample PivotTable based on the *Orders* table imported from the Northwind database. The Chapter07.mdb file includes this table along with several others from the Northwind database. The PivotTable displays the freight and order ID information according to the ship country and shipper. As you can see, the *Ship Country* and *Shipper* fieldsets organize the two detail fieldsets, *Freight* and *Order ID*. The entries at each intersection of a country and a shipper are the freight charges and order ID values for orders transported to a country by a shipper.

Ship Country ▾	Federal Shipping		Speedy Express		United Package		Grand Total	
	Freight ▾	Order ID ▾	Freight ▾	Order ID ▾	Freight ▾	Order ID ▾	Average of Freight	Count of Order ID
Argentina	$1.10	10782	$29.83	10409	$38.82	10448	$37.41	16
	$19.76	10819	$8.12	10531	$17.22	10521		
	$31.51	10937	$90.85	10828	$22.57	10716		
	$3.17	11019	$2.84	10881	$1.27	10898		
			$0.33	11054	$63.77	10916		
					$49.56	10958		
					$217.86	10986		
	$13.89	4	$26.39	5	$58.72	7		
Austria	$146.06	10263	$140.51	10258	$101.95	10368	$184.79	40
	$360.63	10353	$162.33	10351	$67.88	10402		
	$122.46	10392	$94.77	10382	$31.29	10427		
	$73.79	10403	$126.38	10390	$47.94	10442		
	$26.06	10571	$458.78	10430	$5.29	10489		
	$35.12	10597	$96.78	10595	$789.95	10514		
	$477.90	10633	$78.09	10667	$339.22	10530		
	$145.45	10764	$96.50	10686	$11.19	10771		
	$96.43	10773	$272.47	10698	$126.66	10795		
	$351.53	10776	$117.33	10747	$25.22	10844		
	$74.60	10968	$411.88	10836	$100.22	10854		
	$117.61	10990	$162.75	10895	$353.07	10979		
	$79.46	11008			$754.26	11017		
					$53.05	11053		
					$258.64	11072		
	$162.08	13	$184.88	12	$204.39	15		

Figure 7-1   A sample PivotTable based on a copy of the *Orders* table from the Northwind database.

Note   You can open a PivotTable view with the same toolbar control used to expose the more familiar Datasheet view and Design view. This control has a View ToolTip. Click the control in Access 2003 to expose the view types, and notice that there are four selections. In addition to the familiar Design view and Datasheet view, you will see a PivotTable view and a PivotChart view.

In addition to listing raw values, the PivotTable also presents the average freight charge and the count of order IDs. These average and count values appear within the cell at the intersection of each country and shipper as well as in the *Grand Total* columns at the right edge of the PivotTable. The values in the pair of *Grand Total* columns for each row represent the data for all shippers for a particular country. The final row in the PivotTable, which is also named Grand Total, displays the average freight charge and order count for each ship-per for all countries. By default, both the *Grand Total* row and column hide the detail freight charges and order IDs. A user can show and hide these detail val-ues with the Show/Hide Details controls that appear as a plus sign (+) and a minus sign (–) within each row or column of a fieldset, including the *Grand Total* fields. In addition, the toolbar controls in the PivotTable view enable you to expand and contract detail for the entire table. Move the cursor over the toolbar controls to see the ToolTips that indicate which controls support these actions.

A Field List control on the toolbar in the PivotTable view determines the visibility of the PivotTable Field List control. (See Figure 7-2.) This dialog box displays the list of all items available for inclusion in the PivotTable. Items that the PivotTable currently contains appear in a bold font; items not contained in the PivotTable appear in a normal font. The *Order ID*, *Freight*, *Ship Country*, and *Shipper* fields are boldface because the PivotTable currently contains them. In addition, the *Average of Freight* and *Count of Order ID* fields appear in bold-face within the *Totals* fieldset at the top of the dialog box.

Figure 7-2   The PivotTable Field List dialog box for the PivotTable shown in Figure 7-1.

As you've likely gathered, PivotTables work with fieldsets (this topic is examined in more detail later in this chapter). When working with relational tables as data sources, your fieldsets almost always will contain just one field. However, Access automatically breaks date/time field values into hierarchically dependent fieldsets. Expand the *Order Date By Month* fieldset to see the nested fields that Access automatically makes available to you. Of course, you do not have to work with these hierarchical collections of fields. The PivotTable Field List control offers a fieldset item named *Order Date* that has a single item below it as its sole field—also named *Order Date*.

The *Ship Country, Freight*, and *Order ID* fieldset values each corresponds exactly to a matching column value in the *Orders* table, which is the source for the PivotTable in Figure 7-1. In contrast, the *Shipper* fieldset values show ship-per names, but the matching column, *Shipvia* from the *Orders* table, has numeric values instead of names. An expression for the *Shipper* fieldset trans-forms the numbers in the *Shipvia* column to shipper names. You can view the transformation expression by right-clicking *Shipper* in the PivotTable and choosing Properties. Then, click the Calculation tab in the Properties dialog box to view the expression for the fieldset. The formula for converting the *Shipvia* numeric values to shipper names follows:

```
IIf(Shipvia=1, "Speedy Express", IIf(Shipvia=2, "United Package",
"Federal Shipping"))
```

> **Note**   A calculated field, such as *Shipper*, appears in the Field List dialog box only in the PivotTable session initially defining the fieldset. Use the PivotTable, Calculated Totals and Fields, Create Calculated Detail Field command to create the calculated *Shipper* fieldset. You can view the properties for the *Shipper* fieldset by right-clicking the item on the PivotTable and choosing Properties.

The PivotTable Template

As we've discussed, a PivotTable is a view for standard database objects in Access 2003. Therefore, you use the View control on a toolbar to expose the template for constructing and editing a PivotTable. If a database object has no previously saved PivotTable view, you will see a blank template. This tem-plate contains four drop areas into which you can place fieldsets. Click the Field List control on the toolbar in a PivotTable view to open the PivotTable Field List dialog box. The Field List control in a PivotTable view looks identi-cal to the Field List control in a Form Design view. This control exposes all the built-in fieldsets for a database object along with any calculated fields or *Totals* fields. You can add items to a PivotTable by dragging them from the dialog box to a drop area. To remove items from a PivotTable, drag them from the drop area right off the table.

> **Note** For analysts, one of the major benefits of PivotTables is that you can drag items from one drop area to another. A PivotTable automatically recomputes after an item assumes its new position.

Figure 7-3 shows a PivotTable along with a PivotTable Field List dialog box for the *Products* table. Three of the four PivotTable drop areas are empty. These empty drop areas have names of Totals Or Detail Fields, Column Fields, and Filter Fields. A message in each drop area instructs you to drop items into it. The Row Fields area in Figure 7-3 reveals the appearance of the PivotTable immediately after I drop the *Product Name* fieldset into it.

Figure 7-3 You can drag fields from the PivotTable Field List dialog box to drop areas on the PivotTable, as this example for the *Products* table shows.

> **Note** The Filter Fields drop area name is somewhat misleading since you can filter a PivotTable from the Row Fields and Column Fields drop areas as well. Think of the Filter Fields drop area as a third dimension for a PivotTable, with its Row Fields area and Column Fields area comprising the first two dimensions.

You can drag multiple fields to any of the drop areas. For a query based on both the *Categories* and *Products* tables, you can drag both the *Category-Name* and *ProductName* fields to the Row Fields area. The PivotTable Field List dialog box automatically picks up the caption and field name in the table. Therefore, the dialog box shows the *CategoryName* field by its caption, Category Name, but it correctly refers to the field by its name, *CategoryName*.

When you click the Close button to exit a PivotTable view, Access prompts you to save your changes. Choosing to save the changes causes the PivotTable view to open to the current settings the next time a user selects the PivotTable view for that database object. Not choosing to save the changes causes the Pivot-Table to open the next time with the settings that were in effect when you initially opened the view. For example, if the view was blank and contained no fields in its drop areas, it will appear that way the next time you open it.

Overview of PivotCharts

A PivotChart is a chart you can build with the same general approach with which you construct PivotTables. A PivotChart can provide a view to the data in a database object, such as a table or a query.

A PivotChart can graphically represent the data depicted in a PivotTable. As you create a PivotTable with aggregated data, the aggregated values automatically become the data points for a corresponding PivotChart. You can also construct a PivotChart immediately, without first creating a PivotTable. As stated earlier, the Office 2003 Web Components library offers a programmatic interface for managing PivotTable and PivotChart capabilities. PivotCharts offer newer technology than former graphing options. In addition, your PivotChart development skills will directly transfer to Web applications that use PivotCharts on Data Access Pages or on ordinary HTML Web pages. Figure 7-4 shows the PivotChart that corresponds to the PivotTable shown in Figure 7-1. To reveal the chart, all I did was choose the PivotChart view from the View control and choose the Pivot-Chart, Show Legend command. Notice that the chart contains the average freight charge and order count by country for each of the three shippers.

You can modify this chart in a variety of ways. For example, you can filter the data by country to obtain a simpler chart that shows just one or several countries. Click the Ship Country control at the bottom of the chart, clear the All control, and then select the countries that you want to show in the new view. Click OK in the Ship Country drop-down box to close it and display the chart with the selected countries. You can perform the same kind of filtering for the Shipper dialog box as well. To do so, click the Shipper drop-down list to the right of the chart. Then, select just those shippers for which you want the chart to display data. Clicking OK constructs the new view according to your selections.

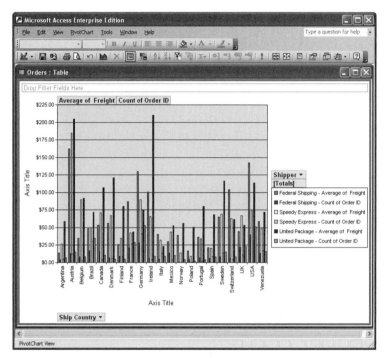

Figure 7-4 A PivotChart automatically generated by the construction of the PivotTable shown in Figure 7-1.

The PivotChart in Figure 7-4 includes default labels for the horizontal and vertical axes. These labels are place markers to help you easily customize the chart. In a finished chart, you can readily edit the horizontal and vertical axis title labels. To do so, simply click on a label to select it. Then, open the Properties dialog box with a control on the toolbar. Next, select the Format tab. Change the entry in the Caption text box on the Format tab. While you have the Format tab selected, you can also modify the boldface, italic, underlining, and font color formatting of the axis title, as well as the font style and size.

Creating PivotTables Programmatically

An easy way to create PivotTables programmatically is by assigning a record source to a form. That way, you can program the PivotTable view for the form. If you specify PivotTable as the form's default view, users will see your Pivot-Table immediately upon opening the form. Alternatively, you can work with a normal Access form. You programmatically create a PivotTable for the form and save it, but you don't make the PivotTable view the form's default view. This approach allows users to open the form and view the data in Form view. Then, when they're ready, users can change the view and examine a PivotTable based on the form's record source. A form can have only one PivotTable at a time. However, since PivotTables are programmable, you can create them dynamically, so that one form can organize data in several PivotTable views.

To manage PivotTable or PivotChart objects programmatically, your VBA project needs a reference to the Microsoft Office 2003 Web Components. An item for the Web components does not appear automatically in the References dialog box generated by the Tools, References command. However, you can use the Browse button on the References dialog box to navigate to the owc11.dll file in the \Program Files\Common Files\Microsoft Shared\Web Components\11 folder. This adds a reference named Microsoft Office Web Components 2003 to the project. Without this reference, any *Dim* statement declaring an object based on a member of the library will fail.

Note   After adding a reference to the Microsoft Office Web Components 2003 library, you can use the Object Browser to discover the objects, properties, methods, and events exposed by the library. Use these elements to add as well as manage PivotTable and PivotChart objects on forms programmatically.

All the samples in this section process the *Invoices* query. This query ties together most of the Northwind tables that have anything to do with orders. The .mdb file for this chapter contains the tables and the *Invoices* SQL string that ties them together. While examining the query's SQL statement, it can be helpful to see a diagram of the relationships between tables that the query specifies. Figure 7-5 shows such a diagram. You can view the SQL code by opening the SQL window for the query.

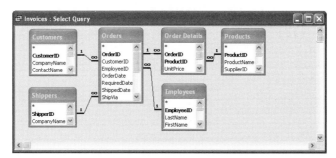

Figure 7-5   A diagram depicting the relationships between tables specified by the *Invoices* query.

Constructing a PivotTable for a Query

To create a form as the basis for a PivotTable, you just need to assign a record source to it. This form's record source then becomes the record source for the PivotTable view. You can programmatically create a form and assign it a record source with just a handful of code lines.

The following sample actually goes beyond the requirements for creating a form as the basis for a PivotTable; the code creates a text box control on the form for each field in the record source behind the form. Though not absolutely necessary, having the text boxes makes it possible to examine the field values for individual records in Form view. This sample is very elementary—it just adds text box controls without adding label controls for each text box. For samples that demonstrate how to add label controls that correspond to text box controls, see Chapter 6. The following sample demonstrates the use of the *CreateControl* method, which follows the same general syntax and conventions as the *CreateReportControl* method used in Chapter 6. However, the *CreateControl* method is used with forms here instead of reports.

The initial sample to build a PivotTable that we'll examine relies on three procedures. The first procedure, *CreateAFormWithPivotTableOnInvoices*, which serves as a main routine, merely calls two other procedures, and it passes a return value from the first called procedure to the second one. The *CreateAFormWithPivotTableOnInvoices* procedure invokes the *FormName* procedure and passes it the name of a query: *Invoices*. The *FormName* procedure is a function procedure, so it returns a value that the *CreateAFormWithPivotTableOnInvoices* procedure stores in *strFormName*. This return value is the name of the custom form, automatically generated by Access, that uses the *Invoices* query as a record source. Next, the main routine invokes the *CreatePivotTableForInvoices* procedure and passes the called procedure the value in *strFormName*. That second called procedure builds a PivotTable view for the record source behind the form whose name is in *strFormName*.

```
Sub CreateAFormWithPivotTableOnInvoices()
Dim strFormName As String

'Create a form with controls for all the fields in
'the Invoices query
strFormName = FormName("Invoices")

'Create a PivotTable view for the new form
'with the selected row, column, and detail fieldset members
CreatePivotTableForInvoices strFormName

End Sub
```

The *FormName* function procedure takes a single argument as a string variable indicating the record source and returns a string value that's the name of the form it creates. The first three lines after the declarations and two lines for saving the form toward the end of the procedure are absolutely necessary here. The first line after the declarations starts by invoking the *Application* object's *CreateForm* method. Because the method belongs to the top-level object in Access, you do not need to precede it with the object's name. The first line establishes *frm1* as a pointer to the form created by the method. The second line assigns the query named in the argument passed to the procedure as the form's *RecordSource* property. The third line designates the PivotTable view as the default view for the form. When users open the form from the Database window, they will automatically see the PivotTable view instead of the Form view.

After constructing the form, the procedure creates an ActiveX Data Objects (ADO) recordset based on the same record source as the form. The procedure loops through the *Fields* collection of the *Recordset* object to add a text box to the form for each field in the recordset. The most important line of code within the *For* loop for the recordset's *Fields* collection invokes the *CreateControl* method. This is another method of the Access *Application* object; its purpose is to add a control to a form. The two arguments for the method designate the form name to add a control to and the type of control to add. Another important line within the loop assigns the current field name value to the *ControlSource* property for the text box control. A third line worthy of special attention is the one assigning the *Name* property to the text box created by the *CreateControl* method. The prefix for the *Name* property setting is always *txt*, and the body of the name setting is the field name for the *ControlSource* property. This is normally just the field name for the underlying table, unless two tables for the *Invoices* query have the same column name. In this situation, Access uses the table name as a qualifier for the column name. The remaining lines within the loop and the four lines before the loop assist in spacing the text box controls evenly along the length of the form.

The first two lines after the loop perform two critical functions. The first of these lines saves the name of the form created by the procedure as the return value from the function procedure. The second line after the loop closes the form and saves the changes. This commits the *RecordSource* and *ControlSource* property assignments. Let's take a look at the procedure now:

```
Function FormName(strSourceName As String) As String
Dim frm1 As Access.Form
Dim txt1 As Access.TextBox
Dim rst1 As ADODB.Recordset
Dim fld1 As ADODB.Field
Dim intLeft As Integer
```

(continued)

```
Dim intLastTop As Integer
Dim intOffset As Integer
Dim intWidth As Integer
Dim intHeight As Integer

'Create a form with the specified record source
Set frm1 = CreateForm
frm1.RecordSource = strSourceName
frm1.DefaultView = acFormPivotTable

'Create a recordset using the specified source
Set rst1 = New ADODB.Recordset
rst1.Open strSourceName, CurrentProject.Connection

'Assign control size and position parameters
intLeft = 144
intOffset = 72
intWidth = 4320
intHeight = 288

'Iterate through recordset fields and create
'corresponding text box controls on the form
For Each fld1 In rst1.Fields
    Set txt1 = CreateControl(frm1.Name, acTextBox)
    With txt1
        .ControlSource = fld1.Name
        .Left = intLeft
        .Top = intLastTop + intHeight + intOffset
        intLastTop = .Top
        .Width = intWidth
        .Height = intHeight
        .Name = "txt" & fld1.Name
    End With
Next fld1

'Close the form, save changes, and pass its name back
FormName = frm1.Name
DoCmd.Close acForm, frm1.Name, acSaveYes

'Clean up objects
rst1.Close
Set rst1 = Nothing
Set frm1 = Nothing
Set txt1 = Nothing

End Function
```

After you have a form with a *RecordSource* setting, you can create a PivotTable view for the data behind the form. The *CreatePivotTableForInvoices* procedure creates a PivotTable view for the form generated by the *FormName* procedure. The procedure begins by opening the form in Design view. This view is necessary to make an assignment for a form's *DefaultView* property. The sample uses the *conPivotTableDefaultView* constant to assign a value of 3 to the property. This property value causes a form to open automatically with a PivotTable view instead of the default Form view from the Access UI. After saving this change to the form, the procedure reopens the form. This time the procedure opens the form in PivotTable view so that it can make changes to the design of the PivotTable.

A PivotTable view organizes selected fields in the record source for a form with a crosstab. The format arranges detail data field values according to their column and row field values. When you programmatically refer to the fields in a record source, your code refers to them as *PivotFieldset* objects.

After referencing a field in the form's record source, use the *InsertFieldset* method to assign the fieldset object to a drop area in the PivotTable. The code sample in *CreatePivotTableForInvoices* invokes the *InsertFieldset* method four times. First, it assigns the *Shippers_CompanyName* field to the column drop area. Visual Basic for Applications (VBA) refers to this area as the *ColumnAxis* property of the *Fieldsets* collection for a PivotTable. Next, the code sample assigns the *ProductName* field to the row drop area (*RowAxis*). Then, the last two assignments assign the *Quantity* and *ExtendedPrice* fields to the detail drop areas (*DataAxis*). The PivotTable organizes the field values in the detail drop areas according to the row and column drop area field values. After making all the fieldset assignments, the procedure commits the changes to the form by closing the form and saving the changes.

```
Sub CreatePivotTableForInvoices(strFormName As String)
Dim frm1 As Access.Form
Dim fset1 As PivotFieldSet
Const conPivotTableDefaultView = 3

'Create reference to form on which to base PivotTable,
'but first set PivotTable as the default view
DoCmd.OpenForm strFormName, acDesign
Set frm1 = Forms(strFormName)
frm1.DefaultView = conPivotTableDefaultView
DoCmd.Close acForm, strFormName, acSaveYes
DoCmd.OpenForm strFormName, acFormPivotTable
Set frm1 = Forms(strFormName)

With frm1.PivotTable.ActiveView
    'Assign fieldset members to the column, row, and detail sections of
    'the PivotTable
    Set fset1 = .FieldSets("Shippers_CompanyName")
```

(continued)

```
       .ColumnAxis.InsertFieldSet fset1
       Set fset1 = .FieldSets("ProductName")
       .RowAxis.InsertFieldSet fset1
       Set fset1 = .FieldSets("Quantity")
       .DataAxis.InsertFieldSet fset1
       Set fset1 = .FieldSets("ExtendedPrice")
       .DataAxis.InsertFieldSet fset1
   End With
   'Close form with its PivotTable view
   DoCmd.Close acForm, strFormName, acSaveYes

   End Sub
```

Figure 7-6 presents an excerpt from the PivotTable view created by the preceding sample. Notice from the window's title bar that the form has the name *Form1*. If *Form1* already exists in the database, the sample creates *Form2*, and so on. Observe that the row, column, and detail field names appear with the control names for the corresponding record source fields. These control names are derived from the record source's field name and have a *txt* prefix. The *FormName* procedure assigns this prefix when it assigns the *Name* property of each text box on a form. You can modify this convention and use any naming rule that meets the requirements of your application.

> **Note** The sample in this section uses default naming conventions for the forms. Code samples in the section "Programmatically Creating PivotCharts" demonstrate how to assign custom form names programmatically. These techniques apply equally to PivotCharts and PivotTables.

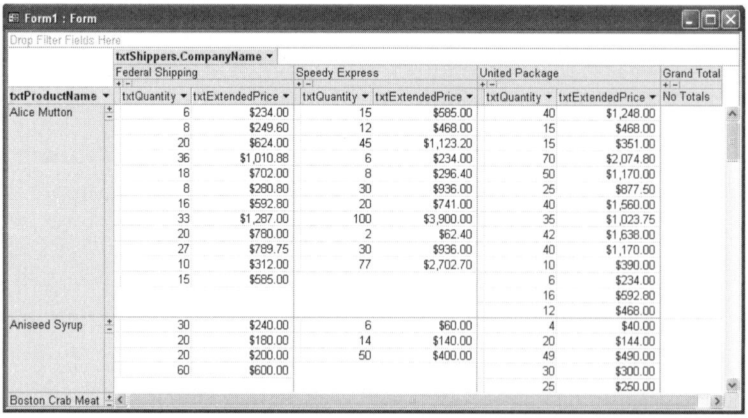

Figure 7-6 An excerpt from the PivotTable created by the *CreateAFormWithPivotTableOnInvoices* sample.

In Figure 7-6, the *No Totals* cells in the Grand Total column are empty by default. By clicking the + Show/Hide Details control, you can display all the values in the preceding columns for each row. If there are more values than can fit in a PivotTable cell, click inside the cell. The PivotTable will display a scroll bar that lets you scroll up and down the list of values for that PivotTable cell. The *ProductName* row values also have + Show/Hide Details controls. Clicking the −control hides all the detail values in any row. However, if any totals were computed in the PivotTable, they would still appear in the row.

Sometimes you might not know the name of a fieldset, which means that you won't be able to use it as an index for *Fieldsets* collection members. Such a fieldset name usually will match the record source field name, but there are exceptions. For example, the *ControlSource* setting for the text box named *txt-Shippers.CompanyName* is *Shippers.CompanyName*. However, the corresponding fieldset name is *Shippers_CompanyName*. If you forget the naming convention for a fieldset, or if you just want to verify the fieldset names on a PivotTable, use the following code sample. The first procedure assigns a form name with a PivotTable view and calls the second procedure, which is a utility that enumerates the fieldset names. This second procedure reports to the Immediate window the total number of members in the *Fieldsets* collection for a PivotTable view and the names of each of those fieldset members.

```
Sub CallUtilityToNameFieldSetMembersForm1()
Dim strFName As String
strFName = "Form1"
UtilityToNameFieldSetMembers strFName
End Sub


Sub UtilityToNameFieldSetMembers(strFName As String)
Dim frm1 As Access.Form
Dim fset1

'Open a form named strFName
DoCmd.OpenForm strFName, acFormPivotTable
Set frm1 = Forms(strFName)


'Enumerate names of elements in the Fieldsets collection.
'This is useful for compound names, such as Shippers_CompanyName.
Debug.Print frm1.PivotTable.ActiveView.FieldSets.Count
For Each fset1 In frm1.PivotTable.ActiveView.FieldSets
    Debug.Print fset1.Name
Next fset1


'Clean up objects
Set frm1 = Nothing


End Sub
```

Adding and Removing PivotTable Totals

The preceding sample application organized the *Quantity* and *ExtendedPrice* fields from the *Invoices* query in a PivotTable. However, it did not develop any summary statistics for the *Quantity* and *ExtendedPrice* field values. One typical reason for composing a PivotTable is to compute summary statistics for the values in the detail drop area. The main vehicle for adding summary statistics to a PivotTable view is the *AddTotal* method. The samples that follow illustrate how to apply this method to the PivotTable returned by the *ActiveView* property of the PivotTable for a form.

The *AddTotal* method creates a new *Totals* field, which contains summary statistics for another field in a PivotTable. The *Totals* field that the method creates appear both in the PivotTable and in the PivotTable Field List through the Access UI for PivotTable views. The *AddTotal* method takes three arguments. First, you name the new *Totals* field. Use a string for this. Next, you reference a field, such as one of the fields in the detail drop area. Then, you specify a function for computing the summary statistic on the field. These functions are the standard aggregate functions available in many contexts throughout Access. They compute the average, count, maximum value, minimum value, and sum, as well as the sample and population standard deviation and variance.

When you attempt to add a new *Totals* field to a PivotTable, the field cannot already exist. Attempting to add a new *Totals* field that has the same name as an existing one generates a run-time error. Because the insertion of a *Totals* field adds it to the PivotTable's detail drop area and the PivotTable Field List, you need to remove it from both locations before attempting to add a new field with the same name.

Adding Totals Fields

The following pair of procedures demonstrates the syntax for adding two *Totals* fields to the PivotTable created by the preceding sample. The *Totals* fields compute the sum of the *Quantity* and the *ExtendedPrice* field values. The corresponding cells in the PivotTable will reflect the total business handled by a shipper for a product. The first procedure names the form to process and passes that name to the second procedure, which actually creates the two *Totals* fields. For this sample to work, you have to verify the name of the form created by the preceding sample. In my sample, the name of this form is *Form1*. However, it could be *Form2*, *Form3*, or *Formx*, depending on how many times you run the sample without deleting the previously created sample forms. In the section "Adding a PivotChart View to a Custom Form," I will show you how to assign a specific name to the form with a PivotTable view that you create. However, you will always have to specify the name of a form when processing its PivotTable view.

The second procedure includes two important variable declarations. First, it specifies *fld1* as a PivotField, which is a field in a PivotTable. Next, the procedure specifies *tot1* as a PivotTotal. A PivotTotal represents a total in a Pivot-Table, such as one created by the *AddTotal* method. The sample reuses the *fld1* and *tot1* variables. First, the code adds the sum of *ExtendedPrice* to the Pivot-Total, and then it adds the sum of *Quantity* to the PivotTotal.

After the declarations, the procedure opens the form corresponding to the name passed to it. Then, the code assigns the form to the *frm1* object reference. This simplifies subsequent code in the sample.

Next, the procedure opens a *With...End With* block of code that operates on the form reference. The block contains two groups of lines. The first group adds the sum of *ExtendedPrice* to the PivotTable, and the second group applies the same function to compute the sum of *Quantity*. Adding a *Totals* field involves three steps. First, you reference the field that the *Totals* field summarizes. Second, you invoke the *AddTotal* method to create the *Totals* field. Third, you assign the new *Totals* field to the PivotTable. The procedure executes this third step in two lines. The first line assigns the *Totals* field to an object reference, *tot1*. The second line inserts that object into the detail section of the PivotTable by using the *InsertTotal* method.

One reason to add *Totals* fields to a PivotTable is to summarize detail data. Often, presenting detail data and summary data in the same PivotTable can be distracting. Therefore, the sample invokes two methods that highlight the display of summary statistics in the resulting PivotTable. First, the code invokes the *HideDetails* method. This forces the suppression of all detail data. With this one step, a user could restore the visibility of the detail data if he so desired. However, as the creator of the PivotTable view, you can disable this capability by assigning a value of *False* to the *AllowDetails* property for the PivotTable. The sample illustrates this optional step.

Whenever you make changes to a PivotTable, you must save them if you want them to persist the next time a user views the PivotTable. Therefore, the procedure concludes by closing the form and saving the changes as it closes. Let's examine the procedure now:

```
Sub CallTotalExtendedPriceAndQuantity()
Dim strFName As String

'Set strFName so that it points at the form with the
'PivotTable view that you want to revise
strFName = "Form1"
```

(continued)

```
TotalExtendedPriceAndQuantity strFName

End Sub

Sub TotalExtendedPriceAndQuantity(strFName As String)
Dim frm1 As Access.Form
Dim fld1 As PivotField
Dim tot1 As PivotTotal

'Open a form named strFName
DoCmd.OpenForm strFName, acFormPivotTable
Set frm1 = Forms(strFName)

With frm1
    'Add total for sum of ExtendedPrice field
    Set fld1 = .PivotTable.ActiveView.FieldSets("ExtendedPrice"). _
        Fields("ExtendedPrice")
    .PivotTable.ActiveView.AddTotal "Sum of Price", fld1, plFunctionSum
    Set tot1 = .PivotTable.ActiveView.Totals("Sum of Price")
    .PivotTable.ActiveView.DataAxis.InsertTotal tot1

    'Add total for sum of Quantity field
    Set fld1 = .PivotTable.ActiveView.FieldSets("Quantity").Fields("Quantity")
    .PivotTable.ActiveView.AddTotal "Sum of Quantity", fld1, plFunctionSum
    Set tot1 = .PivotTable.ActiveView.Totals("Sum of Quantity")
    .PivotTable.ActiveView.DataAxis.InsertTotal tot1
End With

'Hide detail rows
Screen.ActiveDatasheet.PivotTable.ActiveData.HideDetails
frm1.PivotTable.AllowDetails = False

'Save changes as you close the form's PivotTable view
DoCmd.Close acForm, frm1.Name, acSaveYes

End Sub
```

Figure 7-7 shows an excerpt of how *Form1* looks when you open it after running the *CallTotalExtendedPriceAndQuantity* procedure. Recall that the PivotTable is the default view for the form, so this is what a user sees when she initially opens the form. Compare the appearance of the PivotTable in this screen shot with the one shown in Figure 7-6. The new version of the PivotTable suppresses all detail data and presents only summary data. Therefore, it's much easier to identify the differences between cells in the PivotTable shown in Figure 7-7. Invoking the HideDetails method in the procedure suppresses the detail data.

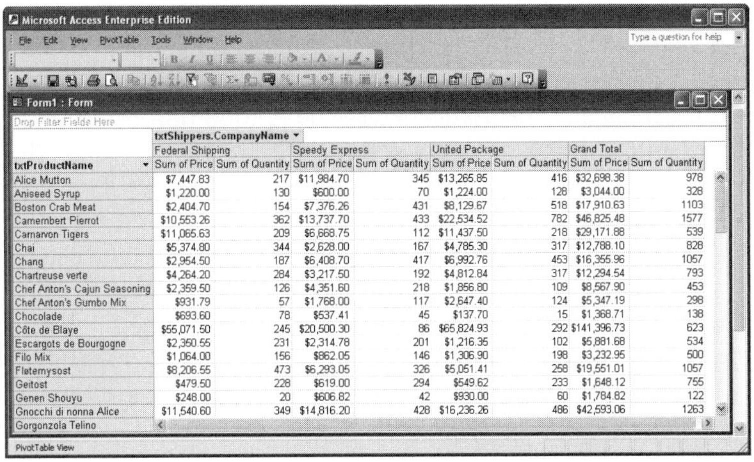

txtProductName	Federal Shipping Sum of Price	Federal Shipping Sum of Quantity	Speedy Express Sum of Price	Speedy Express Sum of Quantity	United Package Sum of Price	United Package Sum of Quantity	Grand Total Sum of Price	Grand Total Sum of Quantity
Alice Mutton	$7,447.83	217	$11,984.70	345	$13,265.85	416	$32,698.38	978
Aniseed Syrup	$1,220.00	130	$600.00	70	$1,224.00	128	$3,044.00	328
Boston Crab Meat	$2,404.70	154	$7,376.26	431	$8,129.67	518	$17,910.63	1103
Camembert Pierrot	$10,553.26	362	$13,737.70	433	$22,534.52	782	$46,825.48	1577
Carnarvon Tigers	$11,065.63	209	$6,668.75	112	$11,437.50	218	$29,171.88	539
Chai	$5,374.80	344	$2,628.00	167	$4,785.30	317	$12,788.10	828
Chang	$2,954.50	187	$6,408.70	417	$6,992.76	453	$16,355.96	1057
Chartreuse verte	$4,264.20	284	$3,217.50	192	$4,812.84	317	$12,294.54	793
Chef Anton's Cajun Seasoning	$2,359.50	126	$4,351.60	218	$1,856.80	109	$8,567.90	453
Chef Anton's Gumbo Mix	$931.79	57	$1,768.00	117	$2,647.40	124	$5,347.19	298
Chocolade	$693.60	78	$537.41	45	$137.70	15	$1,368.71	138
Côte de Blaye	$55,071.50	245	$20,500.30	86	$65,824.93	292	$141,396.73	623
Escargots de Bourgogne	$2,350.55	231	$2,314.78	201	$1,216.35	102	$5,881.68	534
Filo Mix	$1,064.00	156	$862.05	146	$1,306.90	198	$3,232.95	500
Fløtemysost	$8,206.55	473	$6,293.05	326	$5,051.41	258	$19,551.01	1057
Geitost	$479.50	228	$619.00	294	$549.62	233	$1,648.12	755
Genen Shouyu	$248.00	20	$606.82	42	$930.00	60	$1,784.82	122
Gnocchi di nonna Alice	$11,540.60	349	$14,816.20	428	$16,236.26	486	$42,593.06	1263
Gorgonzola Telino								

Figure 7-7 An updated excerpt from our sample PivotTable that shows summary data for the *Quantity* and *ExtendedPrice* fields.

I purposely included the outer Access window in Figure 7-7 so that you could see how many toolbar controls are disabled. The PivotTable does not allow the operation of any controls that expand and collapse rows and columns or that show and hide fields in the detail drop areas. The controls for showing and hiding details on the PivotTable are not visible in this figure. The inoperability of these features is the direct result of setting the *AllowDetails* property to *False*.

Removing Totals Fields

When working with PivotTables, you might want to redefine the formula you use for a *Totals* field. To do this, you must first remove the old *Totals* field from the detail drop area as well as from the collection of *Totals* fields for the PivotTable.

Use the *RemoveTotal* method to eliminate the appearance of a *Totals* field in the detail section of a PivotTable. This method applies to the *DataAxis* property of the PivotTable returned by the *ActiveView* property of a form's PivotTable. *RemoveTotal* takes a single argument, a string variable that names the *Totals* field you want to eliminate from the PivotTable's detail drop area.

A *Totals* field is not completely removed from a PivotTable until you also remove it from the *Totals* fields collection. To do so, invoke the *DeleteTotal* method. This method applies directly to the PivotTable returned by the *ActiveView* property. Like the *RemoveTotal* method, the *DeleteTotal* method takes a single string variable as an argument that names the *Totals* field to strike from the *Totals* fields collection of the PivotTable.

The following pair of procedures demonstrates the correct syntax for the *RemoveTotal* and *DeleteTotal* methods. The first procedure passes a form name to the second procedure. The form has the PivotTable from which the second procedure eliminates the *Totals* fields. The second procedure starts by opening the form and setting an object reference, *frm1*, to it. Next, the procedure removes the two summary fields from the PivotTable detail drop area and from the *Totals* fields collection. This occurs inside a *With...End With* block.

Before closing, the second procedure restores the visibility of detail field values and enables users to show and hide fields as well as expand and collapse rows and columns. The procedure's final line closes the form and saves these changes. After running the *CallRemovePriceAndQuantityTotals* procedure, the PivotTable view for *Form1* returns to its initial condition (the way it appeared after running the sample that created it). Here are the two procedures:

```
Sub CallRemovePriceAndQuantityTotals()
Dim strFName As String

'Set strFName so it points at the form with the
'PivotTable view that you want to revise
strFName = "Form1"
RemovePriceAndQuantityTotals strFName

End Sub

Sub RemovePriceAndQuantityTotals(strFName As String)
Dim frm1 As Access.Form

'Open a form named strFName
DoCmd.OpenForm strFName, acFormPivotTable
Set frm1 = Forms(strFName)

'Remove totals from datasheet and Totals field list setting
With frm1.PivotTable.ActiveView
    .DataAxis.RemoveTotal "Sum of Price"
    .DataAxis.RemoveTotal "Sum of Quantity"
    .DeleteTotal "Sum of Price"
    .DeleteTotal "Sum of Quantity"
End With

'Show Detail Rows
Screen.ActiveDatasheet.PivotTable.ActiveData.ShowDetails
frm1.PivotTable.AllowDetails = True

'Save changes as you close form's PivotTable view
DoCmd.Close acForm, frm1.Name, acSaveYes

End Sub
```

Filtering PivotTables

One of the most valuable features of PivotTables is the ease with which you can include and exclude records for processing. Use the *IncludedMembers* property to specify members that you want to include in a PivotTable. Assign values to the *ExcludedMembers* property to designate fields you want excluded. You can assign an individual field name to these properties, or if you want to filter on more than one field value, you can assign an array of field names. Since the array technique works for individual field names as well as sets of field names, you can use it for all your assignments to the *IncludedMembers* and *Excluded-Members* properties.

The *IncludedMembers* and *ExcludedMembers* properties apply to Pivot-Table *Fields* collections. Recall that these *Fields* collections belong to a *Fieldsets* collection. When working with hierarchical data—such as cities, which reside within states, which reside within countries, which reside within continents—the *Fieldsets* collection represents the top-level node, or *Fields* collection member, and the set of *Fields* collection members denotes the individual members within the *Fieldsets* collection. When working with most columns of a relational table or a query based on relational tables (as in the current sample), the *Field-sets* and *Fields* collection members are identical. Regardless of whether the *Fieldsets* and *Fields* collection members match in a one-to-one fashion or in a one-to-many fashion, you need to designate them separately.

The sample we'll look at next demonstrates the syntax for filtering on a single column field value for the data in the PivotTable for *Form1*. The syntax shows a reference to the *ColumnAxis* property of the PivotTable. Then, the *Fieldsets* and *Fields* collections specifically point at the *Shippers_CompanyName* field in the record source behind the PivotTable. The *IncludedMembers* property next opens a filter for the values the procedure assigns to it. In this sample, the filter designates rows in the *Invoices* query with a shipper value of United Package. You can add another field value by following United Package with a comma and a second field value. For example, the following excerpt from the *FilterFor2Shippers* procedure in the Chapter07.mdb file filters to include rows with a shipper value of either Federal Shipping or Speedy Express:

```
With frm1.PivotTable
    .ActiveView.ColumnAxis.FieldSets("Shippers_CompanyName"). _
        Fields("Shippers_CompanyName").IncludedMembers = _
        Array("Federal Shipping", "Speedy Express")
    .AllowFiltering = False
End With
```

By setting the *AllowFiltering* property for the form's PivotTable to *False*, you remove users' ability to change your filtering setting. You do not need to make this assignment to open a PivotTable with a custom filter. *AllowFiltering* and *AllowDetails* are two independent properties. For example, setting *AllowDetails* to *False* still enables a user to manually filter a PivotTable. Here's the syntax:

```
Sub FilterFor1ShipperAfterPriorFilter()
Dim frm1 As Access.Form
Dim strFormName As String

'Open a form name strFormName
strFormName = "Form1"
DoCmd.OpenForm strFormName, acFormPivotTable
Set frm1 = Forms(strFormName)

'Assign single-shipper filter
With frm1.PivotTable
    .ActiveView.ColumnAxis.FieldSets("Shippers_CompanyName"). _
        Fields("Shippers_CompanyName").IncludedMembers = _
        Array("United Package")
    .AllowFiltering = False
End With

End Sub
```

When you assign fields to the *IncludedMembers* property, you must specify all the items to be included. Therefore, a design such as the preceding sample is awkward because you have to manually edit the procedure by updating the number of members of the *Array* function used to assign values to the *IncludedMembers* property. As a workaround, you could instead designate the *IncludedMembers* values with a parameter array. Then, your code would be able to use the *UBound* function to determine the number of parameters passed, and it would automatically branch to an assignment statement for *IncludedMembers* with the correct number of arguments.

The two procedures in the following sample demonstrate this approach. The first procedure, *CallFilterForShippers*, designates the shipper names to filter for. The second procedure, *FilterForShippers*, opens *Form1* and counts the number of values passed in the parameter array. The procedure then uses a *Select Case* statement to branch to the correct assignment statement for the *IncludedMembers* properties. If a user does not enter any filter values for the parameter array or enters more than three values, the procedure resets the PivotTable to show data for all shippers and reenables manual filtering. In addition, the procedure presents a message box to remind the user that the submitted number of filter values is invalid.

```
Sub CallFilterForShippers()

'Run this to include just two shippers
```

```
FilterForShippers "Federal Shipping", "Speedy Express"

'Run this to restore all shippers by submitting an
'invalid list of shippers
'FilterForShippers "Federal Shipping", "Federal Shipping", _
'    "Federal Shipping", "Federal Shipping"
End Sub

Sub FilterForShippers(ParamArray ShipperArray() As Variant)
'Sub FilterForShippers(strFilter As String)
Dim frm1 As Access.Form
Dim strFormName As String
'Dim ShipperArray As Variant

'Open a form named strFormName
strFormName = "Form1"
DoCmd.OpenForm strFormName, acFormPivotTable
Set frm1 = Forms(strFormName)

'Include one, two, or three shippers
With frm1.PivotTable
    Select Case UBound(ShipperArray())
        Case 0
            .ActiveView.ColumnAxis.FieldSets("Shippers_CompanyName"). _
                Fields("Shippers_CompanyName").IncludedMembers = _
                Array(ShipperArray(0))
        Case 1
            .ActiveView.ColumnAxis.FieldSets("Shippers_CompanyName"). _
                Fields("Shippers_CompanyName").IncludedMembers = _
                Array(ShipperArray(0), ShipperArray(1))
        Case 2
            .ActiveView.ColumnAxis.FieldSets("Shippers_CompanyName"). _
                Fields("Shippers_CompanyName").IncludedMembers = _
                Array(ShipperArray(0), ShipperArray(1), ShipperArray(2))
        Case Else
            .ActiveView.ColumnAxis.FieldSets("Shippers_CompanyName"). _
                Fields("Shippers_CompanyName").IncludedMembers = _
                Array("Federal Shipping", "Speedy Express", _
                    "United Package")
            .AllowFiltering = True
            MsgBox "Not a valid filter.", vbInformation, _
                "Programming Microsoft Access 2003"
            Exit Sub
    End Select
    .AllowFiltering = False
End With

End Sub
```

Programmatically Creating PivotCharts

Creating PivotCharts involves processing a form's *ChartSpace* object, which is returned by the form's *ChartSpace* property. Once you have a reference to the *ChartSpace* object, you can set parameters for that object and its hierarchically dependent objects to format a PivotChart for the data specified in the form's *Record Source* property. As with PivotTables, you can make the PivotChart view the default view for a form so that when a user opens the form, the chart immediately displays. Alternatively, you can leave the Form view as the default view and let users select the PivotChart view for the form when they need it.

Adding a PivotChart View to a Custom Form

The first PivotChart sample we'll examine builds on the PivotTable samples from the previous section and explores the basics of creating a simple bar chart in a form's PivotChart view. This sample involves a main procedure that calls three other procedures. These three procedures create a custom query in an Access database file, base a new form on the custom query, and design a PivotChart view for the new form.

The main procedure, *CreateAPivotChartBasedOnACustomQuery*, starts by assigning names to two string variables. One of these variables represents the custom query's name, *qryExtPriceByShipper*. The second string denotes the name of the form based on the query *frmqryExtPriceByShipper*. Next, the procedure defines the SQL string for a custom query. This query statement uses the *Invoices* query as a record source. It totals *ExtendedPrice* by date, shipper, and product name. In addition, the custom query filters out all records containing orders placed on or after May 1, 1998. This is because the data ends in May 1998, and the *Invoices* query data is incomplete for that month. The field labels for shipper and product name directly originate from corresponding fields in the *Invoices* query. The date field has the name *YearMonth*. This field uses the built-in *DateSerial*, *DatePart*, and *Month* functions to transform the *OrderDate* field in the *Invoices* query so that all dates assume a value of the first day of the month in which they occur. This kind of transformation is useful when you want to plot data by month, as you'll see in the code sample to follow.

After defining the SQL string for the custom query, the procedure calls three other sub procedures that perform most of the work in the sample. Let's take a look at the main procedure first:

```
Sub CreateAPivotChartBasedOnACustomQuery()
Dim strSQL As String
Dim strQName As String
Dim strFName As String
```

```
'Assign names for new query and form
strQName = "qryExtPriceByShipper"
strFName = "frmqryExtPriceByShipper"

'Assign SQL for custom query and create query
strSQL = "SELECT DateSerial(DatePart(" & """" & "yyyy" & """" & _
    ",[OrderDate]), Month([OrderDate]),1) AS YearMonth, " & _
    "Invoices.Shippers.CompanyName, Invoices.ProductName, " & _
    "Sum(Invoices.ExtendedPrice) AS ExtPrice FROM Invoices " & _
    "GROUP BY DateSerial(DatePart(" & """" & "yyyy" & """" & _
    ",[OrderDate]),Month([OrderDate]),1), " & _
    "Invoices.Shippers.CompanyName, Invoices.ProductName " & _
    "HAVING (((DateSerial(DatePart(" & """" & "yyyy" & """" & _
    ", [OrderDate]), Month([OrderDate]), 1)) < #5/1/1998#))"
CreateCustomQuery strSQL, strQName

'Use query as record source for form with value of strFName
CreateFormBasedOnQuery strFName, strQName

'Create PivotChart for data behind form
CreateChart strFName

End Sub
```

The procedure for creating a custom view accepts the SQL string and query name as arguments. This procedure requires a reference to the Microsoft ADO Ext. 2.x for DDL and Security library. This is because the sample uses the ADOX *Catalog* and *View* objects. The procedure begins by instantiating a catalog and assigning its *ActiveConnection* property to the current project. Then, the project attempts to delete any prior query that has the name of the view that it plans to create. If there is no prior view with the same name, the procedure ignores the resulting error. The *On Error GoTo 0* statement restores normal error behavior by Access. The procedure's last block of code starts by instantiating a new ADO *Command* object. Next, it assigns the SQL string passed to the procedure to the *CommandText* property for the command. Finally, the procedure uses the *Catalog* object to append a new view with the name of the query passed to the procedure and the SQL statement associated with the *Command* object. See Chapter 4, "Jet SQL, the ADOX Library, and Queries," for a more thorough review of the techniques for creating custom queries.

```
Sub CreateCustomQuery(strSQL As String, _
    strQName As String)
Dim cat1 As ADOX.Catalog
Dim cmd1 As ADODB.Command
Dim vew1 As ADOX.View
```

(continued)

```
'Create a reference to the catalog for the current project
Set cat1 = New ADOX.Catalog
cat1.ActiveConnection = CurrentProject.Connection

'Remove a query before creating a new copy of it
On Error Resume Next
cat1.Views.Delete strQName
On Error GoTo 0

'Append a select query as a view to the current project
Set cmd1 = New ADODB.Command
cmd1.CommandText = strSQL
cat1.Views.Append strQName, cmd1

'Clean up objects
Set cmd1 = Nothing
Set cat1 = Nothing

End Sub
```

The procedure for basing a form on the custom query also illustrates an approach for assigning a custom name to a form. This sample illustrates one way to avoid accepting the default name for a form as all the preceding samples in this chapter do. The *CreateFormBasedOnQuery* procedure accepts two string arguments. One designates the name of the new form, *strFName*, and the other denotes the name of the query to serve as a record source for the form, *strQName*. This procedure uses the function procedure, *FormName*, for creating a custom form that we discussed earlier in the chapter. The sample starts by iterating through the members of the *AllForms* collection. This iteration searches for an existing form with the same name as the new form the procedure will create. (Chapter 5 discusses the *AllForms* collection and describes several samples that demonstrate how to use it.) If the iteration discovers a form with the same name as the new form, the sample uses the *SelectObject* method of the *DoCmd* object to select the form. Then, the procedure invokes the *DoCmd* object's *DeleteObject* method to remove the form from the current project.

After eliminating a prior version of the form (if one exists), the sample calls the *FormName* function procedure and passes it the name of the custom query. This creates a new form with an arbitrary name, such as *Form2*. The procedure saves the name of the new form returned by the function procedure. Then, the sample uses *DoCmd* object methods to select the form and give it a new custom name as specified by the argument to the procedure. Before saving the form to commit the changes, the procedure uses the *conPivotChartDefaultView* con-

stant to assign a value of 4 to the form's *DefaultView* property. This causes the
form to open automatically with its PivotChart view. Here's the procedure:

```
Sub CreateFormBasedOnQuery(strFName As String, strQName As String)
Dim obj1 As AccessObject
Dim strDefaultName As String
Dim frm1 As Access.Form
Const conPivotChartDefaultView = 4

'Delete any prior form with the name of the new one (if one exists)
For Each obj1 In CurrentProject.AllForms
    If obj1.Name = strFName Then
        DoCmd.SelectObject acForm, obj1.Name, True
        DoCmd.DeleteObject acForm, obj1.Name
        Exit For
    End If
Next obj1

'Create a form with controls for all the fields in
'the custom query
strDefaultName  = FormName(strQName)

'Rename form from default name and assign a
'default view of a PivotChart for manual opening
DoCmd.SelectObject acForm, strDefaultName , True
DoCmd.Rename strFName, acForm, strDefaultName
DoCmd.OpenForm strFName, acDesign
Set frm1 = Forms(strFName)
frm1.DefaultView = conPivotChartDefaultView
DoCmd.Close acForm, frm1.Name, acSaveYes

End Sub
```

Finally, you're ready to create the PivotChart view for the custom form.
The *CreateChart* procedure that accomplishes this starts by opening the custom
form and assigning a reference to it, *frm1*. Next, the procedure invokes the *Set-Data* method twice. The first application of the method sets the *CompanyName*
field of the record source to be represented by the bars in a chart that plots a
series. The second application specifies the *ExtPrice* field as the series that gets
plotted across the *CompanyName* field values represented by the bars. Recall
that *CompanyName* refers to the three shippers that transport goods in the
Northwind sample. After setting the fields for the chart to plot, the procedure
turns off the *DisplayFieldButtons* property. The display field buttons serve as
drop areas for adding fields to a chart. This essentially prevents users from easily changing the chart by adding new fields.

> **Note**   Users can reverse a setting of *False* for the *DisplayFieldButtons* property by resetting the Field Buttons/Drop Zones check box on the Show/Hide tab of the PivotChart's Properties dialog box. A developer can use the techniques for creating a custom startup and programming custom command bars, as illustrated in Chapter 8 to prevent access to the Properties dialog box.

The *SetData* method enables you to designate the data for a chart, including a form's *ChartSpace* object. This object represents a chart workspace where you can programmatically define a form. The *SetData* method takes three arguments. The first argument (the *Dimension* argument) designates the chart object to which the method will assign the data. The sample that follows illustrates the setting for a bar chart and the series it plots. The *SetData* method has 15 possible settings for this argument, which enable you to assign values to different axes of various kinds of charts, such as stock, bubble, and bar charts. The appropriate setting varies according to the type of chart and the chart axis you use. The second argument (the *DataSourceIndex* argument) specifies how the chart object connects with the data source. The third argument (the *DataReference* argument) can name the data source. When working with a database as a data source, this argument typically will be a field name, such as *CompanyName* or *ExtPrice*.

> **Note**   You can discover the argument settings for the *SetData* method as well as for other properties and methods from the Office 2003 Web Components Help file (owcvba11.chm). This Help file resides in the local resource folder of the \Program Files\Common Files\Microsoft Shared\Web Components\11\ path. For those installing the English-language version of Office 2003, this folder is 1033. In addition, you can use the Object Browser to explore the objects, methods, properties, events, and enums in the Office 2003 Web Components library after you make a reference to the Microsoft Office Web Components 11.0 library.

After assigning data to the chart, the procedure moves on to format the chart. This formatting assigns values to the chart that the PivotChart view displays. For example, the procedure assigns string values to the title captions for the vertical and horizontal axes—*Axis(0)* and *Axis(1)*, respectively. To assign a caption to the chart's overall title, you must specify that the chart has a title. Do this by setting the chart's *HasTitle* property to *True*. The default value is *False*. Next, assign a string to the *Caption* property for the chart's title. The *Font* property is another especially useful chart title property. This property returns a *Font* object that you can use to set the chart title's font style, size, and name. The sample that follows illustrates the syntax for designating a 14-point font.

The last step the procedure takes is to close the form and save the changes to the PivotChart view. This action is essential for preserving the settings so that they're available the next time a user opens the form.

```
Sub CreateChart(strFName As String)
Dim frm1 As Access.Form

'Open form to contain PivotChart
DoCmd.OpenForm strFName, acFormPivotChart
Set frm1 = Forms(strFName)

With frm1.ChartSpace
'Open PivotChart without drop areas, and set its categories and values
    .SetData chDimCategories, chDataBound, "CompanyName"
    .SetData chDimValues, chDataBound, "ExtPrice"
    .DisplayFieldButtons = False

'Assign and format titles to axes and overall chart
    With .Charts(0)
        .Axes(1).Title.Caption = "Sales ($)"
        .Axes(0).Title.Caption = "Shippers"
        .HasTitle = True
        .Title.Caption = "Sales By Shipper"
        .Title.Font.Size = 14
    End With
End With

'Close form and save PivotChart view
DoCmd.Close acForm, strFName, acSaveYes

End Sub
```

Figure 7-8 shows the PivotChart view created by the *CreateChart* procedure. Notice that this view has just three bars—one for each of the shippers. A bar chart automatically aggregates the series into its bars. In addition, the bar chart specification automatically gives the bars names that correspond to the *CompanyName* field values. As you've seen, explicit programming actions create the titles for the chart's two axes and the chart as a whole.

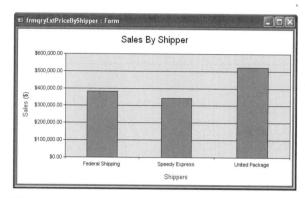

Figure 7-8   The PivotChart view created by the *CreateChart* procedure.

Updating a Bar Chart to a 3-D Bar Chart

The bar chart shown in Figure 7-8 effectively conveys the differences among the values of goods transported by various shippers. Yet charts can be even more powerful when given a dramatic presentation. Your clients won't always seek drama, however; sometimes they'll just want a bit of variety. In any event, by learning to implement all the style variations that PivotCharts offer, you'll be equipped to accommodate your clients' needs for content as well as style.

You can determine the style of a chart by assigning a *ChartChartTypeEnum* value to its *Type* property. The *Type* property has more than 65 enum settings. The full list is available in the Object Browser. A setting of *chChartTypeBar3D* can transform the two-dimensional bar chart shown in Figure 7-8 into a 3-D bar chart, as shown in Figure 7-9. The syntax for this transformation is very straightforward. Just assign the enum constant to the chart's *Type* property.

The following sample demonstrates this syntax. The sample also allows a user to conditionally save the change if they like the appearance of the altered view. The procedure starts by opening the *frmqryExtPriceByShipper* form. Next, the sample assigns the 3-D bar chart constant to the *Type* property. Then, the sample opens a message box that asks the user whether he wants to save the new format. Clicking Yes updates the form's PivotChart view with the new 3-D format, but clicking No preserves the original format.

```
Sub Format3DBarChart()
Dim frm1 As Access.Form

'Open a form in its PivotChart view
DoCmd.OpenForm "frmqryExtPriceByShipper", acFormPivotChart
Set frm1 = Forms("frmqryExtPriceByShipper")

'Assign 3D Bar Chart Format and blank Series axis
frm1.ChartSpace.Charts(0).Type = chChartTypeBar3D
```

```
'Prompt for whether to save with the new format
If MsgBox("Do you want to save the format?", vbYesNo, _
    "Programming Microsoft Access 2003") = vbYes Then
    DoCmd.Close acForm, "frmqryExtPriceByShipper", acSaveYes
Else
    DoCmd.Close acForm, "frmqryExtPriceByShipper", acSaveNo
End If

End Sub
```

Figure 7-9 shows the reformatted PivotChart view. Notice the message box in the lower left corner. With this message box, a user can preserve the new format or revert to the original two-dimensional format that appears in Figure 7-8.

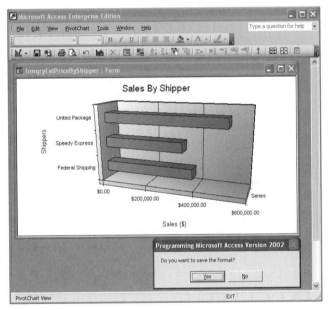

Figure 7-9   The display that results from running the *Format3DBarChart* procedure.

Creating a Time-Based Line Chart

A line chart is similar to a bar chart in two important respects. Therefore, your understanding of the preceding chart sample can help you develop a line chart in a form's PivotChart view. The first similarity is that a line chart contains categories. These categories are the values for grouping a series. When you create a line chart, the categories normally possess some natural order, as is the case with dates. Note that you will often have more categories in a line chart than in a bar chart. The second similarity is that a line chart aggregates a series into its individual categories—just like a bar chart aggregates a series into its bars. Each point along a line chart represents the total of the series for that point. Therefore, if your series is *ExtPrice*, each date (or point) represents the total of *ExtPrice* values for that point.

The main differences between line and bar charts stem from the way each chart type represents aggregated category values. A bar chart uses a bar to signify a category value, whereas a line chart uses points to represent its categories' points, which the chart subsequently connects with a line.

Because of their similarities, you can create a line chart almost the same way that you create a bar chart. Be aware that your category values must have a natural progression and you must group them prior to referencing them with the *SetData* method. For example, the *qryExtPriceByShipper* query created by the preceding sample transforms *OrderDate* field values to create a new *YearMonth* field that reflects just the year and month of the *OrderDate* field value. If you were to use the ungrouped *OrderDate* field values from the *Invoices* query, a line chart would group its series in a PivotChart by day, instead of by month. After you correctly transform the categories, which you can do with a query, you reference the grouped values with a *SetData* method and set the chart's *Type* property to one of the variations of line charts.

The following sample shows the syntax for creating a line chart that displays aggregated *ExtPrice* values by month from the *qryExtPriceByShipper* query. The code starts by naming the source query for the chart and the source form. The PivotChart accesses the data in the query through the form. Next, it creates a form based on the query. This sample uses the same *CreateFormBasedOnQuery* procedure shown earlier in this chapter in the initial sample for creating a bar chart. In this case, the name of the form differs from that of the preceding sample, but the query name remains the same.

After creating the form, the procedure opens it and hides the field buttons for manually adding fields to a PivotChart. Then, the procedure invokes the *SetData* method twice. The first time this sample invokes the *SetData* method, it references the *YearMonth* field as the chart's categories axis. The *YearMonth* field is the transformed field for the *OrderDate* field from the *Invoices* query. The *YearMonth* field value is always the first day of a month. The month and year for the *YearMonth* field correspond to the *OrderDate* field on which it is based. The second time the sample invokes the *SetData* method, the procedure adds the *ExtPrice* field to the line chart the same way it did for the bar chart.

Aside from the first invocation of the *SetData* method, there is one more critical distinction between the processes used to create the bar chart and the line chart. The initial bar chart sample did not specify a chart type. That's because the default type for a chart that assigns values to *chDimCategories* is a bar chart. When you want to create a line chart, you must therefore explicitly assign a value to the chart's *Type* property. The appropriate setting for a line chart with markers for the points is *chChartTypeLineMarkers*.

The formatting for the line chart follows the same pattern as for the bar chart. The only distinction is that different strings define the chart title and the axis title for the categories dimension. Here's the procedure:

```
Sub CreateTimeBasedLineChart()
Dim frm1 As Access.Form
Dim strQName As String
Dim strFName As String

'Assign names for query and form
strQName = "qryExtPriceByShipper"
strFName = "frmqryExtPriceByShipper1"

'Create a form based on query
CreateFormBasedOnQuery strFName, strQName

'Open a form in its PivotChart view
DoCmd.OpenForm strFName, acFormPivotChart
Set frm1 = Forms(strFName)
frm1.ChartSpace.DisplayFieldButtons = False

With frm1.ChartSpace
'Open PiovtChart without drop areas, and set its categories and values
    .SetData chDimCategories, chDataBound, "[YearMonth]"
    .SetData chDimValues, chDataBound, "ExtPrice"
    .Charts(0).Type = chChartTypeLineMarkers

'Assign and format titles to axes and overall chart
    With .Charts(0)
        .Axes(1).Title.Caption = "Sales ($)"
        .Axes(0).Title.Caption = "Dates"
        .HasTitle = True
        .Title.Caption = "Sales By Month"
        .Title.Font.Size = 14
    End With
End With

'Close form and save PivotChart view
DoCmd.Close acForm, strFName, acSaveYes

End Sub
```

Figure 7-10 shows the line chart created by the *CreateTimeBasedLine-Chart* procedure. Notice that it has a single point for each month. Those points represent the total sales during each month. The single line in the chart represents the sales made by all three shippers.

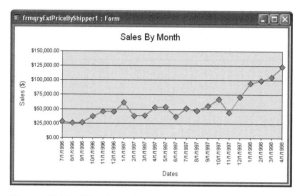

Figure 7-10 The PivotChart that results from running the *CreateTime-BasedLineChart* procedure.

Creating a 3-D Line Chart

This chapter's concluding sample modifies the basic line chart shown in Figure 7-10 in two ways. First, it adds a new series dimension to the chart. The new dimension represents the shippers—namely, the *CompanyName* field in the *qryExtPriceByShipper* query. This new dimension does not replace either of the dimension assignments from the preceding sample. Instead, it refines those dimension assignments. The modified chart contains three lines instead of just one. Each line denotes the sales over time for a different shipper. As a result of the new three-line format, the new chart includes a legend so that viewers can easily identify the shippers. Second, the chart uses a 3-D format for drawing lines. Some users might find that the 3-D lines make it easier to distinguish among the shippers than the two-dimensional line in the preceding sample.

Since this sample modifies an existing chart instead of creating a new one, the code begins by referencing a form and opening it in its PivotChart view. As with the preceding sample, the code hides the Field buttons. Next, the code invokes the *SetData* method to add a new dimension, which represents the *CompanyName* field. This new dimension enables the chart to use a separate line to display the sales transported by each shipper. The line of code after the one invoking the *SetData* method assigns a value of *True* to the chart's *HasLegend* property. Then, the code sets the chart's *Type* property to *chChartTypeLine3D*. This draws a 3-D line for each shipper. The final portion of the sample permits the user to accept the new format or reject it in favor of the original line chart format.

```
Sub UpdateTimeBasedLineChart()
Dim frm1 As Access.Form
Dim strFName As String

'Form to update
strFName = "frmqryExtPriceByShipper1"
```

```
'Open a form in its PivotChart view
DoCmd.OpenForm strFName, acFormPivotChart
Set frm1 = Forms(strFName)
frm1.ChartSpace.DisplayFieldButtons = False

With frm1.ChartSpace
'Add CompanyName series to the chart, draw 3-D lines, and
'add a legend
    .SetData chDimSeriesNames, chDataBound, "CompanyName"
    .Charts(0).HasLegend = True
    .Charts(0).Type = chChartTypeLine3D
End With

'Prompt for whether to save with the new format
If MsgBox("Do you want to save the format?", vbYesNo, _
    "Programming Microsoft Access 2003") = vbYes Then
    DoCmd.Close acForm, strFName, acSaveYes
Else
    DoCmd.Close acForm, strFName, acSaveNo
End If

End Sub
```

Figure 7-11 shows the final chart sample. Take a look at the 3-D line formatting. Do you like being able to easily tell the difference between shippers? Regardless of whether these aesthetic choices appeal to you personally, it's helpful to know how to implement them for your clients.

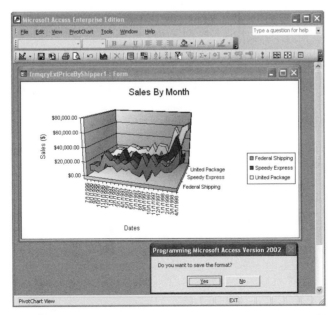

Figure 7-11   The display that results from running the *UpdateTime-BasedLineChart* procedure.

Summary

PivotTables and PivotCharts are two powerful elements for expanding the interface options that you can offer in your custom applications. Microsoft is obviously favoring PivotTables and PivotCharts in Access database files (.mdb) and Access projects (.adp) by making them view objects for all row-returning objects, such as tables, in Access database files (.mdb) and Access projects (.adp). The trick to programmatically creating and formatting PivotTables and PivotCharts in Access 2003 is to learn the Office 2003 Web Components object model. The owc11.dll file implements Office 2003 Web Components, and you can create a reference to the owc11.dll file from a VBA project in your Access database files and Access projects. Because owc11.dll is also used for Web modeling, you have the advantage of one model for work within Access 2003 forms on a LAN as well as within Microsoft FrontPage 2003 Web pages on a Web site. Chapter 14 provides more detail on Office Web Components and FrontPage 2003.

This chapter introduces you to the basics of the object model for Pivot-Tables and PivotCharts through a collection of PivotTable and PivotChart code samples. The PivotTable samples demonstrate techniques for creating a PivotTable, formatting it, controlling how users can edit it, and filtering it. The PivotChart samples illustrate how to create bar charts and line charts, as well as how to reformat base versions of either chart type. In addition, the commentary on the samples equips you for working with other kinds of charts by conveying a basic understanding of the key properties and methods for the PivotChart object and its nested objects.

8

Microsoft Office Objects

As part of Microsoft Office System, Access 2003 shares a select group of objects with the other Office applications. These objects let you carry out such tasks as searching for files, modifying standard menus and toolbars, developing custom menus and toolbars, and manipulating the Office Assistant help feature. In addition, your knowledge of how to program these objects in Access will transfer to the other Office applications—Microsoft Excel, Microsoft Word, and even Microsoft FrontPage. Most of the objects work in all of the Office applications.

This chapter starts with an overview of Office objects. After the overview, you'll examine the *DocumentProperty* object and related Access objects from Access database and Access project files. Within this discussion, I'll focus on techniques for replacing the Database window with a custom startup form. Next, you'll explore two specific objects: *FileSearch*, which you use to programmatically manage file searches, and *CommandBars*, which you use to modify the built-in menu and toolbars as well as create custom toolbars. Those who want to learn more about programming the *Assistant* object can visit my Web site (*http://www.programmingmsaccess.com/ForA2002/AssistantObject.htm*) for text on the subject. Code samples are in the AssistantModule of Chapter08.mdb, which is available with the companion content for this chapter.

Using the Shared Office Objects

The shared Office objects, listed in Table 8-1, provide support in several important areas of functionality. Some of these object models are not available in all Office components (including Access). The table describes the models, mentions when they have restricted availability across Office components, and highlights where you can find further information about them in this book. To get online help and work with any of these objects, you must reference the Microsoft Office 11.0 Object Library. You can do this through the Tools menu in the Microsoft Visual Basic Editor (VBE) or programmatically.

Table 8-1 Shared Office Objects

Object	Description	Comment
CommandBar	You can use this object and its collections to create and modify toolbars, the menu bar, and shortcut menus. You can make design-time changes manually and with Visual Basic for Applications (VBA) code. You can make run-time changes exclusively with VBA code.	See further discussion and samples in this chapter.
Assistant	You use this object to support custom help requirements for the Office Assistant and Office Assistant balloon. Various properties and methods let you control the type and animation of the assistant, as well as the content and behavior of the balloon.	See further discussion and samples on this topic at *www.programmingmsaccess.com /assistantobject.htm.*
FileSearch	You use this object to represent the functionality of the Open dialog box.	When processing files, you can complement the functionality of this object model with the *File-Dialog* object and the *FileSystem-Object* object. See further discussion and samples in this chapter.
DocumentProperty	This object represents a built-in or custom property of an Office document. There are up to 28 built-in properties, which include such document attributes as title, author, comments, last print date, last save time, and total editing time. This object also supports custom document properties.	For Word documents, Excel workbooks, and Microsoft PowerPoint presentations only.
NewFile	This object allows you to add and remove entries on the Office Task Pane toolbar.	This object is available with Access, Excel, FrontPage, PowerPoint, and Word applications, but the route for opening the object changes for each application. See further discussion and samples in the chapter.

Table 8-1   Shared Office Objects

Object	Description	Comment
FileDialog	This object provides a programmatic interface for presenting dialog boxes similar to the File Open and Save As dialog boxes in Microsoft Office.	Available with Access, Word, Excel, and PowerPoint applications.
COMAddin	This is a representation of a COM add-in in Access and other Office host applications.	
LanguageSettings	This object lets you programmatically return information about language installation, user interface, and help settings.	Tracks locale identifier information when deploying Office internationally.
AnswerWizard	You use this object to programmatically manipulate the Answer wizard.	Includes properties and methods for manipulating files returned by the Answer wizard. This wizard is available exclusively through Microsoft Office XP Developer Edition.
MsoEnvelope	This object lets you send documents as e-mail messages.	For Word documents, Excel charts, and Excel worksheets.
OfficeDataSourceObject	This object represents the data source for a mail merge operation. It offers simplified properties and methods for manipulating a data source for a mail merge.	This object is exclusively for use with Microsoft Publisher, but the Office XP documentation refers to it as part of the Office library.
HTMLProject	This object is a top-level project in the Microsoft Script Editor. You use the *HTMLProjectItem* collection to track HTML documents within a project.	For Word documents, Excel workbooks, and PowerPoint presentations only.
Script	This object represents a block of script in the Script Editor.	For Word documents, Excel workbooks, and PowerPoint presentations only.
WebPageFont	This object represents the default font when a document is saved as a Web page.	For Word documents, Excel workbooks, and PowerPoint presentations only.

DocumentProperty, *CurrentDB*, and *CurrentProject* Objects

Although the Microsoft Office *DocumentProperties* collection and the *Properties* collection for the *CurrentDB* object in Data Access Objects (DAO) have similar names, they serve different purposes. The members of the *DocumentProperties* collection are *DocumentProperty* objects. You declare these objects with a *DocumentProperty* variable type. Word, Excel, and PowerPoint store information about documents as *DocumentProperty* objects. Typical *DocumentProperties* collection members point to the author, location, and date created. Developers can use built-in *DocumentProperty* objects as well as add their own custom *DocumentProperty* objects.

A *Property* object in DAO represents a built-in or user-defined characteristic of a DAO object, such as the *CurrentDB* object. The collection of these *Property* objects is the set of built-in and custom properties for the Jet database serving as the current database. You declare a *Property* object for the *CurrentDB* object with a *DAO.Property* variable.

Unlike Access database files, Access project files do not have a *Properties* collection for the *CurrentDB* object. In fact, Access projects do not have a *CurrentDB* object. This is because Access projects do not use DAO. Nevertheless, Access projects store similar information to the members of the *Properties* collections for the *CurrentProject* object. You declare a variable of type *AccessObjectProperty* when designating a pointer for a *Property* object of the *CurrentProject* object. The *Property* object collections for the *CurrentDB* and the *CurrentProject* objects can serve similar roles in helping to manage how an Access application starts.

Printing Access *DocumentProperty* Object Information

Access does not have a shared *DocumentProperty* object as Word, Excel, and PowerPoint do, but it makes much of the same information available using three *Documents* objects: *UserDefined*, *SummaryInfo*, and *MSysDB*. These objects are available exclusively through the DAO Database Container. You can't use these three objects with Microsoft ActiveX Data Objects (ADO). The *UserDefined* object contains all properties on the Custom tab of the Database Properties dialog box. The *SummaryInfo* object contains all properties on the Summary tab of that dialog box. The *MSysDB* object contains all the properties defined under the Tools, Startup menu in a database.

The following sample enumerates the properties collections of each DAO Database Container object:

```
Sub enumDBProps()

Dim db As Database, p As DAO.Property

'Set reference to current database
    Set db = CurrentDb
```

```
'Print heading for results
    Debug.Print "User defined properties"
    Debug.Print "======================="

'Iterate through UserDefined database properties
    For Each p In db.Containers!Databases. _
        Documents!UserDefined.Properties
        Debug.Print p.Name, p.Value
    Next

'Print heading for results
    Debug.Print
    Debug.Print "Summary Properties"
    Debug.Print "=================="

'Iterate through SummaryInfo database properties
    For Each p In db.Containers!Databases. _
        Documents!SummaryInfo.Properties
        Debug.Print p.Name, p.Value
    Next

'Print heading for results
    Debug.Print
    Debug.Print "MSysDB Properties"
    Debug.Print "================="

'Iterate through MSysDB database properties

    For Each p In db.Containers!Databases. _
        Documents!MSysDB.Properties
        Debug.Print p.Name, p.Value
    Next

End Sub
```

Printing the *CurrentDB* and *CurrentProject* Properties

Many of the *CurrentDB* properties designate items you can use to control how an Access application starts. For example, these properties permit you to control whether the Database window appears at startup and which form replaces it. You can even use a special property (*AllowBypassKey*) to suppress a user's ability to bypass your startup settings by holding down the Shift key while the user opens your file. I call this a special property because it's available exclusively through a VBA programmatic interface.

When using the *CurrentDB* property, you'll find it convenient to list the *Properties* collection members. The following code sample illustrates this technique. As with the sample in the sidebar on *DocumentProperty* objects, this procedure bypasses error statements in a loop resulting from attempts to print properties not available from the current Access session.

```
Sub EnumerateCurrentDBProperties()
Dim db As Database
Dim prp1 As DAO.Property

'Set reference to current database
Set db = CurrentDb

Debug.Print CurrentDb.Properties.Count
'Print name and value properties of all
'CurrentDB property objects
For Each prp1 In CurrentDb.Properties
    On Error Resume Next
    Debug.Print prp1.Name, prp1.Value
Next prp1

End Sub
```

Access does not automatically populate *CurrentProject* properties for .mdb files, but the properties are available for you to add, populate, and manipulate as your applications require. The *AccessObjectProperty* object is used to declare the type for a property of the *CurrentProject*. This same kind of declaration applies when referencing *Property* objects of an *AccessObject* object, such as a member of the *AllForms* collection. Each *AccessObjectProperty* of a *CurrentProject* has *Name* and *Value* properties. You can use these properties to designate names and values for properties in the *CurrentProject*. Since the properties of an *AccessObjectProperty* object are read-only, you cannot designate them with an assignment statement. However, the *Add* method for the *Properties* collection of the *CurrentProject* enables you to create properties and assign names and values to them.

Use an *AccessObjectProperty* variable declaration to reference a *Property* object for an Access project's *CurrentProject* object. This same kind of declaration applies when referencing *Property* objects of the *AccessObject* object. The code for referencing the *CurrentProject* and *CurrentDB* properties has slight differences besides the variable used to reference these properties. For example, you use the *Delete* method to remove an item from the *Properties* collection of the *CurrentDB* object, but you use a *Remove* method when working with the properties of a *CurrentProject* object. The following code segment shows how to count the *Property* objects in a *CurrentProject*, instantiate and populate a *Property* object, and loop through the elements of the *Properties* collection of the *CurrentProject* object.

> **Note**   Another version of the *EnumerateCurrentProjectProperties* procedure exists in Module1 of Chapter08.adp, which is available with the sample materials for this book. This version demonstrates that Access automatically populates *Property* objects for the *CurrentProject* in an .adp file, much as it populates *Property* objects in the *CurrentDB* within an .mdb file.

```
Sub EnumerateCurrentProjectProperties()
Dim prp1 As AccessObjectProperty
Dim str1 As String, str2 As String

'Print number of properties defined
'for CurrentProject
Debug.Print CurrentProject.Properties.Count

'Assign values to a Property object for
'the CurrentProject
str1 = "prpTestProperty"
str2 = "test value"
CurrentProject.Properties.Add str1, str2

'Loop through CurrentProject properties
'and print their name and value
For Each prp1 In CurrentProject.Properties
    Debug.Print prp1.Name, prp1.Value
Next prp1

End Sub
```

Building a Custom Startup in an .mdb File

A custom startup permits your custom form to appear instead of the Database window when a user opens your Access database (.mdb) file. A custom startup typically involves three elements.

■   The first element is an Autoexec macro, which fires automatically when a user opens an Access database file or Access project file. Only one Autoexec macro can exist in either type of file.

■   The second element a custom startup requires is a function procedure to set the appropriate *CurrentDB* properties. The discussion of the function procedure code that follows highlights four of these properties.

■ The third element a custom startup needs is a form that serves as the initial user interface (UI) for the custom application. This form replaces the Database window. End users can make selections from this initial form to access all the other features of your application.

Your Autoexec macro should contain just one macro action: the RunCode action. The RunCode action will run a function procedure only. Specify the function procedure name that assigns the *CurrentDB* properties for your custom startup. Figure 8-1 shows an Autoexec macro in Design view that invokes the *HideDBWindowAtStartupInMDB* function procedure. The Build button next to the Function Name argument box indicates that you can use the Expression Builder to select the function name (thus reducing the possibility of typos).

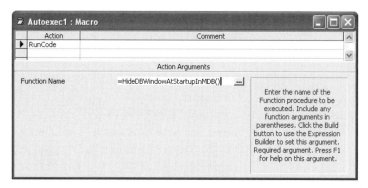

Figure 8-1   Design view of an Autoexec macro for a custom startup.

> **Note**   If you need to invoke a sub procedure or an event procedure from a macro, you must call a function procedure with the RunCode action. In turn, the function procedure can invoke any other types of procedures. This requirement exists because macros can invoke only function procedures.

When setting up a function procedure for a custom startup, you'll typically need to set four of the *CurrentDB* object's properties. First, set the *Startup-ShowDBWindow* property to *False* so that the Database window doesn't show when a user opens the database file. Second, assign *False* to the *AllowBypass-Key* property. This prevents an end user from bypassing your custom startup by holding down the Shift key as the Access database file opens. Third, set the *AllowSpecialKeys* property to *False*. This prohibits an end user from opening the

Database window over your custom startup form by pressing the F11 function key. Fourth, set the *StartupForm* property to a string that specifies the name of your custom startup form.

The function procedure for setting the *CurrentDB* properties for a custom startup appears next. Its error trap is an integral part of the procedure. This is because the first time you run the procedure the *CurrentDB* object might not have all the properties necessary to create a custom startup. The error trap detects when a property does not exist, and it adds the new property as it assigns a value. The startup form for the code sample has the name *frmNotDB-Window*. This form appears instead of the Database window when your application initially appears. Assign the name of your startup form as a string to the *StartupForm* property of the *CurrentDB* object.

```
Function HideDBWindowAtStartupInMDB()
On Error GoTo DAOStartup_Trap
Dim db As Database
Dim prp1 As DAO.Property
Dim str1 As String

'Set reference to current database
Set db = CurrentDb

'Hide Database window the
'next time the database is opened
str1 = "StartupShowDBWindow"
db.Properties(str1) = False
str1 = "AllowBypassKey"
db.Properties(str1) = False
str1 = "AllowSpecialKeys"
db.Properties(str1) = False
str1 = "StartupForm"
db.Properties(str1) = "frmNotDBWindow"

DAOStartup_Exit:
Exit Function

DAOStartup_Trap:

If Err.Number = 3270 And str1 = "StartupShowDBWindow" Then
    Set prp1 = db.CreateProperty("StartupShowDBWindow", dbBoolean, _
        False)
    db.Properties.Append prp1
ElseIf Err.Number = 3270 And str1 = "AllowBypassKey" Then
    Set prp1 = db.CreateProperty("AllowBypassKey", dbBoolean, False)
    db.Properties.Append prp1
```

(continued)

```
ElseIf Err.Number = 3270 And str1 = "AllowSpecialKeys" Then
    Set prp1 = db.CreateProperty("AllowSpecialKeys", dbBoolean, False)
    db.Properties.Append prp1
ElseIf Err.Number = 3270 And str1 = "StartupForm" Then
    Set prp1 = db.CreateProperty("StartupForm", dbText, _
        "frmNotDBWindow")
    db.Properties.Append prp1
Else
    Debug.Print Err.Number, Err.Description
    Exit Function
End If
Resume Next

End Function
```

The startup form for this demonstration contains a lone command button for opening the Database window. In practice, your startup form will include a menu that exposes the functionality of an application through its custom UI. This initial form will typically be unbound, just like the one in my demonstration. Therefore, you'll want to remove any bound data features (such as Navigator buttons) that Access automatically adds to a new form. The *Form_Load* event code handles this. The command button's click event code selects the startup form in the Database window before closing the form. Recall that there is no command for opening the Database window, but you can display the window by selecting an item to show in it. Here's the syntax for the two event procedures:

```
Private Sub Form_Load()

'Set unbound data form properties
Me.RecordSelectors = False
Me.DividingLines = False
Me.NavigationButtons = False

End Sub

Private Sub cmdOpenDBWindow_Click()

'Open Database window by selecting an object in it,
'and close current form
DoCmd.SelectObject acForm, "frmNotDBWindow", True
DoCmd.Close acForm, Me.Name, acSaveNo

End Sub
```

Once you install all the elements just described, you're ready to launch your custom startup process. Run the *HideDBWindowAtStartupInMDB* procedure once before saving the database file. This installs the settings for your custom startup in the Startup dialog box. Then, the next time the database file opens, the *frmNotDBWindow* form appears instead of the Database window. The Autoexec macro fires to refresh your settings for the next time the file opens.

After installing a custom startup, you lose the ability to step through code within the VBE. One way to recover this ability is to remove the special settings on the Startup dialog box and rename the Autoexec macro (for example, by changing it to Autoexec1). By recovering from an error by executing the next line, you guard against an abort caused by the user manually modifying the Startup dialog box settings. Another strategy is to simply lock end users out of the Startup dialog box. "Securing an Application by Programming Command Bars" at the end of this chapter presents techniques for accomplishing this. After you no longer need step mode, you can resume using the custom startup by restoring the name of your Autoexec macro and the Startup dialog box settings. The following two procedures recover step mode and resume using the startup settings:

```
Sub RestoreStepMode()
Dim db As Database, p As DAO.Property

'Set reference to current database
Set db = CurrentDb

'Restore default startup property settings
On Error Resume Next
db.Properties.Delete "StartupShowDBWindow"
db.Properties.Delete "AllowBypassKey"
db.Properties.Delete "AllowSpecialKeys"
db.Properties.Delete "StartupForm"

'Rename Autoexec macro
DoCmd.Rename "Autoexec1", acMacro, "Autoexec"

End Sub

Sub RestoreAutoMode()

'Rename macro and reset startup properties
DoCmd.Rename "Autoexec", acMacro, "Autoexec1"
HideDBWindowAtStartupInMDB

End Sub
```

Building a Custom Startup in an .adp File

The general process for creating a custom startup in an Access project is similar to the one for creating a custom startup in an Access database file. However, the details for setting the startup properties are different. In addition, the process for recovering step mode and resuming the custom startup is similar, but the details vary because your code must deal with the *CurrentProject* object instead of the *CurrentDB* object. In particular, you do not need the DAO library when working with an Access project (.adp) file. However, the Autoexec macro and your custom startup form work identically in .mdb and .adp files.

> **Note** When you open the sample file Chapter08.adp, Access will fail to reestablish the connection to CabSony1. Use the File, Connection menu command to replace CabSony1 with the name of an appropriate SQL server on your network. Chapter 11 discusses .adp files and SQL Server connections in depth.

The following three procedures demonstrate the specific changes that you must make when creating a custom startup in an .adp file. Notice that the syntax for adding and deleting properties is different.

```
Function HideStartupWindowInADP()
On Error GoTo ADPStartup_Trap
Dim str1 As String

'Set CurrentProject properties to hide Database
'window, suppress use of F11 to show it, and
'disallow bypass of startup settings with
'Shift key at startup
str1 = "StartUpShowDBWindow"
CurrentProject.Properties(str1) = False
str1 = "AllowBypassKey"
CurrentProject.Properties("str1") = False
str1 = "AllowSpecialKeys"
CurrentProject.Properties("str1") = False
str1 = "StartupForm"
CurrentProject.Properties("str1") = "frmNotDBWindow"

ADPStartup_Exit:
Exit Function

'If any of three CurrentProject properties do not exist,
```

```
'add them and set their values
ADPStartup_Trap:
If Err.Number = 2455 And str1 = "StartUpShowDBWindow" Then
    CurrentProject.Properties.Add "StartUpShowDBWindow", False
ElseIf Err.Number = 2455 And str1 = "AllowBypassKey" Then
    CurrentProject.Properties.Add "AllowBypasskey", False
ElseIf Err.Number = 2455 And str1 = "AllowSpecialKeys" Then
    CurrentProject.Properties.Add "AllowSpecialKeys", False
ElseIf Err.Number = 2455 And str1 = "StartupForm" Then
    CurrentProject.Properties.Add "StartupForm", "frmNotDBWindow"
Else
    Debug.Print Err.Number, Err.Description
    Exit Function
End If
Resume Next

End Function


Sub RestoreStepMode()

'Remove three startup properties for Database
'window control
On Error Resume Next
CurrentProject.Properties.Remove "StartUpShowDBWindow"
CurrentProject.Properties.Remove "AllowSpecialKeys"
CurrentProject.Properties.Remove "AllowBypassKey"
CurrentProject.Properties.Remove "StartupForm"

'Rename Autoexec macro
DoCmd.Rename "Autoexec1", acMacro, "Autoexec"

End Sub


Sub RestoreAutoMode()

'Rename macro and reset startup properties
DoCmd.Rename "Autoexec", acMacro, "Autoexec1"
HideStartupWindowInADP

End Sub
```

FileSearch Object

You can use the *FileSearch* object model (shown in Figure 8-2) and other selected technologies to integrate file searches into your applications. With Access 2003, the model offers easy access to a broad range of search scopes, including your computer's hard drives, the publicly shared resources on the local area network (LAN) that a computer connects to, Outlook items, and Web files. This object exposes the functionality of the Open and the Find dialog boxes. As Figure 8-2 shows, five collections are dependent on the *FileSearch* object. In addition to the *FoundFiles* and the *PropertyTests* collections from Access 2002, Access 2003 adds the *FileTypes*, *SearchFolders*, and *SearchScopes* collections for the *FileSearch* object.

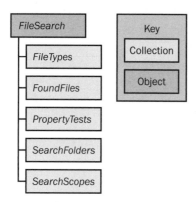

Figure 8-2   The *FileSearch* object is one of the shared Office objects.

> **Note**   Access Help contains code samples that illustrate how to loop through *SearchScopes* to find *SearchFolders* and, ultimately, paths within those folders in which you want to search for files. One major benefit of *SearchScopes* is its ability to search for files that are not on your computer or LAN, such as those located in Web folders. See the "Printing Web Folder Contents" section in Chapter 2 for code samples using the ADODB library that itemize the files on a Web folder.

There are two basic ways to specify a file search, and each approach corresponds to options in the Open dialog box:

- You can designate a single criterion (a filename or pattern, a file type, or a path).

- You can designate multiple search criteria programmatically by using the *PropertyTests* collection.

With the second approach, you specify arguments that serve as input to the Open dialog box. You can use this dialog box to specify multiple search criteria and rules for concatenating them, such as And and Or operators. Use *FoundFiles* to enumerate the result set from either approach. I use the term *result set* because the collection of found files corresponds roughly to the rows of a result set from a *SELECT* statement.

The *FileSearch* object has three methods: *NewSearch*, *Execute*, and *RefreshScopes*. The *NewSearch* method resets all *FileSearch* properties to their default values. You can then edit the properties that require special values for a particular file search. If you do not invoke *NewSearch* at the beginning of a search specification, your new search inherits its property settings from the previous search.

You invoke the *Execute* method to launch a file search after you specify the search parameters. This method can take several arguments that control the arrangement of filenames in the *FoundFiles* object and that control whether to update the file index before conducting a new search. The return value from this method is the number of filenames that match the search specification.

The *RefreshScopes* method updates the *ScopeFolders* collection to reflect the addition or removal of folders since the instantiation of the *FileSearch* object. This method complements the *NewSearch* method as a means of reusing an existing *FileSearch* object. You can programmatically add and drop folders with the *MkDir* and *RmDir* methods for the *FileSystem* class in the VBA library; these methods are available to you as built-in Access functions. Consequently, the *RefreshScopes* method can determine the range of folders in which the *FileSearch* object conducts a search.

Conducting a Basic File Search

Many *FileSearch* properties permit flexible search specifications. The simple code sample that follows specifies a search and retrieves its result set. It creates an instance of the *FileSearch* object by using the *FileSearch* property of the *Application* object. Then it restores all *FileSearch* property settings to their default values by invoking the *NewSearch* method. Next, it assigns the *LookIn* and *FileName* properties, which specify where to look and what to look for. The test machine for this search includes a series of .mdb files with names such as Chapter01 and Chapter02.

The *SearchSubFolders* property accepts a *Boolean* value that indicates whether to restrict the search to the current folder or extend it to subfolders of the *LookIn* property setting. In this instance, the setting matters because the BooksArchive\Access11 folder on the cab2000 computer in my office has a subdirectory for each book chapter. When dealing with folders that can contain many subfolders (such as C:\), you should be careful about how you set the *SearchSubFolders* property because it can lead to some lengthy searches.

```
Sub FileSearch1XP()

'Search in the BooksArchive\Access11 path and
'its subfolders on the c drive of the cab2000
'computer for Chapter*.mdb
With Application.FileSearch
'Start a new search
    .NewSearch
'Set search criteria
    .LookIn = "\\cab2000\c\BooksArchive\Access11"
    .FileName = "Chapter*.mdb"
    .SearchSubFolders = True
End With

With Application.FileSearch
'Execute the search
    If .Execute() > 0 Then
        MsgBox "There were " & .FoundFiles.Count & _
            " file(s) found."
'Display names of all found files
        For i = 1 To .FoundFiles.Count
            MsgBox .FoundFiles(i)
        Next i
    Else
'If no files found, say so
        MsgBox "There were no files found."
    End If
End With

End Sub
```

After creating the specification for the search, the procedure invokes the *Execute* method for the *FileSearch* object. This method has a return value that indicates the number of files that meet the search criteria. If the value is 0, the criteria yield no matching filenames and the procedure issues a message indicating that no files were found. If the criteria yield one or more matching files, the procedure displays the *Count* property of the *FoundFiles* object before presenting each name in *FoundFiles*.

The preceding sample enumerates all the database files from the target folder specified by the *LookIn* setting that have an .mdb extension and start with "Chapter". You can easily broaden the scope of the search to include all database files no matter how their filename starts and regardless of whether they have an .mdb extension. For example, the next piece of code searches for database files in the same folder as the preceding sample. But this code sample retrieves database files with other extensions, such as .adp, .mde, and .ade. Also, the sample places no restrictions on the filename. Therefore, it can find a database filename even if it does not begin with "Chapter".

```
Sub FileSearch1aXP()

'Search in the target path and its subfolders
'for database files
With Application.FileSearch

'Start a new search
    .NewSearch
'Set search criteria
    .LookIn = "\\cab2000\c\BooksArchive\Access11"
    .FileType = msoFileTypeDatabases
    .SearchSubFolders = True
End With

With Application.FileSearch
'Execute the search
    If .Execute() > 0 Then
        MsgBox "There were " & .FoundFiles.Count & _
            " file(s) found."
'Display names of all found files
        For i = 1 To .FoundFiles.Count
            MsgBox .FoundFiles(i)
        Next i
    Else
'If no files found, say so
        MsgBox "There were no files found."
    End If
End With

End Sub
```

Generalizing a Search and Sorting Its Return Set

The following sample sorts the result set from a search by file size. The sample uses two procedures. The first procedure specifies a computer name, a share name, and a pathname. These three parameters can jointly designate the *LookIn* setting for a search. By specifying the parameters in a procedure that passes them to another, we make the procedure that invokes the *Execute* method for the *FileSearch* object more general.

The second procedure accepts the arguments passed to it by the first procedure, and it concatenates them to compute a value for the *LookIn* property of the *FileSearch* object. In addition, the second procedure uses two more parameters when it invokes the *Execute* method. These parameters designate the sort criterion and order, respectively, for arranging the result set from the search. The constant names for the *Execute* method's first parameter indicate the variable on which to sort the returned filenames. These constants are *msoSortByFileName*, *msoSortByFileType*, *msoSortByLastModified*, and *msoSortBySize*. The *Execute* method's second parameter specifies either ascending or descending order. The sample designates a search sorted by file size in descending order. This differs from the previous sample, which returned results in the default ascending order based on filename.

```
Sub CallFileSearch2XP()
Dim str1 As String
Dim str2 As String
Dim str3 As String
'Dim ftp1 As fil

str1 = "\\cab2000\"
str2 = "c\"
str3 = "BooksArchive\Access11"

FileSearch2XP str1, str2, str3

End Sub

Sub FileSearch2XP(ComputerName As String, _
    ShareName As String, PathName As String, _
    Optional FileType)

Dim sngMB As Single

'Search in folder specified by arguments and its
'subfolders for *.mdb
With Application.FileSearch
'Start a new search
    .NewSearch
'Set search criteria
    .LookIn = ComputerName & ShareName & PathName
    .FileName = "*.mdb"
    .SearchSubFolders = True
End With

With Application.FileSearch
'Return found files in descending order by file size
    If .Execute(msoSortBySize, msoSortOrderDescending) > 0 Then
        Debug.Print "There were " & .FoundFiles.Count & _
```

```
                   " file(s) found."
          For i = 1 To .FoundFiles.Count
'Compute file size in MB and display with filename
              sngMB = FileLen(.FoundFiles(i)) / (1024 ^ 2)
              Debug.Print .FoundFiles(i) & vbCrLf & vbTab & _
                  "Filesize (MB): " & Round(CDec(sngMB), 3)
          Next i
      Else
'If no files found, say so
          MsgBox "There were no files found."
      End If
End With

End Sub
```

The sample prints the result set to the Immediate window to show the file sizes and filenames. The code demonstrates the syntax for passing the *FoundFiles* object to the *FileLen* function to determine the file size in bytes. The division by *1024^2* converts the function's return value from bytes to megabytes (MB). Then, by applying the *Round* function, the procedure represents the value to the nearest 1/1000 of a megabyte.

Note   VBA 6 introduced the VBA *Round* function. To derive consistent results with this function, you should first pass its argument to the *CDec* function. The sample just shown uses this syntax.

Searching Based on File Contents

Even with a simple search, as shown in the three previous samples, you can selectively search for specific text, such as ADO, in the document or its *DocumentProperty* object. The sample that follows does this. You use the *FileSearch* object's *TextOrProperty* property to target a text string in the file's body or its *Properties* collection. Notice that you can specify folders on remote computers using the Universal Naming Convention (UNC). There is nothing new about this capability, except now we exercise it to search for text within the files on another computer. This sample uses the same name and path as the preceding samples. (The path \\cab2000\c\BooksArchive\Access11 points to the BooksArchive\Access11 folder in the share named c of a computer named cab2000.) As with other samples in this book, you'll need to change these settings so that they point to the computers, shares, and paths that are relevant to your computing environment.

```
Sub FileSearch3XP()
Dim sngStart As Double
Dim sngEnd As Double
Dim int1 As Integer
Dim str1 As String
#Const AllFiles = False

'Search in a folder on linked computer
'for files containing ADO
With Application.FileSearch
'Start a new search
    .NewSearch
'Set search criteria
    .LookIn = "\\cab2000\c\BooksArchive\Access11"
    .SearchSubFolders = False
'When searching for text, consider
'restricting the files you search
'*.* can require more time
'than msoFileTypeWordDocuments
#If AllFiles = True Then
    .FileName = "*.*"
#Else
    .FileType = msoFileTypeWordDocuments
#End If
    .TextOrProperty = "ADO"
End With

With Application.FileSearch
'Execute the search
    sngStart = Now
    If .Execute() > 0 Then
        sngEnd = Now
        Debug.Print "The file search took " & _
            DateDiff("s", sngStart, sngEnd) & " seconds."
        str1 = "There were " & .FoundFiles.Count & _
            " file(s) found.  Do you want to see " & _
            "them in a series of messages boxes?"
        If MsgBox(str1, vbYesNo, _
            "Programming Microsoft Access 2003") = vbYes Then
'Display names of all found files
            For int1 = 1 To .FoundFiles.Count
                MsgBox .FoundFiles(int1)
            Next int1
        End If
    Else
'If no files found, say so
```

```
        MsgBox "There were no files found."
    End If
End With

End Sub
```

Some file searches are lengthy. By restricting the scope of a *FileSearch* object, you can dramatically improve the performance of the *Execute* method. Three settings that affect search performance include the *Lookin, SearchSub-Folders*, and *FileTypes* properties. A good optimizing rule is to look at the lowest level folder, avoid searching subdirectories, and search for a specific file type. For example, the sample just shown finds all Word documents in a folder that contain a specific string—namely, ADO. On the LAN in my office, this search takes about three seconds. By changing the search settings so the *Execute* method looks at all files (*AllFiles* = True) from the root directory on the c share (*Lookin* = \\cab2000\c) and all its subdirectories (*SearchSubFolders* = True), the search time grows to 10,370 seconds! I got a nice break while the computer timed this search. The two properties that most affect search performance in this example are *Lookin* and *SearchSubFolders*. However, you also can attain meaningful performance gains by using the *FileType* property to search for a specific kind of file (FileType = msoFileTypeWordDocuments) instead of searching for all files (FileName = *.*) in a search path. On the LAN in my office, using a modified version of the preceding sample to search just for Word documents is 14 seconds faster than searching all documents in the BooksArchive folder.

Controlling FileType with a Custom Form and Procedure

In general, your applications will offer file search capabilities through a form. The next sample demonstrates one technique for this while showing how to condition a search on one or more members of the *FileTypes* collection for the *FileSearch* object. The sample's form, which appears in Figure 8-3, allows a user to perform one of three tasks. First, users can specify a new search by designating a single file type for it. The combo box on the form shows the list of possible *FileType* designations. Second, users can add a new member to the *FileTypes* collection for the current *FileSearch* object. Again, users must specify which *FileType* to add via the combo box. Third, they can execute the search with the *FileTypes* collection members showing in the form's list box. This last capability depends, in part, on a procedure named *FileSearch1a3aXP* in a standard module. A module behind the form supports all the form's capabilities, including the call to the procedure in the standard module.

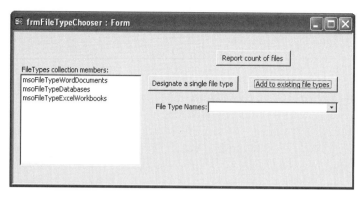

Figure 8-3 A form for adding members to the *FileTypes* collection of a *FileSearch* object. The form also enables executing the search.

The following listing includes all the event procedures and sub procedures behind the form. These procedures provide two classes of services. The first class manages the form by performing tasks such as managing the entries that appear in the list box and responding to command button clicks. The second class of services manages the search. This involves tasks such as managing the members of the *FileTypes* collection for the open *FileSearch* object and launching the search with whatever members are in the list.

The form module starts by declaring three public variables. These variables simplify sharing information across procedures (namely, the settings for the *FileSearch* object). These initial declarations also reduce the need to repetitively declare variables used in standard ways across procedures.

The first procedure is the *Form_Open* event procedure. This procedure handles the formatting and content settings for the form. It also sets a reference to the *FileSearch* object and uses that reference to populate the form's list box with members of the object's *FileTypes* collection. Furthermore, the procedure uses the *AddItem* and *RemoveItem* methods to control the content of the list box. These methods require a list box control to have a *Value List* setting for its *RowSourceType* property.

> **Note** Access 2002 introduced the *AddItem* and *RemoveItem* methods for list boxes and combo boxes. The code behind the form in Figure 8-3 illustrates how to use them. Refer to Access Help for online programmer reference materials. Chapter 5 has a sample illustrating use of the *AddItem* method.

The *Form_Open* event procedure has two loops. A backward-iterating loop that successively invokes the *RemoveItem* method erases any previously existing content from the list box. A forward-iterating loop passes through the members of the *FileTypes* collection. This loop uses the *AddItem* method to add the names of the members to the list box. Office stores members of the *File-Types* collection as intrinsic constant values (numbers). A lookup table (*mso-FileTypeEnum*) in the Chapter08 .mdb file maps the numbers to their intrinsic constant names. A *DLookup* function within the loop operates on the table to extract the intrinsic constant name corresponding to the number for a *FileType* collection member. Notice in the code that *FileTypes* collection members belong to a 1-based collection, but the rows in a list box belong to a 0-based collection.

> **Note**   The form's combo box shows the names of all the intrinsic constants for *FileType* designations but stores a constant's number when a user makes a selection. The combo box uses the same lookup table as the *DLookup* function that decodes an intrinsic constant value to the name for the constant. However, the combo box works the table in reverse from the *DLookup* function in the final loop of the *Form_Open* event procedure.

The *cmdDesignateSingle_Click* and *cmdAddTo_Click* event procedures work in concert with the *RefreshWithNewFileTypeinFileSearch* procedure to keep the list box control rows in synchronicity with the members of the *FileTypes* collection. The two procedures also populate the *FileTypes* collection with members. The event procedure for clicking the *cmdDesignateSingle* button starts by assigning the combo box's value to the *FileTypes* collection for the *FileSearch* object referenced in the *Form_Open* event procedure. The assignment statement clears any prior members of the *FileTypes* collection as it adds the combo box's value to the collection. Next, it removes all row values from the list box in a backward-iterating loop. The call to the *RefreshWithNewFileTypeinFileSearch* procedure passes the last member from the *FileTypes* collection to the list box. In order for the *cmdDesignateSingle_Click* procedure to work properly, users must first make a selection from the combo box. An error trap (*NullSingleTrap*), catches cases where users fail to make a selection and reminds them with a message box.

The *cmdAddTo_Click* event procedure has the same general design as the *cmdDesignateSingle_Click* event procedure, but *cmdAddTo_Click* merely adds an item from the combo box to the *FileTypes* collection and the list box rows. Instead of using an assignment statement to transfer the combo box value to the

FileTypes collection, the *cmdAddTo_Click* procedure uses the collection's *Add* method. This method inserts the combo box's value as the last member of the collection without affecting any other members of the collection. Again, there's an error trap in case users forget to make a selection from the combo box before clicking the button. Let's take a look at the syntax now.

```
Public fls1 As FileSearch
Public int1 As Integer
Public str1 As String

Private Sub Form_Open(Cancel As Integer)

'Set RowSourceType to Value List so you can use
'AddItem and RemoveItem methods
Me.lstExistingFileTypes.RowSourceType = "Value List"

'Set form for unbound data use
Me.RecordSelectors = False
Me.NavigationButtons = False
Me.DividingLines = False

'Remove all existing items from the list box
'showing selected file types
For int1 = Me.lstExistingFileTypes.ListCount - 1 To 0 Step -1
    Me.lstExistingFileTypes.RemoveItem int1
Next int1

'Set FileSearch variable
Set fls1 = Application.FileSearch

'Loop through FileTypes in FileSearch object and
'add them to the list box
'FileTypes collection is 1-based and list box items
'are 0-based
For int1 = 1 To fls1.FileTypes.Count
    str1 = "[msoFileTypeNumber] = " & _
        CStr(fls1.FileTypes.Item(int1))
    Me.lstExistingFileTypes.AddItem _
        Item:=DLookup("[msoFileTypeName]", _
        "msoFileTypeEnum", str1), _
        Index:=Me.lstExistingFileTypes.ListCount
Next int1

End Sub

Private Sub cmdDesignateSingle_Click()
On Error GoTo NullSingleTrap
'Refresh the FileTypes collection of the FileSearch
'object with the combo box selection
fls1.FileType = Combo0
```

```
'Remove all existing items from the list box
'showing selected file types
For int1 = Me.lstExistingFileTypes.ListCount - 1 To 0 Step -1
    Me.lstExistingFileTypes.RemoveItem int1
Next int1

'Refresh the list box with the newly selected item
RefreshWithNewFileTypeinFileSearch

'Blank combo after processing selection
Combo0 = ""

NormalExit:
Exit Sub

NullSingleTrap:
If Err.Number = 94 Then
    MsgBox "Select a file type from the combo " & _
        "box before clicking the button.", vbCritical, _
        "Programming Microsoft Access 2003"
Else
    MsgBox "Call Support to report this problem.", _
        vbCritical, "Programming Microsoft Access 2003"
End If

End Sub

Private Sub cmdAddTo_Click()
On Error GoTo NullAddTrap
'Add the combo box selection to the existing list
'of members in the FileTypes collection of the
'FileSearch object
fls1.FileTypes.Add Combo0

'Refresh the list box with the newly selected item
RefreshWithNewFileTypeinFileSearch

'Blank combo after processing selection
Combo0 = ""

NormalExit:
Exit Sub

NullAddTrap:
If Err.Number = 94 Then
    MsgBox "Select a file type from the combo " & _
        "box before clicking the button.", vbCritical, _
        "Programming Microsoft Access 2003"
Else
    MsgBox "Call Support to report this problem.", _
```

(continued)

```
          vbCritical, "Programming Microsoft Access 2003"
End If

End Sub

Sub RefreshWithNewFileTypeinFileSearch()
'Dim int1 As Integer
'Dim str1 As String

'Find the index for the last item in the FilesTypes collection
int1 = fls1.FileTypes.Count
str1 = "[msoFileTypeNumber] = " & CStr(fls1.FileTypes.Item(int1))

'Add name corresponding to the FileType number to the bottom
'of the list box
Me.lstExistingFileTypes.AddItem _
    Item:=DLookup("[msoFileTypeName]", "msoFileTypeEnum", str1), _
    Index:=Me.lstExistingFileTypes.ListCount

End Sub

Private Sub cmdSearch_Click()

'Launch search with setting from form
Module1.FileSearch1a3aXP

End Sub
```

The last event procedure, *cmdSearch_Click*, in the code behind the form consists of a single line. This line invokes the *FileSearch1a3aXP* procedure in *Module1*, which is a standard module. The *FileSearch1a3aXP* procedure contains elements of the two preceding search procedures in the module whose names end with *1aXP* and *3aXP*. The actual code appears next. One distinction between this procedure and the ones we examined earlier in the section is that it doesn't invoke the *New* method for the *FileSearch* object. This is because the procedure needs to retain the *FileTypes* collection members set by the form.

```
Sub FileSearch1a3aXP()

'Search in Program Files folder and its subfolders
With Application.FileSearch
'Start a new search.
'Set search criteria.
    .LookIn = "C:\PMA Samples"
    .SearchSubFolders = True
End With

With Application.FileSearch
'Execute the search
```

```
        If .Execute() > 0 Then
            str1 = "There were " & .FoundFiles.Count & _
                " file(s) found."
            MsgBox str1, vbInformation, _
                "Programming Microsoft Access 2003"
        Else
    'If no files found, say so
            MsgBox "There were no files found.", vbInformation, _
                "Programming Microsoft Access 2003"
        End If
    End With

    End Sub
```

Specifying Multiple Search Criteria

The advanced search format lets you specify multiple search criteria for your result set in the *FoundFiles* collection. You use the *Add* method two or more times to specify multiple criteria for the *PropertyTests* collection. Your individual criterion specifications must include *Name* and *Condition* settings.

The *Add* method can specify a *Connector* setting as well as one or two *Value* settings. The *Add* method's *Condition* setting determines whether a criterion requires *Value* settings. You can view the members of the *MsoCondition* class in the Object Browser to see all the available options. Figure 8-4 shows an excerpt. Your *Connector* settings can take one of two values to specify how to combine a criterion with other criteria. This setting enables And or Or operators for merging a criterion with other search criteria. You use Or to treat the criterion separately, and you use And to combine the designated criterion with others. The And operator is the default setting. Together, the *Condition*, *Value*, and *Connector* settings offer the same functionality as the Find dialog box.

You can enumerate *PropertyTests* members using a *For...Each* loop. Each member constitutes a unique search criterion. The *Name* property identifies the criterion as you enumerate them.

The file search sample that follows has three segments. The first segment specifies the criteria after setting a reference to a *FileSearch* object. The sample targets all Web files between two dates where the files are located in the \Program Files\Microsoft Office\Office11\Samples folder of the C drive on the current computer. The code shows the correct syntax for invoking the *Add* method for the *PropertyTests* collection. The first criterion designates a Web page file type. The second criterion denotes files last modified between January 1, 2002 and December 31, 2003. The *msoConnectorOr* setting indicates that files must meet both criteria separately to be in the result set. You need not specify a *Connector* property for the second criterion because it adopts the default *msoConnectorAnd* value. Before displaying the result set, the procedure enumerates the *Property-Tests* members in its second segment. The final segment displays the result set.

Figure 8-4 You use the members of the *MsoCondition* enumeration group to specify conditions for advanced criteria in the *PropertyTests* collection of the *FileSearch* object.

```
Sub FileSearch4XP()
Dim fls1 As FileSearch
Dim str1 As String
Dim int1 As Integer

Set fls1 = Application.FileSearch

'Set LookIn and SearchSubFolder properties
With fls1
    .NewSearch
    .LookIn = "\\cab2000\c\Program Files\" & _
    "Microsoft Office\Office10\Samples"
    .SearchSubFolders = False
End With

'Remove default PropertyTest for Office files
fls1.PropertyTests.Remove (1)

'Set a pair of PropertyTests to find all Web pages
```

```
'last modified on either 10/30/2000 or 10/31/2000
With fls1.PropertyTests
    .Add Name:="Files of Type", _
        Condition:=msoConditionFileTypeWebPages, _
        Connector:=msoConnectorOr
    .Add Name:="Last Modified", _
        Condition:=msoConditionAnytimeBetween, _
        Value:="11/1/2002", SecondValue:="12/31/2003"
End With

'Display PropertyTests
For int1 = 1 To fls1.PropertyTests.Count
    With Application.FileSearch.PropertyTests(int1)
    str1 = "This is the search criteria: " & vbCrLf & _
        "The name is: " & .Name & ". " & vbCrLf & _
        "The condition is: " & .Condition
    If .Value <> "" Then
        str1 = str1 & "." & vbCrLf & "The value is: " & .Value
        If .SecondValue <> "" Then
            str1 = str1 _
                & ". " & vbCrLf "The second value is: " _
                & .SecondValue & ", and the connector is " _
                & .Connector
        End If
    End If
    MsgBox str1

    End With
Next int1

'Display return set from property tests
With fls1
'Execute the search
    If .Execute() > 0 Then
        MsgBox "There were " & .FoundFiles.Count & _
            " file(s) found."
'Display names of all found files
        For int1 = 1 To .FoundFiles.Count
            MsgBox .FoundFiles(int1)
        Next int1
    Else
'If no files found, say so
        MsgBox "There were no files found."
    End If
End With

End Sub
```

A Utility for Copying Files Based on *FileSystemObject*

One reason for finding files is to copy them to another destination or save them with a new name. The *FileSearch* object does not facilitate either task, but the *FileSystemObject* object does. This object provides a general model for processing text and binary files. The *CopyFileUtility* procedure described in this section illustrates a simple application of the *FileSystemObject* object that I hope will entice you to explore *FileSystemObject* more fully when your applications require file processing. You can learn more about this tool by searching for *FileSystemObject* in VBScrip5.chm. Perform a search on your computer of the Program Files folder to locate the exact path to the file. The *FileSystemObject* object is an exceedingly robust tool for many Office applications.

The following code sample uses two procedures to manage the operation of the *CopyFile* method. The first procedure sets the computer and share names, the pathname, and the filename for the original file and the copy that the utility attempts to generate. This procedure also sets a *Boolean* variable to determine whether the utility will copy over a file that already exists. The second procedure instantiates a reference to *FileSystemObject* with the *CreateObject* function. The *CreateObject* function is explored in more depth in Chapter 9, and Chapter 1 includes a brief description of its use with *FileSystemObject*. After instantiating the object, the procedure compiles the source and destination arguments for the object's *CopyFile* method.

Users of an application must have appropriate permissions to an original file and the location of a destination file for the *CopyFile* method to function correctly. The most recent Microsoft Windows operating systems, such as Windows XP, do not enable these permissions by default. The basic way to enable read and write permissions in Windows XP is via Simple File Sharing. With Windows XP, you can start to implement Simple File Sharing for a folder by right-clicking it in Windows Explorer and choosing Sharing And Security. From the Network sharing and security group on the Sharing tab of the folder Properties dialog box, permit sharing for the folder by clicking the Share This Folder On The Network check box. Windows makes the folder shared by anyone who knows the share name. By default, the share name is the name of the folder, but you can override this assignment by entering a different name in the Share Name box of the Network Sharing And Security group. You can also disable the ability to change files in a shared folder by clearing the Allow Network Users To Change My Files check box. Figure 8-5 shows Windows Explorer along with the Sharing tab of a folder Properties dialog box. The selection on the tab enables Simple File Sharing, but restricts it to reading. These settings are sufficient for using any file in the folder as the source file for the *CopyFile* method.

> **Note** Because Simple File Sharing provides very unrestricted access to your folders, you should apply it in a highly selective fashion to folders with contents that you deem public. Windows XP has a designated Shared Documents folder. However, by applying Simple File Sharing to a specific folder, you avoid the need to copy or move files from an application folder to a general public folder.

Figure 8-5   The Access11Files Properties dialog box with the settings to implement read-only Simple File Sharing with Windows XP.

The *CallCopyFileUtility* procedure sets the original file and the destination of the copy. The original file is Chapter08.adp in the Access11Files share on the CabSony1 computer. Since the share (Access11Files) contains only one folder, the code designates the share name as the path. The destination of the copied file is the BooksArchive/Access11 folder on the c share of the cab2000 computer. The *CopyFileUtility* procedure instantiates a *FileSystemObject* object with the *CreateObject* function and invokes the *CopyFile* method for the instance. To run this utility application, you'll first need to update the share and path names for your computing environment. By clearing the *Err* object and designating that Access recover from errors by processing the next line, the procedure displays one of three messages after completing the attempt to copy the file. If the *Err* object is still clear, the code announces that the copy attempt succeeded. If the procedure attempts to copy over an existing file without designating that it's OK to do so, the copy attempt fails and the procedure warns the user. Finally, if some unanticipated error occurs, the procedure returns the *Err* object's *Number* and *Description* properties in a message box. Here's the code for the utility.

```
Sub CallCopyFileUtility()
Dim strOrigShare As String
Dim strOrigPath As String
Dim strOrigFlNm As String
Dim strDestShare As String
Dim strDestPath As String
Dim strDestFlNm As String
Dim bolOver As Boolean
#Const ForcePathNotFound = False

'Specify inputs for file copy
strOrigShare = "\\CabSony1\"
strOrigPath = "Access11Files\"
strOrigFlNm = "Chapter08.adp"
#If ForcePathNotFound = False Then
    strDestShare = "\\cab2000\c\"
#Else
    strDestShare = "\\xyz\c\"
#End If
strDestPath = "BooksArchive\Access11\"
strDestFlNm = "Chapter08.adp"

'Setting to False can generate a File already
'exist message if the file is there already
bolOver = True

'Pass arguments to CopyFileUtility
CopyFileUtility strOrigShare, strDestShare, _
    strOrigPath, strDestPath, _
    strOrigFlNm, strDestFlNm, _
    bolOver

End Sub

Sub CopyFileUtility(strOrigShare As String, _
    strDestShare As String, _
    strOrigPath As String, _
    strDestPath As String, _
    strOrigFlNm As String, _
    strDestFlNm As String, _
    Optional bolOver As Boolean = False)
```

```
Dim str1 As String
Dim str2 As String
Dim str3 As String
Dim int1 As Integer
Const msgTitle = "Programming Microsoft Access 2003"

'Reference FileSystemObject
Set fs = CreateObject("Scripting.FileSystemObject")

'Form origin and destination arguments for CopyFile method
str1 = strOrigShare & strOrigPath & strOrigFlNm
str2 = strDestShare & strDestPath & strDestFlNm

'Clear error and resume from error outcome at the next line
'from the CopyFile method
Err.Clear
On Error Resume Next
fs.CopyFile str1, str2, bolOver

'Print message describing CopyFile outcome
Debug.Print Err.Number, Err.Description
Select Case Err.Number
    Case 0
        str3 = "Copy succeeded."
        int1 = vbInformation
    Case 58
        str3 = "File exist at destination already.  Choose new name."
        int1 = vbCritical
    Case Else
        str3 = "Unanticipated error." & vbCr & _
        "Err.number = " & Err.Number & vbCr & _
        "Err.description = " & Err.Description
        int1 = vbCritical
End Select
MsgBox str3, int1, msgTitle

End Sub
```

You can test the error paths of the *CopyFileUtility* procedure by altering the settings for the first procedure in the utility. For example, to generate a message saying that the file already exists, change the assignment for *bolOver* from *True* to *False* and attempt to copy over a file you know exists. One typical unanticipated error occurs when a user attempts to copy to a destination path that does not exist. For example, the user might make a typo when specifying the path. Because it's unlikely that you already have a \\cab2000\c\ computer name and share name in your computing environment, specifying these settings will probably generate a "Path not found" message with an error number of 76. However, even after you update the computer name and share name for your computing environment, users can still generate a "Path not found" message by setting the compiler constant *ForcePathNotFound* to *True* (unless they have a computer named xyz with a share named c on your LAN).

Empowering Users to Create and Open Files from the Task Pane

The Task Pane introduced with Access 2002 as part of the UI was redesigned for Access 2003. The Task Pane now opens on the right side of the Access desktop window and the Task Pane window is a toolbar. The New File section of this toolbar has three sections. In the first section, users can click on shortcuts to launch various actions, such as creating a blank database (.mdb) file, a blank data access page (discussed in Chapter 14), an Access project based on an existing SQL Server or new SQL Server database, or a new database based on an existing .mdb file. The middle section enables users to search for template files on Microsoft.com. The bottom section is for tapping templates installed with Access 2003. These template files have an .mdz extension. Developers can programmatically add and remove shortcuts on the Task Pane to enable users to add (or prevent them from adding) selected files. The Home view of the Task Pane, which you can open with an icon that looks like a house, includes an Open section. By default, the Task Pane uses this section to list links for recently opened files and a link for exposing the Open dialog box for opening new files. Developers can programmatically add links to the Open section on the Home view of the Task Pane with a syntax similar to that used for adding links to the New section in the New File view.

> **Note**   End users can open the Task Pane toolbar by choosing New from the File menu. Developers can program the Task Pane by using the *NewFileTaskPane* property, which returns a *NewFile* object that represents an item in the New section of the New File view of the Task Pane.

The following pair of procedures show how to add and remove a Copy Northwind link from the New From Existing File section of the Task Pane. When a user clicks the link, it creates a new file named Northwind1.mdb, which is a copy of the Northwind.mdb file. The new file appears in the same folder as the original one.

Adding a shortcut to the Task Pane requires managing the Task Pane and the proper shortcut specification. Notice that the *AddCopyNorthwindLink* procedure begins by declaring a *NewFile* object in the Office library. The declared object requires a reference to the Office 11.0 library in the References dialog box of the VBE window. Next, the procedure sets a reference to a *NewFile-TaskPane* object. The Task Pane has three views—one for searching, another for managing the Windows Clipboard, and a third for managing the creation of new files. The *NewFileTaskPane* object references the view of the Task Pane for managing the creation of new files. In between two command bar property assignments, the procedure invokes the *Add* method for the *nftpTemp* instance. Showing and hiding the Task Pane command bar refreshes the Task Pane to show the outcome of the *Add* method.

The *Add* method takes four arguments. Two of these rely on intrinsic constants in enum groups. The action argument specifies what a shortcut does. Its enum group, *msoFileNewAction*, has three members. These members signify adding, editing, and opening a file. The sample that follows uses the constant for adding a file. The second enum group, *msoFileNewSection*, denotes the section of the Task Pane. This group contains a separate intrinsic constant for each Task Pane section. This sample specifies the New From Existing File section. The *FileName* argument designates the source file for the action, and the *DisplayName* setting determines how the shortcut appears on the Task Pane.

```
Sub AddCopyNorthwindLink()
Dim nftpTemp As Office.NewFile

'Instantiate NewFile object for Task Pane
Set nftpTemp = Application.NewFileTaskPane

'Add link to Copy Northwind.mdb database to the New
'From Existing File section of the Task Pane
CommandBars("Task Pane").Visible = False
nftpTemp.Add _
    FileName:="C:\Program Files\Microsoft Office\Office11\" & _
    "Samples\Northwind.mdb", _
    Section:=msoNewfromExistingFile, _
    DisplayName:="Copy Northwind.mdb", _
    Action:=msoCreateNewFile
CommandBars("Task Pane").Visible = True

End Sub

Sub RemoveCopyNorthwindLink()
Dim nftpTemp As Office.NewFile

'Instantiate NewFile object for Task Pane
Set nftpTemp = Application.NewFileTaskPane

'Remove link to Copy Northwind.mdb database from the New
'From Existing File section of the Task Pane
CommandBars("Task Pane").Visible = False
```

(continued)

```
nftpTemp.Remove _
    FileName:="C:\Program Files\Microsoft Office\Office11\" & _
    "Samples\Northwind.mdb", _
    Section:=msoNewfromExistingFile, _
    DisplayName:="Copy Northwind.mdb"
CommandBars("Task Pane").Visible = True

End Sub
```

Removing a shortcut from the Task Pane is especially easy. Just take the procedure for adding the shortcut and replace the *Add* method with the *Remove* method. You can also drop the *Action* argument. That's all it takes!

The following listing illustrates the syntax for adding a link to the Open section of the Home view of the Task Pane. The link in the sample opens the Northwind database when a user clicks the link. The procedure for adding the link has the name *AddOpenNorthwindLink*. Notice the similarity of the syntax to the preceding *AddCopyNorthwindLink* procedure. Critically, the *Section* and *Action* argument values are different for the two procedures. These arguments indicate where the link goes and what the link should do. The Chapter08.mdb contains a procedure named *RemoveOpenNorthwindLink* that corresponds in syntax to the *RemoveCopyNorthwindLink* procedure. However, the procedure for removing the Open Northwind.mdb link fails. The remedy to this problem follows the example.

```
Sub AddOpenNorthwindLink()
Dim nftpTemp As Office.NewFile

'Instantiate NewFile object for Task Pane
Set nftpTemp = Application.NewFileTaskPane

'Add link to Open Northwind.mdb database to
'the Open section of the Task Pane
CommandBars("Task Pane").Visible = False
nftpTemp.Add _
    FileName:="C:\Program Files\Microsoft Office\Office11\" & _
    "Samples\Northwind.mdb", _
    Section:=msoOpenDocument, _
    DisplayName:="Open Northwind.mdb", _
    Action:=msoOpenFile
CommandBars("Task Pane").Visible = True

End Sub
```

As mentioned, there is a problem with the *Remove* method for the Open section of the Task Pane. In this instance, the preceding sample can add a link to the section named Open Northwind.mdb, but a corresponding sample could not remove it. One way to solve this problem is to remove the shortcut via the registry. Start to open the registry by typing *regedit* into the Open box of the Run dialog box from the Windows Start button. Then, click OK. Next, choose Find from the Edit menu. Search for the shortcut text (Open Northwind.mdb, in this example). With the Windows XP operating system, the editor discovers a reference to the shortcut under HKEY_CURRENT_USER, Software, Microsoft, Office, 11.0, Access, New File. In the test computer I used while writing this book, the shortcut was in the Custom1 folder at the end of the path. Delete the custom folder containing the shortcut specification. After removing the registry entry for the shortcut, you might need to close and open the Task Pane or even your Access session. This refreshes the Task Pane to reflect your changed registry settings.

> **Note**   Whenever you make changes to a registry, you first should have a backup copy for restoring it. Detailed commentary on editing, backing up, and restoring registries is beyond the scope of this book.

CommandBar Object

The *CommandBar* object model (shown in Figure 8-6) is rich—it includes both built-in and custom command bars. Command bar is a generic term that refers to a menu bar, a toolbar, or a popup menu bar. *CommandBar* controls enable users to interface with command bars and interact with an application. The three broad classes of *CommandBar* controls are the *CommandBarButton*, *CommandBarComboBox*, and *CommandBarPopup* objects.

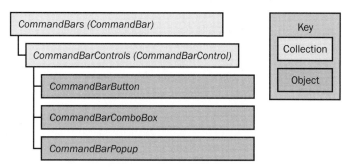

Figure 8-6   You use the *CommandBar* object model to customize built-in command bars and create custom command bars.

Enumerating Command Bar Elements

Enumerating command bar elements is critical to working with command bars. Enumeration provides a vehicle for learning the hierarchy of the *CommandBar* object. The knowledge that you gain through the following samples will help you when you modify built-in command bars and develop custom ones.

The following short procedure gives a count of command bars in an application. If no custom command bars exist, the procedure reports a count of the built-in command bars—178 for Access 2003. The number is higher if an application has custom command bars. There are 140 command bars in Access 2000 and 173 command bars in Access 2002. Access 2002 saw a substantial upgrade in its *CommandBars*, primarily for pivot tables and pivot charts.

```
Sub CountCommandBars()

MsgBox "There are " & CommandBars.Count & _
    " bars in the CommandBars collection."

End Sub
```

> **Note** Access 2003 solutions that draw on command bars may not be compatible with those from Access 2000 or Access 2002, though the default file format is the same in all three versions. Note also that the *CommandBars* object model is a part of the Office Object Library, which updates with each version of Office (the Office 2000 version is different from the Office XP version and that version is different from the library for Office 2003). Therefore, to use programmatically specified custom command bars or customized versions of built-in command bars, plan to move all users to a single version of Access—preferably Access 2003 for its enhanced functionality.

There are three types of command bars. The Office Object Library includes the *msoBarType* constants to reference these as *msoBarTypeNormal*, *msoBarTypeMenuBar*, and *msoBarTypePopup*. You can also distinguish between built-in and custom command bars. The following procedure gives the count by type of command bar for each built-in toolbar. For a complete installation without any custom command bars, the count is one menu bar, 50 toolbars, and 127 popup bars.

```
Sub BuiltinCommandBarCount()
Dim cbr1 As CommandBar
Dim iMbars As Integer
Dim iTbars As Integer
Dim iPbars As Integer
Dim iBuiltin As Integer
```

```
For Each cbr1 In CommandBars
    If cbr1.BuiltIn Then
        iBuiltin = iBuiltin + 1
        If cbr1.Type = msoBarTypeMenuBar Then
            iMbars = iMbars + 1
        ElseIf cbr1.Type = msoBarTypeNormal Then
            iTbars = iTbars + 1
        Else
            iPbars = iPbars + 1
        End If
    End If
Next
MsgBox "There are " & iBuiltin & " command bars. " & _
    iMbars & " is a menu bar, " & iTbars & " are toolbars, and " & _
    iPbars & " are popup bars."

End Sub
```

Listing Visible Command Bars

There are 178 built-in command bars—you probably won't want to enumerate all of them very often. However, subsets of them can be important to an application. For example, your application might want to know which command bars are visible. The following *EnumerateVisibleCommandBars* procedure writes a line to the Immediate window for each visible command bar. The line displays three properties for each command bar—the command bar name, type, and count of controls. A pair of nested *IIf* functions decode the *Type* property. Rather than enumerate the controls on command bars to develop a count, the procedure simply reports the command bar's *Count* property.

```
Sub EnumerateVisibleCommandBars()
Dim cbr1 As CommandBar

For Each cbr1 In CommandBars
    If cbr1.Visible = True Then
        Debug.Print cbr1.Name, _
            (IIf(cbr1.Type = msoBarTypeNormal, _
            "toolbar", _
            IIf(cbr1.Type = msoBarTypeMenuBar, _
            "menu bar", "popup bar"))), _
            cbr1.Controls.Count
    End If
Next cbr1

End Sub
```

It's relatively easy to extend the previous code to enumerate the individual controls on each visible command bar. Command bars have a *Controls* collection, and the elements of this collection are *CommandBarControl* objects. The following procedure applies a *CommandBar* object and a *CommandBarControl* object while listing the captions for the controls on all visible command bars:

```
Sub EnumerateControlCaptions()
Dim cbr1 As CommandBar
Dim ctl1 As CommandBarControl

For Each cbr1 In CommandBars
    If cbr1.Visible = True Then
        Debug.Print "Command bar name: " & cbr1.Name & _
            " and control count: "; cbr1.Controls.Count
        For Each ctl1 In cbr1.Controls
            Debug.Print cbr1.Name, ctl1.Caption
        Next ctl1
    End If
Next cbr1

End Sub
```

Listing Menu Commands

Finally, you might need to list the individual commands on a menu within a *CommandBar* object. This involves treating the menu as a command bar so that the commands expose themselves as controls. You can determine the name for a command bar representing a menu using the *EnumerateControlCaptions* procedure (or a variation of it). Ignore the ampersands (&) in a caption when specifying the command bar's name for a menu. The following pair of procedures loop through the controls on a menu. The first procedure passes a command bar name to the second procedure, which loops through the controls for that command bar. Note that the command bar's name is Help, although its caption is &Help.

```
Sub ListCommands()
EnumerateCommandsOnMenu ("Help")
End Sub

Sub EnumerateCommandsOnMenu(menuName)
Dim cbr1 As CommandBar
Dim ctl1 As CommandBarControl

'Set a reference to a command bar
Set cbr1 = CommandBars(menuName)

'Loop through the controls for that command bar
For Each ctl1 In cbr1.Controls
    Debug.Print ctl1.Caption
Next ctl1

End Sub
```

Disabling and Reenabling Command Bars and Their Controls

You can disable and restore entire command bars. The following two procedures disable the built-in menu bar (called Menu Bar) and then reenable it. To make this command bar inoperable on a form, you simply set its *Enable* property to *False* within a form event procedure. Your applications can condition the disabling of a command bar on various factors, such as a user ID.

```
Sub DisableMenuBar()
Dim cbr1 As CommandBar

For Each cbr1 In CommandBars
    If cbr1.Name = "Menu Bar" Then
        cbr1.Enabled = False
    End If
Next cbr1

End Sub

Sub EnableMenuBar()
Dim cbr1 As CommandBar

For Each cbr1 In CommandBars
    If cbr1.Name = "Menu Bar" Then
        cbr1.Enabled = True
    End If
Next cbr1

End Sub
```

You can also disable individual commands on a menu bar or toolbar. The first procedure in the following pair disables the View command on the Menu Bar menu bar and the Form View toolbar. This helps to secure a form's design by removing two familiar routes for switching from Form view to Design view. In addition to disabling the View control, the first procedure protects the change by setting the command bar's *Protection* property to *msoBarNoCustomize*. This setting dims the Reset button in the Customize dialog box for the Menu Bar and Form View command bars. The second procedure reenables the commands on both command bars and clears protection by setting the command bar *Protection* property to 0.

```
Sub DisableViewMenuAndControl()
Dim ctl1 As CommandBarControl

'Disable and protect View menu
Set ctl1 = CommandBars("Menu Bar").Controls("View")
ctl1.Enabled = False
CommandBars("Menu Bar").Protection = msoBarNoCustomize
```

(continued)

```
'Disable and protect View control
Set ctl1 = CommandBars("Form View").Controls("View")
ctl1.Enabled = False
CommandBars("Form View").Protection = msoBarNoCustomize

End Sub

Sub EnableViewMenuAndControl()
Dim ctl1 As CommandBarControl

'Enable View menu
Set ctl1 = CommandBars("Menu Bar").Controls("View")
ctl1.Enabled = True
CommandBars("Menu Bar").Protection = 0

'Enable View control
Set ctl1 = CommandBars("Form View").Controls("View")
ctl1.Enabled = True
CommandBars("Form View").Protection = 0

End Sub
```

Making Invisible Command Bars Visible

Another simple but powerful manipulation you can perform is to expose a built-in menu that does not normally appear. The following procedure displays the name, type, and number of controls on each visible command bar. If the Web toolbar is not visible, the procedure resets its *Visible* property and leaves a record of it in the Immediate window by printing its name, type, and control count. You can make the Web toolbar disappear by resetting its *Visible* property to *False*.

```
Sub ShowWebBar()
Dim cbr1 As CommandBar

    For Each cbr1 In CommandBars
        If cbr1.Visible = True Then
            Debug.Print cbr1.Name, cbr1.Type, cbr1.Controls.Count
        ElseIf cbr1.Name = "Web" Then
            cbr1.Visible = True
            Debug.Print cbr1.Name, cbr1.Type, cbr1.Controls.Count
        End If
    Next cbr1

End Sub
```

> **Note**   The Chapter08.mdb file in the companion materials for this book includes a procedure named *HideWebBar*. This procedure makes the Web toolbar invisible again. With a collection of simple procedures like those discussed throughout the *"CommandBar* Object" section, you can build your own interface for managing built-in and custom command bars. This allows for tighter limits on user capabilities than the built-in toolbar management tools allow. If you want to secure changes to the *CommandBars* collection, you will almost surely enable manipulation of the toolbars through your own interface, which issues a subset of the built-in commands available from it.

Securing an Application by Programming Command Bars

Earlier in this chapter, I presented an example containing a custom startup form. This approach suppresses the appearance of the Database window. However, a user can easily show the Database window by using the Unhide command on the Window menu. This next sample demonstrates the code for making the Unhide command unavailable as a menu selection and preventing a user from reversing the process.

The *NoHideUnhideToolbars* procedure that follows has two parts. First, it iterates through the controls on the Window menu of the menu bar. The procedure assigns *False* to the *Enabled* and *Visible* properties of controls with the captions "&Hide" or "&Unhide…". This essentially makes the controls unavailable. If we were to stop here, the user could simply choose View, Toolbars, Customize, and then expose the command again through the Customize dialog box. Although it's possible to lock the changes to a command bar by setting its *Protection* property, you might want to remove the ability of end users to invoke the Customize dialog box from the View, Toolbars menu or any shortcut menu. The *DisableCustomize* property of the *CommandBars* collection enables you to do this. Simply set the property to *True* to prevent end users from opening the Customize dialog box from any menu. By calling the *NoHideUnhide* procedure from a custom startup form, you make the Hide and Unhide commands on the Window menu unavailable and you block end users from changing your settings. This can effectively lock users out of the Database window when you use it in combination with a custom startup technique.

```
Sub NoHideUnhide()
Dim cbr1 As CommandBar
Dim ctl1 As CommandBarControl
```

(continued)

```
'Disable and make invisible Hide and Unhide
'commands on the Window menu
Set cbr1 = CommandBars("Window")
For Each ctl1 In cbr1.Controls
    If ctl1.Caption = "&Hide" Or _
        ctl1.Caption = "&Unhide..." Then
        ctl1.Enabled = False
        ctl1.Visible = False
    End If
Next ctl1

'Disable ability to open Customize dialog box
Application.CommandBars.DisableCustomize = True

End Sub
```

> **Note**   The Chapter08.mdb file includes a utility procedure for making the Hide and Unhide commands available again on the Window menu as well as for restoring the ability to open the Customize dialog box. In addition, another procedure named *HideDBWindowAtStartupinMDB2* illustrates how to call the *NoHideUnhide* procedure while presenting a custom startup form. The *HideDBWindowAtStartupinMDB2* utility application in Chapter08.mdb effectively presents a custom form at startup while disabling the ability of users to get to the Database window through the Window, Unhide menu item.

Adding Commands to Built-In Command Bars

Besides manipulating built-in members of the *CommandBars* collection, you can add custom commands to any built-in toolbar. One simple way to do this is to add a *CommandBarButton* object. You must know the precise name of a command bar to add a new button to it with the *Add* method. (Recall that you can run the *EnumerateControlCaptions* procedure to list the command bar names.) After adding the button, you set properties for the new *CommandBar-Button* object so that it points at a custom procedure or function.

The *NewMenuItem* procedure and three related procedures shown next add new menu items to the Tools menu. The *NewMenuItem* procedure adds *CommandBarButton* objects to the end of a Tools command bar. The three related procedures let users specify whether the assistant appears as Clippit, Rocky, or F1. The new *CommandBarButton* objects let users invoke the procedures that control which assistant to display. Whether you like the assistant or not is immaterial. The menu commands in the sample perform a simple task that you can readily verify (by showing the assistant). The point of the sample is to demonstrate that you can add a custom menu item to any menu. In addition, you can implement a new menu item with any procedure.

```
Sub NewMenuItem()
Dim newItem As CommandBarButton

'Set reference to new control on the Tools command bar
Set newItem = CommandBars("Tools").Controls. _
    Add(Type:=msoControlButton)
'Start new group with command to invoke showClippit
With newItem
    .BeginGroup = True
    .Caption = "Show Clippit"
    .OnAction = "ShowClippit"
End With

'Set reference to new control on the Tools command bar
Set newItem = CommandBars("Tools").Controls. _
    Add(Type:=msoControlButton)
'Assign command to invoke showRocky
With newItem
    .Caption = "Show Rocky"
    .OnAction = "ShowRocky"
End With

'Set reference to new control on the Tools command bar
Set newItem = CommandBars("Tools").Controls. _
    Add(Type:=msoControlButton)
'Assign command to invoke showRocky
With newItem
    .Caption = "Show F1"
    .OnAction = "ShowF1"
End With

End Sub

Sub ShowRocky()

With Assistant
    .Visible = True
    .FileName = "Rocky.acs"
    .On = True
End With

End Sub

Sub ShowClippit()
```

(continued)

```
With Assistant
    .Visible = True
    .FileName = "Clippit.acs"
    .On = True
End With

End Sub

Sub ShowF1()

With Assistant
    .Visible = True
    .FileName = "F1.acs"
    .On = True
End With

End Sub
```

You use the *Add* method for the *Controls* collection of a command bar to insert a new control on a built-in menu. This method takes several arguments, including a *Type* parameter. In addition to the button control (*msoControlButton*) in the sample, you can specify a simple text box (*msoConrolEdit*), a combo box (*msoControlComboBox*), and more. By default, the *Add* method inserts your new control at the end of a command bar, but you can override this feature so that the control appears elsewhere on the command bar. Another parameter, *ID*, facilitates the addition of built-in commands relative to other menus on your customized command bar.

After adding a control to a built-in command bar, you can tie it to a custom function using the *OnAction* property. You set the property's value equal to the name of a procedure you want your new control to invoke. The control's *Caption* property offers an easy way to label the new control. You can use the *CopyFace* and *PasteFace* methods to mark your custom controls. When the *BeginGroup* property is set to *True*, a control appears on a command bar with a divider line before it. The sample sets this property to *True* for the first of the three custom controls, but it leaves it at the default value of *False* for the remaining two controls.

As you refine custom applications, you'll sometimes want to remove custom controls on built-in menus. You can do this using the *Reset* method. The following procedure clears any custom controls on the Tools command bar:

```
Sub removeMenuItem()
CommandBars("Tools").Reset
End Sub
```

Creating Custom Command Bars

Creating a custom command bar involves at least three steps:

1. Adding a new command bar to your application. It will be blank when your code initially inserts it.

2. Positioning controls on the command bar. This is similar to placing controls on a built-in command bar.

3. Setting the *Visible* property of the command bar to *True* when you want to show it. You can also let users expose your custom command bar using standard features (such as the Customize dialog box).

The following two procedures add a custom command bar with a single button control to make Rocky appear as the assistant. The *NewCommand-BarAndButton* procedure passes off the first two steps of creating command bars to the procedure *AddShowAssistantsAndRocky*. Placing these steps in a separate procedure has advantages for a subsequent sample. The *AddShowAssistants-AndRocky* procedure names the new custom command bar Show Assistants. Next, the procedure adds a custom control. When you specify controls for custom command bars, you must assign a value to the *Style* property as well as to the other properties that you set with built-in command bars. Failing to do so in the procedure *AddShowAssistantsAndRocky* can cause the button on the command bar to appear blank.

```
Sub NewCommandBarAndButton()
On Error GoTo CBarBtnTrap
Dim cbr1 As CommandBar
Dim cbr1btn1 As CommandBarButton
Dim cbr1Name As String

'Add command bar to show Rocky
AddShowAssistantsAndRocky

'Make command bar visible
Set cbr1 = CommandBars("Show Assistants")
cbr1.Visible = True

CBarBtnExit:
Exit Sub

CBarBtnTrap:
Debug.Print Err.Number; Err.Description
Resume CBarBtnExit

End Sub

Sub AddShowAssistantsAndRocky()
Dim cbr1 As CommandBar
Dim cbr1btn1 As CommandBarButton
```

(continued)

```
'Add a command bar named Show Assistants
Set cbr1 = CommandBars.Add("Show Assistants", _
    msoBarTop, , True)

'Add a button control to the command bar
Set cbr1btn1 = cbr1.Controls _
    .Add(msoControlButton, , , , True)
'Set button properties
With cbr1btn1
    .Caption = "Show Rocky"
    .BeginGroup = True
    .OnAction = "ShowRocky"
    .Style = msoButtonCaption
End With

End Sub
```

After the *NewCommandBarAndButton* procedure regains control, it sets the control's *Visible* property to *True*. Without this step, the only way a user can view the new custom command bar is by explicitly showing it (for instance, by right-clicking a command bar and selecting the name of the command bar you want to show). The error-trapping logic in the *NewCommandBarAndButton* procedure allows the application to invoke the procedure even when the command bar is already present. Without the error-trapping logic, the *addShowAssistantsAndRocky* procedure generates a fatal error when it tries to add a command bar that already exists. Because this error is not critical—after all, the command bar is there already—it's reasonable to ignore it.

Modifying Custom Command Bars

The following three procedures add new controls to an existing custom command bar. They also reveal another approach to handling the problem of an existing command bar. The *AddCbrBtns* procedure inserts another pair of buttons on the Show Assistants command bar created in the previous sample. If that command bar does not already exist, this procedure is smart enough to run the *AddShowAssistantsAndRocky* procedure. *AddCbrBtns* conditionally calls the procedure that creates the Show Assistants command bar based on the return value of the *DoesCbrExist* function procedure. This function procedure checks for the existence of a command bar. Whether or not the Show Assistants command bar exists, the initial *If...Then...Else* statement sets a reference to it. The rest of the procedure adds two more buttons to the command bar. *AddCbrBtns* closes by making the command bar visible if it isn't already.

```
Sub MoreButtons()
    AddCbrBtns "Show Assistants"
```

```
End Sub

Sub AddCbrBtns(cbrName As String)
Dim cbr1 As CommandBar
Dim cbr1btn1 As CommandBarButton

'Optionally create Show Assistants command bar.
'Reference it with a variable.
If Not doesCbrExist(cbrName) Then
    AddShowAssistantsAndRocky
    Set cbr1 = CommandBars(cbrName)
Else
    Set cbr1 = CommandBars(cbrName)
End If

'Add a new button to Show Assistants command bar
Set cbr1btn1 = cbr1.Controls _
    .Add(msoControlButton, , , , True)
'Set properties for button to show Clippit
With cbr1btn1
    .Caption = "Show Clippit"
    .OnAction = "ShowClippit"
    .Style = msoButtonCaption
End With

'Add a new button to Show Assistants command bar
Set cbr1btn1 = cbr1.Controls _
    .Add(msoControlButton, , , , True)
'Set properties for button to show F1
With cbr1btn1
    .Caption = "Show F1"
    .OnAction = "ShowF1"
    .Style = msoButtonCaption
End With

'Make the Show Assistants command bar visible
If Not cbr1.Visible = True Then cbr1.Visible = True

End Sub

Function doesCbrExist(cbrName As String) As Boolean
Dim cbr1 As CommandBar

doesCbrExist = False
For Each cbr1 In CommandBars
    If cbr1.Name = cbrName Then
        doesCbrExist = True
    End If
Next cbr1

End Function
```

Creating Popup Command Bars

The first sample procedure that follows enables a combo box control on a custom command bar and makes the command bar a popup menu bar. Figure 8-7 shows the behavior of the popup menu bar on a form. You click anywhere on the form to bring up a custom command bar with a single control. This control is a combo box with entries for selecting the Clippit, Rocky, or F1 assistant. The process starts with a click event for the form's Detail section. The next three procedures implement the sample depicted in Figure 8-7.

Figure 8-7 A custom popup menu bar with a combo box control. You click anywhere on the form to open the custom menu bar.

```
'From module behind form with popup toolbar
Private Sub Detail_Click()
    ShowAndProcessComboBox
End Sub

'From standard module in Access database file
'with form containing popup toolbar
Sub ShowAndProcessComboBox()
Dim cbr1 As CommandBar
```

```
'Call from click event in form

    If doesCbrExist("Custom1") Then
        CommandBars("Custom1").ShowPopup
    Else
        CreateAndShowPopUpMenu
    End If

End Sub

Sub CreateAndShowPopUpMenu()
Dim cbr1 As CommandBar

'Add command bar named Custom1
    Set cbr1 = CommandBars _
        .Add(Name:="Custom1", Position:=msoBarPopup, Temporary:=True)

    With cbr1
        .Controls.Add Type:=msoControlComboBox
        With .Controls(1)
            .Style = msoComboLabel
            .Caption = "Pick an Assistant."
            .AddItem "Show Clippit"
            .AddItem "Show Rocky"
            .AddItem "Show F1"
            .OnAction = "processComboBoxChoice"
        End With
    End With

    cbr1.ShowPopup

End Sub

Sub ProcessComboBoxChoice()

'Decode selected item and implement corresponding method
    Select Case _
        CommandBars("custom1").Controls(1).ListIndex
        Case 1
            ShowClippit
        Case 2
            ShowRocky
        Case 3
            ShowF1
    End Select

End Sub
```

The first procedure is the event procedure behind the form. It calls *ShowAndProcessComboBox*, a procedure that resides in a standard module. This procedure determines whether the Custom1 command bar already exists. If the command bar exists, the procedure invokes the *ShowPopup* method to display the command bar as a popup menu bar. Otherwise, it creates the Custom1 command bar with a call to *CreateAndShowPopUpMenu*. As the name of this third procedure implies, it creates the custom command bar just before displaying it as a popup menu bar. The *CreateAndShowPopUpMenu* procedure is compact, but it uses interesting techniques. First, it contains nested *With…End With* statements. The outer statement adds a new member to the *CommandBars* collection, and the inner one adds a control to that member. The property assignments within the inner *With…End With* statement specify a combo box style for the control, define the elements in the combo box list, and denote a procedure, *ProcessComboBoxChoice*, that fires after a selection from the combo box. This final procedure uses a *Select Case* statement based on the selected element from the combo box list to invoke one of three custom procedures that display an assistant.

Deleting Custom Command Bars

If you build custom command bars, you'll eventually need to remove one or more of them within an application. The following sample does this by looping through all the command bars to find the custom ones—those with a *BuiltIn* property of *False*. When the procedure finds a custom command bar, it asks the user whether it should delete the command bar. If the user replies Yes, the procedure deletes that command bar and adds one to the count of deleted command bars. In any event, the procedure increments a variable that tallies custom command bars.

```
Sub DeleteCustomCbr()
Dim cbr1 As CommandBar, delFlag As Boolean
Dim delBars As Integer, cusBars As Integer

'Not necessary to initialize delFlag, delBars, or
'cusBars because their default values (False and 0)
'are OK

'Conditionally delete custom menu bars
    For Each cbr1 In CommandBars
        If (cbr1.BuiltIn = False) Then
            If MsgBox("Are you sure that you want to " & _
```

```
                    "delete the " & cbr1.Name & " command bar?", _
                    vbYesNo, _
                    "Programming Microsoft Access 2003") = _
                        vbYes Then
                        cbr1.Delete
                        delFlag = True
                        delBars = delBars + 1
                End If
                cusBars = cusBars + 1
            End If
        Next cbr1

'Report outcome of command bar enumeration
    If Not delFlag Then
        If cusBars > 0 Then
            MsgBox "No custom command bars deleted " & _
                "out of a total of " & cusBars & ".", _
                vbInformation, _
                "Programming Microsoft Access 2003"
        Else
            MsgBox "No custom command bars.", vbInformation, _
                "Programming Microsoft Access 2003"
        End If
    Else
        MsgBox delBars & " custom command bar(s) deleted.", _
            vbInformation, _
            "Programming Microsoft Access 2003"
    End If

End Sub
```

The *DeleteCustomCbr* procedure closes by presenting one of three possible statements based on the number of deletions and the number of custom command bars. A pair of nested *If…Then…Else* statements handles the routing to the correct message box statement. If there are no deletions but at least one custom command bar, the statement displays a message reporting that no custom command bars were deleted and showing the total number of custom command bars. If there are no deletions and no custom command bars, the procedure presents a message to that effect. Finally, if the procedure deleted any command bars, the message box reports that number.

Summary

This chapter covers three main topics and provides bonus content outside the textbook through a module (AssistantModule) in the Chapter08.mdb file and an excerpt from a prior version of this book (*www.programmingmsaccess.com /ForA2002/AssistantObject.htm*). The three main topics covered in the chapter are an overview and comparison of *DocumentProperty*, *CurrentDB*, and *Current-Project* objects, an examination of the *FileSearch* object, and a careful review of the *CommandBar* object model. All three of these topics are rich in code samples for performing typical chores that you are likely to require in the applications that you build.

The highlight of the first section are two samples that show how to present a custom form instead of the Database window. These two samples are special because they essentially lock out the ability of the user to override the custom start with any special keys. In addition, the process is different in important ways for .mdb files versus .adp files. Therefore, the chapter presents a separate sample for each type of file. The *CommandBar* object model discussion revisits the topic to show how to make unavailable menu options that would allow users to bypass the custom form to get to the Database window.

The *FileSearch* object is a programmatic interface to the File Search capability in Office. You can manually access this capability from the Database toolbar in Access; its default control position is the fourth control from the left. The programming samples in this section illustrate the basics along with a couple of tips for optimizing programmatic searches. In addition, one sample demonstrates how to design a custom form that enables custom file searches. This design approach permits your applications to offer an alternative to the built-in File Search interface. The section closes with several samples that go beyond the *FileSearch* object. One sample illustrates how to apply *FileSystemObject* to develop a utility application for copying any file from one location to another on a LAN. The last two applications in the section demonstrate how to modify the Task Pane with links for creating files and opening files.

The closing section drills down on the *CommandBars* object model. The section commences by introducing the basics of object enumeration for command bars, menus, and menu items. Next, it presents how to modify the built-in commands by adding and making unavailable *CommandBar* and *Command-BarControl* objects. The chapter closes with a series of samples that demonstrates different approaches to building custom *CommandBar* objects and populating them with *CommandBarControl* objects.

9

Integrating Access with Other Office Applications

The Microsoft Access user interface shares many elements with the user interfaces of the other Office applications, and it's relatively easy to transfer data between Access and the other Office components. In addition, Access can be integrated with the other Office components in custom applications, which allows you to combine the strengths of a database package with the familiar and friendly environment of word processor and spreadsheet programs.

This chapter explains how to programmatically integrate Access 2003 with the other Office 2003 applications using built-in Access features. For instance, your applications can tap installable indexed sequential access method (ISAM) drivers through the *Connection* object to work with the data in a Microsoft Excel spreadsheet. A *Connection* object based on an ISAM driver can serve as a two-way data-sharing channel between Access and Excel. An ISAM driver also enables Access developers to build solutions that retrieve data from Microsoft Outlook.

Furthermore, you can tap Access data sources programmatically with the Microsoft Word mail merge capability to facilitate creation of mailing labels, form letters, and product catalogs. Developers familiar with programming conventions for Word's rich formatting options can employ Word as a reporting vehicle for data otherwise managed by Access.

Using Automation, your applications can exploit the object model from one application with a solution created in another application. Access developers can take advantage of Automation and extend the capabilities of their solutions by tapping the object model of other Office packages. For example, an Access application can export names and addresses from an Access data store to an Outlook Contacts folder. Similarly, you can populate values to tables in a

Word document from an Access data source. The samples in this chapter focus on the interoperability of Access with Excel, Outlook, and Word, but the general principles extend to Office applications as well as third-party packages that expose their object models through Automation and that enable manipulation using Microsoft Visual Basic for Applications (VBA).

Linking Access to Other Office Applications

This section introduces three techniques for making Access work with other Office applications: using installable ISAM drivers, employing the *OpenData-Source* method of the *MailMerge* object, and implementing Automation. Subsequent sections will apply these techniques in practical contexts.

Installable ISAM Drivers

You use the familiar Microsoft ActiveX Data Objects (ADO) *Connection* object to link to other data sources through installable ISAM drivers. These data sources can include non-Jet, non-ODBC data sources such as Excel, dBASE, and Paradox. This section will demonstrate how Access developers can use the Excel ISAM driver for linking to Excel workbooks and the Outlook ISAM driver for linking to Outlook folders. Similar techniques apply to ISAM drivers for dBASE, Paradox, Lotus 1-2-3, text, and HTML files, but each driver has its unique features and restrictions.

> **Note**   Installable ISAM support continues to change with user requirements and technology developments. ISAM support for Microsoft FoxPro databases was discontinued with Access 2000 in favor of the Microsoft ODBC FoxPro driver. The traditional ISAM drivers still provide import/export/read access for dBASE and Paradox data in version 5 and earlier. If you need read-write access to these versions of dBASE and Paradox files, you must independently acquire the Borland Database Engine through Inprise Inc. or verify the installation of Jet 4.0 SP5. See Microsoft Knowledge Base article 230125 for additional details. You can find any Knowledge Base article by going to *http://support.microsoft.com* and searching for its article number.

Using ISAM Drivers with Excel

When you use an ISAM driver, your connection string has three arguments, each of which must terminate with a semicolon. First you designate a provider.

When you use an installable ISAM driver, start your connection string with a reference to the Jet 4.0 provider. Follow this reference with a specification that points at the file for the data source. In the case of Excel, this specification includes the drive, path, and filename. In certain other cases, you can designate just the drive and the path. You designate the final parameter by setting the extended properties parameter equal to the name of the ISAM driver. There are specific drivers for different versions of Excel and for the other types of data sources you can link to. You reference any recent version of an Excel workbook (from Excel 97 through Excel 2003) using the string "*Excel 8.0*" followed by a semicolon.

The following simple sample uses an ISAM driver to link to an Excel 2003 workbook in an Access 2003 application. The *Dim* statement declares and creates a new *Connection* object. The next statement opens the connection by pointing it at an Excel workbook through the Excel 8.0 ISAM driver. After creating the connection to the data source, your application must specify a range of cells in the workbook. This sample assigns the customers range within the file to a *Recordset* object named *rst1*. Access uses this link to work with the data in the workbook. The sample concludes by printing the first two columns of the first row from the range in the Excel workbook to the Immediate window in Access.

```
Sub Connect2XLPrintFromFirst()
Dim cnn1 As New ADODB.Connection, rst1 As ADODB.Recordset

'Make connection to Excel source
cnn1.Open "Provider=Microsoft.Jet.OLEDB.4.0;" & _
    "Data Source=C:\Access2003Files\Customers.xls;" & _
    "Extended Properties=Excel 8.0;"

'Open read-only recordset based on Excel source
Set rst1 = New ADODB.Recordset
rst1.CursorType = adOpenForwardOnly
rst1.LockType = adLockReadOnly
rst1.Open "customers", cnn1, , , adCmdTable

'Print selected fields from first record
Debug.Print rst1.Fields(0).Value, rst1.Fields(1).Value

'Close connection to source
cnn1.Close

End Sub
```

When you work with an ISAM driver, the Excel data source (or even Excel itself) need not be open. Your application also doesn't require a reference to the Excel object model. Despite the Excel ISAM driver's minimal requirements, you can use it to both read and update Excel data sources.

Using ISAM Drivers with Outlook

You can use ISAM drivers to examine the contents of Outlook folders on the current machine from within Access. With this approach, you can read but not update the contents of Outlook folders through an ADO object, such as a recordset. A SQL *SELECT* statement can serve as the source for the *Recordset* object, and the recordset can reference the *CurrentProject* object's connection. No matter which cursor settings you assign the recordset, it will not let you update Outlook folder items.

The SQL string that serves as the source for the recordset requires three elements. First, you must designate a collection of columns to extract from the folder record source. Precede the string specifying the columns you want with the *SELECT* keyword. You can use an asterisk (*), but performance will be faster if you designate a specific subset of columns. Second, you must designate a folder name and a path to Outlook. Preface the folder name with the *FROM* keyword. For example, if you want incoming messages, reference the Inbox folder. Third, you need to specify a path name and an Outlook ISAM driver name. Designate the name for the top-level Outlook folder. (Unless you change the default, this is the Personal Folders collection.) Identify the start of the third element with the *IN* keyword.

The following sample prints the first record in the Contacts folder of Outlook's Personal Folders collection. Use the Outlook 9.0 ISAM driver for Outlook 2003, Outlook 2002, or Outlook 2000. The sample extracts the *First*, *Last*, and *E-mail Address* fields from the Contacts folder. Although you cannot update Outlook through the Outlook ISAM driver, you can view changes (such as updated values) to the underlying recordset.

You will get the same results if you use either of the two paths that you can reference by setting your compiler constant to *True* or *False*. On the system that I am running, the E:\ folder points at a CD drive. Demonstrating this capability confirms that it doesn't matter what path you specify, so long as you designate a path.

```
Sub Connect2OutlookPrintFromFirst()
Dim rst1 As ADODB.Recordset
#Const AnyPath = False

'Instantiate recordset
Set rst1 = New ADODB.Recordset

'Open recordset on Contacts folder with either of
'two path designations
#If AnyPath = False Then
    rst1.Open "SELECT First, Last, [Email Address] " & _
```

```
          "FROM Contacts IN 'C:\Windows\Temp\;'" & _
          "[Outlook 9.0;MAPILEVEL=Personal Folders|;];", _
          CurrentProject.Connection
#Else
      rst1.Open "SELECT First, Last, [Email Address] " & _
          "FROM Contacts IN 'E:\;'" & _
          "[Outlook 9.0;MAPILEVEL=Personal Folders|;];", _
          CurrentProject.Connection
#End If

'Print first row of Contacts folder
Debug.Print rst1(0), rst1(1), rst1(2)

'Clean up objects
rst1.Close
Set rst1 = Nothing

End Sub
```

The *OpenDataSource* Method

You can use the *OpenDataSource* method of the *MailMerge* object to link to an Access data source from within a Word application. You use Access—or more specifically, Jet—as a data store for mail merge applications that create mailing labels, form letters, product catalogs, and so on. While Access can do some of this through its *Report* object, Word is a more natural environment for composing content. It also has excellent text-formatting tools and WYSIWYG features that the Access *Report* object does not have (see Chapter 6 for more information on the *Report* object). You can tap these resources with Word-based VBA procedures, as well as through Automation from within Access.

> **Note**   The most appropriate development environment for database reports and mail merge documents might be a matter of developer preference. Although Word is a more natural environment for developing text documents, using Word from Access requires Automation. This means that a developer has to program two object models and that a computer needs to manage two Office applications. You might be able to achieve greater efficiency for sets of standard messages sent regularly in large volumes by building solutions entirely within Access. Refer to Chapter 6 for sample reports that illustrate the options available from Access.

When you reference an Access data source using the *OpenDataSource* method, you must first reference a Word document file and the Word *MailMerge* object. You specify two parameters for the method with Access: the *Name* parameter, which indicates the drive, path, and filename for the Access data source; and the *Connection* parameter, which designates either a Table or Query data source type, and the name of the Access database object. Your Word document must have either bookmarks or mail merge fields that point to the fields in the Jet database. You invoke the *Execute* method for the *MailMerge* object to launch a merge that pulls data from a designated data source, such as an Access table, into a Word document.

You can filter values that appear in a Word mail merge document in several ways. For example, you can use the *OpenDataSource* method's *SQLStatement* parameter to specify which records to extract from a data source. When you do this with a Jet data source, you reference Access through an ODBC driver and specify *constr* as the *Connection* setting. You use SQL statement syntax to filter records from an Access table or query.

A second approach to filtering is to use a special query within a Word macro that you activate from Access. The *OpenDataSource* method's *Connect* parameter merely references that query. You use the *FirstRecord* and *Last-Record* properties of the *MailMergeDataSource* object to specify the first and last records to appear in a merged Word document. The *MailMergeDataSource* object points to a target specified by the *OpenDataSource* method.

Automation

Using Automation, you can enable one application to control another. Component Object Model (COM) defines the protocol for this capability. The controlling application interacts with the controlled application by manipulating its exposed properties and methods and responding to its events. To do this, the controlling application must have a reference to the other application's object library and must create an instance of that application. (See Chapter 8 for instruction on how to create and manage references programmatically.) The controlling application invokes methods and assigns property values through that instance of the controlled application.

Figure 9-1 shows a References dialog box from an Access application with references to Excel, Outlook, and Word as well as the Office library with the shared object models. In a sense, Automation makes all the Office component object models shared. Access can expose its object model as an Automation server, and it can tap the object models of other applications by acting as an Automation client.

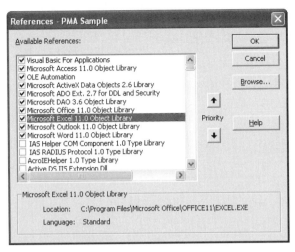

Figure 9-1   A References dialog box in Access showing references to Excel, Outlook, and Word.

CreateObject vs. *GetObject*

You use the *CreateObject* and *GetObject* functions to generate instances of other applications. You use *GetObject* to determine whether an instance of an application is already open. If it is, you can create a reference to it. If a user is not actively working with the instance, using an open instance might be acceptable. If the Automation server application is not already open or if you prefer not to use an open instance, you can use the *CreateObject* function to create a new instance of an application. You can also use *GetObject* to open an instance of an application with a particular file open in it.

The following two procedures create an instance of Excel from within an Access application. The second procedure, *IsAppThere*, uses late binding to test for an instance of any Office application. An *objApp* variable with a generic *Object* declaration can represent any Office application (or even another COM object). The first procedure, *XLThere*, uses early binding to designate a pointer for an Excel instance. If the application creates a new instance of Excel, the instance lasts only as long as the application. If the application uses an existing instance of Excel (for example, one based on an open version of the Customers.xls file), then the instance can have a scope beyond the application. The option pursued depends on how a user responds to a prompt from the application. One response to the prompt closes the Excel session pointed at by *xlApp* whether or not the application opened the session.

The *xlApp* variable can only represent an Excel *Application* object, because its declaration uses early binding. You cannot replace *Excel.Application* in either the *CreateObject* or *GetObject* functions with another Office *Application* object, such as *Word.Application*. However, you can create another procedure altogether—for example, one named *WordThere*—that includes a variable declared as a *Word.Application* object type. This new procedure can reference the generic *IsAppThere* procedure in the same way as *XLThere*.

```
Sub XLThere()
Dim xlApp As Excel.Application

If IsAppThere("Excel.Application") = False Then
'If not, create a new instance
    Set xlApp = CreateObject("Excel.Application")
    xlApp.Visible = True
Else
'Otherwise, reference the existing instance
    Set xlApp = GetObject(, "Excel.Application")
End If

'If user wants instance closed, close application
'and set reference to Nothing
If MsgBox("Close XL ?", vbYesNo, _
    "Programming Microsoft Access 2003") = vbYes Then
    xlApp.Quit
    Set xlApp = Nothing
End If

End Sub

Function IsAppThere(appName) As Boolean
On Error Resume Next
Dim objApp As Object

IsAppThere = True

Set objApp = GetObject(, appName)
If Err.Number <> 0 Then IsAppThere = False

End Function
```

Automation does not normally make an Office application visible when opening it. If you want an application to display, you must normally set its *Visible* property to *True*. Different applications expose different objects for you to automate. Excel causes objects such as *Application*, *Workbook*, and *Worksheet* to display. The latter two, of course, are not available with other Office applications.

Closing an Automation Reference

The *XLThere* procedure conditionally disposes of a reference to another Office application. First, you close or quit the application. (Excel supports a *Quit* method.) Then, you set the reference to *Nothing*. Both steps are required to release the resources consumed by the Automation reference. As with many object references, *XLThere* closes the reference, but the application doesn't free the resource for the object reference until setting the reference to *Nothing*. Failing to set an object to *Nothing* can cause Windows to not release the resources for the object even when the object goes out of scope because a procedure ends. This is the worst of all possibilities. You do not have the resource available in your application, but Windows deprives your application of the resources allocated to the object instance.

Working with Excel from Access

The first two samples in this section demonstrate capabilities that the Excel installable ISAM can add to an application. The third sample shows a simple but powerful way to use Automation. Instead of directly manipulating detailed elements of the object model of an Automation server, the procedure launches a procedure within the Automation server. The second procedure in the Excel Automation server, in turn, updates the spreadsheet file, but at the time and in the manner that an Access application determines. The section closes with a fourth sample that enables navigation through Excel data with an Access form.

Working with Values from Excel Worksheets

All three samples work with the Excel workbook depicted in Figure 9-2. The file is MyGas.xls. The first four columns of Sheet1 contain manually entered data, and the next four columns contain expressions based on the first four. The formula bar shows the expression for the first value in the *MPG* (miles per gallon) column. The data resides in a range named gas. The Define Name dialog box shows the extent of the range in Sheet1. The sample application utilizes this named range. When you apply this model application to your data, you will need a corresponding range in your adaptation of the application.

> **Note**   The macro security level for the MyGas.xls file is set at Low. This setting is convenient for any .xls file in which you want to run macros via Automation from another application. From the Excel menu, choose Tools, Macros, Security to open the Security dialog box for macros. Select the Security level tab to expose the security settings. Then, choose High, Medium, or Low.

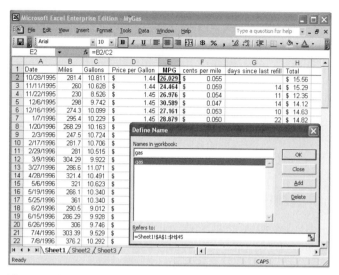

Figure 9-2 An Excel spreadsheet with a named range, Gas, extending over cells A1 through H45.

The first sample reads the entries from Excel, performs some calculations in Access, and prints the results to the Immediate window. After establishing a connection to the Excel data source, your application can programmatically treat the data source just like an internal Access table. For example, you can enumerate records in the table or compute values based on the entries in the record source. The sample prints to the Immediate window the existing entries in the Excel worksheet alongside the results of expressions computed in Access. This, incidentally, confirms that Access computations can generate results identical to those in Excel. This capability can reduce the amount of data that your application must read from a computationally intensive spreadsheet.

```
Sub OpenXLComputePrint()
Dim cnn1 As New ADODB.Connection
Dim rst1 As ADODB.Recordset
Dim computedMPG As Double
Dim computedTotal As Currency

'Make connection to Excel source
cnn1.Open "Provider=Microsoft.Jet.OLEDB.4.0;" & _
    "Data Source=C:\Access2003Files\Mygas.xls;" & _
    "Extended Properties=Excel 8.0;"

'Open read-only recordset based on Excel source.
'Recall default is read-only.
Set rst1 = New ADODB.Recordset
```

```
rst1.Open "gas", cnn1, , , adCmdTable

'Enumerate records and compute with field values
Do Until rst1.EOF
computedMPG = rst1.Fields("Miles") / _
    rst1.Fields("Gallons")
computedTotal = rst1.Fields("Gallons") * _
    rst1.Fields("Price per Gallon")
Debug.Print rst1.Fields("Date"), _
    rst1.Fields("Miles"), _
    rst1.Fields("Gallons"), _
    rst1.Fields("Price per Gallon"), _
    rst1.Fields("MPG"), computedMPG, _
    rst1.Fields("days since last refill"), _
    rst1.Fields("Total"), computedTotal
rst1.MoveNext
Loop

'Clean up objects
rst1.Close
Set rst1 = Nothing
cnn1.Close
Set cnn1 = Nothing

End Sub
```

The sub procedure declares and creates a new *Connection* object, and then it opens the *Connection* object. This is critical when you work with most ISAM drivers because this is how you manage your link to the data source outside of Access. The connection string points the object at the Excel file MyGas.xls. (Figure 9-2 displays an excerpt of the data from the workbook file.) You must conclude the connection string with an Extended Properties specification that points at the ISAM driver that your application uses. The sample uses the syntax for the Extended Properties specification (Excel 8.0) that works with Excel 2003 through Excel 97 workbook files.

The *Recordset* sample that follows illustrates another critical and relatively standard feature of ISAM applications. By defining a recordset on the connection, your application can gain the ability to read from and write to the remote data source. The ability to update data depends on the functionality available through the ISAM driver. If your Access application links to the Excel data source, you can use the *Recordset* object's *AddNew* and *Update* methods to add new rows to a worksheet from Access. The recordset specification must also designate which portion of the workbook to link. If you reference the gas range, the recordset can use the built-in range for the worksheet. The syntax for referencing an external Excel table is identical to that for referencing an internal Access table.

> **Note** If your application must write to or revise an Excel data source from Access, be sure to define a cursor that supports this functionality. (For example, pass the *adOpenKeyset* constant for the cursor type and the *adLockOptimistic* constant for the lock type.) Unlike Data Access Objects (DAO), the default ADO cursor does not support updating.

The next major element of the procedure is a *Do* loop that enumerates all the records in the gas range. The first two lines in the loop evaluate expressions for two computed values. The *computedMPG* and *computedTotal* variables compare Access to Excel arithmetic as they confirm your ability to read and manipulate data from an Excel data source. The next seven lines within the *Do* loop print to the Immediate window Excel table field values along with the two computed variables for each row. You navigate through an Excel table exactly as you do through an internal table. Of course, you must invoke a *MoveNext* method within the loop to progress through the spreadsheet rows.

Figure 9-3 shows the five rightmost columns of the output from the preceding sample. The first two columns show identical results for MPG from Excel (the first column) and Access (the second column). The same is true for the total gas bill for each gas fill-up. This confirms that the double and currency data types from Access can duplicate results from Excel.

26.0290444917214	26.0290444917214	Null	15.557	15.557
24.4636808430561	24.4636808430561	14	15.2937	15.2937
26.9763077644851	26.9763077644851	11	12.3542	12.3542
30.5892013960172	30.5892013960172	14	14.1162	14.1162
27.1611050599069	27.1611050599069	10	14.6335	14.6335
28.8786782676703	28.8786782676704	22	14.8218	14.8218
26.3987011709141	26.3987011709141	13	14.6246	14.6246
23.0790749720254	23.0790749720254	14	13.287	13.287
26.3123482159537	26.3123482159537	14	13.0506	13.0506
26.7237280076082	26.7237280076082	12	12.8178	12.8178
30.6682120540214	30.6682120540214	9	12.2934	12.2934
25.8874537078855	25.8874537078855	18	13.6063	13.6063
30.6357830521399	30.6357830521399	32	14.6769	14.6769
30.2174526969783	30.2174526969783	8	15.2865	15.2865
25.7350096711799	25.7350096711799	13	15.1895	15.1895
34.9129593810445	34.9129593810445	6	15.0861	15.0861
32.2347980470484	32.2347980470484	8	13.1485	13.1485
28.8366236905721	28.8366236905721	13	14.3857	14.3857
31.3974964087831	31.3974964087831	11	14.122	14.122
31.8385979641096	31.8385979641096	8	13.7122	13.7122

Figure 9-3 An excerpt from the output of the *OpenXLComputePrint* procedure. Notice the identical computational results from Access and Excel.

Dynamically Creating Access Tables Based on Excel Worksheets

The preceding sample exposes the values in a spreadsheet through a recordset. If your application must regularly work with the data in a spreadsheet, you can improve performance by copying the spreadsheet values to a local table within Access. In addition, an application can reduce its demand for connection resources by copying spreadsheet values to local tables when it requires simultaneous access to several different spreadsheet ranges. The following sample programmatically creates a table that has an index for a spreadsheet range and then populates the table with values from the range. Incidentally, the sample uses the Identity data type to specify the start and step values for the table's index field (*MyID*).

```
Sub CreateTableFromXL()
On Error GoTo createTableTrap
Dim cnn1 As ADODB.Connection
Dim cnn2 As New ADODB.Connection
Dim rst1 As ADODB.Recordset
Dim rst2 As ADODB.Recordset
Dim cat1 As ADOX.Catalog
Dim tbl1 As ADOX.Table
Dim pk1 As ADOX.Index
Dim strSQL As String

'Set Connection, Catalog, and Table objects
Set cnn1 = CurrentProject.Connection
Set cat1 = New ADOX.Catalog
cat1.ActiveConnection = cnn1
Set tbl1 = New ADOX.Table

'Define table named "gas" and append it
'to the Tables collection
With tbl1
    .Name = "gas"
    .Columns.Append "Date", adDate
    .Columns.Append "Miles", adDouble
    .Columns.Append "Gallons", adDouble
    .Columns.Append "PricePerGallon", adCurrency
End With
cat1.Tables.Append tbl1

strSQL = "ALTER TABLE Gas ADD COLUMN MyID Identity(2,2)"
cnn1.Execute strSQL

Set pk1 = New ADOX.Index
With pk1
    .Name = "MyPrimaryKey"
    .PrimaryKey = True
    .Unique = True
    .IndexNulls = adIndexNullsDisallow
End With
```

(continued)

```
pk1.Columns.Append "MyID"
tbl1.Indexes.Append pk1

'Make connection to Excel source
cnn2.Open "Provider=Microsoft.Jet.OLEDB.4.0;" & _
    "Data Source=C:\Access2003Files\MyGas.xls;" & _
    "Extended Properties=Excel 8.0;"

'Open read-only recordset based on Excel source.
'Recall default is read-only.
Set rst1 = New ADODB.Recordset
rst1.Open "gas", cnn2, , , adCmdTable


'Open read-write recordset based on local table
'named "gas"
Set rst2 = New ADODB.Recordset
rst2.ActiveConnection = cnn1
rst2.CursorType = adOpenKeyset
rst2.LockType = adLockOptimistic
rst2.Open "gas", cnn1, , , adCmdTable

Do Until rst1.EOF
    With rst2
        .AddNew
        .Fields("Date") = rst1.Fields("Date")
        .Fields("Miles") = rst1.Fields("Miles")
        .Fields("Gallons") = rst1.Fields("Gallons")
        .Fields("PricePerGallon") = _
            rst1.Fields("Price Per Gallon")
        .Update
    End With
    rst1.MoveNext
Loop

createTableExit:
Set pk1 = Nothing
Set tbl1 = Nothing
Set cat1 = Nothing
rst1.Close
rst2.Close
Set rst1 = Nothing
Set rst2 = Nothing
cnn1.Close
cnn2.Close
Set cnn1 = Nothing
Set cnn2 = Nothing
Exit Sub
```

```
createTableTrap:
If Err.Number = -2147217857 Then
'If the gas table already exists, delete it
    cat1.Tables.Delete "gas"
    Resume
Else
'Else print the Err object Number
'and Description properties
    Debug.Print Err.Number; Err.Description
End If

End Sub
```

The previous procedure is lengthy because it performs several discrete but related functions. To create a local table with Excel spreadsheet values, the sample needs a pair of *Connection* and *Recordset* objects. These objects provide simultaneous connectivity to the spreadsheet and the local table so that the procedure can copy a row from one data source to the other. To define a local table programmatically within Access, the code declares *Catalog*, *Table*, and *Index* objects.

Before copying the data from Excel, the procedure prepares a local table to accept them. It starts by assigning the connection for the current project to the cnn1 reference. Because *cnn1* refers to the native project connection, there is no need to include the *New* keyword in its declaration. On the other hand, the procedure does create new instances of the *Catalog* and *Table* objects (and their declarations reflect this by the inclusion of *New*). The procedure then uses ADO code to define and append fields for holding spreadsheet values. However, it reverts to SQL code for specifying the start and step values for the index. This capability depends completely on built-in Jet engine functionality. Therefore, the SQL code is specific to the Jet database engine. After completing the definition of the index and appending it to the table, the procedure opens a connection to the spreadsheet. (This sample uses the same spreadsheet as the preceding one.)

Any attempt to redefine an existing table generates error number –2147217857. In the event of such an error, the procedure deletes the old table and resumes adding the new table. In a full-scale application, you might want to archive the old table.

The procedure prepares for copying values by creating two *Recordset* objects—one for the spreadsheet and one for the local table. The code uses the default cursor for the spreadsheet because it just reads values sequentially from it, but it uses a keyset cursor type for the link to the local table so that it can add records. Because Access can exactly duplicate the computations of Excel, there is no need to copy computed fields. In addition, not copying computed fields keeps your table's field values independent of one another so that your table is normalized.

Running Excel Procedures from an Access Procedure

In the following procedure, *runXL*, Access uses the *GetObject* function to create an instance of the Excel *Application* object that contains the MyGas workbook shown in Figure 9-2. It sets the *Visible* property of the *Application* and *Window* objects to *True*. Then, it invokes the *Application* object's *Run* method for the *ComputeOnGas* procedure in the ThisWorkbook folder of the MyGas.xls file.

The security level for running Excel macros can be set with the steps described in a Note in the "Working with Values from Excel Worksheets" section of this chapter. The Security dialog box for macros in Excel permits you to choose High, Medium, or Low, depending on your needs and the policies of your organization. If the Medium security level is selected, you will see a prompt when you attempt to run a macro in a workbook file. Choose Enable Macros to run the *ComputeOnGas* procedure. If you select the Low security level (as I did for the MyGas.xls file), the macros behind the worksheet will run without a prompt. Do not run the procedure with the High security level selected because it will disable the code in the unsigned module within the workbook file.

After the *ComputeOnGas* procedure from the Excel file returns control to Access, the *runXL* procedure invokes the *Save* method for the *ActiveWorkbook* object in Excel. This commits the changes to storage and avoids a prompt asking whether to do so when the next line invokes the *Quit* method. If you want to close Excel without saving the changes and without a prompt that asks whether to save them, you set the workbook's *Saved* property to *True* before invoking the *Quit* method. (See the commented line for the correct syntax.) You retrieve the Automation resources by setting the Automation object reference to *Nothing*.

> **Note**   For your convenience when rerunning this sample, the .mdb file for this chapter includes a procedure called *RunRestoreXLSheet*. This procedure restores the MyGas.xls workbook to the state it was in prior to invoking *RunXL*.

```
Sub RunXL()
Dim myXLWrkBk As Excel.Workbook

'Open connection to XL workbook and make it visible
Set myXLWrkBk = GetObject("C:\Access2003Files\MyGas.xls")
myXLWrkBk.Application.Visible = True
myXLWrkBk.Application.Windows("MyGas.xls").Visible = True

'Run procedure in ThisWorkBook folder
myXLWrkBk.Application.Run "ThisWorkBook.computeOnGas"
```

```
'Close Automation object.
'Either invoke the Save method or set the Saved
'property to True to avoid a prompt about saving changes.
myXLWrkBk.Application.ActiveWorkbook.Save
'myXLWrkBk.Application.ActiveWorkbook.Saved = True
myXLWrkBk.Application.Quit
Set myXLWrkBk = Nothing

End Sub
```

Figure 9-4 shows the worksheet after *ComputeOnGas* runs. Notice that the worksheet computes summary information two rows below the table's last row, and it adds a new column that displays the miles traveled per day between refills. The procedure also resizes the columns so that they can contain their widest entry.

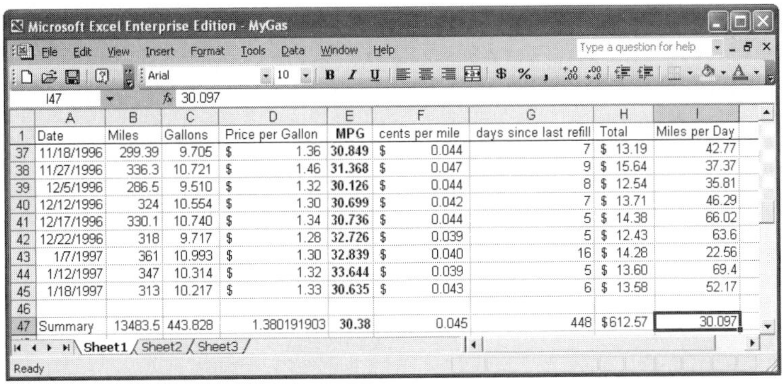

	A	B	C	D	E	F	G	H	I
1	Date	Miles	Gallons	Price per Gallon	MPG	cents per mile	days since last refill	Total	Miles per Day
37	11/18/1996	299.39	9.705	$ 1.36	30.849	$ 0.044	7	$ 13.19	42.77
38	11/27/1996	336.3	10.721	$ 1.46	31.368	$ 0.047	9	$ 15.64	37.37
39	12/5/1996	286.5	9.510	$ 1.32	30.126	$ 0.044	8	$ 12.54	35.81
40	12/12/1996	324	10.554	$ 1.30	30.699	$ 0.042	7	$ 13.71	46.29
41	12/17/1996	330.1	10.740	$ 1.34	30.736	$ 0.044	5	$ 14.38	66.02
42	12/22/1996	318	9.717	$ 1.28	32.726	$ 0.039	5	$ 12.43	63.6
43	1/7/1997	361	10.993	$ 1.30	32.839	$ 0.040	16	$ 14.28	22.56
44	1/12/1997	347	10.314	$ 1.32	33.644	$ 0.039	5	$ 13.60	69.4
45	1/18/1997	313	10.217	$ 1.33	30.635	$ 0.043	6	$ 13.58	52.17
46									
47	Summary	13483.5	443.828	1.380191903	30.38	0.045	448	$612.57	30.097

Figure 9-4 An excerpt from the output of the *ComputeOnGas* procedure. Notice the new column of data and the resized columns.

The *ComputeOnGas* procedure involves nothing more than standard VBA, but it uses objects, properties, and methods that are unique to Excel. When you perform Automation, you inevitably require some knowledge of at least one other object model—namely, the object model for the Office application that you're automating. One advantage of using the *Run* method, as in the *RunXL* procedure, is that it lets individual developers specialize in particular object models. When a developer wants to use a standard function in an unfamiliar application, he or she can copy a procedure designed by another developer. Even without detailed knowledge of an application, a developer can invoke the *Run* method for the copied procedure.

```
Sub ComputeOnGas()
Dim mySheet As Worksheet
Dim iRow As Integer, lastRow As Integer
Dim sumDays As Long

'Set reference to first worksheet
```

(continued)

```
    Set mySheet = Worksheets(1)
    With mySheet
        lastRow = Range("gas").Rows.Count

    'Assign column heading
        .Cells(1, 9) = "Miles per Day"

    'Compute miles per day
        For iRow = 3 To lastRow
            .Cells(iRow, 9) = _
                Format(Range("gas").Cells(iRow, 2) / _
                Range("gas").Cells(iRow, 7), _
                "0.##")
            sumDays = sumDays + .Cells(iRow, 7)
        Next iRow


    'Compute summary statistics
        .Cells(Range("gas").Rows.Count + 2, 1).Select
        ActiveCell.Formula = "Summary"
    'Compute total miles
        ActiveCell.Offset(0, 1).Activate
        ActiveCell.Formula = "=Sum(b2:b" & lastRow & ")" & ""
    'Compute total gallons
        ActiveCell.Offset(0, 1).Activate
        ActiveCell.Formula = "=Sum(c2:c" & lastRow & ")" & ""
    'Compute total gas dollars
        ActiveCell.Offset(0, 5).Activate
        ActiveCell.Formula = "=Sum(h2:h" & lastRow & ")" & ""
    'Compute days since last refill
        ActiveCell.Offset(0, -1).Activate
        ActiveCell.Formula = "=Sum(g3:g" & lastRow & ")" & ""
    'Compute price per gallon and format cell like column D
        .Cells(Range("gas").Rows.Count + 2, 4).Select
        ActiveCell.Formula = "=H" & (lastRow + 2) & "/C" & (lastRow + 2)
    'Compute miles per gallon
        ActiveCell.Offset(0, 1).Activate
        ActiveCell = Format(.Cells(lastRow + 2, 2) / _
            .Cells(lastRow + 2, 3), "0.###")
        ActiveCell.Font.Bold = True
    'Compute cents per mile
        ActiveCell.Offset(0, 1).Activate
        ActiveCell = Format(.Cells(lastRow + 2, 8) / _
            .Cells(lastRow + 2, 2), "0.###")
    'Compute miles per day
        ActiveCell.Offset(0, 3).Activate
        ActiveCell = Format(.Cells(lastRow + 2, 2) / sumDays, "0.###")
    End With
    'Resize columns to show values
    Worksheets("Sheet1").Columns("a:I").AutoFit

End Sub
```

Navigating Imported Excel Data with an Access Form

The ability to show Excel data in an Access form is a common request. This functionality enables spreadsheet analysts to work with data in Excel even while your application shows the same data within an Access form. Figure 9-5 shows an excerpt from Sheet1 in the Customers.xls file open above the frmCustomers form from the Chapter09.mdb file. The .xls and .mdb files are open concurrently. The workbook file shows the first customer selected. The Access form displays the same data from a concurrent Access session. The buttons below the text boxes enable an Access user to navigate backward and forward through the Excel data.

> **Note**   Figure 9-5 (on the next page) shows Excel opening Customers.xls, and then Access opening the frmCustomers form. Attempting to concurrently display data in Excel and Access applications by other methods can result in faulty displays.

The frmCustomers form is an unbound form that depends on an ISAM link to the Customers.xls file. The code behind the form enables three tasks. First, it populates the recordset and assigns the first row in the recordset to the text boxes on the form. Second, it permits clicks to the button with a right arrowhead to move forward through the data. Third, it permits clicks to the button with a left arrowhead to move backward through the data. The form has built-in intelligence to disable either arrowhead button when the action the button permits is not legitimate. The following listing shows the three event procedures that respond to the button clicks.

The *Form_Open* event procedure starts by creating a *Connection* object (*cnn1*) to the Excel workbook file (Customers.xls) and creating a *Recordset* object (*rst1*) based, in part, on *cnn1*. The first row of column values from *rst1* is copied to the *TextBox* controls on the form. Although *rst1* has a keyset cursor, the form does not enable an updated value in a text box to flow through to Sheet1 in Customers.xls. This capability depends on the state of the workbook file and additional code that you can add behind the form. Essentially, the code must implement any kind of database maintenance tasks that you decide to enable from the form. See the sample in the "Running Excel Procedures from an Access Procedure" section of this chapter for one approach to modifying a spreadsheet from Access. The *Form_Open* event procedure closes with code that manages the appearance of the form. Namely, the next to the last section disables the button for moving backward beyond the first record, and the closing section removes three selected design features, such as the built-in navigation buttons.

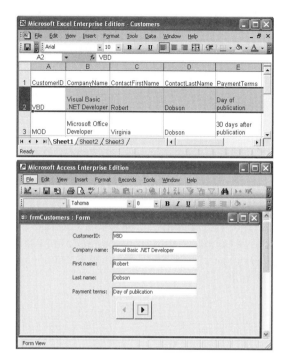

Figure 9-5   A display of Excel data in concurrent Excel and Access applications.

Note   The application declares the *rst1* variable with a *Public* keyword so that any of the three procedures in the application can refer to it.

The button for moving forward through *rst1* has the name *cmdNext*. Therefore, the *cmdNext_Click* procedure begins by moving to the next record and re-populating the *Value* property of the *TextBox* controls with the current row in *rst1*. Before closing, the *cmdNext_Click* procedure manages the Enabled value of the navigation buttons and sets the focus if necessary. For example, if the values displayed are for the last row in *rst1*, then the procedure disables the *cmdNext* button and sets the focus to the *cmdPrevious* button for moving backward through *rst1*.

The *cmdPrevious_Click* procedure has the same general design as the *cmdNext_Click* procedure. For the *cmdPrevious_Click* procedure, the application moves backward through *rst1*. In addition, it shifts the focus to *cmdNext* if appropriate.

```
Public rst1 as ADODB.Recordset

Private Sub Form_Open(Cancel As Integer)

Dim cnn1 As New ADODB.Connection
Dim fld1 As ADODB.Field
Dim str1 As String
Dim frm1 As Access.Form

'Create connection
cnn1.Open "Provider=Microsoft.Jet.OLEDB.4.0;" & _
   "Data Source=C:\Access2003Files\Customers.xls;" & _
   "Extended Properties=Excel 8.0;"

'Create recordset
'requires named range of customers in .xls file and
'adCmdTable argument to reference object instead of
'SQL string
Set rst1 = New ADODB.Recordset
With rst1
    .CursorType = adOpenKeyset
    .LockType = adLockOptimistic
    .Open "customers", cnn1, , , adCmdTable
End With

'Assign selected columns from first row of
'recordset to text box controls on form
With Me
    .Text0.Value = rst1("CustomerID")
    .Text2.Value = rst1("CompanyName")
    .Text4.Value = rst1("ContactFirstName")
    .Text6.Value = rst1("ContactLastName")
    .Text8.Value = rst1("PaymentTerms")
End With

'Disable cmdPrevious button initially
Me.cmdPrevious.Enabled = False

'Format form on open to leave out
'built-in navigation buttons, record
'selector, and dividing lines
Me.NavigationButtons = False
Me.RecordSelectors = False
Me.DividingLines = False

End Sub

Private Sub cmdNext_Click()

'Move to next row and populate form controls
```

(continued)

```
rst1.MoveNext
With Me
    .Text0.Value = rst1("CustomerID")
    .Text2.Value = rst1("CompanyName")
    .Text4.Value = rst1("ContactFirstName")
    .Text6.Value = rst1("ContactLastName")
    .Text8.Value = rst1("PaymentTerms")
End With

'Disable cmdNext button if at last record
If rst1.AbsolutePosition = rst1.RecordCount Then
    Me.cmdPrevious.SetFocus
    Me.cmdNext.Enabled = False
End If

'Enable cmdPrevious button if it is disabled
If Me.cmdPrevious.Enabled = False Then _
    Me.cmdPrevious.Enabled = True

End Sub

Private Sub cmdPrevious_Click()

'Move to previous row and populate form controls
rst1.MovePrevious
With Me
    .Text0.Value = rst1("CustomerID")
    .Text2.Value = rst1("CompanyName")
    .Text4.Value = rst1("ContactFirstName")
    .Text6.Value = rst1("ContactLastName")
    .Text8.Value = rst1("PaymentTerms")
End With

'Disable cmdPrevious button if at first record
If rst1.AbsolutePosition = 1 Then
    Me.cmdNext.SetFocus
    Me.cmdPrevious.Enabled = False
End If

'Enable cmdNext button if it is disabled
If Me.cmdNext.Enabled = False Then _
    Me.cmdNext.Enabled = True

End Sub
```

Working with Outlook from Access

Outlook comes with a standard set of folders, including folders for its calendar, contacts, deleted items, drafts, e-mail Inbox, journal, notes, e-mail Outbox, sent e-mail, and tasks. Users can also add custom folders and can nest folders within one another. Users work with items within their folders—adding, deleting, viewing, and performing other functions.

The initial version of Outlook shipped with programmatic support only through Microsoft Visual Basic Scripting Edition (VBScript). Outlook 2003 supports scripting with either VBA or VBScript. For compatibility with the rest of the book, this section focuses on scripting Outlook from Access using VBA. In addition, most of the samples use the Contacts folder to provide a familiar context.

This section starts with two samples that build on the Outlook ISAM driver sample you saw in the earlier section, "Linking Access to Other Office Applications." Using the ISAM driver offers a quick, convenient way to look at data in different Outlook folders. The two ISAM driver samples we'll examine momentarily manipulate the Inbox and Contacts folders. The sample that processes the Contacts folder demonstrates how easy it is to consolidate Outlook contents across multiple computers. However, this technique might not be obvious at first because the Outlook ISAM driver returns information for the local computer only.

You can establish an object reference to an instance of Outlook in Access with the *CreateObject* function. Before you can reference a particular folder, you typically must apply the *GetNameSpace* method to the *Application* object. The *NameSpace* object is an abstract root object that exists between the *Application* object and individual folders. The method (*GetNameSpace*) takes a single argument, which must be *MAPI* (Mail Application Programming Interface). You apply the *GetDefaultFolder* method to the *NameSpace* object to get the default folder of a certain type. You use a constant to designate which default folder your application will manipulate. The Contacts folder constant is *olFolderContacts*. Our Outlook Automation samples focus on the Contacts and Outbox folders as well as techniques for creating custom folders and populating them with items.

> **Note**   You can use the familiar Object Browser to probe the Outlook 2003 object model. Start by opening a Visual Basic Editor session in Outlook. For example, choose Tools, Macro, Visual Basic Editor, or just press Alt+F11. Then, select a class item, such as Application or Namespace. Next, select a class member and click the Help icon (?) for more information about the class member.

Viewing Outlook Inbox Items in an Access Form

Outlook has its own explorers for examining items in its folders. Nevertheless, you might find it useful to use an Access-based explorer for Outlook items. First of all, this is easy to do. Second, it offers an application better control over functionality and allows users to work in your application while using Outlook data. (The built-in Outlook explorers require users to exit your application while using Outlook data.) Third, when you build your own custom forms for exploring Outlook items, you can readily filter Outlook data and even merge it with data from other sources.

The form depicted in Figure 9-6 shows a custom explorer built in Access for Outlook items with the string "Access mail explorer" in the *Subject* field of any item in the Outlook Personal Folders collection. This collection contains all personal folders available to an Outlook user, including the Inbox folder. When I ran this form, my Inbox had three items, but only two of them contained the string "Access mail explorer" in the *Subject* field. Notice the form's navigator buttons show that it's displaying the first of two records—these are the two items that match the search criterion.

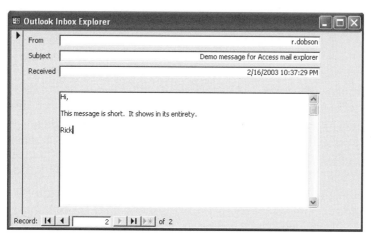

Figure 9-6 An Access form used to browse filtered Outlook Inbox items.

The form's Properties dialog box shows the Record Source property setting is *Null*, but the fields have Control Source settings that correspond to *Inbox* fields. The top three text boxes refer to the *From*, *Subject*, and *Received* fields, and the bottom text box with a vertical scroll bar references the *Contents* field. To simplify the presentation, I made these design settings manually, but you can also program them. (See Chapter 5 and Chapter 6 for more information on programming controls.) When the controls point at fields but the form itself does not reference a particular record source, it's easy to use a single form to explore Inbox items with different filter specifications. At the very least, you must explicitly designate a record source for the form in order for it to show any data at all. The sample code we'll examine in a moment assigns an ADO recordset to the form's *Recordset* property.

The code sets the form's recordset and opens the form. Because the code sets the form's *Recordset* property and no default Record Source setting exists, you cannot use the form to browse data without first running the code. The code sample performs two functions. First, it defines a recordset, which will become the record source for the form. The recordset uses the ISAM driver for Outlook as discussed in the "Linking Access to Other Office Applications" section in this chapter. Second, the application's code opens the form and assigns the recordset to the form's *Recordset* property. The code for defining the recordset has three distinctive features. First, the recordset must have its *CursorLocation* property set to *adUseClient* if you plan to use it as input to a form. This is unnecessary if you just want to print results to the Immediate window. Second, the fields after the *SELECT* keyword in the recordset's source statement delimit *FROM* with square brackets ([ ]). This is because *FROM* is both a SQL keyword and an Outlook Inbox item field name. To specify the field name, you need the brackets. Third, the SQL string for the recordset includes a *WHERE* clause. The *WHERE* clause filters out all records that don't have the string "Access mail explorer" in the *Subject* field. Notice that the *WHERE* clause appears after the *IN* keyword, which is an element of the *FROM* clause for the SQL statement.

After defining the recordset, the procedure opens the form. Next, the procedure assigns the recordset to the form's *Recordset* property. To help you understand the values returned by the recordset, the application prints in the Immediate window the *Name*, *ActualSize*, and *Value* properties for each field within each row of the recordset. This simple demonstration resides in a standard module. In order to demonstrate the sample application, you need to open the form by running the *ShowDemoMessages* procedure instead of directly opening the frmInboxExplorer form from the Access database window. Return to the Access window to view the form after running the procedure in the Visual Basic Editor. In order to see any messages on the form, you will need to update the search string in the procedure ("Access mail explorer") to match that the string from one or more messages in your Outlook folders.

> **Note**   The application can show multiple lines, but each line must end in a new-line character on or before its two hundred fifty-sixth character. Therefore, the mail explorer in this application can show no more than the initial 256 characters in each mail item matching the criterion until it encounters a new-line character, such as a carriage return. If there is no new-line character within a block of 256 characters, the procedure does not extract additional characters. A subsequent sample in the "Viewing Outlook Items in an Access Form" section in this chapter demonstrates a more general approach to the task that does not require new-line characters.

```
'Click the View Microsoft Access control on the
'VBE Standard toolbar immediately after running this to
'see the form
Sub ShowDemoMessages()
Dim rst1 As ADODB.Recordset

'Instantiate recordset and open it on a subset
'of the columns and rows in the Outlook Inbox
'on the current computer
Set rst1 = New ADODB.Recordset
rst1.CursorLocation = adUseClient
rst1.Open "SELECT [From], Subject, Received, Contents " & _
    "FROM Inbox IN'C:\Windows\Temp\;'" & _
    "[Outlook 9.0;MAPILEVEL=Personal Folders|;]" & _
    "WHERE INSTR(Subject,'Access mail explorer')>0;", _
    CurrentProject.Connection, , , adCmdText

'Open frmInboxExplorer and assign rst1 to it
DoCmd.OpenForm "frmInboxExplorer"
Set Application.Forms("frmInboxExplorer").Recordset = rst1

'Print the name, actual size, and value for each row
'in the recordset; delimit rows from one another
Dim i As Integer
Do Until rst1.EOF

    For i = 0 To rst1.Fields.Count - 1
        Debug.Print rst1.Fields(i).Name, _
            rst1.Fields(i).ActualSize, _
            rst1.Fields(i).Value
    Next i

    Debug.Print "-----"
    rst1.MoveNext

Loop

'Cleanup objects
rst1.Close
Set rst1 = Nothing

End Sub
```

Enumerating Items in the Contacts Folder

The following procedure uses Automation to manipulate the Outlook Contacts folder to enumerate all its items. You can set up a sample Contacts folder with a few entries to evaluate this and subsequent samples. This book's companion content also includes some sample contact information for populating a Contacts folder (see the *AddContacts* procedure discussed in the "Adding Multiple Items to the Contacts Folder" section of this chapter). When manipulating or even enumerating items in Outlook, it is convenient to have Outlook open so that there is no delay in the effect of a manipulation, such as adding or deleting a contact item in the Contacts folder.

Microsoft Outlook Security Prompts and Express ClickYes

Several Outlook Automation samples in this chapter directly manipulate the contents of your Outlook contact items. Because such manipulation might be the result of a virus attack, Outlook by default prompts you through a popup dialog box whenever a user attempts to manipulate a contact item or other type of Outlook item. The prompt lets you authorize the use of a single item or Outlook items generally for a designated interval of up to 10 minutes.

Microsoft offers workarounds to these built-in security rules for Microsoft Exchange administrators, but sophisticated individual users and small businesses not running Microsoft Exchange might be frustrated by the security prompt that requires a click every time a VBA macro attempts to manipulate an Outlook item. Often times, the user simply has to click Yes on the security prompt. ExpressSoft Inc. offers a free utility program (Express ClickYes) that runs in the background and automatically clicks Yes in response to an Outlook security prompt. This program is suitable for Outlook users who have legitimate Automation needs, but do not run Microsoft Exchange (computers running Outlook in Internet Mode Only are candidates for this utility). The download URL for the Express ClickYes utility is *http://www.express-soft.com/mailmate/clickyes.html*.

After downloading the utility, a computer operator can turn the Express ClickYes utility off and on. This allows an operator to benefit from the built-in Outlook security prompt except for when a custom VBA macro can explicitly benefit from an automatic response to the security prompt. I tested all the Outlook Automation samples in this chapter with the Express ClickYes utility running in the background.

```
Sub ListContacts()
Dim myOlApp As Outlook.Application
Dim myNameSpace As NameSpace
Dim myContacts As Items
Dim myItem As ContactItem

'Create an instance of Outlook.
'Reference its MAPI NameSpace.
'Reference MAPI's Contact folder.
Set myOlApp = CreateObject("Outlook.Application")
Set myNameSpace = myOlApp.GetNamespace("MAPI")
Set myContacts = _
    myNameSpace.GetDefaultFolder(olFolderContacts).Items

'Enumerate items in Contact folder and
'print selected fields
For Each myItem In myContacts
    Debug.Print myItem.FirstName, myItem.LastName, _
        myItem.EmaillAddress
Next

'Clean up objects
Set myOlApp = Nothing

End Sub
```

The procedure starts by declaring four variables: one for the Outlook application, one for its *NameSpace* object, one for the collection of items in the Contacts folder, and one for enumerating those items. It takes three *Set* statements to display the items in the Contacts folder. The last of these statements uses the *GetDefaultFolder* method to return the Contacts folder, and it uses the *Items* property to return the individual items from within the Contacts folder. The enumeration takes place within a *For...Each* loop. The items in the Contact folder have a series of properties that identify information about contacts. The sample uses three of these properties to print the first name, last name, and first e-mail address for each entry in the Contacts folder. These property names differ from the field names for the return sets from the Outlook ISAM driver, even when both types of names refer to the same data elements.

Adding an Item to the Contacts Folder

You can also build Access-based solutions that manipulate the contents of the Contacts folder. The first of the next three procedures, *AddOneContact*, inserts a new contact into the folder. It uses string constants to define the first name, last name, and e-mail address for a contact, but you can easily modify the procedure to pass these as arguments. The next two procedures, *Remove-OneEmail* and *DeleteAContact*, do just that. The *RemoveOneEmail* procedure passes an e-mail address to the *DeleteAContact* procedure, finds a contact item with a matching e-mail address, and then deletes it.

```
Sub AddOneContact()
Dim myOlApp As Outlook.Application
Dim myItem As ContactItem

'Create an instance of Outlook
Set myOlApp = CreateObject("Outlook.Application")

'Create an item for the Contacts folder.
'Populate the item with values.
'Save the item.
Set myItem = myOlApp.CreateItem(olContactItem)
With myItem
    .FirstName = "foo"
    .LastName = "bar"
    .EmailAddress = "foobar@yourcompany.com"
    .Save
End With

'Clean up objects
Set myItem = Nothing
Set myOlApp = Nothing

End Sub

Sub RemoveOneEmail()

DeleteAContact ("foobar@yourcompany.com")

End Sub

Sub DeleteAContact(strEmail)
Dim myOlApp As Outlook.Application
Dim myNameSpace As NameSpace
Dim myContacts As Items
Dim myItem As ContactItem

'Create an instance of Outlook.
'Reference its MAPI Namespace.
'Reference MAPI's Contact folder.
Set myOlApp = CreateObject("Outlook.Application")
Set myNameSpace = myOlApp.GetNamespace("MAPI")
Set myContacts = _
    myNameSpace.GetDefaultFolder(olFolderContacts).Items

'Enumerate to search for item to delete
For Each myItem In myContacts
    If myItem.EmailAddress = strEmail Then
        myItem.Delete
```

(continued)

```
        Exit Sub
    End If
Next

'No entry found
MsgBox "No entry found with email of " & strEmail, vbCritical, _
    "Programming Microsoft Access 2003"

'Clean up objects
Set myOlApp = Nothing

End Sub
```

The *AddOneContact* procedure requires just two objects—the Outlook *Application* object and a *ContactItem* object to represent an item in the Contacts folder. The procedure creates a reference to the *Application* object with the *CreateObject* function. This reference supports the *CreateItem* method, which creates an empty instance of an item for any specified folder. You designate the type of folder for the item by using an argument that you pass to the *CreateItem* method. You can choose from more than 140 properties to specify the characteristics of a contact. The sample assigns string constants for the *FirstName*, *LastName*, and *Email1Address* properties. (Yes, each contact can have more than one e-mail address.) Then, the sample invokes the *Save* method to store the new entry in the Contacts folder.

Deleting an Item from the Contacts Folder

The *DeleteAContact* procedure accepts a string argument that is the value of the *Email1Address* property of the contact item to delete. The procedure enumerates members of the Contacts folder until it finds one with an *Email1Address* property that matches the passed argument. When the procedure finds a match, it removes the item by invoking the *Delete* method and exits to eliminate further searching. If the procedure enumerates the entire contents of the Contacts folder without discovering a match, control passes to a message box statement, which reports that no entries match the e-mail address passed to it.

Adding Multiple Items to the Contacts Folder

One common task performed with a database manager such as Access is adding multiple contact items to the Contacts folder. These contacts can come from any source, such as the Contacts folder on another computer, addresses entered over the Internet, or even an old Access contact file. The *AddContacts* procedure that follows uses one approach to updating an Outlook Contacts folder with the contact information in an Access table:

```
Sub AddContacts()
Dim myOlApp As Outlook.Application
```

```
Dim myItem As ContactItem
Dim rst1 As New Recordset

'Open the Contacts folder in Outlook
Set myOlApp = CreateObject("Outlook.Application")

'Open the table with the new contacts
With rst1
    .ActiveConnection = CurrentProject.Connection
    .Open "oe4pab"
End With

'Create a contact item for adding contacts and
'loop through the table records to add them to the folder
AssistantWorkingOn
Do Until rst1.EOF
    Set myItem = myOlApp.CreateItem(olContactItem)
    With myItem
        .FirstName = IIf(IsNull(rst1.Fields(0)), _
            "", rst1.Fields(0))
        .LastName = rst1.Fields(1)
        .EmailAddress = rst1.Fields(2)
        .Save
    End With
    rst1.MoveNext
Loop
AssistantIdleOn

'Clean up objects
Set myItem = Nothing
Set myOlApp = Nothing

End Sub
```

The procedure sets a reference to the Outlook application and then opens a recordset based on the *oe4pab* table. This is the local table in the Access Tables folder. The table contains just 35 entries, but the procedure can accommodate a much longer list of addresses. For this reason, the procedure calls another procedure that turns on the Assistant with a working animation and leaves it on until Access and Outlook finish updating the Outlook Contacts folder with the entries in the *oe4pab* table. In between the two calls to turn Assistant animation on and off, a *Do* loop iterates through all the records in the *oe4pab* table. The loop creates a new *ContactItem* object on each pass, and then it assigns the records for that pass to the item and saves the item.

Deleting Multiple Items from the Contacts Folder

The following procedure, *RemoveEmails*, is an adaptation of the *DeleteAContact* procedure shown earlier in the section. *RemoveEmails* deletes multiple records from a Contacts folder. It removes one item at a time by successively calling *DeleteAContact* with different e-mail addresses. The sample uses the addresses in the *oe4pab* table as the source for the arguments. This procedure offers two advantages: it is easy to write, and it reuses the *DeleteAContact* procedure.

```
Sub RemoveEmails()
Dim rst1 As New Recordset

'Open the table with the new contacts
    With rst1
        .ActiveConnection = CurrentProject.Connection
        .Open "oe4pab"
    End With

'Loop through the table records to move them to the folder
    AssistantWorkingOn
    Do Until rst1.EOF
        DeleteAContact (rst1.Fields(2))
        rst1.MoveNext
    Loop
    AssistantIdleOn

'Clean up objects
rst1.Close
Set rst1 = Nothing

End Sub
```

While this procedure can get the job done, it has at least two deficiencies. First, it searches through the Contacts folder for each item that it wants to remove. This gets increasingly costly as the number of items to delete grows, the number of items in the Contacts folder grows, or both. Second, if there is no match for an item, the procedure pauses with a message box that requires the user to click a button to continue. If numerous entries in the list of items to delete are already missing from the Contacts folder, having to click a button for each item not present in the folder can become tedious. One solution to these weaknesses is to replace the call to *DeleteAContact* with a call to *DeleteAContact2*, shown here:

```
Sub DeleteAContact2(strEmail)
On Error GoTo delete2Trap
Dim myOlApp As Outlook.Application
Dim myNameSpace As NameSpace
Dim myContacts As Items
Dim myItem As ContactItem
Dim strFilter As String

'Create an instance of Outlook.
'Reference its MAPI NameSpace.
'Reference MAPI's Contact folder.
```

```
      Set myOlApp = CreateObject("Outlook.Application")
      Set myNameSpace = myOlApp.GetNamespace("MAPI")
      Set myContacts = _
          myNameSpace.GetDefaultFolder(olFolderContacts).Items

'Find target item and remove it
      strFilter = "[Email1Address] = """ & strEmail & """"
      Set myItem = myContacts.Find(strFilter)
      myItem.Delete

delete2Exit:
      Exit Sub

delete2Trap:
      If Err.Number = 91 Then
'If item is not there, keep on going
          Resume Next
      Else
'Otherwise, pause with a message box
          MsgBox Err.Number & ": " & vbCrLf & _
              Err.Description, vbCritical, _
              "Programming Microsoft Access 2003"
          Resume Next
      End If

'Clean up objects
Set myOlApp = Nothing

End Sub
```

This procedure expedites the search for an item to delete by using the *Find* method. It constructs a criterion for the *Find* method based on the e-mail address passed to it. After finding an item with a matching e-mail address, the procedure applies the *Delete* method to that item. The speed advantage from using the *Find* method grows along with the number of e-mail addresses in the Contact folders and the total number of items in the Contacts folder. The procedure also traps failures of the *Find* method to return an item, which happens when there is no matching item for an e-mail address in the Contacts folder. In this situation, *DeleteAContact2* silently returns control to the calling routine so it can search again for a new e-mail address without operator intervention.

Merging Access Contacts with an Outlook Message

The Outlook mail item is the primary device for holding a message. Individual mail items have the properties *Subject*, *Body*, and *Recipients*. The *Body* property is a string representing the body of a message. If you prefer, you can designate the body of a message through its *HTMLBody* property, which represents the HTML content for a message. Mail items have numerous other properties that allow you to control the content of individual e-mail messages. Furthermore, a mail item has a variety of methods that correspond to what folks do with messages. The next sample demonstrates the invocation of the *Send* method. However, mail items include many additional methods, such as *Reply*, *ReplyAll*, *Copy*, and *Delete*.

The e-mail merge sample combines a subset of records from an Access table with a standard message for all members of the subset. An ADO recordset makes the table's contents available for inclusion in individual messages. A *WHERE* clause in the SQL string for the recordset allows the selection of a subset of records from a much lengthier record source. The mail item's body is a string, so you can vary its content based on the values in the Access table. For example, the sample shows how to personalize a message by addressing individuals by their first name. This name comes from the Access table. After setting a message's properties, the procedure sends the message and advances to the next row in the recordset.

```
Sub MergeEmail()
Dim myOlApp As Outlook.Application
Dim myNameSpace As Outlook.NameSpace
Dim myFolders As Outlook.Folders
Dim myFolder As Outlook.MAPIFolder
Dim myMailItem As Outlook.MailItem
Dim str1 As String
Dim rst1 As Recordset

'Set reference to Outlook, NameSpace object,
'and the first-level folders collection
Set myOlApp = CreateObject("Outlook.Application")
Set myNameSpace = myOlApp.GetNamespace("MAPI")
Set myFolders = myNameSpace.Folders.Item(1).Folders

'Set a reference to the PMAMail folder and
'select a subset from a table containing contacts
Set myFolder = _
    myFolders.Item("PMADemo").Folders.Item("PMAMail")
Set rst1 = New ADODB.Recordset
rst1.Open _
    "SELECT * FROM WebBasedList WHERE " & _
    "StateOrProvince='NY' OR " & _
    "StateOrProvince='NJ' OR " & _
    "StateOrProvince='CT'", _
    CurrentProject.Connection

'Loop through rst1 and assign the FirstName
'field to the body of the message
AssistantWorkingOn
Do Until rst1.EOF
    Set myMailItem = myFolder.Items.Add(olMailItem)
    str1 = "Dear " & rst1.Fields("FirstName")
    str1 = str1 & "," & vbCrLf & vbCrLf
    str1 = str1 & "On October 1, 2002, CAB, Inc. "
```

```
        str1 = str1 & "will be holding a seminar at the "
        str1 = str1 & "Hilton just this side of heaven.  "
        str1 = str1 & "You are cordially invited to attend "
        str1 = str1 & "the complimentary continental "
        str1 = str1 & "breakfast, with healthy servings of "
        str1 = str1 & "manna and water from 7:30 to 8:30 AM.  "
        str1 = str1 & "An enlightening multimedia "
        str1 = str1 & "presentation and demo follows "
        str1 = str1 & "from 8:30 to 11:30 AM." & vbCrLf
        str1 = str1 & vbCrLf & "Rick Dobson" & vbCrLf
        str1 = str1 & "President" & vbCrLf & "CAB, Inc."
        str1 = str1 & vbCrLf & vbCrLf & "PS: Please "
        str1 = str1 & "RSVP via a reply to this "
        str1 = str1 & "message.  Thanks."
        myMailItem.Body = str1
        myMailItem.Subject = "Seminar Invitation"
        myMailItem.Recipients.Add rst1.Fields("EmailAddress")
        myMailItem.Send
        rst1.MoveNext
Loop
AssistantIdleOn

'Clean up objects
rst1.Close
Set rst1 = Nothing
Set myOlApp = Nothing

End Sub
```

Working with Word from Access

The first sample in this section demonstrates how to build, design, and populate a table in Word based on data in an Access table. It uses Automation to control Word from Access, and it even includes a simple Access form for invoking the Automation procedure. The second and third samples tackle two mail merge tasks programmatically: generating mailing labels and generating a form letter.

The form letter sample in this chapter facilitates mailing a form letter to a list of recipients, which is the same task tackled in Chapter 6 by other means. You can compare the two approaches to see which best fits your needs. In general, the philosophy behind having multiple components is that you should use each to do what it does best. The sample in this chapter enables Access to store data and Word to generate form letters for printing. If you find it easy to work with the Word object model and the *MailMerge* object, the approach demonstrated in this chapter offers opportunities to expand your skills in pursuit of automating common business requirements. If you prefer to concentrate on becoming expert in Access by itself, the approach in Chapter 6 is more suitable for you.

Automating Word from Access

The following Automation sample transfers contents from a recordset based on a table in Access to a table in Word. When you have references to multiple object models with similar terms, you should include a prefix before the object data type designation in its declaration—you should use *Word.Table* instead of *Table*, for example. Recall that the ADOX library supports a *Table* class as well. Specifying *Word.Table* tells the VBA interpreter which kind of *Table* object you want. Access can also declare a *Table* object from the ADOX library. Also, note that the *Range* object in Word behaves differently than the one in Excel. VBA and IntelliSense facilitate building cross-application solutions, but they do not relieve you from learning the object models for individual applications.

```
Sub fromAccessToWordTable()
Dim myWDApp As Word.Application
Dim myRange As Word.Range, myTable As Word.Table
Dim acell As Word.Cell, emailCol As Integer
Dim rst1 As New Recordset, irow As Integer

'Open the table with the new contacts
With rst1
    .ActiveConnection = CurrentProject.Connection
    .Open "oe4pab", , adOpenKeyset, adLockOptimistic, adCmdTable
End With

'Create a Word application instance and turn on
'the Assistant's working animation
AssistantWorkingOn
Set myWDApp = CreateObject("Word.Application")

'Add a document to the application and a table to the document.
'Specify rows to equal one more than number of rows in e-mail
'address table in Access.
myWDApp.Documents.Add
Set myRange = myWDApp.ActiveDocument.Range(0, 0)
myWDApp.ActiveDocument.Tables.Add Range:=myRange, _
    NumRows:=rst1.RecordCount + 1, NumColumns:=3

'Insert column headings for table
With myWDApp.ActiveDocument.Tables(1).Rows(1)
    .Cells(1).Range.Text = rst1.Fields(0).Name
    .Cells(2).Range.Text = rst1.Fields(1).Name
    .Cells(3).Range.Text = rst1.Fields(2).Name
End With

'Insert first name, last name, and e-mail from Access table.
'Insert contact information in the second through the last row.
For irow = 2 To myWDApp.ActiveDocument.Tables(1).Rows.Count
emailCol = 0
```

```
    For Each acell In _
        myWDApp.ActiveDocument.Tables(1).Rows(irow).Cells
        acell.Range.Text = IIf(IsNull(rst1.Fields(emailCol)), _
            "", rst1.Fields(emailCol))
        emailCol = emailCol + 1
    Next acell
rst1.MoveNext
Next irow

'Format table to fit content, turn on idle animation, and
'make Word visible so that user can see table in Word
myWDApp.ActiveDocument.Tables(1).AutoFitBehavior wdAutoFitContent
AssistantIdleOn
myWDApp.Visible = True

End Sub
```

The procedure starts by opening a *Recordset* object based on a table in Access—the familiar *oe4pab* table that you saw in the Outlook samples in "Working with Outlook from Access" in this chapter. Because the application needs the *RecordCount* property, the sample code uses the *adOpenKeyset* constant for the cursor type specification. After opening the recordset, the application turns on the working animation for the Assistant and runs the *CreateObject* function to create a fresh instance of Word.

The procedure then constructs the table in Word. It adds a new document and then adds a table to the document's top left corner. The parameters of the *Add* method for the *Table* object specify that the table will have one more row than there are rows in the Access table. This allows one row of column headers plus all the data in the *oe4pab* table. Before starting to work with the recordset values, the procedure writes the column headers in the first row. These are the field names for the table in Access.

A pair of nested *For* loops navigate through the cells in the table. The outer loop progresses sequentially through the rows. The inner one marches across the columns within a row. Notice that Word has a *Cells* collection for the columns within the row of a table. The inner loop navigates to individual cells within a row of a Word table. The reference to a cell starts with the Automation object, *myWDApp*, and then hierarchically moves to the *ActiveDocument* object, the first table on the document, and the row in the table. After identifying a cell within a row to process, an *IIf* function based on the recordset values computes a value for the *Text* property of the cell. The *emailcol* integer value coordinates with the *rst1* variable to deposit recordset column values into the columns for the Word table.

After iterating through all of the table's cells, the procedure closes by performing three steps. First it reformats the columns' widths so that they're wide enough to display column values without wrapping. Then, it assigns an idle animation to the Assistant. This essentially turns off the working animation that starts just before the Word *Application* object launches. Finally the procedure sets the *Application* object's *Visible* property to *True*. This changes the focus from Access to Word.

Figure 9-7 shows the *frmAutomationSample* Access form in the Chapter09.mdb file that lets users start the *fromAccessToWordTable* procedure by clicking a button. The code behind the form merely invokes the *fromAccessToWordTable* procedure for the button's click event. After the event procedure concludes, Word opens with a table of values from Access.

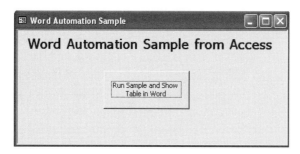

Figure 9-7   This form invokes the *fromAccessToWordTable* procedure.

Producing Mailing Labels

The built-in Word mail merge feature can draw on an Access database table or query as a record source for generating mailing labels. While you can programmatically lay out the mail merge fields or bookmarks to support the placement of Access data on Word documents, it's often much simpler to lay them out manually where you want data inserted on a document. In addition, you can use built-in wizards to help with the layout of controls for forms with multiple labels per page. For example, choose Tools, Letters And Mailings, Mail Merge Wizard to launch the Mail Merge Wizard in Word 2003.

Figure 9-8 shows an excerpt from the mlabels.doc file. The mail merge fields were positioned with the built-in Mail Merge Wizard that you can invoke from the Tools menu. I found it convenient to lay out the controls for the label with the help of the Insert Merge Fields control on the Mail Merge toolbar. After laying out the controls, you can programmatically control the printing of labels based on Access tables or queries through the *MailMerge* object.

The following Word procedure is designed to run from the ThisDocument folder of the Normal template. It starts by opening the mlabels.doc file that contains the mail merge fields depicted in Figure 9-8. Then, it sets a reference, *myDoc*, to a document based on the file. The mlabels.doc file actually contains no code of its own.

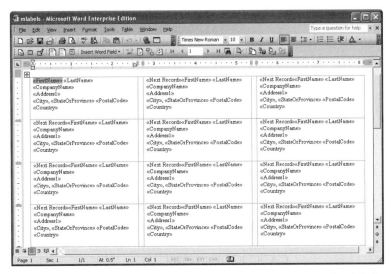

Figure 9-8   An excerpt from a Word document for printing mailing labels on Avery 5260 laser forms.

> **Note**   To run the mailing sample and the form letter sample shown later in this section, you must first update your Normal template in Word 2003 with two VBA scripts for mailing labels and form letters. The advantage of putting VBA procedures in the Normal template is that you can run them from any document. The scripts appear in this book's companion content, along with a Readme.txt file with step-by-step instructions on how to update your Normal template with the sample scripts. You also will need the mlabels.doc and formletter.doc files, which are also contained in the companion content.

```
Sub PrintPreviewLabels()
Dim myDoc As Document

'Set reference to the document
Documents.Open FileName:="C:\Access2003Files\mlabels.doc"
Set myDoc = Documents("mlabels.doc")

'Reference the data source in Access
myDoc.MailMerge.OpenDataSource _
    Name:="C:\Access2003Files\Chapter09.mdb", _
    Connection:="TABLE WebBasedList"
'Send the labels to a new document
```

(continued)

```
With myDoc.MailMerge
    .Destination = wdSendToNewDocument
    .Execute Pause:=True
End With

'Either preview or print labels
If MsgBox("Do you want to preview before printing?", _
    vbYesNo, _
    "Programming Microsoft Access 2003") = vbYes Then
    ActiveDocument.PrintPreview
Else
    ActiveDocument.PrintOut
End If

End Sub
```

The key to performing any mail merge with data from Access is to invoke the *OpenDataSource* method for the *MailMerge* object within a document, such as the document that the *myDoc* reference points to. You often must assign two arguments, *Name* and *Connection*. You point the *Name* argument at the Access source file containing the data for the mail merge. The *PrintPreviewLabels* procedure references Chapter09.mdb. You use the *Connection* argument to designate a type of database object and its name. Your code can designate either a *Table* or a *Query*. The sample points to a table named *WebBasedList*.

You can use the Word *MailMerge* object to write over the template with the mail merge fields or create a new document with the merged data. You use the *MailMerge* object's *Destination* property to designate your choice. The sample uses the constant to create a new document for the merged data. After setting all the *MailMerge* properties that you want, you apply the *Execute* method to the *MailMerge* object. This merges the Access data into a Word document that creates your mailing labels. The sample presents a message box asking whether to print or preview the labels. After you no longer need the document with the merged fields and the one controlling the layout of the fields in a document, you can close both of them manually or with another program.

Note A bug in the shipping version of Word 2003 prompts the user to select a table from the data source even though the code denotes one in its *Connection* parameter for the *OpenDataSource* method. This prompt appears before the message box mentioned in the preceding paragraph. For this sample, select *WebBasedList*. In general, users should choose whatever record source is appropriate for the current merge task.

You can easily invoke a procedure such as *PrintPreviewLabels* from within Access. The next procedure does this in just three lines. This sample runs from a standard module in an Access file:

```
Sub RunMLabels()
Dim myWDApp As Word.Application

'Open connection to Word and make Word visible
Set myWDApp = CreateObject("Word.Application")
myWDApp.Application.Visible = True

'Run mailing label procedure
myWDApp.Application.Run "PrintPreviewLabels"

End Sub
```

Producing Form Letters

The procedure for producing form letters is essentially the same as the one for producing mailing labels except that the layout of mail merge fields is more straightforward. This is because you typically have just one occurrence of a record per page instead of multiple records on a page. Figure 9-9 shows the layout of a form letter in Word. It is easy to include a mail merge field within the body of a letter. The figure shows this in its bottom panel.

Do not use the full Mail Merge Wizard if you plan to programmatically control the printing of labels. The code that the wizard generates has many extra parameters and is designed explicitly for use with the wizard, not necessarily with custom applications. The sample that follows and the one in the previous section are designed for use from the ThisDocument folder of the Normal template. Both are good starting points for your own custom form letter or mailing label applications. However, you should start the Mail Merge Wizard to add the Mail Merge toolbar to the window of a document. Once you have the toolbar displayed, you can freely insert mail merge fields anywhere in a document. In fact, the Mail Merge Wizard that ships with Word 2003 includes tools for simplifying and speeding up the layout and formatting of address and greeting blocks within a form letter. However, you can still lay out the fields individually as the sample shows.

The following procedure works with the document depicted in Figure 9-9, which shows excerpts from the top and bottom of the formletter.doc file. The procedure opens this file. The use of the *OpenDataSource* method is the same for both a form letter and mailing labels. This sample, however, designates values for the *FirstRecord* and *LastRecord* properties of the *DataSource* object. The

OpenDataSource method specifies parameters pointing at the data source that the *DataSource* object represents. Setting the *FirstRecord* and *LastRecord* properties establishes a range of records for which to print form letters. This sample works with the default sort order for the records in the data source.

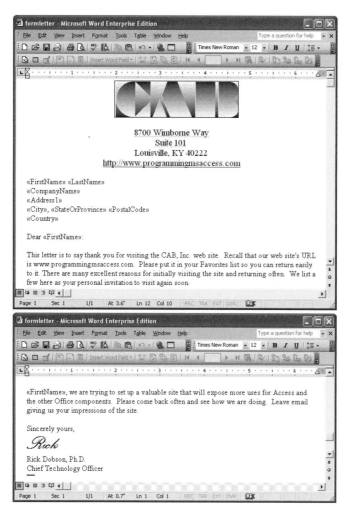

Figure 9-9 Excerpts from a Word document for printing form letters.

```
Sub PrintPreviewLetters()
Dim myDoc As Document

'Load file and set a reference to it
Documents.Open FileName:="C:\Access2003Files\formletter.doc"
Set myDoc = Documents("formletter.doc")
```

```
'Reference the data source in Access
myDoc.MailMerge.OpenDataSource _
    Name:="C:\Access2003Files\Chapter09.mdb", _
    Connection:="TABLE WebBasedList"

'Send the labels to a new document
With myDoc.MailMerge
    .Destination = wdSendToNewDocument
    With .DataSource
        .FirstRecord = 5
        .LastRecord = 9
    End With
    .Execute Pause:=True
End With

'Either preview or print labels
If MsgBox("Do you want to preview before printing?", _
    vbYesNo, _
    "Programming Microsoft Access 2003") = vbYes Then
    ActiveDocument.PrintPreview
Else
    ActiveDocument.PrintOut
End If

End Sub
```

You can invoke the procedure from within Access by invoking the *Run* method for the Word *Application* object, as shown in the following procedure. This takes just three lines. While the *RunFormLetters* and *RunLabels* procedures apply to a standard module in Access, you can place either or both of them behind an Access form and invoke them from command buttons (for a sample of how to do this, see the code behind the frmAutomationSample form in Chapter09.mdb). If your code designates a query in the *OpenDataSource Connection* parameter, you can modify the query before invoking the Word mail merge operation to further enhance your control of the mail merge.

Note   The same Word 2003 bug that afflicts the mailing label sample affects this one. Basically, Word prompts you to select a table to serve as a record source even though the code already denotes one. The remedies are also the same. You manually designate the proper table to serve as a record source.

```
Sub RunFormLetters()
Dim myWDApp As Word.Application

'Open connection to Word and make Word visible
Set myWDApp = CreateObject("Word.Application")
myWDApp.Application.Visible = True

'Run form letter procedure
myWDApp.Application.Run "PrintPreviewLetters"

End Sub
```

Summary

The tight integration of Access with its siblings in the Office suite enables Office developers to take advantage of the great resources in Access. In addition, Access developers can tap the power of the other Office components.

This chapter presents a series of case-study examples with detailed instructions and sample code for making Access interoperate with Excel, Outlook, and Word. In the review of techniques for Access/Outlook interoperability, the chapter highlights a workaround to an Outlook security issue that prompts before granting programmatic access to Outlook items. While blocking selected viruses, this security technique also inhibits the operation of valid Automation procedures. By learning the samples in this chapter, you prepare yourself to create Access solutions that interoperate with any other package exposing its object model as a COM object and allowing programming via VBA.

10

Database Security

This chapter focuses on security issues for Microsoft Access database files (.mdb), while the next chapter considers special techniques for securing SQL Server databases via Access projects (.adp files). Material in the last section of this chapter also highlights security issues for both .mdb and .adp files.

Database security has several important facets. One is to authenticate users before they gain access to a database. The user authentication process asks: Is this user who he or she claims to be? Another database security consideration pertains to permissions, which ascertain whether an authenticated user can perform certain tasks. For example, you can use database permissions to define who can view or modify rows in a table containing sensitive data, such as employee salaries. Developers with proprietary technologies often care about securing applications so that clients can use their technologies, but cannot view the code. Machine security is yet another consideration. In these days of rampant computer crimes, it is important that database solutions do not expose a machine to malicious acts by others, such as the potential for erasing or gathering information from files on a hard drive.

This chapter explores database security from three perspectives. First, it presents a miscellany of security techniques other than user-level security. While user-level security provides the most advanced form of security for .mdb files, these other techniques are generally easier to understand and implement. In many situations, these other techniques provide sufficient security for an application. Next, the chapter reviews user-level security in three distinct sections. The first section presents an overview of user-level security, steps for setting it up manually, and demonstrations of how it operates. The second section covers ADOX techniques for programmatically administering user-level security. The third section highlights Jet SQL techniques for programmatically managing user-level security. The chapter closes with a review of the Jet SandBox mode and macro security features. These features manage threats from potentially unsafe VBA and Access functions in Access 2003 applications.

Securing Files Without User-Level Security

Access offers a rich array of security features to support the needs of different types of Access applications. Many multiuser Access applications can benefit from user-level security, which lets developers assign database permissions to individual users and groups of users. Other applications have more specialized needs. This section offers a brief overview of security techniques other than user-level security.

One of the strengths of Access is its ability to serve different audiences. Some applications are code intensive, so you need to secure your investment in source code. Other applications serve small workgroups with limited technical capabilities but still require minimum levels of security to restrict access to data. Still other applications benefit from a custom user interface (UI) that restricts functionality simply by exposing a restricted set of commands.

Using a Custom Interface

Sometimes you can adequately secure an application by simply replacing the standard Access interface with a custom one. Choose Startup from the Tools menu to open a dialog box that lets you specify a custom application title and icon, a custom startup form, and custom menus to replace the standard Access ones. This dialog box also lets you suppress the Database window and the status bar. You can also manipulate the features of the Startup dialog box programmatically. If this type of manipulation is suitable for your security needs, consider augmenting it with the *Show* and *Hide* methods, the *Visible* property, and the *Hidden* property for objects in the Database window.

Note   See earlier chapters for creating custom features. Chapter 5 introduces building a custom startup form, and Chapter 8 demonstrates how to eliminate access to the Database window when your application has a custom startup form. Chapter 8 also illustrates programming techniques for building custom menus and adapting the built-in menus with the *CommandBars* object model.

Setting a Database Password Manually

You can require users to enter a password to gain unrestricted access to all Access data and database objects. Passwords are easy to administer compared to user-level security. Password security is appropriate if you have a group whose members need equal access to all elements of a database file but not everyone in the office is a member of that group.

You cannot use a password-protected file as a member in a replica set because Jet database replication cannot synchronize with a password-protected file. You should also be careful about linking to database files with password protection because anyone who can access the file that links to the protected file has unrestricted access to the protected file. Furthermore, Access stores an encrypted version of the password along with other information about the linked file. Finally, if a user changes the password for a linked file, Access prompts for the new password the next time another database file links to it.

To assign and remove a database password, you need exclusive access to the file. You obtain exclusive access when you open a file by choosing Open Exclusive from the Open button's drop-down menu in the Open dialog box.

To assign a database password perform the following steps:

1. On the Tools menu, point to Security then choose Set Database Password.

2. In the Set Database Password dialog box, enter your password of choice in the Password and Verify boxes and then click OK. The application will ask for the password the next time a user opens the file.

To remove a database password, do the following:

1. On the Tools menu, point to Security and choose Unset Database Password.

2. Type the password in the Unset Database Password dialog box. This removes the initial prompt for a password before a database is made available.

Setting a Database Password Programmatically

You can also programmatically initialize, change, and remove a database password. The next three samples draw on Jet SQL, offering a simple approach to managing the security for Jet databases. Use the *ALTER DATABASE PASSWORD* statement to set and remove database passwords. The first argument signifies the new password, and the second argument denotes the old password. You represent the passwords as strings delimited by square brackets ([ ]), except in two cases. As with all SQL terms and expressions, you should leave a blank space between SQL statement arguments, such as the delimited old and new passwords. When initializing a database password, use *NULL* to signify the old password. When removing a database password, designate *NULL* as the new password. The keyword *NULL* should not appear within square brackets.

The *CreateDBPassword* procedure shown next initializes a database password for a database by performing three main steps. First the code constructs the string based on Jet SQL to assign a password to a database for the first time. The password is the word *password* and is the first argument after the *ALTER DATABASE PASSWORD* keyword. Notice that *NULL* appears as the second argument. This is because there is no password to replace. The next block of code creates a connection to the database for which the procedure assigns a password. Notice that the procedure opens the database file exclusively (see the assignment for the *Mode* property). This is imperative when you manipulate the password for a database. The sample assigns a password to the UserLevel.mdb file. The UserLevel.mdb file serves double duty for user-level security and password-protected file demonstrations. If you haven't copied the file from the book's companion content, you'll need to do it now to run this sample. When you do so, remember to remove the read-only file property setting. You can, of course, use any other file you choose, but you must revise the listing accordingly. The third step executes the SQL string with the ADO *Connection* object created in the second step. This takes just one line.

```
Sub CreateDBPassword()
Dim cnn1 As ADODB.Connection
Dim str1 As String

'SQL string to initialize the database password
'to password
str1 = "ALTER DATABASE PASSWORD [password] NULL;"

'Open unsecured database
Set cnn1 = New ADODB.Connection
With cnn1
    .Mode = adModeShareExclusive
    .Open "Provider=Microsoft.Jet.OLEDB.4.0;Data " & _
        "Source=C:\Access11Files\UserLevel.mdb;"

'Execute SQL in str1 to secure database with a password
    .Execute (str1)
End With

'Clean up objects
cnn1.Close
Set cnn1 = Nothing

End Sub
```

When your application changes the password for a database, you have to log in with the old password (see the next code sample). To do this, you assign the old password to the *Database Password* property of the *Connection* object for the database whose password will change. This is one of the extended properties for the *Connection* object, so you need to use a special syntax, as the sample demonstrates. The sample also confirms the Jet SQL syntax for replacing one password with another. In this instance, "foo" replaces the password. Aside from these two modifications, the code sample has the same structure as the preceding one; both initialize a database password for an Access database file.

```
Sub ChangeDBPassword()
Dim cnn1 As ADODB.Connection
Dim str1 As String

'SQL string to change the database password
'from password to foo
str1 = "ALTER DATABASE PASSWORD [foo] [password]"

'Open secured database with password for its
'database password
Set cnn1 = New ADODB.Connection
With cnn1
    .Mode = adModeShareExclusive
    .Provider = "Microsoft.Jet.OLEDB.4.0"
    .Properties("Jet OLEDB:Database Password") = "password"
    .Open "Data Source= C:\Access11Files\UserLevel.mdb;"

'Execute SQL in str1 to change database password from
'password to foo
    .Execute (str1)
End With

'Clean up objects
cnn1.Close
Set cnn1 = Nothing

End Sub
```

The next code sample demonstrates how to remove a database password from an Access database file. This sample borrows heavily from both of the preceding ones. In fact, the only way that this sample differs from the preceding two is in its definition of the SQL string. When you remove a password from a database, make the first argument for the *ALTER DATABASE PASSWORD* keyword *NULL*. The second argument password should be the current password for the database. This is the same password that you use to connect to the database. If you've been following the progression of these code samples, you already know that this password will be "foo."

```
Sub RemoveDBPassword()
Dim cnn1 As ADODB.Connection
Dim str1 As String

'SQL string to clear the database password
'from a database file
str1 = "ALTER DATABASE PASSWORD NULL [foo]"

'Open secured database with foo for its
'database password
Set cnn1 = New ADODB.Connection
With cnn1
    .Mode = adModeShareExclusive
    .Provider = "Microsoft.Jet.OLEDB.4.0"
    .Properties("Jet OLEDB:Database Password") = "foo"
    .Open "Data Source= C:\Access11Files\UserLevel.mdb;"

'Execute SQL in str1 to clear database password
'from a database file
    .Execute (str1)
End With

'Clean up objects
cnn1.Close
Set cnn1 = Nothing

End Sub
```

Setting a Module Password

Since its 2000 version, the Access UI has enabled password security for modules instead of offering user-level security. This new approach makes Access consistent with the other Office 2000 components. It applies to all standard and standalone class modules as well as the modules behind forms and reports.

> **Note**   In the "User-Level Security via Jet SQL and ADO" section that appears later in this chapter, you will read about user-level security for module containers. This feature is available through Jet SQL and the Jet Engine rather than the Access UI.

You set password security once for all the modules in a Microsoft Visual Basic for Applications (VBA) project from the Visual Basic Editor (VBE). Choose the Properties command for the project from the Tools menu to open the

Project Properties dialog box. The Protection tab (shown in Figure 10-1) offers the Lock Project For Viewing check box and text boxes for entering and confirming a password for the module. Assigning a password for viewing modules in a project does not prevent your code from running as though it were not protected. If you assign a password but do not select the Lock Project For Viewing check box, anyone can edit the code but the Project Properties dialog box will be protected. You remove password security from the modules in a project by clearing all entries on the Protection tab.

Figure 10-1   You use the Protection tab of the Project Properties dialog box to set password security for the modules in a project.

After securing your modules with a password, you must enter the password once per session before you can view, edit, or add new code. You can secure forms and reports with both user-level security and module password security. User-level security applies to designing and using forms and reports. You can require a user to have Modify Design permission to add controls to forms. That user will also need the password for modules in a project to write event procedures for the control. Conversely, knowing the password for the modules in a project does not enable a user to add controls to or remove controls from a form. Also, Modify Design permission does not allow a user to change the *HasModule* property of forms and reports to No; the user must first enter the password for the modules in a project.

Using .mde Files

An .mde file totally secures the code for an Access database file. When you convert an .mdb file to an .mde file, Access compiles all your modules, removes editable code, and compacts the destination database while preserving the original .mdb file. The size of your database will shrink because of the removal of editable code. Also, because the conversion optimizes memory usage, your code will run faster.

To convert an .mdb file to an .mde file, you must have exclusive access to the file. (See the "Setting a Database Password Manually" section in this chapter for instructions on how to open a database exclusively.) In addition, the database file must have a 2002 file format; Access 2003 and Access 2002 share this file format, although the Access 2000 file format is the default file format for Access 2000 through Access 2003. On the Tools menu, point to Database Utilities and then choose Make MDE File. After saving the converted file, be sure to save your original file. The only way to edit or add to the code in a database file is to modify the original file and then convert it to an .mde file. After making an .mde file based on an .mdb file, you will have two files with the same file name but with different extensions (the original one with .mdb and the new one with .mde). Save the original .mdb to make the underlying code visible and available for editing.

> **Note**   You can use the Advanced tab of the Options dialog box to select the file format for the next database that you create. Use the drop-down box for the default file format to select the file format.

An .mde file has some restrictions:

- You cannot modify or add forms, reports, or modules.

- You cannot import or export forms, reports, or modules to a standard .mdb file. You can, however, freely import and export tables, queries, macros, and shortcuts for data access pages with other database files.

- You cannot add, delete, or change references to other object libraries or databases.

- You cannot dynamically change code because .mde files contain no editable code.

- You cannot convert any existing member of a replica set to an .mde file, but an .mde file can participate in a replica set.

- An .mde file can reference another database file only if that file is also an .mde file. You must start converting .mdb files (or .mda add-in files) that are referenced before you convert the .mdb file that references them. The new reference must point at the new .mde file.

Overview of User-Level Security

This section introduces the basics of user-level security, with a special emphasis on techniques for managing it manually. First, we'll look at core notions, such as the Admin user and workgroups. Second, a three-step process to implement user-level security is described. The section closes with a brief review of the impact of the settings made during the three-step process. This review acquaints you with the kinds of security that can be enforced with user-level security.

What Is User-Level Security?

User-level security manages the security of Jet database files through the interaction of two files. One of these is the traditional .mdb file. This file tracks objects in a database, such as tables and queries, as well as permissions to use those objects. The second file is an .mdw file, which is commonly referred to as a workgroup information file. The .mdw file stores information about individual users and groups of users in a workgroup. User-level security tracks identification codes for the users and groups within a workgroup as well as the overall workgroup in the .mdw file. When an .mdb file joins an .mdw file, the users and groups defined in the .mdw file inherit the permissions specified for them in the .mdb file. Figure 10-2 graphically depicts the relationship between the two files as well as major functions of each file type.

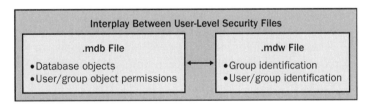

Figure 10-2   A graphical depiction of the interaction of .mdb and .mdw files in user-level security.

Besides the .mdb and .mdw files, there are several other core concepts to grasp as you begin to apply user-level security.

■   These concepts start with the definition of a workgroup administrator. You can think of the workgroup administrator as a user within the workgroup who has unlimited permissions, including permission to assign permissions to other users.

■   A second core notion is that every workgroup must have a workgroup administrator. By default, Access designates the Admin user as the workgroup administrator. To customize the security of your user-level security architecture, I recommend that you always designate another user as the workgroup administrator.

■   The third core notion is that the Admin user account should be stripped of all the permissions because of its status as the default workgroup administrator. In addition, you need to assign a password to the Admin account. This assignment is necessary for the popup dialog that asks for a user name and password when logging on to a database file. If anyone can log on as the Admin user because the account does not have a password and you have not stripped it of permissions, then anyone can enjoy unrestricted permissions in the database.

User-level security does not use passwords to track users. Instead, user-level security relies on a user name and a personal identifier (PID). A workgroup administrator, or other user empowered to administer a workgroup, must assign these when creating a user account for a workgroup information file. User-level security stores the user account information in the workgroup information file (.mdw), but you create a user account from the database file (.mdb). The password is an extra identifier in addition to the user name requested for identifying a user at logon. Users can change their passwords, but not their PIDs. If a user has no password or erases the password for a user account, that person can still log on by leaving the Password box empty in the Logon dialog box.

> **Note**   A workgroup information file can become unavailable for a variety of reasons, including erasure or corruption. When this happens, you need to obtain a new copy of the workgroup information file to gain access to the database file. For this reason, it is good practice to back up a workgroup information file on a regular basis. See the following Web site for tips on recovering from an unavailable .mdw file and other links that drill down on selected user-level security topics: *http://msdn.microsoft.com/library/default.asp?url=/library/en-us/off2000 /html/achowRebuildCorruptedDeletedMSAccessWorkgroupS.asp.*

Three-Step Process for Instituting User-Level Security

In three relatively easy steps, you can create a database file guarded with user-level security. The overall process requires you to start Access from the Windows Start button twice. Each step involves multiple actions. Collectively, the actions in each step contribute to achieving the goal for a step.

Step 1 Create Workgroup and Administrator and Force Logon

Start this first step by opening a new Access session from the Windows Start button. From an empty Access session with no database, choose Tools, Security, Workgroup Administrator. Click Create in the Workgroup Administrator dialog box.

When Create is clicked, the Workgroup Owner Information dialog box opens. This dialog offers three boxes for you to create a unique identification for your workgroup. By default, the Workgroup Administrator populates the Name and Organization boxes with values used when you installed Access. Since it is relatively easy to guess the default Name and Organization entries, you should change these and type a value in the Workgroup ID box. User-level security combines the contents of all three text boxes to create a unique identification code for the workgroup. Therefore, it is wise to record these values if you need to recreate the Workgroup file later.

> **Note**   The *Workgroup ID* field must contain between four and 20 characters. It is case sensitive.

After specifying the values identifying a workgroup and clicking OK, designate path and file names for the workgroup information file in the Workgroup Information File dialog box. If you created an Access11Files folder off your root directory of the C: drive, you could specify C:\Access11Files\SystemDemo.mdw. By default, Access locates .mdw files in the ApplicationData\Microsoft\Access folder for the current user profile. In addition, it names a new .mdw file, System*x*, where *x* is a sequential number based on the last System*x*.mdw file in the default folder. You can override both the default folder and the file name (as the instructions for this example do). You should record the path and file name. This is because a computer using a database file secured by a workgroup must join the workgroup. In order to accomplish this, a computer user (or at least the application) needs to know the path and file name of the .mdw file. Before creating the workgroup information file, Access gives you a final chance to confirm the workgroup identification field values as well as the path and file names for the .mdw file containing the workgroup information. Figure 10-3 shows the Confirm Workgroup Information dialog box for the current example. It can be convenient to copy the confirmation dialog box image, because if necessary you can use the vital information in this image for re-creating the workgroup information file. Once a new workgroup information file is completed, the current Access session is automatically joined to the workgroup.

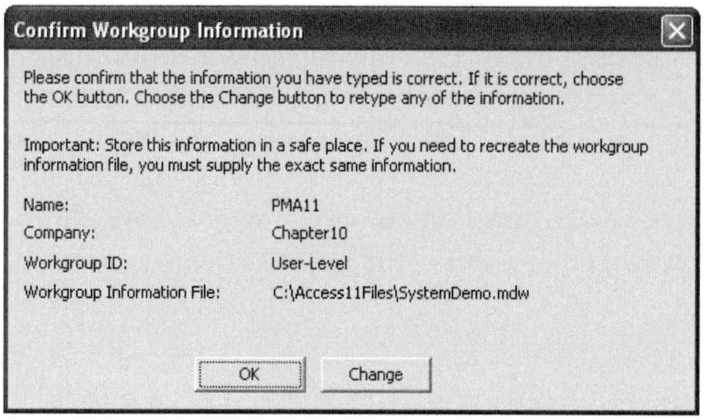

Figure 10-3   Confirmation screen for a newly created workgroup information file.

The next task in the first step involves designating a new administrator for the workgroup. Start the task by choosing Tools, Security, User And Group Accounts. You can start to create a new user to serve as an administrator by clicking New on the Users tab of the User And Group Accounts dialog box. In this example, I assigned Chap10Admin as the name and PMA11 as the personal ID for the user. Then, I used the arrows between the Available Groups and Member Of lists to add the Chap10Admin user to the Admins group. This completes the task of creating a new workgroup administrator named Chap10Admin. Figure 10-4 shows the User And Group Account dialog box after adding the new member to the Admins group.

Figure 10-4   The User And Group Accounts dialog box for creating a workgroup administrator named Chap10Admin.

The concluding element of the first step is to manipulate settings for the Admin user in ways permitted by the User And Group Accounts dialog box.

This dialog box allows you to perform two actions for the Admin user. First, you can remove the Admin account from the Admins group. This deprives the account of its built-in status as an administrator for the workgroup. Second, you can assign a password to the Admin user. By default, the Admin user has no password. After you assign a password to the Admin user, Access automatically prompts with a Logon dialog box the first time a user attempts to perform some action guarded by user-level security.

Note   Clearing the password for the Admin user is a simple way to disable user-level security.

To remove the Admin user from the Admins group, you must select the Admin user from the Name drop-down list. Then, with Admins selected in the Member Of list, click the << Remove button.

You can assign a password to the Admin on the Change Logon Password tab of the User And Group Accounts dialog box. Since you are assigning an initial password, leave the Old Password box empty and populate the New Password and Verify boxes with the same string value, such as *password*. After assigning a password to the Admin user, exit Access and close the window for the Access session.

You cannot assign a password to the Chap10Admin user from the User And Group Accounts dialog box in the session for Step 1. This is because you used the default user account of Admin when you opened the Access session, and you can assign a password with this dialog box only for the user in the current session. Since Step 1 does not assign a password to the Chap10Admin user, the administrator for the workgroup has a blank password. Recall that the assignment of passwords to user accounts is optional for all accounts except the Admin user when you invoke user-level security.

Step 2 Create a Secure Database with at Least One Table
The second step creates a new database with Chap10Admin as the owner. In this example, I call the database ManualDemo.mdb. The example continues to add a table to the database. Step 3 creates a couple of users and then assigns distinct permissions for the table to the users. A subsequent section demonstrates how the different permissions enable one user to perform tasks that another user is unable to perform.

Start a new Access session and click the Blank database link on the New File Task Pane. Assign the name ManualDemo to the database and select a Save

In folder of Access11Files (if you created such a folder to follow along with the demonstrations in this book). In the Logon dialog box, enter Chap10Admin in the Name box and leave the Password box empty. These steps create the ManualDemo.mdb file with Chap10Admin as the owner.

Before adding a table to the database, it is necessary to strip the Admin user and any groups to which it belongs of permissions for new database objects. While the Admin user does not enjoy any direct permissions for new objects in the ManualDemo database, it still belongs to the Users group (recall that you cannot delete the Admin user in a workgroup). By default, Access grants members of the Users group all permissions that apply to any new tables or queries (see Figure 10-5). Since the Admin user belongs to the Users group, it inherits these permissions. Therefore, to strip the Admin user of all permissions for tables, you have to remove all permissions from the Users group. This operation has the side benefit of eliminating unlimited permissions from other users that you may add to the workgroup. You can strip the Users group of all permissions by clicking the Read Design check box. This clears the other check boxes in the dialog box shown in Figure 10-5.

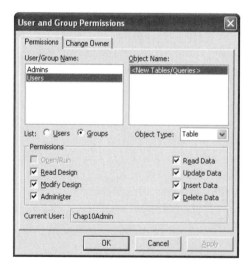

Figure 10-5 The Users group permissions for new tables and queries with the default permission settings.

Next, use the File, Import command to add the *Shippers* table from the Northwind database to the ManualDemo database. This operation makes available a database object for which different users can have different permissions. You can create your own table manually or programmatically instead of importing it. Importing the *Shippers* table from the Northwind database concludes the second step.

Step 3 Create Other Users with Different Permissions

The third step adds two users and then assigns different permissions to each user. It is not necessary to restart Access for this step. In fact, you should stay in the same database in which you concluded Step 2.

Start to add the users by opening the User And Group Accounts dialog box as described in Step 1. Add two new users named ReadOnly and ReadUpdate. These users automatically belong to the Users group. However, since we stripped that group of all permissions for new tables and queries before adding the *Shippers* table to the ManualDemo database, the two users have no permissions yet for the *Shippers* table.

Next, open the User And Group Permissions dialog box as described in Step 2. In Step 3, the instructions apply to users instead of groups. Therefore, select the Users option for List, if it is not already selected. Then, select Read-Only in the User/Group Name list. In addition, make sure the *Shippers* table is selected from the Object Name list. These selections let you apply permissions for the *Shippers* table to the ReadOnly user. Assign the permission by selecting the Read Data check box. This action automatically selects the Read Design check box as well. Click Apply to confirm your permission settings for the ReadOnly user. Next, select the ReadUpdate user. Then, select the Update Data check box. In this case, Access automatically selects the Read Data and Read Design check boxes as well. Confirm your permission assignments for the ReadUpdate user by clicking Apply. This completes the steps for assigning the permissions to the two new users. You can exit Access at this point.

If you want to do so, you can add passwords for the other users in the workgroup besides the Admin user. Recall that users do not require passwords, and they can always change or remove them on their own. The process of adding a new password to any user is the same as for the Admin user. However, you must initially open Access by logging on as that user first. To do this, you can open a new Access session from the Windows Start button. Then, choose Tools, Security, User And Group Accounts. Before Access opens the dialog box for the command, it prompts with a Logon dialog box. Enter the name of the user for which you want to assign a password. From the Change Logon Password tab of the User And Group Accounts dialog box, complete the process of assigning a password. To assign a password to another user, you must exit Access. Then, open Access again from the Windows Start button. Log on to Access as the user for which you want to assign a password. In this example, we leave the password for all users unset, except for the Admin user.

Demonstrating the Effects of Permission Settings

After completing the preceding three steps, you will have four users with different permissions for the *Shippers* table in the ManualDemo.mdb file. Because each has different permissions, the users' experiences will be unique from one other. The following table lists the users, passwords (if they exist), and permissions for the *Shippers* table in the ManualDemo database.

Table 10-1 Users, Permissions, and Passwords for the ManualDemo Database

User name	Permission Summary	Password
Chap10Admin	Unlimited permissions because of its status as workgroup administrator	*Null*
ReadUpdate	Permission to view and update values in the *Shippers* table	*Null*
ReadOnly	Permission to view, but not update, values in the *Shippers* table	*Null*
Admin	No permission (not even to view) for the *Shippers* table	password
User name	Permission Summary	Password
Chap10Admin	Unlimited permissions because of its status as workgroup administrator	*Null*
ReadUpdate	Permission to view and update values in the *Shippers* table	*Null*
ReadOnly	Permission to view, but not update, values in the *Shippers* table	*Null*
Admin	No permission (not even to view) for the *Shippers* table	password
User name	Permission Summary	Password
Chap10Admin	Unlimited permissions because of its status as workgroup administrator	*Null*
ReadUpdate	Permission to view and update values in the *Shippers* table	*Null*
ReadOnly	Permission to view, but not update, values in the *Shippers* table	*Null*
Admin	No permission (not even to view) for the *Shippers* table	password
User name	Permission Summary	Password
Chap10Admin	Unlimited permissions because of its status as workgroup administrator	*Null*
ReadUpdate	Permission to view and update values in the *Shippers* table	*Null*
ReadOnly	Permission to view, but not update, values in the *Shippers* table	*Null*
Admin	No permission (not even to view) for the *Shippers* table	password

How a user opens the ManualDemo database varies depending on whether the user has a password. For example, the ReadOnly user can open the database by starting an Access session and clicking the ManualDemo link in the Getting Started task pane or by choosing File, Open, and then navigating to the Manual-Demo.mdb file. In the Logon dialog box, the ReadOnly user needs only to populate the Name box and click OK. The Admin user, who has a password, must enter Admin in the Name box and the Admin password in the Password box.

Although Admin has no permissions in the ManualDemo database, the Admin user can still open the database. This is because Access is a file-based database manager. Its security cannot begin to take effect until a user opens a database. By entering Admin in the Logon name box, the Admin user specifies a set of permissions for objects in the ManualDemo database. The permissions do not allow any permissions for the *Shippers* table. Therefore, if the user tried to open the *Shippers* table, Access would respond with an error message saying the user could not read the definitions for the table.

The ReadOnly user has a different kind of experience. This user can open the *Shippers* table. However, ReadOnly cannot edit the column values within the rows of the *Shippers* table. Attempts to edit data results in no effect other than a reminder sound. There is no error message as there is when the Admin user attempts to open the *Shippers* table.

The ReadUpdate user has permissions that are midway between those for the ReadOnly user and the Chap10Admin user. The ReadUpdate user can open and edit column values in the *Shippers* table, but cannot add new rows or remove existing rows to the table. The Chap10Admin user enjoys permission to view all rows, edit any column value, insert new rows, and delete existing rows. In fact, as the workgroup administrator, Chap10Admin can perform any task in the database and delegate permission to perform those tasks to other users.

User-Level Security via ADOX

As you have seen, user-level security enables you to define a workgroup composed of user accounts. You can also create group accounts. A group account can have zero or more user accounts associated with it. This section demonstrates how to create user and group accounts as well as assign permissions to those accounts programmatically. The ADOX model supports this functionality through its *Catalog* object as well as its *Users* and *Groups* collection objects. Figure 10-6 shows the hierarchy: groups can belong to users, and users can belong to groups; users and groups both belong to the *Catalog* object.

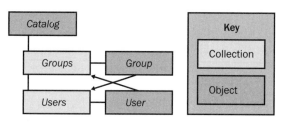

Figure 10-6   The relationship of the *User* and *Group* objects to the *Catalog* object and the *Users* and *Groups* collections.

You can assign permissions to users, groups, or both. It is generally most efficient to assign permissions to groups when a workgroup has a large number of users with frequent additions and deletions of user accounts. You clear all default permissions from existing individual user accounts as well as the Users group account, and then assign users to all appropriate groups. With this type of user-level design, you can administer permissions by assigning users to groups and assigning permissions to groups. Recall that users inherit all permissions from the groups to which they belong. By restricting permission assignments to groups, this design provides a single focal point for managing permissions.

The upcoming samples show how to code typical user-level administration tasks. Because they are meant to highlight basic security management procedures, only a couple of the samples demonstrate error-trapping logic. The samples assume you have a working knowledge of Access security concepts, such as those reviewed in the "Overview of User-Level Security" section in this chapter. To learn more about the basics of Access user-level security, search Access Help for the topics "Manage user and group accounts" and "Types of permissions."

Connecting to a Secure Database

The following procedure connects to a secured Jet database named UserLevel. I created the database with the Chap10Admin user while I was joined to the SystemDemo.mdw workgroup created earlier in this chapter. The database has a single table name *WebBasedList*. This is the same table used in the "Producing Form Letters" section of Chapter 9. I stripped the Users group of all table/view permissions in the database so that no user had any permissions for the *WebBasedList* table except the Chap10Admin user. The UserLevel.mdb and the SystemDemo.mdw files for the workgroup are available in the book's companion materials.

The string for connecting to a database protected with user-level security requires four phrases. The first phrase designates the *Provider* property for the procedure's *Connection* object. It specifies the Jet 4.0 OLE DB provider. The second phrase assigns the system database property for the connection. This is the name and path to the workgroup information file. This file is System-Demo.mdw in the Access11Files folder (or wherever you saved it). The third phrase specifies the data source, which in this case is the secured database file, UserLevel.mdb. The fourth phrase denotes user ID and password values for logging into the secure database. In this sample, the procedure logs on as the Chap10Admin user with a *Null* password. No other user in the workgroup has any permissions for the *WebBasedList* table.

> **Note**   Before attempting to run the following sample or any others in this section, you must copy the Systemdemo.mdw file from the book's companion content to your hard drive and join the workgroup it defines. As with any file copied from the companion content, clear the read-only property setting. To join the workgroup, choose the Tools, Security, Workgroup Administrator menu command, then click the Join button and select the SystemDemo.mdw file in the Access11Files folder (or wherever you saved it). In addition, turn on the Access logon feature; see the "Three-Step Process for Instituting User-Level Security" section in this chapter for instructions on accomplishing this. By the way, you can restore the Access default workgroup by joining the System.mdw. Perform a search for this file because it resides in different folders depending on your Windows user profile and Windows operating system.

```
Sub OpenUserLevel()
Dim cnn1 As New ADODB.Connection
Dim rst1 As New ADODB.Recordset

'Open connection to target user-level secured data
'source; specify path for workgroup information
'file; designate logon ID and password (if appropriate)
cnn1.Provider = "Microsoft.Jet.OLEDB.4.0"
cnn1.Properties("Jet OLEDB:System database") = _
    "C:\Access11Files\SystemDemo.mdw"
cnn1.Open "Data Source=C:\Access11Files\UserLevel.mdb;" & _
    "User ID=Chap10Admin;Password=;"

'Print first field from first record to confirm connection
rst1.Open "WebBasedList", cnn1, , , adCmdTable
```

(continued)

```
Debug.Print rst1.Fields(0)

'Clean up objects
cnn1.Close
Set cnn1 = Nothing

End Sub
```

The two lines following the comment open a recordset based on the connection and print the first field's value from the first record. This simply confirms the operation of the sample. The table, *WebBasedList*, is the same one used in the earlier multiuser sample.

Adding and Deleting Users

When you develop and manage a custom application with user-level security, you are likely to add and delete users. Before you can add users, you must log on as a member of the Admins group, such as Chap10Admin. You can use the *Append* method of the *Users* collection to add users to a catalog or group. You must specify a name for the new user, and you can designate a password. ADO lets you assign a password later using the *ChangePassword* method for the *User* object. Unfortunately, you cannot assign a personal ID (PID) with this approach. Instead, ADO picks one randomly.

> **Note** In the section "User-Level Security via Jet SQL and ADO," I'll show you another approach based on Jet SQL and ADO that enables you to set the PID. The discussion of that approach mentions why the ability to set the PID is important (as does the Access Help file).

The following two procedures show one approach to invoking the *Append* method to add a new user to an application. The *CallMakeUser* procedure launches the *MakeUser* procedure as it passes along two arguments. The first argument designates a new user's name. The second argument sends a password. In the sample, the string "*password*" is the value of the password argument.

```
'Make sure NewUser account does not exist prior to running
'this procedure; for example, run callDeleteUser first

Sub CallMakeUser()
MakeUser "NewUser", "password"
```

```
End Sub

Sub MakeUser(usrName As String, secureWord As String)
Dim cat1 As ADOX.Catalog
Dim usr1 As ADOX.User

'Instantiate catalog
Set cat1 = New ADOX.Catalog

'Set ActiveConnection property for catalog for
'use in adding a new user
cat1.ActiveConnection = _
    "Provider=Microsoft.Jet.OLEDB.4.0;" & _
    "Data Source=C:\Access11Files\UserLevel.mdb;" & _
    "Jet OLEDB:System database=C:\Access11Files\SystemDemo.mdw;" & _
    "User Id=Chap10Admin;Password=;"

'Append user passed from calling routine
'and assign password
Set usr1 = New ADOX.User
usr1.Name = usrName
cat1.Users.Append usr1
cat1.Users(usr1.Name).ChangePassword "", secureWord

'Clean up objects
Set usr1 = Nothing
Set cat1 = Nothing

End Sub
```

The *MakeUser* procedure specifies a target for the new group using the *Catalog* object's *ActiveConnection* setting. Note that it designates a user ID with the authority to make a new user, and it points to a workgroup information file. The *Append* method in *MakeUser* adds a new member to the *Catalog* object. Therefore, this new user is not yet a member of any groups. The user created by *MakeUser* does not have any permissions for database objects. You can also add a member to a *Group* object so that the user has immediate membership in that group. One of the samples to follow uses this technique.

Even without any permissions for database objects in a database, the *NewUser* user can connect programmatically to any database in the System-Demo.mdw workgroup. The user has a name and a password, and the *Logon-NewUser* procedure demonstrates the syntax for connecting *NewUser* securely to the UserLevel database in the SystemDemo.mdw workgroup. Later in the chapter, after a demonstration of how to assign database object permissions and group memberships, you'll see another procedure demonstrate more advanced functionality from a programmatically created user.

```
Sub LogonNewUser()
Dim cnn1 As New ADODB.Connection
Dim rst1 As New ADODB.Recordset
Dim str1 As String

'Open connection to target user-level secured data
'source; specify path for workgroup information
'file; designate logon ID and password
With cnn1
    .Provider = "Microsoft.Jet.OLEDB.4.0"
    .Mode = adModeShareDenyNone
    .Properties("Jet OLEDB:System database") = _
        "C:\Access11Files\SystemDemo.mdw"
    .Open "Data Source=C:\Access11Files\UserLevel.mdb;" & _
        "User ID=NewUser;Password=password;"
End With

'Clean up objects
cnn1.Close
Set cnn1 = Nothing

End Sub
```

The next two procedures remove a user from the catalog for a database. The *Delete* method for the *Users* collection has the same syntax as the *Delete* method for the *Tables*, *Procedures*, and *Views* collection objects. The first procedure, *CallDeleteUser*, passes a single argument—the user name—to the second procedure, *DeleteUser*. The second procedure removes the user from the catalog and concurrently removes the user from any groups as well.

```
'Make sure NewUser account exists prior to running this
'procedure; for example, run callMakeUser

Sub CallDeleteUser()
DeleteUser "NewUser"
End Sub

Sub DeleteUser(usrName As String)
Dim cat1 As ADOX.Catalog

'Instantiate catalog
Set cat1 = New ADOX.Catalog

'Set ActiveConnection property for catalog for
'use in dropping a user
cat1.ActiveConnection = _
    "Provider=Microsoft.Jet.OLEDB.4.0;" & _
    "Data Source=C:\Access11Files\UserLevel.mdb;" & _
```

```
    "Jet OLEDB:System database=C:\Access11Files\SystemDemo.mdw;" & _
    "User Id=Chap10Admin;Password=;"

'Remove user from workgroup
cat1.Users.Delete usrName

'Clean up objects
Set cat1 = Nothing

End Sub
```

You must log on to a database as a member of the Admins group to delete a user. The *Delete* method does not require a password. All that the second procedure needs is a string argument naming the user to delete.

Assigning Groups to Users

One common technique for administering permissions is to assign groups to users and manage permissions for groups. Users can derive all their permissions implicitly through their group memberships. The samples in this discussion add and remove group memberships from a user account. Both samples use the built-in Users group, but the same techniques work for custom groups.

The following two procedures add a group to a user account called NewUser. Make sure the user account exists before running the procedure (for example, run the *CallMakeUser* procedure if the user account does not exist). The first procedure, *CallAddGroupToUser*, passes a user name and a group name to the second procedure, *AddGroupToUser*, which uses the *Append* method to add the *Group* object to the *Groups* collection for the user. The sample passes arguments to the second procedure that tell it to add the new group to the *Groups* collection for a particular *User* object.

```
Sub CallAddGroupToUser()
AddGroupToUser "NewUser", "Users"
'AddGroupToUser "Admin", "MySecretGroup1"
End Sub

Sub AddGroupToUser(usrName As String, grpName As String)
On Error GoTo AddTrap
Dim cat1 As New ADOX.Catalog
Const acctNameAlreadyExist = -2147467259

'Instantiate catalog
Set cat1 = New ADOX.Catalog

'Set ActiveConnection property for catalog for
'use in adding a new group to an existing user
cat1.ActiveConnection = _
```

(continued)

```
                "Provider=Microsoft.Jet.OLEDB.4.0;" & _
                "Data Source=C:\Access11Files\UserLevel.mdb;" & _
                "Jet OLEDB:System database=C:\Access11Files\SystemDemo.mdw;" & _
                "User Id=Chap10Admin;Password=;"

        'Append new group to Groups collection for the
        'workgroup and then add group to the Groups
        'collection for a user account passed in as an argument
        cat1.Groups.Append grpName
        cat1.Users(usrName).Groups.Append grpName

    AddExit:
        Set cat1 = Nothing
        Exit Sub

    AddTrap:
        If Err.Number = acctNameAlreadyExist Then
        'If account already exists, ignore the run-time error
            Resume Next
        Else
            Debug.Print Err.Number; Err.Description
        End If

    End Sub
```

The second procedure invokes the *Append* method in an attempt to create a group with the name of the second argument passed to it. This procedure works for groups whether or not they already exist. Because Users is a built-in group account, it will always exist. If a group with the name of the second argument does not already exist, the *Append* method succeeds; otherwise, the procedure falls into an error trap with error number –2147467259 and moves on to the next statement. Then, the procedure appends the group to the *Groups* collection for the *NewUser* object. Again, if the group is already in the *Groups* collection for the user, the procedure progresses to the next statement.

The next two procedures remove a group from a user's *Groups* collection. The first procedure, *CallRemoveUserFromGroup*, passes user and group name parameters to the second procedure, *RemoveUserFromGroup*, which does the work. There is no error checking in this sample, so make sure the group belongs to the user. You can do this by running the preceding sample.

```
    'Make sure the group account exists for the user
    'prior to running this procedure
    'For example, run CallAddGroupToUser

    Sub CallRemoveUserFromGroup()
    RemoveUserFromGroup "NewUser", "Users"
    End Sub
```

```
Sub RemoveUserFromGroup(usrName As String, grpName As String)
Dim cat1 As ADOX.Catalog

'Instantiate catalog
Set cat1 = New ADOX.Catalog

'Set ActiveConnection property for catalog for
'use in dropping a group from the Groups collection for
'an existing user
cat1.ActiveConnection = _
    "Provider=Microsoft.Jet.OLEDB.4.0;" & _
    "Data Source=C:\Access11Files\UserLevel.mdb;" & _
    "Jet OLEDB:System database=C:\Access11Files\SystemDemo.mdw;" & _
    "User Id=Chap10Admin;Password=;"

'Drop the group from the Groups collection for a user
cat1.Users(usrName).Groups.Delete grpName

'Clean up objects
Set cat1 = Nothing

End Sub
```

You invoke the *Delete* method to remove a group from the *Groups* collection for a *User* object. Notice the hierarchical specification for an individual user. After identifying a user, the syntax requires the designation of the *Groups* collection and, finally, the *Delete* method. The syntax designates the group name as a parameter for the *Delete* method.

Creating, Deleting, and Tracking Groups in a Catalog

When you develop custom user-level solutions, you'll probably want to create custom groups with names that are meaningful to your clients and whose permissions fit the special requirements of your custom application. The four upcoming samples do the following:

- Create a custom group

- Delete a custom group

- Prepare a report itemizing all the groups in a catalog and the groups associated with each user account

- Toggle the membership of a user in the Admins group

- The next two procedures add a group named MySecretGroup1. After referencing a database file with a user ID sufficient to make the addition, the procedure invokes the *Append* method of the *Groups* collection. You must specify a container for the *Groups* collection.

When you add a new group to the project's *Users* collection, the container is a *Catalog* object. When you assign a group to the *Groups* collection of a *User* object, you must specify the user as the root object for the *Groups* collection.

```
'Make sure MySecretGroup1 does not exist before running
'this procedure; for example, run callDeleteGroup

Sub CallMakeGroup()
MakeGroup "MySecretGroup1"
End Sub

Sub MakeGroup(grpName As String)
Dim cat1 As ADOX.Catalog

'Instantiate catalog
Set cat1 = New ADOX.Catalog

'Set ActiveConnection property for catalog for
'creating a custom group
cat1.ActiveConnection = _
    "Provider=Microsoft.Jet.OLEDB.4.0;" & _
    "Data Source=C:\Access11Files\UserLevel.mdb;" & _
    "Jet OLEDB:System database=C:\Access11Files\SystemDemo.mdw;" & _
    "User Id=Chap10Admin;Password=;"

'Add custom group to the catalog's Groups collection
cat1.Groups.Append grpName

'Clean up objects
Set cat1 = Nothing

End Sub
```

The following two procedures remove a group from a catalog. You must make sure that the group already exists in the catalog before running the procedures. You can do this by running the preceding sample. In fact, the next sample removes the group added in the preceding one.

```
'Make sure MySecretGroup1 exists prior to running this
'procedure; for example, run callMakeGroup

Sub CallDeleteGroup()
DeleteGroup "MySecretGroup1"
End Sub

Sub DeleteGroup(grpName As String)
Dim cat1 As ADOX.Catalog

'Instantiate catalog
```

```
Set cat1 = New ADOX.Catalog

'Set ActiveConnection property for catalog for
'dropping a custom group
cat1.ActiveConnection = _
    "Provider=Microsoft.Jet.OLEDB.4.0;" & _
    "Data Source=C:\Access11Files\UserLevel.mdb;" & _
    "Jet OLEDB:System database=C:\Access11Files\SystemDemo.mdw;" & _
    "User Id=Chap10Admin;Password=;"

'Drop a group from the catalog's Groups collection
cat1.Groups.Delete grpName

'Clean up objects
Set cat1 = Nothing

End Sub
```

The syntax for deleting a group closely parallels that for adding a group.
The code invokes the *Delete* method of the catalog's *Groups* collection. You
pass the method a single parameter—the name of the group to delete.

As you add and delete groups and users and reassign groups to users, you
can easily create a custom report that tracks the group memberships for the
Catalog and individual *User* objects. The following procedure itemizes the
groups in a *Catalog* object that points at a specific database. Then it itemizes the
Groups collection members for each user in the catalog's *Users* collection.

```
Sub ListGroupsInCat()
Dim cat1 As ADOX.Catalog
Dim grp1 As New ADOX.Group
Dim usr1 As ADOX.User

'Instantiate catalog
Set cat1 = New ADOX.Catalog
Set usr1 = New User

'Set ActiveConnection property for catalog for
'looping through groups and users
cat1.ActiveConnection = _
    "Provider=Microsoft.Jet.OLEDB.4.0;" & _
    "Data Source=C:\Access11Files\UserLevel.mdb;" & _
    "Jet OLEDB:System database=C:\Access11Files\SystemDemo.mdw;" & _
    "User Id=Chap10Admin;Password=;"

'Groups in overall catalog
Debug.Print cat1.Groups.Count & " groups are in the catalog"
For Each grp1 In cat1.Groups
    Debug.Print String(3, " ") & "* " & grp1.Name
Next grp1
Debug.Print
```

(continued)

```
'Groups in each user
'Creator and Engine are special users that appear in the
'Users collection but do not need to be tracked
For Each usr1 In cat1.Users
    If usr1.Name <> "Creator" And usr1.Name <> "Engine" Then
        Debug.Print String(5, " ") & usr1.Groups.Count & _
            " group(s) are in  " & usr1.Name
        For Each grp1 In cat1.Users(usr1.Name).Groups
            Debug.Print String(8, " ") & "* " & grp1.Name
        Next grp1
        Debug.Print
    End If
Next usr1

'Clean up objects
Set usr1 = Nothing
Set cat1 = Nothing

End Sub
```

The report generated from this procedure appears in Figure 10-7. The report displays the total number of groups in the workgroup information file, and it lists the names of those groups. Then, the procedure reports the number of groups to which each user belongs. If a user does belong to any groups, the procedure prints their names. The Admin user belongs to the built-in Users groups, but the Chap10Admin user, which serves as a workgroup administrator, belongs to the built-in Users and Admins groups. The NewUser user does not belong to any group, but the ReadOnly and ReadUpdate users, which were created for the manual user-level security demonstrations, both belong to the Users groups. You can use the samples just discussed to create and delete users, groups, and user membership in groups.

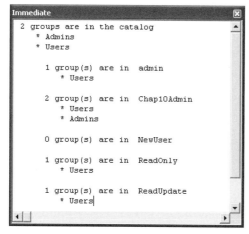

Figure 10-7   A group membership report from the *ListGroupsInCat* procedure.

The following procedure shows one possible application of the *List-GroupsInCat* procedure shown a moment ago. The *ToggleNewUserInAdmins-Group* procedure does what its name implies. It toggles the membership of the *NewUser* object in the Admins group. It also documents the current status of the *NewUser* object in the Admins group by calling the *ListGroupsInCat* procedure.

```
Sub ToggleNewUserInAdminsGroup()
On Error GoTo ToggleTrap
Dim cat1 As ADOX.Catalog
Const notInAdmins = 3265

'Instantiate catalog
Set cat1 = New ADOX.Catalog

'Set ActiveConnection property for catalog
cat1.ActiveConnection = _
    "Provider=Microsoft.Jet.OLEDB.4.0;" & _
    "Data Source=C:\Access11Files\UserLevel.mdb;" & _
    "Jet OLEDB:System database=C:\Access11Files\SystemDemo.mdw;" & _
    "User Id=Chap10Admin;Password=;"

'Attempt to delete membership of user in the Admins group
cat1.Users("NewUser").Groups.Delete ("Admins")

ToggleExit:
Set cat1 = Nothing
ListGroupsInCat
Exit Sub

ToggleTrap:
If Err.Number = notInAdmins Then
'If user not in Admins group, add it to the group
    cat1.Users("NewUser").Groups.Append "Admins"
Else
    Debug.Print Err.Number; Err.Description
End If
Resume Next

End Sub
```

Notice that the toggling procedure relies on error trapping. After connecting to the target database and the workgroup information file through the *cat1* object reference, the procedure attempts to delete *Admins* from the *Groups* collection of *NewUser*. If it is successful, the procedure closes by calling *List-GroupsInCat* and exiting. Otherwise, an error occurs. If the error occurs because the group is not in the user's *Groups* collection, the procedure adds *Admins* to the *NewUser Groups* collection. Then it closes by resuming as though no error had occurred.

Setting Permissions

You can use the *SetPermissions* method for *Group* and *User* objects to manage the permissions available to a security account. You invoke the *GetPermissions* method for these objects to return a *Long* value that specifies the types of permissions assigned to a group or to a user. Both methods offer a wide array of outcomes; they can assign and report various permissions for a number of database object types. In addition, you can use the *SetPermissions* method to assign, revoke, and deny permissions as well as audit their use.

The two procedures that follow grant a group full permissions for any new table. Setting the permission for new tables has no impact for existing tables. Therefore, a group can have full permissions for all new tables and no permissions for existing tables.

```
'Make sure MySecretGroup1 exists before running procedure
Sub CallSetAllTablePermissionsForGroup()
SetAllTablePermissionsForGroup "MySecretGroup1"
End Sub

Sub SetAllTablePermissionsForGroup(grpName As String)
Dim cat1 As ADOX.Catalog

'Instantiate catalog, group, and user
Set cat1 = New ADOX.Catalog

'Set ActiveConnection property for catalog
cat1.ActiveConnection = _
    "Provider=Microsoft.Jet.OLEDB.4.0;" & _
    "Data Source=C:\Access11Files\UserLevel.mdb;" & _
    "Jet OLEDB:System database=C:\Access11Files\SystemDemo.mdw;" & _
    "User Id=Chap10Admin;Password=;"

'Assign full rights to new tables to grpName group
cat1.Groups(grpName).SetPermissions Null, adPermObjTable, _
    adAccessSet, adRightFull

'Clean up objects
Set cat1 = Nothing

End Sub
```

The first procedure passes a group name, *MySecretGroup1*, to the second procedure. The second procedure invokes the *SetPermissions* method for the group member with that name. Therefore, you must make sure that the group exists before you run the procedure or add error-trapping logic. The method's first parameter has an explicit *Null* value. This parameter normally specifies the name of a database object, such as a table. A *Null* value indicates that you should set permissions for any new database objects. The second parameter designates a *Table* object type. The third parameter serves as a verb; it indicates that the command will set a permission. Other constants indicate different actions that the method can launch, such as revoking permissions. The fourth parameter grants the user full rights. Other rights grant data manipulation privileges, such as insert, update, and delete rights, as well as data definition privileges, such as create and drop rights for objects such as tables. The method and its parameters grant *MySecretGroup1* full rights for all new tables in the UserLevel.mdb database file with the SystemDemo.mdw workgroup information file.

This basic design is flexible and can serve in many different situations. For example, to revoke all rights for new tables, you change the third parameter for the *SetPermissions* method from *adAccessSet* to *adAccessRevoke*. To set rights for an existing database object, you replace the *Null* for the first parameter with the database object's name.

> **Note**   The book's companion content contains more VBA samples illustrating how to revoke permissions for new objects and how to set and revoke permissions for existing objects.

Putting It All Together

The following two procedures tap a cross-section of prior samples and show a new twist to the *SetPermissions* method. The first procedure calls the *Make-Group* procedure to create a new group in the SystemDemo.mdw workgroup information file. Then, it invokes the second procedure and passes along the new group's name as well as the name of a database object for which it wants to assign permissions. The last two lines in the first procedure create a new user named NewUser2 and add MySecretGroup2 to its *Groups* collection. In this way, NewUser2 inherits the permissions assigned to MySecretGroup2 by the second procedure.

```
Sub CallSetRIDTablePermissionsForGroupTable()

'This procedure makes a group called MySecretGroup2
'Assigns Read/Insert/Delete permissions for
'WebBasedList table to MySecretGroup2
'Next, it creates NewUser2 and assigns
'MySecretGroup2 to NewUser2

'Before running this, delete MySecretGroup2 and
'NewUser2 from UserLevel.mdb if they exist
```

(continued)

```
    MakeGroup "MySecretGroup2"
    SetRIDTablePermissionsForGroupTable "MySecretGroup2", "WebBasedList"
    MakeUser "NewUser2", "password"
    AddGroupToUser "NewUser2", "MySecretGroup2"

End Sub

Sub SetRIDTablePermissionsForGroupTable(grpName As String, tblName)
Dim cat1 As New ADOX.Catalog
Dim grp1 As New ADOX.Group, usr1 As New ADOX.User

'Instantiate catalog
Set cat1 = New ADOX.Catalog

'Set ActiveConnection property for catalog
cat1.ActiveConnection = _
    "Provider=Microsoft.Jet.OLEDB.4.0;" & _
    "Data Source=C:\Access11Files\UserLevel.mdb;" & _
    "Jet OLEDB:System database=C:\Access11Files\SystemDemo.mdw;" & _
    "User Id=Chap10Admin;Password=;"

'Assign read, insert, and delete rights to an existing table
'for grpName group
cat1.Groups(grpName).SetPermissions tblName, adPermObjTable, _
 adAccessSet, adRightRead Or adRightInsert Or adRightDelete

'Clean up objects
Set cat1 = Nothing

End Sub
```

The second procedure assigns read, insert, and delete permissions for the *WebBasedList* table in UserLevel.mdb to MySecretGroup2. Notice update permissions are missing from the list of rights. This procedure is similar to the earlier sample that applied rights for a specific database object, but this one illustrates how to concatenate three separate rights to get a combined set of permissions. Notice that the syntax uses an Or operator for concatenating rights.

The major substantive outcome of the preceding pair of procedures is that NewUser2 has select, insert, and delete permissions through its membership in the MySecretGroup2 group. The following *SelectInsertDeleteAndUpdateWithNewUser2* procedure demonstrates how to connect NewUser2 to the UserLevel database and invoke its rights in the database for the *WebBasedList* table. The procedure starts by connecting to the database. Then it successively selects, inserts a record, and deletes the added record. Finally, it attempts to update the last record. This attempt fails since NewUser2 does not have an update right for the *WebBasedList* table. However, you can manually or programmatically add this right, and the attempt will succeed. A sample in the "User-Level Security via Jet SQL and ADO" section of this chapter demonstrates one approach to this task.

```
Sub SelectInsertDeleteAndUpdateWithNewUser2()
Dim cnn1 As New ADODB.Connection
Dim rst1 As New ADODB.Recordset
Dim str1 As String

'Open connection to target user-level secured data
'source; specify path for workgroup information
'file; designate logon ID and password
cnn1.Provider = "Microsoft.Jet.OLEDB.4.0"
cnn1.Mode = adModeShareDenyNone
cnn1.Properties("Jet OLEDB:System database") = _
    "C:\Access11Files\SystemDemo.mdw"
cnn1.Open "Data Source=C:\Access11Files\UserLevel.mdb;" & _
    "User ID=NewUser2;Password=password;"

'Select and print LastName field from last record
rst1.Open "WebBasedList", cnn1, adOpenKeyset, _
    adLockOptimistic, adCmdTable
rst1.MoveLast
Debug.Print "Last Name before update: " & rst1("LastName")

'Add a new record
rst1.AddNew
    rst1.Fields(1) = "Rick"
    rst1.Fields(2) = "Doe114"
rst1.Update

'Print LastName field from last record
rst1.MoveLast
Debug.Print "Last Name before update: " & rst1("LastName")

'Delete previously added record
rst1.MoveLast
rst1.Find "LastName = 'Doe114'", , adSearchBackward
rst1.Delete

'Print LastName field from last record
rst1.MoveLast
Debug.Print "Last Name before update: " & rst1("LastName")

'Clear Err object and trap for error with attempt to update
Err.Clear
On Error Resume Next

'Save FirstName field before attempting to update its value
str1 = rst1("LastName")
rst1("LastName") = str1 & "updated"
```

(continued)

```
'Check results in Err object and respond appropriately
If Err.Number = -2147217911 Then
'Print no permission message
    Debug.Print "No UPDATE permission for WebBasedList table"
ElseIf Err.Number <> 0 Then
'Print alternate message for another error
    Debug.Print Err.Number, Err.Description
    Exit Sub
Else
'For LastName field update table, print updated value
'and restore original LastName field value
    rst1.Update
    Debug.Print "Last Name after update: " & _
        rst1("LastName")
    rst1("LastName") = str1
    rst1.Update
End If

'Clean up objects
cnn1.Close
Set cnn1 = Nothing

End Sub
```

User-Level Security via Jet SQL and ADO

Jet SQL is the language of the Jet database engine. Selected Jet 4.0 language features target user-level security issues. This section commences with an overview of Jet SQL statements and keywords for managing security and then moves on to present two samples. The first sample illustrates how to add and drop users. The second sample shows how to manage permissions for a user.

Jet SQL Statements and Keywords for User-Level Security

Four Jet SQL statements enable the management of user and group accounts: *CREATE*, *ADD*, *ALTER*, and *DROP*. Use these statements with the *USER* and *GROUP* keywords to create and drop user and group accounts. You can assign both a password and a PID when you initially create either type of user-level security account. Invoke *ALTER* statements to modify initial settings for user and group accounts. You add and remove users from groups with *ADD* and *DROP* statements. *DROP* statements also permit you to remove individual group accounts and user accounts from the currently active workgroup.

You can execute these statements from a VBA procedure via ADO *Connection* or *Command* objects. The *USER* and *GROUP* keywords fail in the Access SQL View window. Additionally, Data Access Objects (DAO) does not enable the use of the *USER* and *GROUP* keywords.

Use the *GRANT* and *REVOKE* statements to manage assigning and removing permissions for objects to user and group accounts. Typical objects include tables and stored queries (either views or procedures). However, you also have the capability to assign permissions to a whole database file; to its forms, reports, and macros; and to its containers, which behave similarly to *AccessObject* objects. The range of permissions that you can grant and revoke includes those available through the Access security permissions interface (by choosing Tools, Security, User And Group Permissions). The complete list of permissions available for Jet 4.0, which ships with Access 2003, is in the Help JETSQL40.chm file under the *Grant* statement topic. This file can be found in a different location from one computer to the next; use a Windows Search to locate it on your computer.

Adding a New User

One advantage of adding a new user with Jet SQL and the ADO *Connection* object (rather than using ADOX) is that you can set the PID. When you create a new user with ADOX, Access randomly assigns the PID. Because Jet uses the PID and user name to compute a security identifier (SID) for tracking users, the ability to specify a PID is critical to recovering user accounts when the workgroup information file is destroyed, corrupted, or otherwise unavailable. Without the ability to recover user SIDs, you will have to re-create all the security settings for each user and group account.

The following pair of procedures adds and drops a new user, NewUser2, to the UserLevel.mdb database file. The first procedure, *AddNewUser2*, adds and drops the new user and calls the second procedure. The second procedure, *CountAndListUsers*, generates a user report. The procedures generate three reports that give the count of users and their names. The first report documents the baseline number of users and their names. The second report confirms the addition of the new user. The last report confirms the return to the baseline number of users.

Notice the syntax for creating a new user. The PID appears after the password. Like a database password, the password for a user appears in square brackets. However, unlike a database password, the password for a user doesn't contain blank spaces or other special characters. All SQL strings execute from the *cnn1 Connection* object. Let's take a look at the syntax now:

```
'Make sure that the workgroup information file does
'not contain a user named NewUser2

Sub AddNewUser2()
Dim cnn1 As ADODB.Connection
Dim str1 As String

'Make secure connection to target database
```

(continued)

```
Set cnn1 = New ADODB.Connection
With cnn1
    .Provider = "Microsoft.Jet.OLEDB.4.0"
    .Properties("Jet OLEDB:System database") = _
        "C:\Access11Files\SystemDemo.mdw"
    .Open "Data Source=C:\Access11Files\UserLevel.mdb;" & _
        "User ID=Chap10Admin;Password=;"

'Count and enumerate users before adding a user
    CountAndListUsers cnn1

'Set SQL string to add a new user and execute it.
'Notice the specification of a PID after the password.
    str1 = "CREATE USER NewUser2 [password] pidcode"
    .Execute (str1)

'Count and enumerate users again to confirm addition
'of the new user
    CountAndListUsers cnn1

'Set SQL string to drop a user and execute it
    str1 = "DROP USER NewUser2"
    .Execute (str1)

End With

'Count and enumerate users again to confirm dropping
'of previously added new user
CountAndListUsers cnn1

'Clean up objects
cnn1.Close
Set cnn1 = Nothing

End Sub

Sub CountAndListUsers(cnn1 As ADODB.Connection)
Dim cat1 As ADOX.Catalog
Dim usr1 As ADOX.User

'Instantiate catalog and set its ActiveConnection property
'to the passed Connection object
Set cat1 = New ADOX.Catalog
cat1.ActiveConnection = cnn1

'Print count of users (less Creator and Engine)
'and enumerate their names
Debug.Print "Total number of users is = " & _
    cat1.Users.Count - 2
For Each usr1 In cat1.Users
```

```
        If usr1.Name <> "Creator" And usr1.Name <> "Engine" Then _
            Debug.Print usr1.Name
Next usr1

'Clean up objects
Set cat1 = Nothing

End Sub
```

Granting and Revoking Permissions

The next sample we'll look at contrasts permissions for a new user. Like the previous sample, this one uses two procedures. The *AssignUpdatePermissions-ToNewUser2* procedure creates a new user account and grants and revokes user permissions. This procedure calls the *SelectInsertDeleteAndUpdateWithNew-User2* procedure discussed in the "Putting It All Together" section of this chapter. In particular, the *AssignUpdatePermissionsToNewUser2* procedure grants *SELECT*, *INSERT*, *DELETE*, and *UPDATE* permissions. It subsequently revokes the *UPDATE* permission. After initially granting all permissions and then revoking just the *UPDATE* permission, the *AssignUpdatePermissionsToNewUser2* procedure invokes the *SelectInsertDeleteAndUpdateWithNewUser2* procedure. An error trap in *SelectInsertDeleteAndUpdateWithNewUser2* responds when the user does not have permission to update a value from the *WebBasedList* table in the UserLevel.mdb database file.

The *AssignUpdatePermissionsToNewUser2* procedure starts by making a connection to the UserLevel.mdb file. Then, it defines the SQL string for adding a new user and executes the string through the connection. Next, the procedure grants the new user Select permission for the *MSysAccessObjects* table. This step is not absolutely necessary in the sample application. However, if a user manually attempts to open the database with the new user account, the Database window won't be viewable without receiving Select permission for the table.

> **Note**   The ADOX technique for adding a user shown in the "Adding and Deleting Users" section of this chapter does not grant Select permission for the *MSysAccessObjects* system table. Therefore, you need to supplement the technique to grant permission if you want users to log on manually. Alternatively, this is a good technique for forcing users to log on through your interface instead of using the built-in Access interface.

The critical part of the *AssignUpdatePermissionsToNewUser2* procedure is the execution of the next two SQL strings. The first of these SQL strings grants the new user *SELECT, INSERT, DELETE,* and *UPDATE* permissions to the *WebBasedList* table in the UserLevel.mdb file. After granting these two permissions, the procedure invokes the *SelectInsertDeleteAndUpdateWithNewUser2* procedure. This procedure exercises all the permissions and prints results reflecting the outcome. Next, the *AssignUpdatePermissionsToNewUser2* procedure revokes the *UPDATE* permission of NewUser2 to the *WebBasedList* table. The procedure follows this action with a call to the *SelectAndUpdateWithNewUser2* procedure. This second call prints results for all valid permissions and traps the error resulting from the revoked permission. The error trap prints a message explaining the problem instead of printing the updated value. Figure 10-8 shows the results printed to the Immediate window.

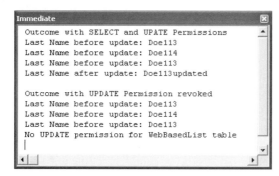

Figure 10-8 Output to the Immediate window from the *AssignUpdatePermissionsToNewUser2* procedure.

```
'Make sure that the workgroup information file does
'not contain a user named NewUser2

Sub AssignUpdatePermissionsToNewUser2()
Dim cnn1 As ADODB.Connection
Dim str1 As String

'Make secure connection to target database
Set cnn1 = New ADODB.Connection
With cnn1
    .Provider = "Microsoft.Jet.OLEDB.4.0"
    .Properties("Jet OLEDB:System database") = _
        "C:\Access11Files\SystemDemo.mdw"
    .Open "Data Source=C:\Access11Files\UserLevel.mdb;" & _
        "User ID=Chap10Admin;Password=;"

'Set SQL string to add a new user and execute it
    str1 = "CREATE USER NewUser2 [password] pidcode"
```

```
    .Execute (str1)

'Needed for viewing with manual opening of database
    str1 = "GRANT SELECT ON TABLE MSysAccessObjects TO NewUser2"
    .Execute (str1)

'Grant SELECT and UPDATE permissions for WebBasedList table
'and attempt to select and update from the table
    str1 = "GRANT SELECT, DELETE, INSERT, UPDATE " & _
        "ON TABLE WebBasedList TO NewUser2"
    .Execute (str1)
    Debug.Print "Outcome with SELECT and UPATE Permissions"
    SelectInsertDeleteAndUpdateWithNewUser2

'Revoke UPDATE permission for WebBasedList table
'and attempt to select and update from the table
    str1 = "REVOKE UPDATE " & _
        "ON TABLE WebBasedList FROM NewUser2"
    .Execute (str1)
    Debug.Print vbLf & "Outcome with UPDATE Permission revoked"
    SelectInsertDeleteAndUpdateWithNewUser2

End With

End Sub
```

Access 2003 Security Innovations

Access 2003 implements two security features that were not included in prior versions of Access. Both of these features help you manage potentially unsafe code. The Jet SandBox mode security targets Access queries and controls on Access forms and reports. Macro security offers Access developers and their clients the same security against VBA macros that has been available for other Office applications since Office 2000.

The final design of both these features was yet to be determined when this book went to press. However, this section provides general information about the two new security features as a heads up to prepare you for the final implementation of the product and its description in the Access 2003 Help file. In this section you will discover selected code samples and step-by-step instructions that demonstrate how you can take advantage of the new features.

Jet SandBox

The Jet SandBox helps insure that you do not run unsafe code from queries using the Jet engine or from controls in Access forms and reports. This section describes what the Jet SandBox does and specifically what it blocks. Finally, you learn how to disable and re-enable the Jet SandBox so that you can precisely determine when the Jet SandBox will run on a computer.

Why Have a SandBox?

Selected commands that you can run through Jet or in expressions on Access forms are potentially unsafe. These commands can pose a threat to the security of the files on a computer. A *SELECT* statement operating in Jet with the *Shell* function can run any instruction available from a Command window. Access form controls expose the same vulnerability. In other words, your database applications through Jet and expressions in controls on Access forms and reports can lead to the damage or the loss of files on your computer. The growing use of Jet for Web applications, such as in data access pages, further contributes to the risk of allowing these unsafe commands to be available, such as the Shell function, through Jet and in expressions for control default values and control sources.

The Jet SandBox was redesigned from Access 2002 (*http://support. microsoft.com/default.aspx?scid=kb;en-us;294698*) so that it could become the default mode for the operation of Jet 4.0 in Access 2003. In the version before Access 2003 Jet SandBox mode was an optional, nondefault mode. In Access 2003, Jet SandBox mode is the default mode, though you still have the option of disabling it. With one exception (the *Eval* function), the Jet SandBox does not apply to VBA code in a VBA project. In fact, use of *Public* functions implemented in a VBA project for an .mdb or an .adp file is one way to enjoy the security offered by the Jet SandBox and still maintain the functionality provided by potentially unsafe VBA and Access functions in queries. That is, you can replace references to unsafe built-in functions in queries with references to custom functions designed with VBA code. This VBA code defining the custom function should reside in an Access project with queries that need to reference the custom function.

What Gets Blocked by the Jet SandBox?

The Jet SandBox blocks selected VBA and Access functions from executing in Jet queries, as well as any expression in a property, such as the *Default Value* and *Control Source* properties, for Access controls. This SandBox action protects your clients from the potentially harmful effects of these actions.

Figure 10-9 shows an Access form with a text box and two buttons. The text box contains the path to the currently selected folder. Showing this path can help someone without authority to map a hard drive—exposing the paths on a hard drive is a step on the way to compromising the security of the files on the hard drive. *Form1* also includes two button controls. These controls invoke queries that illustrate other aspects of Jet SandBox operation.

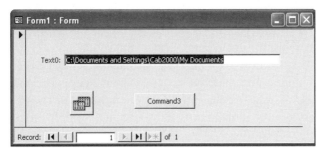

Figure 10-9   *Form1* from Chapter10.mdb illustrates operational features
of the Jet SandBox.

Although showing a path might or might not be a risk, the ability to invoke VBA and Access functions in response to click events is a clear risk. For example, the button on the left in *Form1* opens *Query1*. The query has the following SQL statement, which references the VBA *Shell* function to run the Calc.exe file from the system32 directory within the Windows folder. While Calc.exe opens only the Windows calculator, the same directory contains many .exe files and related file types, including the disk format utility format.com.

```
SELECT Shell("calc")
FROM WebBasedList;
```

Even with the Jet SandBox invoked, you can still run the *Shell* command along with any of the other VBA or Access functions blocked for Jet queries and control expressions. The workaround to the blocking capabilities of the Jet SandBox requires a *Public* user-defined function. The *Public* declaration makes the function available throughout the application, including in Jet queries. The button on the right in *Form1* opens *Query2*. The SQL for this query references a *Public* user-defined function named *MyCalc*. The exact SQL string for the query is:

```
SELECT =MyCalc() AS Expr1;
```

The VBA code for the *MyCalc* function appears in Module1 of the Chapter10.mdb file. This user-defined function invokes the *Shell* function to open the Calc.exe file. In a VBA procedure, the *Shell* function requires a return value.

```
Public Function MyCalc()
Dim ret

ret = Shell("C:\WINDOWS\SYSTEM32\CALC.EXE", 1)

End Function
```

By requiring the movement of code to a module, the Jet SandBox delivers three benefits. First, you avoid the potential risk of users inputting spurious code that can run from the Jet engine. This can happen when you allow a text box on a form to contribute to a SQL string that the Jet engine runs. Second, you can better maintain and manage your VBA and Access code from the VBA project in an .mdb or .adp file than in a Jet SQL window or the Zoom window for control expressions. Third, you gain the new macro security feature described in the next section.

Two rich text files in this book's companion content contain the list of VBA and Access functions blocked by the Jet SandBox (as of the time that I write this chapter). The Table10-2.rtf file includes the full list of nearly 50 blocked VBA functions. The Table10-3.rtf file includes the list of Access functions blocked by the Jet SandBox. The table in this file includes two columns with just over 100 rows. Each row contains an object in the Object column and a property or function of the object in the Property/Function Blocked column. The properties of the objects behave like functions in that they return property values. The Table10-3 list makes it clear that the Jet SandBox applies to both Access database files (.mdb) and Access projects (.adp).

How Do You Disable and Enable the Jet SandBox?

The Jet SandBox operates by default when you install Office 2003. However, you can also explicitly disable and enable the Jet SandBox. The registry key for managing the operation of the Jet SandBox is:

```
HKEY_LOCAL-MACHINE\SOFTWARE\Microsoft\Jet\4.0\Engines\SandBoxMode
```

This registry key can take one of four possible values. The meaning of the settings evolved over the years so that now there are only two possible security states, but there are still four possible settings, which appear below.

1. 0 disables the Jet SandBox in Access

2. 1 enables Jet SandBox at all times

3. 2 disables Jet SandBox in Access

4. 3 enables Jet SandBox at all times

Macro Security

Macro is a generic term used by the Microsoft Office development team to describe programmatic extensibility features. In Access, those feature pertain to VBA code, macro objects, action queries, and SQL pass-through queries. Macro security offers you a means of controlling what programmatic features can be executed by Office 2003 applications. Digital signatures refine this capability and help verify the authenticity of the code in your Office 2003 documents. This section begins with a review of core macro security concepts. Next, it describes the three macro security settings. The section ends with a closer look at digital signatures and how they interact with macro security. An example demonstrates how to use the two concepts together.

What Is Macro Security?

VBA macros are procedures and even classes in the VBA project associated with Office applications, such as Access, Word, and Excel. VBA macros are a lingua franca programming language for Office applications and even many non-Microsoft applications. The power and widespread availability of VBA macros contribute to their popularity as a means of spreading viruses. In response, Microsoft offers two means of managing macro security. First, Access 2003 introduces a macro security menu item (Tools, Macro, Security). You open the Security dialog box for this menu item from the menu bar in Access—not from the menu bar in Visual Basic Editor. Access 2003 is the first Access version to implement this feature that has been available for other Office components, such as Word and Excel, since Office 2000. Macro security offers a means of controlling how or if VBA code or other programmatic features, such as action queries or macros, can run in an .mdb or .adp file. Second, you can now digitally sign your code in a VBA project. The macro security feature calls the contents of a VBA project macro code. Digitally signed macro code gives you a means of accurately determining who is the provider of the code in a file. Organizations can use digital signatures as a means of verifying the source of the code in an Office 2003 file, such as an .mdb file. If an organization chooses to enforce the highest level of macro security, digitally signed .mdb and .adp files are the only way for applications to run VBA code or other programmatic features (the next section discusses the three possible macro security settings).

If you have used the macro security feature in any of the other Office components, then you are already mostly familiar with how the feature works in Access files. Macro security in Access applies to VBA macros (code), Access macros, and action queries. In addition, the Jet SandBox can require the migration of VBA code that used to be in queries and Access controls into the VBA project for an Access application. Therefore, macro security interacts with the Jet SandBox because you can now precisely manage how that code operates. Choosing Tools, Macro, Security opens the Security dialog box, which allows you to concurrently manage the functionality of all these objects within an Access application. In addition, digitally signing an Access application file can automatically enable all VBA code even with the highest level of macro security enforced.

What Are the Macro Security Settings?

There are three macro security settings: High, Medium, and Low. You can expose the macro security settings with the Tools, Macro, Security command.

These settings apply to an application, such as Access. Different Office applications can have different macro security settings.

The High macro security setting automatically blocks any applications from running with unsigned VBA projects. The High setting guarantees that a user cannot run any code from an unsigned, untrusted source. The High setting is particularly appropriate for organizations with many desktop and laptop computers that run code supplied by a wide variety of different developers. Although a digital signature does not guarantee that a file is virus-free, the digital signature provides a mechanism for at least discovering the author of any applications containing macros and holding the supplier of an application responsible for its safe operation.

In organizations with a small number of desktop and laptop computers running applications from one or a small number of highly trusted suppliers, the use of the Medium or Low macro security settings may be appropriate. For Medium macro security, a dialog box appears when a user attempts to open an Access database file or Access project with a VBA project. If the project has a digital signature, the dialog box shows a signature identifier, such as to whom the digital signature was issued to. The dialog box also displays buttons labeled Cancel, Open, and More Info. Clicking Open opens the Access database file or Access project so users can run the code in the VBA project. With Medium macro security, users can also choose to enable macros for VBA projects with no digital signature (recall that this is not possible with High macro security).

The Low setting is not generally recommended because no security prompt pops up for Access 2003 applications containing code and all code runs whether or not a file is digitally signed. The Low setting is convenient for experienced developers who are using virus protection software and fully understand the risks associated with viruses. This setting might also be appropriate when a single developer manages all the Access software development in an organizational unit, such as a department or small business. Organizations and individuals selecting the Low setting do so at their own risk. The Microsoft Office development team generally recommends not using this setting.

Note   I recommend a Medium or a Low security setting for running the code samples for this book that you download from the Microsoft Press site. The Low security will not remind you with a prompt that you are opening Access files with VBA code. The Medium security setting will remind that your are opening a file with VBA code. If you do use a Low setting, consider using the selfcert.exe program (see the next section) to sign the VBA project yourself and then assign Medium security. The High security setting will not allow you to run the Access database files and Access projects in this book.

What Are Digital Signatures and How Do I Use Them?

A digital signature binds the holder of the digital signature to a file – much like a traditional signature on a contract binds the person to the terms of a contract. You can digitally sign a document with a digital certificate. There are three broad sources for digital certificates. First, you can create one on your computer. Office 2003 ships with a utility program (selfcert.exe) for creating this kind of digital certificate. A digital certificate created with selfcert.exe is appropriate for testing purposes or for single-user databases because the certificate is only recognized on the computer used to create it. In a sense, a holder self-certifies his identity. Second, you can use the Microsoft Certificate Service as a means of generating valid digital certificates that can be used on any computer. With this approach, a company can generate its own digital certificates. Third, you can obtain a certificate from a firm whose business is issuing certificates and validating the identity of certificate holders. Verisign (*http://www.verisign.com*) and Thawte (*http://www.thawte.com*) are two well-known sources that provide these services, but there are others. These firms are called certifying authorities (CAs). Because certification and identity validation demand the expenditure of resources, there is a fee associated with certificates from these firms. However, in exchange, you obtain a third-party validation of the identity associated with a digital certificate. To ensure the encryption for a digital certificate cannot be decrypted in the lifetime of the certificate, digital certificates are normally issued for a specific duration and must be renewed on a regular basis, such as annually.

> **Note**   To view a list of sources for obtaining valid digital certificates, go to *http://officeupdate.microsoft.com/office/redirect/fromOffice9/cert.htm*.

The certificates have two keys. The private key signs a file with an encrypted code, which acts like an electronic signature. A recipient of the file with a corresponding public key can verify the encrypted code for the electronic signature. If a document is altered by a third party after its signing, the public key cannot verify the electronic signature. The organization issuing the private/public key pairs is responsible for verifying the identity of the individuals to which it issues certificates.

> **Tip**   For those who are new to digital certificates and signatures, a particularly friendly explanation of the topic can be found at *http://www.youdzone.com/signature.html*.

I close the chapter with a demonstration to make macro security and digital signatures easier to grasp. The step-by-step instructions create a digital certificate, use the certificate to sign a VBA project, and open an Access database file with the signed project. You can start the demonstration by creating a digital certificate with selfcert.exe. Begin by opening selfcert.exe, which you can do with the following command sequence: Start, Programs, Microsoft Office, Microsoft Office Tools, Digital Certificate for VBA Projects. Enter your name in the Create Digital Certificate dialog box. Figure 10-10 shows the selfcert program dialog box with my name entered. To run this demonstration, you need to create your own digital certificate using selfcert.exe.

Figure 10-10   Selfcert.exe dialog box for creating a digital certificate for Rick Dobson.

Next, create a new Access database file named db1.mdb with a sub procedure in Module1 that displays via a *MsgBox* function "Hello, World!" Then, from the Visual Basic Editor choose Tools, Digital Signature. Click Choose in the Digital Signature dialog box to sign the VBA project with the signature created above. You will be prompted to select a digital signature if more than one digital signature is registered on your computer. Next, Click OK to commit your digital signature to the VBA project and close the Digital Signature dialog box. Save your VBA project to persist your signed VBA project to a storage device. The procedure displaying "Hello, World!" and the Digital Signature dialog box appear within Figure 10-11.

> **Note**   I am not including a db1.mdb file in the companion content for this chapter because you will have to create your own version and sign it with a certificate created on your machine (or one from a CA, such as Thawte).

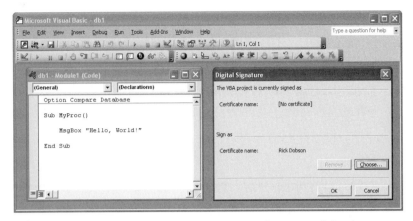

Figure 10-11   A VBA procedure and the Digital Signature dialog box.

To demonstrate the operation of the digital signature, open a new Access session. Choose Tools, Macro, Security and in the Security dialog box, select Medium macro security. You might receive a prompt to restart Access again for the new security level to take effect. Start a new Access session for the db1.mdb file created as described above. This presents the security warning that appears in Figure 10-12. Click Open to open the Access database file so that you can invoke the code in its VBA project. If you click the check box whose label starts with Always trust files from this publisher, subsequent attempts to open db1.mdb automatically trust the publisher and bypass the Security Warning dialog box. The Cancel button will cancel the file from being opened.

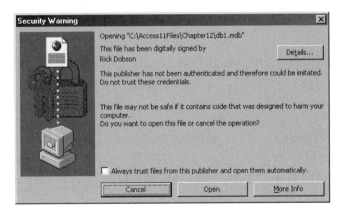

Figure 10-12   The Security Warning dialog box.

> **Note** Figure 10-12 appears with a Windows 2000 dialog box style, instead of the Windows XP dialog box style like all the other screen shots in the book. In order to get you the most likely Security Warning dialog box for the final version of Access 2003, I had to borrow a screen shot from a remote computer running Windows 2000.

Summary

This chapter's goal is to equip you with a basic understanding of Access 2003 solutions for each of your security needs. The initial section quickly reviews techniques for handling security with Access database files. These are basic techniques, but they can be especially effective for specialized needs, such as using .mde files to secure VBA code. Three sections within the chapter focus on user-level security. User-level security traditionally has been one of the most robust means of authenticating database users and determining what they could do in a Jet database. The chapter closes with an examination of two new security features introduced with Access 2003.

11

Using Access to Build SQL Server Solutions: Part I

Access 2003 has an ability to build and manage Microsoft SQL Server 2000 solutions. Microsoft implements this exciting new feature through Access projects, which offer Access developers a new file type: .adp files. With .adp files, Access developers can create their own SQL Server databases, populate them with tables, queries, and other database objects, and add data to the tables. These new capabilities free Access developers to create database objects for their own solutions instead of having to depend on SQL Server database administrators (DBAs). Access projects gives Access developers the same kinds of abilities for SQL Server databases that you use for Jet databases.

These advances in administering SQL Server solutions deliver substantial benefits to Access developers and others dealing with SQL Server databases. For starters, a friendly user interface (UI) and many powerful wizards dramatically drive down the cost of deploying SQL Server solutions by providing the solutions more quickly and easily. Second, Access enables intermediate and advanced developers a means to start building more powerful solutions than they could with Jet databases. Third, Access gives SQL Server DBAs a rapid application development environment for creating forms, reports, and Web pages for their database clients at the same time that it supports selected database administration features. And finally, Access gives current SQL Server programmers a powerful, flexible development alternative that avoids the complexity of n-tier architectures.

Access 2003 and Access 2002 offer tight integration with SQL Server 2000, while Access 2000 has a feature set tailored for SQL Server 7. The Access project is your key to unlocking the resources of SQL Server, but Access 2003 and

Access 2002 are tuned to SQL Server 2000 and Access 2000 is tuned for SQL Server 7. You can obtain upgrades and patches to make Access 2000 compatible with SQL Server 2000.

This chapter focuses on using Access 2003 with either SQL Server 2000 or the Microsoft SQL Server 2000 Desktop Engine (MSDE 2000). MSDE 2000 ships with any version of Microsoft Office 2003 that includes Access 2003. This engine is an upgrade to the Microsoft Data Engine (MSDE) that shipped with Office 2000. MSDE 2000 is compatible with SQL Server 2000, while its predecessor—MSDE—is compatible with SQL Server 7.

Tip See Chapter 12 in *Programming Microsoft Access 2000* (Microsoft Press, 1999) for coverage of how to build SQL Server 7 solutions with Access 2000. Another of my books, *Professional SQL Server Development with Access 2000* (Wrox Press, 2000), provides in-depth coverage of SQL Server development techniques—especially those that apply to SQL Server 7.

This chapter introduces Access projects and the SQL Server objects you can create with them. You will learn about creating and opening SQL Server databases with Access projects. Specific SQL Server database objects covered include tables, database diagrams, views, stored procedures, triggers, and user-defined functions.

Access Projects and SQL Server Versions

To understand how Access 2003 interoperates with SQL Server, you need to learn about Access projects. Access projects dramatically enhance the ability of developers to use Access to create, manage, and deploy SQL Server solutions. This section describes what an Access project is and presents the basic architecture of an Access project. It also examines the versions of SQL Server with which Access projects interoperate.

Understanding Access Projects

An Access project is a new Access file type that offers an alternative to the traditional Access database file. The new file type has an .adp extension, which differentiates it from the traditional .mdb file. Both file types feature a Database window for opening and designing database objects, such as tables, and application objects, such as forms and reports. The .mdb file is optimized for processing Jet databases in a file/server environment. The .adp file is optimized for working with SQL Server in a client/server environment.

> **Note**   Prior to Access 2000, Access developers typically worked with SQL Server databases by using linked tables from Access database files. The introduction of Access projects with Access 2000 did not eliminate this linked table capability, but its functionality is dwarfed by the vastly superior capabilities of Access projects. What I find most exciting about Access projects is their ability to easily create SQL Server objects. Access 2003 provides visual designers for creating databases, tables, views, stored procedures, and user-defined functions, which appeared initially with SQL Server 2000. In addition, through database diagrams, you can create primary keys, indexes, constraints, and relationships between tables. A database diagram is similar to the Access database file Relationship window, but you can do more with a database diagram and you can have more than one diagram per database. Access 2003 makes basing forms and reports on SQL Server objects straightforward. By using server-side filters, you can improve the performance of your forms because less data will move over a network.

You probably will be happy to learn that it's now much easier to program SQL Server from Access thanks to text-based design environments for creating and editing stored procedures and user-defined functions. This chapter demonstrates use of these environments with Transact SQL (T-SQL), which is a SQL dialect optimized for SQL Server.

> **Note**   Transact-SQL (T-SQL) is an extension of the SQL standards authorized by the American National Standards Institute (ANSI) and the International Organization for Standards (ISO). This extension conforms with all SQL Server versions, enabling you to optimize and simplify your code for any SQL Server version you use. The T-SQL extension for SQL Server is analogous to Jet SQL for Jet databases.

Access Project Architecture

The Access project represents the client side of a client/server application. The SQL Server database to which the Access project connects represents the server side of the client/server application. An OLE DB connection links the client and server sides of this application. Notice that there isn't a database file as in a traditional Access application. Instead, the connection to the database, the OLE DB connection, serves as a conduit through which an Access project provides data access.

Figure 11-1 depicts the Database window for an Access project connected to the NorthwindCS SQL Server database that ships with Office 2003. This database is a client/server version of the classic Northwind sample database. The left panel in the figure displays the Data Link Properties dialog box for the connection. You can open this dialog box by choosing File, Connection for an Access project connected to the NorthwindCS database. The panel on the right shows the Database window for the Access project. From the title bar of the Database window, you can see that the Access project file name is adp1.adp and that the project connects to the NorthwindCS database.

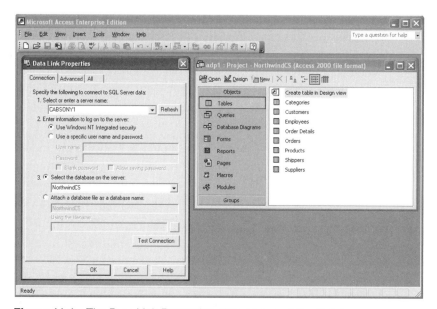

Figure 11-1 The Data Link Properties dialog box and the Database window for an Access project.

The Data Link Properties dialog box represents the OLE DB connection element of the Access project architecture. It shows that the NorthwindCS database for the Access project resides on a SQL server named CabSony1. You can have other versions of the NorthwindCS database on different servers, but the database names on any one server must be unique. The CabSony1 SQL server in my office network is running SQL Server Developer Edition on a computer running Microsoft Windows XP. The Access project authenticates itself to the SQL server through Windows NT integrated security. Authentication is the process by which a SQL server verifies that a user has permission to access the server. This is the MSDE 2000 default mode of authentication on Windows NT, Windows 2000, and Windows XP computers.

The Database window in the right panel of Figure 11-1 shows the table names in the database connection for the Access project. The Database window for the Access project closely aligns with the Database window in traditional Access database files. Notice the entries for Tables and Queries in the Objects bar. The Queries entries group together three kinds of SQL Server objects: views, stored procedures, and user-defined functions. Views and stored procedures in SQL Server correspond generally to the ADOX objects with those names (see Chapter 4). User-defined functions enable you to use T-SQL to code custom functions that perform like built-in functions in many ways. These functions are described more fully later in the chapter.

The first three object classes in the Objects bar shown in Figure 11-1 are Tables, Queries, and Database Diagrams. These are server-side elements of the client/server architecture for an Access project. In other words, the objects in these classes do not reside within the Access project file, which is adp1.adp in this example. These objects reside within the NorthwindCS database on the CabSony1 server. You can use the Database window to open collections of the *Forms*, *Reports*, *Pages*, *Macros*, and *Modules* classes. The objects in these classes reside within the Access project file. They are client-side objects. If I had another Access project file (for example, adp2.adp) connected to the NorthwindCS database on the CabSony1 server, it could have a different collection of forms than the one in adp1.adp.

Table 11-1 provides a summary of the object classes available from the Database window of an Access project, along with their location on the server or client side of the client/server application. Developers migrating to Access projects from Access database files will need to learn new SQL Server data types to create their own SQL Server tables (just as developers had to learn the Jet data types to create tables for Jet databases). The Database Diagrams object class is not available with traditional Access database files. If you find programming SQL Server databases more of a challenge than you prefer (or if you just want a break from programming), learn to use these diagrams. They offer a graphical approach to designing tables and the relationships between them. The Tables, Queries, and Database Diagrams collections contain all the server-side objects in an Access project.

The *Forms*, *Reports*, *Pages*, *Macros*, and *Modules* collection members for Access projects comprise the set of client-side objects in an Access project. These client-side objects work almost identically in Access projects to the way Access database files do. This is one of the main reasons Access projects are such an attractive model for developing SQL Server solutions. Whether you're an old hand at Access or a SQL Server DBA with limited Access experience, you can easily and quickly start generating custom forms and reports.

Table 11-1 Object Bar Classes in the Database Window of an Access Project

Class Name	Comment	Location
Tables	Tables for SQL Server databases work similarly to the way they do in traditional Access database files. However, you will have to learn some new designations for data types in order to specify columns. In addition, you will have to learn a new way to specify a column with the *AutoNumbers* data type.	Server
Queries	Although Access 2003 removes views and stored procedures from the Objects bar (where they used to be in Access 2000), it retains these objects. They are available from the Queries item in the Objects bar. You can also see user-defined functions from the Queries object class.	Server
Database Diagrams	SQL Server databases permit more than one database diagram per database. This is particularly handy when you want to break a large database application into parts. You can also use database diagrams to create other objects, such as tables.	Server
Forms	Works generally the same way as it does in a traditional Access database file.	Client
Reports	Works generally the same way as it does in a traditional Access database file.	Client
Pages	Works generally the same way as it does in a traditional Access database file.	Client
Macros	Works generally the same way as it does in a traditional Access database file.	Client
Modules	Works generally the same way as it does in a traditional Access database file.	Client

Supported SQL Server Databases

Microsoft designed Access 2003 to work especially well with SQL Server 2000 and MSDE 2000 on Windows 2000 or a later version of Windows. However, Access 2000 supports a wide range of SQL Server versions on a variety of operating systems. Table 11-2 summarizes the three groups of SQL Server installations with which Access projects are compatible. Notice that if you use SQL Server 2000 or MSDE 2000, you cannot use Windows 95. However, Access projects do support working with SQL Server 7 and MSDE on Windows 95.

Table 11-2   SQL Server and Windows Versions Supported by Access Projects

SQL Server Version	Operating System Version
SQL Server 2000 or MSDE 2000	Works on Windows 2000, Windows NT (Service Pack 6 or later), or Windows 98
SQL Server 7 or MSDE	Works on Windows 2000, Windows NT (Service Pack 4 or later), and Windows 95 (or later)
SQL Server 6.5 (Service Pack 5 or later)	Works on Windows 2000, Windows NT (Service Pack 4 or later), and Windows 95 (or later)

Using MSDE 2000 is a great way to start learning SQL Server development techniques. MSDE 2000 is free with any version of Office 2003 that includes Access. Its T-SQL and SQL-DMO programming syntax is compatible with SQL Server 2000. Its file format is compatible with SQL Server 2000, meaning you can reattach the MSDE 2000 database files to a SQL Server 2000 database for greater processing power and access to better graphical client management tools. These graphical tools can dramatically simplify the administration and use of a SQL Server database.

Like its predecessor, MSDE, MSDE 2000 has a built-in performance degrader after five users connect, but there is no hard limit on the number of users. Nevertheless, if you have many more than five users, you can boost performance by switching to the standard or enterprise edition of SQL Server 2000. By switching to either version of SQL Server 2000, you also gain the client management tools, Enterprise Manager and Query Analyzer. These easy-to-use yet powerful tools enable you to administer one or more SQL servers (Enterprise

Manager) as well as an integrated development environment for debugging and running T-SQL (Query Analyzer). The full version of SQL Server 2000 delivers other SQL Server components that are unavailable with MSDE 2000. These include the Full-Text Search and Indexing tools as well as Online Analytical Services for data warehousing applications. In addition, you cannot use MSDE 2000 as a transactional replication server. However, the standard edition of SQL Server 2000 (as well as the developer edition that ships with Microsoft Access 2003 Developer Edition, ADE) can support this function.

Installing and Using MSDE 2000

MSDE 2000 ships with any version of Office 2003 that includes Access 2003, but it does not install with the standard Office 2003 setup.exe program. To install MSDE 2000 so that it can operate side by side with the Jet database engine, run setup.exe from the MSDE2000 folder in the Office 2003 installation CD. If you have a network installation of Office 2003, you can run the MSDE 2000 setup.exe application from the network installation. Complete the installation by restarting the computer. This launches MSDE 2000 as a service on Windows XP, Windows 2000, and Windows NT computers.

If MSDE does not start automatically, run the Service Manager from the Startup folder of the Windows Start button. On Windows 98 computers, you might need to select the Auto-Start check box if you want MSDE 2000 to launch automatically when the computer boots. This check box appears at the bottom of the SQL Server Service Manager dialog box. You can use this same dialog box to pause and stop the SQL Server service.

Note   You can customize the installation of MSDE 2000 by assigning values for named switches when you invoke setup.exe. Search Access Help for "Install and Configure SQL Server 2000 Desktop Engine" for details on a subset of the switches and their settings. Additional settings not documented in Access Help appear in the readme.txt file within the \MSDE2000 folder on your Office 2003 installation CD. Look under headings 3.1.4 and 3.1.23 for setup parameters that enable you to customize MSDE 2000 authentication at startup and database file recovery from a prior MSDE version.

Creating and Opening Access Projects

There are three ways to open Access projects. First, you can open an existing Access project with a link to a SQL Server database. This is typically the way users work with Access projects. Second, you can create a new Access project to connect to an existing SQL Server database. Third, you can create a new Access project and concurrently create a new SQL Server database for it.

Note   This book often uses the term *SQL Server database* to refer generically to a database maintained by one of the versions of SQL Server 2000 or MSDE 2000.

Opening an Existing Access Project

An existing Access project is stored in an .adp file just like an Access database file is stored in an .mdb file. You can find an existing Access project to open through the File, Open command. This command presents the Open dialog box. Specify files of type Microsoft Access Projects to search for .adp files. If you previously compressed an .adp file to an .ade file like an .mdb file to an .mde, then you can specify ADE Files as the file type. See the "Using .mde Files" section in Chapter 10 for more detail on compressed files.

If you opened an Access project recently, you can click on its name in the Open section of the Getting Started task pane. The Open section depicts the most recently used files as links along with another link, named More, which presents the Open dialog box. See Chapter 8 for more programming samples that manage the task pane.

Figure 11-2 shows the Database window for the NorthwindCS Access project. This project is a sample file that you can load with the Office 2003 setup installation program. You should have MSDE 2000 or SQL Server 2000 on your workstation before loading the NorthwindCS sample. This is because the sample Access project installs the NorthwindCS database the first time that you open it if no other version of the Northwind database exists on the local SQL Server machine. In any event, you must have a version of either the NorthwindCS or Northwind database installed on the local SQL Server machine for the NorthwindCS Access project file to open successfully the first time. After the Access project file connects to a database on a server, you can open it from another computer or you can make a copy of the Access project file and then open that copy from another computer.

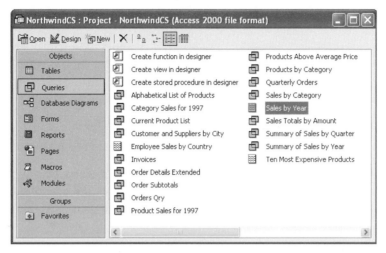

Figure 11-2   The Database window for the NorthwindCS Access project.

> **Note**   If the NorthwindCS project file does not successfully open the first time because you do not have SQL Server installed on the current computer, you can manually specify the project's connection to a SQL Server database on another computer. Use the File, Connection command to open the Data Link Properties dialog box. Then complete the dialog box by typing the remote server's name, your authentication information, and the name of the database to which you want to connect the project.

Do not confuse the reference to the Northwind database in the preceding paragraph with a reference to the Access Northwind database file. When you install SQL Server 2000, the setup program automatically installs a Northwind database. This SQL Server database has the same data tables as the Access Northwind database file. However, it does not have all the same queries. The SQL Server Northwind database contains no forms, reports, or Web pages because these are not SQL Server database objects. The Database window shown in Figure 11-2 has its *Queries* class selected in the Objects bar. Notice that the list of objects shows two types of icons next to the object names. The icon comprised of two datasheets represents views. The icon depicting text on a page represents stored procedures. In T-SQL, views return the output from a single *SELECT* statement that has no parameters or *ORDER BY* clause, unless the *SELECT* statement includes a *TOP* clause. Although stored procedures enable this function, they also permit parameters and an *ORDER BY* clause without a *TOP* clause, as well as some additional capabilities. If the NorthwindCS database contained any user-defined functions, they would appear in the Database window shown in Figure 11-2. Just before the listing of objects, you'll notice three list items for launching wizards that permit you to graphically design views and some types of stored procedures and user-defined functions. We'll take a closer look at these components later in the chapter, in the sections, "SQL Server Views," "Creating and Using Stored Procedures," and "User-Defined Functions."

When you use Access projects in a multiuser application, every user should have his or her own copy of the Access project file. This is because Access opens these files exclusively. If two users open the same Access project, the second user to open the file gains read-only access. Recall that the Access project file is the client component of a client/server application. Every user needs his or her own copy of the client component. The sharing takes place from the server component.

Opening an Access Project for an Existing Database

To open a new Access project for an existing database, click the Project Using Existing Data link on the Getting Started task pane. If you do not see the link, click the More link. The Task Pane opens by default when you start Access 2003. Clicking the Project Using Existing Data link opens the File New Database dialog box (see Figure 11-3). Access assigns a default name to the Access project file in the style of adp*x*.adp. You can override adp*x* with a custom name of your choice, and you can change the destination folder for the file by changing the selection in the Save In drop-down list. By clicking Create in the dialog box shown in Figure 11-3, the user creates an Access project with a filename of adp2.adp in the My Documents folder.

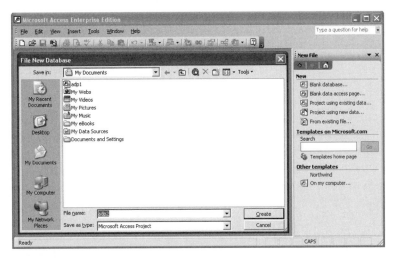

Figure 11-3   The File New Database dialog box in an Access window immediately after a click on the Project Using Existing Data link on the Getting Started task pane.

At this point, the project has no connection to a database. Therefore, Access automatically opens the Data Link Properties dialog box. Fill in the server name, user authentication information, and database name to link the project to a database. Figure 11-4 shows a completed Data Link Properties dialog box that connects an Access project to the Northwind database on the OfficeDeveloper SQL Server instance on the cab2000 server with Windows NT integrated security. Windows NT integrated security becomes particularly convenient when organizations can readily manage a single login account for Windows and SQL Server.

Figure 11-4   The Data Link Properties dialog box for connecting a new Access project to the Northwind database on the cab2000 server.

SQL Server supports the installation of multiple SQL Server instances on a single computer. The first installed SQL Server is the default installation. Its name is the name of the computer, such as the CabSony1 SQL Server on the CabSony1 computer. Subsequent installs of other SQL Server editions or versions, such as MSDE 2000 installed after the SQL Server Standard Edition, take a two-part name where a backslash (\) delimits each part of the name. In Figure 11-4, the default instance is cab2000, and the nondefault instance to which the Data Properties dialog box refers is the cab2000\OfficeDeveloper. This edition of SQL Server 2000 is the one that shipped with the Microsoft Office XP Developer Edition. Since I did not install the NorthwindCS database on this SQL Server instance, I pointed the Access project at the Northwind SQL Server database.

If you fail to specify the Data Link Properties dialog box entries correctly or you don't complete the dialog box, the new Access project will be disconnected from a data source when it opens. An Access project can be disconnected from a data source upon opening because your server is stopped. Once you get the

Access project to connect to a server, you can open the Data Link Properties dialog box with the File, Connection command and respecify its settings.

Manually Opening an Access Project for a New Database

Perhaps the most powerful way to open a new project is to open one that creates a new SQL Server database at the same time. To do this, click the Project Using New Data link on the New File task pane. This opens the File New Database dialog box. Use the dialog box to designate the destination folder and the filename for the new Access project. For this example, I named the file Chapter11 and clicked Create. Access automatically added the .adp file extension so that the file name is Chapter11.adp.

Except for clicking the Project Using New Data link, this process is identical to the one for creating a new Access project to connect to an existing database. After you click Project Using New Data, Access presents the initial dialog box for the Microsoft SQL Server Database Wizard. This dialog box enables you to specify the parameters for a new SQL Server database. These parameters include the name of the server on which you will store your new database, the type of authentication you will use for the SQL Server user ID that creates the new database, and the name of the new database.

Figure 11-5 shows an example of a completed dialog box for creating a new database. This dialog box specifies the local server. This example assumes you have SQL Server or MSDE 2000 running on the local server. The drop-down list that initially displays "(local)" enables you to select the name of any other SQL server to which you are connected. To connect to an instance of MSDE 2000 running on a Windows 98 computer, you must type the name of the server into the box. Notice that you can use either a trusted connection or an account with *CREATE DATABASE* privileges on a server. Your Windows account has these privileges if you install SQL Server on your computer with the default selections. This example selects the Use Trusted Connection check box, which designates the Windows account of the person attempting to create the database. Chapter 10 will discuss SQL Server security, including accounts and permissions. The database creation wizard automatically names the database after the Access project by appending a suffix of SQL to the Access project name. In this case, the resulting name for the new database is Chapter11SQL. You can override this default name with any other you prefer.

After completing the entries referenced in the preceding paragraph, click Next on the initial wizard dialog box. Then click Finish on the second wizard dialog box. This creates the new database for the new Access project. When the process completes, your new Access project opens with a connection to the newly created SQL Server database on the server indicated in the Microsoft SQL Server Database Wizard dialog box for the database creation wizard.

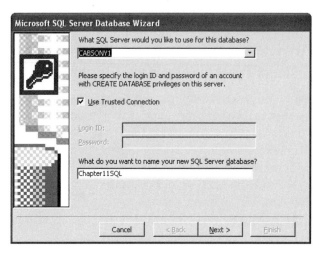

Figure 11-5   The initial dialog box of the Microsoft SQL Server Database Wizard.

Programming an Access Project for a New Database

You can also program the creation of a new SQL Server database and link it to an Access project without using the Microsoft SQL Server Database Wizard. Managing this process programmatically allows you to automatically create Access projects with attached databases. In addition, enabling the task programmatically allows you to fine-tune the process so that it meets your clients' precise requirements.

Creating a SQL Server database for an Access project requires two distinct steps. First, you need to create a new database. Then you need to assign that database to an Access project. This second step is analogous to entering the database settings into the Data Link Properties dialog box, and it creates the OLE DB connection between an Access project and the SQL Server database. You can also persist your changes to an Access project on a hard drive.

The following four procedures comprise an application for creating a new SQL Server database and assigning it to the current project. The first procedure, *CreateDBForAccessProject*, is the main routine. It designates the database name and a path for the database files—namely, its .mdf and .ldf files. The second procedure, *CreateDBOnCurrentProjectServer*, uses the information the first routine passes to it to create the database files. The third procedure, *AssignConnectionForNewDB*, assigns the new database to the current project. The fourth procedure, *PersistNewAccessProject*, is called from the third procedure. This fourth procedure creates a new Access project file in a path and assigns a connection pointing at the new database created by the *CreateDBOnCurrentProjectServer* procedure.

> **Note**   The .mdf file type is the primary file for a SQL Server database. In many applications, this file holds all the database objects in a SQL Server database, but SQL Server does permit other secondary database files to hold database objects. The .ldf file stores changes to a SQL Server database. The .ldf file can be used to recover a database. Each database must have a .mdf file and a .ldf file.

As you can see, the first procedure assigns the name foo2 to the new database. This name must conform to SQL Server conventions for identifiers as well as to a special restriction for database names in the *CREATE DATABASE T-SQL* statement. Your database name must be no more than 123 characters. The path can follow standard Windows path requirements. After assigning the database name and path to the database files, the main routine passes both parameters to the procedure for creating a new database but passes only the database name to the procedure.

The second procedure in the following code invokes the *CREATE DATABASE T-SQL* statement with an ActiveX Data Objects (ADO) *Connection* object. The procedure accepts the database name and path for the creation of the .mdf and .ldf files. You aren't required to store database files in the default directory, but it's a good practice that makes finding your database files easy. The *CREATE DATABASE* statement creates a database based on the SQL Server model database. The model database is one of the ones that SQL Server sets up upon installation. If you have special requirements for your databases, you can modify the model database's design. For example, you can create a special table design or even a special table that is populated with preset values. The sample procedure accepts the default model database settings for the initial database size, its maximum size, and the amount that the database grows when nearing its current size limit.

What's a SQL Server Identifier?

Every object in SQL Server, including a database and its elements, can have an identifier. The identifier is the name by which you reference the object. Identifiers have four general rules, and individual objects and special settings can further impact the valid names for SQL Server objects.

The first rule states that an identifier must begin with a letter from the Unicode Standard 2.0. These include but are not limited to the uppercase

(continued)

and lowercase letters of the English alphabet and those of other languages. It's good practice to avoid starting identifiers with characters that SQL Server uses for special purposes—such as the underscore (_), at sign (@), pound sign (#), double at sign (@@), and double pound sign (##)—unless you explicitly mean to reference the special purpose. For example, @ is a prefix for denoting a local variable in a stored procedure. A local variable in a stored procedure functions similarly to a memory variable that's local to a single procedure in Microsoft Visual Basic for Applications (VBA). In some contexts, starting a table name with @ invites SQL Server to treat the table as a local variable instead of a table.

The second rule for identifiers is that all characters after the first one can be letters, decimal numbers, or any of the following symbols: @, $, #, or _. Again, the letters and numbers are specified by the Unicode Standard 2.0. Third, you cannot specify object identifiers that are SQL Server reserved words. This page on the Microsoft Web site lists the SQL Server 2000 reserved words: *http://msdn.microsoft.com/library/psdk/sql/ts_ra-rz_9oj7.htm*. And finally, identifiers cannot contain embedded spaces or other special characters.

You can circumvent some of these rules by using double quotes or brackets, but you will create more universally acceptable identifiers by following all four rules.

The third procedure uses the *BaseConnectionString* property for the current project as a basis for specifying the connection string for a project connected to a new database—namely, the one created by the second procedure. A significant advantage of this approach is that it doesn't need to specify a valid connection string from scratch for an Access project. The "Initial Catalog" setting in the connection string points at the database name. Therefore, the procedure excises "Initial Catalog" and its setting and replaces the connection string with a setting that points at the new database. After composing the new connection string in *str1*, the procedure invokes the *OpenConnection* method for the *CurrentProject* object. The method takes a single argument, which is the name of the string with the edited *BaseConnectionString* property value.

In its last line, the third procedure calls the *PersistNewAccessProject* procedure while passing the edited *BaseConnectionString* property value as *str1*. This fourth procedure uses automation to launch another Access session. Then, with the *NewAccessProject* method, the procedure persists the session to disk as an Access project pointing at the database specified within *str1*.

```
Sub CreateDBForAccessProject()
Dim DBName As String
```

```
Dim DBFilename As String
Dim LogFilename As String
Dim DBFilePath As String

'Set string constants
DBName = "foo2"
DBFilePath = "c:\program files\microsoft sql server\mssql\data\"

'Create a database
CreateDBOnCurrentProjectServer DBName, DBFilePath

'Open the current project to the database
AssignConnectionForNewDB DBName

End Sub

Sub CreateDBOnCurrentProjectServer(DBName As String, _
    DBFilePath As String)
Dim cnn1 As ADODB.Connection
Dim str1 As String

'Accept Model DB defaults for initial size,
'maximum size, and growth steps
str1 = "CREATE DATABASE " & DBName & " " & _
    "ON " & _
    "( NAME = " & DBName & "_dat, " & _
    "FILENAME = '" & DBFilePath & DBName & "dat.mdf') " & _
    "LOG ON " & _
    "( NAME = '" & DBName & "_log', " & _
    "FILENAME = '" & DBFilePath & DBName & "log.ldf')"

'Point Connection object at current project and
'execute SQL string in str1
Set cnn1 = CurrentProject.Connection
cnn1.Execute (str1)

End Sub

Sub AssignConnectionForNewDB(DBName As String)
Dim str1 As String
Dim Beginpos As Integer
Dim Endpos As Integer

'Save BaseConnectionString for editing
str1 = CurrentProject.BaseConnectionString

'Optional printout to see the line being edited;
'remove comment prefix to see line in the Immediate window
Debug.Print str1

'Extract starting and ending positions for database assignment
'in the BaseConnectionString
```

(continued)

```
Beginpos = InStr(1, str1, "Initial Catalog", 1)
Endpos = InStr(Beginpos, str1, ";")

'Replace the old database assignment with a new one
str1 = Left(str1, Beginpos - 1) & "Initial Catalog=" & _
    DBName & Right(str1, Len(str1) - Endpos + 1)

'Pass updated connection string to CurrentProject
'and persisted Access project
CurrentProject.OpenConnection str1
PersistNewAccessProject str1

End Sub

Sub PersistNewAccessProject(str1)
Dim obj1 As Access.Application

'Instantiate Access session
Set obj1 = CreateObject("Access.application")

'Save Access session as Access project pointing
'at str1
obj1.NewAccessProject "c:\access11files\foo2", str1

'Clean up objects
obj1.Quit
Set obj1 = Nothing

End Sub
```

The preceding sample uses specific paths and file names that are written into the code, so as not to obscure the main points of this section on creating databases with T-SQL and managing connections for current and new Access projects. You probably will need to edit one or more hard-coded settings for the procedure to work in your environment. In addition, after you run the sample once, it will fail if you try to run it again. This failure stems from all the changes to settings that the sample makes. You can program around these failures, but that just adds to the sample's length while obscuring its main point. As I tested the application, it became useful to reset the settings altered by the sample. The following procedure illustrates logic for restoring the settings. First, it makes the current project point back at the Chapter11SQL database instead of the foo2 database. Second, it kills the persisted Access project file. Third, it drops the foo2 database from the SQL Server for the current project. After running *ResetFromCreateDB-ForAccessProject*, you will be able to rerun the initial sample successfully. Even if you don't rerun the initial sample, the Chapter11.adp file will point at the database used for most of the samples throughout the remainder of this chapter.

```
Sub ResetFromCreateDBForAccessProject()
Dim str1 As String
Dim Beginpos As Integer
Dim Endpos As Integer
Dim cnn1 As ADODB.Connection

'Reset CurrentProject to Chapter11SQL
str1 = CurrentProject.BaseConnectionString
Beginpos = InStr(1, str1, "Initial Catalog", 1)
Endpos = InStr(Beginpos, str1, ";")
str1 = Left(str1, Beginpos - 1) & "Initial Catalog=" & _
    "Chapter11SQL" & Right(str1, Len(str1) - Endpos + 1)
CurrentProject.OpenConnection str1

'Kill created Access project file
Kill "c:\access11files\foo2.adp"

'Drop created database
Set cnn1 = CurrentProject.Connection
cnn1.Execute ("DROP DATABASE foo2")

End Sub
```

Books Online and Other SQL Server Learning Resources

After you open an Access project and create a new SQL Server database, you need to learn how to use them. This chapter, along with Chapter 12 and Chapter 13, gets you started by providing fundamental instruction and helpful code samples. Because the topic is monumental in scope, these chapters are meant to complement existing developer resources. *Books Online* is the definitive Microsoft-supplied SQL Server reference source. The sample database applications that Microsoft makes available, such as the NorthwindCS project and its matching database, are another great resource. The pubs database is another database sample, though it is less widely available to Access developers than NorthwindCS. The pubs database relates to SQL Server much as the Northwind database relates to Access.

> **Note**   Those who want to learn more about T-SQL may derive value from *Programming Microsoft SQL Server 2000 with Microsoft Visual Basic .NET* (Microsoft Press, 2002), which I also authored. This book presents numerous T-SQL programming samples for typical developer tasks.

Getting Books Online

Books Online is a valuable documentation resource that discusses SQL Server administrative issues and T-SQL code samples. T-SQL code samples in Books Online primarily target Query Analyzer, one of the SQL Server Client Tools that ships with all commercial editions of SQL Server 2000. Neither Query Analyzer nor Books Online ship with MSDE 2000. In addition, most editions of Office 2003 will not have the SQL Client Tools either. However, both of these resources plus other resources, such as the pubs database mentioned below, ship with the SQL Client Tools. One edition of Office 2003 will have the SQL Client Tools through the SQL Server 2000 Developer Edition. I highly recommend this edition for any Access developer doing a significant amount of work with SQL Server 2000.

If you do not have ADE, you can still use Books Online. Be aware that there is a distinct version of Books Online for each version of SQL Server. All the Books Online samples apply to MSDE 2000 and SQL Server 2000. The SQL Server 2000 version of Books Online is available for download from the Microsoft Web site *http://www.microsoft.com/SQL/techinfo/productdoc/2000/books.asp*. The ADE also includes Books Online as part of its client tools for SQL Server.

Adapting Books Online Code for the SQL Pane

The following excerpt is the first T-SQL code sample (titled example A) for the *CREATE VIEW* statement in the SQL Server 2000 version of Books Online. The sample works perfectly from Query Analyzer, but it fails when you copy the code into the SQL pane of a view member in the *Views* collection of an Access project. (Later in the chapter, in "SQL Server Views," I will explain how to work with the SQL pane in an Access project.) When you click the Run button after copying the code into the SQL pane and accept the prompt to save T-SQL, Access can report a succession of errors. The first of these errors results from the fact that the SQL Server view template in Access does not support the *USE* keyword. The fundamental issue is that an Access project is a different kind of SQL Server client than Query Analyzer.

```
USE pubs
IF EXISTS (SELECT TABLE_NAME FROM INFORMATION_SCHEMA.VIEWS
    WHERE TABLE_NAME = 'titles_view')
    DROP VIEW titles_view
GO
CREATE VIEW titles_view
AS
SELECT title, type, price, pubdate
FROM titles
GO
```

The sample performs two tasks that can cause errors. First, the code deletes any existing view in the database with the identifier "titles_view". Second, it invokes the *CREATE VIEW* statement, which Access views do not support. There's no need to conditionally execute a *DROP VIEW* statement or unconditionally execute a *CREATE VIEW* statement from an Access project because the File, Save As and File, Save commands handle these tasks automatically. In addition, view templates in Access projects do not process the *USE* and *GO* keywords that Query Analyzer needs for many code samples.

To make the preceding sample work from a view in an Access project, simply copy two lines from the sample into the view's SQL pane: the *SELECT* statement after the *AS* keyword, and the *SELECT* statement before the trailing *GO* keyword. If you're running this sample from an Access project that doesn't link to the pubs database, such as Chapter11.adp, you can still reference the *titles* table as the source for the query. When the pubs database resides on the server, you can specify the source for the query as *pubs..titles*. The first name represents the database. This database name qualifier replaces the need for the *USE* statement. The last name represents the table within the database. The complete syntax for the view follows:

```
SELECT title, type, price, pubdate
FROM pubs..titles
```

The syntax for specifying the source omits an intervening name for the database owner, which is implicitly dbo. As long as a user doesn't create a table named *titles* in the pubs database, it's acceptable to omit the owner when specifying a database source owned by the dbo. If a user does create a table named *titles*, it is necessary to explicitly introduce an intervening owner name (such as dbo) to reference the table.

> **Note**   The database owner, or dbo, can be any member of the sysadmin group. This special security group of logins has broad authority in any database on a server, including the ability to create objects, such as tables. As long as a user connects to a database with one of the special logins in the sysadmin group, any objects he or she creates during a session will have dbo as their owner. If a user logs on with a login that's not in the sysadmin group, that object will always require an explicit owner name that refers to the login whenever anyone other than the object's owner refers to it. Database owners are a security topic that we'll cover in more detail in Chapter 13.

If the pubs database is not on the server for the current project, you can still reference the table. However, you'll have to reference the server name explicitly. SQL Server offers a couple of different approaches to this, which I'll cover later in this chapter in "SQL Server Views."

Adapting Books Online Code for a VBA Project

You can run the previous Books Online sample in the code window of a VBA project pretty much as is. The following sample shows an adaptation of the immediately preceding sample that works from a VBA code window. As you can see, this sample uses a lot more of the original Books Online sample. But it still has some changes. For example, the *GO* keyword after the *DROP VIEW* statement is commented out. Leaving it in would generate an error. The *USE* statement is removed so that the new view enters the database for the current project instead of the pubs database. Although the sample excludes the *GO* keywords, it follows their batching conventions for lines of T-SQL code. This is essential for the *CREATE VIEW* statement to succeed.

```
Sub CreateTitleViewInCurrentProject()
Dim cnn1 As ADODB.Connection
Dim str1 As String

'Point the Connection object at the current project
Set cnn1 = CurrentProject.Connection

'The code purposely leaves out the USE statement to create the
'view in the database for the current project, and it comments
'out the GO statement
str1 = "" & _
    "IF EXISTS (SELECT TABLE_NAME FROM INFORMATION_SCHEMA.VIEWS " & _
    "WHERE TABLE_NAME = 'titles_view') " & _
    "DROP VIEW titles_view " & _
    "--GO "
cnn1.Execute str1

'The code breaks here so that the CREATE VIEW statement is the first
'statement in its batch; comment prefix removes GO statement
str1 = "CREATE VIEW titles_view " & _
    "AS " & _
    "SELECT title, type, price, pubdate " & _
    "FROM pubs..titles " & _
    "--GO "
cnn1.Execute str1

End Sub
```

By the conclusion of the sample, your current project has a new view with an identifier of titles_view. This new object might not appear immediately in the Database window. In this case, select Queries from the Object bar in the Database window, and choose View, Refresh. Alternatively, you can write a pair of short VBA procedures that loop through the members of the *Views* collection and print their names to the Immediate window (see the next code sample). The members will include one named *title_view*. The procedure uses SQL-DMO objects, so your VBA project needs a reference to the Microsoft SQLDMO Object Library. The VBA project for the Chapter11.adp file has this reference already. The following pair of procedures demonstrates the syntax for looping through the members of the *Views* collection. This sample assumes your sa user has a password equal to the string password. You might need to update the procedure if the password is different.

```
Sub CallPrintViewsInADBOnLocalServer()
Dim DBName As String

DBName = "Chapter11SQL"
PrintViewsInADBOnLocalServer DBName

End Sub


'A utility routine for printing views in a database
'on the local server
Sub PrintViewsInADBOnLocalServer(DBName)
Dim srv1 As New SQLDMO.SQLServer

srv1.Connect "(local)", "sa", "password"

For Each vew1 In srv1.Databases(DBName).Views
    Debug.Print vew1.Name
Next vew1

End Sub
```

Sample Databases

The NorthwindCS and pubs databases are the two most readily available databases that you can use as models for your custom application development. The NorthwindCS database ships as part of Office 2003. Office 2003 also includes a NorthwindCS Access project that links to the NorthwindCS database. As mentioned earlier in this chapter, the NorthwindCS Access project includes a script for automatically loading the NorthwindCS database to a local server if the Northwind database isn't already installed. Otherwise, the script connects to the SQL Server Northwind database if it's available locally. The script for managing the first-time startup of the NorthwindCS project resides in its Startup module.

Working with the NorthwindCS Database

The NorthwindCS database is so attractive as a resource because nearly all Access developers have some familiarity with the Northwind database. The NorthwindCS Access project offers the same functionality as the Northwind Access database file. Therefore, you can use the NorthwindCS Access project as a model for performing any task in SQL Server that the Northwind Access database file performs for Jet databases. For example, the *Ten Most Expensive Products* stored procedure selects just the top 10 products in terms of unit price and lists them in descending order. The T-SQL script for this stored procedure follows:

```
ALTER PROCEDURE [Ten Most Expensive Products]
AS
SET ROWCOUNT 10
SELECT Products.ProductName AS TenMostExpensiveProducts,
Products.UnitPrice
FROM Products
ORDER BY Products.UnitPrice DESC
```

> **Note** The preceding script is edited slightly (for ease of reading) from the version that appears when you open the stored procedure by selecting it in the Database window and clicking Design. The script initially appears as one long line because Microsoft does not ship the script with built-in carriage returns. As you add the carriage returns to improve readability, remember to leave a blank space after all keywords. Then save and reopen the stored procedure with the revised format.

The syntax for this stored procedure is different than the corresponding query in the Access Northwind database file. That sample uses the *TOP* clause to moderate the behavior of the *SELECT* statement. However, this sample achieves the same result with a *SET ROWCOUNT* statement. This statement causes SQL Server to halt the processing of a *SELECT* statement after it returns a specified number of records—10, in the case of the sample script. The *ORDER BY* clause arranges those rows in descending order based on UnitPrice.

If you're a SQL Server DBA or developer, you might be confused about why the script begins with an *ALTER PROCEDURE* statement instead of a *CREATE PROCEDURE* statement (as is common in the Books Online samples). When you design a stored procedure within an Access project's stored procedure template, you use *CREATE PROCEDURE* the very first time that you input and save the stored procedure. Thereafter, Access automatically changes the *CREATE PROCEDURE* statement to an *ALTER PROCEDURE* statement. This prevents you from having to drop the old stored procedure before re-creating a new one with the changes you make in Design view. In fact, Access projects do not permit you to drop and then re-create stored procedures from their stored procedure templates.

When you work with a stored procedure based on a single *SELECT* statement, Access permits you to create the query statement in its graphical Design view. This relieves you of some syntax requirements otherwise associated with specifying stored procedures. The following code comes from the SQL pane of the Design view for a stored procedure. The stored procedure's T-SQL representation appears without *ALTER PROCEDURE*, *AS*, or parameter declarations. To me, the most exciting aspect of the script is that it demonstrates the use of parameters without the bother of explicitly declaring them. The *@Beginning_ Date* and *@Ending_Date* parameters control the range of orders about which the stored procedure returns records. Notice also that the syntax uses a three-part naming convention for the identifying fields. The field identifiers start with a reference to the owner (dbo), move on to specifying the source table, and conclude with the column name.

```
SELECT dbo.Orders.ShippedDate, dbo.Orders.OrderID,
    dbo.[Order Subtotals].Subtotal,
    DATENAME(yy, dbo.Orders.ShippedDate)
    AS Year
FROM dbo.Orders INNER JOIN dbo.[Order Subtotals]
    ON dbo.Orders.OrderID = dbo.[Order Subtotals].OrderID
WHERE (dbo.Orders.ShippedDate IS NOT NULL)
    AND (dbo.Orders.ShippedDate BETWEEN @Beginning_Date AND @Ending_Date)
```

The Access 2003 innovations for stored procedures based on a single *SELECT* statement are even better. Now you can design them with a graphical query designer—even when they contain parameters. Figure 11-6 depicts the graphical view of the *Sales by Year* stored procedure, represented in the preceding code sample from the NorthwindCS database. Notice that the code enables a join and the specification of parameters.

Figure 11-6   A graphical view of the *Sales by Year* stored procedure in the NorthwindCS database.

The graphical view in Figure 11-6 is the default for stored procedures based on a single *SELECT* statement. You can open a SQL pane in the query designer or open the stored procedure in SQL View. Using SQL View shows the syntax of the *ALTER PROCEDURE* statement, including its *AS* keyword. This view is necessary when a stored procedure relies on more than a single *SELECT* statement.

Working with the Pubs Database

Many Access developers will be less familiar with the pubs database than with the NorthwindCS database, a look-alike of the Northwind Access database file. Nevertheless, the pubs database is the source for many samples in Books Online. For this reason, Access developers can boost their learning of SQL Server by getting comfortable with the pubs database. SQL Server DBAs and developers will likely have firsthand experience working with the pubs database.

No matter what your background, you need a version of SQL Server other than MSDE 2000 to work with the pubs database. This is because the database does not ship with MSDE 2000. Office developers planning to do extensive SQL Server work should consider getting ADE because this version ships with a Developer Edition of SQL Server 2000. For this reason, ADE offers an opportunity to readily gain experience with pubs database samples.

One way to get started with pubs is to open an Access project for an existing database and then point that project at the pubs database on a server. After opening the Access project, you can examine the members of its *Tables* and *Queries* classes. Figure 11-7 displays the Database window and the Data Link Properties dialog box for an Access project connected to the pubs database. The Access project file has the name Forpubs.adp and connects to the local SQL Server. Therefore, for this Access project to open properly you must have the pubs database on your local SQL Server default instance. The Database window shows the names of the view and four stored procedures that ship as part of the pubs sample. By clicking Tables in the Objects bar for the Database window, you can display the names of all the tables in the pubs database. All the other object classes for the Access project will be empty because the pubs database does not ship with a database diagram, and the project has no client-side objects such as forms and reports.

One of the best ways to learn about a database is through a database diagram that indicates all the tables in the database and their relationships with other tables. You can create such a diagram for the pubs database by selecting Database Diagrams in the Objects bar and then clicking New on the Database window. This opens the Add Table dialog box. Successively click the Add button on the dialog box until all the tables appear in the diagram, and then close the Add Table dialog box. As an option, you can drag and rearrange the icons representing tables to improve the ease of viewing all tables in one database diagram display.

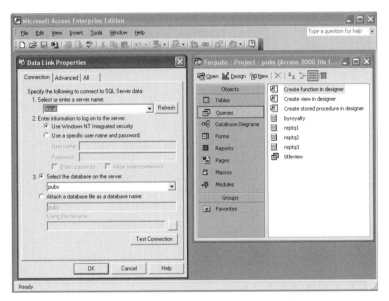

Figure 11-7   The Data Link Properties dialog box and Database window for an Access project connected to the pubs database.

Figure 11-8 shows a diagram for the pubs database after it's been saved with the name CustomizedDiagram. Notice that it includes the database's tables as well as the columns within them. In addition, the diagram also shows the relationships between tables. The line connecting the *stores* and *sales* tables indicates that any one store row can have many corresponding sales rows. The *authors* and *titles* tables have a many-to-many relationship. The *titleauthor* table serves as the junction between these two tables. The *publishers* and *pub_ info* tables have a one-to-one relationship. As you gain familiarity with the database diagram UI, you can probe relationships and table definitions. We'll discuss database diagrams in more detail in the next section. These diagrams provide a way to graphically perform data definition for tables. Database diagrams offer a means of circumventing programming tasks that do not require highly customized code development. This reserves the programming resources available to an assignment, saving them for the most demanding development tasks.

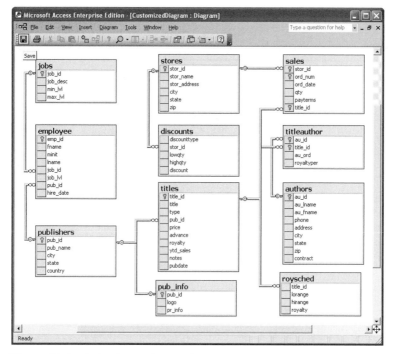

Figure 11-8   A database diagram for the pubs database.

The following code sample comes from example B for the *AVG* function in Books Online. The Books Online example, which is for the pubs database, demonstrates the behavior of the *AVG* and *SUM* aggregate functions with a *GROUP BY* clause. The code computes the average advance and the total advance by type of book.

```
USE pubs

SELECT type, AVG(advance), SUM(ytd_sales)
FROM titles
GROUP BY type
ORDER BY type
```

Copying the sample to the SQL Server database can result in a change or two. First, I copied the T-SQL script to a new stored procedure template. Next, I edited the code so that it would reference the pubs database even while running from a stored procedure in another database, such as Chapter11SQL. I could have copied the sample directly into the Forpubs Access project, in which case it would run exactly as is, except for removing the *USE* statement. In this instance, I wanted to provide as much code as possible in the chapter's Access project.

Figure 11-9 shows the edited T-SQL script in a stored procedure template. In addition to the modification to the *FROM* clause argument, the sample starts with an *ALTER PROCEDURE* keyword followed by the procedure's name and the *AS* keyword to signal the start of the procedure's T-SQL. The result set from the stored procedure's *SELECT* statement appears in the window on the right. You can flip to this view by selecting Datasheet View for the stored procedure.

Figure 11-9 An adapted T-SQL sample (along with its return values) from Books Online for the pubs database in an Access project.

Tables and Database Diagrams

This section orients you to some of the table design issues you can expect to encounter as you move from Access database files to SQL Server files. The presentation pays particular attention to the SQL Server data types. It also introduces you to the *CREATE TABLE* statement so that you can design your own custom tables programmatically. A pair of code samples demonstrates how to use one or more *INSERT* statements after a *CREATE TABLE* statement to populate a new table with values. These samples demonstrate techniques for working with contact data and graphic images in SQL Server databases. The section concludes with a brief introduction to database diagrams. The examples you'll see convey the simplicity and power of this graphical data definition tool.

SQL Server Column Data Types

Because the basics of designing a database are similar in Access and SQL Server, experienced Access developers will easily grasp the basics of designing SQL Server solutions. However, the data type names for table columns vary substantially in these two applications. In some cases, the same names point to different data types. In other cases, data types available in SQL Server are missing in Access. There's even one Access data type that's missing in SQL Server.

As Access developers migrate to SQL Server, specifying the right data type grows in importance. This is because SQL Server tables often have many more rows than Access tables. In fact, expanding tables are a big motivation for moving from an Access database solution to one based on SQL Server. Therefore, as you design your SQL database, specifying the column data type so that it is the smallest size possible can dramatically improve performance. Make your data types just large enough to hold the largest value possible for a column. If your numbers do not have fractional values, use one of the data types for whole numbers. Look for opportunities to take advantage of the *Smalldatetime* and *Smallmoney* data types if a column's values fall within their ranges. These data types require 4 bytes less per column value than their siblings, *Datetime* and *Money*. When working with character data, use a fixed-length data type if all column values are the same length. This saves SQL Server from having to look for the end of the string.

Table 11-3 summarizes the SQL Server data types along with the closest matching Access data types. When a SQL Server data type is missing from Access, the corresponding Access data type column reads "Not applicable."

Table 11-3 SQL Server Column Data Types

SQL Server Data Type	Closest Matching Access Data Type	Bytes	SQL Server Data Type Description
Bit	Yes/No	1	If you have multiple *Bit* data type fields per record, SQL Server groups them into units of eight so that an individual column value can take less than 1 byte. SQL Server represents Yes as 1 and No as 0. In contrast, Access represents Yes and No as -1 and 0.
Tinyint	Number (byte)	1	This data type is the same in SQL Server and Access databases; integers from 0 through $(2^8) - 1$.
Smallint	Integer	2	Integers in the range of -2^{15} through $(2^{15}) - 1$.
Integer	Long integer	4	Integers in the range of -2^{31} through $(2^{31}) - 1$.
Bigint	Not applicable	8	Integers in the range of -2^{63} through $(2^{63}) - 1$.
Real	Number (single)	4	Positive and negative numbers with whole and fractional parts, including 0. Positive numbers range from 1.18E - 38 through 3.40E + 38. Negative numbers range from -1.18E - 38 through -3.40E + 38.
Float	Number (double)	8	Positive and negative numbers with whole and fractional parts, including 0. Positive numbers range from 2.23E - 308 through 1.79E + 308. Negative numbers range from -2.23E - 308 through -1.79E + 308.
Money	Number (currency)	8	Values range from -922,337,203,685,477.5707 through 922,337,203,685,477.5807. Arithmetic with this data type is accurate to the nearest ten-thousandth of a unit within the specified range.

Table 11-3   **SQL Server Column Data Types**

SQL Server Data Type	Closest Matching Access Data Type	Bytes	SQL Server Data Type Description
Smallmoney	Number (currency)	4	Values range from -214,748.3648 through 214,748.3647. Arithmetic with this data type is accurate to the nearest ten-thousandth of a unit within the specified range.
Decimal	Number (decimal)	Varies based on digits for scale and precision	Exactly represents values from -10^{38} through $(10^{38}) - 1$. You can use the range to independently specify the total number of digits and the number of digits after the decimal. *Numeric* is a SQL Server synonym for the *Decimal* data type.
Datetime	Date/Time	8	A value capable of representing dates from January 1, 1753, through December 31, 9999, to an accuracy of 3.33 milliseconds.
Smalldatetime	Date/Time	4	A value capable of representing dates from January 1, 1900, through June 6, 2079, to an accuracy of within 1 minute.
Varchar	Text	Varies based on number of characters	A variable-length text string of up to 8,000 non-Unicode characters.
Nvarchar	Text	Varies based on number of characters	A variable-length text string of up to 4,000 Unicode characters.
Text	Memo	Varies depending on content	Can hold up to $(2^{31}) - 1$ non-Unicode characters. This data type is not valid for variables or parameters.
Ntext	Memo	Varies depending on content	Can hold up to $(2^{30}) - 1$ Unicode characters. This data type is not valid for variables or parameters.
Image	OLE Object	Varies depending on content	Can hold up to $(2^{31}) - 1$ bytes of binary data. Use it for binary data that exceeds the limits of the *Varbinary* data type.
Unique-identifier	Number (replication ID)	16	A globally unique identifier (GUID). Carefully evaluate whether you need this data type because it is long (16 bytes) and has a format that isn't easy to read or manipulate.

(continued)

Table 11-3 SQL Server Column Data Types *(continued)*

SQL Server Data Type	Closest Matching Access Data Type	Bytes	SQL Server Data Type Description
Char	Not applicable	Varies depending on content	A fixed-length text string of up to 8,000 non-Unicode characters.
Nchar	Not applicable	Varies depending on content	A fixed-length text string of up to 4,000 Unicode characters.
Varbinary	Not applicable	Varies depending on content	Can hold up to 8,000 bytes of binary data in a variable-length format.
Timestamp	Not applicable	8	A binary value that increments by 1 whenever any table with a column of the *Timestamp* data type has an insertion or an update. This data type does not store *Datetime* values.
Sql_variant	Not applicable	Varies depending on content	A data type that accommodates multiple data types within a single column in a table. Can contain all other data types, except *Text*, *Ntext*, *Image*, and *Timestamp*.

The Access data type for table columns that's missing from SQL Server is the *Hyperlink* data type. Recall that this data type permits you to link to different parts of the same or a different Office document as well as Web pages. The *Hyperlink* data type is a text string comprised of up to four separate components: the link's display, main URL address, subaddress, and appearance when a mouse moves over it. Access projects enable the functions for this data type through form fields.

The visual Table Designer in Access 2003 offers a Lookup tab in Table Design view. Although Access project files do not offer an explicit *Lookup* data type like Access database files do, Access projects provide a Lookup tab. You can use this tab to set the parameters for a lookup field. This graphical process mirrors the settings you make for a combo box but causes the table to display the lookup value. Any forms you base on the table will show the lookup value and can offer a drop-down list for changing existing values as well as inputting new ones.

> **Note**   The sample files for this chapter include the *Orders_with_lookup* table, which demonstrates one way to make the lookup column settings. You can show Help for the Lookup tab in the visual Table Designer by resting your cursor in the Display Control box and pressing F1.

Setting and Looking Up Column Data Types

When you first work with SQL Server, the easiest way to start creating table columns is with the visual Table Designer. Even experienced developers frequently use a designer to create tables. You can invoke the Access 2003 Table Designer from the Database window. Just select Tables from the Objects bar and then click New. Figure 11-10 shows a table in the designer with a column named after each of the SQL Server column data types. I constructed this table by typing data type names into the *Column Name* column. You can populate the Data Type column by making a selection from its drop-down list. I chose the data type corresponding to the entry to the *Column Name* column. The only SQL Server column data type the table fails to include is the *Numeric* data type, which is synonymous with the *Decimal* data type.

Figure 11-10   A view of the *data_types* table in the new Access 2003 Table Designer.

The specification for the *data_types* table shown in Figure 11-10 accepts the defaults for Length and Allow Nulls settings, with two exceptions. The first exception is the *pk* column. This column does not allow nulls. You can make a column the primary key (as you can with the *pk* column) by clicking the Primary Key button with the cursor resting on the row containing the column specification. The second exception is the column named *int_with_identity*. This column also does not accept nulls. Figure 11-10 shows the cursor resting on the row containing the specification for this column. As a result, the Columns tab offers additional column properties. In this case, you see the Identity setting equals Yes, and the default values of 1 for both the Identity Seed and Identity Increment settings. You can override these defaults by entering new values for the settings.

Mapping SQL Server to Access and ADO Data Types

Mapping between data types for different data stores can help you understand when to use which data type in which context. This kind of information is critical when migrating data from one database to another. The following code sample takes each of the columns in the *data_types* table shown in Figure 11-10 and prints their SQL Server, Access, and ADO data type names, as well as their defined size. The Access and ADO data type names and the *DefinedSize* property uniquely distinguish most SQL Server data types. However, the SQL Server *Money*, *Smallmoney*, *Datetime*, and *Smalldatetime* data types require you to provide more information to distinguish them. Although the SQL Server *Datetime* and *Smalldatetime* data types have identical ADO *DefinedSize* settings, their *Precision* properties are different. This is because *Datetime* column values have more precision that *Smalldatetime* column values.

The following three procedures map the SQL Server data types in the *data_types* table to their Access data type names and ADO enum names. The report also prints the *DefinedSize* property for each column in the table. In the case of the *Money*, *Smallmoney*, *Datetime*, and *Smalldatetime* data types, the report also includes the precision of the columns. This helps to differentiate between data types that are otherwise identical in the report's other columns.

The main routine, *ReportDataTypes*, starts by printing a heading and setting it off with a line of equal signs below the report's column headings. Next, it opens a recordset for the *data_types* table. Then it loops through all the fields in the recordset. Within the loop, an *If...Then...Else* statement directs the reporting to one of two *Debug.Print* statements. The *Then* clause prints results for the two sets of fields that require *Precision* to distinguish between them. The *Else* clause processes all the remaining data types. The two other procedures are function procedures that return the name of the Access data type and the enum name for the ADO data type value corresponding to the SQL Server

data type. ADO automatically maps the SQL Server data types into its own data
types to create a field *Type* property value.

```
Sub ReportDataTypes()
Dim rst1 As ADODB.Recordset
Dim fld1 As ADODB.Field

'Print and separate column headings from the rest
'of the report
Debug.Print "SQL Server name" & String(3, " ") & _
    "Access name" & String(12, " ") & _
    "ADO Enum name" & String(5, " ") & _
    "DefinedSize" & " " & "Precision"
Debug.Print String(17, "=") & " " & String(22, "=") & " " & _
    String(17, "=") & " " & String(11, "=") & " " & _
    String(9, "=")

'Base a recordset on the data_types table
Set rst1 = New ADODB.Recordset
rst1.Open "data_types", CurrentProject.Connection

'Loop through the columns in the data_types table and
'report their name, Access data type, ADO data type,
'DefinedSize, and Precision, if appropriate
For Each fld1 In rst1.Fields
    If (fld1.Type = adCurrency Or _
        fld1.Type = adDBTimeStamp) Then
        Debug.Print fld1.Name & _
            String(18 - Len(fld1.Name), " ") & _
            AccessDataTypeName(fld1.Type) & _
            String(23 - Len(AccessDataTypeName(fld1.Type)), " ") & _
            ADODataTypeName(fld1.Type) & _
            String(18 - Len(ADODataTypeName(fld1.Type)), " ") & _
            fld1.DefinedSize, fld1.Precision
    Else
        Debug.Print fld1.Name & _
            String(18 - Len(fld1.Name), " ") & _
            AccessDataTypeName(fld1.Type) & _
            String(23 - Len(AccessDataTypeName(fld1.Type)), " ") & _
            ADODataTypeName(fld1.Type) & _
            String(18 - Len(ADODataTypeName(fld1.Type)), " ") & _
            fld1.DefinedSize

    End If
Next fld1

'Clean up objects
rst1.Close
Set rst1 = Nothing

End Sub
```

(continued)

```
Function AccessDataTypeName(DataTypeEnum As Integer) As String

'Decodes SQL Server data type to Access data type
'based on the ADO enum value for the data type
Select Case DataTypeEnum
    Case 2
        AccessDataTypeName = "Number(Integer)"
    Case 3
        AccessDataTypeName = "Number(Long Integer)"
    Case 4
        AccessDataTypeName = "Number(Single)"
    Case 5
        AccessDataTypeName = "Number(Double)"
    Case 6
        AccessDataTypeName = "Number(Currency)"
    Case 11
        AccessDataTypeName = "Yes/No"
    Case 12
        AccessDataTypeName = "Not applicable"
    Case 17
        AccessDataTypeName = "Number(Byte)"
    Case 20
        AccessDataTypeName = "Not applicable"
    Case 72
        AccessDataTypeName = "Number(Replication ID)"
    Case 128
        AccessDataTypeName = "Not applicable"
    Case 129
        AccessDataTypeName = "Not applicable"
    Case 130
        AccessDataTypeName = "Not applicable"
    Case 131
        AccessDataTypeName = "Number(Decimal)"
    Case 135
        AccessDataTypeName = "Date/Time"
    Case 200
        AccessDataTypeName = "Text"
    Case 201
        AccessDataTypeName = "Memo"
    Case 202
        AccessDataTypeName = "Text"
    Case 203
        AccessDataTypeName = "Memo"
    Case 204
        AccessDataTypeName = "Not applicable"
    Case 205
        AccessDataTypeName = "OLE Object"
    Case Else
        AccessDataTypeName = "Data Type Not Decoded"
End Select

End Function
```

```
Function ADODataTypeName(DataTypeEnum As Integer) As String

'Decodes SQL Server data type to ADO data type
'based on the ADO enum value for the data type
Select Case DataTypeEnum
    Case 2
        ADODataTypeName = "adSmallInt"
    Case 3
        ADODataTypeName = "adInteger"
    Case 4
        ADODataTypeName = "adSingle"
    Case 5
        ADODataTypeName = "adDouble"
    Case 6
        ADODataTypeName = "adCurrency"
    Case 11
        ADODataTypeName = "adBoolean"
    Case 12
        ADODataTypeName = "adVariant"
    Case 17
        ADODataTypeName = "adUnsignedTinyInt"
    Case 20
        ADODataTypeName = "adBigInt"
    Case 72
        ADODataTypeName = "adGUID"
    Case 128
        ADODataTypeName = "adBinary"
    Case 129
        ADODataTypeName = "adChar"
    Case 130
        ADODataTypeName = "adWChar"
    Case 131
        ADODataTypeName = "adNumeric"
    Case 135
        ADODataTypeName = "adDBTimeStamp"
    Case 200
        ADODataTypeName = "adVarChar"
    Case 201
        ADODataTypeName = "adLongVarChar"
    Case 202
        ADODataTypeName = "adVarWChar"
    Case 203
        ADODataTypeName = "adLongVarWChar"
    Case 204
        ADODataTypeName = "adVarBinary"
    Case 205
        ADODataTypeName = "adLongVarBinary"
    Case Else
        ADODataTypeName = "Data Type Not Decoded"
End Select

End Function
```

Figure 11-11 shows the output from the *ReportDataTypes* procedure. It includes a row for each column in the *data_types* table. You can use this printout as a convenient mapping tool for naming data types. The *DefinedSize* property values are the default settings for the data types when the number of bytes used to store an entry varies according to each entry's content, as it does for *Nvarchar* and *Nchar*. As you can see, the *Money* and *Smallmoney* SQL Server data types have the same ADO enum name, *adCurrency*. They differ only in their *Precision* property. The same pattern holds for *Datetime* and *Smalldatetime*. In addition, the SQL Server *Datetime* and *Smalldatetime* data types translate into the same ADO enum name, *adDBTimeStamp*. However, neither data type is related to the SQL Server *Timestamp* data type, which is a binary value.

Immediate

SQL Server name	Access name	ADO Enum name	DefinedSize	Precision
pk	Number(Long Integer)	adInteger	4	
bit	Yes/No	adBoolean	2	
tinyint	Number(Byte)	adUnsignedTinyInt	1	
smallint	Number(Integer)	adSmallInt	2	
bigint	Not applicable	adBigInt	8	
real	Number(Single)	adSingle	4	
float	Number(Double)	adDouble	8	
money	Number(Currency)	adCurrency	8	19
smallmoney	Number(Currency)	adCurrency	8	10
decimal	Number(Decimal)	adNumeric	19	
datetime	Date/Time	adDBTimeStamp	16	23
smalldatetime	Date/Time	adDBTimeStamp	16	16
int_with_identity	Number(Long Integer)	adInteger	4	
varchar	Text	adVarChar	50	
nvarchar	Text	adVarWChar	50	
text	Memo	adLongVarChar	2147483647	
ntext	Memo	adLongVarWChar	1073741823	
image	OLE Object	adLongVarBinary	2147483647	
uniqueidentifier	Number(Replication ID)	adGUID	16	
char	Not applicable	adChar	50	
nchar	Not applicable	adWChar	50	
varbinary	Not applicable	adVarBinary	50	
timestamp	Not applicable	adBinary	8	
sql_variant	Not applicable	adVariant	16	

Figure 11-11 The output generated by the *ReportDataTypes* procedure.

Defining Tables and Inserting Rows

One typical application for column data types is to create the columns in a table. To create a table, use the T-SQL *CREATE TABLE* statement. This statement lets you specify the table name and then declare each of the columns within the table. You must specify a data type for each table column. You can optionally specify various constraints, such as one for a table's primary key. Although SQL Server doesn't require a primary key, you should always declare one when migrating to SQL Server from Access because SQL Server doesn't allow manual input to tables without a primary key. Another special feature of primary keys in SQL Server is that they can be clustered. A clustered primary key orders the records on a storage device according to the primary key values. A clustered index can dramatically improve sort and search activities for a clustered key versus columns without a clustered primary key or index. Primary keys are unclustered unless you explicitly declare them as clustered.

After you create a table, you probably will want to populate it with values. You can do this programmatically with the *INSERT* statement. This statement lets you populate all or a subset of the fields in a target table. You can specify the column values for each new row with a new *INSERT* statement. The source of the records can be individual values, another SQL Server table in the same or a different database, or data based on a legacy Access database file.

The next sample demonstrates the correct syntax for the *CREATE TABLE* and *INSERT* statements. Before using these statements, the sample removes any table, if one exists, that has the same name as the table it's about to create in a database. The sample demonstrates the use of an InformationSchema view to determine whether a prior version of a table exists. You can use the system-defined *sysobjects* table to determine whether a table or other database object exists already, but Microsoft recommends using InformationSchema views instead. Using InformationSchema views enables your applications to work properly, even if Microsoft changes the design of system-defined tables such as *sysobjects*.

The *MyExtensions* table name and the *EmployeeID, FirstName, LastName,* and *Extension* column names are hardcoded in the sample. Hardcoding is more typical when working with a table's design than with other coding tasks. This is because your application is likely to have custom requirements. However, if you plan to use one procedure to create many tables with the same basic design, it's trivial to generalize the procedure. Again, what to leave fixed and what to make variable will depend on the requirements of your custom applications.

Note   Wondering why you would ever need to know how to create a table programmatically? After all, weren't visual designers invented to make programming tables unnecessary? The preceding paragraph indicates one occasion when it makes sense to bypass the designer—you need one table and you want many copies, all to the exact same spec, of its basic design. Creating a table programmatically also makes sense when you want to create the same table design on more than one computer. If you have multiple tables to create on two or more computers, the savings are even greater. Yet another use for programming tables is to create them at run time in response to user input. This capability allows a user to specify the content for a table to store dynamically at run time.

After setting a *Connection* object for the current project, the *CreateMyExtensions* procedure features three main sections. Each of these sections demonstrates the use of T-SQL code to perform an independent task for creating and populating the *MyExtensions* table. The procedure repeatedly invokes the *Execute* method of the *Connection* object to run each of the sample's T-SQL code segments.

The first T-SQL segment uses an *IF* statement with an *EXISTS* keyword. This keyword permits the *IF* statement to conditionally execute a *DROP TABLE* statement if a prior version of the table exists. The sample uses an Information-Schema view to detect whether a table already exists in the database. If the table exists, the application simply drops the old version of it. In a production environment with critical operations or financial data, you might want to archive the table's data before dropping it. I'll illustrate a data archiving strategy later in the chapter in the "Triggers" section.

The second code segment invokes the *CREATE TABLE* statement to create the *MyExtensions* table. Because the column serves as the primary key, its declaration explicitly excludes nulls. In addition, the *EmployeeID* declaration includes an *IDENTITY* setting with a default value of 1 for its seed and 1 for its increment. The other three table columns permit nulls.

The third code segment invokes the *INSERT* statement three times. The first two instances of the statement populate all three nonidentity columns. SQL Server automatically populates the identity column value based on the last identity column value and the incremental value for the *IDENTITY* setting. Because the first two invocations of the *INSERT* statement specify values for all three nonidentity columns, the *INSERT* statements do not require a field list before the *VALUES* keyword. (This list indicates the fields for which the *VALUES* keyword designates values.) However, the third instance of the *INSERT* statement specifies only the *LastName* and *Extension* column values. Therefore, this instance of *INSERT* requires a field list before the *VALUES* keyword.

The procedure closes by invoking the *RefreshDatabaseWindow* method. This method refreshes the Database window so that the user can immediately see the newly added table. If the procedure did not include this method, the user might not see the new table in the Database window.

```
Sub CreateMyExtensions()
Dim str1 As String
Dim cnn1 As ADODB.Connection

'Point a Connection object at the current project
Set cnn1 = CurrentProject.Connection

'Delete the MyExtensions table if it exists already
str1 = "IF EXISTS(SELECT TABLE_NAME " & _
    "FROM INFORMATION_SCHEMA.TABLES " & _
    "WHERE TABLE_NAME = 'MyExtensions') " & _
    "DROP TABLE MyExtensions"
cnn1.Execute str1
```

```
'Create the MyExtensions table with an unclustered primary key
str1 = "CREATE TABLE MyExtensions " & _
    "( " & _
    "EmployeeID int IDENTITY(1,1) NOT NULL PRIMARY KEY, " & _
    "FirstName nvarchar(10) NULL, " & _
    "LastName nvarchar(20) NULL, " & _
    "Extension nvarchar(4) NULL " & _
    ")"
cnn1.Execute str1

'Populate the MyExtensions table with data; populate one record
'with a subset of the input fields
str1 = "INSERT INTO MyExtensions Values('Rick', 'Dobson', '8629')" & _
    "INSERT INTO MyExtensions Values('Virginia', 'Dobson', '9294')" & _
    "INSERT INTO MyExtensions (LastName, Extension) Values('Hill','3743')"
cnn1.Execute str1

'Refresh Database window to show new table
RefreshDatabaseWindow

End Sub
```

The next sample uses a nearly identical approach to create and populate a table of picture descriptions and file addresses for picture images. You can use this kind of table to display photographs, diagrams, or any graphically formatted file. By storing the file address instead of the image, you speed up the image retrieval time and shorten the image processing time. In Chapter 12, you'll see a sample that illustrates how to use this kind of table to populate controls on a form that contain photos.

The sample table in this next application is structurally unique from the one in the preceding sample because it uses a clustered primary key. Access database files do not support this kind of primary key. Recall that when an application specifies this type of primary key, SQL Server orders the records on the storage medium according to their primary key values. Each table can have just one clustered index, and it doesn't have to be the primary key. Because a clustered index substantially expedites record retrieval, you should reserve the clustered index setting for the key that users are most likely to work with.

The following code sample contains the same three main phases as the preceding sample, but the column names are different. In addition, this sample conditionally drops any prior version of the table by calling a sub procedure. Although table designs and data tend to be unique from one table to the next, the process of dropping a table doesn't vary much. Therefore, the main procedure calls the *Drop_a_table* procedure by passing a connection argument and a string representing the table name.

When working with image files, it's common to store them with the operating system and store only their locations in the database. You can maintain the security of your image files by placing them on a read-only file share. This allows users to query the table, but prevents them from adding, updating, and deleting image files. Some images are included with this chapter's sample materials so that you can experiment with displaying them. See Chapter 12 for a code sample that demonstrates how to display the images from an Access form.

```
Sub CreatPic_Addresses()
Dim str1 As String
Dim cnn1 As ADODB.Connection
Dim TableName As String

'Point a connection object at the current project
Set cnn1 = CurrentProject.Connection

'Delete the Pic_Addresses table if it exists already
TableName = "Pic_Addresses"
Drop_a_table cnn1, TableName

'Create the Pic_Addresses table with a clustered primary key
str1 = "CREATE TABLE " & TableName & " " & _
    "( " & _
    "PictureID int IDENTITY NOT NULL PRIMARY KEY CLUSTERED, " & _
    "Pic_description nvarchar(50), " & _
    "Pic_address nvarchar(256) " & _
    ") "
cnn1.Execute str1

'Insert descriptions and addresses for four pictures
str1 = "INSERT INTO " & TableName & " " & _
    "Values('Rick munches glasses', " & _
        "'C:\Access11Files\Picture1.jpg')" & _
    "INSERT INTO Pic_Addresses " & _
        "Values('Rick not working at computer', " & _
        "'C:\Access11Files\Picture2.jpg')" & _
    "INSERT INTO Pic_Addresses " & _
        "Values('Rick finally working at computer', " & _
        "'C:\Access11Files\Picture3.jpg')" & _
    "INSERT INTO Pic_Addresses " & _
        "Values('Rick gets reward for working', " & _
        "'C:\Access11Files\Picture4.jpg')"
cnn1.Execute str1

'Refresh Database window to show new table
RefreshDatabaseWindow

End Sub
```

```
Sub Drop_a_table(cnn1 As ADODB.Connection, TableName As String)
Dim str1 As String

'Delete the table if it exists already
str1 = "IF EXISTS (SELECT TABLE_NAME " & _
    "FROM INFORMATION_SCHEMA.TABLES " & _
    "WHERE TABLE_NAME = '" & TableName & "') " & _
    "DROP TABLE " & TableName
cnn1.Execute str1

End Sub
```

Adding a Table from a Database Diagram

When you first migrate to SQL Server, you might want to use graphical approaches with the programmatic ones to help expedite your solution development. Database diagrams are a graphical development aid that resemble the Relationship window in Access. However, you can have multiple database diagrams for the same database. In addition, database diagrams have a much richer set of data definition capabilities than the Relationship window does. Think of database diagrams as the Relationship window on steroids!

This section introduces these data definition capabilities by building a new table. Database diagrams are graphical, so I'll present the example with step-by-step instructions. The sample table, *Orders_linked_to_MyExtensions*, will have three columns, *OrderID*, *OrderDate*, and *EmployeeID*. The *OrderID* column will be the table's primary key, with an *IDENTITY* property setting of 10 for its seed and 2 for its increment.

To create a new table with a database diagram, you have to open either a new or an existing diagram. To open a new diagram for a new table from the Database window, follow these steps:

1. Open a diagram by selecting Database Diagrams in the Database window and clicking New.

2. Click Close in the Add Table dialog box because you won't need an existing table to create a new one.

3. Right-click anywhere in the empty diagram, and choose New Table from the shortcut menu.

4. Type the name **Orders_linked_to_MyExtensions** in the Choose Name dialog box, and click OK.

These steps open a blank table grid that you can use to help design your new table. The grid has a title with the name you assigned to the table, but otherwise it's empty. You can add columns to the table with these steps:

1. Type **OrderID** in the first Column Name row of the grid. Then select an *int* data type and clear the Allow Nulls check box because this field will serve as the primary key.

2. Type **OrderDate** in the second Column Name row. Choose a *smalldate* data type for this column because this application will be outdated well before 2079 (the last represented by the *Smalldate* data type) and you don't need to track orders that are less than a minute apart (the most precise *Smalldate* time unit). Leave the Allow Nulls check box selected.

3. Finish entering columns by typing **EmployeeID** in the third row of the *EmployeeID* column. Because this column will eventually serve as a foreign key for linking this table to the *MyExtensions* table, choose *int* as the data type so that it matches the data type for *EmployeeID* in the *MyExtensions* table.

You're almost finished defining your new table. However, you need to make *OrderID* the primary key. In addition, if you want the column to automatically populate itself with values, you need to give it an *IDENTITY* setting. After making these refinements, you can add the new table to the database. Follow these steps to finish creating the table:

1. Right-click anywhere on the *OrderID* row. Choose Primary Key from the shortcut menu.

2. Click the record selector for *OrderID*. Right-click a second time in the *OrderID* row, and choose Properties from the shortcut menu.

3. Select the Columns tab for the Properties dialog box, and confirm that the Column Name setting is *OrderID*. If not, use the drop-down list for the setting to select *OrderID*.

4. Next, change the Identity setting to Yes. Then assign the Identity Seed a value of 10 and the Identity Increment a value of 2. (See Figure 11-12.) This will cause *OrderID* to start at 10 and grow by increments of two for each new record. After making these settings, close the Properties dialog box by clicking Close in the top right corner.

Figure 11-12   The Properties dialog box for the *OrderID* column that shows the setting for the Identity, Identity Seed, and Identity Increment.

5. Then, click Close for the diagram. Click Yes when prompted about saving changes. Then assign a name to the diagram, such as Adding_Orders_linked_to_MyExtensions.

Linking Two Tables in a Database Diagram

Now let's create a new database diagram that links the *Orders_linked_to_MyExtensions* table to the *MyExtensions* table. You can use the diagram to set up referential integrity and cascading updates and deletes. In this example, you don't want to throw away orders based on the status of an employee, but you do want to be able to switch accounts from one employee to the next. Therefore, you enable cascading updates but not cascading deletes.

Let's start the process of linking the tables by creating a new database diagram. (We could use the old diagram, but it is more instructive to start from scratch.) Use the steps on the following page.

1. Open a diagram by selecting Database Diagrams in the Database window and clicking New.

2. From the Add Table dialog box, select *MyExtensions*. Then click Add.

3. Repeat this process for the *Orders_linked_to_MyExtensions* table.

4. Click the Close button in the Add Table dialog box.

After rearranging the boxes representing the tables so that they're easy to use, you're ready to start linking the two tables. Follow these steps:

1. Click the record selector for *EmployeeID* in the *MyExtensions* table.

2. Drag the *EmployeeID* field from the *MyExtensions* table to the *EmployeeID* field in the *Orders_linked_to_MyExtensions* table. (See Figure 11-13.)

3. In the Create Relationship dialog box that appears, verify that the primary key table is *MyExtensions* and that its linking field is *EmployeeID*. In addition, verify that the foreign key table is *Orders_linked_to_MyExtensions* and that its linking field is also *EmployeeID*.

4. Verify that the Enforce Relationship For INSERTs And UPDATEs check box is selected.

5. Select the Cascade Update Related Fields check box.

6. Verify that the Cascade Delete Related Records check box is clear.

7. Click OK to assign the settings in the dialog box.

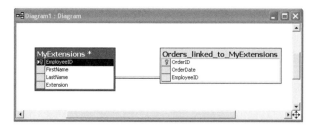

Figure 11-13   This database diagram shows the graphical link between the *EmployeeID* field from the *MyExtensions* table and the *EmployeeID* field in the *Orders_linked_to_MyExtensions* table after the Create Relationship dialog box opens but before the establishment of a relationship.

In the last sequence, you specified a foreign key for the *Orders_linked_to_MyExtensions* table that points at the *MyExtensions* table. However, Access hasn't yet saved the relationship to the database. You can facilitate this by closing the diagram and saving it. Before you close the diagram, Access will ask whether you want to save your changes. Follow these steps to save the relationship:

1. Click the Close button on your database diagram to close it.

2. Click Yes when prompted about saving your changes.

3. Assign the diagram a name, such as *Adding_a_Relationship*.

4. Access again asks whether you want to save changes. Click Yes. This prompt also allows you to write the changes to a text file.

There's a lot more to database diagrams, but these two examples can acquaint you with some of the basics and allow you to determine whether using database diagrams fits your personal style of developing. Some Access developers love to code, but others prefer graphical design techniques. If you're in the latter camp, database diagrams might be a good topic for you to explore further.

The following code sample resets the database to remove the objects created with the two database diagram examples you've seen. This permits you to review the steps from scratch, without having to work around previously defined objects, relationships, and diagrams. It also gives you some insight into programmatically managing database diagrams.

This sample has two components. First, it conditionally drops the *Orders_ linked_to_MyExtensions* table. Dropping the table also eliminates its relationship to the *MyExtensions* table. Then the procedure removes all the diagrams in the database. SQL Server stores information describing its database diagram collection members in the *dtproperties* table. Although SQL Server defines this as a user-defined table, it's typically managed by SQL Server. In addition, SQL Server provides no explicit means for programmatically referencing database diagrams. However, you can delete the rows in the *dtproperties* table. Doing so removes the diagrams associated with those rows. This procedure removes the diagrams created in this chapter. The procedure refreshes the Database window with the *RefreshDatabaseWindow* method.

```
Sub Drop_Orders_linked_table_and_Diagrams()
Dim str1 As String
Dim cnn1 As ADODB.Connection
Dim TableName As String

'Point a connection object at the current project
Set cnn1 = CurrentProject.Connection

'Delete the Order_linked_to_MyExtensions table if it exists already
TableName = "Orders_linked_to_MyExtensions"
Drop_a_table cnn1, TableName

'Drop all database diagrams
str1 = "DELETE FROM dtProperties"
cnn1.Execute str1

'Refresh Database window to show new table
RefreshDatabaseWindow

End Sub
```

SQL Server Views

SQL Server views are a subset of the traditional Access queries that you know from Access database files and the T-SQL samples that you find in Books Online. A view is an object in a SQL Server database. However, SQL Server does not save the view as a table of data values. Instead, SQL Server stores a T-SQL *SELECT* statement and related properties that define the view. The purpose of a view is to act as a virtual table. Once you understand the purpose of a view in a database, some of its apparent limitations (when compared to other database objects and T-SQL statements) generally seem reasonable.

At its core, a SQL Server view is a single *SELECT* statement. The result set returned by this statement is the view's virtual table. The *SELECT* statement can include all the standard clauses of a typical *SELECT* statement except the *ORDER BY* clause. (The *ORDER BY* clause is permissible, but you must also include the *TOP* clause in the *SELECT* statement so that SQL Server can interpret the view and return a result set.) Although a view does permit a *WHERE* clause, its arguments cannot be parameters. In addition, you cannot include multiple *SELECT* statements in a view, and a view cannot process *INSERT, UPDATE*, and *DELETE* statements.

These limitations of views stem from their basic purpose—to represent a single, virtual table in T-SQL code. When you need to accomplish this, the view is an able tool. In addition, Access projects offer a Query Designer for constructing and editing views that resembles the Query Designer available in Access database files for stored queries. The Access project Query Designer can make designing views fast. Furthermore, you can use this tool to teach yourself T-SQL syntax by graphically designing views and then examining the T-SQL underlying them in the Query Designer's SQL pane.

Creating Sample Tables

This section uses the *Orders* table and the *Shippers* table, which are based on the corresponding tables in the NorthwindCS database. As mentioned earlier in the chapter, if you don't have the NorthwindCS database on your server, you probably have the Northwind database. Recall that the NorthwindCS sample Access project automatically installs the NorthwindCS database on the local server the first time you open the project if a copy of the Northwind database doesn't already exist on the local server.

The following two procedures show the code for creating the tables and populating them with values. Each procedure handles the creation and data population of one table. The procedures start by conditionally removing a prior version of the table (if one exists). Next, the procedures invoke a *CRE-*

ATE TABLE statement to define the table structure. After executing the *CREATE TABLE* statement, the database for the current project will have a new empty table. Then the procedures run a stored procedure that copies data from the NorthwindCS *Orders* table or the *Shippers* table to the local table of the same name. I discuss these stored procedures later in this chapter so that you can modify them as needed.

```
Sub CreateAndPopulateOrdersTable()
Dim str1 As String
Dim cnn1 As ADODB.Connection
Dim TableName As String

'Point a Connection object at the current project
Set cnn1 = CurrentProject.Connection

'Delete the table if it exists already
TableName = "Orders"
Drop_a_table cnn1, TableName

'Create the table
str1 = "CREATE TABLE Orders " & _
    "( " & _
    "OrderID int IDENTITY (1, 1) NOT NULL PRIMARY KEY CLUSTERED, " & _
    "OrderDate datetime NULL , " & _
    "ShipVia int NULL , " & _
    "Freight money NULL " & _
    ")"
cnn1.Execute str1

'Run custom stored procedure to populate table based
'on NorthwindCS database
str1 = "EXEC Copy_from_NorthwindCS_Orders"
cnn1.Execute str1

'Refresh Database window to show new table
RefreshDatabaseWindow

End Sub

Sub CreateAndPopulateShippersTable()
Dim str1 As String
Dim cnn1 As ADODB.Connection
Dim TableName As String
```

(continued)

```
'Point a Connection object at the current project
Set cnn1 = CurrentProject.Connection

'Delete the table if it exists already
TableName = "Shippers"
Drop_a_table cnn1, TableName

'Create the table
str1 = "CREATE TABLE Shippers " & _
    "( " & _
    "ShipperID int IDENTITY (1, 1) NOT NULL PRIMARY KEY CLUSTERED, " & _
    "CompanyName varchar(40) NOT NULL , " & _
    "Phone varchar(24) NULL " & _
    ")"
cnn1.Execute str1

'Run custom stored procedure to populate table based
'on NorthwindCS database
str1 = "EXEC Copy_from_NorthwindCS_Shippers"
cnn1.Execute str1

'Refresh Database window to show new table
RefreshDatabaseWindow

End Sub
```

Using the Access Project Query Designer

You can launch the Query Designer by selecting Queries in the Objects bar and clicking New. This opens the New Query dialog box. Select Design View, and click OK. Next, you will see the Show Table dialog box. You can choose from previously defined tables, views, and user-defined functions. The dialog box contains a tab for each of these objects. You can select objects from these tabs and click Add to include them as record sources for your view. When you are done, click Close to close the Show Table dialog box. Alternatively, you can just click Close. This frees you to write T-SQL code directly into the SQL pane without having to use the graphical UI.

Figure 11-14 shows the graphical UI and code specifications for a view. I added the *Orders* table to this view, which, as you can see, offers three panes. The toolbar buttons let you independently show or hide each of these panes in Design View. The top pane, which has an *Orders* table icon, is the Diagram pane. This pane can depict any joins between tables that serve as the record source for a view. In this case, just one table serves as the record source. You can add table columns from the Diagram pane to a view by selecting the check box next to the column you want.

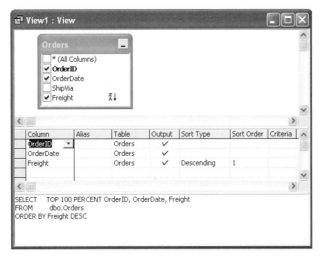

Figure 11-14   The three panes for the Access project Query Designer
with a view that sorts orders by *Freight* column values in descending order.

The Query Designer automatically adds the column name for a checked box
to the middle panel, called the Grid pane. The Grid pane contains a row for each
column in the view's virtual table. Note that you can designate the order in which
the view sorts its records. Figure 11-14 shows the *Freight* column being sorted in
descending order. Because the view has only one sort key, its *Sort Order* column
has a value of 1 and the *Sort Order* values for the other columns are blank.

The bottom pane is the SQL pane. This pane does not open by default,
but you can manually open it with the SQL button on the Design view toolbar.
The Query Designer automatically populates this pane with code when you
commit changes to either of the other two panes. In addition, you can type T-
SQL code into the SQL pane, and the Query Designer will revise the other two
panes accordingly. Type your T-SQL syntax directly into this pane to avoid having to work with the graphical UI for the Query Designer.

When you're ready to examine the result set from a view, you must save
the view before looking at the rows that it returns. The view depicted in Figure
11-14 appears in the sample database for this chapter as *Orders_sorted_by_
Freight*. Whenever you edit a view's design, you must resave the view before
you can see its result set. Click Run or choose Datasheet View from the View
drop-down menu on the toolbar to examine the result set. If you haven't saved
the view since the last change, Access automatically prompts you to save it. If
you're examining a view's result set for the first time, you must assign it a name.
Access prompts with a name such as *View1*, but you can override this default
name with one that is meaningful for your application.

Filtering by Date

SQL Server stores *datetime* and *smalldatetime* data type values internally in a format similar to that used for Access database files. However, SQL Server normally displays dates in a string format, such as *Varchar* or *Char*. Indeed, you can filter SQL Server fields with dates by using a string. Alternatively, you can also use various functions to help specify filtering criteria. The *DATEPART* function is particularly useful for this purpose.

The following T-SQL statement shows the syntax for using a string filter employed in the *Orders_in_1996_1* view. The statement specifies the return of rows that are less than or equal to the last day in 1996. The statement is from the SQL pane of the Query Designer. You do not necessarily need the dbo qualifier for the *Orders* table in the *FROM* clause, but the Query Designer forces its inclusion. Notice that the string for the date uses single quotes. Access developers migrating to SQL Server will have to get used to delimiting text strings with single rather than double quote marks.

```
SELECT    OrderID, OrderDate, ShipVia, Freight
FROM      dbo.Orders
WHERE     (OrderDate <= '1996-12-31')
```

Figure 11-15 shows an excerpt from the result set for the view. Notice that it contains just 152 rows, instead of the 830 rows in the original *Orders* table. This reduced number of rows stems directly from the filter in the *WHERE* clause's argument. Of the full set of 830 records in the *Orders* table, only 152 are from 1996. (This is the first year of data for the NorthwindCS database.)

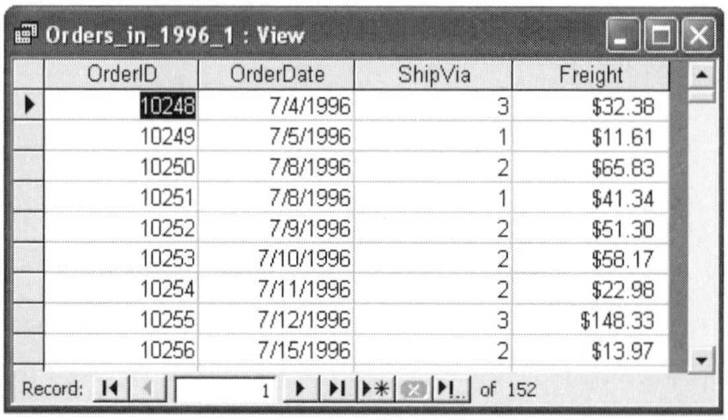

OrderID	OrderDate	ShipVia	Freight
10248	7/4/1996	3	$32.38
10249	7/5/1996	1	$11.61
10250	7/8/1996	2	$65.83
10251	7/8/1996	1	$41.34
10252	7/9/1996	2	$51.30
10253	7/10/1996	2	$58.17
10254	7/11/1996	2	$22.98
10255	7/12/1996	3	$148.33
10256	7/15/1996	2	$13.97

Figure 11-15 An excerpt from the result set for *Orders_in_1996_1*.

The following syntax for the *Orders_in_1996_2* view shows another piece of T-SQL syntax that generates the same result set as the one shown in Figure 11-15. Instead of filtering on a string value, the T-SQL code for this view applies the *DATEPART* function to the *OrderDate* column values. This function returns an integer with the value of a specified part in a specified date. In the context of this demonstration, the function returns a value of 1996. Only rows that have an *OrderDate* column value in the year 1996 pass through the filter into the result set for the *Orders_in_1996_2* view.

```
SELECT    OrderID, OrderDate, ShipVia, Freight
FROM      dbo.Orders
WHERE     (DATEPART(yyyy, OrderDate) = 1996)
```

If your work requires you to filter on different dates or units of time, you should get to know the *DATEPART* function. It works similarly though not identically to its counterpart for Access database files. The SQL Server *DATEPART* function lets you extract from columns of *datetime* values any of 11 different time parts, from the year down to the millisecond. Table 11-4 shows the *DATEPART* arguments that permit you to extract different time units from a *datetime* or *smalldatetime* value. The day of year and day of month numbering starts at 1 for the first respective day of the year or the month. The day of week runs from 1 (for Sunday) to 7 (for Saturday). This is the default setting for U.S. English. Use the *SET DATEFIRST* statement to alter the default day for the start of a week. (See Books Online for the syntax.)

Table 11-4   *DATEPART* Arguments for Extracting Time Units

Time Unit	*DATEPART* Argument
Year	*yy* or *yyyy*
Quarter	*qq* or *q*
Month	*mm* or *m*
Day of year	*dy* or *y*
Day of month	*dd* or *d*
Week of year	*wk* or *ww*
Day of week	*dw*
Hour	*hh*
Minute	*mi* or *n*
Second	*ss* or *s*
Millisecond	*ms*

Joining Tables for a Lookup

Although Access offers a Query Designer for inputting the T-SQL code for a view, you are not forced to create views graphically at design time. You can use the ADO *Connection* object to execute T-SQL statements to create a view. This approach offers several advantages. First, it automatically creates an archive of the script for a view in a location that typical users aren't likely to access. Second, if users inadvertently corrupt a view's T-SQL by opening and modifying it in the Database window, you can restore the view by rerunning the procedure to create the view. The third advantage is that your code more closely follows the samples in Books Online. For example, you must use a *CREATE VIEW* statement to create a view with the *Connection* object's *Execute* method. However, you cannot use a *CREATE VIEW* statement in the Query Designer. Fourth, the T-SQL code for a view will be easier to maintain when you prepare it to run with the *Connection* object, because you write the code according to your preferred styles. Recall that the Query Designer forces a dbo qualifier whether or not you want to use it.

The next sample demonstrates the syntax for creating a SQL Server view without the use of the Query Designer. This particular view joins the *Shippers* table to the *Orders* table so that a listing of orders shows a shipper's name instead of an ID code. The code for this simulates the behavior of the Lookup tab settings for a table. Because you control the view through code, you have substantial flexibility regarding which shipper names you show and how you show them. For example, you could use a *WHERE* clause to decode only some names but hide others that require special permission for examination.

The next sample performs a simple equijoin that shows a shipper's name for every row in the *Orders* table with a *ShipperID* value. The sample uses a main procedure and a sub procedure to create a new version of the *Orders_with_lookup_from_view* view. The main procedure starts by dropping any prior version of the view with a call to the *Drop_a_view* procedure. The call passes an ADO *Connection* object that points at a database and a string denoting the name of the view to remove from the database. Next, the main procedure defines a SQL string that includes a *CREATE VIEW* statement. The *SELECT* statement element of the *CREATE VIEW* statement performs an inner join of the *Orders* table with the *Shippers* table by the *ShipperID* column values. This join permits the view to show the *CompanyName* field from the *Shippers* table—which contains the shipper's name—in place of the *ShipperID* field from the *Orders* table. This is the lookup behavior that we want. Notice that the *SELECT* statement for the view includes an *ORDER BY* clause. This is only possible because the *SELECT* statement also includes a *TOP* clause immediately after the *SELECT* keyword. The sort by *OrderID* is necessary because the inner join sorts the result set based on the *ShipperID* field from the *Shippers* table. The *ORDER BY* clause reorders the returned rows based on *OrderID* values.

```
Sub CreateOrders_with_lookup_from_view()
Dim str1 As String
Dim cnn1 As ADODB.Connection
Dim ViewName As String
```

```
'Point a Connection object at the current project
Set cnn1 = CurrentProject.Connection

'Delete the view if it exists already
ViewName = "Orders_with_lookup_from_view"
Drop_a_view cnn1, ViewName

'Use TOP 100 PERCENT to permit use of ORDER BY clause in T-SQL for
'a view
str1 = "CREATE VIEW Orders_with_lookup_from_view " & _
    "AS " & _
    "SELECT TOP 100 PERCENT Orders.OrderID, Orders.OrderDate, " & _
    "Shippers.CompanyName as Shipvia, Orders.Freight " & _
    "FROM  Orders INNER JOIN " & _
    "Shippers ON Orders.ShipVia = Shippers.ShipperID " & _
    "ORDER BY Orders.OrderID "
cnn1.Execute str1

'Refresh Database window to show new table
RefreshDatabaseWindow

End Sub

Sub Drop_a_view(cnn1 As ADODB.Connection, ViewName As String)

'Delete the view if it exists already
str1 = "IF EXISTS (SELECT TABLE_NAME " & _
    "FROM INFORMATION_SCHEMA.VIEWS " & _
    "WHERE TABLE_NAME = '" & ViewName & "') " & _
    "DROP VIEW " & ViewName
cnn1.Execute str1

End Sub
```

After creating a view, it's natural to want to examine all or a subset of its records. The following sample demonstrates one technique for doing this. The sample's first procedure specifies a *Connection* object that points at a database, the view's name from which to print rows, and the maximum number of rows to print. The *Connection* object needs to point at the database with the view. The first procedure passes these parameters to the second one, making the specified subset of the view's records available.

The second procedure opens a recordset on the view in the database specified. Next this procedure determines whether the recordset has the maximum number of records requested. If this number is less than the maximum, the procedure computes a new limit based on the number of records in the view. Because the numeric index for records in a recordset starts at 0, the procedure loops from 0 to one less than the maximum number of records to print. Inside the loop for the records, a nested loop passes through all the fields for the current record.

```
Sub CallOpenSubsetOfView()
Dim cnn1 As ADODB.Connection
Dim VName As String
Dim LimitToPrint As Byte

Set cnn1 = CurrentProject.Connection
VName = "Orders_with_lookup_from_view"
LimitToPrint = 10

OpenSubsetOfView cnn1, VName, LimitToPrint

End Sub

Sub OpenSubsetOfView(cnn1 As ADODB.Connection, VName As String, _
    LimitToPrint As Byte)
Dim rst1 As ADODB.Recordset
Dim byt1 As Byte
Dim byt2 As Byte

'Instantiate recordset, and open it on view
Set rst1 = New ADODB.Recordset
rst1.Open VName, CurrentProject.Connection, _
    adOpenKeyset, adLockOptimistic, adCmdTable

'Loop through all fields for the desired subset of records
byt1 = IIf(rst1.RecordCount < LimitToPrint, _
    rst1.RecordCount - 1, LimitToPrint - 1)
For byt2 = 0 To byt1
    Debug.Print "Results for record " & (byt2 + 1)
    For Each fld1 In rst1.Fields
        Debug.Print "    " & fld1.Name & " = " & rst1.Fields(fld1.Name)
    Next fld1
    rst1.MoveNext
    Debug.Print
Next byt2

End Sub
```

When working with SQL Server databases by using Access, it's common for the tables in a database to have a large number of rows. This can result in degraded performance for applications that attempt to open all the records without taking any special steps. One step you can take is to limit the number of records that a recordset retrieves. The built-in default for Access projects is

10,000 records. This setting applies to the whole database. You can manually update this setting from the Advanced tab of the Options dialog box. You can programmatically read and write this setting for any recordset by using the *MaxRecords* property. The following adaptation of the *OpenSubsetOfView* procedure retrieves only the maximum number of records to print. This approach provides a simple way to improve performance when a recordset based on a view has many rows and your application requires only a small set from the beginning of the view.

```
Sub OpenSubsetOfView1(cnn1 As ADODB.Connection, VName As String, _
    LimitToPrint As Byte)
Dim rst1 As ADODB.Recordset
Dim byt1 As Byte

'Instantiate recordset, and open it on view for just
'a subset of records
Set rst1 = New ADODB.Recordset
rst1.MaxRecords = LimitToPrint
rst1.Open VName, cnn1, adOpenKeyset, adLockOptimistic, adCmdTable

'Loop through all fields for the desired subset of records
byt1 = 0
Do Until rst1.EOF
    Debug.Print "Results for record " & (byt1 + 1)
    For Each fld1 In rst1.Fields
        Debug.Print "    " & fld1.Name & " = " & rst1.Fields(fld1.Name)
    Next fld1
    rst1.MoveNext
    byt1 = byt1 + 1
    Debug.Print
Loop

End Sub
```

Aggregating Records in a View

If you have a basic understanding of SQL, aggregating inside a view is straightforward. Refer back to Chapter 4 for an examination of Jet SQL syntax. This syntax is broadly applicable to SQL Server for select queries—especially for simple aggregations. The following sample reuses code from the preceding sample, which set the *MaxRecords* property for a recordset before opening it. Because this sample generates a view that has just three records, the *Byte* data type specification for the *MaxRecords* property, which has an upper limit of 10 records, won't prevent you from retrieving all the view's records.

This sample aggregates the *Freight* column values in the *Orders* table by year. The T-SQL syntax for the view generates just three rows because the

Orders table contains data for 1996 through 1998 only. The *SELECT* statement's column list reveals a couple of interesting T-SQL features. First, it uses the *DATEPART* function to transform the *OrderDate* field to a year. This same function specification appears in the *GROUP BY* clause, aggregating the data by year. Second, the *SUM* function has an alias with internal spaces. The default T-SQL delimiters for such identifiers are square brackets. After creating the view by executing the SQL string as the argument of a *Connection* object, the procedure opens the view and prints its contents to the Immediate window with a call to the *OpenSubsetofView1* procedure.

```
Sub CreateSum_of_Freight_by_year()
Dim str1 As String
Dim cnn1 As ADODB.Connection
Dim ViewName As String
Dim LimitToPrint As Byte

'Point a Connection object at the current project
Set cnn1 = CurrentProject.Connection

'Delete the view if it exists already
ViewName = "Sum_of_Freight_by_year"
Drop_a_view cnn1, ViewName

 'Use TOP 100 PERCENT to permit use of ORDER BY clause in T-SQL for
'a view
str1 = "CREATE VIEW " & ViewName & " " & _
    "AS " & _
    "SELECT DATEPART(yyyy, OrderDate) AS Year, " & _
    "SUM(Freight) AS [Sum of Freight] " & _
    "FROM Orders " & _
    "GROUP BY DATEPART(yyyy, OrderDate) "
cnn1.Execute str1

'Print result set
LimitToPrint = 10
OpenSubsetOfView1 cnn1, ViewName, LimitToPrint

End Sub
```

Converting Dates and Times to Different Formats

CAST and *CONVERT* are two SQL Server system–defined functions that let you convert between data types. The *CAST* function is consistent with the ANSI SQL specification, but the *CONVERT* function is optimized more for use with SQL Server. If you don't plan to generate applications designed to run across multiple database servers from different vendors, *CONVERT* will deliver more simplicity and power to your data conversion tasks.

One of the nice things about the *CONVERT* function is its ability to represent *datetime* and *smalldatetime* column values in a variety of formats. For example, *CONVERT* can represent times in the U.S., British/French, German, Italian, or Japanese date formats. This can be very useful for applications that need to display dates in the formats of several different countries. The *CONVERT* function takes three arguments for this kind of transformation. First, it takes the data type to which you are converting the *datetime* value. This value will typically be *Varchar* or *Char*. Second, it takes an expression that evaluates to a *datetime* value. This can be a column value with a *Datetime* data type, a function that returns a *datetime* value, or an expression based on either or both of these. Third, the function takes a style parameter that designates the format for the output. (See the *CAST* and *CONVERT* topic in Books Online for a list of style parameter values and the results that they return.)

The next sample shows how to return the results from the system-defined *GETDATE* function in five distinct formats, depending on country. The sample relies on two procedures. The first procedure calls the second procedure five times. Each time the first procedure calls the second procedure, it passes a different style parameter for the *CONVERT* function. The second procedure is a function procedure that returns its value as a string for use in a *Debug.print* statement in the first procedure. The second procedure invokes the *CONVERT* function with the style parameter passed to it by the first procedure.

```
Sub CallReturnDateStyle()
Dim str1 As String

'U.S. date style
str1 = "101"
Debug.Print "Date in the U.S. is: " & ReturnDateStyle(str1)

'British/French date style
str1 = "103"
Debug.Print "Date in Britain/France is: " & ReturnDateStyle(str1)

'German date style
str1 = "104"
Debug.Print "Date in Germany is: " & ReturnDateStyle(str1)

'Italian date style
str1 = "105"
Debug.Print "Date in Italy is: " & ReturnDateStyle(str1)

'Japanese date style
str1 = "111"
Debug.Print "Date in Japan is: " & ReturnDateStyle(str1)

End Sub
```

(continued)

```
Function ReturnDateStyle(StyleNumber As String) As String
Dim str1 As String
Dim cnn1 As ADODB.Connection
Dim rst1 As ADODB.Recordset

'Point a Connection object at the current project, and create
'a recordset based on the connection
Set cnn1 = CurrentProject.Connection
Set rst1 = New ADODB.Recordset
rst1.ActiveConnection = cnn1

'Create SQL string with CONVERT function and date style
'parameter for a country
str1 = "SELECT Convert(varchar,GETDATE()," & _
    StyleNumber & ")"
rst1.Open str1, cnn1

'Pass back value
ReturnDateStyle = rst1(0)

 'Clean up objects
rst1.Close
Set rst1 = Nothing

End Function
```

One of the easiest ways to understand this sample is to examine its output to the Immediate window. Figure 11-16 shows this output. Notice that it includes five lines—one for each country-specific date representation. A remarkable feature of the *CONVERT* function is that the syntax for these distinct date formats is identical for all five of them. All the *CONVERT* function needs to switch from one format to another is a different style parameter. As you can see, this is a string value that the first procedure passes to the second one.

Figure 11-16 The output from the date conversion sample.

The *CONVERT* function can also use the time portion of a *datetime* value to represent time values in different formats. For example, you can express the time portion of the *GETDATE* function either in hours and minutes (as well as specifying A.M. or P.M., referred to as *day parts* in the following code), or in hours, min-

utes, seconds, and milliseconds (again specifying A.M. or P.M.). Again, using one
format over the other is as simple as passing a different style parameter to the
CONVERT function. The next sample shows a pair of procedures that demonstrates this, along with the specific style parameters for each time format.

In this sample, the second procedure needs to do a little more processing
than it did in the preceding sample. This is because the *CONVERT* function
returns a full *datetime* value, with both a date and a time concatenated together.
The second procedure extracts all the characters to the right of the date. These
characters represent a time value. Then the procedure trims the result to
remove any leading blanks. As with the previous sample, examining the output
of the *CONVERT* function and its style parameters can help you understand
how they work. Figure 11-17 shows the result of applying the two different time
formats to the *GETDATE* function.

```
Sub CallReturnTimeStyle()
Dim str1 As String

'Hours, minutes, day part style
str1 = "100"
Debug.Print "Time to hours:minutes day part is: " & _
    ReturnTimeStyle(str1)

'Hours, minutes, seconds, milliseconds, day part style
str1 = "109"
Debug.Print "Time to hours:minutes:seconds:milliseconds " & _
    "day part is: " & ReturnTimeStyle(str1)

End Sub

Function ReturnTimeStyle(StyleNumber As String) As String
Dim str1 As String
Dim cnn1 As ADODB.Connection
Dim rst1 As ADODB.Recordset

'Point a Connection object at the current project, and create
'a recordset based on the connection
Set cnn1 = CurrentProject.Connection
Set rst1 = New ADODB.Recordset
rst1.ActiveConnection = cnn1

str1 = "SELECT LTRIM(RIGHT (CONVERT " & _
    "(varchar, GETDATE(), " & StyleNumber & "), " & _
    "LEN(CONVERT (varchar, GETDATE(), " & StyleNumber & _
    ")) - 11))"
rst1.Open str1, cnn1
```

(continued)

```
'Pass back value
ReturnTimeStyle = rst1(0)

'Clean up objects
rst1.Close
Set rst1 = Nothing

End Function
```

```
Immediate                                                    ✕
  Time to hours:minutes day part is: 12:55PM                  ▲
  Time to hours:minutes:seconds:milliseconds day part is: 12:55:53:097PM
                                                             ▼
 ◄ |       |                                                ►
```

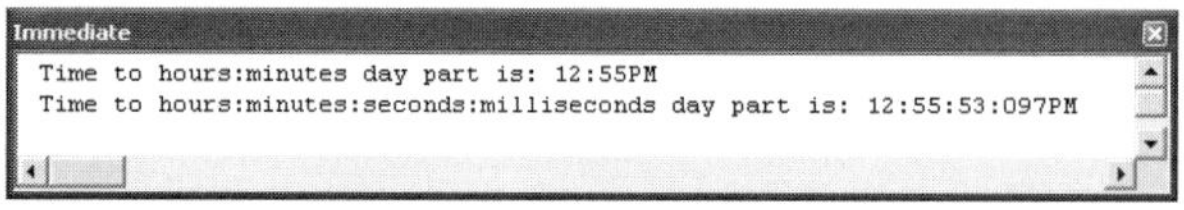

Figure 11-17   The output from the time conversion sample.

Creating and Using Stored Procedures

A stored procedure is a set of compiled T-SQL statements. Although these statements can return a result set just like a view, stored procedures offer many more capabilities. At the most basic level, you can use an *ORDER BY* clause in a stored procedure without also having to specify a *TOP* clause for a *SELECT* statement. Stored procedures enable basic programming capabilities, such as allowing *IF...ELSE* statements and parameters to facilitate the reuse of code. Parameters are particularly useful for stored procedures that maintain databases; parameters can enable the inserting, updating, and deleting of table records. You can also perform data definition with stored procedures. For example, you can create tables.

Because stored procedures are compiled T-SQL statements, they are ideal for increasing the performance of your database administration tasks. Instead of having to compile T-SQL statements to perform a task, SQL Server can immediately process the compiled code. Because you can specify the code with parameters, it's possible to modify the behavior of stored procedures through the values that you assign to their parameters at run time.

Stored procedures offer a variety of ways to accept input and return values. The input parameters for stored procedures work much like the parameters for stored queries for traditional database files. However, SQL Server parameters readily permit the return of values from a stored procedure. Of course, a stored procedure can return a result set. In fact, it can return multiple result sets. You also can pass back values from a stored procedure by using output parameters. These parameters can handle the return of scalar values instead of result sets. Additionally, you can use the *RETURN* statement in a stored procedure to pass back an integer value to the procedure that invokes it. The syntax rules for *RETURN* enable the use of a constant or an expression. Output parameters can return all kinds of data types—not just integer values. You will typically use an expression to specify an output parameter's value, but your T-SQL code can also designate a constant.

The Access UI for Stored Procedures

Access 2003 offers a couple of user interfaces for specifying stored procedures. You can view the different options by selecting Queries in the Objects bar in the Database window and clicking New. The New Query dialog box shows two options for creating a stored procedure. One option has the name Create Text Stored Procedure. The stored procedure template associated with this option facilitates typing T-SQL code into it. The template's layout and operation facilitate the creation and maintenance of stored procedures. Design Stored Procedure is the other option in the New Query dialog box for creating a stored procedure. This option presents a visual designer that is similar to the one you use for views. This designer is appropriate when you want to develop a result set from a single *SELECT* statement without any other T-SQL statements. This graphical designer is also available for stored procedures that insert, update, and delete records. However, it is not appropriate for stored procedures that perform data definition tasks, such as creating a new table or altering an existing one.

The two options for creating stored procedures are also available for maintaining them. To view the graphical or text-based version of an existing stored procedure, select the stored procedure in the Database window. Then click Design. If you open a stored procedure that returns a result set based on a single *SELECT* statement, you will see the visual designer for the stored procedure. If you open a procedure based on another kind of stored procedure (for example, one with more than a single *SELECT* statement), the text-based stored procedure template appears. Even if Access opens the visual designer view for a stored procedure, you can navigate to the text-based stored procedure template with the View drop-down menu on the toolbar. Although stored procedures with a single *SELECT* statement let you navigate freely between the two views, other kinds of stored procedures that open initially in the text-based template cannot be represented by the visual designer.

> **Note**   You can run a stored procedure by selecting it in the Database window and clicking Open. The Open button used to have the label Run In Access 2000. However, because Access 2003 offers a single mode for displaying views, stored procedures, and user-defined functions, you now click Open to run a stored procedure.

You can also manipulate stored procedures programmatically. This is more flexible and compatible with Books Online. For example, when you choose Create Text Stored Procedure, Access opens the stored procedure template with the *CREATE PROCEDURE* keyword phrase. After you initially save the stored procedure, it always opens with an *ALTER PROCEDURE* keyword phrase. This change in the keyword phrase makes it easy to modify a stored procedure, but the approach is at odds with most samples in Books Online. These samples typically drop the previously existing procedure and then execute a new *CREATE PROCEDURE* statement. When you create a stored procedure from a VBA module (as I will show you in subsequent samples in this section), you can follow the design guidelines in Books Online. In addition, creating the SQL Server stored procedure in a VBA procedure gives you more flexibility in using the stored procedure. For example, you can fire the stored procedure immediately after creating it. Whether you create the stored procedure with VBA or from the Access stored procedure template, you can invoke the stored procedure from an event procedure, such as a procedure that runs after a user clicks a button.

Using the *LIKE* Operator with *datetime* Column Values

Figure 11-18 shows the Design view for a stored procedure named *Orders_in_like_1996*. It uses the *LIKE* operator to specify a criterion for *OrderDate* column values. The rows with *OrderDate* column values that include 1996 pass through the filter for membership in the stored procedure's result set. Recall that SQL Server represents *datetime* values internally as numbers, but it displays and filters them as string values. This feature makes it possible to use the *LIKE* operator to filter rows based on their column values.

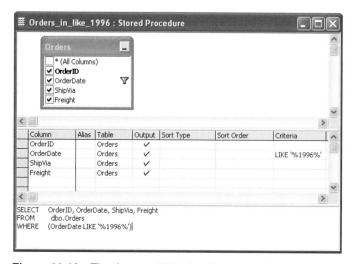

Figure 11-18   The Access 2003 visual designer for stored procedures.

As you can see, the visual designer for stored procedures has the same look and feel as the visual designer for views. Both designers enable the specification of a result set based on a single *SELECT* statement. However, one designer creates and maintains a stored procedure object, and the other manages a view. The visual designer for stored procedures offers special features, such as the ability to represent *INSERT*, *UPDATE*, and *DELETE* statements. Although this chapter describes and illustrates how to program these statements, you can examine the programming samples with the visual designer to see how the designer handles *INSERT*, *UPDATE*, and *DELETE*.

Although most stored procedures such as the one shown in Figure 11-18 open to the visual designer by default, you can switch to the text-based template. Click the View down arrow on the toolbar and choose SQL View. This capability to switch between views lets you begin designing a stored procedure in the visual designer and then refine it in the text-based designer. Figure 11-19 presents a second stored procedure that filters the *Orders* table for rows with an order date occurring in 1997.

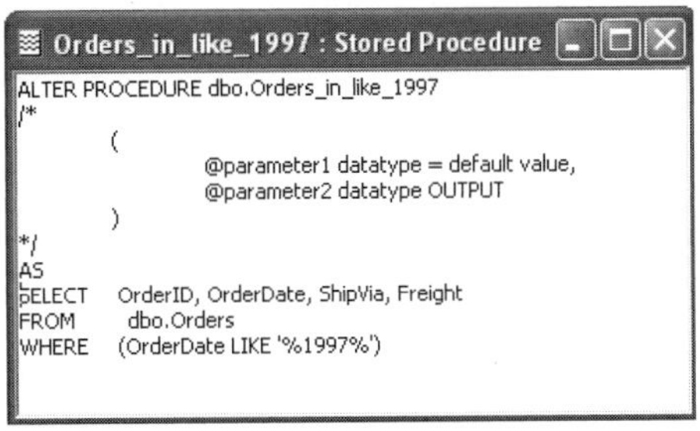

```
Orders_in_like_1997 : Stored Procedure
ALTER PROCEDURE dbo.Orders_in_like_1997
/*
        (
                @parameter1 datatype = default value,
                @parameter2 datatype OUTPUT
        )
*/
AS
SELECT   OrderID, OrderDate, ShipVia, Freight
FROM     dbo.Orders
WHERE    (OrderDate LIKE '%1997%')
```

Figure 11-19   The Access 2003 text-based designer for stored procedures.

The text-based designer has a look and feel that Access developers who aren't familiar with SQL Server might find foreign. If you are familiar with SQL Server, you might notice that this designer is somewhat similar to the Query Analyzer. The sample in Figure 11-19 starts with *ALTER PROCEDURE*, followed by the stored procedure's name, because the sample is based on a previously created stored procedure. On your initial attempt to create a stored procedure, the first line reads `CREATE PROCEDURE "StoredProcedurex"`, where *x* is a number such as 1, 2, or whatever. You can overwrite this default name with one that is more meaningful for your application.

The next group of lines before the *AS* keyword occurs within block comment markers (/* and */). The template includes these lines in comments to remind you of the format and location for parameters. The parentheses for parameters within the comment markers are optional. Subsequent samples in this section discuss and demonstrate the syntax for specifying parameters.

The T-SQL syntax after the *AS* keyword specifies the operation and the result set from a stored procedure. The text-based stored procedure template gives you more precise control over the layout and formatting of a stored procedure's T-SQL code than the visual designer's SQL pane. For example, in the text-based stored procedure template, you can drop the dbo qualifier for Orders in the *FROM* clause if it's not necessary. You can also insert comment lines. Use two contiguous hyphens (--) at the start of a line to mark it as a comment.

Specifying Parameters in the Text-Based Designer

The preceding two samples show how to extract all rows from the *Orders* table for a particular year. Without parameters, you're forced to create a separate stored procedure for each year for which you want to filter. The code sample that follows shows how to filter the rows for any year at run time. Instead of using the *LIKE* operator, this *Orders_in_@year* stored procedure relies on the *DATEPART* function to extract just the year from the *OrderDate* column value. Specifying the function extracts a four-digit field. Therefore, the sample specifies an *int* data type for the parameter. The four *y*'s in the *DATEPART* mean that instead of using, say, 96, you must use 1996.

```
ALTER PROCEDURE Orders_in_@year
@year int
AS
SELECT OrderID, OrderDate, ShipVia, Freight
FROM Orders
WHERE DATEPART(yyyy, OrderDate) = @year
```

When you select the *Orders_in_@year* stored procedure in the Database window and click Open, Access displays a dialog box for you to type a parameter value into. (See Figure 11-20.) You are prompted for the parameter name that follows the @ sign in the stored procedure. Therefore, the prompt for the parameter in *Orders_in_@year* is for the year. This is how a typical parameter query from an Access database file would work.

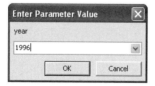

Figure 11-20   A prompt for a stored procedure parameter value.

The preceding sample requires you to input a value each time you run the stored procedure. However, sometimes it's useful to have a default value for a parameter so that users have the opportunity to omit specifying one. By specifying a default value for a parameter, users can either accept the default value or override it with another one that they input.

The following code sample shows the syntax for designating a default value for a parameter. The *Orders_in_@year_96default* stored procedure shows how to assign a value in the parameter's declaration. Essentially, an assignment statement is all you need.

```
ALTER PROCEDURE Orders_in_@year_96default
@year int = 1996
AS
SELECT OrderID, OrderDate, ShipVia, Freight
FROM Orders
WHERE DATEPART(yyyy, OrderDate) = @year
```

If you run this stored procedure from the Database window by selecting *Orders_in_@year_96default* and clicking Open, the result set always contains rows for 1996. No prompt appears for a parameter with a default value. To override the default setting, you must invoke the stored procedure from another procedure that explicitly passes an alternative parameter value to the stored procedure's default setting. The following sample demonstrates this approach by passing a parameter of 1997 to override the default value of 1996:

```
ALTER PROCEDURE Exec_96default_with_1997
AS
EXEC Orders_in_@year_96default 1997
```

Sorting Result Sets

Although you can sort the result set from a view, it's probably more natural to sort the result set from a stored procedure. There are a couple of reasons for this. First, the syntax is more straightforward in stored procedures. Recall that you do not need to include a *TOP* clause in a *SELECT* statement. Second, you can make the sort order dynamic by assigning it at run time through a parameter. This capability is unavailable with a view.

Figure 11-21 presents two Design views. The top window shows a view, and the other shows a stored procedure. Both the view and the stored procedure sort the *Orders* table rows by freight in descending order. The top window, for the view, shows the *TOP* clause. Notice that you have to choose the top 100 percent—namely all the rows in the result set. It doesn't make sense to do this other than for the fact that the syntax requires this formulation to enable sorting within a view. With the stored procedure, you can simply specify an *ORDER BY* clause for the columns on which you need to sort a result set. In addition, the stored procedure formulation (shown in the next sample) lends itself to an extension that isn't possible with a view.

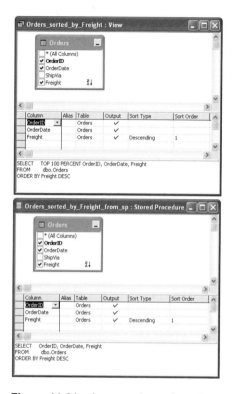

Figure 11-21 A comparison of two Design views that sort records: one for a view, and one for a stored procedure.

The following stored procedure illustrates an extension of the sample shown in the bottom window of Figure 11-21. This extension lets a user control the sort order at run time. The default calls for an ascending sort on *Freight*. However, if a user assigns a value of 1 to the parameters for the stored procedure, the code sorts on *Freight* in descending order. As you can see, the design of the *Orders_sorted_by_Freight_Up_Or_Down* stored procedure uses an *IF...ELSE* statement to branch to one of two blocks of code. *BEGIN* and *END* keywords mark the start and conclusion of each block. You need to repeat the code once for a descending order sort and a second time for an ascending order sort because of the T-SQL syntax. You can't specify the sort order (*DESC* or *ASC*) with a parameter.

```
ALTER PROCEDURE Orders_sorted_by_Freight_Up_Or_Down
@za bit = 0
AS

IF @za = 1
    BEGIN
        SELECT   OrderID, OrderDate, Freight
        FROM     dbo.Orders
        ORDER BY Freight DESC
```

```
      END
ELSE
    BEGIN
        SELECT    OrderID, OrderDate, Freight
        FROM      dbo.Orders
        ORDER BY Freight ASC
    END
```

You can use an Access application to invoke this SQL Server stored procedure and to return the values in its result set. The trick is to assign a value to the *@za* parameter. There are three basic steps to this process. First, you point an ADO *Command* object at the stored procedure. You need a *Command* object instead of a *Connection* object, because the approach requires you to set parameter values and a *Connection* object does not have a *Parameters* collection. Second, you need to create the parameter for *@za*, assign it a value, and append it to the *Command* object that points at the stored procedure. Third, you need to execute the stored procedure referenced by the *Command* object and print a subset of its records to confirm the order of the sort.

> **Note**   The section on user-defined functions at the end of the chapter illustrates how to run T-SQL statements that require parameters without using *Command* objects. Although this alternative syntax is generally simpler, it forfeits the ability to specify the data type for an input parameter. Once you know how to execute both approaches, you can make an informed decision about which is appropriate for you.

The following pair of VBA procedures illustrates the syntax to run the *Orders_sorted_by_Freight_Up_Or_Down* stored procedure. The first procedure points a *Command* object at the stored procedure and assigns a parameter to the command. This parameter sets a value for the *@za* parameter and passes it to the stored procedure when the code executes the command. Notice that the command's *CommandType* property is *adCmdStoredProc*. This is necessary when running a stored procedure from a command. The *CommandText* property designates the name of the stored procedure. The first procedure calls the second procedure and passes it the *Command* object, signifying the number of records to print. The second procedure executes the command, passes a subset of the records in the result set to a *Recordset* object, and prints the values to the Immediate window.

```
Sub AssignFreightSortOrder()
Dim cmd1 As ADODB.Command
Dim prm1 As ADODB.Parameter
```

(continued)

```
'Instantiate command and set up for use with stored proc,
'and create parameter, assign value, and append to command
Set cmd1 = New ADODB.Command
With cmd1
    .ActiveConnection = CurrentProject.Connection
    .CommandType = adCmdStoredProc
    .CommandText = "Orders_sorted_by_Freight_Up_Or_Down"
    Set prm1 = _
        .CreateParameter("@za", adBoolean, adParamInput)
    prm1.Value = _
        InputBox("Enter 1 for Descending or 0 for " & _
    "Ascending.", _
        "Programming Microsoft Access 2003", 0)
    .Parameters.Append prm1
End With

'Print subset of results set from the command
OpenSubsetOfCmd cmd1, 10

'Clean up objects
Set cmd1 = Nothing

End Sub

Sub OpenSubsetOfCmd(cmd1 As ADODB.Command, LimitToPrint As Byte)
'cmd1 As ADODB.Comand, LimitToPrint As Byte
Dim rst1 As ADODB.Recordset
Dim byt1 As Byte
Dim fld1 As Field

'Assign cmd1 results set to rst1
Set rst1 = New ADODB.Recordset
Set rst1 = cmd1.Execute

'Limit results set recordcount and loop through
'all fields for the desired subset of records
With rst1
    .Close
    .MaxRecords = LimitToPrint
    .Open
    byt1 = 0
    Do Until .EOF
        Debug.Print _
            "Results for record " & (byt1 + 1)
        For Each fld1 In .Fields
            Debug.Print "    " & fld1.Name & _
                " = " & .Fields(fld1.Name)
        Next fld1
        .MoveNext
        byt1 = byt1 + 1
        Debug.Print
    Loop
```

```
End With

'Clean up objects
rst1.Close
Set rst1 = Nothing

End Sub
```

Managing Input Parameters, Output Parameters, and Return Values

One of the ways that stored procedures in SQL Server databases differ from stored queries in Jet database files is in their ability to pass back scalar values as output parameters and return values. The next sample illustrates the syntax for concurrently handling an input parameter, an output parameter, and a return value. You have already seen samples demonstrating the use of input parameters, but the samples become more complicated when combined with output parameters and return values.

Recall that an output parameter is just a scalar value passed back from a stored procedure. It could be a datetime, string, number, or binary value, such as an image. A return value is the value passed back from a stored procedure that is the argument of a *RETURN* statement in the stored procedure. This argument can be a constant or an expression, but it must be an integer.

VBA parameters treat input parameters, output parameters, and return values as parameters. However, a few distinctions between these three entities might not be so obvious at first glance. First, whenever you use a return value along with either an input parameter or an output parameter, you must reserve the first ADO parameter for the return value. Second, the order in which you declare parameters in the stored procedure must match the order in which you create the parameters within a VBA procedure that invokes a command based on the stored procedure. It does not matter if you declare an input parameter before an output parameter. However, it does matter that you use the same order in both the stored procedure and the VBA procedure.

The following T-SQL script shows a SQL Server stored procedure from the text-based Access template for the sample that demonstrates the concurrent use of input and output parameters along with a return value. This stored procedure builds on one presented earlier that extracts the rows from the *Orders* table for a year that the user specifies at run time. The parameter that designates the year is an input parameter. The *@sum_of_freight* parameter is an output parameter. Notice that its declaration includes the keyword *OUTPUT*. T-SQL lets you compute scalar values, such as the one for the *@sum_of_freight* output parameter with a *SELECT* statement. In this instance, the statement computes the sum of *Freight* column values across the year the user specifies in the *@year* input parameter.

The *RETURN* statement is always the last one that a stored procedure processes. This is because *RETURN* transfers control back to the entity that called the current stored procedure. You can insert one or more *RETURN* statements in an *IF...ELSE* statement or any other branching logic statement to reflect which path a stored procedure took. If a VBA procedure initiated the stored procedure, the stored procedure passes back to the VBA procedure an argument for the *RETURN* statement. In the following stored procedure, the return value denotes the number of orders for the year in the *@year* input parameter:

```
ALTER PROCEDURE Orders_in_@year_in_out_return

--Input and output parameter declarations
@sum_of_freight money OUTPUT,
@year int

AS

--Develop result set
SELECT OrderID, OrderDate, ShipVia, Freight
FROM Orders
WHERE DATEPART(yyyy,OrderDate) = @year

--Develop output parameter
SELECT @sum_of_freight =
SUM(Freight) FROM Orders
WHERE DATEPART(yyyy,OrderDate) = @year

--Develop return value
RETURN (SELECT COUNT(OrderID) FROM Orders
WHERE DATEPART(yyyy,OrderDate) = @year)
```

The following VBA procedure illustrates the syntax for invoking the preceding SQL Server stored procedure. Use the sample as a model for setting ADO parameters that denote a return value, an output parameter, and an input parameter. The VBA code assigns a value to the input parameter, executes the command pointing at the procedure, and captures the output parameter and return value. The sample also returns a subset of the result set from the *SELECT* statement for the stored procedure.

The sample begins by pointing a *Command* object at the preceding SQL Server stored procedure. Next, it creates three parameters and appends each one to the parameter collection of the *Command* object. As indicated previously, the order of parameter declarations is important. The return value goes first. This value recovers the number of order IDs in the result set for the stored procedure. The second parameter points to the *@sum_of_freight* output parameter. This parameter must go before the input parameter because the stored procedure declares it first. Also notice that the data types match those inside the stored procedure. It's not always necessary that a parameter in a VBA procedure and a stored procedure coincide precisely, but it's a good practice.

After declaring and appending the parameters, the VBA procedure executes the command and assigns its result set to a *Recordset* object. These two steps make the output parameter and return value available to the VBA procedure. The sample uses these values to display the total freight, total orders, and average freight per order for whichever year the VBA procedure specifies as the input for the stored procedure. Then the sample reexecutes the command to recover the first three records in the result set for the stored procedure's result set. The sample takes this approach to reuse the *OpenSubsetOfCmd* procedure from the preceding VBA sample. In a production environment with a large result set, you might just reprocess the *rst1* procedure that's already available and save your time for reexecuting the stored procedure's *SELECT* statement.

```
Sub InOutReturnDemo()
Dim cmd1 As ADODB.Command
Dim prm1 As ADODB.Parameter
Dim prm2 As ADODB.Parameter
Dim prm3 As ADODB.Parameter
Dim rst1 As New ADODB.Recordset

'Instantiate command and set up for use with stored procedure
Set cmd1 = New ADODB.Command
cmd1.ActiveConnection = CurrentProject.Connection
cmd1.CommandType = adCmdStoredProc
cmd1.CommandText = "Orders_in_@year_in_out_return"

'Set up a return parameter
Set prm1 = cmd1.CreateParameter("RETURN", adInteger, _
    adParamReturnValue)
cmd1.Parameters.Append prm1

'Set up an output parameter
Set prm2 = cmd1.CreateParameter("@sum_of_freight", _
    adCurrency, adParamOutput)
cmd1.Parameters.Append prm2

'Create parameter, assign value, and append to command
Set prm3 = cmd1.CreateParameter("@year", adChar, _
    adParamInput, 4)
prm3.Value = "1996"
cmd1.Parameters.Append prm3

'Execute the command to recover the return value (cmd1(0))
'and the output parameter (cmd1(1))
Set rst1 = New ADODB.Recordset
Set rst1 = cmd1.Execute
```

(continued)

```
Debug.Print "Results for " & prm3.Value
Debug.Print "Total Freight = " & FormatCurrency(cmd1(1))
Debug.Print "Total Orders = " & cmd1(0)
Debug.Print "Average Freight/Order = " & _
    FormatCurrency(cmd1(1) / cmd1(0))

'Print subset of result set from the command
Debug.Print vbCr & "Partial list of Orders for " & prm3.Value
OpenSubsetOfCmd cmd1, 3

'Clean up objects
rst1.Close
Set rst1 = Nothing

End Sub
```

Figure 11-22 shows the output for the preceding VBA sample. Its header dynamically portrays the year for which it returns results. The year in the header title comes from the value for *prm3*. The next three lines signify the output parameter, the stored procedure's return value, and the ratio of the two. Next the listing shows the first three records in the result set from running the stored procedure to which the *Command* object in the preceding sample points.

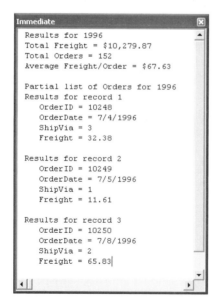

Figure 11-22 The output to the Immediate window for the *InOutReturn-Demo* VBA procedure.

Inserting, Updating, and Deleting Records

Inserting, updating, and deleting records are the three classic database mainte-nance tasks. There are at least two ways to use stored procedures when inserting records into a table. One method takes advantage of T-SQL to populate one table from all or a subset of another table's records. The source can reside in the same database, a different database, or even a database on a different server. Another way to facilitate inserting records into a table with a stored procedure is to use parameters. This permits you to reuse the stored procedure to input different records into the same table. This reuse model also enables you to update and delete records from a database. Again, one stored procedure can support an indefinite number of updates or deletions.

Inserting Records from a Source Table

Earlier in the section "Creating Sample Tables," we covered the stored procedures *CreateAndPopulateShippersTable* and *CreateAndPopulateOrdersTable*. These procedures execute a T-SQL statement to create a table. Then they invoke another stored procedure that copies data from one table to another. When the procedures were initially discussed, it was premature to examine the code for populating the tables. So let's take a look at the syntax now.

The stored procedures for populating the *Orders* and *Shippers* tables have the same basic design, except that they refer to different source and destination tables. In the case of the *Orders* table, the source is the *Orders* table from the NorthwindCS database and the destination is the *Orders* table in the Chapter11SQL database—the sample database for this chapter. In the case of the *Shippers* table, the source is the *Shippers* table from NorthwindCS and the destination is the *Shippers* table in Chapter11SQL. Aside from different field designations, the two stored procedures are identical. One has the name *Copy_from_NorthwindCS_Orders*, and the other is named *Copy_from_NorthwindCS_Shippers*.

The sample stored procedure for the *Orders* table follows. It starts by checking whether the *Orders* table in the current database has any records. If the number of records is greater than zero, the stored procedure deletes all records from the *Orders* table. Next, the procedure executes the *SET IDENTITY_INSERT* statement and sets it to ON. This permits a stored procedure or other collection of T-SQL statements to add records that populate the column in a table with an *IDENTITY* value. Without this setting, you wouldn't be able to specify that the original *IDENTITY* values serving as primary key values in the source table populate the primary key in the destination table.

The most important statement in the *Copy_from_NorthwindCS_Orders* stored procedure is the *INSERT* statement. This statement has three sets of arguments. Its first argument set is the name of the source table, *Orders*. This set consists of a single member. The second argument set consists of the column names for the destination table into which to deposit data. And the statement's third argument set comprises the table column names from which to collect data for the destination table. The statement can transfer one or more rows from the source table to the destination table. The syntax for the *SELECT* statement in the *INSERT* statement determines which rows transfer from the source to the destination table.

After performing the *INSERT* statement, the stored procedure restores the *SET IDENTITY_INSERT* to OFF, its default value. This is critical because only one table in a SQL Server session can have a setting of ON for *SET IDENTITY_INSERT*. The second table to attempt the assignment of ON in a single SQL Server session generates a run-time error.

```
ALTER PROCEDURE Copy_from_NorthwindCS_Orders
AS

--Remove any records already present in local Orders table
IF (SELECT COUNT(*) FROM Orders) > 0
    DELETE FROM Orders

--Allow writing to IDENTITY column
SET IDENTITY_INSERT Chapter11SQL..Orders ON

--Specify target and source columns for INSERT
INSERT INTO Orders (OrderID, OrderDate, Shipvia, Freight)
SELECT OrderID, OrderDate, Shipvia, Freight
    FROM NorthwindCS..Orders

--Reset IDENTITY column
SET IDENTITY_INSERT Chapter11SQL..Orders OFF
```

Inserting Records from Parameter Values

The next three VBA procedures (shown in the following code) create a SQL Server stored procedure for inserting new records and then use that stored procedure to add a new record. The sample isolates each of these actions in its own batch of T-SQL statements. If the stored procedure for inserting new records exists already, the sample removes the prior version with a third stored procedure. After creating a new stored procedure named *Insert_a_new_shipper*, you can invoke it by running the VBA procedure named *InsertANewShipper*. This VBA procedure passes parameter values to and starts the *Insert_a_new_shipper* stored procedure.

The first procedure, *CreateInsert_a_new_shipperProcedure*, illustrates how to use VBA to create a SQL Server stored procedure. SQL Server uses the *CREATE PROCEDURE* statement to create new stored procedures. Then SQL Server syntax calls for additional statements with parameter declarations and T-SQL code that comprise the body of the stored procedure. You can designate these statements with strings in VBA. Next, executing the *CREATE PROCEDURE* statement with its embedded T-SQL statements saves the batch of embedded T-SQL statements as a stored procedure. The sample uses a *Connection* object to execute the *CREATE PROCEDURE* statement. The first procedure concludes with the invocation of the *RefreshDatabaseWindow* method. The method attempts to update the Database window to show the newly created stored procedure. If the procedure still does not appear, you can manually invoke the View-Refresh command from the Database window.

Before actually attempting to create a new stored procedure, the first procedure calls the *Drop_a_procedure* VBA procedure. *Drop_a_procedure* is the last of the three procedures shown in the following sample. The first procedure passes two parameters to *Drop_a_procedure*. The initial parameter designates the *Connection* object that points at a database to remove a stored procedure from (if it exists already). The second parameter is the name of the procedure. In the following sample, this is *Insert_a_new_shipper*. The *Drop_a_procedure* procedure invokes the *DROP PROCEDURE* statement only if it detects a stored procedure with the target name in the *INFORMATION_SCHEMA.ROUTINES* view. This view contains information about the stored procedure and user-defined functions in a database.

InsertANewShipper, the second procedure in the following sample, uses the stored procedure created by the first VBA procedure to add a new record to the *Shippers* table. *InsertANewShipper* commences by instantiating a new *Command* object and pointing it at the stored procedure for inserting new records. Next, the *InsertANewShipper* procedure specifies and adds parameters to the *Command* object. Notice that both the *@CompanyName* and *@Phone* parameters have a *Varchar* data type. This kind of data type requires that you specify the maximum number of characters for the parameter. Other parameter data types, such as *Numeric*, *Datetime*, and *Currency*, do not require a length specification. The procedure for inserting a new record concludes by running the *Command* object. This executes the stored procedure for adding a new record with the values specified for the parameters.

```
Sub CreateInsert_a_new_shipperProcedure()
Dim str1 As String
Dim cnn1 As ADODB.Connection
Dim ProcedureName As String

'Point a Connection object at the current project
Set cnn1 = CurrentProject.Connection

'Delete the procedure if it exists already
ProcedureName = "Insert_a_new_shipper"
Drop_a_procedure cnn1, ProcedureName

'Create the procedure
str1 = "CREATE PROCEDURE " & ProcedureName & " " & vbLf & _
    " " & vbLf & _
```

(continued)

```
        "@CompanyName varchar(40), " & vbLf & _
        "@phone varchar(24) " & vbLf & _
        " " & vbLf & _
        "AS " & vbLf & _
        "INSERT Shippers VALUES(@CompanyName, @Phone) "
    cnn1.Execute str1

    'Refresh Database window to show new procedure
    RefreshDatabaseWindow

End Sub

Sub Drop_a_procedure(cnn1 As ADODB.Connection, _
        ProcedureName As String)
Dim str1 As String

    'If the procedure name exists in the
    'INFORMATION_SCHEMA.ROUTINES view, drop it
    str1 = "IF EXISTS (SELECT ROUTINE_NAME " & _
        "FROM INFORMATION_SCHEMA.ROUTINES " & _
        "WHERE ROUTINE_NAME = '" & ProcedureName & "') " & _
        "DROP PROCEDURE " & ProcedureName
    cnn1.Execute str1

End Sub

Sub InsertANewShipper()
Dim cmd1 As ADODB.Command
Dim prm1 As ADODB.Parameter
Dim prm2 As ADODB.Parameter

    'Point a Connection object at the stored procedure
    Set cmd1 = New ADODB.Command
    cmd1.ActiveConnection = CurrentProject.Connection
    cmd1.CommandType = adCmdStoredProc
    cmd1.CommandText = "Insert_a_new_shipper"

    'Create and append parameters
    Set prm1 = cmd1.CreateParameter("@CompanyName", adVarChar, _
        adParamInput, 40)
    prm1.Value = "CAB Delivers"
    cmd1.Parameters.Append prm1

    Set prm2 = cmd1.CreateParameter("@Phone", adVarChar, _
        adParamInput, 24)
    prm2.Value = "(123) 456-7890"
    cmd1.Parameters.Append prm2
```

```
'Invoke a stored procedure by executing a command
cmd1.Execute

End Sub
```

Updating and Deleting Records from Parameter Values

The following VBA procedure illustrates one approach to creating a stored procedure that revises a shipper's name in the *Shippers* table. To perform the revision, the update needs two pieces of information. The *Update_a_shipper* stored procedure represents these two pieces of information with parameters. One parameter is the *ShipperID* value for the shipper that will receive the new value. The second parameter represents the new company name for the shipper associated with the *ShipperID* value. The VBA procedure shows the syntax using these two parameters with the *UPDATE* statement in T-SQL within a stored procedure.

The *Create_Update_a_shipperProcedure* procedure that appears next shows the correct syntax for using a trusted connection to connect to a server. The Server and Database terms in the *str1* string should reflect the name of the server and the database in which you want to create the stored procedure. When running this sample on your computer, you will probably need to revise the server name. If you adapt this sample for your custom projects, you'll also need to update the database name. This general approach is very flexible because it works with any server and database for which the current user has permission to create new database objects.

```
Sub CreateUpdate_a_shipperProcedure()
Dim str1 As String
Dim cnn1 As ADODB.Connection
Dim ProcedureName As String

'Point a connection object at the Chapter11SQL
'database on the CabSony1 server with a trusted connection
Set cnn1 = New ADODB.Connection
cnn1.Provider = "sqloledb"
str1 = "Server=CabSony1;Database=Chapter11SQL;" & _
    "Trusted_Connection=yes"
cnn1.Open str1

'Delete the table if it exists already
ProcedureName = "Update_a_shipper"
Drop_a_procedure cnn1, ProcedureName

'Create the procedure
str1 = "CREATE PROCEDURE " & ProcedureName & " " & vbLf & _
    " " & vbLf & _
```

(continued)

```
        "@id_for_update int, " & vbLf & _
        "@new_name varchar(40) " & vbLf & _
        " " & vbLf & _
        "AS " & vbLf & _
        "UPDATE Shippers " & vbLf & _
        "SET CompanyName = @new_name " & vbLf & _
        "WHERE ShipperID = @id_for_update "
    cnn1.Execute str1

    'Refresh Database window to show new procedure
    RefreshDatabaseWindow

End Sub
```

The next sample applies the *Update_a_shipper* stored procedure created by the preceding VBA sample. The *UpdateAShipper* VBA procedure reverts to referring to the current project's connection. This syntax for specifying a connection is less general than the preceding one, which used a trusted connection. However, designating the current project's connection is more straightforward. The sample procedure revises the name of the shipper that has a shipper ID of 4. If you ran the *InsertANewShipper* VBA procedure from the preceding sample, the *Shippers* table likely has a record with a *ShipperID* value of 4. If not, update the *prm1.Value* assignment so that it points to a row that you want to revise in the *Shippers* table.

```
Sub UpdateAShipper()
Dim cmd1 As ADODB.Command
Dim prm1 As ADODB.Parameter
Dim prm2 As ADODB.Parameter

'Point a Connection object at the stored procedure
Set cmd1 = New ADODB.Command
cmd1.ActiveConnection = CurrentProject.Connection
cmd1.CommandType = adCmdStoredProc
cmd1.CommandText = "Update_a_shipper"

'Create and append parameters
Set prm1 = cmd1.CreateParameter("@id_for_update", _
    adInteger, adParamInput)
prm1.Value = 4
cmd1.Parameters.Append prm1

Set prm2 = cmd1.CreateParameter("@new_name", adVarChar, _
    adParamInput, 40)
prm2.Value = "CAB Shipping Co."
cmd1.Parameters.Append prm2

'Invoke a stored procedure by executing a command
```

```
cmd1.Execute

End Sub
```

The next pair of procedures illustrates the VBA syntax for creating a stored procedure that deletes a record from the *Shippers* table and then invoking that stored procedure. This stored procedure follows the same basic design as the samples for inserting and updating records with parameters. In this case, the procedure for creating the *Delete_a_shipper* stored procedure reveals the T-SQL syntax to remove a single record from a table based on its *ShipperID* column value. The *@id_to_delete* parameter points to this column value.

```
Sub CreateDelete_a_shipperProcedure()
Dim str1 As String
Dim cnn1 As ADODB.Connection
Dim ProcedureName As String

'Point a Connection object at the current project
Set cnn1 = CurrentProject.Connection

'Delete the procedure if it exists already
ProcedureName = "Delete_a_shipper"
Drop_a_procedure cnn1, ProcedureName

'Create the procedure
str1 = "CREATE PROCEDURE " & ProcedureName & " " & vbLf & _
    " " & vbLf & _
    "@id_to_delete int " & vbLf & _
    " " & vbLf & _
    "AS " & vbLf & _
    "DELETE FROM Shippers " & vbLf & _
    "WHERE ShipperID = @id_to_delete "
cnn1.Execute str1

'Refresh Database window to show new procedure
RefreshDatabaseWindow

End Sub

Sub DeleteAShipper()
Dim cmd1 As ADODB.Command
Dim prm1 As ADODB.Parameter
Dim prm2 As ADODB.Parameter

'Point a Connection object at the stored procedure
Set cmd1 = New ADODB.Command
cmd1.ActiveConnection = CurrentProject.Connection
cmd1.CommandType = adCmdStoredProc
```

(continued)

```
cmd1.CommandText = "Delete_a_shipper"

'Create and append parameter
Set prm1 = cmd1.CreateParameter("@id_to_delete", _
    adInteger, adParamInput)
prm1.Value = 4
cmd1.Parameters.Append prm1

'Invoke a stored procedure by executing a command
cmd1.Execute

End Sub
```

Triggers

A trigger is a special kind of stored procedure attached to a table. Triggers work for tables much like event procedures work for forms. You can place T-SQL code in a trigger that fires when a user attempts to modify a table.

Access 2003 offers support for SQL Server triggers through its UI as well as in VBA procedures. With SQL Server 2000, Microsoft introduced a new kind of trigger called an *INSTEAD OF* trigger and renamed traditional triggers *AFTER* triggers. When present, an *INSTEAD OF* trigger operates instead of any *AFTER* triggers attached to a table. The Access UI has a special interface for working with *AFTER* triggers. Due to this special interface and the fact that you need to understand *AFTER* triggers before you can appreciate *INSTEAD OF* triggers, this discussion focuses exclusively on *AFTER* triggers (which the UI calls triggers). See Books Online for more in-depth coverage of *INSTEAD OF* triggers.

When you create a trigger for a table, all database maintenance operations for the table occur within a transaction. You can specify triggers for insert, update, and delete actions. You can even specify multiple triggers for the same kind of action. For example, you can have two or more delete triggers for the same table. SQL Server 2000 introduces the capability to specify which trigger fires first and which fires last. However, any triggers that fire between the first and last ones will occur in an indeterminate order.

Within the transaction for a trigger, revisions to the table are available from two special temporary tables named *deleted* and *inserted*. All deleted records are in the *deleted* table, and all inserted records are in the *inserted* table. Updated records move the old version of the record to the *deleted* table and add the new version to the *inserted* table. Changes are not committed to a table with a trigger until the trigger transaction concludes. Within the trigger transaction, your T-SQL code can change the operation so that it performs none, some, or more of the action that initiated the trigger. For example, you can roll back a delete, copy a deleted record to another table in the same database, or maintain referential integrity with a table in another database. SQL Server declarative referential integrity does not support referential integrity across two different databases.

Creating and Using Triggers from the Access UI

The next set of instructions will guide you through creating and testing the operation of a trigger for the *Shippers* table. Start by creating a fresh version of the table. The easiest and most reliable way to do this is to run the *CreateAnd-PopulateShippersTable* VBA procedure. This procedure is available from Module1 of the Chapter11SQL.adp file in this book's companion content.

After creating a new version of the *Shippers* table, select Tables in the Database window and right-click *Shippers*. Choose Triggers from the menu, and then click New on the Triggers For Table: Shippers dialog box. This creates a template like the one that follows this paragraph. You can use this template as a guide for creating your own custom trigger. For example, suppose you wanted to roll back all attempts to modify the *Shippers* table. To do so, you could invoke a T-SQL statement and print a message to inform the user of what was happening.

```
CREATE TRIGGER Shippers_Trigger1
ON dbo.Shippers
FOR /* INSERT, UPDATE, DELETE */
AS
    /* IF UPDATE (column_name) ...*/
```

The next T-SQL script shows the text of a trigger for the *Shippers* table that blocks all changes to the table. Users can still open the table and examine its contents. However, if they try to change the table by inserting a new record, updating an existing record, or deleting a record, the trigger rolls back the action and prints a message that says, "I am untouchable!" The *ROLLBACK TRAN* statement rolls back any attempt to modify the table, and the *RAISERROR* statement presents a message to Access from SQL Server.

As with a stored procedure, Access opens the template with a *CREATE* statement for a trigger. However, any attempt to view the trigger after saving it changes the *CREATE* keyword to *ALTER*. The default name for the trigger is *Shippers_Trigger1*. You can override this default and use a name that's more meaningful for your application.

```
CREATE TRIGGER Shippers_Trigger1
ON Shippers
FOR INSERT, UPDATE, DELETE
AS
ROLLBACK TRAN
RAISERROR 50000 'I am untouchable!'
```

Figure 11-23 shows the error message generated by the *Shippers_Trigger1* trigger. Notice that the *Shippers* table shows an attempt to update the *CompanyName* field from *Speedy Express* to *Speedy Expressx*. This attempt generates the error message box. This rollback action is a cool, powerful feature: With just a couple of lines of T-SQL code, you can protect a table from being changed. The protection applies even if users try to make a change directly in the table without using one of your Access forms.

Figure 11-23 An error message generated by the *Shippers_Trigger1* trigger.

You can clear the attempted change to the table by pressing Escape twice. Then close the table.

Programmatically Changing a Table with a Trigger

Recall that we have three VBA procedures for making changes to the *Shippers* table. These are the procedures that use parameters for inserting, updating, and deleting records in a table. Run the *InsertANewShipper* procedure from Module1 of the Chapter11SQL.adp file. Notice that it fails with a run-time error. The message that accompanies the error message reads, "I am untouchable!" This message confirms that the *Shippers_Trigger1* trigger is preventing the *InsertANewShipper* procedure from adding a new record to the *Shippers* table. As you'll recall, this procedure ran successfully earlier in the chapter.

> **Note** A sample in the "User-Defined Functions" section at the end of this chapter shows how to trap an error and retrieve its message without relinquishing control to the error.

You might need to temporarily disable a trigger to make some changes to a table that it's blocking. One way to do this is with an *ALTER TABLE* statement that includes a *DISABLE TRIGGER* statement. Recall that a trigger applies to a table. Therefore, you need to modify a table when you want to disable a trigger that applies to it. Follow the *DISABLE TRIGGER* keyword phrase with the name of the trigger that you want to disable. After making your changes to the table, you should reenable the trigger. To do so, you can embed an *ENABLE TRIGGER* statement inside another *ALTER TABLE* statement.

The following VBA procedure shows an updated version of the VBA procedure for inserting a record into the *Shippers* table. This procedure uses the *DISABLE TRIGGER* and *ENABLE TRIGGER* statements to determine when the trigger operates and to make a change to the table when the trigger is disabled. The sample runs the *ALTER TABLE* statements with a *Command* object because it's already available, thanks to the approach that inserts a new record by using the parameters.

```
Sub InsertANewShipper2()
Dim cmd1 As ADODB.Command
Dim prm1 As ADODB.Parameter
Dim prm2 As ADODB.Parameter

'Disable Shippers_Trigger1
Set cmd1 = New ADODB.Command
cmd1.ActiveConnection = CurrentProject.Connection
cmd1.CommandText = _
    "ALTER TABLE Shippers DISABLE TRIGGER Shippers_Trigger1"
cmd1.CommandType = adCmdText
cmd1.Execute

'Point a Connection object at the stored procedure
cmd1.CommandType = adCmdStoredProc
cmd1.CommandText = "Insert_a_new_shipper"

'Create and append parameters
Set prm1 = cmd1.CreateParameter("@CompanyName", adVarChar, _
    adParamInput, 40)
prm1.Value = "CAB Delivers"
cmd1.Parameters.Append prm1

Set prm2 = cmd1.CreateParameter("@Phone", adVarChar, _
    adParamInput, 24)
prm2.Value = "(123) 456-7890"
cmd1.Parameters.Append prm2

'Invoke a stored procedure by executing a command
cmd1.Execute

'Reenable Shippers_Trigger1
cmd1.CommandText = _
"ALTER TABLE Shippers ENABLE TRIGGER Shippers_Trigger1"
cmd1.CommandType = adCmdText
cmd1.Execute

End Sub
```

Problem and Fix for Manual Trigger Creation

If you create even a moderately sized collection of triggers manually, your code will be in jeopardy. There are a couple of reasons for this. First, users can readily update the triggers through the Access UI if they have permission. In cases where you have no backup for the triggers, diagnosing the problem and developing a solution can be time consuming. Second, if you need to drop a table, your application loses all triggers associated with that table. When you manually enter triggers using the Access UI, you make your code vulnerable to both problems. In addition, you have no way to automate a recovery from the problem after it occurs.

An alternative is to create your triggers in VBA programmatically. This still does not stop either problem from occurring. However, recovering a lost or corrupted trigger is as simple as dropping an existing version of the trigger and then running the code to create a new version of it. The next pair of VBA procedures modifies the *CreateAndPopulateShippersTable* procedure discussed earlier in this chapter so that it automatically creates the *Shippers_Trigger1* sample just presented. Before actually creating the new trigger, the procedure deletes a prior version if one is available. A call to the *Drop_a_trigger* procedure performs this. The *Drop_a_trigger* procedure demonstrates how to use the *Exists* keyword to test for such a condition—for example, the existence of a trigger with the target name in a database's *sysobjects* table. This system-defined table maintains one row for each object within a database. The *Type* column of this table denotes the type of object for each row, and the *Name* column represents an object's name.

```
Sub CreateAndPopulateShippersTable2()
Dim str1 As String
Dim cnn1 As ADODB.Connection
Dim TableName As String
Dim TriggerName As String

'Point a Connection object at the current project
Set cnn1 = CurrentProject.Connection

'Delete the table if it exists already
TableName = "Shippers"
Drop_a_table cnn1, TableName

'Create the table
str1 = "CREATE TABLE " & TableName & " " & _
    "( " & _
    "ShipperID int IDENTITY (1, 1) NOT NULL PRIMARY KEY CLUSTERED, " & _
    "CompanyName varchar(40) NOT NULL , " & _
```

```
    "Phone varchar(24) NULL " & _
    ")"
cnn1.Execute str1

'Run custom stored procedure to populate table based
'on NorthwindCS database
str1 = "EXEC Copy_from_NorthwindCS_Shippers"
cnn1.Execute str1

'Delete the trigger if it exists already
TriggerName = "Shippers_Trigger1"
Drop_a_trigger cnn1, TriggerName

'Add the trigger after populating the table
str1 = "CREATE TRIGGER " & TriggerName & " " & vbLf & _
    "ON Shippers " & vbLf & _
    "FOR INSERT, UPDATE, DELETE " & vbLf & _
    "AS " & vbLf & _
    "ROLLBACK TRAN " & vbLf & _
    "RAISERROR 50000 'I am untouchable!'"
cnn1.Execute str1

'Refresh Database window to show new table
RefreshDatabaseWindow

End Sub

Sub Drop_a_trigger(cnn1 As ADODB.Connection, _
    TriggerName As String)
Dim str1 As String

'Point a Connection object at the current project
Set cnn1 = CurrentProject.Connection

'Search sysobjects for TriggerName, and drop
'the trigger if it exists
str1 = "IF EXISTS (SELECT name FROM sysobjects " & _
    "WHERE name = '" & TriggerName & "' AND type = 'TR') " & _
    "DROP TRIGGER " & TriggerName
cnn1.Execute str1

End Sub
```

Archiving Updated and Deleted Records

Instead of blocking changes, we can use triggers to archive them. The table of archived records provides a source of changes to a table that's easy to examine.

To perform this kind of task, we need a table to hold the archived changes as well as a trigger to write the changes to that table.

The following procedure illustrates one approach to creating a table of archived records for the *Shippers* table. The *ArchivedShippers* table will store the *ShipperID*, *CompanyName*, and *Phone* column values for any updated or deleted records in the *Shippers* table. The *ArchivedShippers* table also includes a primary key with an *IDENTITY* property setting. This column provides a convenient way of tracking the order of changes to the *Shippers* table.

```
Sub CreateArchivedShippersTable()
Dim str1 As String
Dim cnn1 As ADODB.Connection
Dim TableName As String

'Point a Connection object at the current project
Set cnn1 = CurrentProject.Connection

'Delete the table if it exists already
TableName = "ArchivedShippers"
Drop_a_table cnn1, TableName

'Create the table
str1 = "CREATE TABLE " & TableName & " " & _
    "( " & _
    "ArchiveID int IDENTITY (1, 1) NOT NULL PRIMARY KEY CLUSTERED, " & _
    "ShipperID int NOT NULL, " & _
    "CompanyName varchar(40) NOT NULL , " & _
    "Phone varchar(24) NULL " & _
    ")"
cnn1.Execute str1

End Sub
```

The next code sample shows the VBA procedure to create the new trigger that does the archiving. This new version of the *Shippers_Trigger1* trigger fires whenever an attempt to update or delete a record in the *Shippers* table occurs. The *INSERT INTO* statement in the trigger copies the values from the deleted table to the *ArchivedShippers* table. This action preserves the records before the delete or update action takes effect.

```
Sub CreateArchivingTrigger()
Dim str1 As String
Dim cnn1 As ADODB.Connection
Dim TriggerName As String

'Point a Connection object at the current project
Set cnn1 = CurrentProject.Connection
```

```
'Delete the table if it exists already
TriggerName = "Shippers_Trigger1"
Drop_a_trigger cnn1, TriggerName

'Add a trigger to archive deleted or updated records
str1 = "CREATE TRIGGER Shippers_Trigger1 " & vbLf & _
    "ON Shippers " & vbLf & _
    "FOR UPDATE, DELETE " & vbLf & _
    "AS " & vbLf & _
    "INSERT INTO ArchivedShippers " & _
        "(ShipperID, CompanyName, Phone) " & vbLf & _
    "SELECT ShipperID, CompanyName, Phone FROM deleted "
cnn1.Execute str1

End Sub
```

Our example concludes with a procedure that demonstrates the operation of the *Shippers_Trigger1* trigger and the *ArchivedShippers* table. The next procedure merely calls procedures we've already discussed in this chapter. However, through the *Shippers_Trigger1* trigger these procedures now preserve the unchanged values of records updated or deleted from the *Shippers* table.

The sample begins by creating a fresh copy of the *Shippers* table with a call to the *CreateAndPopulateShippersTable* procedure. Next it invokes the two procedures just discussed to create a fresh copy of the *Archived Shippers* table and the *Shippers_Trigger1* trigger. Then the procedure successively invokes the *InsertANewShipper*, *UpdateAShipper*, and *DeleteAShipper* procedures. We discussed the operation of these procedures earlier in the chapter. In this demonstration, these three procedures add a new record to the original *Shippers* table and then modify and delete that record. This creates two records in the *ArchivedShippers* table. The first record represents the newly added record just before it gets modified. The second record in the *ArchivedShippers* table represents the changed record just before it's deleted from the *Shippers* table. The sample procedure concludes by opening the *ArchivedShippers* table so that you can click the View Microsoft Access button on the VBA code window toolbar and confirm the availability of the two records in the *ArchivedShippers* table.

```
Sub DemoArchivingWithTrigger()

'Generate a fresh copy of the Shippers table
CreateAndPopulateShippersTable

'Create the table for archiving deleted and
'updated records, and the trigger to populate
'the table
CreateArchivedShippersTable
CreateArchivingTrigger
```

(continued)

```
'Add a record, then update to generate an archived record.
'Next, delete the updated record to generate a second
'archived record.
InsertANewShipper
UpdateAShipper
DeleteAShipper

'Open the archived table for viewing.
'Click View Microsoft Access toolbar control to see table.
DoCmd.OpenTable "ArchivedShippers"

End Sub
```

User-Defined Functions

User-defined functions are a SQL Server 2000 innovation, and Access 2003 inter-operates well with this new capability on several different levels. With user-defined functions, you can define your own custom functions and use them similarly to the way you use the built-in SQL Server functions. User-defined functions contain collections of T-SQL statements that determine their behavior.

User-defined functions come in three different varieties. The first type of user-defined function returns a scalar value. This type of function can optionally take one or more arguments. Although the output from a scalar function is always a single item value, its input can comprise scalar values or one or more tables. The second type of user-defined function is an in-line table-valued function. This type allows you to return a table from a function based on a single *SELECT* statement. SQL Server offers a data type that specifically accommodates the return values from this kind of user-defined function as well as the third kind. The third type of user-defined function relies on multiple statements and returns a table. You can explicitly declare this function's column data type. You also can conditionally define its result set by using an *IF...ELSE* statement based on a record source defined in the function or by using parameters passed to the function.

User-defined functions have a variety of features that affect how you use them. First, you can nest functions within one another, and you can use them in other database objects, such as views and stored procedures. In addition, you can invoke a function from a T-SQL statement, such as the source for a *Record-set* object within a VBA procedure. Second, you must always include at least a dbo qualifier in a function's identifier, as in *dbo.myfunction()*. As the last code sample in the previous section demonstrates, you must follow a function name with parentheses even if it takes no arguments. If the function does take arguments, you can position them within the parentheses. Comma-delimit the arguments when a function has more than one. Third, use the *CREATE FUNCTION*,

ALTER FUNCTION, and *DROP FUNCTION* statements to define, revise, and remove user-defined functions from a database, respectively. This feature allows you to manipulate functions such as those in the earlier samples for tables, views, and stored procedures.

Scalar User-Defined Functions

Scalar user-defined functions will often return a value based on one or more arguments passed to them. For example, you can develop scalar functions to convert from one unit of measurement to another, such as Fahrenheit to centigrade, degrees to radians, feet to meters, and dollars to pounds. Another type of application for user-defined functions is the computation of complicated formulas. This type application is appropriate in situations where all the units within an organization must identically perform a mission-critical calculation.

You can launch the creation of a user-defined function by selecting Queries in the Objects bar of the Database window and clicking New. From the New Query dialog box, you can choose Create Text Scalar Function, Design In-Line Function, or Create Text Table-Valued Function. These correspond to the first, second, and third types of user-defined functions.

If you choose Create Text Scalar Function, Access responds by presenting a template such as the one that follows for constructing a scalar user-defined function. Notice that this template has a space for inserting arguments in parentheses after the function name. In addition, the template includes a mandatory *RETURNS* statement. Use this statement to specify the data type of the scalar value returned by a function. An *AS* keyword marks the beginning of the user-defined code. All T-SQL statements for the function must reside between *BEGIN* and *END* statements. The T-SQL code within these statements must include at least one *RETURN* statement. The argument for this statement determines the return value of the function.

```
CREATE FUNCTION "Function1"
    (
    /*
    @parameter1 datatype = default value,
    @parameter2 datatype
    */
    )
RETURNS /* datatype */
AS
    BEGIN
        /* sql statement ... */
    RETURN /* value */
    END
```

The next T-SQL script is a very simple scalar function. Notice that the function starts with an *ALTER FUNCTION* statement. Access automatically converts a *CREATE FUNCTION* statement into an *ALTER FUNCTION* statement after you initially save the function from one of the Access user-defined function templates. The following function returns a single value. This value derives from the built-in *AVG* function applied to the *Freight* column values of the *Orders* table. Although the source for the function is a table, it returns a scalar value—the average *Freight* value from the *Orders* table. This value returns with a *Money* data type.

```
ALTER FUNCTION dbo.AVG_Freight_overall()
RETURNS money
AS
BEGIN
    RETURN (SELECT AVG(Freight) FROM Orders)
END
```

As long as the values in the *Freight* column do not change, this function will always return the identical value. Users cannot directly alter the function's return value based on arguments they submit to the function. However, functions often incorporate additional functions that determine what their output will be. For example, you can define a function that returns the average freight for just one year—instead of all the years combined as the preceding sample does. The following function illustrates the syntax for this kind of user-defined function. Notice the specification of the parameter to accept an argument in the parentheses after the function name. An argument declaration must always include a name and a data type specification. The *SELECT* statement for this function includes a *WHERE* clause that uses the argument to restrict the range of values over which the *AVG* function computes the average freight.

```
ALTER FUNCTION dbo.Avg_Freight_in_@year (@year int)
RETURNS money
AS
BEGIN
    RETURN (
        SELECT AVG(Freight)
        FROM Orders
        WHERE DATEPART(yyyy,OrderDate) = @year
        )
END
```

You can also base scalar user-defined functions exclusively on scalar inputs—without relying on a tabular row source. The next sample computes the percentage of change between two positive numbers. Both input values have a *Float* data type. The return value is a *Decimal* data type with a scale of 6 and a precision of 3. This function illustrates the use of a local variable named *@change* with a *Float* data type. SQL Server local variables in functions and stored procedures have scope (or visibility) only within the function or procedure in which you define them. The local variable saves the difference between the two arguments for use in the percent change expression, which is the argument for the *RETURN* statement. This expression returns a percent with a value of 0.1 as 10 percent because it multiplies the percent change by 100.

```
ALTER FUNCTION dbo.Percent_change (@firstnumber float,
    @secondnumber float)
RETURNS decimal(6,3)
AS
BEGIN
DECLARE @change float
    SET @change = @secondnumber-@firstnumber
    RETURN @change/@firstnumber*100
END
```

You can invoke user-defined functions from other SQL Server database objects, such as stored procedures, or from VBA procedures. The following stored procedure invokes the preceding two user-defined functions to compute the average freight in each of two different years as well as the percent change between those two years. Because the functions return numeric data types, it's necessary to convert them for use as the argument of the *RAISERROR* statement. The *CONVERT* functions in the stored procedure require a character data type specification for the *@year1* and *@year2* parameters. This statement, which concludes the stored procedure, presents a message box when you run the stored procedure from the Database window. If you run the stored procedure from a VBA procedure, it passes back its computed string as an error message to the VBA procedure.

```
ALTER PROCEDURE ComputePercentChangeBetweenYears
    @year1 char(4),
    @year2 char(4)
AS
DECLARE @str1 as varchar(100)

--Compute a string expression based on the Avg_Freight_in_@year
--and Percent_change functions
SET @str1 =
    'Freight in ' + @year1 + ' = $'
        + CONVERT(varchar(7),dbo.Avg_Freight_in_@year(@year1))
        + CHAR(10) +
    'Freight in ' + @year2 + ' = $'
        + CONVERT(varchar(7),dbo.Avg_Freight_in_@year(@year2))
        + CHAR(10) +
    'Percent change = '
        + CONVERT(varchar(7),
        dbo.Percent_change(dbo.Avg_Freight_in_@year(@year1),
        dbo.Avg_Freight_in_@year(@year2))) + '%'

--Return the string from the stored procedure
RAISERROR 50000 @str1
```

If you invoke this stored procedure from the Database window, it sequentially presents a pair of prompts for its two arguments. Insert 1996, 1997, or 1998, because those are the only years for which the *Orders* table has data. Figure 11-24 shows the format of the message box that the procedure generates when it concludes. This message box shows the average freight in 1996 and 1997, along with the percent change from 1996 to 1997.

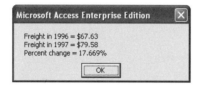

Microsoft Access Enterprise Edition

Freight in 1996 = $67.63
Freight in 1997 = $79.58
Percent change = 17.669%

OK

Figure 11-24   A message box generated by the *ComputePercentChangeBetweenYears* stored procedure when it's run from the Database window.

When you run the same procedure from a VBA procedure, no message box appears. In fact, the procedure returns a run-time error. The *Description* property of the *Err* object for the error contains the same content shown in Figure 11-24. Therefore, you can print the *Err* object's *Description* property to the Immediate window to display this content. The following pair of procedures shows one approach to accomplishing this. The first procedure specifies the year parameters that serve as arguments for the stored procedure. It passes these values to the second procedure, which constructs a SQL string (*str1*) for a *Connection* object to execute. Before invoking the *Connection* object's *Execute* method, the procedure opens an error trap that passes control to the next line of code. Because the stored procedure in the SQL string passes back its content through an error message, this error trap—which prints the *Err* object's *Description* property—retrieves the message. Without the error trap, an error box would still appear with the content but the procedure would lose control of the session.

```
Sub CallVBAPercentChange()
Dim str1 As String
Dim str2 As String

'Assign string values of 1996, 1997, or 1998
'to str1 and str2
str1 = "1996"
str2 = "1998"

'Call procedure to invoke stored procedure
'that returns values from user-defined functions
VBAPercentChange str1, str2

End Sub

Sub VBAPercentChange(year1 As String, year2 As String)
```

```
Dim str1 As String
Dim cnn1 As ADODB.Connection

'Point cnn1 at current project's database connection
Set cnn1 = CurrentProject.Connection

'Invoke stored procedure, pass arguments, and print return
str1 = "Exec ComputePercentChangeBetweenYears " & year1 & _
    ", " & year2
On Error Resume Next
cnn1.Execute str1
Debug.Print Err.Description

End Sub
```

In-Line User-Defined Functions

In-line functions return a table of values in the result set for a single *SELECT* statement. In addition, in-line functions have a simplified syntax. They do not require *BEGIN* and *END* statements, and they must have only one *RETURN* statement for their single *SELECT* statement.

In-line functions can behave like views. In addition, you can assign parameters to their *WHERE* clauses—a feature that views lack. Stored procedures do possess this functionality, but you cannot use a stored procedure as a *FROM* clause argument like you can with an in-line function procedure.

Because an in-line function depends on a single *SELECT* statement, Access 2003 offers a graphical design tool that is very similar to the visual designer for views. You can create an in-line function by selecting Queries in the Objects bar on the Database window and clicking New. Then you double-click Design In-Line Function. This opens the visual designer for in-line functions that appears in Figure 11-25. Notice that you can use tables, views, and other table-returning functions as sources for in-line functions. You can build the query similarly to the way you build a view, but you can specify criteria with parameters (as with stored procedures). In addition, the View drop-down menu on the toolbar offers a SQL View option as well as a SQL pane. With the SQL pane, you can see the T-SQL syntax for the *SELECT* statement underlying an in-line function's graphical view. With the SQL View window, you can see the full *ALTER FUNCTION* statement defining the in-line function.

Figure 11-26 shows the visual designer for an in-line function that returns all rows from the *Orders* table with a *Freight* column value greater than the average of the *Freight* values for all rows in that table. The function also sorts its result set in ascending order. The T-SQL code appears in the bottom SQL pane. Notice that it follows the view syntax for defining a sort—in other words, the *SELECT* statement must include a *TOP* clause. This syntax also shows the code for nesting one user-defined function within another. This is because the average *Freight* column value across all rows in the *Orders* table is based on the *AVG_Freight_overall* function. Notice that this function's identifier includes a user qualifier that points to the dbo user. Function identifiers must be unique within their respective owners. A pair of parentheses follows the function name even though the function takes no arguments. As mentioned previously, these parentheses are mandatory.

Figure 11-25 The visual designer for in-line functions lets you base a function on tables, views, or other table-returning functions.

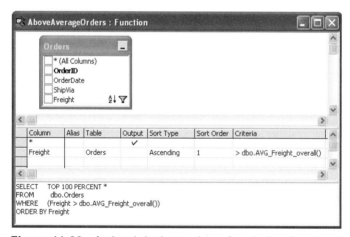

Figure 11-26 A visual designer view of an in-line function that has another user-defined function nested within it.

The following code listing shows the SQL View window of the in-line function whose design appears in Figure 11-26. The SQL View window exposes the *ALTER FUNCTION, RETURNS,* and *RETURN* statements. These statements serve as a shell and a conduit for returning the table defined by the function's *SELECT* statement. The *ALTER FUNCTION* is the outside wrapper for the T-SQL code. The *RETURNS* statement specifies that the function returns a *TABLE.* The *RETURN* statement is a wrapper for the *SELECT* statement that specifies the result set for the function.

```
ALTER FUNCTION dbo.AboveAverageOrders
()
RETURNS TABLE
AS
RETURN ( SELECT TOP 100 PERCENT *
FROM    dbo.Orders
WHERE   (Freight > dbo.AVG_Freight_overall())
ORDER BY Freight )
```

The following VBA procedure offers one approach to extracting values from the result set for an in-line function. The trick here is to use a T-SQL statement that returns all columns from the result set for the function. This statement becomes the source for the *Open* method of a *Recordset* object. By setting the recordset's *MaxRecord* property to 5, we return a small subset of the entire result set to loop through and list in the Immediate window. If you want to retrieve the full result set, omit the *MaxRecord* property setting. Be aware that if you do so, you might need to change the data type setting for *byt1* to a data type that can accommodate a larger limit.

```
Sub ReturnResultsSetFromInlineFunction()
Dim rst1 As ADODB.Recordset
Dim byt1 As Byte

'Get a subset of the results set from an in-line function
Set rst1 = New ADODB.Recordset
rst1.MaxRecords = 5
rst1.Open "SELECT * FROM dbo.AboveAverageOrders()", _
    CurrentProject.Connection

'Print a subset of results set record from the in-line function
Do Until rst1.EOF
    Debug.Print "Results for record " & (byt1 + 1)
    For Each fld1 In rst1.Fields
        Debug.Print "    " & fld1.Name & " = " & rst1.Fields(fld1.Name)
    Next fld1
    rst1.MoveNext
    byt1 = byt1 + 1
    Debug.Print
Loop

End Sub
```

Multistatement User-Defined Functions

User-defined functions returning tables can also contain multiple statements—instead of just the single *SELECT* statement in a typical user-defined function. Books Online calls this type of user-defined function a multistatement table-valued function. This long description accurately reflects the structure of this kind of user-defined function. This kind of function lets you use many different types of T-SQL statements to define its result set. At a minimum, using this function will require you to specify the data types for columns and the record sources for the result set. Additionally, you will need to include one or more *INSERT* statements for copying values from one or more record sources into the return set.

Summary

This chapter examines how to use Access projects (.adp files) to create database objects, such as tables, views, stored procedures, triggers, and user-defined functions in SQL Server databases. You also gain exposure to the Access Upsizing Wizard, a graphical tool for creating SQL Server databases and database objects based on existing Access databases (.mdb files).

The chapter's first three sections introduce Access projects and cover graphical means of creating them and the SQL Server databases to which they connect. In addition, the initial three sections introduce Access developers to resources for learning more about SQL Server, including Books Online, sample databases, and MSDE 2000, which is an edition of SQL Server 2000 that ships with Office 2003. Beyond that, you learn of special SQL Server resources that ship with one edition of Office 2003—Chapter 12 explores these resources in greater depth.

The chapter compares and contrasts database objects in Access and SQL Server databases. In addition, you gain exposure to graphical techniques for creating and using these objects. The graphical interfaces start with the Access project Database window that permits you to explore the database objects in the SQL Server database to which an Access project points. You also learn how to graphically create tables, views, stored procedures, and user-defined functions as well as database diagrams for representing whole database schemas.

Although the chapter covers graphical means for creating objects, there is also a strong emphasis on programmatically creating database objects. For example, you learn T-SQL coding techniques. The chapter shows you how to run this code from templates accessible through the Access project Database window as well as via ADO in the VBA project associated with an Access project. Although the VBA samples generally take advantage of running from an Access project, many of these samples can run with slight modification from the VBA project for an Access database file.

12

Using Access to Build SQL Server Solutions: Part II

Microsoft Access projects are impressive development tools for at least two key reasons. First, they expose many of the most powerful features of Microsoft SQL Server. Also, Access projects facilitate the application of many of the most powerful Access development capabilities to SQL Server databases. Chapter 11 focused on the user interface (UI) and database objects, such as tables, views, stored procedures, and user-defined functions. These topics are all server-side objects in a client/server solution supported by Access projects.

This chapter continues the saga of how to build client/server solutions with Access projects. However, this chapter switches the spotlight to the client-side tools. Several early sections in the chapter examine how to use forms with SQL Server record sources. These are followed by another section on building solutions with reports. Do not feel that you are limited to the form and report techniques covered in this chapter. In fact, most techniques for applying forms and reports in Access database files also apply in Access projects; this chapter describes selected differences. This capability to use forms and reports means that you can refer back to coverage of these topics in earlier chapters (see especially Chapter 5) for more ways to create SQL Server solutions with Access.

Creating a Form Based on a Table with One Click

One of the most remarkable features of Access projects is the ease and power that they bring to developing form-based solutions for SQL Server databases. For example, the AutoForm Wizard enables you to create a form based on a table with just a single click. When working with the AutoForm Wizard, remember that you do not select Forms in the Objects bar. Instead, you select a class, such as Tables. Then you highlight the database object to serve as the source for the form and click the AutoForm button on the toolbar.

A single click of the AutoForm Wizard creates a form that's bound to the table. If the table has a parent-child relationship with another table, the wizard automatically creates a form that has a main form control for the parent record and a subform control for its child records. If the table for the subform also has a parent-child relationship with a third table, the wizard automatically creates subdatasheets for the rows to represent the child records of the subform's parent records.

The automatic capturing of subform and subdatasheet relationships in Access 2003 is an improvement upon the first Access projects in Access 2000. The earlier version of Access allowed you to manually construct subforms, but it did not construct them automatically. In addition, Access 2000 did not manage subdatasheet relationships. However, Access 2003 and Access 2002 manage subdatasheets for tables and use that information when constructing forms.

All the samples in this chapter use the Chapter12.adp file, which needs to connect to the Chapter12SQL database on a SQL Server instance. The companion materials for this chapter include an .mdf file to enable installing the Chapter12SQL database on a SQL Server instance available to you. Detailed instructions for initially running Chapter12.adp and installing the Chapter12SQL database on your local SQL Server accompany this chapter in the "Opening an Access Project for an .mdf File" sidebar. You can adapt these instructions for moving a database between any two servers, such as the one in your office to the one in your client's office. To create a copy of an .mdf file from the current database to which an Access project connects, choose Tools, Database Utilities, Copy Database File. If your current database is Chapter12SQL, this creates a file named Copy of Chapter12SQL_dat.mdf. Rename and copy the resulting .mdf file for the database as your needs dictate.

Opening an Access Project for an .mdf File

Recall from Chapter 11 that an .mdf holds all the database objects, including their data, in a SQL Server database. This feature makes it easy to open an Access project on an .mdf file, such as the one in the companion content for this chapter (Chapter12SQL_dat.mdf). The Access project can be a new project with no client-side objects or an existing one with client-side objects, such as Chapter12.adp. When using a new project, the process is a little unusual because you start by clicking the link for a new Project using existing data—yet, you create a new database on the server to which you connect. If you have an existing Access project with client-side objects, then you can just open the project. In either case, you need to open the Data Link Properties dialog box with the File, Connection command.

To work with the samples in this chapter, attach the Chapter12SQL database to your local SQL Server through the Data Link Properties dialog box for the Chapter12.adp file. Designate (local) as the server name. Choose the Use Windows NT Integrated security radio button. Do not select a database on the server because the one you want is not there the first time that you open Chapter12.adp. Instead, choose the Attach a database file as a database name option. Then type the name **Chapter12SQL** in the text box below the option. In the Using The Filename box, enter the path for the Chapter12SQL_dat.mdf; for example, C:\Access11Files\Chapter12\Chapter12SQL_dat.mdf. If your files are properly specified and your Windows login has permission to create a database on the local server, clicking the Test Connection button will confirm that your connection succeeded. Click OK to close the Data Link Properties dialog box, and click OK again to connect Chapter12.adp to Chapter12SQL on your local database server. When you subsequently open the Chapter12.adp file, it will connect to the Chapter12SQL database on your local server.

Once you create a new database on your local server, your local SQL Server instance will create a companion file, Chapter12SQL_log.ldf for your .mdf file. The SQL Server instance will actively manage the .mdf and .ldf files so they will not be available for use by other processes as long as the files stay attached to the SQL Server instance and the instance remains running.

Using the AutoForm Wizard with an Unrelated Table

The main sample database for this chapter (Chapter12SQL) includes a subset of database objects from the NorthwindCS database, as well as other database objects created specifically for this chapter. One of these objects is the *Order Details* table. This table contains a row with five columns of information. The *OrderID* column value repeats for as many rows as there are line items in the order denoted by the order ID. Figure 12-1 shows a form based on the *Order Details* table. You can generate a form like this by selecting the *Order Details* table in the Database window and clicking the AutoForm tool. The form permits users to browse, update, add, and delete records from the underlying table. You can save that form by clicking File-Save. Then type a name for the form (such as frmOrderDetails) in the Save As dialog box and click OK.

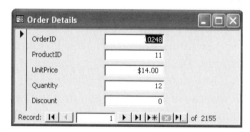

Figure 12-1   A form created with one click for the *Order Details* table in a SQL Server database.

The form depicted in Figure 12-1 is available in the sample Access project for this chapter as *frmOrderDetails*. This form resides with the Access project, Chapter12.adp. The project references its own custom database, which is Chapter12SQL.

Creating a Main/Subform with a Bound Image

Creating a main form with a subform control using the AutoForm Wizard is no more complicated than generating a form with one click, as just described. In fact, your main form can even display bound graphic images if they're saved as bitmap (.eps) files in the database. Figure 12-2 shows a main/subform based on the *Categories* table in the sample database for this chapter. The form is available in the Access project for this file as *frmCategories*. Notice that *frmCategories* includes a bound graphic image depicting the products in a category. The image that appears on each record originates from the *Picture* column of the *Categories* table. A Bound Object Frame control renders the image on the form. The AutoForm Wizard automatically selects the control based on the *Picture* column's data type and contents.

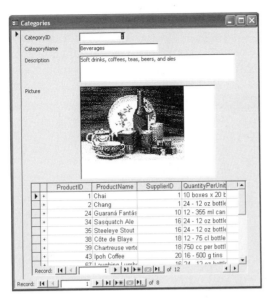

Figure 12-2 A main/subform generated by the AutoForm Wizard for the *Categories* table.

The *Categories* table in the Chapter12SQL database has a subdatasheet based on the *Products* table. This subdatasheet allows users to view the products within a category. The *Products* subdatasheet for the *Categories* table, in turn, has its own subdatasheet that shows rows in the *Order Details* table that reference the *ProductID* column value in the *Products* table. The form depicted in Figure 12-2 accurately reflects the relationship between the *Categories* and *Products* tables.

The subform in the figure presents the products within the current category on the main form. The subform navigator control is on Chai, the first of 12 products in the Beverages category. Clicking the expand indicator (the plus sign) on the row containing Chai displays a subdatasheet of rows from the *Order Details* table that reference the product ID for Chai.

All the functionality of *frmCategories* was obtained by a single click of the AutoForm Wizard. Remember to highlight the *Categories* table before clicking the AutoForm Wizard. After the wizard generates the form, choose File, Save and assign a name to the form, such as *frmCategories*.

Another Main/Subform Example

The AutoForm Wizard is a great tool, but it has its limitations. The next main/subform example we'll discuss illustrates two of these drawbacks. Figure 12-3 displays the output from the AutoForm Wizard for the *Employees* table. This form is available in the chapter's project as *frmEmployees*. The *Employees* table, which is the record source for the main form in *frmEmployees*, has a sub-datasheet that points at the *Orders* table. Users can open this subdatasheet to examine the orders made by any employee. The *Orders* table, in turn, has a subdatasheet that points at the *Order Details* table.

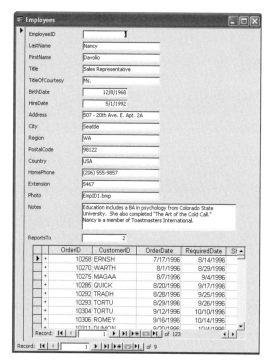

Figure 12-3   A main/subform generated by the AutoForm Wizard for the *Employees* table.

The *frmEmployees* form reflects the data relationships for the *Employees* table. The main form shows all the fields in the *Employees* table. The subform shows all the orders made by the current employee on the main form. The expand indicator allows a user to expand the view to include the line items for a particular order.

Figure 12-3 highlights two limitations of the AutoForm Wizard. Fortunately, a little programming can easily resolve both of these problems. The first limitation is that the Photo row shows an image address rather than an image. Notice that the contents of the Photo cell reads EmpID1.eps. This is the filename for the bitmap file depicting an employee named Nancy Davolio. When working with large collections of graphic images, a popular development option is to leave the images as files outside of a database and store the image filenames in a database. This speeds up performance, but it requires an extra step when displaying the graphic image. Happily, that extra step is quick and easy. The second limitation is that the AutoForm Wizard includes no prompts for automatically selecting or aggregating subform values on the main form. However, selecting or aggregating subform values is a common requirement for main/subform designs.

Extending AutoForm-Generated Forms

This section tackles two issues. First, it shows how to reference items on a subform programmatically from the code behind a main form. This enables you to compute values based on subform fields or just extract a particular subform field value (which can eliminate the need to scroll a subform). Second, this section explains how to show pictures in a form when the table serving as the form's record source contains image file addresses instead of bound images.

Referencing Subform Fields from a Main Form

Figure 12-4 shows an adaptation of the form depicted in Figure 12-3. The new form has the name *frmEmployees1*. The adaptation drops the Notes text box and adds two others in its place. The Notes text box in *frmEmployees* is bound to the *Notes* column in the *Employees* table. The two new text boxes are both unbound. Their captions are Total Freight and Last Order Date.

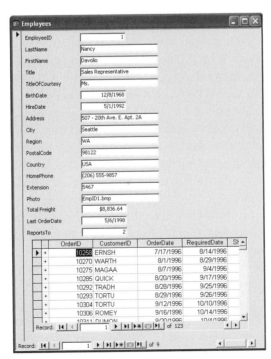

Figure 12-4 A main/subform based on the *Employees* table with two unbound text boxes that display subform content on the main form.

It's easy to edit the AutoForm-generated form in Figure 12-3 so that it adopts the design of the form in Figure 12-4. You use the same techniques as you would with standard Access database files. First select the Notes text box in Design view. Then click the Delete key on the keyboard to remove the form control and its corresponding label, which is a caption for the Notes text box. Second open the Toolbox. Third drag a couple of text boxes to the form from the Toolbox. Assign *txtTotalFreight* as the name for the first new text box and *txtLastOrderDate* as the name for the second new text box. Then select the label for each text box and assign its *Caption* property a name similar to the one in Figure 12-4. Finally align and size the labels and text boxes with the other controls already on the form.

After these steps, you will have two text boxes that appear blank in Form view. In Design view, the forms contain the word *Unbound*. You can insert values into the unbound text boxes using any of the standard form development techniques. For example, you can programmatically assign values to the text boxes. One of the most common places to insert code that programmatically modifies a form is in the event procedures behind a form and its controls.

The following sample uses two form events: *Current* and *Open*. The *Current* event fires whenever a form accesses a new record. The form can access a new record when a user opens the form, navigates from one record to the next, or requeries the form. The sample code populates the *txtTotalFreight* and *txtLastOrderDate* controls with the *Current* event procedure for the form. After a form event procedure populates a text box, it will have the default formatting unless you explicitly program another format. The sample uses an *Open* event procedure to assign formats to the two unbound controls that match the content developed by the *Current* event procedure. The *Open* event fires whenever a form opens. This can happen when a user opens a closed form or a developer switches from Design view to Form view. You can open a template for a form event procedure in an Access project just as you would for an Access database file. Select the form in Design view. (See Chapter 5 to review how to do this.) Then open its Properties dialog box. Select the Event tab on the dialog box. Then click the Build button (…) next to the *Event* property that matches the event procedure you want to program. For example, click the Build button for the *On Current* event property to open a template for the *Current* event. Choose Code Builder in the Choose Builder dialog box, and then click OK to open the template.

The next two VBA scripts show the *Form_Current* and *Form_Open* event procedures for the *frmEmployees1* form. The *Form_Current* event procedure uses the *ctl1* object reference to point at the *sbfOrders* control on the *frmEmployees1* form. This control contains the subform. The procedure uses the *Form* property of the *sbfOrders* control to reference individual control values on the subform. For example, the event procedure points *ctl2* at the *Freight* control on the subform.

Next the event procedure opens a loop on the recordset behind the subform. The syntax for pointing at the recordset behind a subform is *ctl1.Form.Recordset*. In this instance, *ctl1* points at the subform control. *Form* displays the collection of form properties behind the subform control, and *Recordset* specifies the particular property of interest. The loop travels through the records behind the subform until it encounters an *EOF* flag. During each pass through the loop, the code accumulates the value of the *Freight* control in the *cur1* local variable. The code within the loop also saves the current value of the *OrderDate* control in the *dat1* local memory variable. During the last pass through the loop, *dat1* receives the value of the last *OrderDate* value for the current employee. After exiting the loop, the procedure saves the values of *cur1* and *dat1* in the *txtTotalFreight* and *txtLastOrderDate* text boxes on the main form. This way, the procedure reflects subform control values on the main form.

The procedure makes the subform invisible during its operation. Setting the subform control's visibility property to *False* hides updates to the control at the procedure's start, and a closing property setting of *True* restores the visibility of the subform at the end of the procedure. In between, the procedure moves from one record to the next on the subform. Setting the subform control's *Visible* property to *False* hides this movement between records on the subform. Just before restoring the subform's visibility, the procedure moves the current record in the subform back to the first record in the recordset.

```
Private Sub Form_Current()
Dim ctl1 As Control
Dim ctl2 As Control
Dim cur1 As Currency
Dim dat1 As Date

'Set reference for subform control
Set ctl1 = Me.sbfOrders
ctl1.Visible = False

'Set reference to Freight control on subform
Set ctl2 = Me.sbfOrders.Form("Freight")

'Loop through subform rows in subform recordset.
'Accumulate total freight.
'Save OrderDate values for last subform row.
Do Until ctl1.Form.Recordset.EOF
    cur1 = cur1 + ctl2.Value
    dat1 = Me.sbfOrders.Form("OrderDate")
    ctl1.Form.Recordset.MoveNext
Loop
Me.txtTotalFreight = cur1
Me.txtLastOrderDate = dat1
```

(continued)

```
'Reposition current record at top of recordset
ctl1.Form.Recordset.MoveFirst

ctl1.Visible = True

End Sub
```

The following *Form_Open* event procedure formats the two unbound controls added to *frmEmployees1*. The assignment of <;$QD>*Currency*<;$QD> to the *Format* property of the *txtTotalFreight* control represents its quantity as a currency. This assignment adds a leading currency sign, and it aligns the total value so that it appears on the box's right-hand side. The second assignment right-justifies the date in the *txtLastOrderDate* control. Access does not have enum members to represent the *TextAlign* formatting settings. Therefore, the procedure assigns a constant naming the correct value for right alignment. This makes the code easier to read and maintain. Without the *TextAlign* property assignment, the date value in *txtLastOrderDate* appears as a left-justified label.

```
Private Sub Form_Open(Cancel As Integer)

'Set the Format and TextAlign properties for the
'two unbound text boxes
Const conRightAlign = 3

Me.txtTotalFreight.Format = "Currency"
Me.txtLastOrderDate.TextAlign = conRightAlign

End Sub
```

Showing Images Based on Image Addresses

One problem with the form shown in Figure 12-3 is that it displays the address of the photo image, but not the image itself. The AutoForm Wizard assigned the file address for the image to a control, but it didn't put code behind the form to display the image that corresponds to an address on each record. (It's fixing little things like this that helps you justify getting paid the big bucks by your clients.) This section takes two approaches to the task. First, it shows how to work with the addresses in the *Employees* table. These point at bitmap images. Although this image format is acceptable for many purposes, Web applications often use different image formats, such as files with a .gif or .jpg extension. The second sample in this section demonstrates the use of images with a .jpg format.

To use image files from the *Employees* table, I build a simple query statement in a view. The view's name is *Employee_Pic_addresses*. This view contains three fields: *EmployeeID, EmployeeName,* and *Photo*. The *Photo* column contains the image filenames. The *EmployeeName* field is computed as the *FirstName* field, plus a space, plus the *LastName* field. Notice from the following T-SQL statement that SQL Server syntax uses a plus sign (+) to concatenate strings:

```
SELECT EmployeeID, FirstName + ' ' + LastName AS EmployeeName, Photo
FROM dbo.Employees
```

To create a form that displays the three column values in the *Employee_Pic_addresses* view and the images corresponding to the filenames in the *Photo* column, you can create a form based on the view. Use the AutoForm Wizard to get off to a quick start. Then, in Design view, click the Image control in the Toolbox and select the location where you want the control in the form's top-left corner. When the Insert Image dialog box appears, choose EmpID1.eps. This file will reside in the folder where you store the image files. For example, Microsoft Office XP installs the image files for the Employees table by default at C:\program files\microsoft office\office11\samples\. When the form initially opens, it will automatically show this image. Any code you run from event procedures can substitute a new image. Assign *pic_image* to the Image control's *Name* property by using the Properties dialog box for the control. Insert the following script for the form's current event procedure. This procedure starts by assigning a value to a path, which represents the path to the image files. You can use any path you have for the image files. If the *Photo* column value is not *Null*, the procedure assigns the concatenation of the path and filename to the image control's *Picture* property. This branch of the *If…Then…Else…End If* statement also assigns a value of *True* to the image control's *Visible* property. This property is *True* by default, but the procedure assigns *False* to the property when the filename for the image is *Null*. Therefore, setting the *Visible* property to *True* when an image exists ensures that the employee's picture appears on the form.

```
Private Sub Form_Current()
'Assign a path for the image filename files
Const path _
    = "C:\program files\microsoft office\office11\samples\"

'If the image exists, assign the path and photo address
'to the pic_image's Picture property. Otherwise, make
'pic_image invisible.
If IsNull(Me.Photo) Then
    Me.pic_image.Visible = False
Else
    Me.pic_image.Picture = path & Me.Photo
    Me.pic_image.Visible = True
End If

End Sub
```

Figure 12-5 shows the *frmEmployee_Pic_addresses* form with the image of the first employee. Users can move through the records with the normal navigation controls at the bottom of the form. With each new record, the image changes. The table contains only nine records. As a developer, you can add new employees and photo addresses to the table to enable the form to show additional employee pictures. With a very modest amount of code, you can enable end users to add images for display on the form.

Figure 12-5   A form containing employee photo images that correspond to the photo filenames in the *Employees* table.

The next sample uses a very similar design. But instead of showing the employee photos from the Northwind database, this sample shows the photos for the *Pic_Addresses* table initially developed in Chapter 11. Recall that the table has three columns: *PictureID*, *Pic_description*, and *Pic_address*. These columns roughly correspond to those in the *Employees* table, with two important exceptions. First, the addresses in the *Pic_address* column include both the path and filename. Second, the addresses in *Pic_Addresses* point at .jpg files. This file type is popular for Web applications that show photo images. Therefore, bitmap files tend to have a larger file size for comparable images and resolutions. Using the Image control, you can display bitmap as well as JPEG files (those with a .jpg extension).

> **Note**   The *Pic_address* column references the C:\Access11Files path instead of the folder for either Chapter 11 or Chapter 12. Your image files need to be in the C:\Access11Files path location for the following sample to work properly.

Because the *Pic_address* column includes both a path and filename for an image file, the *Form_Current* event procedure doesn't need a path specification for the image filenames. Aside from this minor distinction (based on the *Pic_address* column values and the name of the column containing image filenames), the *Form_Current* event for the *Employees* photos and the *Pic_Addresses* table are identical. The script for the form showing images from the *Pic_Addresses* table appears next:

```
Private Sub Form_Current()

'If the image exists, assign the Pic_address value
'to the pic_image's Picture property. Otherwise, make
'pic_image invisible.
If IsNull(Me.Pic_address) Then
    Me.pic_image.Visible = False
Else
    Me.pic_image.Picture = Me.Pic_address
    Me.pic_image.Visible = True
End If

End Sub
```

Figure 12-6 shows the *frmPic_Addresses* form during the transition from the first to the second record. This dialog box alerts you to the fact that the .jpg file is being imported. The *PictureID* value points at the third record.

Figure 12-6   Importing a .jpg file into an Image control on a form.

> **Note** The Image control prompts with an importing dialog box when it loads a .jpg file. I've never discovered a way to present .jpg image files that suppresses this dialog box. In any event, this dialog box appears only briefly, so it's not a major distraction. Moreover, it doesn't appear for bitmap images.

Creating Unbound Combo Boxes on Forms

Creating an unbound combo box on a form is a very popular technique for controlling the flow of an application. Users make a selection from a combo box to launch a second form. When the list of values for a combo box is very large, your application can use multiple combo boxes so that users pick from two or more combo boxes to control the flow of an application. Replacing a single combo box with two combo boxes can speed the operation of an application by avoiding a long wait for a single combo box to display a list.

This section illustrates several different approaches to working with unbound combo boxes. An unbound combo box shows the values from a field in a record source, but it doesn't enter values into that field when users make selections from the control. The section initially revisits using the Combo Box Wizard with SQL Server. Being able to use such a lowly tool with a database as advanced as SQL Server is a major breakthrough. This capability minimizes the complexity of building solutions based on an advanced database manager such as SQL Server. This section also illustrates multiple ways to build combo box solutions with code, including writing a procedure that actually creates an event procedure.

Using the Combo Box Wizard with SQL Server

You can invoke the Combo Box Wizard from a blank form in Design view. Open the Toolbox, and select the Control Wizards button. Recall that you can show the name for a control in the Toolbox, on toolbars, and elsewhere by holding the cursor over the control. Next click the Combo Box control in the Toolbox, and then click on a central area on the blank form. The Combo Box Wizard dialog box opens. The features of this dialog box are mostly identical to those in the dialog box for Access database files. Make the selections for a combo box that shows the *CategoryName* but saves the *CategoryID* column values from the *Categories* table. Instead of having a check box to hide the first column with *CategoryID*, you must drag the column width to an extent of zero to hide the column. See Figure 12-7 for an illustration of this process. By dragging the *CategoryID* column border to the left margin, you hide this column even while Access saves the *CategoryID* value after a selection from the combo box.

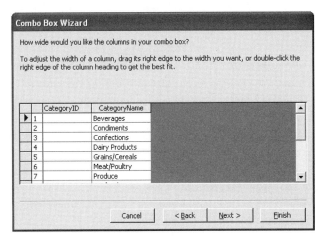

Figure 12-7   Collapsing the first column to hide it with a combo box list, even while the combo box binds to the column value after a selection.

After using the Combo Box Wizard as just described, you'll have a form that resembles Form1, contained in the Access project for this chapter. Figure 12-8 shows the sample combo box created by this process. Although the combo box allows you to select items from a list, nothing happens after you do so. To enable some action based on a selection from the combo box, you need an *AfterUpdate* event procedure. In this section, I'll describe a couple of approaches to building this type of event procedure, and I'll show the event procedure performing a couple of different tasks.

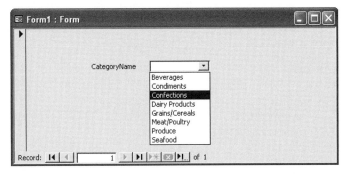

Figure 12-8   A combo box created with the Combo Box Wizard against a SQL Server database that shows items from the *CategoryName* table but saves the corresponding *CategoryID*.

Programming a Combo Box with an Event Procedure

Programming a combo box with an event procedure on a form involves three steps. First, you create the form. Second, you add the combo box control to the form. Third, you program the addition of an event procedure for the combo box.

The next VBA sample contains three procedures for programmatically creating a blank form with a designated name. The main routine, *Createfrm-ForCbo*, calls the other two procedures. The first called procedure drops a prior version of the form, if it exists. The second called procedure creates the new form and assigns it a specific name. Before calling either of the other procedures, the main routine assigns the string variable *frmName*, the name of the new form.

The *Drop_a_form* procedure loops through the *AllForms* collection. If the procedure finds a form that has the name created by the sample, it attempts to delete the form from the Access Database window by using the *DeleteObject* method for the *DoCmd* object. Before invoking the method, the procedure closes the form. This step is necessary because Access cannot delete an open form. If the form is already closed, Access ignores the request to close it.

The *Create_a_form* procedure adds a form to the application based on the default template. The *CreateForm* method accomplishes this task but doesn't offer a way to assign a name to the form. Therefore, the procedure saves the default name and closes the form to save it. Next the procedure selects the form with the default name in the Database window and renames the form with the value of the string saved in *frmName*. In this instance, the new form assumes the name *frmForCbo*.

```
Sub CreatefrmForCbo()
Dim frmName As String

'Create a form for programmatically specified
'combo box
frmName = "frmForCbo"
Drop_a_form frmName
Create_a_form frmName

End Sub

Sub Drop_a_form(frmName As String)
Dim obj1 As AccessObject

'If form exists, close it and delete it
For Each obj1 In CurrentProject.AllForms
    If obj1.Name = frmName Then
        DoCmd.Close acForm, obj1.Name
        DoCmd.DeleteObject acForm, obj1.Name
```

```
      End If
Next obj1

End Sub

Sub Create_a_form(frmName As String)
Dim frm1 As Form
Dim str1 As String

'Create form and close it with a default name
Set frm1 = CreateForm
str1 = frm1.Name
DoCmd.Close acForm, str1, acSaveYes

'Change from default (str1) to custom name (frmName)
DoCmd.SelectObject acForm, str1, True
DoCmd.Rename frmName, acForm, str1

End Sub
```

The next step is to add a combo box to the programmatically created form. The two procedures in the next sample illustrate this. The first procedure simply passes a name to the second procedure. Then the second procedure uses the name to open a form to which it will add a combo box. If the code is passed the name of a form with controls that already exist, the procedure removes each control on the form by invoking the *DeleteControl* method. When the procedure finishes looping through any existing controls on the form, it invokes the *CreateControl* method to add a new combo box to the form named by the value *frmName*. After adding the combo box control, the procedure makes two types of settings for the combo box. The first pair of settings positions the combo box on the form. The settings for the control's *Left* and *Top* properties are offsets in twips from the form's left and top borders. The next five settings for the combo box control specify a combo box that shows *CategoryName* but saves *CategoryID* from the *Categories* table. Once the combo box settings are complete, the procedure saves the changes to the form. Just before closing, the procedure asks whether the user wants to show the form. Because the procedure can add a control to a form in Design view only, this final prompt gives Access an opportunity to reopen the form in Normal view if the user wants to preview the form with its new combo box control.

```
Sub CallAddUnboundCboToForm()
Dim frmName As String

'Call a procedure to add a combo box to form
frmName = "frmForCbo"
AddUnboundCboToForm frmName
```

(continued)

```
End Sub

Sub AddUnboundCboToForm(frmName As String)
Dim frm1 As Form
Dim ct11 As Control
Dim cbo1 As ComboBox

'Open the form in Design view
DoCmd.OpenForm frmName, acDesign
Set frm1 = Forms(frmName)

'Remove all controls from the form
For Each ct11 In Forms(frmName).Controls
    DeleteControl frmName, ct11.Name
Next ct11

'Add a new combo box
Set cbo1 = CreateControl(frmName, acComboBox)
cbo1.Left = 2880
cbo1.Top = 720

'Assign combo box settings
cbo1.RowSourceType = "Table/View/StoredProc"
cbo1.RowSource = _
    "SELECT CategoryID, CategoryName FROM Categories"
cbo1.ColumnCount = 2
cbo1.ColumnWidths = "0,2"
cbo1.BoundColumn = 1

'Save settings
DoCmd.Close acForm, frm1.Name, acSaveYes

If MsgBox("Do you want to show form?", _
    vbYesNo, _
    "Programming Microsoft Access 2003") = vbYes Then
    DoCmd.OpenForm frmName
End If

End Sub
```

The last step is to add an event procedure to the combo box programmatically. The next sample illustrates one direct way to accomplish this. Again, the first procedure just passes a form name to the second procedure, which programs the event procedure for a combo box on the form.

The second procedure in this sample starts by opening the form with the name passed to it. Next the procedure clears any lines of code in the module behind the form. Then it searches through the controls on the form for a combo box. Actually, it searches for all the combo boxes on the form, but because the form has just one combo box, the set of all combo boxes contains just that one combo box. When the procedure finds the combo box, it invokes the *CreateEventProc* method to add an *AfterUpdate* event procedure to the combo box. This method takes two arguments. One is a string that names the type of event procedure. The second argument is another string that represents the name of the control to which you'll add the event procedure. The *InsertLines* method for a module object writes the code to the module behind the control's form. The procedure's first line creates a string that denotes a filter for opening a form based on the selected item in the combo box. The procedure's second line specifies the opening of the *frmProducts* form and references the filter from the first line. This event procedure programs the *frmProducts* form to display only products from the category selected in the combo box.

The second procedure concludes by opening the form with the combo box so that you can try out the application. Switch from the Code window to the Access application environment so that you can use the combo box to open the *frmProducts* table for a single category of products. Here's the syntax for the procedures just described.

```
Sub CallAddAfterUpdateEvent()
Dim frmName As String

'Call a procedure to add an AfterUpdate event procedure
'to a combo box
frmName = "frmForCbo"
AddAfterUpdateEventToCbo frmName

End Sub

Sub AddAfterUpdateEventToCbo(frmName As String)
Dim frm1 As Form
Dim cbo1 As ComboBox
Dim ctl1 As Control
Dim mdl1 As Module
Dim str1 As String

'Open the form in Design view
DoCmd.OpenForm frmName, acDesign
Set frm1 = Forms(frmName)

'Set reference to module for form, and delete
'all previously existing procedures
Set mdl1 = frm1.Module
mdl1.DeleteLines 1, mdl1.CountOfLines

'Add event procedure to open frmProducts for the
```

(continued)

```
'category selected in the combo box; loop through form
'controls to find combo box
For Each ctl1 In frm1.Controls
    If TypeOf ctl1 Is ComboBox Then
        lngReturn = mdl1.CreateEventProc("AfterUpdate", ctl1.Name)
        mdl1.InsertLines lngReturn + 2, _
        "str1 = " & _
        """"CategoryID = """ & " & Cstr(" & ctl1.Name & ".Value)"
        mdl1.InsertLines lngReturn + 3, _
         "DoCmd.OpenForm ""frmProducts"", , , str1" & vbCr
    End If
Next ctl1

'Save settings and reopen form in Normal view
DoCmd.Close acForm, frm1.Name, acSaveYes
DoCmd.OpenForm frmName

End Sub
```

This sample writes the *AfterUpdate* event procedure listed next for the combo box named Combo3. The procedure that writes the event procedure never actually searches for a control with this specific name. It merely searches for combo boxes. If you want to update a specific combo box, you can reference its name as well as the type of the control inside the loop within the procedure that writes the event procedure. Notice that the completed event procedure has two lines. Compare their construction with that of the sample that writes them, to see the string syntax rules for constructing event procedures programmatically.

```
Private Sub Combo3_AfterUpdate()

str1 = "CategoryID = " & CStr(Combo3.Value)
DoCmd.OpenForm "frmProducts", , , str1

End Sub
```

Programming Conditional Combo Boxes

Instead of opening a form based directly on a combo box selection, you sometimes will want to base a form (either directly or indirectly) on two or more combo box selections. The sample in this section shows how to generate the list for a second combo box depending upon the selection made in an initial combo box. Only the selection from the second combo box is directly used to open the form.

The *frmTwoCboOpenForm* form in the sample Access project for this chapter contains a couple of combo boxes. The first combo box lets a user pick from a list of category names. The list for the second combo box shows products just for the category selected in the first combo box. After a user selects a product from the second combo box, *frmTwoCboOpenForm* opens *frmProducts* for the specific product selected. Figure 12-9 shows how the combo boxes and forms work together. In the figure, the user initially picks the Confections category from the first combo box. This sets the source for the second combo box to show only products in the Confections category. If a user chooses Chocolade in the second combo box on *frmTwoCboOpenForm*, *frmProducts* will open and display detailed product data for Chocolade. The caption for *frmProducts* is Products.

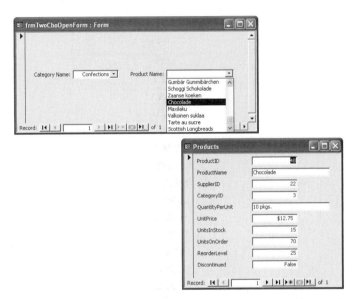

Figure 12-9   A combo box that's conditional upon another and opens a second form.

To make the *frmProducts* form show another product, close the form by clicking its top right Close control. Then make new selections from first and second combo boxes on *frmTwoCboOpenForm*. Making a selection from the first combo box is optional. If you do make a new selection in the first combo box, it will alter the selection list for the second combo box. After making a selection from the second combo box, *frmProducts* will reopen to the new product selection for the second box.

I created this sample by adding two combo boxes to a form (without using the Combo Box Wizard). In fact, the second combo box is just a duplicate of the first one. You can create such a copy with the Edit, Duplicate command from the form Design view menu bar. Figure 12-10 shows the combo boxes in Design view. Because you're just creating one combo box and then duplicating it, this design is quick to set up manually. The code behind the form does all the formatting and makes all the data assignments for the combo boxes.

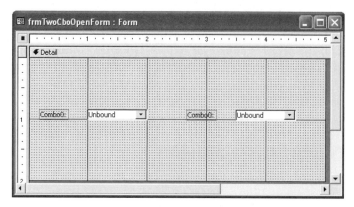

Figure 12-10 Design view of the *frmTwoCboOpenForm* form.

Aside from adding the combo boxes and positioning them in the style of those shown in Figure 12-10, the sample depicted in Figure 12-9 requires one more manual setup step—assigning names to the combo boxes and their labels. Use the *Name* property setting on a control's Properties dialog box to assign the control a name. The names for the first label and combo box are *lblCategoryName* and *cboCategoryName*, respectively. The names for the second label and its combo box are *lblProductName* and *cboProductName*.

The following three event procedures drive the application. The *Form_Open* event procedure formats the two combo boxes and makes the data assignments for the first combo box, which displays the list of categories. Recall that this combo box displays values from the *CategoryName* column in the *Categories* table but saves values from the *CategoryID* column. The code for this in the *Form_Open* event procedure relieves a developer from having to use the Combo Box Wizard to add the control. It also eliminates the need to manually make assignments in the combo box's Properties dialog box to control its selection list.

Formatting the combo boxes might be the most novel feature of the *Form_Open* event procedure. This is because of the way the code positions controls in relation to one another. In addition, this event procedure uses an assortment of combo box and label control properties. The procedure positions the label control for the first combo box 60 twips from the form's left border. It also assigns a width and caption for the label and right aligns the caption in the control. Next the procedure arranges the first combo box so that its left border begins 60 twips beyond where its label ends. After setting the selection for the first combo box, the procedure positions the label for the second combo box. This label starts 40 twips to the right of where the first combo box ends. The label control width for the second combo box matches the width of the label control for the first combo box. The code right aligns the caption for the second label—just like the first one. The second combo box itself is wider than any of the other three controls, but the second combo box begins 60 twips beyond the right edge of its label control—just like the first combo box. After setting the position of the second combo box, the procedure concludes by clearing the combo box *Value* property, which reveals its display.

```
Private Sub Form_Open(Cancel As Integer)
Dim ctl1 As Control
Dim cbo1 As ComboBox
Const conAlignRight = 3

'Position CategoryName label 60 twips from form's
'left border and 1 inch (1440 twips) wide
Set ctl1 = Me.lblCategoryName
ctl1.Left = 60
ctl1.Width = 1440
ctl1.Caption = "Category Name:"
ctl1.TextAlign = conAlignRight

'Set CategoryName combo box to start where text box ends,
'and set combo box's width to 1 inch (1440 twips)
Set ctl1 = Me.cboCategoryName
ctl1.Left = 60 + Me.lblCategoryName.Left + _
    Me.lblCategoryName.Width

'Assign data/display settings for CategoryName combo box
ctl1.RowSourceType = "Table/View/StoredProc"
ctl1.RowSource = _
    "SELECT CategoryID, CategoryName FROM Categories"
ctl1.ColumnCount = 2
ctl1.ColumnWidths = "0,2"
ctl1.BoundColumn = 1

'Position ProductName label 40 twips from right edge of
'cboCategoryName and 1 inch (1440 twips) wide
Set ctl1 = Me.lblProductName
ctl1.Left = Me.cboCategoryName.Left + _
    Me.cboCategoryName.Width + 40
ctl1.Width = Me.lblCategoryName.Width
ctl1.Caption = "Product Name:"
ctl1.TextAlign = conAlignRight

'Set ProductName combo box to start where text box ends,
'and lengthen combo box to 1.5 inches (2160 twips)
Set ctl1 = Me.cboProductName
ctl1.Width = 2160
ctl1.Left = 60 + Me.lblProductName.Left + Me.lblProductName.Width
ctl1.Value = ""

End Sub
```

Whereas the *Form_Open* event procedure configures the layout of controls and the contents of the selection list for the first combo box, the two *AfterUpdate* event procedures make the form responsive to user input. Making a selection from the *cboCategoryName* combo box assigns an SQL string as the *RowSource* property to the *cboProductName* combo box. The *cboCategoryName_AfterUpdate* event procedure enables this as well as other actions. The SQL string for the *cboProductName RowSource* property relies on the value in the *cboCategoryName* combo box to filter the product names that appear in the *cboProductName* combo box. Other assignments in the *cboCategoryName_AfterUpdate* event procedure enable the *cboProductName* control to show *ProductName* column values but save *ProductID* column values.

```
Private Sub cboCategoryName_AfterUpdate()
Dim ctl1 As Control

'Assign data/display settings for ProductName combo box
'based on CategoryName combo box selection
Set ctl1 = Me.cboProductName
ctl1.RowSourceType = "Table/View/StoredProc"
ctl1.RowSource = _
    "SELECT ProductID, ProductName FROM Products " & _
    "WHERE CategoryID = " & Me.cboCategoryName
ctl1.ColumnCount = 2
ctl1.ColumnWidths = "0,2"
ctl1.BoundColumn = 1

End Sub
```

The *cboProductName_AfterUpdate* event procedure is very simple. It creates a string for identifying a single product that appears in the *frmProducts* form. This string depends on the value a user selects from the *cboProductName* list. The event procedure uses that string as an argument for the *OpenForm* method to show the *frmProducts* form with the selected item from the *cboProductName* list.

```
Private Sub cboProductName_AfterUpdate()
Dim str1 As String

'Open frmProducts based on cboProductName selection
str1 = "ProductID = " & Me.cboProductName
DoCmd.OpenForm "frmProducts", , , str1

End Sub
```

SQL Server Form Issues

As noted earlier, one of the great strengths of Access projects is that you can program them in a way that's very similar to programming Access database files.

Therefore, many of the topics covered in Chapter 5 apply to the use of forms in Access projects. However, some issues are unique to Access projects. (This section considers two of these issues—see the first two subsection titles.) In addition, although not solely applicable to Access projects, some other topics are more salient for them. Server filters, which we'll discuss in this section, is such a subject.

Specifying a Form's *RecordsetType* Property in Access Projects

Forms have a *RecordsetType* property in both Access projects and Access database files, but the settings for this property—along with the capabilities they provide—differ between the two kinds of files. Access projects offer two settings for a form's *RecordsetType* property. The default setting is an updatable snapshot. This setting allows a user to edit all fields bound to any table. You can programmatically assign this setting with a value of 4. A form's *RecordsetType* property settings do not belong to an enum class. Therefore, you have to use a numeric constant. When your applications call for read-only access to data, you can use the snapshot setting, which has a numeric value of 3. With this setting, users can use a form to browse data, but they cannot edit it. In addition, they cannot add or delete records from the record source for a form.

The following procedure illustrates the syntax for working with a form's *RecordsetType* property. Although you can run the procedure automatically and have it provide feedback, I urge you to step through the code. This will give you a better feel for the performance of the *RecordsetType* settings.

The procedure has a compiler flag that simplifies working with the *frmOrderDetails* form in two ways. When you run the *ReadWriteOrReadOnly* procedure using a value of *True* for the *ReadOnly* compiler constant, as in the following code listing, the procedure assigns a snapshot setting to the form. This makes it impossible to update the *Order Details* table through the form. If you change the *ReadOnly* compiler constant to *False*, the form opens with an updatable snapshot setting for its *RecordsetType* property. This enables users to manually modify the *Orders Details* table through the *frmOrderDetails* form.

The procedure simulates a manual update of the data through the form by attempting to modify the *Quantity* field on the form's first record. If the form has an updatable snapshot setting, the update succeeds. Otherwise, the initial attempt to update the form fails. However, the procedure asks the user whether she is sure she wants to edit the quantity. When the user responds yes, the procedure resets the *RecordsetType* property so that the form provides read-write access to its data. Then the procedure tries again.

The following procedure begins by opening the *frmOrderDetails* form. Then it sets the form's *RecordsetType* property to *conReadOnly*. A *Const* declaration assigns a value of 3 to *conReadOnly*. This is the *RecordsetType* setting for a snapshot that does not permit updates, additions, or deletions from a form's record source. Then the sample multiplies the value of the *Quantity* field by 100 and stores the result in the text box. Next the code invokes the form's *Refresh* method, updating the database on the server with the value in the form's *Quantity* text box. After updating the server, the procedure ends with an *Exit Sub* statement. If you run the sample with the code listing's value for the *ReadOnly* compiler constant, it won't take the main path through the program. Instead, when the procedure attempts to write over the Quantity value in the text box, it will generate error number −2147352567. The procedure traps this error and prompts the user, asking whether he's sure about wanting to edit the value. If the user responds yes, the procedure resets the form's *RecordsetType* property to *conReadWrite*, which has a numeric value of 4. This setting permits the procedure to succeed at updating the record source behind the form.

If you run this procedure a second time without restoring the *Quantity* field for the first record to its initial value (or some other relatively small value), you can generate an overflow. This is easy to do because *Quantity* has a *Small-int* data type with a maximum value of 32,767 and the expression for revising the value of *Quantity* multiplies it by 100. The procedure traps this overflow error and prints a message to remind the user that one common cause of this error is failing to reset the value of *Quantity* for the first record to its initial value of 12. The procedure leaves the reset process to the user. However, it does offer another procedure for accomplishing this process automatically.

```
'Step through this procedure to see the flow and understand
'its logic
Sub ReadWriteOrReadOnly()
On Error GoTo ReadWrite_Trap

Dim frm1 As Form
Dim int1 As Integer
Const conReadOnly = 3
Const conReadWrite = 4
#Const ReadOnly = True

'Open frmOrderDetails, set reference to it, and
'assign ReadOnly setting to RecordsetType property
DoCmd.OpenForm "frmOrderDetails"
Set frm1 = Forms("frmOrderDetails")
#If ReadOnly = True Then
    frm1.RecordsetType = conReadOnly
#Else
    frm1.RecordsetType = conReadWrite
#End If
```

```
'Multiply the value of Quantity for the first record by 100,
'and refresh value on server
int1 = frm1.Quantity
frm1.Quantity = 100 * int1
frm1.Refresh

'Close form and exit sub
ReadWrite_Exit:
DoCmd.Close acForm, frm1.Name
Exit Sub

ReadWrite_Trap:
If Err.Number = -2147352567 And frm1.RecordsetType = conReadOnly Then
'If data is not updatable and RecordsetType is ReadOnly,
'offer option to change setting
    If MsgBox("Are you sure you want to edit quantity?", _
        vbYesNo, _
        "Programming Microsoft Access 2003") = vbYes Then
        frm1.RecordsetType = conReadWrite
        Resume
    Else
        Resume ReadWrite_Exit
    End If
ElseIf Err.Number = 6 Then
'If it is an overflow error, you might be able to recover
'by restoring Quantity to its initial value
    MsgBox "Quantity may exceed its limit; " & _
        "its current value is " & frm1.Quantity & ".  " & _
        "Consider running RestoreFirstQuantityTo12", _
        vbInformation, _
        "Programming Microsoft Access 2003"
Else
    Debug.Print Err.Number; Err.Description
End If

End Sub
```

If a user runs this procedure with a *ReadOnly* compiler constant of *True* but doesn't accept the option to revise the value of the *Quantity* field, the sample leaves the *RecordsetType* property equal to *conReadOnly*. This complicates working with the form because you cannot update its data manually without first resetting the *RecordsetType* property to an updatable snapshot. This is especially important when your application requires you to update form field values, such as when you want to restore the value of *Quantity* in the first record. The following code sample, *RestoreFirstQuantityTo12*, illustrates this process of attempting to restore the *Quantity* field in the first record to its initial value of 12.

```
Sub RestoreFirstQuantityTo12()
On Error GoTo RestoreFirstQuantity_Trap
Dim frm1 As Form
Const conReadOnly = 3
Const conReadWrite = 4

'Open frmOrderDetails, set reference to it, and
'assign ReadOnly setting to RecordsetType property
DoCmd.OpenForm "frmOrderDetails"
Set frm1 = Forms("frmOrderDetails")

'Restore Quantity with saved value
frm1.Quantity = 12
frm1.Refresh

'Close form
DoCmd.Close acForm, frm1.Name

RestoreFirstQuantity_Exit:
Exit Sub

RestoreFirstQuantity_Trap:
If Err.Number = -2147352567 And frm1.RecordsetType = conReadOnly Then
'If data is not updatable and RecordsetType is ReadOnly,
'offer option to change setting
    If MsgBox("Are you sure you want to restore quantity to 12?", _
        vbYesNo, _
        "Programming Microsoft Access 2003") = vbYes Then
        frm1.RecordsetType = conReadWrite
        Resume
    End If
Else
    Debug.Print Err.Number, Err.Description
End If

End Sub
```

Processing Hyperlinks in an Access Project Form

Access database files permit a *Hyperlink* data type that embraces and extends the standard hyperlinks found on Web pages. Recall from Chapter 5 that the *Hyperlink* data type permits you to navigate from Access to Web pages on a local intranet or the Internet. Additionally, applications can use hyperlinks to let users navigate between database objects in the current database file, another Access database file, or any Office document file. A hyperlink data value can also open the e-mail package on a workstation with a specified recipient and subject. Access projects do not offer a *Hyperlink* data type. This is because SQL

Server does not directly support such a data type. However, Access projects do permit the setting of an *IsHyperlink* property for form fields in text box and combo box controls. When the value of this property is *True*, Access interprets the value in a control as though it were a hyperlink. When the *IsHyperlink* property is *False*, the control's contents appear as a normal text field.

Recall that a *Hyperlink* data type can have up to four segments. The pound sign (#) delimits the segments (or elements) from one another within a field. The first segment is the text that a hyperlink displays. By default, a hyperlink field displays the combination of its second and third segments, but you can override this setting with a text label for the first segment. The second and third elements of a hyperlink value designate the destination to which the link navigates. These two elements can take on different meanings depending on the type of destination. The links that appear in the next sample illustrate the broad range of possibilities. The final hyperlink segment represents the text that appears when the cursor hovers over a link. (Search Access Help for "About Hyperlinks" for more in-depth coverage of hyperlink parts, and see Chapter 5 for a couple of practical uses for hyperlinks within Access applications.)

Before you can use hyperlinks in an Access project, you need a table of hyperlink values. The following code sample demonstrates one approach to creating such a table. The sample also includes the *Drop_a_table* procedure. This short procedure initially appeared in Chapter 11. The following sample repeats the listing so that you have it readily available as you move through the other samples in this chapter. This sample starts by referencing the current project with a *Connection* object and then drops any prior version of the *Links* table.

This *Links* table stores the hyperlinks that the sample creates. After dropping an earlier version of the table, the code creates a new table that has four columns. The first of these is an *autonumber* field that serves as the table's primary key. The second column holds a descriptive name for the field. This serves the same purpose as the first hyperlink element, but it's not a physical part of the hyperlink. The third column contains the actual hyperlink data value. This field is 128 characters long, which is sufficient for the sample data. Keep in mind, however, that each hyperlink segment can contain up to 2,000 characters. The fourth column designates the purposes of the hyperlink—for example, to open a Web page, an e-mail message, or a database object. This column is limited to six characters.

The sample procedure concludes by exercising the *INSERT INTO* statement five times. Each instance of the *INSERT INTO* statement adds another link to the *Links* table. The first link in the table illustrates the format for specifying a hyperlink to a Web page. This link assigns ProgrammingMSAccess.com as the display text that appears when a user navigates to *http://www.programmingmsaccess. com.* The second link starts the e-mail package on a workstation. This link specifies my e-mail address and a subject line of "Your book is great!" (Feel free to use this link to send me messages with feedback about the book or suggestions for ways that I can improve it in future editions.) The third link indicates the format of a hyperlink that points at the *Links* table in the current project. The fourth link points at the *Employees* table in the Northwind.mdb file. This link specifies the default location for the file. The final hyperlink navigates to a bookmark on a Web page. A bookmark is a reference location on a page. In this instance, the bookmark points to descriptive materials for the prior edition of this book.

```
Sub CreateLinksTable()
Dim str1 As String
Dim cnn1 As ADODB.Connection
Dim TableName As String

'Point a connection object at the current project
Set cnn1 = CurrentProject.Connection

'Delete the table if it exists already
TableName = "Links"
Drop_a_table cnn1, TableName

'Create the table
str1 = "CREATE TABLE " & TableName & " " & _
    "( " & _
    "LinkID int IDENTITY (1, 1) NOT NULL PRIMARY KEY CLUSTERED, " & _
    "LinkName varchar(96) NULL , " & _
    "LinkURL varchar(128) NOT NULL , " & _
    "LinkType varchar(6) NULL " & _
    ")"
cnn1.Execute str1

str1 = "INSERT INTO " & TableName & " " & _
    "VALUES('Link to Web page', " & _
        "'ProgrammingMSAccess.com#" & _
        "http://www.programmingmsaccess.com', " & _
        "'page') " & _
    "INSERT INTO " & TableName & " " & _
    "VALUES('Start email for praise', " & _
        "'Link for email#mailto:rickd@cabinc.net" & _
        "?subject=Your book is great!#', " & _
        "'email') " & _
    "INSERT INTO " & TableName & " " & _
    "VALUES('Link for tables in current project', " & _
        "'Links##Table Links', " & _
        "'object') " & _
    "INSERT INTO " & TableName & " " & _
    "VALUES('Link to a table in a database file', " & _
        "'Link to Access database file table#" & _
        "../../Program Files/Microsoft Office/" & _
        "Office11/Samples/Northwind.mdb#Table Employees', " & _
```

```
                "'object') " & _
        "INSERT INTO " & TableName & " " & _
        "VALUES('Link for bookmark on a Web page', " & _
            "'Bookmark link#http://www.programmingmsaccess.com/thebook/" & _
            "#A2002', 'page') "
cnn1.Execute str1

'Refresh Database window to show new table
RefreshDatabaseWindow

End Sub

Sub Drop_a_table(cnn1 As ADODB.Connection, TableName As String)

'Delete the table if it exists already
str1 = "IF EXISTS (SELECT TABLE_NAME " & _
        "FROM INFORMATION_SCHEMA.TABLES " & _
        "WHERE TABLE_NAME = '" & TableName & "') " & _
        "DROP TABLE " & TableName
cnn1.Execute str1

End Sub
```

Figure 12-11 shows an excerpt from the *Links* table that contains the five column values in the third column. Recall that this column holds the actual hyperlink data values. Use these sample hyperlinks to gain an appreciation of the various formatting options offered by the Access *Hyperlink* data type. Also, notice that the links in this table are not active. This is because SQL Server has no *Hyperlink* data type. SQL Server tables can hold hyperlink data, but they can't interpret its segments. Therefore, Access displays the values in the third column of the *Links* table as text values.

Figure 12-11   Column values containing hyperlink data from the *CreateLinksTable* procedure.

Figure 12-12 shows the *frmLinks* table that you can create with the Auto-Form Wizard for the *Links* table. The most obvious feature is that the *LinkURL* field appears as a hyperlink. Unlike the third column in the *Links* table, the *LinkURL* field on the form is an active hyperlink (meaning users can activate the link by clicking it). To activate the table's links, you can set the LinkURL control's *IsHyperlink* property to *True* in VBA, or you can select Yes from the control's Properties dialog box for its *IsHyperlink* property. If you don't perform either of these steps, the form displays the *LinkURL* column values as ordinary text rather than as functioning links.

Figure 12-12   The *frmLinks* form that displays values from the *Links* table.

Programming Form Server Filters

Server filters operate at the database server, independently of the traditional form *Filter* property and the ActiveX Data Objects (ADO) recordset *Filter* property. In addition, the programming interface is different for all three of these filtering techniques. A server filter also operates differently than the *WHERE* clause syntax for the *OpenForm* method. Recall that the *WHERE* clause syntax for the *OpenForm* method lets you determine the records available to a form when it loads. The other filter methods allow an application to dynamically change the filtered records after the form loads.

Unlike a traditional filter, which operates on a form's local data cache, a server filter operates at the server. With a server filter, your applications can speed up performance by downloading smaller record sources for a form. When users finish working with a subset of a larger record source, they can filter for a new subset from the larger source. Server filters for forms apply to bound forms. This makes a server filter easier to use than the ADO *Filter* property, which applies to an ADO recordset rather than a form. Unlike the ADO *Filter* property, a server filter can accept SQL strings that reference multiple fields.

Figure 12-13 presents a sample form that we'll use to examine programming techniques for the form's server filter property. One good way to familiarize yourself with the flexibility provided by the server filter is to use this form. The name of the sample form is *frmvwEmployeesOrderDetails*, and you'll find it in Chapter12.adp. The record source for this sample form is the vwEmployeesOrderDetails view. The view merely links the *Employees* table to the *Order Details* table and then selects a subset of the columns from both tables. The form always opens without any filters. The sample in Figure 12-13 shows a total of 2,155 records in the record source for the form. You can elect to filter by the employee last name, the discount for an order, or both. Any filtering reduces the form record count to those records that satisfy the filter.

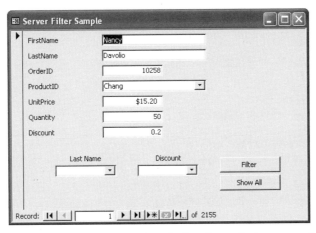

Figure 12-13   A sample form in the chapter's Access project that demonstrates how to program the *ServerFilter* property.

You can launch filtering by making selections from one or both combo boxes at the bottom of the form and clicking the command button with the caption Filter. When the form opens, the combo boxes show all employees and all discount percents. After a user selects an employee from the Last Name combo box, the other combo box shows just the discount percents for that employee. This prevents you from specifying a filter that returns no records. Clicking the command button labeled Show All clears any existing filters. The Show All button also clears both combo boxes and resets the combo box for discount percents so that it shows the discounts for all employees.

A server filter setting doesn't take effect until you refresh a form against the server. Recall that the filter operates at the server level. The invocation of the *Refresh* method makes a filter property operate. When you load a form that was closed with a filter in place, the filter setting persists. The sample form in Figure 12-13 addresses this behavior by clearing the server filter property setting when the form opens. This synchronizes the server filter setting with a newly opened form.

The following set of event procedures shows the code controlling the form that appears in Figure 12-13. The *Form_Open* event procedure prepares the form for filtering. After setting the caption, the code clears any existing filter from a prior session by setting the form's *ServerFilter* property to a zero-length string and refreshing the form against the server. Next the procedure sets the *RowSource* property for the two combo boxes. These settings display all employees and all distinct discount percents. To maintain the integrity of the filter criteria settings, the procedure limits the combo boxes to the items in their row source specification. The *Form_Open* event concludes by clearing the two filter combo boxes. This brings the display in line with the *ServerFilter* property setting made at the top of the procedure.

```
Private Sub Form_Open(Cancel As Integer)
Dim str1 As String

'Assign form's caption
Me.Caption = "Server Filter Sample"

'Clear any filter from a prior session
Me.ServerFilter = ""
Me.Refresh

'Develop row source string for cboLastNames
'and assign it
str1 = "SELECT LastName " & _
    "FROM Employees "
Me.cboLastNames.RowSource = str1

'Develop row source string for cboDiscounts
'independent of cboLastNames and assign it
str1 = "SELECT DISTINCT Discount " & _
    "FROM vwEmployeesOrderDetails "
Me.cboDiscounts.RowSource = str1

'Restrict combo boxes to list and clear them
Me.cboDiscounts.LimitToList = True
Me.cboLastNames.LimitToList = True
Me.cboDiscounts = Null
Me.cboLastNames = Null

End Sub
```

The *cboLastNames_AfterUpdate* event procedure revises the *RowSource* property setting for the combo box that shows discount percents. After a user selects an employee's last name, this event procedure restricts the selection list from the second combo box to just those discount percents that the selected employee offered on one or more occasions. The procedure also clears the combo box for showing discounts. This setting was relevant when the user previously filtered by discount percent.

```
Private Sub cboLastNames_AfterUpdate()
Dim str1

'Develop row source string for cboDiscounts
'and assign it
```

```
str1 = "SELECT DISTINCT Discount " & _
    "FROM vwEmployeesOrderDetails " & _
    "WHERE LastName = '" & cboLastNames & "'"
Me.cboDiscounts.RowSource = str1

'Clear prior setting from cboDiscounts
Me.cboDiscounts = ""

End Sub
```

The heart of the application is the *cmdFilter_Click* event procedure. This procedure reads the two combo box settings and assigns a value to the form's *ServerFilter* property based on the combo box values. The procedure closes by refreshing the form against the server to apply the *ServerFilter* property for the form. The procedure offers four possible paths for setting the *ServerFilter* property. The first applies to cases in which the Discount combo box has a selection but the Last Name combo box is blank. The second path is for the reverse scenario—a user selects an employee name but does not specify a discount amount. The third path uses both an employee last name and a discount percent to designate a filter. The final path clears the filter when both combo boxes are set to *Null*. This situation can occur when a user manually clears both boxes of their previous filter selections and clicks the Filter command button.

```
Private Sub cmdFilter_Click()
Dim str1 As String

'Set filter based on combo box settings
If IsNull(Me.cboLastNames) And _
    IsNull(Me.cboDiscounts) = False Then
    Me.ServerFilter = "Discount = " & cboDiscounts
ElseIf IsNull(Me.cboLastNames) = False And _
    IsNull(Me.cboDiscounts) Then
    Me.ServerFilter = "LastName = '" & cboLastNames & "'"
ElseIf IsNull(Me.cboLastNames) = False And _
    IsNull(Me.cboDiscounts) = False Then
    str1 = "LastName = '" & cboLastNames & "'"
    str1 = str1 & " AND Discount = " & cboDiscounts
    Me.ServerFilter = str1
ElseIf IsNull(Me.cboLastNames) And _
    IsNull(Me.cboDiscounts) Then
    Me.ServerFilter = ""
End If

'Apply the filter
Me.Refresh

End Sub
```

The *cmdRemoveFilter_Click* event procedure removes all existing filters. It also clears the combo boxes to synchronize them with the filter setting and resets the *RowSource* property setting for the combo box showing discount percents. The new setting shows discounts offered by any employee.

```
Private Sub cmdRemoveFilter_Click()

'Clear filter and combo boxes
Me.ServerFilter = ""
Me.Refresh

'Clear both combo boxes
Me.cboLastNames = Null
Me.cboDiscounts = Null

'Restore initial row source for cboDiscounts
str1 = "SELECT DISTINCT Discount " & _
    "FROM vwEmployeesOrderDetails "
Me.cboDiscounts.RowSource = str1

End Sub
```

Programming Reports in Access Projects

You can program reports in Access projects similarly to the way that you program reports in Access database files. In addition, nearly all the same wizards you know about from Access database files are available for building reports based on SQL Server database objects. Although you aren't likely to find these reports suitable for creating a final, professional report, they're definitely a useful starting point for creating a custom report. Due to the extreme similarity between Access reports in Access database files and Access projects, I recommend you revisit Chapter 6. That chapter demonstrates many useful techniques for generating reports for Access projects.

Both samples in this section cover interesting report topics. The first sample illustrates how to create a report that lets a user specify the sort key and sort direction at run time. The ability to set report features at run time is a topic that has wide appeal. The key to setting report features at run time is knowing the structure of reports and report objects. This sort sample demonstrates the use of two report properties. The second sample reveals how to set and restore input parameters for the record source behind a report. This sample fires a procedure to restore an *InputParameters* report property after a report closes. Firing a procedure after closing a report is necessary because you cannot modify a report's *InputParameters* property while it's open in Preview or Print modes. This solution comes in handy for any report application in which you need to restore report properties after a report finishes printing.

Sorting on Any Field in Any Direction

One of the many uses for reports in SQL Server applications is to sort the result set from views (and other database objects) at run time. Unless you specify a *TOP* clause in the *SELECT* statement for a SQL Server view, the view's statement will not support an *ORDER BY* clause. Even if you do anticipate this need and include the *TOP* clause for a particular sort order, different end users, or even the same user at different points in time, may require the same report sorted in different ways.

The following sample shows how to dynamically control the sort order of a result set from a view when you show that result set in a report. Start with a tabular report for the view. If your view's columns fit nicely on one page, you can use the AutoReport: Tabular Wizard to create the report's layout. You can access this wizard by selecting Reports in the Objects bar on the Database window and clicking New. Then highlight AutoReport: Tabular, and select a view from the drop-down list below the report types in the New Report dialog box. Launch the creation of the report by clicking OK. This technique applies equally well to tables, row-returning stored procedures, and user-defined functions that can also serve as record sources for reports.

If the report's columns do not fit on a single page, choose the Report Wizard in the New Report dialog box. Choose as many columns as you need from the wizard's first screen, and then accept the defaults for the second and third screens by choosing Next. On the Report Wizard's fourth screen, clear the check box with the label Adjust The Width So All Fields Fit On A Page. Then click Finish to create a tabular report that spreads the report's columns across multiple pages.

I created and saved a tabular report named rptvwEmployeesOrderDetails based on the vwEmployeesOrderDetails view. This view served as the source for the form sample in the preceding section and is available in the Access project for this chapter. The custom view displays columns from the *Employees* and *Order Details* tables. The column name qualifiers denote the table owners and table names. To merge fields from the *Employees* and *Order Details* tables, the SQL statement for the view requires the *Orders* table. The following T-SQL statement represents the view that serves as the source for the report:

```
SELECT dbo.Employees.FirstName, dbo.Employees.LastName,
dbo.[Order Details].OrderID, dbo.[Order Details].ProductID,
dbo.[Order Details].UnitPrice, dbo.[Order Details].Quantity,
dbo.[Order Details].Discount
FROM dbo.Employees INNER JOIN
dbo.Orders ON dbo.Employees.EmployeeID =
dbo.Orders.EmployeeID INNER JOIN
dbo.[Order Details] ON dbo.Orders.OrderID =
dbo.[Order Details].OrderID
```

The report sorts rows natively first by *EmployeeID*, second by *OrderID*, and third by *ProductID*. (See Figure 12-14.) This arrangement of records reflects the primary keys for the *Employees* and *Order Details* tables. However, sometimes you might prefer to show the output in another order. The next sample, which is based on a pair of procedures, implements the core logic for assigning a sort at run time on any field in a report's record source. In addition, the sample lets you sort in either ascending or descending order on any key. Before analyzing the code, you might find it useful to review how a report handles sorting programmatically. A *Report* object has two properties to facilitate sorting: *OrderBy* and *OrderByOn*. The *OrderBy* property is a string that represents the *ORDER BY* clause of an SQL statement without the *ORDER BY* keyword. Therefore, the *OrderBy* property should contain a string of field names, followed by an optional keyword designating the sort order on each key field. If you have more than one sort key, separate them by commas. Setting a report's *OrderBy* property does not by itself establish a sort order based on a list of fields. You must also set the *OrderByOn* property to *True*.

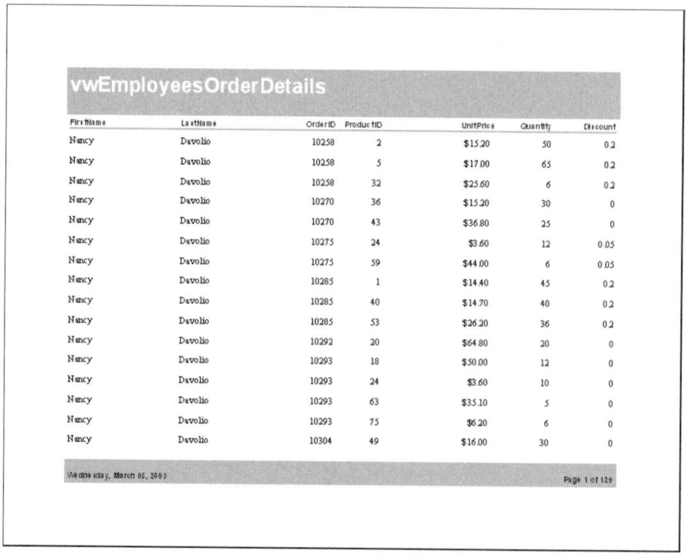

vwEmployeesOrderDetails

FirstName	LastName	OrderID	ProductID	UnitPrice	Quantity	Discount
Nancy	Davolio	10258	2	$15.20	50	0.2
Nancy	Davolio	10258	5	$17.00	65	0.2
Nancy	Davolio	10258	32	$25.60	6	0.2
Nancy	Davolio	10270	36	$15.20	30	0
Nancy	Davolio	10270	43	$36.80	25	0
Nancy	Davolio	10275	24	$3.60	12	0.05
Nancy	Davolio	10275	59	$44.00	6	0.05
Nancy	Davolio	10285	1	$14.40	45	0.2
Nancy	Davolio	10285	40	$14.70	40	0.2
Nancy	Davolio	10285	53	$26.20	36	0.2
Nancy	Davolio	10292	20	$64.80	20	0
Nancy	Davolio	10293	18	$50.00	12	0
Nancy	Davolio	10293	24	$3.60	10	0
Nancy	Davolio	10293	63	$35.10	5	0
Nancy	Davolio	10293	75	$6.20	6	0
Nancy	Davolio	10304	49	$16.00	30	0

Wednesday, March 05, 2003 Page 1 of 129

Figure 12-14 An excerpt from the rptvwEmployeesOrderDetails report. It shows the sort of *OrderID* and *ProductID* within *EmployeeID*.

Access permits you to set both the *OrderBy* and *OrderByOn* properties in Preview mode after a report is open. Settings made this way do not persist until the next time the report opens. This feature makes the properties ideal for assigning sort keys at run time. Your property settings apply exclusively to the current Preview session for a report.

The following code listing represents one combination of settings for this sample's functionality. The first procedure allows a user to specify the report name and the field name on which to perform a sort. As an option, you can specify a third argument in the first procedure that designates either an ascending or a descending sort order. If you do specify a sort order argument, the application sorts in ascending order by default. This default assignment takes place in the second procedure. After setting the argument values, the first procedure passes them to the second procedure.

The second procedure accepts three arguments, but the last of these is preceded by the *Optional* keyword. This keyword applies to the *Asc* argument. This argument is a *Boolean* value for designating an ascending sort order. Its default value is *True* in its declarations for the second procedure. The sample listing doesn't designate a third argument, so the default value for *Asc* applies. You can designate a descending sort order by specifying a value of *False* for the third argument in the first procedure, which passes the arguments to the second procedure. The second procedure begins by opening a report. The first argument passed to the second procedure names the report. After creating a reference to the report, the procedure starts an *If...Then...Else...End If* statement. The *Then* clause assigns the second argument as the value of the report's *OrderBy* property. This argument is the field name on which to perform the sort. Because the default order is ascending and there isn't any order specification, the *Then* clause assigns an ascending sort. The *Else* clause designates a descending sort order. Before closing, the procedure sets the report's *OrderByOn* property to *True*. This assignment activates the *OrderBy* property setting.

```
Sub CallSortReport()
Dim rptName As String
Dim fldName As String
Dim bolAsc As Boolean

'Specify sort name and sort field
rptName = "rptvwEmployeesOrderDetails"
fldName = "Discount"

'Pass arguments to procedure to
'prepare sorted report
SortReport rptName, fldName

End Sub

Sub SortReport(rptName As String, SortKey As String, _
    Optional Asc As Boolean = True)
Dim rpt1 As Report
```

(continued)

```
Dim str1 As String

'Open the report
DoCmd.OpenReport rptName, acViewPreview
Set rpt1 = Reports(rptName)

'Sort in ascending or descending order on sort
'key according to optional argument value
If Asc = True Then
    rpt1.OrderBy = SortKey
Else
    str1 = SortKey & " DESC"
    rpt1.OrderBy = str1
End If

rpt1.OrderByOn = True

End Sub
```

Figure 12-15 shows an excerpt from the report. Notice that this excerpt sorts rows on the *Discount* value before the primary key settings for the view's source tables. Contrast this with the report excerpt in Figure 12-14 to see the effects of the sort. The primary key settings for the source still apply, but only after the sort specification in the sample code. By resetting the *Fieldname* argument, users can sort the report on any column containing numeric or string values in the view. You can adapt this sample to permit run-time sorts on more than one field.

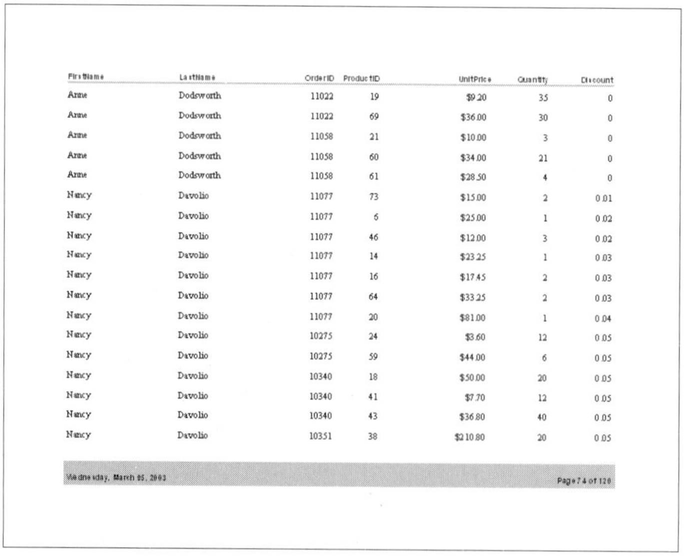

FirstName	LastName	OrderID	ProductID	UnitPrice	Quantity	Discount
Anne	Dodsworth	11022	19	$9.20	35	0
Anne	Dodsworth	11022	69	$36.00	30	0
Anne	Dodsworth	11058	21	$10.00	3	0
Anne	Dodsworth	11058	60	$34.00	21	0
Anne	Dodsworth	11058	61	$28.50	4	0
Nancy	Davolio	11077	73	$15.00	2	0.01
Nancy	Davolio	11077	6	$25.00	1	0.02
Nancy	Davolio	11077	46	$12.00	3	0.02
Nancy	Davolio	11077	14	$23.25	1	0.03
Nancy	Davolio	11077	16	$17.45	2	0.03
Nancy	Davolio	11077	64	$33.25	2	0.03
Nancy	Davolio	11077	20	$81.00	1	0.04
Nancy	Davolio	10275	24	$3.60	12	0.05
Nancy	Davolio	10275	59	$44.00	6	0.05
Nancy	Davolio	10340	18	$50.00	20	0.05
Nancy	Davolio	10340	41	$7.70	12	0.05
Nancy	Davolio	10340	43	$36.80	40	0.05
Nancy	Davolio	10351	38	$210.80	20	0.05

Wednesday, March 05, 2003   Page 74 of 120

Figure 12-15   An excerpt from the rptvwEmployeesOrderDetails report after sorting by the preceding code sample.

Setting and Restoring the *InputParameters* Property

Another typical run-time request is to make the record source for a report dynamic. Instead of just re-sorting the same records on different criteria, users might need to specify different subsets from a record source at run time. One way to do this is to define a stored procedure with parameters. For example, a user might want to view specifications for all cars in a given price range—for example, $20,000 to $30,000. Another user might want to examine the same specifications report but might need to see cars priced above $50,000. Database consultants often have to make the same report available to different users with different needs. This section shows you how to do this for your clients.

The sample in this section relies on a stored procedure named *Employee Sales by Country*. This procedure ships with the NorthwindCS database. It returns the sales amount for each order by employee and by the customer's country. Users can specify a start date and an end date that indicate the period for which the procedure should return this data.

The *Employee Sales by Country* stored procedure is available on the Access project for this chapter along with the view and tables that it references. The T-SQL script from an Access template for the stored procedure appears next. Note that it contains two parameters: *@Beginning_Date* and *@Ending_Date*. By setting these parameters just before calling the procedure, users can restrict the range of dates indicating when the stored procedure returns data. If you have a report based on the stored procedure, that report will display only data for the range specified by the *@Beginning_Date* and *@Ending_Date* parameters.

```
ALTER PROCEDURE dbo.[Employee Sales by Country]
@Beginning_Date datetime,
@Ending_Date datetime)
AS
SELECT dbo.Employees.Country, dbo.Employees.LastName,
dbo.Employees.FirstName, dbo.Orders.ShippedDate,
dbo.Orders.OrderID, dbo.[Order Subtotals].Subtotal AS SaleAmount
FROM dbo.Employees INNER JOIN
dbo.Orders INNER JOIN
dbo.[Order Subtotals] ON dbo.Orders.OrderID =
dbo.[Order Subtotals].OrderID ON dbo.Employees.EmployeeID =
dbo.Orders.EmployeeID
WHERE (dbo.Orders.ShippedDate BETWEEN @Beginning_Date AND @Ending_Date)
```

The sample Access project for this chapter includes an Access report named rptEmployeeSalesbyCountry that's based on the previous stored procedure. You can create a tabular report such as rptEmployeeSalesbyCountry with steps similar to those used for the preceding report example. However, Access will prompt you for a starting and ending date as you build the report. If you save the report as is, every time a user runs it he or she will have to respond to prompts for the beginning and ending dates for the report data.

You might need to specify some default start and end dates so that these prompts do not appear when a user is willing to accept a default range of dates. More importantly, you will definitely want the ability to specify the starting and ending dates for a report without requiring the user to respond to the report prompts. For example, you might want end users to select values from a custom form in your application. When a user specifies parameter values that differ from the default ones, you will want their selections to override the default values. In any event, you'll probably want your application to restore the default parameter settings after the report closes. The sample application in this section illustrates how to manage these processes.

There are several elements to the application. First, it needs to specify default values for the stored procedure through the report. By specifying the default values through the report, you preserve the integrity of the stored procedure's design for other applications. Second, the sample needs to override the default specification for the starting and ending dates. Third, the sample needs to restore the default parameter settings after the report closes. This is trickier than it might seem at first because you cannot modify the input parameters for a report other than in Design view. However, the report will open and close in Print or Preview mode. Therefore, the solution needs to reopen the report after it closes and then reset its parameter settings in Design view.

Use the Input Parameters setting on the Data tab of a report's Properties dialog box to set default parameters for a stored procedure that serves as the record source for a report. Developers can devise programs that override these default parameters. However, a user opening a report through the Database window will always have the default parameters assigned to the stored procedure. Figure 12-16 shows some settings for the sample application that cause the report to return data for all of 1998. The format for a parameter assignment is `parametername datatype = value`. If the stored procedure for a report has more than one parameter, you must delimit the setting for each parameter with a comma. Recall from Chapter 11 that SQL Server permits you to set a date parameter with a string. Figure 12-16 demonstrates this syntax.

Figure 12-16   The Data tab for a report's Properties dialog box reveals the syntax for assigning parameter values to the *Employee Sales by Country* stored procedure.

Although it can be useful to have default settings for the parameters, programmatically setting the parameters at run time is more flexible. The following two procedures demonstrate such an approach. Notice that I include the specification of two public variables. You must declare public variables at the top of a module, before declaring any procedures. These public variable declarations aren't absolutely necessary for setting the parameters at run time, but they're very useful for restoring the original default parameters. I'll discuss restoring the default parameters immediately after I explain how to set parameters programmatically.

The first procedure starts by assigning the report name to one of the public variables, *pubrepName*. Next the code assigns values to two string variables, denoting the start and end dates for which you want the report to display data. These are local variables. The first procedure uses two different mechanisms for passing its variable assignments to the second procedure. The local variables, *strStart* and *strEnd*, travel between procedures as passed arguments. Notice that the public variable, *pubrepName*, does not appear in the argument list. This is because public variables are within the scope of all procedures in all modules and even all projects (if you're concurrently working with more than one project). Therefore, the second procedure can detect the value of *pubrepName* even though the first procedure assigned the variable a value.

The second procedure opens in Design view the report whose name is in *pubrepName* and sets a reference (*rpt1*) to the report. You must use Design view because Access doesn't permit the specification of the *InputParameters* property from Print mode or Preview mode. Next the procedure saves the setting for the report's *InputParameters* property in *initialparams*. (Notice from the declarations before the procedures that *initialparams* is the name of the second public variable.) After saving the initial *InputParameters* property value, the procedure makes a new assignment for the property based on the start and end dates passed from the first to the second procedure. The procedure next saves the report with the new *InputParameters* setting. This step prevents Access from prompting users about whether they want to commit the report changes when the second procedure's last line opens the report in Preview mode.

The last line leaves the report open so that you can examine the values in the report. These values will all be for 1997. Recall from Figure 12-16 that the default parameter settings specify values for 1998. The assignment of arguments passed to the second procedure overrides the default parameter settings.

```
Public pubrepName As String
Public initialparams As String

Sub CallPreviewrptEmployeeSalesbyCountry()
Dim strStart As String
Dim strEnd As String
```

(continued)

```
'Set report name as public variable
pubrepName = "rptEmployeeSalesByCountry"

'Set start and end dates for report
strStart = "1/1/1997"
strEnd = "12/31/1997"

'Pass arguments to procedure for opening report
PreviewrptEmployeeSalesbyCountry pubrepName, strStart, strEnd

End Sub

Sub PreviewrptEmployeeSalesbyCountry _
    (repName As String, strStart As String, _
    strEnd As String)
Dim rpt1 As Report
Dim str1 As String

'Set the InputParameters property in Design view
DoCmd.OpenReport repName, acViewDesign
Set rpt1 = Reports(repName)
initialparams = rpt1.InputParameters
rpt1.InputParameters = "@Beginning_Date DateTime = '" & _
    strStart & "', @Ending_Date DateTime = '" & strEnd & "'"
DoCmd.Close acReport, rpt1.Name, acSaveYes

'Then examine the output based on the parameters
'in Print Preview
DoCmd.OpenReport repName, acViewPreview

End Sub
```

When you're done examining the results from the parameter assignment, close the report. Closing the report starts a process that restores the default parameter settings. This process starts with the report's *Close* event. The report's *Close* event procedure opens a form named *frmToResetReportParameters*. This form has a timer event that concludes after the report closes. The *Close* event is the last to execute before physically closing the report. The following script shows the event procedure:

```
Private Sub Report_Close()

'Start timer that concludes after report closes
DoCmd.OpenForm "frmToResetReportParameters"

End Sub
```

The *frmToResetReportParameters* form has two event procedures and a label on it. The label explains the purpose of the form: to reset the parameters. The first event procedure handles the *Load* event. The procedure sets the form's *TimerInterval* property to 5000. This schedules a timer event five seconds after the form loads. Because the *Close* event procedure for the rptEmployeeSalesbyCountry report opens the form, the form's timer event occurs five seconds after the report closes. You can shorten this interval if you find it excessive. In turn, the timer event invokes the *RestoreReportParameters* procedure in Module1. As an option, you can add code to make sure the rptEmployeeSalesbyCountry report closed successfully. Recall that the *AllReports* collection supports this function. The two form event procedures appear next.

> **Note**   The Module1 qualifier for the *RestoreReportParameters* procedure is optional, unless you have a procedure with the same name in a different module.

```
Private Sub Form_Load()

'Set timer interval to delay after deactivation
'of report before resetting parameters
Me.TimerInterval = 5000

End Sub

Private Sub Form_Timer()

'Invoke procedure to restore parameters
'in a report
Module1.RestoreReportParameters

End Sub
```

The final and crucial step for restoring the default parameters occurs in the *RestoreReportParameters* procedure, whose listing appears next. This procedure reopens the rptEmployeeSalesbyCountry report in Design view. Next it assigns the saved default parameter settings in *initialparams* to the report's *InputParameters* property. Then it closes the report and saves the changes. The last step is to close the *frmToResetReportParameters* form. This step concludes the application.

```
Sub RestoreReportParameters()
Dim rpt1 As Report
Dim repName As String

'Assign public repName variable as report for
'which to restore parameters
```

(continued)

```
repName = pubrepName

'Open report and make reference to it
DoCmd.OpenReport repName, _
    acViewDesign
Set rpt1 = Reports(repName)

'Restore initial parameters and save changes
rpt1.InputParameters = initialparams
DoCmd.Close acReport, rpt1.Name, acSaveYes

'Close form that resets parameters
DoCmd.Close acForm, "frmToResetReportParameters", _
    acSaveNo

End Sub
```

Summary

Because they bring rapid application development to SQL Server databases, Access projects are a powerful tool for creating SQL Server solutions. The many Access wizards and builders for SQL Server databases empower Access developers who are new to SQL Server. The availability of these wizards and builders also help traditional SQL Server developers and DBAs, who want to extend the reach of their databases via Access client-side tools, such as forms and reports.

The good news for Access developers is that if you know Access forms and reports for Access databases (.mdb files) all that knowledge transfers over to SQL Server objects, such as tables, views, and stored procedures. This chapter highlights special form and report features that target SQL Server databases. The good news for the SQL Server development community is that Access projects provide an easy way to deliver benefits to the clients of your SQL Server databases. Access projects combine basic SQL Server database administration features with easy and powerful report and form development capabilities. This chapter focuses on form and report capabilities. If you have a SQL Server background, you will probably benefit from a close study of Chapter 5 and Chapter 6 to get additional background on Access form and report capabilities.

13

Using Access to Build SQL Server Solutions: Part III

There is no such thing as too much security. The days of valuing ease of use over security are past. Code samples in computer articles and books from an earlier time often described how to log into SQL Server with the sa login and no password. Nowadays, database developers and DBAs acknowledge that such practices jeopardize the safety of corporate networks.

Building secure solutions is similar to any other computer topic. You have to learn the concepts, discover how to implement those concepts, and then refine your security designs, just as you do the layout and behavior of your databases and forms. Furthermore, practice makes perfect. No database application should be put on a network without being secure. Therefore, you will have many opportunities to enhance your understanding of and ability to implement secure database solutions.

This chapter offers four sections to help you along your way to building secure solutions. The chapter commences with an overview of SQL Server security concepts. This first section aims to introduce you to core security notions and show how they interact with Access projects. Next, the chapter presents an introduction to SQL-DMO (SQL Distributed Management Objects). This is a hierarchical object model in the style of many Office object models that you can use to administer SQL Server instances. The SQL-DMO review illustrates database security and other uses for the object model, such as exploring database objects as well as attaching and detaching database files. The last two sections deal with logins, users, roles, and permissions. These concepts interact to determine who can do what on a SQL Server instance and its databases.

Overview of SQL Server Database Security Concepts

This chapter provides a conceptual introduction to SQL Server security topics. It also touches on how SQL Server security interacts with the functionality available from Access projects, such as connecting to a SQL Server database, creating a new SQL Server database, or making a new table or other database object in a database. Subsequent sections in this chapter present code samples for selected content from this section.

> **Note** SQL Server security is a broad topic that can easily consume a book all by itself. This chapter focuses on a subset of security features relating to database access and manipulation. Many security issues, including the Slammer worm outbreak in late January 2003, are best addressed by server administration policies and practices. As of this writing, the definitive Microsoft statement on SQL Server security tools for DBAs is available at *http://www.microsoft.com /downloads/details.aspx?familyid=9552D43B-04EB-4AF9-9E24 -6CDE4D933600&displaylang=en*. By the way, it was the Slammer worm that taught many organizations that an operator of a computer running MSDE 2000 with a Web connection is a DBA.

Authentication

Authentication is the process by which SQL Server recognizes users trying to gain access to a SQL Server instance. SQL Server 2000 permits two authentication modes: Microsoft Windows-only authentication and mixed-mode authentication supporting both SQL Server and Windows logins. In either style, the SQL Server DBA must create a SQL Server login.

Windows-only authentication is the default mode after you initially install a SQL Server 2000 instance. With this mode, users can gain access to a SQL Server only after successfully logging into a Windows operating system, such as Windows NT, Windows 2000, Windows XP, or Windows 2003. This approach simplifies connecting to a SQL Server database because a user does not require an additional login and password for SQL Server. A user can present a Windows login credential, and SQL Server trusts Windows to authenticate the user. With this authentication mode, users can gain access to a SQL Server instance via their individual Windows login account or via a Windows group to which they belong. The DBA must explicitly recognize a Windows user account or a Windows group account in order for the Windows account to gain access to a SQL Server instance. The DBA recognizes a Windows account by assigning a SQL Server login to represent the Windows account.

SQL Server or mixed-mode authentication assigns the DBA more responsibility for managing SQL Server security. This is because the SQL Server DBA uniquely controls the logins for a SQL Server instance. With SQL Server authentication, users can log in with the built-in sa login and other custom SQL Server login accounts created by a SQL Server DBA and connect to a SQL Server instance. Because the sa login has unrestricted permissions in a SQL Server instance, it is important to assign a password to the login so that you can protect your SQL Server instance.

Enabling SQL Server authentication is valid in circumstances where it is convenient for SQL Server DBAs to have exclusive control of logins due to the sensitive nature of database contents or administrative obstacles to coordinating Windows logins with SQL Server logins. There are at least three circumstances when SQL Server authentication is the only option available to a SQL Server DBA. They are:

- SQL Server is running on a Windows 98 computer

- Your application is running on a Windows workstation in standalone mode from a network server

- You do not have a Windows server managing logins to your network

Login and User Accounts

Login and user accounts apply to users as opposed to SQL Server instances. If you think of authentication as the lock for a SQL Server instance and its databases, then login and user accounts are the keys to the authentication locks. SQL Server documentation frequently shortens the name for login and user accounts to logins and users. A login grants access to a SQL Server instance. Therefore, this kind of security object belongs to a SQL Server database server. A user account grants access to a particular database on a SQL Server instance. Any one login can have multiple user accounts associated with it. Generally, a login will have one user account for each database to which it has access. In fact, when you grant database access to a login account, you automatically create a user in the database for that login. User objects therefore belong to databases and not to SQL Server instances.

Login accounts can apply to a SQL Server login without a connection to a Windows login or a SQL Server login granted to a Windows user or a Windows group. The Windows server administrator will create Windows user and

Windows group accounts. A Windows group account represents a collection of Windows user accounts. A SQL Server DBA creates a SQL Server login by managing the account name and setting a password and a database password. The DBA also controls the permissions that a SQL Server login can have. Although a SQL Server DBA does not create a Windows user or a Windows group, the DBA must create the SQL Server login account that corresponds to a Windows user or a Windows group. Without this, a Windows user or members of the Windows group have no ability to connect to a SQL Server instance or any database on a SQL Server instance.

After installing SQL Server 2000, you will have several built-in accounts, including the Administrator, sa, and BUILTIN\Administrators login accounts. If you accept the default installation choices, the startup account for the SQL Server instance will be the Windows Administrator account on the computer running SQL Server. The default installation choices map this Windows account to the SQL Server Administrator login. In addition, the default installation choices turn on the Windows-only authentication mode.

The Administrator account belongs to a SQL Server role that grants the login unlimited permissions on a SQL Server instance. The sa login is another login account set up during SQL Server installation. The sa login name stands for Systems Administrator. This login is disabled with the default installation choices, but it can function if you enable mixed-mode authentication.

The BUILTIN\Administrators login account is the third account that is created automatically. Both the Administrator and sa login accounts are standard SQL Server logins, while the BUILTIN\Administrators login account is a Windows group account. This account grants SQL Server access to members in the Windows Administrators group on the computer running SQL Server. As with the Administrator and sa logins, the default installation choices set up the BUILTIN\Administrators login with unlimited permissions on a SQL Server. Since the BUILTIN\Administrators login is for a Windows group, it functions with either Windows or mixed-mode authentication.

You should create logins other than the three automatically created accounts to enable users to perform the tasks they need with a SQL Server instance or one of its databases. You'll learn how to create logins later in this chapter in the "Programming Login and User Accounts" section. All the automatically created accounts can be dropped or have their permissions altered, except for the sa login. These automatically created logins might expose a SQL Server to attack by a hacker. Since you cannot drop the sa login, you should always assign a password to it during installation.

You should use the startup account when you log into SQL Server after installation. If you accept all the default choices during installation, the SQL Server instance grants a login to the Windows Administrator account. This is the startup login. Also, the SQL Server instance has Windows-only authentication. Therefore, you should log into your computer as the Administrator, and choose Use Windows NT Integrated security on the Data Link Properties dialog box. If an installation enabled mixed-mode authentication, then you can also use the sa login. To do this, select the Use A Specific User Name And Password option on the Data Link Properties dialog box. Then enter the sa login as the user name with the password assigned to the sa login during installation (see Figure 13-1). If no password was assigned during installation, then leave the Password text box empty. After opening an Access project by clicking OK, you should immediately assign a password to the sa login. Choose the Tools, Security, Set Login Password command to open the Change Password dialog box. Click the Help button for instructions on using the dialog to assign a password to a login.

Figure 13-1   The Data Link Properties dialog box for an Access project ready to connect to the Northwind database with an sa login that has a password.

Notice in Figure 13-1 that sa is the user name. Login names serve as user names in the Data Link Properties dialog box. The sa login has automatic access to any database on a SQL Server instance. User accounts are for logins that do not belong to the sysadmin fixed server role. The sa and other logins automatically created during installation belong to the sysadmin fixed server role, but other user-defined logins may or may not belong to the sysadmin role. These other login accounts are typically created after the installation for those in an organization who require access to one or more databases on a SQL Server instance. One organizational member may require access to just one database, another may need access to two databases, and a third may need access to one database, but one that is different from that of the first user. A login account grants access to a SQL Server instance, and a user account grants access to a specific database on a SQL Server instance.

Roles

Roles and permissions are the two mechanisms for enabling login accounts to perform actions within a SQL Server instance and the databases managed by a SQL Server instance. You can think of a role as a cluster of individual permissions. There are four types of roles. Two of the four are fixed roles specified by SQL Server. Within each of these two roles are individual roles that convey permissions to logins and users that belong to them. Fixed server roles convey different clusters of permissions for a SQL Server instance to logins (not users). Fixed database roles convey different clusters of permissions within a database to users (not logins). Assigning logins and users to these fixed roles is a convenient way to manage which permissions logins and users have, so long as the permissions you need to manage are specified by one of the fixed server or database roles. When this is not the case, then you can create custom roles, which are the third kind of role, and assign specific permissions that meet the requirements of your application. Then you can assign users to these custom roles just as with the fixed database roles.

The fourth kind of role is an application role. This role is different from the other three in that it does not have logins or users associated with it. Instead, an application role has a name, password, and permissions for a specific application. An application role is a gateway into which any user can enter (so long as the user knows the name and password for the application role). This kind of role does not depend on SQL Server user accounts. However, application roles are best demonstrated with the Query Analyzer, a SQL Server client tool.

The fixed server roles target permissions to perform tasks within a SQL Server instance, such as creating a database. There are eight fixed server roles. Because these roles especially target permissions for administering a SQL Server instance, many of them have only passing interest to developers. Nevertheless, it is important to know about them generally, and a few of them can be vitally important. When you are in an environment where you serve as database developer and DBA, then it is useful to learn the full array of fixed server roles. A code sample in the T-SQL Help for Roles section offers a way for learning more about fixed server roles.

The sysadmin, dbcreator, and securityadmin roles are three of the eight fixed server roles that are likely to have special value to database developers. Logins belonging to the sysadmin role have special value to developers serving a dual developer/DBA function within an organization. Members of the sysadmin role can perform any function on a SQL Server instance. This is especially important for managing DBA tasks, but it is convenient for many developer tasks. For example, you cannot create a new SQL Server database from an Access project unless your login belongs to either the sysadmin or dbcreator role. In general, it is good practice to assign the lowest level permission appropriate for a task. Therefore, if a login does not need the more general permissions of the sysadmin role, assign the dbcreator role instead. The securityadmin role is convenient for logins that must manage logins. Logins in the securityadmin role can create new logins, assign logins membership in roles, and assign individual permissions to other logins.

There are nine fixed database roles. These roles convey permissions to perform tasks in or for a database. You assign membership in these roles to users. Users can have membership in multiple roles within a single database. In addition, a single login can have membership in different sets of fixed database roles for two or more different databases. Just as members of the sysadmin roles have unlimited authority within a SQL Server instance so does the db_owner role have unlimited permissions within a database. The db_datareader role grants permission to read all tables and views within a database. The db_datawriter role enables permission to insert, update, and delete rows for any table or view in a database. The db_denydatawriter denies permission to insert, update, or delete from any table or view in a database.

Fixed database roles are likely to affect the ability of those using Access projects to perform typical tasks. For example, you cannot open a table unless you have *SELECT* permission for the table. One way to gain this permission is through membership in the db_datareader role. Update queries will not work from an Access project unless the login for the Access project has an associated user account with update permission. One way to get this permission is for the user account to have membership in the db_datawriter role.

SQL Server security allows a single user account to belong to multiple roles that can have conflicting permissions. A denied permission always trumps a granted permission. For example, if a single user belongs to both the db_datawriter and db_denydatawriter roles, then the user cannot insert, update, or delete from any table or view in a database. This situation can exist if a user has a login for an individual Windows account, and the individual also belongs to a Windows group with a SQL Server login. This kind of conflict can additionally occur with the granting and denying of individual permissions.

You can learn more about roles from many topics in Books Online. The Roles topic is my favorite topic in Books Online for beginning to grasp security via fixed server and fixed database roles. Do not limit your study of roles to the

Roles topic, however. For example, the public Role topic in Books Online introduces the operation of the default role in a database. All users in a database belong to a public role. You can assign permissions to a public role just as you can to any custom or fixed database role. However, since all users belong to the public role, it is good practice to strip it of permissions so that the only way users can receive permissions is through membership in fixed database roles or custom roles that you create for the assignment of permissions.

Note   Recall from Chapter 11 that Books Online is the official source for Microsoft SQL Server documentation and help. It offers definitive presentations of conceptual issues, code samples for T-SQL and SQL-DMO, as well as coverage of SQL Server administration topics, such as database security.

There are several special user accounts you should get to know. This topic is raised here because understanding these special user accounts require a basic grasp of roles. The dbo user can perform any function in any database. Any login in the sysadmin role is a dbo user. Therefore, a login belonging to the sysadmin role does not require a user account in any database. Do not confuse the dbo user with members of the db_owner fixed database role. Members of the db_owner role have unlimited permissions within a particular database, but they do not need to be members of the sysadmin group. In fact, a member of the sysadmin role can grant a user account associated with another login membership in the db_owner role. That role enables a user to create tables and views in a database. The guest user account is an optional account. It enables logins without a database user account to gain access to a database anyway. You do not have to specify a guest account for a database. The account exists in the Northwind and pubs sample databases, but not in the NorthwindCS sample database. You should carefully evaluate the permissions that you assign to the guest user account because users who do not have permission to enter a database can perform tasks based on permissions for the guest account.

Managing Permissions

You can manage two main types of permissions for standard SQL Server logins, logins granted for Windows users or Windows groups, and for custom SQL Server roles. Permissions are specific rights to perform actions. These permissions can stand alone or compliment permissions conveyed through membership in a fixed server or fixed database role. For example, you can grant a user the right to perform a *SELECT* query from all tables in a database by associating a user account with the db_datareader role, but then use the T-SQL *DENY* keyword to disallow the ability to read a specific table, such as one containing private personnel information.

SQL Server lets you manage three classes of permissions. These include object permissions, such as the ability to select a result set from a table or execute a stored procedure. SQL Server also supports statement permissions, such as *CREATE DATABASE, CREATE DEFAULT, CREATE TABLE,* and *CREATE PROCEDURE*. Without a login that has statement permissions for *CREATE DATABASE* and *CREATE DEFAULT* or membership in roles conveying those permissions, you cannot use the Access Upsizing Wizard to create a new SQL Server database based on an Access database file. The third group of permissions are called implied permissions. Implied permissions involve managing permissions through the assignment of logins to fixed server roles and users to fixed database roles.

The list of statements for which you can grant permissions is relatively short. The items on the list include:

- *CREATE DATABASE*

- *CREATE DEFAULT*

- *CREATE FUNCTION*

- *CREATE PROCEDURE*

- *CREATE RULE*

- *CREATE TABLE*

- *CREATE VIEW*

- *BACKUP DATABASE*

- *BACKUP LOG*

Developers and DBAs can often satisfy their needs for statement permissions by assigning login accounts to fixed server roles and user accounts to fixed database roles. Use the *sp_srvrolepermission* system stored procedure to itemize the statements associated with fixed database roles. You can invoke the *sp_srvrolepermission* system stored procedure from a stored procedure template in an Access project. To invoke the system stored procedure, precede it with the *EXEC* keyword. You might need to save and reopen the stored procedure in an Access project to view the list of statements associated with each fixed server role.

Similarly, you can run the *sp_dbfixedrolepermission* system stored procedure to enumerate the statements associated with fixed database roles.

The list of object permissions vary according to the type of object. You can manage *SELECT, INSERT, UPDATE,* and *DELETE* statement permissions for tables and views. SQL Server allows you to specify a subset of these statements, namely *SELECT* and *UPDATE*, to individual columns within a table or view. In the case of user-defined functions that return tables, you can only specify *SELECT* permissions. The *EXECUTE* permission applies to both stored procedures and user-defined functions. The *REFERENCES* permission has two primary uses for typical Access developers creating SQL Server solutions. When two tables in a database have different owners, and one table needs to reference the other for a foreign key constraint, you need to assign *REFERENCES* permission to the owner of the table that contains the foreign key constraint. In addition, the non-owner of user-defined functions must be granted *REFERENCES* permission for those functions when they help to define check constraints, defaults, or computed columns for a table.

You can use three T-SQL keywords to manage object and statement permissions. All these statements can manage permissions for individual users as well as custom roles. Use the *GRANT* keyword to assign a permission to a specific security account, such as a login, a user, or a custom role. Invoke the *DENY* keyword to disallow a permission for a security account. Recall that denying a permission trumps granting a permission. Security settings can grant a user a permission through one security account, say a login for an individual Windows user, but deny the same permission for a user through a login for a Windows group. These conflicting permission assignments cause the user to not have the permission. You can retract either a *GRANT* or a *DENY* statement with the *REVOKE* keyword. Therefore, any permission for a security account can have one of three states: granted, denied, or neither granted nor denied.

SQL-DMO Programming

As mentioned in Chapter 11, SQL-DMO, or SQL Distributed Management Objects, is a hierarchical programming model for SQL Server administration and data definition tasks. You can use SQL-DMO to enumerate databases and their objects on a server. With this capability, you can perform such tasks as referencing all the databases on a server or all the stored procedures within a database. You can also view and edit the contents of databases and the objects they contain, as well as create new objects. With SQL-DMO, developers can view and edit the design of tables, triggers, views, and stored procedures within databases. In addition, you can create new instances of SQL-DMO objects. For example, you can create a new table within a database. You can even copy the script for a table from one database to create a duplicate table within another database. In fact, you use SQL-DMO programming to copy the contents between different instances of SQL Server on different computers. For example, you can detach a database from one server, copy its files to another server, and then attach those database files for use on a second server. Chapter 12 described how to do this manually, but it took more than a couple of steps—which is enough steps for a casual user to cause a failure. With SQL-DMO, you can create a solution that completes the process with the press of a button.

There are three main reasons for Access developers (and other developers using Microsoft SQL Server 2000 Desktop Engine) to become familiar with SQL-DMO:

- Administration is much more important for SQL Server databases than Access databases. By programmatically performing database administration chores, you improve your ability to manage SQL Server databases. You can even write Access applications that enable others to edit SQL Server databases in ways that you prescribe.

- Neither Microsoft SQL Server 2000 Desktop Engine (MSDE 2000) nor Microsoft Data Engine (MSDE) ships with Enterprise Manager, a graphical client management tool that offers many more database administration features than the Access project UI. This tool is available to users of all other SQL Server editions. Because Microsoft programmed Enterprise Manager with SQL-DMO, you can incorporate selective subsets of Enterprise Manager functionality into your custom applications.

- SQL-DMO is a hierarchical model for SQL Server components. Access developers who have a history of working with hierarchical models will feel comfortable adapting to its programming conventions as opposed to the more procedurally oriented T-SQL programming environment.

SQL-DMO installs with either MSDE 2000 or any other version of SQL Server 2000. Installing either MSDE 2000 or SQL Server 2000 adds sqldmo.dll and sqldmo.rll to a workstation. The .dll file implements SQL-DMO, and the .rll file is a localized resource file. Except for MSDE 2000, all versions of SQL Server 2000 ship with sqldmo80.hlp, the file that provides context-sensitive help. However, MSDE 2000 developers can get support for SQL-DMO from the downloadable version of Books Online (*http://www.microsoft.com/sql/techinfo/productdoc/2000 /books.asp*). To reference the SQL-DMO object model, your project must have a reference to the Microsoft SQLDMO Object Library in the References dialog box that the Tools-References command opens. SQL-DMO files also ship with SQL Server 7 and MSDE. SQL-DMO scripts developed with the SQL Server 7 version will run in SQL Server 2000 and MSDE 2000. Because of new features and an incompatible type library file, SQL-DMO scripts developed for SQL Server 2000 do not run in SQL Server 7. On the other hand, the SQL Server 2000 version of SQL-DMO provides new capabilities and features not available with SQL Server 7. For example, SQL-DMO for SQL Server 2000 supports user-defined functions. To tap the features associated with the latest version of SQL-DMO, you must use new object class names. One of this chapter's SQL-DMO samples demonstrates an approach to this task.

Figure 13-2 presents an excerpt from the SQL-DMO object model for SQL Server 2000. Your SQL-DMO applications will frequently start by connecting to a *SQLServer* object. The *SQLServer* object represents your application's connection to a SQL Server database server. SQL-DMO doesn't share this connection with ADO or other SQL Server client software. This is because the objects from the ADODB and SQLDMO libraries are not compatible. After specifying a connection to a server, your application can "walk the model" to return information about individual databases on a server and the objects within them. For example, SQL-DMO makes it easy to enumerate the databases on a server or the views within those databases. You can easily list and update the T-SQL script for a view.

Note   SQL-DMO for SQL Server 2000 readily supports multiple instances of SQL Server running on a single computer. This feature is only available with the version of SQL-DMO that comes with SQL Server 2000. (However, you can install a SQL Server 2000 instance alongside a SQL Server 7 installation.) The topic of installing and managing multiple instances of SQL Server on a single computer is outside the scope of this book. See Books Online for more coverage of this topic, which, by the way, is easy to accomplish.

Chapter 11 offered detailed coverage of several objects and collections portrayed in Figure 13-2. In fact, SQL Server databases, tables, views, stored procedures, and user-defined functions all received extensive coverage in that chapter. The *Users* collection and *DatabaseRoles* collection support SQL Server security. The remaining collections and individual objects from Figure 13-2 pertain to SQL Server database administration and data definition features. See Books Online for coverage of these topics.

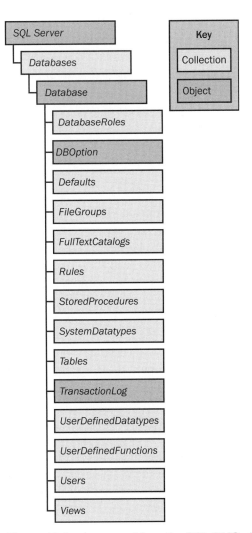

Figure 13-2   An excerpt from the SQL-DMO object model.

Ensuring Secure Login and Enumerating Databases

When you connect to a server, you can use either of two types of authentication: Microsoft Windows authentication or SQL Server authentication. Authentication is the process by which a client application verifies its credentials to connect to a SQL server. The "Authentication" section in this chapter is an overview of the topic.

When a SQL-DMO application connects to a SQL server instance with the login for a Windows user, the application must assign *True* to the *SecureLogin* property for the *SQL Server* object representing the instance. The following sample illustrates the syntax for doing this as well as enumerating the databases on a server. The first procedure merely specifies the name of a SQL Server instance and passes the information along to the second procedure as an argument. The name for a SQL Server instance is typically the name of the computer on which the program runs. This sample designates the SQL server named CabSony1. If you move the application from one computer to another, you'll have to specify a new instance name when you reference the local server on the second computer. Alternatively, you can designate the server name as the string "*(local)*". This second approach ensures that you always reference the local default SQL Server instance. But what if you want to connect to a specific server regardless of the workstation your application runs from? To do so, you must name the specific server to which your application needs to connect. There are advantages to both ways of designating a computer. Use the one that best suits your needs.

The second procedure in the next sample begins by instantiating an instance of the *SQLServer* object as *srv1*. Then the sample sets the *LoginSecure* property of *srv1* to *True*. This property sets the authentication method that a login attempt uses to connect to SQL Server instance with Windows authentication. The next line invokes the *Connect* method for the *srv1* object instance. This method attempts to connect to a server. The method can take up to three arguments. The sample uses a single argument to represent the *Name* property of the *SQLServer* object. If you don't use any arguments for the *Connect* method, the code attempts to point the *SQLServer* object at the main instance of SQL Server running on the local computer. A subsequent sample demonstrates the use of additional arguments.

After making a connection to the CabSony1 server, the sample prints the number of databases on the server by referencing the *Count* property of the *Databases* collection for *srv1*. Then the second procedure uses a *For...Next* loop to enumerate the members of the *Databases* collection.

```
Sub CallLoginSecureAndListDBs()
Dim srvName As String

'Assign name to server
srvName = "CabSony1"

'Pass server name to login routine
LoginSecureAndListDBs srvName

End Sub


Sub LoginSecureAndListDBs(srvName As String)
Dim srv1 As SQLDMO.SQLServer
Dim dbs1 As SQLDMO.Database
```

```
'Instantiate a SQLServer object, and connect
'using integrated security
Set srv1 = New SQLDMO.SQLServer
srv1.LoginSecure = True
srv1.Connect srvName

'Report the count of the databases on a server
Debug.Print "Server " & srv1.Name & " has " & _
    srv1.Databases.Count & " on it." & vbCr & _
    "Their names are:" & vbCr

'Enumerate the names of databases
For Each dbs1 In srv1.Databases
    Debug.Print vbTab & dbs1.Name
Next dbs1

'Clean up objects
srv1.DisConnect
set srv1 = Nothing

End Sub
```

Setting Mixed Authentication

When an organization's IT structure or resources make using mixed authentication desirable, you might need to change from a Windows-only authentication mode to a mixed mode that lets users connect to a SQL Server instance with login accounts managed by SQL Server or Windows. The next sample shows how to create and manage this transition. If you install MSDE 2000 on a Windows NT or Windows 2000 computer, your installation automatically starts with Windows-only authentication. If you prefer to use mixed authentication, you can use the following sample to set up the sa login account and your server for mixed authentication. Recall that the sa account has broad control within a SQL Server instance, and that it is impossible to delete the sa login.

This sample uses four procedures. The first one designates the server's name and demonstrates the syntax for explicitly referencing a computer's local SQL server. The first procedure passes the name of the server to the second procedure.

The second procedure attempts to log in to the server with SQL Server credentials. In other words, the *Connect* method specifies a login account and password for SQL Server. There are at least two ways that the attempt to log in can fail. First, the authentication mode can be set to Windows-only authentication. You can fix this by changing the server's authentication style. Second, the password for the sa login might be incorrect. You can remedy this problem by assigning a new password to the login and then using it. The second procedure uses error traps to detect either of these conditions. If the attempt to log in fails because the login request designates SQL Server credentials when the SQL Server instance is in Windows-authentication mode, the second procedure calls the *WindowsToMixedAuthentication* procedure. This procedure changes the security mode from Windows to mixed-mode authentication, permitting the use of logins authenticated by either SQL Server or Windows. If the attempt to log in fails because of a faulty password, the second procedure calls *AssignNew-Password*. This procedure assigns a known password to the sa login. For both error conditions, the second procedure tries to log in again after fixing the detected error. The second procedure starts by assigning a string to *NewPassword*. The value of the string in the listing is *password*. You can change this to any string that your needs dictate. This string contains the new password that the procedure will assign to the sa login account. The second procedure then instantiates an instance of the *SQLServer* object and attempts to log in with SQL Server credentials. Notice that the procedure doesn't set the *LoginSecure* property of *srv1* to *True*; a property setting of *True* is necessary only for a Windows user or group account with Windows authentication. The property's default value is *False* when designating SQL Server authentication. The *Connect* method specifies sa as the login account, and it references the value of *New-Password* for sa's password. If the attempt succeeds, the procedure exits normally. This happens when the server permits mixed-mode security and the sa password equals the value set for *NewPassword*.

When the authentication mode for the server is Windows-only, you have to alter the security mode to accommodate SQL Server authentication. The second procedure detects the need for this alteration when the *Connect* method generates an error number of −2147203052. The second procedure calls *WindowsToMixedAuthentication* and passes the server name. The called procedure requires the name of the server to change the authentication mode for a SQL Server instance. After control returns to the second procedure, the second procedure attempts to log in again with SQL Server authentication by invoking the *Resume* method. If this second attempt fails, it can generate an error number of −2147203048. This number is consistent with the error generated by a bad password. Therefore, the procedure updates the password for the sa account by calling the *AssignNewPassword* procedure. Then the second procedure passes the server name and the string value for the new password. When control returns from the called procedure, the second procedure tries to connect again to the local server. If this attempt succeeds, the procedure exits normally. Otherwise, you get another error, and the procedure writes a message to the Immediate window. (For example, the Connect method can fail because of a faulty physical connection.)

```
Sub CallAddSQLServerAuthentication()
Dim srvName As String

'Specify server name
srvName = "(local)"

'Pass server name
AddSQLServerAuthentication srvName

End Sub

Sub AddSQLServerAuthentication(srvName As String)
On Error GoTo SQLAuth_Trap
Dim srv1 As SQLDMO.SQLServer
Dim NewPassword As String

'Override assigned password, if you prefer
NewPassword = "password"

'Attempt to log in with sa and assigned password
Set srv1 = New SQLDMO.SQLServer
srv1.Connect srvName, "sa", NewPassword

SQLAuth_Exit:
srv1.DisConnect
Set srv1 = Nothing
Exit Sub

SQLAuth_Trap:
Select Case Err.Number
    Case -2147203052
'If no trusted connection, enable
'SQL Server authentication
        WindowsToMixedAuthentication srvName
        Resume
    Case -2147203048
'If sa login fails, set password for sa to password
        AssignNewPassword srvName, NewPassword
        Resume
    Case Else
        Debug.Print Err.Number, Err.Description
End Select

'Clean up objects
srv1.DisConnect
Set srv1 = Nothing

End Sub
```

The *WindowsToMixedAuthentication* procedure opens a connection using Windows authentication to the server named in the argument passed to it. This permits the *Connection* method to succeed even when SQL Server authentication is not in place. Next, the procedure sets the *SecurityMode* property to *SQLDMOSecurity_Mixed*. This property assignment applies to the *IntegratedSecurity* object instead of the *SQLServer* object. This assignment denotes mixed authentication to permit connections with logins authenticated by either SQL Server or Windows. Two other possible *SecurityMode* property settings include *SQLDMOSecurity_Integrated* for Windows authentication and *SQLDMOSecurity_Normal* for exclusive SQL Server authentication.

> **Note** Developers who are familiar with Enterprise Manager might be pleased to discover that SQL-DMO provides more flexibility for authentication than does the Security tab of the Database Server Properties dialog box. SQL-DMO offers three valid authentication modes, whereas the Security tab of the Database Server Properties dialog box exposes just two possible choices for setting authentication mode.

Just making the property assignment does not enforce the setting. You must stop and restart the server for the setting to become active. This involves several steps, which the balance of the procedure manages. The trickiest of these steps is the loop after the invocation of the *Stop* method. When your code issues the *Stop* method, the SQL server does not instantly stop. Therefore, trying to restart the computer can result in a situation in which your code attempts to restart a server that's still running, which causes a run-time error. The *Status* property of the *SQLServer* object can detect when a server stops. After issuing the *Stop* method, the procedure loops until the server's *Status* property indicates that the procedure responded completely to the invocation of the method. Next, the procedure restarts the server. This is essential if you plan to use the server any further because SQL-DMO cannot use the *Connect* method to connect to a stopped server.

```
Sub WindowsToMixedAuthentication(srvName As String)
Dim srv1 As SQLDMO.SQLServer

'Instantiate a SQLServer object and connect
'using integrated security
Set srv1 = New SQLDMO.SQLServer
srv1.LoginSecure = True
srv1.Connect srvName
```

```
'Set security mode to mixed Windows/SQL Server
'authentication
srv1.IntegratedSecurity.SecurityMode = _
    SQLDMOSecurity_Mixed
srv1.DisConnect

'Invoke command to stop server and wait
'until it stops
srv1.Stop
Do Until srv1.Status = SQLDMOSvc_Stopped
Loop

'Restart server with SecurityMode setting
srv1.Start True, srvName

'Clean up objects
srv1.DisConnect
Set srv1 = Nothing

End Sub
```

The *AssignNewPassword* procedure takes as many as three arguments, but it only requires two: the server name and the string for the new password. The third password is the login account name. This is an optional argument with a default value of *sa*. This value will automatically change the password for the sa login unless the calling procedure explicitly specifies another login. Because the *AddSQLServerAuthentication* procedure does not change the password, the *AssignNewPassword* procedure sets the sa password to *password*.

```
Sub AssignNewPassword(srvName As String, _
    NewPassword As String, _
    Optional lgnName As String = "sa")
Dim srv1 As SQLDMO.SQLServer

'Instantiate a SQLServer object, and connect
'using integrated security
Set srv1 = New SQLDMO.SQLServer
srv1.LoginSecure = True
srv1.Connect srvName

'Assign new password to login
srv1.Logins(lgnName).SetPassword "", NewPassword

 'Clean up objects
srv1.DisConnect
Set srv1 = Nothing

End Sub
```

Without much comment, I give you two other utility procedures for managing security mode and password. I found these utilities useful while developing the preceding sample, and you might find them useful for other purposes. The first utility procedure has the name *MixedToWindowsAuthentication*. It does what its name implies. The second procedure, *BlankPasswordForsa*, assigns a blank password to the sa login for the local SQL server. Although you definitely should not run a production system with a blank password for sa, some developers find it convenient to build an application with at least one account that has no password.

> **Note** If you are going to run a SQL server with an sa login that has no password, you should restrict the connectivity of the server so that it exists on a network that is not accessible from the Internet. The best practice is to always assign a password to the sa login.

```
Sub MixedToWindowsAuthentication()
Dim srv1 As SQLDMO.SQLServer

'Assign whatever server name you like;
'default is (local)
srvName = "(local)"

'Instantiate a SQLServer object, and connect
'using integrated security
Set srv1 = New SQLDMO.SQLServer
srv1.LoginSecure = True
srv1.Connect srvName

'Set security mode to mixed Windows/SQL Server
'authentication
srv1.IntegratedSecurity.SecurityMode = SQLDMOSecurity_Integrated
srv1.DisConnect

'Invoke command to stop server and wait
'until it stops
srv1.Stop
Do Until srv1.Status = SQLDMOSvc_Stopped
Loop

'Restart server with mixed security
srv1.Start True, srvName

'Clean up objects
```

```
    srv1.DisConnect
    Set srv1 = Nothing

End Sub

Sub BlankPasswordForsa()
Dim NewPassword As String
Dim lgnName As String

NewPassword = ""

AssignNewPassword "(local)", NewPassword

End Sub
```

Building a SQL Server Object Navigator

Because of its hierarchical design, SQL-DMO is particularly convenient for enumerating the objects within a database. An earlier sample showed how to enumerate the databases on a server to the Immediate window. This is easy to do with SQL-DMO because the *Databases* collection is hierarchically dependent on the server. You also can enumerate the tables, views, stored procedures, and user-defined functions within a database easily because collections for these objects are hierarchically dependent on a database. The next sample shows how to do this with a custom Access form.

Figure 13-3 shows an Access form, *frmSQLObjectNavigator*, that illustrates one approach to browsing the database objects on the local server. When the form opens, it automatically displays the names of the databases on the local SQL server in its first list box. Users can display the names of tables, views, stored procedures, and user-defined functions on the local SQL server in the last list box by following three steps. First, select a database name from the list box on the left. Second, click an option button to select a type of object from the option group control. Third, click the button above the list box on the right. The second step is optional because the form automatically selects Tables as the default database object type. However, users must select a database name for the browser to return the names of an object type in a database.

The form's layout has three critical input controls and one critical output control. I added the first and last list boxes without using the Controls Wizard. The only customization I performed was the sizing and positioning of the list boxes. Event procedures behind the form set the sources for both list boxes. The first list box, lstDBs, is an input control because a user must make a selection from it. The last box, lstDBObjects, is an output control that displays the objects on the local server when a user clicks the button above it. The opgDBObjectTypes option group control always displays the same four objects, so I used the Controls Wizard for its design. However, I chose not to select a default value when building the control. This is because the sample application uses an event procedure behind the form to assign a default value to the control. By making the assignment in the event procedure, your application can adjust the default setting for the option group control along with any other desired settings. The last critical control is the command button above lstDBObjects. A click to the cmdRefreshList command button updates the display in lstDBObjects according to the values of lstDBs and opgDBObjectTypes.

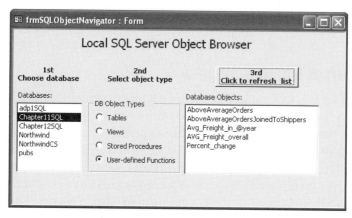

Figure 13-3   An Access form that lets a user browse selected database objects on the local SQL server.

With just two short event procedures, you can manage the contents of the controls. However, the event procedures rely on two function procedures in Module1 of the VBA project for the Access project with the samples for this chapter (Chapter13.adp).

> **Note**   Chapter13.adp connects to the Chapter11SQL database created in Chapter 11. The Access project needs this connection in order for code samples that draw on the *Connection* property of the *Current-Project* object (*CurrentProject.Connection*) to point at the right database. Alternatively, you can update these samples with explicit *Connection* objects pointing at the Chapter11SQL database.

The *Form_Open* event procedure (shown next) performs three main tasks. First, it populates the *lstDBs* control by setting its *RowSourceType* and

RowSource properties. Notice that the *RowSourceType* property is set to "Value List". The procedures makes this assignment because it sets the *RowSource* property for *lstDBs* to the return value for the *LoginSecureandListDBs2* function. This function takes a single argument, the name of a server. It returns a semicolon-delimited list of names for the databases on the server specified in its argument. This is a valid format for a *RowSourceType* property setting of Value List. Second, the *Form_Open* event procedure assigns a value of 1 to the *opgDBObjectTypes* control. You can change this value to 2, 3, or 4, which respectively designate views, stored procedures, and user-defined functions. Finally, the *Form_Open* event procedure performs some minor formatting to remove form display elements for data selection and record navigation—functions that do not apply to this form.

Note   The module behind the *frmSQLObjectNavigator* form declares *srvName* at the module level. This makes the *srvName* variable available in both the *Form_Open* and *cmdRefreshList_Click* event procedures. In this application, when the *Form_Open* event procedure assigns a value to the variable, the *cmdRefreshList_Click* event procedure can access the variable's value without the need for a passed argument.

```
Private Sub Form_Open(Cancel As Integer)

'Populate database object list box with
'names of databases on local server
Me.lstDBs.RowSourceType = "Value List"
srvName = "(local)"
Me.lstDBs.RowSource = LoginSecureAndListDBs2(srvName)

'Set Tables as the default database type
opgDBObjectTypes = 1

'Perform selected minor formatting
Me.NavigationButtons = False
Me.RecordSelectors = False
Me.DividingLines = False

End Sub
```

The Click event procedure for the *cmdRefreshList* command button performs just two tasks. First, it checks the value of *lstDBs*. The sample requires the user to make a selection from the first list box. If the user does not make this selection, the attempt to develop a list of objects within a database can generate a run-time error. When the event procedure doesn't detect a selection, it prints a message reminding the user to make this selection and exits before the command generates the error. Second, the procedure uses the *DBObjectsList* function in Module1 to populate the *RowSource* property for the *lstDBObjects* control. The function procedure returns a semicolon-delimited list of objects based on the selections for database name and object type from the local server.

```
Private Sub cmdRefreshList_Click()

'Abort if user did not select a database
If IsNull(Me.lstDBs) Then
    MsgBox "Please select a database before " & _
        "attempting to list the objects within it.", _
        vbInformation, _
        "Programming Microsoft Access 2003"
    Exit Sub
End If


'Populate database object list box based on
'server name, database name, and object type
Me.lstDBObjects.RowSourceType = _
    "Value List"
Me.lstDBObjects.RowSource = _
    DBObjectList(srvName, lstDBs, opgDBObjectTypes)

End Sub
```

LoginSecureAndListDBs2 is an adaptation of a procedure described earlier in this section that had the same name except for the trailing 2. The adaptation uses a function procedure format instead of the sub procedure format of the earlier version. There are two additional distinctions between the two procedures. This version of the procedure uses the *SystemObject* property to exclude system databases. This prevents users from browsing the objects in system databases such as the master database. Exposing the contents of the master database without a specific need is not recommended. Also, the function procedure constructs its return value in a format suitable for the *RowSource* property to a list box with a Value List *RowSourceType* setting. This simply involves appending a trailing semicolon and a space to each database name. After passing through the list of databases on the server, the procedure clips off the last semicolon and space by using the *Left* function.

```
Function LoginSecureAndListDBs2(srvName As String) As String
Dim srv1 As SQLDMO.SQLServer
Dim dbs1 As SQLDMO.Database
```

```
'Instantiate a SQLServer object, and connect
'using integrated security
Set srv1 = New SQLDMO.SQLServer
srv1.LoginSecure = True
srv1.Connect srvName

'Store delimited names of databases in function
For Each dbs1 In srv1.Databases
    If dbs1.SystemObject = False Then
        LoginSecureAndListDBs2 = _
            LoginSecureAndListDBs2 & dbs1.Name & "; "
    End If
Next dbs1

'Strip trailing delimiter
LoginSecureAndListDBs2 = _
    Left(LoginSecureAndListDBs2, _
        Len(LoginSecureAndListDBs2) - 2)

'Clean up objects
srv1.DisConnect
Set srv1 = Nothing

End Function
```

The *DBObjectList* function procedure appears next. This procedure returns a semicolon-delimited list of database objects based on the database name and object type selected in the *frmSQLObjectNavigator* form shown in Figure 13-3. The argument list accepts the value of the *opgDBObjectTypes* control as *bytObjectType*, which has a *Byte* data type declaration. This procedure begins by making a selection to the server name passed to it. The sample's *Form_Open* event procedure designates the local server, but you can change the code to reference another server. When you change the assignment in the *Form_Open* event procedure, it automatically affects the *DBObjectList* and *LoginSecureAndListDBs2* function procedures.

The heart of the *DBObjectList* procedure is a *Select Case* statement that has a separate case for each of the four values that the *opgDBObjectTypes* control can return. When I created the *opgDBObjectTypes* control, I set these values to 1 through 4. If you change the Option button control settings within the option group control so that they return other values, be sure to update the *Case* values accordingly.

When the *opgDBObjectTypes* control equals 1 in the sample, the procedure enumerates the user-defined *Tables* collection within the database name selected on the form. If the *opgDBObjectTypes* control value is either 2 or 3, the procedure enumerates user-defined views or stored procedures, respectively.

The code for enumerating views and stored procedures must exclude some object names that begin with ~TMPCLP. Although SQL Server generates objects with this prefix for its own internal use, it considers such objects user defined.

An *opgDBObjectTypes* control value of 4 causes the code to enumerate user-defined functions. SQL Server 2000 is the first version of SQL Server to introduce this object class. Therefore, SQL-DMO must use the *Database2* object as opposed to the default *Database* object used for the other object collections. The declaration for *dbs2* at the beginning of the procedure illustrates the syntax for an object reference to the new *Database2* object class. The code for the clause when the *Case bytObjectType* value equals 4 illustrates how to use this object to enumerate the user-defined functions in a database.

```
Function DBObjectList(srvName As String, _
    DBname As String, _
    bytObjectType As Byte) As String
Dim tbl1 As SQLDMO.Table
Dim vew1 As SQLDMO.View
Dim spr1 As SQLDMO.StoredProcedure
Dim dbs2 As SQLDMO.Database2
Dim udf1 As SQLDMO.UserDefinedFunction

'Instantiate a SQLServer object, and connect
'using integrated security
Set srv1 = New SQLDMO.SQLServer
srv1.LoginSecure = True
srv1.Connect srvName

'Pass back from function-delimited object names function.
'All objects used are available with Databases collection
'(default of SQL Server 7), except for UserDefinedFunctions,
'which require a Database2 object.
Select Case bytObjectType
    Case 1
        For Each tbl1 In srv1.Databases(DBname).Tables
            If tbl1.SystemObject = False Then
                DBObjectList = _
                    DBObjectList & tbl1.Name & "; "
            End If
        Next tbl1
    Case 2
        For Each vew1 In srv1.Databases(DBname).Views
            If vew1.SystemObject = _
                False And Left(vew1.Name, 7) <> "~TMPCLP" Then
                DBObjectList = _
                    DBObjectList & vew1.Name & "; "
            End If
```

```
            Next vew1
        Case 3
            For Each spr1 In srv1.Databases(DBname).StoredProcedures
                If spr1.SystemObject = _
                    False And Left(spr1.Name, 7) <> "~TMPCLP" Then
                    DBObjectList = _
                        DBObjectList & spr1.Name & "; "
                End If
            Next spr1
        Case 4
            Set dbs2 = srv1.Databases(DBname)
            For Each udf1 In dbs2.UserDefinedFunctions
                If udf1.SystemObject = False Then
                    DBObjectList = _
                        DBObjectList & udf1.Name & "; "
                End If
            Next udf1
End Select

'Strip trailing delimiter
If DBObjectList <> "" Then
    DBObjectList = _
        Left(DBObjectList, _
        Len(DBObjectList) - 2)
Else
        DBObjectList = "None"
        Exit Function
End If

'Clean up objects
srv1.DisConnect
Set srv1 = Nothing

End Function
```

Copying a Table's Design from One Database to Another

If you become even moderately handy with SQL-DMO, you can get it to do your T-SQL programming for you. The following sample demonstrates how to use SQL-DMO to copy a table's design from one database to another. In this particular instance, the code copies the *Pic_Addresses* table initially created in Chapter 11. The sample re-creates the table in the database for this chapter's Access project by copying the T-SQL for the table from the Chapter11SQL database, editing it slightly, and then running the altered code in the current database. After the code generates a new table, the procedure next copies the data from the table in the other database. Although both Access projects and

SQL Server offer graphical means of achieving the same objectives, this code sample shows how to tightly integrate the functionality within applications that you program for clients.

The sample first opens a connection to the server with the database containing the table we plan to copy. In my environment, this is the CabSony1 server. You can use any server that maintains the database for Chapter 11 (Chapter11SQL.) If you haven't run the samples for creating the database and the *Pic_Addresses* table along with populating the table, now is a good time to do so. The code uses SQL Server authentication with the sa login and a password string of *password*. You can change the login style, login name, and password string to match the setup of your database server and the password for the sa login.

The trick to getting SQL-DMO to write the T-SQL syntax for a database object is to use the *Script* method. This method returns the T-SQL batch to re-create an object. *Script* automatically creates the T-SQL batch for any object to which you apply it. Unfortunately, the T-SQL batch ends with a GO command for Query Analyzer, a SQL Server client management tool we discussed in Chapter 11. To use the batch in a VBA module, we need to strip the trailing GO command, which appears in the last eight characters of the script. The following sample demonstrates the use of this technique for the *Pic_Addresses* table in the Chapter11SQL database. After editing the script, this sample removes any prior version of the *Pic_Addresses* table from the current database. Then it runs the edited T-SQL statement for creating a new copy of the *Pic_Addresses* table. Notice that the procedure uses an ADO *Connection* object to execute the T-SQL strip. Chapter 11 demonstrated and described this technique.

After creating the table based on the script, you're left with an empty table. The next step is to populate the table with data from the original table in the other database, Chapter11SQL. An *INSERT INTO* statement can facilitate this. Use a *SELECT* statement instead of a *VALUES* list as the source for the data to insert. In the *FROM* clause of the *SELECT* statement, specify the table in the source database. After constructing the string, the sample invokes the statement with an ADO *Connection* object.

```
Sub CreatePic_Addresses()
Dim srv1 As SQLDMO.SQLServer
Dim str1 As String
Dim cnn1 As ADODB.Connection
Dim int1 As Integer
#Const PrintScript = True

'Assign server name
srvName = "CabSony1"
```

```
'Make connection to remote server
Set srv1 = New SQLDMO.SQLServer
srv1.Connect srvName, "sa", "password"

'Copy, optionally print, and edit script for table
str1 = srv1.Databases("Chapter11SQL"). _
    Tables("Pic_Addresses").Script
#If PrintScript Then
    Debug.Print str1
#End If
int1 = Len(str1) - 8
str1 = Left(str1, int1)

'Execute edited script for table;
'drop prior version of table, if necessary
Set cnn1 = CurrentProject.Connection
Drop_a_table cnn1, "Pic_Addresses"
cnn1.Execute str1

'Insert descriptions and addresses from Pic_addresses
'in Chapter11SQL database on CabSony1 server
str1 = "INSERT INTO Pic_Addresses " & _
    "SELECT Pic_description, Pic_address " & _
    "FROM Chapter11SQL.dbo.Pic_Addresses"
cnn1.Execute str1

'Refresh Database window to show new table
RefreshDatabaseWindow

'Clean up objects
srv1.DisConnect
Set srv1 = Nothing

End Sub

Sub Drop_a_table(cnn1 As ADODB.Connection, TableName As String)
Dim str1 As String

'Delete the table if it exists already
str1 = "IF EXISTS (SELECT TABLE_NAME " & _
    "FROM INFORMATION_SCHEMA.TABLES " & _
    "WHERE TABLE_NAME = '" & TableName & "') " & _
    "DROP TABLE " & TableName
cnn1.Execute str1

End Sub
```

If you want to populate the table with new data, you'll need a slightly different version of the VBA procedure to create *Pic_Addresses*. This alternate version will still use the *Script* method to derive the T-SQL for the *Pic_Addresses* table. However, the alternate procedure uses a simple *VALUES* list, as in the samples shown in Chapter 11. The alternate procedure, *CreatePic_Addresses2*, appears in Chapter13.adp, which is with the companion content for this book.

As I developed this sample, it was useful to scan the end of the T-SQL batch statement generated by the *Script* method. In particular, I needed to examine the characters toward the end of the method's return value. The following pair of procedures demonstrates one approach to printing an index number and a string value for each of the last 50 characters in the string returned from the *Script* method. You can use this code sample to verify the number of characters to cut from the end of the *Script* method's return value. You can easily adapt this code sample to examine any number of characters at the end of any string.

```
Sub CallTrailingCharactersInString()
Dim srv1 As SQLDMO.SQLServer
Dim str1 As String

'Assign server name
srvName = "CabSony1"

'Make connection to remote server with sa login
Set srv1 = New SQLDMO.SQLServer
srv1.Connect srvName, "sa", "password"

'Copy script for table to str1
str1 = srv1.Databases("Chapter11SQL"). _
    Tables("Pic_Addresses").Script

'Print trailing 50 characters in table script
TrailingCharactersInString str1, 50

'Clean up objects
srv1.DisConnect
Set srv1 = Nothing

End Sub

Sub TrailingCharactersInString(str1 As String, _
    bytCharacters As Byte)
Dim int1 As Integer
Dim int2 As Integer
```

```
int1 = Len(str1)

'Print bytCharacter trailing characters in str1
For int2 = 1 To int1
    If (int1 - int2) <= bytCharacters Then _
        Debug.Print int2, Mid(str1, int2, 1)
Next int2

Debug.Print "Total number of characters in str1: " & int1

End Sub
```

Attaching and Detaching Database Files

Attaching and detaching database files is a flexible way to transfer databases between different SQL servers. Chapter 12 describes how to attach a database file (actually, an .mdf file) with manual techniques based on the Database menu for an Access project. Because this is an administrative function, SQL-DMO also offers good support for this kind of activity. In fact, you can easily automate working with sets of files. This section starts with a pair of samples for attaching and detaching individual files. Then it moves on to manipulate a set of database files all at once.

> **Note**   T-SQL also offers support for managing the attaching and detaching of database files. For example, see the "sp_attach_db" topic in Books Online.

The following pair of procedures shows how to attach a single SQL Server database file with an .mdf extension to the local server. Access developers are used to thinking of an .mdb file as a database. However, with SQL Server, the database file is not visible until you attach it to a server. Once you do, users interact with the database by addressing the server. They never have direct access to the file as is common with Access file-server applications.

The sample's first procedure specifies the database name and the .mdf file name. Then it passes this information to the *AttachADB* procedure. This second procedure starts by making a connection to the local server. Then it invokes the *SQLServer* object's *AttachDB* method. This method requires a function specification in which you set the function's return value to a string.

```
Sub CallAttachADB()
Dim DBName As String
Dim MdfFilePath As String

'Specify database name and filepath to .mdf
DBName = "adp4SQL"
MdfFilePath = "C:\Access11Files\Chapter13\adp4sql.mdf"
AttachADB DBName, MdfFilePath

End Sub

Sub AttachADB(DBName As String, MdfFilePath)
Dim srv1 As New SQLDMO.SQLServer
Dim str1 As String

'Connect to local server
srv1.LoginSecure = True
srv1.Connect "(local)"

'Attach database with passed arguments
str1 = srv1.AttachDB(DBName, MdfFilePath)

End Sub
```

The *AttachDB* method is very flexible. For example, its argument list can optionally include a log file with an .ldf extension. If the database spans multiple operating system files, you can specify up to 16 files for it. You can also use this method to attach database files to a server other than the one on your workstation.

Detaching a database file is even easier than attaching one. First, use the *DetachDB* method for a server. Then specify the name of the databases on the server. The following code shows a sample that detaches adp4SQL from the local server:

```
Sub CallDetachADB()
Dim DBName As String

'Specify database name
DBName = "adp4SQL"
DetachADB DBName

End Sub

Sub DetachADB(DBName As String)
Dim srv1 As New SQLDMO.SQLServer

srv1.LoginSecure = True
srv1.Connect "(local)"
```

```
srv1.DetachDB (DBName)
End Sub
```

If you're attaching a file to another database, it's common to derive the file by detaching it from another server. You cannot copy or move a database file until you first detach it from a server. After processing a database file for use on another server (for example, to make a copy of it), you can reattach the original .mdf file to the server from which you detached it.

Attaching and Detaching Multiple Files

The *AttachDB* method can be particularly handy when you want to attach a set of database files between servers on the same or a different computer. After detaching the files that you need from a server, copy the .mdf file for each database to a destination folder. Then reattach the original files to their server. The "Opening an Access Project for an .mdf File" sidebar and the reference to it in the "Creating a Form Based on a Table with One Click" section of Chapter 12 describe a manual approach for opening an Access project connected to the database corresponding to an .mdf file. The process described in the sidebar creates a database on a server for the .mdf file. You can repeat this process manually for each .mdf file for which you want to create a corresponding database on a server. This section includes a sample for attaching and detaching a set of files programmatically.

The next sample consists of a couple of procedures that demonstrate how to attach multiple .mdf files from a target folder. The first procedure requires a reference to the Microsoft Scripting Runtime library. This procedure uses the library to facilitate looping through the files in a target folder, which in this case is the C:\Access11Files\Chapter13\ directory. For each .mdf file that the procedure discovers in the target folder, the sample creates a database name (DBName) based on the filename (less the extension). In addition, the procedure assigns a value to the *MdfFilePath* variable and the filename for the .mdf database file (including the extension). The second procedure in the sample is the *AttachADB* procedure discussed earlier. The sample calls this procedure once for each .mdf in the target folder.

```
'Requires Microsoft Scripting Runtime reference
Sub AttachDataFiles()
Dim fso1 As Scripting.FileSystemObject
Dim str1 As String
Dim fil1 As Scripting.File
Dim DBName As String
Dim MdfFilePath As String

'Set reference to FileSystemObject
```

(continued)

```
Set fso1 = New Scripting.FileSystemObject

'Loop through files in target folder
'attempt to attach .mdf files to local
'database server
str1 = "C:\Access11Files\Chapter13\"
For Each fil1 In fso1.GetFolder(str1).Files
    If fil1.Type = "Database File" And _
        Right(fil1.Name, 3) <> "ldf" Then
        DBName = Left(fil1.Name, Len(fil1.Name) - 4)
        MdfFilePath = str1 & fil1.Name
        AttachADB DBName, MdfFilePath
    End If
Next fil1

End Sub
```

The code in the preceding sample excludes the processing of files with an .ldf extension in the target folder. This is purely a convenience for the sample. As mentioned in the preceding section, the *AttachDB* method can process multiple types of database files, including .ldf files. This requires that your application pass the method a SQL-DMO multistring with the names of all files comprising the database. See the "Using SQL-DMO Multistrings" topic in Books Online for instruction on how to work with multistrings.

You can also automatically detach a collection of databases. The sample that demonstrates an approach to the detaching process also serves as a sample for attaching a set of files; the difference is that you repeatedly invoke *DetachADB* instead of the *AttachADB* procedure. Because the process is so similar to attaching multiple database files, refer to Module1 of the Chapter13.adp file for the program listing. The sample procedure has the name *DetachDatabaseFiles*.

Programming Login and User Accounts

SQL Server has a different security model than the one covered for Jet databases in Chapter 10. In addition, the Access project UI changed from Access 2000 to Access 2003 to remove some screens for manually controlling SQL Server security. As a consequence, the programmatic solutions for managing SQL Server security are more important than ever.

There are at least two programmatic interfaces for managing SQL Server security. The first of these is T-SQL. Using T-SQL to administer SQL Server security is often straightforward because T-SQL includes many commands tailored for managing security. In addition, Books Online offers numerous detailed samples that illustrate the use of T-SQL for programming database security. SQL-DMO, a hierarchical programming language for SQL Server, is another programmatic interface you can use to manage SQL Server security. Your experience with the Office hierarchical models transfers readily to SQL-DMO programming of SQL Server security. This section emphasizes SQL-DMO programming, but it includes some examples of T-SQL programming as well.

SQL Server security is a huge topic. The goal of this section is to acquaint you with selected SQL Server security issues. Once you have this foundation, you can advance your knowledge of the topic as much as your circumstances warrant.

Setting Up the SQL Server Security Demonstrations

This book's presentation of SQL Server security programming techniques relies on a new database, SecurityDemo1, which has a pair of tables, *Pic_Addresses* and *Employees*. This simple database design will help you understand the basics of security programming. The security code samples all operate from the Access project for this chapter. These samples demonstrate how to programmatically control the security for one database from an Access project connected to a second database. Chapter 10 showed the same kind of programming technique for Jet security.

Several heavily commented procedures in the Access project for this chapter create the SecurityDemo1 database and its two tables. The main procedure names are *CallCreateDBOnFilePath*, *CreatePic_Addresses3*, and *CreateEmployees*. These procedures borrow from and sometimes extend the programming methods presented in Chapter 11 and earlier in this chapter. Run *CallCreateDBOnFilePath* before either of the other two main procedures. *CallCreateDBOnFilePath* calls two others: one that drops a prior version of the SecurityDemo1 database if it exists, and another to create a new copy of the SecurityDemo1 database. When you run *CallCreateDBOnFile-Path*, make sure there are no active users for the SecurityDemo1 database, such as another Access project connected to the database. You can run the other two procedures in either order. They create the *Pic_Addresses* and *Employees* tables in the SecurityDemo1 database. The *CreatePic_Addresses3* procedure relies on the prior installation of the Chapter11SQL database on your server, and the *CreateEmployees* procedure requires that you have the Chapter12SQL database attached to your server.

The SecurityDemo1 database file is included with the companion content for this book. If you prefer, you can attach the sample procedures to your server instead of running them to create the sample security database with its tables.

Creating Login and User Accounts with SQL-DMO

Creating a new SQL Server user for a database requires several steps. First, you have to add a login account. This account permits an individual to log on to the server. SQL-DMO represents a login account with a *Login* object. This object is a member of the *Logins* collection that belongs to a *SQLServer* object. Second, you can create a user account for a database. This user account should reference the login account that you just created. SQL-DMO represents a user account with a *User* object. This object is a member of the *Users* collection that belongs to the *Database* object. Third, you can assign the user account to a database role. This lets the user account inherit the permissions assigned to the role by SQL Server (for fixed database roles) or you (for custom roles). SQL-DMO represents a database role with a *DatabaseRole* object. This object is a member of the *DatabaseRoles* collection that belongs to a *Database* object.

The following sample shows a general procedure for creating a new login account in a server with a corresponding user account in a database on the server. The procedure also makes the user a member in a fixed database role. You must supply five arguments to target the procedure's behavior. The *srvName* argument designates the server for the login account. The *dbsName* argument specifies the database name for the user account. The *lgnName* and *usrName* arguments designate the names for the login and user accounts. The *dbrName* argument is the name of a database role. The procedure makes the user account a member of this role.

The procedure has a main flow and an error trap flow. After creating a *SQLServer* object that points at the server named *srvName*, the procedure's main flow immediately attempts to remove a prior user account with the name of *usrName* and a prior login account with the name *lgnName*. The error flow accounts for various run-time errors that can occur when you attempt to remove a *Login* or a *User* object. For example, the object might not exist.

The procedure starts to create a new login account by instantiating a login object (*lgn1*). Then it assigns a name to the object. Unless you explicitly specify otherwise, all logins have a SQL Server standard type by default. This type property is for SQL Server authentication. Two other login *Type* property settings can designate a login for Windows NT authentication. The sample invokes the *SetPassword* method to assign the login a password equal to the string password. You can override this default password in the procedure. Regardless of whether you change this password, users can change it once you make the login account available to them. For example, users can invoke the Tools, Security, Set Login Password command in an Access project to change their password. After designating the login properties, the code adds the new *Login* object to the *Logins* collection for the server instantiated at the start of the procedure.

> **Note**   If you change the password setting for the login in this proce-
> dure, you should revise it in the other procedures (discussed next) that
> reference it.

Next, the procedure moves on to creating a new user account. The procedure begins this process by instantiating a new *User* object. The next two lines
of code assign a name property to the user and associate the user with a login,
which is the login just created. After specifying these core user properties, the
procedure appends the *User* object to the *Users* collection for the database
named in *dbsName*.

The procedure's final step before exiting is to add the new user to a database role. This step lets the user inherit the permissions that belong to the role.
The *AddMember* method of the *DatabaseRole* object enables the assignment of
a user to a role. The argument takes a string with the name of the user that it
adds to a role.

```
Sub AddLoginAndUserToDBRole(srvName As String, _
    dbsName As String, _
    lgnName As String, _
    usrName As String, _
    dbrName As String)
On Error GoTo AddLogin_Trap
Dim srv1 As SQLDMO.SQLServer
Dim lgn1 As SQLDMO.Login
Dim usr1 As SQLDMO.User
Dim cnn1 As ADODB.Connection

'Instantiate a SQLServer object, and connect
'using integrated security
Set srv1 = New SQLDMO.SQLServer
srv1.LoginSecure = True
srv1.Connect srvName

'Remove prior user and login accounts, if they exist,
'by first removing user object and then removing
'login object
srv1.Databases(dbsName).Users(usrName).Remove
srv1.Logins(lgnName).Remove

'Add login by instantiating a login object, giving it a
'name, assigning it a default database, setting its
'password, and adding it to a server's Logins collection
```

(continued)

```
    Set lgn1 = New SQLDMO.Login
    lgn1.Name = lgnName
    lgn1.SetPassword "", "password"
    srv1.Logins.Add lgn1

    'Add a user by instantiating it, giving it a name,
    'assigning a corresponding login, and adding it to
    'a database's Users collection
    Set usr1 = New SQLDMO.User
    usr1.Name = usrName
    usr1.Login = lgn1.Name
    srv1.Databases(dbsName).Users.Add usr1

    'Assign database permissions to user by adding
    'the user to fixed database role
    srv1.Databases(dbsName). _
        DatabaseRoles(dbrName).AddMember usr1.Name

AddLogin_Exit:
Set usr1 = Nothing
Set lgn1 = Nothing
srv1.DisConnect
Set srv1 = Nothing
Exit Sub

AddLogin_Trap:
If Err.Number = -2147199728 Then
'User does not exist
    Resume Next
ElseIf Err.Number = -2147206330 Then
'lngCanSelectOnly still logged on
    Set cnn1 = New ADODB.Connection
    cnn1.Open "Provider=sqloledb;Data Source=(local);" & _
        "Initial Catalog=SecurityDemo1; " & _
        "User Id=lgnCanSelectOnly;" & _

        "Password=password;"
    cnn1.Close
    Set cnn1 = Nothing
    Resume Next
ElseIf Err.Number = -2147200496 Then
'Login does not exist
    Resume Next
Else
    Debug.Print Err.Number, Err.Description
End If

End Sub
```

Testing User Accounts

The preceding sample, which was based on the *AddLoginAndUserToDBRole* procedure, needs another procedure to call it. At a minimum, this second procedure must supply values for the sample that creates the login and user accounts. The following sample accomplishes this, and it verifies the operation of a user account with membership in the db_datareader role. This role authorizes the ability to use a *SELECT* statement with any table or view in a database.

The sample procedure for this section, *TestSelectPermissionLogin*, performs several tasks. First, it invokes the *AddLoginAndUserToDBRole* procedure. Using the arguments passed to the procedure in the preceding sample, the code creates a login named *lgnCanSelectOnly* with a corresponding user named *usrCanSelectOnly*. The user belongs to the SecurityDemo1 database and is a member of the db_datareader fixed database role. It is common to name the user corresponding to a login with the same name as the login. However, using different names helps to highlight the unique role of the *Login* object and the *User* object in this sample.

After creating the login and user, the code starts to use them. It begins by making a connection to the SecurityDemo1 database on the local server. Notice that you use the value of *lgnName* (rather than *usrName*) for the user ID in the connection string. Next, the code opens a recordset with a T-SQL *SELECT* statement for the *Pic_Addresses* table. This is one of the two tables in the SecurityDemo1 database. To confirm the selection, the procedure prints the number of records in the *Pic_Addresses* table to the Immediate window. Then the procedure closes the recordset and connection before removing both of them from memory.

The success of the attempt to select from the *Pic_Addresses* table depends on the status of the *usrCanSelectOnly* user as a member of the db_datareader role. By dropping the *User* object from the role, you can invalidate an attempt by the *usrCanSelectOnly* user to select from the *Pic_Addresses* table. The next segment of code in *TextSelectPermissionLogin* drops the user from the db_datareader role and then tries to execute the T-SQL statement that previously succeeded. An inline error trap catches the error from the attempt to open the recordset. If the error is the one that points to a missing *SELECT* permission, the procedure opens a message box informing the user and suggesting she contact the DBA.

```
Sub TestSelectPermissionLogin()
Dim cnn1 As ADODB.Connection
Dim rst1 As ADODB.Recordset
Dim srv1 As SQLDMO.SQLServer
Dim srvName As String
```

(continued)

```
Dim dbsName As String
Dim lgnName As String
Dim usrName As String
Dim dbrName As String

'Create lgnName on srvName and usrName in dbsName
'with dbrName database role
srvName = "(local)"
dbsName = "SecurityDemo1"
lgnName = "lgnCanSelectOnly"
usrName = "usrCanSelectOnly"
dbrName = "db_datareader"
AddLoginAndUserToDBRole srvName, dbsName, _
    lgnName, usrName, dbrName

'Connect using lgnName login to dbsName database with
'password equal to password
Set cnn1 = New ADODB.Connection
cnn1.Open "Provider=sqloledb;Data Source=" & srvName & ";" & _
    "Initial Catalog=" & dbsName & "; " & _
    "User Id=" & lgnName & ";" & _
    "Password=password;"

'Open Pic_Addresses table and return record count
Set rst1 = New ADODB.Recordset
rst1.Open "SELECT * FROM Pic_Addresses", cnn1, _
    adOpenKeyset, adLockOptimistic, adCmdText
Debug.Print "Count of records is: " & rst1.RecordCount & _
    ".  Attempt to open succeeds when user belongs to " & _
    "db_datareader role."

'Close and remove from memory recordset and connection
rst1.Close
Set rst1 = Nothing
cnn1.Close
Set cnn1 = Nothing

'Instantiate a SQLServer object, and connect
'using integrated security; drop usrCanSelectOnly from
'db_datareader role for SecurityDemo1
srvName = "(local)"
Set srv1 = New SQLDMO.SQLServer
srv1.LoginSecure = True
srv1.Connect srvName
srv1.Databases(dbsName). _
    DatabaseRoles(dbrName).DropMember usrName
srv1.DisConnect
Set srv1 = Nothing
```

```
'Connect using lgnName login to dbsName database with
'password equal to password
Set cnn1 = New ADODB.Connection
cnn1.Open "Provider=sqloledb;Data Source=" & srvName & ";" & _
    "Initial Catalog=" & dbsName & "; " & _
    "User Id=" & lgnName & ";" & _
    "Password=password;"

'See if usrCanSelectOnly can select after it is removed
'from db_datareader role
Set rst1 = New ADODB.Recordset
On Error Resume Next
rst1.Open "SELECT * FROM Pic_Addresses", cnn1, _
    adOpenKeyset, adLockOptimistic, adCmdText

'Simple trap for no SELECT permission error
If Err.Number = -2147217911 Then
    MsgBox "No SELECT permission for Pic_Addresses " & _
    "table.  See DBA for assignment of SELECT permission " & _
    "to user account: usrCanSelectOnly.", vbCritical, _
    "Programming Microsoft Access 2003"
    Exit Sub
End If

End Sub
```

Creating Login and User Accounts with T-SQL

You need to invoke two T-SQL system stored procedures to create a new user in a database based on a SQL Server login. The *sp_addlogin* system stored procedure can add a login for accessing a SQL Server instance if you are invoking the procedure from a connection with a user ID that has authority to process security accounts, such as a login in the sysadmin fixed server role. The *sp_addlogin* has one required argument and a maximum number of six arguments. The required argument is *@loginame* (the argument name is not a typo; it is spelled with a single n), whose value names the login account created by the system stored procedure. The *@passwd* argument value is a password for the login. If you do not set this argument, then your new login has a null password. The *@defdb* argument sets the default database for the new login. The default database is the database to which an account connects immediately after connecting to a server. The samples in this chapter assign a user-defined database to the *@defdb* argument for a new login. The default value for this argument is the master database, which is a system-defined database that controls the operation of a SQL Server instance. Other *sp_addlogin* arguments allow you to manage more specialized features of logins. Again, you only have to set one argument (*@loginame*) for the *sp_addlogin* system stored procedure.

> **Note** A system stored procedure is a built-in stored procedure that SQL Server supplies for performing tasks. Chapter 11 describes how to create stored procedures from an Access project. These are user-defined stored procedures. System stored procedures are system-defined stored procedures. Since system stored procedures begin with an *sp_* prefix, it is good practice to avoid using this prefix as the name for your user-defined stored procedures.

After creating a login, you need to give it database access so that it will have a user account in a database. The *sp_grantdbaccess* system stored procedure performs this function. This procedure takes as many as two arguments, but if the user name is the same as the login name, then you can use a single argument to denote the user name. In addition, you do not have to explicitly designate argument names, you can just trail *sp_grantdbaccess* with the name of the user. When a user name is something other than the corresponding login name, you must explicitly specify both arguments with a comma delimiter. The *@loginame* argument denotes the login to which a user corresponds. The *@name_in_db* argument value denotes the user name. Specify *@loginame* before *@name_in_db*.

Just as adding a user takes two system stored procedures, so does removing a login with a user account in a database. In fact, the process of dropping a login can require more than two invocations of system stored procedures. T-SQL requires that you remove all user accounts corresponding to a login before you can successfully drop a login. Invoke the *sp_revokedbaccess* system stored procedure to remove each user account for a login that you want to drop. This procedure takes a single argument, which is the name of the user account that you want removed from a database. After removing all the user accounts in any database for a user, you can reference the *sp_droplogin* system stored procedure to eliminate a login from the security accounts for a database. As with the *sp_revokedbaccess* procedure, the *sp_droplogin* procedure requires just one argument. In this case, the argument is the name of the login to drop.

The following procedure listing for the *AddRemoveSQLUsers* VBA procedure illustrates an approach for applying the system stored procedures for managing login and user accounts with T-SQL. The declarations at the top of the procedure declare and instantiate *Connection* and *Recordset* objects. The VBA procedure performs two main tasks. First, it creates a login with a corresponding user account for the Northwind database. This is the database that provides a context for manipulating login and user accounts. Second, the VBA procedure removes the user and login accounts created in the first step. After each step, the procedure enumerates the user accounts in the Northwind database.

The *AddRemoveSQLUsers* procedure begins by declaring and instantiating *cnn1* as a *Connection* object and *rst1* as a *Recordset* object. Through the use of an *Open* method, the procedure points *cnn1* at the Northwind database with sa as the login. Because this login belongs to the sysadmin fixed server role, it can manipulate logins and users. The *Execute* method for a *Connection* object permits you to invoke a SQL statement. This method works for T-SQL as well as Jet SQL. You can construct a T-SQL statement to invoke a system stored procedure, such as *sp_addlogin*, by preceding the statement with the *EXEC* T-SQL keyword. After opening the *cnn1* object, the procedure listing shows the syntax for invoking the *sp_addlogin* system stored procedure to create a login named Access11User. Next, the code sample uses the same general approach to invoking the *sp_grantdbaccess* system stored procedure. This application of *sp_grantdbaccess* creates a user named Access11User. With the *sp_helpuser* system stored procedure, the sample generates a recordset based on the users in the Northwind database. The sample code enumerates these users by their login and user names. After listing the users in the Immediate window, the sample revokes the Access11User in the Northwind database and drops its corresponding login. To confirm the effect, the procedure again lists the users in the database. In the second listing of users, there are only two users as opposed to three immediately after the addition of the Access11User (see Figure 13-4).

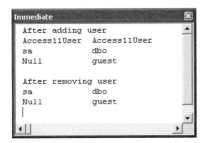

Figure 13-4   The Immediate window showing the users in the Northwind database after adding the Access11User and then removing the user.

```
Sub AddRemoveSQLUsers()

Dim cnn1 As New ADODB.Connection
Dim rst1 As New ADODB.Recordset
Dim str1 As String
```

(continued)

```
'Specify a connection for a database to which
'you want to grant the user access with a login
'that can manage logins
cnn1.Open "Provider=sqloledb;Data Source=(local);" & _
    "Initial Catalog=Northwind;" & _
    "User Id=sa; Password=password;"

'Create a SQL Server login
str1 = "EXEC sp_addlogin " & _
    "@loginame = 'Access11User', " & _
    "@passwd = 'password', " & _
    "@defdb = 'Northwind'"
cnn1.Execute str1

'Create a user for the login
str1 = "EXEC sp_grantdbaccess 'Access11User'"
cnn1.Execute str1

'Open a recordset of users for the database
'to which cnn1 points; print login and
'user names
rst1.Open "EXEC sp_helpuser", _
    cnn1, adOpenKeyset, adLockOptimistic
Debug.Print "After adding user"
Do Until rst1.EOF
    Debug.Print rst1("LoginName"), rst1("UserName")
    rst1.MoveNext
Loop

'Remove user and associate login added above
str1 = "EXEC sp_revokedbaccess 'Access11User' " & _
    "EXEC sp_droplogin @loginame = 'Access11User'"
cnn1.Execute str1

'Open a recordset of users for the database
'to which cnn1 points; print login and
'user names
rst1.Close
rst1.Open "EXEC sp_helpuser", _
    cnn1, adOpenKeyset, adLockOptimistic
Debug.Print vbLf & "After removing user"
Do Until rst1.EOF
    Debug.Print rst1("LoginName"), rst1("UserName")
    rst1.MoveNext
Loop

'Clean up objects
rst1.Close
```

```
Set rst1 = Nothing
cnn1.Close
Set cnn1 = Nothing

End Sub
```

Adding a login and user that map to a Windows user or Windows group follows a set of steps similar to that for adding a login and user that SQL Server manages. The sole difference is that you invoke the *sp_grantlogin* system stored procedure instead of the *sp_addlogin* system stored procedure. With *sp_grantlogin*, you can create a login for a Windows user or Windows group account. The *sp_grantlogin* system stored procedure takes a single argument, which is the name of the Windows account for the user or group. In the *AddRemoveWindowsUsers* procedure within Chapter13.adp, you can see the syntax for designating a Windows user or Windows group account. You must denote the account with a two-part name. Use a backslash (\) to delimit the parts. The first part denotes the server name, and the second part represents the user name or group name. In the *AddRemoveWindowsUsers* procedure, the argument CabSony1\PMA11 points at the PMA11 Windows user on the CabSony1 Windows server. After replacing the *sp_addlogin* with *sp_grantlogin*, the process for managing logins and users based on SQL Server logins versus Windows user and Windows group accounts is the same. Because the *AddRemoveWindowsUsers* procedure is nearly identical to the listing for the *AddRemoveSQLUsers* procedure, you can refer to Module1 in Chapter13.adp for the full listing for the *AddRemoveWindowsUsers* procedure. In order to run the *AddRemoveWindowsUsers* procedure, you will need to update the code to reflect your local Windows server and a Windows user account on it.

Programming Roles and Permissions

Roles are an easy way to manage permissions for logins and users. You can programmatically create custom roles and assign permissions to your custom roles. Then logins and users can inherit permissions from your custom roles just as they do when you add logins to fixed server roles and users to fixed database roles. This section presents three samples to illustrate techniques for managing role membership and permissions.

T-SQL Help for Roles

Two system stored procedures remind you about the different fixed server roles and their capabilities. The *sp_helpsrvrole* system stored procedure returns a list of the fixed server roles along with a brief description of each role. The *sp_srvrolepermission* stored procedure can return the server permissions associated with all the fixed server roles or with a specific one. You can run either stored procedure from the Create Text Stored Procedure template in an Access project or from a VBA procedure. It may be necessary to save and then open the procedures that you create before you can view the results sets generated by *sp_helpsrvrole* and *sp_srvrolepermission*. When you use a VBA procedure instead of the Create Text Stored Procedure template, you can run these two stored procedures from the *Command* object and then pass the result set to a *Recordset* object for display in the Immediate window or elsewhere in an Access application.

The following sample demonstrates the syntax for running both the *sp_helpsrvrole* and *sp_srvrolepermission* system stored procedures in a single VBA procedure. The output from this procedure is a convenient, top-level, detailed report documenting the functionality provided by each fixed server role. The procedure instantiates a command and then uses it to run a T-SQL statement that invokes the *sp_helpsrvrole* system stored procedure. After transferring the result to a recordset, the procedure loops through the recordset's rows to enumerate the fixed server names and descriptions. Next, the VBA procedure reuses the command and recordset to enumerate detailed permissions for the fixed server roles.

```
Sub SummarizeFixedServerRoles()
Dim cmd1 As ADODB.Command
Dim rst1 As ADODB.Recordset

'Instantiate a Command object and let it use
'the connection for the current project
Set cmd1 = New ADODB.Command
cmd1.ActiveConnection = CurrentProject.Connection

'Summarize fixed server roles
cmd1.CommandText = "Exec sp_helpsrvrole"
Set rst1 = New ADODB.Recordset
Set rst1 = cmd1.Execute
Debug.Print "Print Fixed Server Roles and Descriptions"
Do Until rst1.EOF
    Debug.Print rst1(0), rst1(1)
    rst1.MoveNext
Loop
Debug.Print String(2, vbCr)

'Provide detailed permissions
cmd1.CommandText = "EXEC sp_srvrolepermission"
Set rst1 = cmd1.Execute
Debug.Print "Print Fixed Server Roles and Permissions"
```

```
Do Until rst1.EOF
    Debug.Print rst1(0), rst1(1)
    rst1.MoveNext
Loop

'Clean up objects
rst1.Close
Set rst1 = Nothing
Set cmd1 = Nothing

End Sub
```

The next sample shows application of the same basic logic for documenting the fixed database roles. In this case, the *sp_helpdbfixedrole* system stored procedure enumerates the individual fixed database roles along with brief descriptions. The *sp_dbfixedrolepermission* system stored procedure lists the individual permission descriptions for each fixed database role. Because the names for the fixed database roles vary more in length than they do for fixed server roles, the code sample pads the end of the names with spaces so that the second column of descriptions aligns evenly across all fixed database role names.

```
Sub SummarizeFixedDBRoles()
Dim cmd1 As ADODB.Command
Dim rst1 As ADODB.Recordset

'Instantiate a Command object and let it use
'the connection for the current project
Set cmd1 = New ADODB.Command
cmd1.ActiveConnection = CurrentProject.Connection

'Summarize fixed database roles
cmd1.CommandText = "Exec sp_helpdbfixedrole"
Set rst1 = New ADODB.Recordset
Set rst1 = cmd1.Execute
Debug.Print "Print Fixed Database Roles and Descriptions"
Do Until rst1.EOF
    Debug.Print rst1(0) & _
        String(18 - Len(rst1(0)), " ") & rst1(1)
    rst1.MoveNext
Loop
Debug.Print String(2, vbCr)

'Provide detailed permissions
cmd1.CommandText = "EXEC sp_dbfixedrolepermission"
Set rst1 = cmd1.Execute
Debug.Print "Print Fixed Database Roles and Permissions"
Do Until rst1.EOF
```

(continued)

```
        Debug.Print rst1(0) & _
            String(18 - Len(rst1(0)), " ") & rst1(1)
        rst1.MoveNext
    Loop

    End Sub
```

Dynamically Adding Permissions to a User Account

Instead of sending a user to the DBA to get permission, you can dynamically add permissions to a user account when your application discovers that the account has insufficient permissions to perform some task. Of course, you need a login with appropriate fixed server role status to process the permissions you wish to assign. The next sample procedure, *DynamicallyAddUpdatePermission*, offers an approach to handling the dynamic assignment of a permission.

This sample starts by setting up the login and user accounts for *lgnName* and *usrName*. These accounts are endowed with *SELECT* permission for the tables in the SecurityDemo1 database. To this point, this code sample is similar to the *TestSelectPermissionLogin* procedure from the "Testing User Accounts" section in this chapter. The two procedures diverge after the invocation of the *Open* method for the recordset. This sample's code assigns a new value to the recordset value with the statement rst1(1) = "foo". At this point in the procedure, the change is still local. However, the *rst1.Update* statement alerts the server to the client application's desire to modify a value on the server.

The attempt to invoke the *Update* method generates a run-time error. This run-time error occurs because the *usrCanSelectOnly* user belongs to just one fixed database role, db_datareader. This role conveys *SELECT* permission for any table or view in a database, but the role does not authorize its members to update any record source. On the other hand, the db_datawriter role does grant the ability to modify any updatable record source tied to a SQL Server database. The remainder of the procedure lets the user know about the problem and provides the user with a way to dynamically add the *usrCanSelectOnly* user to the db_datawriter role.

This approach to dynamically adding a *User* object to a new database role starts just before the line of code that triggers the run-time error *rst1.Update*. Notice that the preceding line opens an inline error trap with an *On Error Resume Next* statement. The line after the attempt to update the record source is merely an *If...Then...Else...End If* statement. This statement permits the execution of the code within the block when the *Number* property value for the *Err* object matches the value of a run-time error resulting from an attempt to update a value without *UPDATE* permission. The code within the *Then* clause of the *If...Then...Else...End If* statement first presents an error message briefly explaining the problem in a message box. Then the code uses an *InputBox* function to ask for the secret word that will upgrade the user account to include the *UPDATE* permission. Users responding with the secret word *update* have the *usrCanSelectOnly User* object upgraded to include membership in the db_datawriter role. After this upgrade occurs, the procedure executes the *Update* method a second time just before printing a message about the success of the update. If a user does not reply to the prompt from the *InputBox* function with the correct secret word, the procedure tells him to get help from the DBA.

```
Sub DynamicallyAddUpdatePermission()
Dim cnn1 As ADODB.Connection
Dim rst1 As ADODB.Recordset
Dim str1 As String
Dim srv1 As SQLDMO.SQLServer
Dim srvName As String
Dim dbsName As String
Dim lgnName As String
Dim usrName As String
Dim dbrName As String
Dim str2 As String

'Create lgnName on srvName and usrName in dbsName
'with dbrName database role
srvName = "(local)"
dbsName = "SecurityDemo1"
lgnName = "lgnCanSelectOnly"
usrName = "usrCanSelectOnly"
dbrName = "db_datareader"
AddLoginAndUserToDBRole srvName, dbsName, _
    lgnName, usrName, dbrName

'Connect using lgnName login to dbsName database with
'password equal to password
Set cnn1 = New ADODB.Connection
cnn1.Open "Provider=sqloledb;Data Source=" & srvName & ";" & _
    "Initial Catalog=" & dbsName & "; " & _
    "User Id=" & lgnName & ";" & _
    "Password=password;"

'Attempt to update a table with a user account that has
'only SELECT permission
Set rst1 = New ADODB.Recordset
rst1.Open "SELECT * FROM Pic_Addresses", cnn1, _
    adOpenKeyset, adLockOptimistic, adCmdText
str1 = rst1(1)
Debug.Print rst1(1)
rst1(1) = "foo"
```

(continued)

```
'Setup to process error from attempt to update a table
'with a user account that has only SELECT permission
On Error Resume Next
rst1.Update
If Err.Number = -2147217911 Then
    MsgBox "No UPDATE permission for Pic_Addresses " & _
    "table.", vbCritical, _
    "Programming Microsoft Access Version 2003"
    str2 = InputBox("Do you know the secret word for UPDATE " & _
    "permission?", _
    "Programming Microsoft Access 2003", _
    "I don't know.")
    If str2 = "update" Then
'If user knows secret word, add permission to user account
'immediately and perform update
        srvName = "(local)"
        Set srv1 = New SQLDMO.SQLServer
        srv1.LoginSecure = True
        srv1.Connect srvName
        srv1.Databases("SecurityDemo1"). _
            DatabaseRoles("db_datawriter").AddMember _
            "usrCanSelectOnly"
        srv1.DisConnect
        Set srv1 = Nothing
        rst1.Update
        str2 = "Update from " & """" & str1 & """" & " to " & _
            """" & rst1(1) & """" & " succeeded."
        MsgBox str2, vbInformation, _
            "Programming Microsoft Access 2003"
    Else
'If user does not know the secret word, refer to DBA
        str2 = "Wrong secret word; see your DBA for " & _
            "UPDATE permission."
        MsgBox str2, vbCritical, _
            "Programming Microsoft Access 2003"
    End If
End If

End Sub
```

Selectively Applying Object Permissions

The db_datareader and db_datawriter roles, along with the other fixed database
roles, apply permissions indiscriminately to all database objects. However, it's
common for security needs to selectively apply to database objects. For example, a typical requirement is for users to be able to select from all tables—

except those containing salaries and other sensitive information. To accommodate this need, you must create user-defined roles with custom permissions for individual database objects.

The code in the next sample demonstrates how to set up a user-defined role and then add a user to it. This may or may not be sufficient for your security requirements. This is because user accounts can belong to multiple database roles. Therefore, if a user cannot accomplish a task with the permissions for one database role membership, that person might be able to succeed with membership in another database role. The syntax for creating a user-defined database role and assigning a new user will be the focus as I walk you through the sample code. You also will learn how to drop a user from a database role. The sample concludes by conditionally executing one of two *SELECT* query statements for a recordset. When the user takes the path associated with a value of *True* for the *UseWrongSelect* compiler constant, the program generates a runtime error but the other path leads to a normal exit. This sample demonstrates the behavior of user accounts based on roles and adds to the spectacle value of the outcome by not building an error trap for taking the wrong path.

The procedure starts by pointing a *SQLServer* object at the local server. Then the code instantiates a *DatabaseRole* object, gives it a name, and assigns the object to the *DatabaseRoles* collection for the database at which the *dbsName* string points. The new role's name is SelectEmployeesNotPics. After adding the *DatabaseRole* object, the procedure invokes the *Grant* method for the *Employees* table. With this method, the procedure adds a *SELECT* permission for the table to the SelectEmployeesNotPics database role. The sample references this role with *dbr1*. Next, the sample adds the *usrCanSelectOnly* user, represented by *usrName*, to the SelectEmployeesNotPics user-defined role. Notice that the *dbr1* role has no permission for the *Pic_Addresses* table.

Now the procedure is ready to start testing the security of the database. First, it opens a connection to the SecurityDemo1 database for the *usrCanSelectOnly* user. Then it uses the *Connection* object to open a recordset based on a *SELECT* query for the *Pic_Addresses* table. Although the SelectEmployeesNotPics database role grants *SELECT* permission for just the *Employees* table, the recordset for the *Pic_Addresses* table still opens. This is because the *usrCanSelectOnly* user belongs to the db_datareader role, which grants *SELECT* permission for all tables and views.

After successfully executing the *SELECT* query, the sample performs one more database definition. The next statement drops *usrCanSelectOnly* from the db_datareader role. This completes the steps necessary to restrict *usrCanSelectOnly SELECT* privileges to the *Employees* table. The final statement in the sample is a *#If...Then...#Else...#End If* statement that runs one of two recordset

Open method statements based on the value of the *UseWrongSelect* compiler constant. When the constant's value is *False*, as in the next sample, the procedure ends normally.

When you change the constant's value to *True*, the procedure can fail in a couple of ways that do not illustrate the impact of the compiler constant setting. For this reason, run the *DropSelectEmployeesNotPics* procedure after each execution of the following procedure. The *DropSelectEmployeesNotPics* procedure—the last sample procedure in the chapter—removes the SelectEmployeesNotPics role and restores the membership of the *usrCanSelectOnly* user in the db_datareader role. With these two fixes, the following procedure is ready to run again and show the effects of a changed compiler constant setting. When you run the procedure with a compiler constant of *True*, the procedure fails in the *Then* clause of the *#If…Then…#Else…#End If* statement because the code tries to run a *SELECT* query against the *Pic_Addresses* table.

```
'Run after DynamicallyAddUpdatePermission procedure so that
'usrCanSelectOnly has db_datareader and db_datawriter
'role memberships
Sub CreateDBRoleAndGrantSelectPermission()
Dim srvName As String
Dim dbsName As String
Dim lgnName As String
Dim usrName As String
Dim srv1 As SQLDMO.SQLServer
Dim dbr1 As SQLDMO.DatabaseRole
#Const UseWrongSelect = False

'Assign selected string names
srvName = "(local)"
dbsName = "SecurityDemo1"
lgnName = "lgnCanSelectOnly"
usrName = "usrCanSelectOnly"

'Connect to server
Set srv1 = New SQLDMO.SQLServer
srv1.LoginSecure = True
srv1.Connect srvName

'Instantiate, name, and add new custom database role
Set dbr1 = New SQLDMO.DatabaseRole
dbr1.Name = "SelectEmployeesNotPics"
srv1.Databases(dbsName).DatabaseRoles.Add dbr1

'Grant SELECT permission to the Employees table but not
'the Pic_Addresses table to dbr1 role, and add user
'account with usrName to dbr1 database role
```

```
srv1.Databases(dbsName).Tables("Employees"). _
    Grant SQLDMOPriv_Select, dbr1.Name
srv1.Databases(dbsName). _
    DatabaseRoles("SelectEmployeesNotPics"). _
    AddMember usrName

'Connect using lgnName login to dbsName database with
'password equal to password
Set cnn1 = New ADODB.Connection
cnn1.Open "Provider=sqloledb;Data Source=" & srvName & ";" & _
    "Initial Catalog=" & dbsName & "; " & _
    "User Id=" & lgnName & ";" & _
    "Password=password;"

'Attempt to select a table with a user account that belongs
'to the the db_datareader and db_datawrite roles
Set rst1 = New ADODB.Recordset
rst1.Open "SELECT * FROM Pic_Addresses", cnn1, _
    adOpenKeyset, adLockOptimistic, adCmdText

'Drop usrName user account from db_datareader role
srv1.Databases(dbsName). _
    DatabaseRoles("db_datareader"). _
    DropMember usrName

'If UseWrongSelect is True, click End on error message dialog box
#If UseWrongSelect = True Then
    Set rst1 = New ADODB.Recordset
    rst1.Open "SELECT * FROM Pic_Addresses", cnn1, _

        adOpenKeyset, adLockOptimistic, adCmdText
#Else
    Set rst1 = New ADODB.Recordset
    rst1.Open "SELECT * FROM Employees", cnn1, _
        adOpenKeyset, adLockOptimistic, adCmdText
#End If

End Sub


'Utility to restore security after running
'the CreateDBRoleAndGrantSelectPermission procedure
Sub DropSelectEmployeesNotPics()
Dim srv1 As SQLDMO.SQLServer

'Connect to server
Set srv1 = New SQLDMO.SQLServer
```

(continued)

```
    srv1.LoginSecure = True
    srv1.Connect "(local)"

    'Remove member, and then drop role
    srv1.Databases("SecurityDemo1"). _
        DatabaseRoles("SelectEmployeesNotPics"). _
        DropMember "usrCanSelectOnly"
    srv1.Databases("SecurityDemo1"). _
        DatabaseRoles("SelectEmployeesNotPics").Remove

    srv1.Databases("SecurityDemo1"). _
        DatabaseRoles("db_datareader"). _
        AddMember "usrCanSelectOnly"

End Sub
```

Summary

Building secure solutions is a vital activity for any database developer. Chapter 10 explores and demonstrates techniques for building secure Jet database solutions. This chapter does the same for SQL Server solutions. In addition, you learn about uses for SQL-DMO that extend beyond SQL Server security. In particular, the chapter presents a database and object explorer that lets a user explore databases and objects on the local SQL Server instance from an Access form. In addition, the chapter presents programmatic means for attaching and detaching databases via SQL-DMO. These techniques are convenient when you want to move databases from one computer to another.

14

Access Does the Web

For many businesses, computing over the Web is the way of the future. However, Web development techniques are often novel and unintuitive to typical Microsoft Access developers. Access 2003 addresses the need of Access developers to deliver powerful, full-featured Web applications in an easy and familiar development environment. Access 2003 offers rapid application development (RAD) techniques for the Web based on enhanced data access pages, the Microsoft Office 2003 Web Components, and FrontPage 2003. This chapter shows you how to tap into all these capabilities to create productive Web solutions.

After providing a brief overview of Web development techniques targeting the special needs of Access developers, this chapter introduces Microsoft FrontPage 2003. FrontPage 2003 integrates tightly with Office 2003, but it is not available as part of any Microsoft Office 2003 Editions (and must be purchased separately). FrontPage is a natural tool for managing the Web sites that make your Jet and SQL Server databases available to users. The chapter next presents step-by-step examples of graphical design techniques for creating forms and reports on a special kind of Web page known as a data access page. These forms and reports bind directly to Jet and Microsoft SQL Server databases. You'll learn how to make these forms and reports dynamic and interactive through the integrated development environment (IDE) behind them. Several samples in the chapter illustrate how to build event procedures with the IDE. Furthermore, you'll learn some easy ways to tackle advanced topics, such as programmatically creating Web-based forms and reports. Access 2003 enables you to create new Web-based forms and reports based on existing Access forms and reports.

Overview of Web Technologies

Access developers can readily build Web solutions with data access pages and Office Web Components. These two technologies assist you in creating Web solutions that share data with many users, but both have characteristics that make it better suited for particular scenarios. This section provides brief summaries of these technologies to help you evaluate which tools best meet the needs of your clients.

When building Web solutions with either of the technologies just mentioned, you will typically deploy files to a Web site where others can access them. FrontPage is a Web site management tool that ships with Office. It has a look and feel that resembles other Office components. Therefore, FrontPage enables Office users to readily contribute content to a Web site and developers with limited Web experience can serve as Web site administrators.

Data Access Pages

A data access page is a Web page with special ties to Access 2003. It makes available graphical tools for building Web solutions that resemble Access forms and reports. A Web solution can consist of one or more data access pages, or it can contain a mix of data access pages, other kinds of Web pages, and additional files, such as those with graphic images. In addition, you can publish some Access reports and forms as data access pages. This makes it possible to build a form or report in Access and then publish it as a data access page. Access also offers a programming environment that complements and extends the graphical development tools that make data access pages so easy to create solutions with.

You need to understand that, unlike Access forms and reports residing within Access database files and Access projects, a data access page is a stand-alone file. The Access Database window shows a *Pages* collection just like the *Forms* and *Reports* collections. However, the items in the Database window representing pages are links that point at external files.

Like forms, data access pages have two key views. Page view shows the data, if any, on the page. For example, if a page represents a form tied to a table, you can use the form to navigate the table records. You can also open a data access page in a browser by pointing the browser at the URL of the standalone file for the data access page. Design view reveals the objects within a data access page. These objects are controls, many of which are similar to those for forms, and other design objects for the data access page, such as a navigation bar. However, some of these controls are especially tailored for the Web environment. Both the Page view and Design view are available directly from the Database window. Just select the page name in the Database window, and click Open for the Page view or Design for the Design view. A third view, named Web Page Preview, is available from either of the first two views. Selecting this third view opens a browser session as a container for the data access page. This view shows a Web page designer exactly how the page looks in a browser. You can access the Web Page Preview from the standard View control on the toolbar.

The data access page format is different in Access 2000, Access 2002, and Access 2003. Therefore, you must upgrade the Access version on workstations if you want to open data access pages created with Access 2003 in Page view. You must install Office Web Components for Office 2003 if you want to view data access pages created with Access 2003 from Access 2000 or Access 2002 workstations. However, this upgrade does not permit you to open Access 2002 data access pages in Design view on a workstation running either Access 2000 or Access 2003. To gain that functionality, you must install Access 2003 as a part of Office 2003. You can have Access 2003 running simultaneously with Access 2000 and Access 2002 on the same workstation. These same version compatibility guidelines apply to Office Web Components discussed in the next section.

> **Note**   Office 2000, Office 2002, and Office 2003 can run side by side on a single computer, therefore, there is no need to upgrade solutions that work in a prior Office version so long as you have that version on a computer.

Office Web Components

There are four Office Web Components: the Data Source Control object, the Chart control, the PivotTable list control, and the Spreadsheet control. The Data Source Control object is the data engine behind data access pages. A separate ActiveX control implements each of the Office Web Components. You can use these components in isolation on Web pages or in combination. For example, one Web page can use the Data Source Control object to include a form based on data in a table. You can also use the Spreadsheet control to build a spreadsheet on the Web page that can create projections based on the data that displays in the form. And you can use the Chart control to create a chart on the page that can graph the projections in the spreadsheet.

The PivotTable list control mainly targets solutions for business decision analysts. Many business analysts are already familiar with PivotTable reports from Microsoft Excel. The PivotTable list control enables developers to publish subsets of data from a database. Developers can enable end users to manipulate the data from browsers by publishing subsets of it on Web pages containing PivotTable list controls. By publishing the data in a PivotTable, developers save end users from having to write queries whenever they want to process data. Developers can also precisely specify the scope of data to which end users have access by restricting the record sources that contribute to a PivotTable list. In addition to supporting security, this capability can improve performance by avoiding poorly constructed and overly broad queries.

Office Web Components is distributed through the installation of Office XP. Two .dll files, MSOWCW.DLL and OCW11.DLL, implement the components. You can get programming help for Office Web Components from OWCVBA11.CHM, which is installed by default in the local resources folder at C:\Program Files\Common Files\Microsoft Shared\Web Components\11\. On my computer, the local resources folder is 1033.

Active Server Pages

Active Server Pages (ASP) is a Microsoft Internet Information Services (IIS) technology that lets you script pages on a server for client browsers. ASP files are popularly used to present dynamic Web pages, including those that reflect ongoing data updates. You can also use ASP files to process forms in a Web environment.

Though data access pages offer a rich graphical environment through Access, ASP files aren't considered a strong graphical development tool. You can populate ASP files with HTML and a scripting language, such as Microsoft Visual Basic Scripting Edition (VBScript). The script and HTML run on the Web server to create a file for the server to send to a browser. The page for the browser doesn't contain any server-side script and can include pure HTML. The client environment is one of the main distinctions between data access pages and ASP files. Because ASP files can write pure HTML, their output can be appropriate for any browser that reads HTML (essentially all browsers). By contrast, data access pages work exclusively in Microsoft Internet Explorer 5 or later.

ASP development can be code intensive and unfamiliar to Access developers. In addition, the availability of ASP.NET, a .NET Framework alternative to traditional ASP Web pages, suggests that traditional ASP development might be coming to an end. If you know ASP already, you can use it, so long as you can live without the benefits of ASP.NET. For those who care to learn more about integrating ASP with Access database files, a chapter on the topic can be found at *http://www.programmingmsaccess.com/ForA2002/Ch17A2002.htm*.

FrontPage 2003

FrontPage 2003 is available in a standalone edition that supports Web development with Office 2003. FrontPage 2003 integrates tightly with IIS and is a graceful extension of FrontPage 2002.

FrontPage enables you to create a Web site and manage its pages. For example, you can save your data access pages and Web pages containing Office Web Components at a FrontPage Web site. Users can access any of these files from a URL. This lets your Web-based solutions serve large communities of users from a FrontPage Web site.

FrontPage includes a variety of tools for creating and editing Web pages. For example, the Insert, Database, Results command opens a wizard for simplifying the creation of ASP pages that use databases. Invoke this wizard to represent data from any ODBC-compliant data source. In addition, FrontPage features tools for simplifying the creation of Web-based forms that connect to Access database files and SQL Server databases via ASP (visit the URL at the close of the preceding section for additional details).

Using FrontPage 2003

If you plan to manage a Web site, you need a Web server and a Web site management tool. While writing this book, I ran IIS 5.1 on a computer running Microsoft Windows XP Professional. IIS is the Web server for Windows XP Professional, Windows 2000 Server, and Windows 2000 Professional. You can also access a Web server from an Internet host provider, a firm that runs a Web server shared by many Web sites. The host provider manages the Web server, the setup of Web sites, and the installation of a Web site manager. Additional details on the installation and management of a Web server are beyond the scope of this book. Check with your system administrator regarding the proper installation of operating systems and Web server software. Microsoft maintains a list of registered Web hosting service providers; see *http://www.microsoftwpp.com/default.asp* for further details.

FrontPage 2003 is a Web site manager and Web authoring tool. If you are managing a Web site on a Web server with FrontPage 2003, you typically will want to install the FrontPage 2003 Server Extensions on the computer running your Web server. These server extensions let you perform select advanced features, such as creating a Web site and using the Database Wizard to create ASP files. These extensions aren't installed as part of the typical installation. However, you can use the standard Office 2003 setup program to select the server extensions for installation, or you can run a complete install of all of Office 2003 to install the FrontPage 2002 Server Extensions.

> **Note**   The FrontPage 2003 Server Extensions run on Windows XP, Windows 2000, and Windows NT computers only. Windows NT computers require the installation of Service Pack 5. You cannot install the FrontPage 2003 Server Extensions on Windows 98, Windows ME, or Windows 95 computers.

Creating a Web Site

A Web site serves as a folder within the computer running your Web server; it acts as a file collector and an administration point. This folder typically resides under the wwwroot directory of the Inetpub folder for a computer's root directory. Although the files for a Web site reside in a standard Windows folder, you do not create or administer the files from Windows Explorer.

You can use FrontPage 2003 to create a new Web site and manage an existing one. To create a new Web site with FrontPage 2003, choose File, New. This opens the Task Pane found in all Office 2003 applications. Click the More Web Site Templates link in the New Web Site group on the New Task Pane. This opens the Web Site Templates dialog box. Select the Empty Web Site icon from the General tab, as shown in Figure 14-1. In the drop-down box for specifying a Web location, you must specify a URL for your new Web site. Then click OK to launch the site creation process. If your Web server has the proper FrontPage Extensions, if you have a valid connection to the server, and if your URL for the Web site is valid, the process completes successfully.

When you work with a Web server on your intranet, you can type **http://yourservername/yoursitename** in the Web Site Templates dialog box to specify the location of the new Web site. For example, the Web server I used in my office while writing this book has the name cabSony1. The Web site for this book has the name pma11. Therefore, I typed **http:/cabSony1/pma11** when creating the Web site for the book. If your Web site exists on the Internet, you can specify your new site name with a syntax such as *http://www.yourcompany.com /yoursitename*. The first part, *www.yourcompany.com*, designates the main Web access entry point or portal into your company. The *yoursitename* trailer denotes a destination available from the portal.

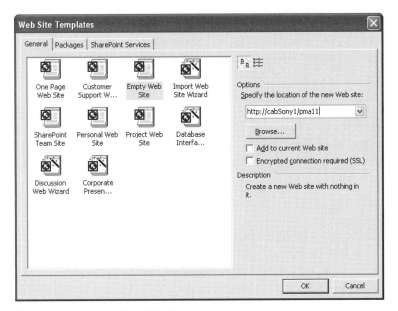

Figure 14-1   The Web Site Templates dialog box for creating a new Empty Web Site with FrontPage 2003.

Choose View, Folders to present a split pane view that shows folders on the left, and files and folders on the right. When you initially create a Web site with the instructions just outlined, your site will include two default folders and no pages. The _private folder is used for confidential files that you don't want visitors browsing through. The images folder can contain images that your site uses. Note that you can place images anywhere else within your Web site.

Click the toolbar control for creating a new normal page. When you perform this task immediately after creating a Web site, FrontPage names the page Default.htm when you save it. Click the Save button on the Standard toolbar to open the Save As dialog box. FrontPage automatically selects the root folder of your Web site for the destination of this page. When users navigate to your site with their browser, this, the first page they encounter; is your home page. Therefore, it is wise to have content on the page to let visitors know they reached your site. You should assign a meaningful name for other Web page files that you create after the first page. These page files are stored in the root folder for your site unless you explicitly create other folders within the root folder and designate one of those folders in the Save In drop-down control of the Save As dialog box.

Begin to populate the home page by double-clicking Default.htm in the Folder List on the left pane in FrontPage. If the Folder List does not appear on the left, click the Toggle Pane button on the Standard toolbar. This opens a horizontal split-pane view. The left pane shows the folders for the Web site and the files in the root folder; you can expand any folder nested in the root folder to reveal the contents of a nested folder. Double-clicking Default.htm opens the page in the right pane. You'll notice a tab at the top of the pane on the right labeled Default.htm. Include any content on this page that you want visitors to see when they initially arrive at your site. For example, you could type **This is the home page for the pma11 Web site**. Save the page by clicking the Save button on the Standard toolbar. The current open page, Default.htm, appears in the right pane. Choose File, Exit to close FrontPage.

> **Note**   Four tabs just below the view of a page determine the type of view that FrontPage presents. FrontPage 2003 renames the Normal and HTML tabs from FrontPage 2002 as Design and Code. The Preview tab retains its name. In addition, FrontPage 2003 introduces a new Split tab that shows the Code view in a pane on top of another pane that shows the Design view. With the Split tab, you can enter data in the Design pane of a page and concurrently view changes occurring in the Code pane, and vice versa. If you are new to HTML, this is an easy way to learn HTML as you edit pages manually. The Preview pane does not allow editing; its view is optimized for the currently configured browser or for whatever browser you select from browsers of different types or with different window sizes.

Opening an Existing Web Site

The next time you open FrontPage, it automatically resumes with the last Web site on which you worked. You can manage multiple Web sites with a single version of FrontPage. If you need to open another Web site besides the one with which you worked most recently, you can choose it from the File, Recent Webs menu. To open a Web site that doesn't appear in the menu, choose File, Open Site. Then type the URL for the Web site, such as **http://cabSony1/pma11**, and click Open in the Open Site dialog box. Opening a Web site in any of these ways does so with the window arrangement from the last time that you were on the Web site.

Editing a Web Page

One of the most popular ways to edit a Web page is to add hyperlinks. FrontPage offers an Insert Hyperlink control on its Standard toolbar that resembles the one in Access. To add a hyperlink, select some text or an image to which you want to apply a link. Then click the Insert Hyperlink tool to open the dialog box with the same name. At this point, you can choose to link to an existing file or Web page, a bookmark inside the current Web page, or a new Web page. You can also specify an e-mail address with which the e-mail package opens in the To field.

Figure 14-2 shows the pma11 site after multiple pages have been added to it. The figure shows the construction of a link to another page (dapEmployee-Pics.htm) on the site. The new link will add to the existing ones on the site's home page, whose name (Default.htm) appears on the tab at its top. You can also set the text for a ScreenTip that appears when the cursor hovers over a hyperlink. Click the ScreenTip button on the Insert Hyperlink dialog box to open the Set Hyperlink ScreenTip dialog box. However, if you do not care about setting ScreenTip text for the hyperlink, then you can click OK to the Insert Hyperlink dialog box in Figure 14-2. The page will be dirty after you commit your change in memory—that is, it has a committed change that is not saved to disk.

> **Note**   An asterisk (*) appears after the tab title for a page name with changes that are not yet saved to a disk (dirty pages). You can have multiple pages open for viewing and can navigate among them by selecting their tabs. The tabs for dirty pages have an asterisk. The asterisk serves as a reminder to save the pages to commit your changes to a disk. Figure 14-2 shows an asterisk on its Default.htm tab title. Click OK, and then save the page to remove the asterisk from the tab title.

The home page also includes links to sites other than the current one. You can click on the Browse The Web control in the Insert Hyperlink dialog box, or you can type a URL in the Address text box within the dialog box to add a link to another Web site.

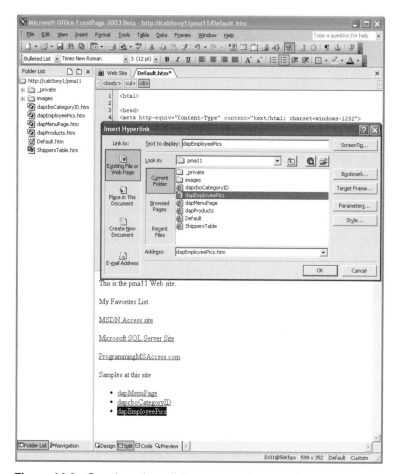

Figure 14-2   Creating a hyperlink on a page by using FrontPage.

If you select an existing hyperlink and click the Insert Hyperlink control, FrontPage opens the Edit Hyperlink dialog box with all settings for the selected link. You can edit those settings as your needs dictate. For example, if the URL for a link changes, you can type in the new URL.

Just below the Insert Hyperlink dialog box in Figure 14-2 you'll notice four tab controls. FrontPage names these tabs Design, Split, Code, and Preview. The role of these tabs is discussed in the "Creating a Web Site" section of this chapter. The page shows a Split view with the Insert Hyperlink dialog box obscuring most of the contents from the Code view of the Split tab.

The following HTML block shows the complete script for the page in Figure 14-2. Notice the pattern of symmetric tags. The page starts with an <html> tag and ends with an </html> tag. This is characteristic of HTML syntax, although not all tag types require—or even allow—opening and closing tags. Because of the way the text is entered at the top of the page announcing the pma11 Web site, the sentence appears on two lines in the HTML code. However, since there are no HTML tags delimiting the text on each line, the text appears as a single line with no special formatting in Figure 14-2.

The following script shows a couple of ways to represent hyperlinks in HTML. The URLs shown include the full address of the Internet location as the argument for an href attribute of the <a> tag. The <a> tag is an anchor tag that specifies a link. The href attribute setting designates the destination for the link. After the first anchor tag completes, some normal text outside the tag indicates how the link displays on a page. The trailing anchor tag (</a>) completes the hyperlink specification. The trailing </p> tags after </a> tags denote the end of a paragraph. These tags (</p>) place each hyperlink in the first block on a line by itself.

The three sample links in the second block on the Default.htm page use the same general format that's used for links to Internet locations, except that the href attribute merely specifies a page's filename. Notice that attribute values, such as for href appear within quotes. Using quote marks to delimit field assignment values is common for many arguments in HTML—even when dealing with numeric values. The three links for the current site appear as bulleted text. The <ul> tag marks a block of text as bulleted, and the <li> tags denote the insertion of individual bullets within a block of text.

```html
<html>

<head>
<meta http-equiv="Content-Type" content="text/html; charset=windows-1252">
</head>

<body>
This is the
pma11 Web site.<p>My Favorites List</p>
<a href="http://msdn.microsoft.com/access/">MSDN Access site</a><p>
<a href="http://www.microsoft.com/sql/">Microsoft SQL Server Site</a></p>
<a href="http://www.programmingmsaccess.com/">ProgrammingMSAccess.com</a><p>
Samples at this site</p>
<ul>
    <li><a href="dapMenuPage.htm">dapMenuPage</a></li>
    <li><a href="dapcboCategoryID.htm">dapcboCategoryID</a></li>
    <li><a href="dapEmployeePics.htm">dapEmployeePics</a></li>
</ul>
</body>

</html>
```

Getting Started with Forms on Data Access Pages

Data access pages can exhibit behavior similar to traditional Access forms and reports, except that they work across a web. When all clients use Internet Explorer 5 or later and you can install the Office 2003 Web Components on all workstation clients, data access pages offer a quick and easy route to developing forms that work across the Web.

In many ways, building solutions with forms for data access pages is similar to building a solution for forms within Access. This similarity makes data access pages an attractive technology for Access developers who want to begin building Web solutions. Despite the fact that building data access pages is similar to creating forms, data access pages are Web pages. This means that the appropriate browsers can open them just as they would any other Web page. Of course, Access forms and reports do not have this characteristic.

The sample application for this section creates a form on a data access page that displays selected fields from the *Products* table. Then it creates another form on another data access page that allows users to filter the products that the first data access page shows.

Creating a Product Tracking Form

The sample database file for this chapter, Chapter14.mdb, has links to the Northwind database. Chapter14.mdb is available with the companion content for this chapter. This means you can readily exhibit data from the *Products* table, which includes inventory information about products. One common way to view data, especially if users might need to update it, is with a form. You can build a data access page that lets Web users browse and update the contents of the *Products* table.

There are at least two graphical ways you can build a form for the *Products* table. One relies on a wizard similar to the Form Wizard. You can launch the Page Wizard by selecting Pages on the Objects bar in the Database window and then double-clicking Create Data Access Page By Using Wizard. This way of building pages targets end users and beginning developers. The second approach lets you construct a form in an environment that is similar but not identical to the Design view for Access forms. This approach shows more basic functionality than using the Page Wizard does. This section and much of the remaining discussion about data access pages highlight managing data access pages in Design view.

Begin creating a form on a data access page for the *Products* table by highlighting Pages in the Objects bar on the Database window and double-clicking Create data access page in Design view. When you get to the Design view, you will see a grid for positioning controls on your form (unless you changed the default setting) as well as a title area above the grid. You can optionally click in the title area and type text for the page's title. Otherwise, the area appears blank. Since our task is to build a form for the *Products* table, we need to bind the form to this table.

> **Note**   The visibility of the grid that denotes the area for positioning controls is optional. You can control the visibility of the grid by using the View, Grid command.

The grid area is the area that you bind to a record source for your form. If you click anywhere inside the grid, handle controls appear around the grid to indicate that you've selected it. Display the properties for the grid by clicking the Properties tool on the Design view toolbar. Notice that the grid is a *Section* object with an assigned name of *SectionUnbound*; this name changes as you specify the design of your page. Select the Data tab on the Properties dialog box, and observe the *RecordSource* property setting control. Clicking the down arrow lets you specify any table or row-returning query as a record source for the grid.

After selecting the *Products* table as a record source, Access divides the original grid into two sections. A navigation control appears in a section below a blank grid. If you select each section and examine their Properties dialog boxes, you will discover that they have section *Id* settings: *HeaderProducts* for the top grid area, and *NavigationProducts* for the control below the grid area. These names appear in the title bar for the Properties dialog box. Captions appear in bars at the top of each similarly named section on the data access page. These bars and captions appear only in Design view. Each section with data has a *RecordSource* property. The setting for both sections is Recordset: Products. If the Field List isn't already visible from the design session for a previous page, you can click the Field List control on the Page Design toolbar. This click opens a Field list to the right of the data access page with data sources in the connection for the current .mdb or .adp file.

You can add individual controls to the grid to help design a form. There are at least two approaches to this. First, you can open the Toolbox and then position controls from it to the grid to specify a form's layout. This works similarly to the Design view of an Access form, except that some different controls are available. When you take this first approach, you must individually specify a *ControlSource* property for all bound text box controls that you add. The

ControlSource setting binds the text box to a field in the *RecordSource* property for the section. The second approach is to move items from the Field List to the top area of the grid. One easy way to do this is to successively double-click the fields in the Field List that you want to add to your form. This technique automatically creates bound controls and aligns them in a columnar fashion.

> **Note** Before double-clicking fields in the Field List to add them to a data access page, be sure to select the section to which you want to add the fields as controls.

If you click the *ProductID*, *ProductName*, *UnitsInStock*, *ReorderLevel*, and *Discontinued* fields, your top section will contain four text boxes and a check box for the *Discontinued* field. Each bound data control on the form has a matching label control as well. However, the text boxes appear in a default width that is too small for several product names. You can update the *Width* property of the ProductName text box by selecting it and then dragging its right edge to make it wider. Alternatively, you can type a number followed by a unit of measurement in the *Width* setting on the Format tab of the Properties dialog box for the ProductName text box. For example, type **2in** to designate a width of 2 inches.

There are two possible metrics for specifying the width: inch and pixel. However, pixel is the default. If you type a number without designating a unit of measurement, Access assumes that the number represents the width of the text box in pixels. When you drag the width of the text box, Access converts the setting from its default value of 1 inch to some other width specified in the unit of measurement used before resizing started.

You can resize the other text box controls to match the width of the ProductName text box. However, it's not necessary to manually reset the width for each of the other three text boxes to match that of ProductName. Instead, you can use the Alignment And Sizing toolbar (display the toolbar if it does not already show). Next, select the ProductName text box if it isn't already selected. Then double-click the Size Width control on the Alignment And Sizing toolbar. This double-click causes the cursor to include a representation of the Size Width control. Next, click each of the remaining three text boxes in the top section. Then move the cursor back to the Size Width control and click it once to unlatch the control, returning the cursor to its normal function. It's faster to latch the control when making several other controls match the position or size of one particular control. The alternative is to reselect the standard control and an item on the Alignment And Sizing toolbar before clicking each additional control that you want to match the standard control you've selected. Figure 14-3 shows the data access page just before the widening of the ReorderLevel text box. As you're constructing the page, you will see the cursor appear as a Size Width control when you hover it over a text box.

> **Note**   If the Alignment And Sizing toolbar is not open, you can show it by choosing View, Toolbars, Customize, Alignment And Sizing. Click Close in the Customize dialog box to return the focus to a data access page.

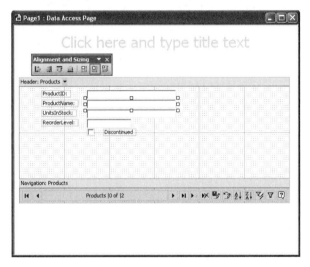

Figure 14-3   Latch controls on the Alignment And Sizing toolbar speed up the process of making new settings to controls.

As in Design view for Access forms, you can preview your layout by leaving Design view. There are two alternatives to Design view: Page view and Web Page Preview. You are restricted to using Page view until you commit your design by saving the data access page. However, switching to Page view opens the page within Access. It also lets you examine the form's layout and manipulate the data on the page with the help of the controls and the navigation bar.

Figure 14-4 shows the page from Figure 14-3 open in Page view. Notice that the form is on record 1 of 77 from the *Products* table. Besides controlling the flow from one record to the next and adding or deleting records, the navigation bar performs multiple other functions. Figure 14-4 depicts an edit to the contents of the ProductName text box (notice the three trailing x characters). After making a change to the contents of a cell, you can undo that change by clicking the Undo control on the navigation bar (this control is highlighted in Figure 14-4 and its ScreenTip legend shows). The control to the immediate left of the Undo control commits a change on the current record. Moving off the current record also commits any pending change to the *ControlSource* for a control. Users can additionally sort the records behind a form in ascending or descending order on the field behind any control. The records return to their native order the next time the form opens, and one user's sort does not affect the order of the records for another simultaneous user. Another pair of navigation bar controls let users filter by form and clear an active filter. Finally, a Help control on the navigation bar opens a file that explains how users can take advantage of data access pages as well as Office Web Components.

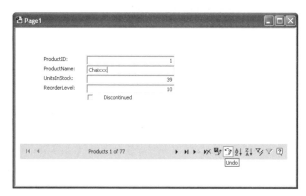

Figure 14-4   By using the navigation bar, end users can navigate, update, add, and delete records as well as sort and filter the data behind a form.

Saving a Data Access Page

Once you design a data access page to be the way you want it, you need to save it so that others can use it. This is where a Web site comes in handy. It's not essential to have a Web site, because data access pages open over a local area network (LAN) even with a browser. However, a Web location gives you the convenience of making your data access pages available with the other Web pages for a project. No matter where you store your data access pages, users with a browser can open and interact with data access pages as long as they have a license for Office 2003 and Office 2003 Web Components installed on a workstation. In addition, you can open data access pages with a link in the Pages collection of the Database window of any Access project (.mdb or .adp files). In order to edit data access pages, a workstation must have Access 2003 installed. This is the only environment in which a data access page opens in Design view. An easy way to exploit the full functionality of data access pages is to install any version of Office 2003 with Access 2003 on a workstation. Remember, you can install Access 2003 along with Access 2002 and/or Access 2000 on the same computer.

> **Note**   Although you can start editing the design of a data access page from a browser, the browser actually opens Access 2003. Before saving the file for a data access page, you need to remember two things. First, you must revise the path to the Access database file to Uniform Naming Convention (UNC) notation. By default, Access references a local path using drive letters to specify that path to the data source behind a data access page. However, users from other workstations are unlikely to map the same letters to drives on your workstation. Using UNC notation (for example, *computername**sharename**filename*) enables other users to reference the data source for a data access page independent from how they map physical drives to drive letters. Second, when you save a data access page, you store a standalone file. A convenient but not a mandatory location for this file is at a Web site, such as the pma11 Web site created earlier in this chapter. However, if you save only this file, there is no immediate way for the current Access project to reference the data access page. Therefore, Access also saves a shortcut for the page in the Database window.

I recommend a two-step approach to saving the file for a data access page that references an Access database on the local computer. First, save the data access page file with the default local drive letter designation. (This is how Access automatically creates a specification for the database file with the record source for the page.) This initial step enables Access to reliably create a shortcut in the Access database file for the standalone data access page file. Then use the shortcut to reopen the page. Edit the connection path to reflect the UNC path, and resave the file.

> **Note**   When you create a data access page for a database file on a different workstation, Access specifies the path to the database with UNC notation automatically. You can save the page with that designation, and Access reliably creates a link to the page in the Database window of the Access database file.

To change the path designation for a data access page, you can start by opening its Field List in Design view. Then click the Page connection properties control on the upper-left edge of the Field List. (Recall that you can also discover the name for a control by moving your cursor over the control until its ToolTip appears.) This opens a Data Link Properties dialog box. From the Select or enter a database name text box on the dialog box, revise the path designation to UNC notation. For example, if the database name is

```
C:\path1\databasename.mdb
```

you should change it to

```
\\workstationname\sharenamefordriveC\path1\databasename.mdb
```

> **Note**   When it's time to delete a data access page from the Database window, Access asks whether you want to delete the link only or the link and the file. The link refers to the shortcut to a data access page in a Database window. Choosing to remove the link only enables you to delete a link to a data access page within a database; you retain the data access page for use with other databases.

Opening and Filtering Forms with Links

When saving the preceding sample, I assigned it the name dapProducts in the root folder of the pma11 Web site. Since Access automatically assigns an .htm extension and the pma11 Web site is on the cabSony1 Web server in my office, the URL for the page in my office environment is *http://cabSony1/pma11/dapProducts.htm*. Typing this address into an Address box in Internet Explorer 5 or later opens the form in a browser with the full set of functionality presented in Figure 14-4. Any user who can connect to the pma11 server and has the Office 2003 Web Components running on their workstation can open the page.

Web applications normally don't require users to type URLs into a browser's Address box. Instead, developers typically create pages with links. By clicking a link, users automatically navigate from one page to another.

The example in the "Editing a Web Page" section demonstrated how to create links with FrontPage for a collection of URLs. You can also create links directly in data access pages. The tool for creating hyperlinks in data access pages has a special feature to facilitate filtering the records that appear on a form. This makes it easy to create links that display different records from the same form. In the current example, a hyperlink can optionally filter the records in the form on the dapProducts page by *CategoryID* value. Although *CategoryID* does not appear on the form, it's available for filtering because the form references the whole *Products* table as its *RecordSource* property setting. *CategoryID* is a column in the *Products* table. The trick is the setting of the *ServerFilter* property for the record source. Access database files do not support this property, except for data access pages. Recall that this property is always available for use with Access projects for SQL Server databases.

You add a hyperlink to a data access page in Design view with the Hyperlink tool in the Toolbox. A hyperlink on a data access page has *Href* and *ServerFilter* properties. You can assign settings to these properties from the Anchor tab of the Properties dialog box for the hyperlink. Because a hyperlink is essentially a label with some special settings for page navigation, you can also set properties that control its appearance on a data access page, such as its *FontSize* property. This property appears on the Format tab of its Properties dialog box. Two other property settings on the Other tab of a hyperlink Properties dialog box are critical for mastering the use of hyperlinks on data access pages. The *InnerText* property designates the display text for a hyperlink. By default, this is the same as the *Href* property, but you will typically want to override this default setting to provide a friendlier text that has more meaning to a typical user. The *Id* property denotes a name for the hyperlink. This name appears in the title for a hyperlink's Properties dialog box. When your application programmatically references hyperlinks on a page, it uses the *Id* property setting as the name for the link.

Figure 14-5 shows a collection of hyperlinks on a data access page. This page, which exists in this chapter's sample files as dapMenuPage.htm, has nine hyperlinks. All the hyperlinks open the same page, dapProducts.htm, but they show different records. Since all the hyperlinks open the same page, their *Href* property settings are identical (*http://cabSonycabSony1/pma11/dapProducts.htm*). The center hyperlink (All Products) has the largest font. This hyperlink opens the form on the dapProducts.htm page for all the records in the *Products* table. Therefore, this hyperlink has no *ServerFilter* property setting associated with it.

The links on either side of the center link all have a *ServerFilter* property setting that points at a single *CategoryID* value. For example, the hyperlink with an *InnerText* property setting of Beverages has a *ServerFilter* property value of *CategoryID=1*. Figure 14-5 shows the syntax for this assignment. The other seven links on the page, which appear to either side of the center link, have different *CategoryID* assignments that range from 2 through 8.

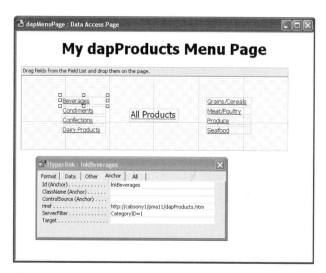

Figure 14-5   Use the *ServerFilter* property of a hyperlink to control the data that a form displays.

Figure 14-6 shows the link and filter operation in action as the application transfers control from the dapMenuPage.htm file to the dapProducts.htm file. In dapMenuPage.htm, the user clicks the Seafood hyperlink, which has a *ServerFilter* property of *CategoryID=8* (see the status bar). When the link executes, it filters the data on the form for dapProducts.htm so that only seafood products appear. Notice that the ServerFilter setting transfers as a parameter that follows the URL in the Address box. A question mark (?) signifies the end of the URL and the start of the passed parameter. Built-in software on the data access page properly interprets the parameter assignment. At *http://www.programmingmsaccess.com /ForA2002/Ch17A2002.htm* you can learn how to write your own application software to accept parameters. Keep in mind that the beauty of data access pages is that they let you save your programming efforts for other application requirements when their built-in capabilities are sufficient.

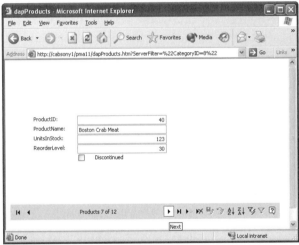

Figure 14-6   Hyperlinks can transmit a *ServerFilter* property assignment after the URL as a parameter.

Programming Events on Data Access Pages

Programming events involves two steps. First you place objects on a page. Then you design code that runs when events fire for those objects or for the page itself. Access developers have experience with both of these requirements for Access forms. However, implementing these requirements is a little different for data access pages than for Access forms. The sample in this section describes the implementation of a typical event procedure for a data access page. You'll also see an event procedure sample in this chapter's "Creating Interactive Reports with Computed Fields" section.

Adding a Drop-Down List Control

Although links are a common tool in Web-based solutions, unbound drop-down list controls offer several attractive advantages as well. First, you can base a drop-down list on a record source. Therefore, you can alter the items in the list without having to redesign the form; instead, you just update the SQL statement for the record source. Second, developers are used to creating combo box controls in Access solutions. With data access pages, the drop-down list is a comparable type of control. The wizard for creating drop-down list controls further invites Access developers to try this approach. Third, the ability to create event procedures for these controls is another motivator for using them. Access developers have substantial familiarity with these powerful and often compact pieces of code.

There are two main tasks for using unbound drop-down list controls on a data access page. First, you must physically add the control to the page and specify what it shows and what it saves. Happily, the Toolbox and its Control Wizards simplify this. By the way, the Toolbox calls a drop-down list control a Dropdown List. Second you must create an event procedure that reads the value a user selects with the control and performs some action based on it. For an example, open another data access page that contains a form whose values are filtered by a selection from the drop-down list control.

The easiest way to add an unbound drop-down list control to a data access page is to invoke the Control Wizards. Click and engage the Control Wizards button within the Toolbox before clicking the Dropdown List button. Then click on the grid within the data access page where you want the control to appear. The similarities between the drop-down list and the more familiar Access combo box will be apparent immediately. This is because the wizard's first screen has the caption Combo Box Wizard in its title bar. Make your selections for the instance of the drop-down list on the page as you normally would for a combo box on an Access form.

After responding to the Combo Box Wizard dialog boxes, you'll have a drop-down list control that displays some items from a record source. Users will be able to select items from the control, but nothing will happen as a result. Use an event procedure to cause an action based on a user choice.

For this example, I added a drop-down list control to a page. This type of control specifies its source via its *ListRowSource* property. The property for the control was the *Categories* table. The control displays category names, but it saves the corresponding *CategoryID* value for the name a user selects. I assigned an *Id* setting of *cboCategoryID* to the control. Although I created all these settings (except for the *Id* property value) with the Combo Box Wizard, you can set them easily on your own. Merely add the drop-down list control with the Control Wizards turned off. Then open the Properties dialog box for the control, and select the Data tab. Type *CategoryID* for *ListBoundField* and *CategoryName* for *ListDisplayField*. Select Table: Categories for *ListRowSource*. Access automatically converts the last selection to Recordset: Categories. Specify *cboCategoryID*, or whatever name you choose for your control, to the *Id* property setting box on the Other tab. Any event procedures you create for the control will reference the control by its *Id* setting.

Figure 14-7 shows the Design view for the drop-down list control on the data access page. The display shows the *cboCategoryID* control selected. To the right of the *cboCategoryID* control is the Properties dialog box for the control. You also can see all four settings discussed in the preceding paragraph.

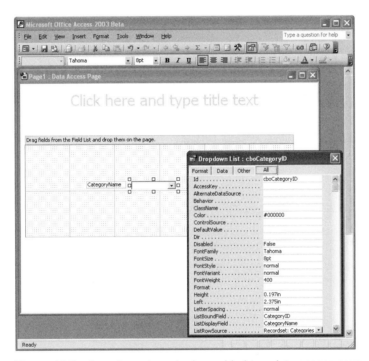

Figure 14-7   An unbound combo box added to a data access page.

Before ending this section, I'd like to note that there's more to data access pages than their drop-down list controls and labels with a caption for the control. For example, the control sits on a grid. The grid is a *Section* object from the Office Web Component model that can represent a hierarchical element within a data access page. The *Section* object in Figure 14-7 contains the drop-down list control and its label, but the section resides within the body of the page. The caption on top of the grid that starts with the words Drag fields resides in a banner for the section sitting below it. The large, gray text above the banner for the section is the page's heading text. The caption in the page's title bar indicates that Page1 is the top-level object in the data access page.

Using the Microsoft Script Editor

There's good news and bad news about using event procedures for controls on data access pages. The good news is that you can create event procedures using a language much like the one you already know in an environment that bears some similarity to the integrated development environment (IDE) that you're already accustomed to. The bad news is that the language is not exactly Visual Basic for Applications (VBA) and the IDE is not the Visual Basic Editor (VBE) window. Of the two popular languages for scripting data access pages, the one you're likely to find easiest is VBScript. The IDE for the code behind a data access page is the Microsoft Script Editor. If you programmed data access pages much in Access 2000 or you used Microsoft Visual InterDev 6 or later, you probably have some familiarity with the layout and operation of the IDE for data access pages.

To open the Script Editor, click the Microsoft Script Editor tool on the toolbar for the Design view of a data access page. The Script Editor displays the data access page in HTML and scripts. Not only can a page have multiple scripts to make it dynamic and interactive, each script can be programmed in a different language. The two scripting languages that are readily available for this are VBScript and JScript.

Note There's plenty of help for learning about the Script Editor. From the Script Editor, you can open the Help system by choosing Help, Microsoft Script Editor Help. This takes you to a Help system with information about the Script Editor, HTML, VBScript, and JavaScript. This Help file primarily features content on the Microsoft Script Editor IDE. Meanwhile, I have found the Help files in \Program Files\Common Files\Microsoft Shared\Web Components\1033 to be useful for increasing my understanding of programming techniques for data access pages and Office Web Components generally. The last folder (1033) in the path for the Help files is a language-specific resource folder. If your primary language is something other than English, another folder will replace 1033.

After you initially open the Script Editor for a data access page and return to the Design view of the page, a control on the Windows status bar (with the symbol for the Script Editor) permits you to toggle between Design view in Access and the Script Editor. In addition, you can navigate between windows using other standard techniques, such as with the Alt+Tab key combination. Making a change in one representation knocks that representation out of sync with the other one. You need to switch between these two views because doing so resynchronizes the two representations of the data access page.

Figure 14-8 presents a collection of three windows within the Script Editor for the data access page shown in Figure 14-7. These are the Document Outline, Properties, and Document windows. The Document Outline window offers two representations of a data access page. The view appearing in Figure 14-8 is for the HTML Outline. It depicts the hierarchical relationship among the objects that comprise a page. At the top level is Page1, the name for the data access page. Within Page1 are three objects: the Data Source Control (MSODSC), a *Script* object representing a script for the page, and a *Body* object that contains other top-level HTML tags defining the data access page. MSODSC contains the specification of the data source for the drop-down list control. The *Script* object contains two built-in scripts that check for the availability of an appropriate browser and a version of Office Web Components.

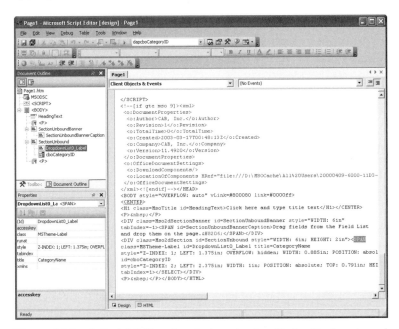

Figure 14-8   A Script Editor view that contrasts with the Design view of the data access page shown in Figure 14-7.

The items within the *Body* object show the HTML tags that lay out content on the data access page. The Document Outline window denotes these tags by their *Id* setting, when one exists. Otherwise, the window just references the tags. In order of appearance, the items within the *Body* object are a *Heading-Text* object, a paragraph tag (<p>), a banner for an unbound section, the unbound section, and another paragraph tag (<p>). Additional hierarchical elements, such as the drop-down list control (*cboCategoryID*) and its label, reside within the unbound section banner and objects.

The highlighted object in the Document Outline window also controls the focus in the Properties and Document windows. The Properties window appears directly below the Document Outline window. Since the Document Outline window depicts the *DropdownList0_Label* element selected, the Properties window indicates properties for that element. This selection is convenient for changing the *Id* value from its default setting to one that more precisely defines its purpose, such as *cboCategoryID_Label*. The Document window appears to the right of both the Document Outline and Properties windows. You can use this window to improve the appearance of the label so that it reads Category Name instead of CategoryName. Just insert a space between the words *Category* and *Name*, which appear between the <span> and </span> tags. These tags can denote a label, and the text between the tags comprises the *InnerText* property value for the label control.

The suggested updates in the Document window will cause the *Id* and *InnerText* property values for the label to revise in Design view when you synchronize the two data access page representations. Click the Page1 Script Editor control on the Windows status bar to toggle control back to Design view for the data access page. After a while, Access updates the view with the changes made in the Script Editor.

Adding an Event Procedure to a Control

Recall that *cboCategoryID*, the drop-down list control on the data access page we're building, lets a user choose a category name and stores the corresponding *CategoryID* value for the selected category name. However, nothing happens after that. With the help of an event procedure attached to the control, you can open the dapProducts data access page filtered by the *CategoryID* value in *cboCategoryID*. This section shows how to build an event procedure that accomplishes this.

You start to build event procedures for the objects on a data access page from the Document Outline window. This window offers two views. You saw the first of these, the HTML Outline view, in Figure 14-8. An alternative view is the Script Outline view, which can display all the client objects with their events and any existing client scripts in a data access page. Two controls just below the title bar for the Document Outline window allow you to switch between the two views.

Figure 14-9 shows the Document Outline window in its Script Outline view after you click the *onchange* event for the *cboCategoryID* object. You can expose the events for other objects by clicking the plus sign (+) next to them. Each client object has a set of events appropriate to it. The *onchange* event for drop-down list controls on data access pages works like an *afterupdate* event for combo boxes on Access forms. Therefore, the *onchange* event fires right after the user changes the value saved in the *cboCategoryID* control by making a selection from it.

Figure 14-9   A Document Outline window with the *onchange* event for the *cboCategoryID* control selected.

Double-click *onchange* in the Document Outline window to make the Script Editor insert the shell for an *onchange* event procedure for the *cboCategoryID* object in the Document window. The shell appears as shown below. Notice that the *for* and *event* attributes denote the purpose of the *Script* object. The language attribute is the default one, vbscript. The <!-- and --> markers denote comments. These comment markers cause the text for the event procedure to disappear from a page when the browser reading the page cannot interpret VBScript. If the browser can interpret VBScript, the code executes.

```
<script language=vbscript for=cboCategoryID event=onchange>
<!--


-->
</script>
```

The following script shows the code for the event procedure. Insert the code between the comment markers shown in the preceding shell. The code checks the value of the *cboCategoryID* control. If the control has a value of 1 through 8, it transfers control to the dapProducts data access page with a server filter setting for the control's current value. If the control returns a different value because the *Categories* table has changed, the procedure presents a message reminding the user to update the filter code and to make another selection in the meantime.

The expression *window.location.href* transfers control to a URL. The value of the expression determines the location and any filters that apply to the transferred location. Notice that the URL specifications start with a protocol (http) followed by a Web address, namely the dapProducts.htm file on the pma11 Web site at the cabSony1 Web server. A question mark (?) follows the address, and the filter specification begins. The general form for a filter expression is *ServerFilter="filter string"*. In this instance, the expression cannot use quote marks (") because the whole URL appears in quotes. Therefore, the expression uses the HTML code for quote marks (%22) to avoid a run-time error caused by embedding quote marks within quote marks.

```
If cboCategoryID.value=1 Then
    window.location.href="http://cabSony1/pma11/dapProducts.htm" & _
    "?ServerFilter=%22CategoryID=1%22"
ElseIf cboCategoryID.value=2 Then
    window.location.href="http://cabSony1/pma11/dapProducts.htm" & _
    "?ServerFilter=%22CategoryID=2%22"
ElseIf cboCategoryID.value=3 Then
    window.location.href="http://cabSony1/pma11/dapProducts.htm" & _
    "?ServerFilter=%22CategoryID=3%22"
ElseIf cboCategoryID.value=4 Then
    window.location.href="http://cabSony1/pma11/dapProducts.htm" & _
    "?ServerFilter=%22CategoryID=4%22"
ElseIf cboCategoryID.value=5 Then
    window.location.href="http://cabSony1/pma11/dapProducts.htm" & _
    "?ServerFilter=%22CategoryID=5%22"
ElseIf cboCategoryID.value=6 Then
    window.location.href="http://cabSony1/pma11/dapProducts.htm" & _
    "?ServerFilter=%22CategoryID=6%22"
ElseIf cboCategoryID.value=7 Then
    window.location.href="http://cabSony1/pma11/dapProducts.htm" & _
    "?ServerFilter=%22CategoryID=7%22"
ElseIf cboCategoryID.value=8 Then
    window.location.href="http://cabSony1/pma11/dapProducts.htm" & _
    "?ServerFilter=%22CategoryID=8%22"
Else
    MsgBox "Requires update to filter code. Make another selection.",, _
    "Programming Microsoft Access 2003"
End If
```

After inserting the code into the event procedure shell, you can return to Design view for the data access page under construction. This gives the environment a chance to update with any changes made to the page in the Script Editor.

In this chapter's sample page (dapcboCategoryID.htm) with the chapter's companion content, I added some instructions on how to use the page in the

<headingtext> tag. You can make the instructions in either the Design view or the Script Editor representations of the data access page. When using Design view, click in the gray text at the top of the page and type your replacement text. In the Script Editor, replace the text between the <h1> and </h1> tags with the *Id* setting of *HeadingText*. In addition, clear the value for the assignment to the class attribute—that is, change it from "MsoTitle" to "". The initial setting references a style that causes the text between the tags with an *Id* of *HeadingText* to disappear.

Managing Images on a Data Access Page

Displaying images on data access pages has several commonalities with displaying images on forms in Access, with some qualifying distinctions. Happily, you can use an image control to display your image on a data access page. But instead of directing the control at the filename and path for an image, you're likely to use the URL for an image that can specify a protocol, path, and filename.

And just as with a LAN-based solution for an Access form, you're likely to maintain your image addresses in a separate table with a primary key that matches the primary key for the rest of the data about your entities (items that the pictures represent). However, when using data access pages, you join the two tables directly behind the page instead of in a separate query. This is because using a standalone query as the record source for a form on a data access page makes the form read-only. This is not necessarily the case for Access forms on LANs.

A third distinction between presenting images on data access pages and presenting them on Access forms is that data access pages save you from having to rely on event procedures to manage the display of images. You can merely designate a field with a URL as the *ControlSource* property for the Image control. The navigation bar controls on data access pages are smart enough to eliminate the need for any custom coding. With Access forms, to avoid an error, event procedures typically must detect whether a user is moving beyond the first or last record.

Creating Your Image Files for the Web

The sample described in this section works with a variation of the employee pictures that ship with the Access database file for the Northwind sample. Although the picture images ship with the sample, they are standalone files. As you'll recall, these files have a bitmap image format, which is uncommon in Web applications. Alternative graphic formats, such as those with a .jpg file type, represent images with fewer bytes than bitmap files. I used the Picture Library package that ships with Office 2003 to create another set of employee image files based on the original images that ship with the Northwind database. Picture Library permits you to open a folder of bitmap (.bmp) files and save the image files in another file type, such as .jpg. I specified a compression setting of 50 percent, which reduced the file size of the images from around 40 KB each to slightly under 10 KB each with only a modest reduction in clarity.

Note If Picture Library is unavailable, you can use the .jpg image files included with the companion content for this chapter. You can also convert image file types with your favorite graphics package. When applying the techniques just discussed to image files other than those in the example, request an appropriate format from the supplier of the images if you don't have a package for performing the conversion.

After you save your new image files in a format appropriate for the Web, copy them to a Web site. You can do this differently for an intranet to which you have LAN access than you would for a remote Web site that you must connect to over the Internet. However, Picture Library is well suited to this kind of task—it can compress and copy the full set of nine images in one step to either a LAN or a remote Web site location. To use a remote Web site, create a shortcut to the Web site with the Add Network Place Wizard in Windows XP. Then browse to the shortcut in the My Network Places folder from Picture Library. When working with an intranet to which you have LAN access, use Picture Library to specify the destination folder on your LAN for the images. The steps with Picture Library include:

- Designating a Picture Shortcut that points at the folder with the images that you want to copy and/or convert by choosing File, Add Picture Shortcut and then navigating to the folder with the images.

- Choosing File, Export to open a pane for managing the export process.

- Selecting all the image files that you want to convert and copy.

- Browsing to a destination folder or network shortcut.

- Specifying an export file format and optionally specifying JPEG options.

- Clicking OK.

If you are working without Picture Library, use your favorite graphics package for the conversion. If it can copy the files like Picture Library does, you're done. Otherwise, use another program to move the converted files to a destination folder. For example, Windows Explorer for a LAN or FrontPage for a Web site with FrontPage extensions. To use FrontPage to copy the converted image files to a remote Web site, follow these steps:

- Open FrontPage to the Web site to which you want to import the image files.

- From the Folder List, select a location where you want to import the image files.

- Choose File, Import.

- Use the Add File button to successively select as many files as you want to import to the Web site from your local workstation or LAN. If all the files that you want to import reside in one folder, use the Add Folder button to specify the whole folder in one step.

- When you finish specifying the location of the files to import to the Web site, click OK.

- When the import completes, click Close to remove the Import dialog box.

After copying the image files to this book's sample Web site, the images folder of the pma11 Web site has nine image files (plus one—thumbs.db—to facilitate the presentation of the images in a thumbnail view). The names for the image files range from EMPID1.jpg to EMPID9.jpg. Figure 14-10 shows the Folder List window with the Web Site tab to its right providing more detail on the image folder contents.

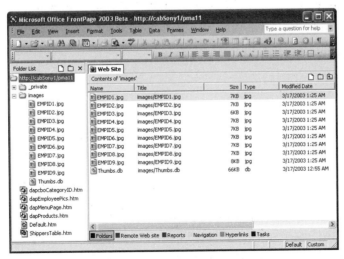

Figure 14-10   A collection of .jpg files in the images folder of a Web site for use as images on a data access page.

Creating a Record Source with Picture Addresses

The sample application for displaying images on a data access page shows selected column values from the *Employees* table, along with the image for each employee. There are several ways to organize this data for use as the record source for a data access page. This presentation opts for simplicity and read/write functionality for the bound fields.

Create a table with a name such as *EmployeePic_Addresses* that contains *EmployeeID* and *URL* fields for the image of each employee. For example, the URL for the first employee in the current sample is cabSony1/pma11/images /empid1.jpg. Name the column of URL values for images *Pic_Address*. You will need an application for adding, deleting, and possibly updating records in the table. Review Chapter 4 for sample code that describes how to create and maintain the table with Jet SQL statements.

> **Note**   A complete version of the *EmployeePic_Addresses* table is in this chapter's sample Access database file in the companion content for this chapter. It's imperative that the table have a primary key with values matching rows from the *Employees* table.

Creating a Page to Display Images

There are several different approaches to developing data access pages on record sources. This example illustrates some variations on the preceding example for the dapProducts page. Start by generating a blank data access page for editing in Design view. To do this, select Pages in the Objects bar of the Database window. Then click New on the Database window, and click OK in the New DataAccess Page dialog box. If the Field List does not show, click its control on the toolbar to make it appear. This completes the generation of a blank data access page and prepares it for editing.

Next, populate the page with fields from the *Employees* table. Open the Tables folder, and click the expand control for the *Employees* table in that folder. Successively double-click the fields to add to the form. These are *EmployeeID*, *FirstName*, *LastName*, *Country*, *HomePhone*, and *Extension*. These steps add a subset of fields from the *Employees* table for display on the data access page.

It will be helpful to show the URL for the image that the form will ultimately display. You can do this with a text box bound to the *Pic_Address* column in the *EmployeePic_Addresses* table. To add this text box to the page, select the text box with a *ControlSource* property setting of Extension. Selecting this text box enables Access to add a new text box below it. Then click the plus sign (+) to expand the *EmployeePic_Addresses* table in the Field List. Finally, double-click the *Pic_Address* column name. If the Layout Wizard dialog box appears, select Columnar and click OK. Access automatically opens a Relationship Wizard dialog box to link the *EmployeePic_Addresses* table to the *Employees* table. (See Figure 14-11.) Accepting the default setting is important for preserving the ability to update *Employee* table fields through the form on the page. The wizard specifies that the *EmployeePic_Addresses* table is in a one-to-many relationship with the *Employees* table and that the *EmployeePic_Addresses* table is on the many side of the relationship.

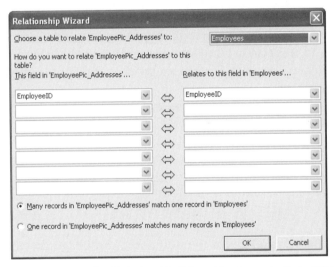

Figure 14-11   The Relationship Wizard for dynamically building relationships for the tables behind a form on a data access page.

The steps in the preceding paragraph complete the specification of a form with a set of text boxes similar in design to the dapProducts page. However, this example demonstrates how to make a couple of changes to this basic form. First, the example replaces the text box for the *Country* field with a bound drop-down list control. This makes it easy for users to change the *Country* field to another legitimate value. Second, the example illustrates how to add an image control to a form and base its display on a field in the current row on the record source for the data access page.

The drop-down list control for this data access page is different from the one in the preceding sample. The preceding data access page illustrated how to create an unbound control, but the drop-down list control for this data access page is bound to the *Country* column. Therefore, the control always shows the value of the column for the current row in the data access page's record source. In addition, you can use the drop-down list to update that value.

To add a bound drop-down list control for the *Country* field, delete the text box for the *Country* field so that the drop-down list control can take its place. Remove the text box by selecting it and then pressing the Delete key on the keyboard. Next, open the Toolbox and clear the Control Wizard's button if it's selected. Then add a drop-down list control from the Toolbox to the data access page. Select *Country* as the *ControlSource* property setting on the Data tab of the drop-down list control's Properties dialog box. This binds the control to the *Country* column in the record source for the page. Next, type *SELECT DISTINCT Country FROM Employees* into the *ListRowSource* property setting. This statement enables the drop-down list to show each country in the *Employees* table without duplicating any country. Then select *Country* as the *ListBoundField* and the *ListDisplayField* property values. This completes the control property settings that determines whether the control displays values and permits updates.

There are some additional settings that the control needs. Change the *Id* setting on the Other tab from *DropdownList0* to *cboCountry*. Next, select the label for the drop-down list control. Make two changes on the Other tab of its Properties dialog box. First, type *cboCountry_Label* as the *Id* setting. Second, type *Country:* as the *InnerText* property setting. Finish the insertion of the bound drop-down list control into the form on the page by moving its label and control so that they take the empty slot left by the deleted text box for the *Country* field.

The form is now ready for the addition of an image control. Click the image control in the Toolbox, and then click the upper-left corner where you want your image to appear. At this point, a dialog box prompts you to insert a picture. It's not mandatory that you designate a picture, but choosing a file that contains an image with the right dimensions sizes the image control for you automatically. This is convenient when you don't want the image control to clip or distort the dimensions of your images. You can type the address of the image for the first employee, such as *http://cabSony1/pma11/empid1.jpg*. This creates a static image for the control no matter which record shows, but the control does have the right size for the image file. Next, open the Properties dialog box for the image control. Then highlight *Pic_Address* from the drop-down list for the *ControlSource* property on the Data tab. This assignment allows the image control to reflect the image for the current employee.

Complete the layout of the data access page by dragging the lower edge of the section above the navigation bar so that there is sufficient space to move the *Pic_Address* text box below the image control. Then drag the text box below the image control, and resize the text box so that it's wide enough to show the URLs for images. Complete the example by saving the page. The page is available as dapEmployeesPics.htm in the companion content for this chapter. Figure 14-12 shows the page in Page view.

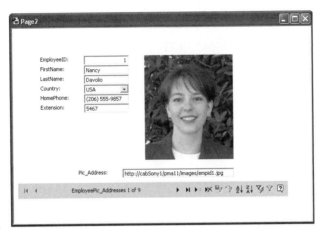

Figure 14-12   A data access page featuring an image control that updates the picture it shows as users navigate through *Employees*.

Creating Interactive Reports with Computed Fields

Data access pages support another use for controls: using interactive reports. An interactive report lets you represent a parent-child relationship. Interactive reports have a section-based architecture that resembles the sections in Access reports. These Web-based reports are considered interactive because they feature controls that let users expand a parent record and see the child records associated with it. In Design view, you can promote a field so that it becomes a parent. This capability is particularly appropriate for foreign key fields that repeat across many rows in a record source. The parent fields group the repetitions as child records. Just as with forms on data access pages, you can base interactive reports on multiple record sources. The first version of data access pages in Access 2000 didn't let you edit values in interactive reports. However, the Access 2003 version supports the editing of field values within a report.

This section gives step-by-step instructions on building two-level reports and three-level reports. You will also learn techniques for improving the appearance of data access pages by using calculated fields. The section closes with a code sample for an event procedure that illustrates how to implement conditional formatting for the data values on a data access page.

Building a Two-Level Report

You populate a data access page with controls the same way whether you're building an interactive report or a form. When adding fields to an interactive report, it's important to have one field serve as a parent for the other fields on the report. For example, most of the fields in the *Products* table relate to individual products; however, the *CategoryID* field in the *Products* table is a parent field that can have one or more products below it.

When you build multilevel reports, you can add all fields to a report at the same level. With this approach, all fields are siblings to one another. Then you promote at least one field above the others. In the case of the *Products* table, promoting *CategoryID* will lead to a grouping of product records with the same *CategoryID* field value. If users interactively expand a *CategoryID* value, they will see the products with that *CategoryID* value.

You can start to build a two-level report with fields from the *Products* table by adding *CategoryID*, *ProductName*, *UnitsInStock*, and *ReorderLevel* to a blank data access page. This creates a form on a page similar to several of the preceding examples in this chapter—namely, it contains what looks like a form with text boxes for the fields. Next, select the *CategoryID* text box and choose Promote on the Page Design toolbar. This creates a new section on the page with the banner Header: Products-CategoryID. Clicking Promote also moves the *CategoryID* text box into the new section and revises the *Id* property of the text box from *Category* to *GroupOfCategoryID*. The label for the text box also changes to Group Of CategoryID. The new label aptly describes the section, since it groups products with the same category ID value.

Figure 14-13 shows a Page view for the data access page (dapExpandCategoryIDForProducts.htm) after some rearrangement of the fields to make the report layout more compact. The *CategoryID* groups for 1–5 and 7–8 are collapsed so that you cannot see the detail records below them. However, the detail records for products with a category ID value of 6 show on the report. This is because I expanded this group. The Collapse/Expand control shows a minus sign ([–]) to signify it is expanded. Clicking the minus sign will hide the detail records for products with a category ID value of 6 and transform the control so that it shows as a plus sign [+].

Notice that the report contains two navigation bars. The one with the label of Products 1–6 Of 6 is the inner navigation bar. This bar does not appear unless a user expands at least one *CategoryID* group. By default, the maximum number of records that the bar shows at one time is 10. You can increase or decrease this amount by using the Properties dialog box for the navigation bar. The outer navigation bar appears whenever the data access page opens. Again, all 8 category ID values show at one time since there are fewer than 11.

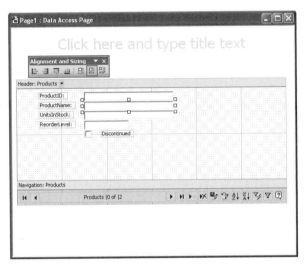

Figure 14-13   A two-level interactive report (dapExpandCategoryIDFor-Products.htm) with an expanded group for the category ID of 6.

Building a Three-Level Report

You can build multilevel reports from multiple record sources. Figure 14-14 shows a three-level report with *CustomerID* on the outer level, *OrderID* on the middle level, and fields from the *Order Details* table on the inner level. The complete report is available in this chapter's companion content. The stand-alone file is for the report dapThreeLevelReport.htm, which appears as dapThreeLevelReport in the Database window for Chapter14.mdb. This report design lets a user open the order details for any customer order. This interactive report depicted in Figure 14-14 shows the three line items for *OrderID* 10643 for the customer whose *CustomerID* is ALFKI. The figure displays the two inner navigation bars. The third outer navigation bar isn't visible in the figure. However, the outer navigation bar shows that there are 89 customers. This is two customers less than the number of rows in the *Customers* table since two customers have no orders.

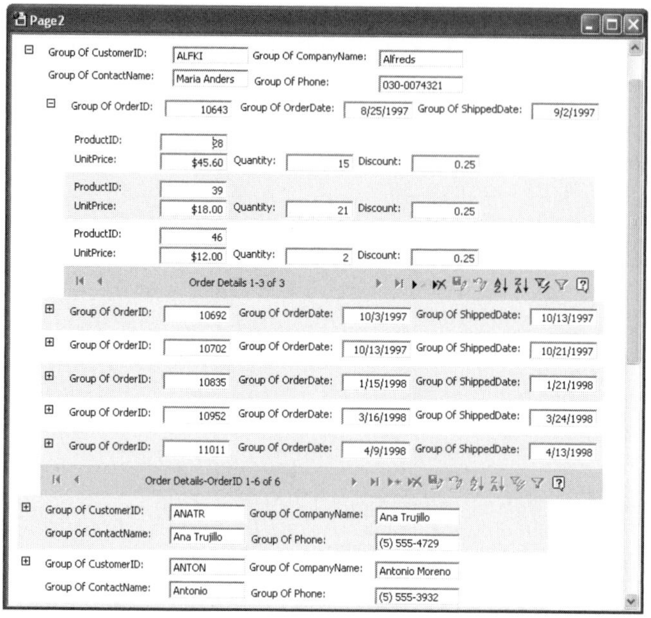

Figure 14-14 A three-level interactive report with an expanded group showing line items within *OrderID* groups, within *CustomerID* groups.

You can build a report like this one with three basic steps. A fourth step performs any report layout editing needed. These steps are as follows:

1. Add all the fields that you need in your report. Use the Relationship Wizard dialog box to define relationships between tables when you add the first field from a new record source. Don't try to add a table as a record source unless it already has a relationship to an existing record source for the report.

2. Select a field that you want to serve as the top-level field, and click the Promote tool. This creates a new section in the report and inserts the selected field into it. In the report shown in Figure 14-14, the top-level field is *CustomerID*. Move fields related to the top-level field—such as *CompanyName*, *ContactName*, and *Phone*—into the new section.

3. Select a field that you want to serve as the key field for the report's second tier. In this example, that field is *OrderID*. Then click Promote. This adds another new section to the report containing the selected field. Again, add related fields to the new section.

4.   Perform whatever rearrangement and editing of control labels your application requires. For example, the sample report in Figure 14-14 aligned controls horizontally to conserve space so that you could see as much information as possible in a single screen.

Adding Calculated Fields to a Report

Including calculated fields in a report can improve the report's usefulness by providing summary information before a user expands a control or by deriving conclusions based on the available data. This section demonstrates how to use calculated fields in interactive reports to benefit from these advantages. In addition, this section shows how to replace numeric fields used for grouping with string values that are easier to read and interpret.

The starting point for this section is the dapExpandCategoryIDForProducts report we developed earlier. The example saves the report under a new name, dapCalculatedFields. It then makes three main edits to the report before resaving it. If you're authoring the report from the same workstation that stores the data access page for the interactive report, you'll have to revert from UNC notation for specifying the connection to a local drive designation. To achieve this, save the dapExpandCategoryIDForProducts report with a local drive designation and a name of dapCalculatedFields.

Once you have your copy of dapExpandCategoryIDForProducts saved as dapCalculatedFields, you can start editing the copy. Begin by replacing the text box that displays a different category ID value with the actual name of the category. This will make it easier for users unfamiliar with the category ID codes to interact with the report. Since the *Products* table does not include a *CategoryName* field, it's necessary to add a new record source to the data source control that manages data for the report.

Before adding a new record source, remove the text box and its label in the Products-CategoryID report section. Next, click the expand control for the *Categories* table in the Field List, and drag the *CategoryName* field just to the right of the expand control in the Products-CategoryID section. Then drag the edges of the bound span control for *CategoryName* and its label so that you can easily select either control. A bound span control displays the contents of a text or memo field, but it doesn't enable editing. This limitation is acceptable for a field that acts as a label. Select the bound span control, and change its *Total-Type* setting on the Data tab of its Properties dialog box to *dscNone*. Use the drop-down list for the *ControlSource* property to select *CategoryName*. Update the *Id* setting on the Other tab of the Properties dialog box to *bspCategoryName*. Next, select the label for the bound span control. On its Other tab, type *bspCategoryName_Label* as its *Id* setting and *Category Name:* as its *InnerText* setting. Finish the editing for the bound span control and its label by positioning and sizing them the way you want on the report.

Using a SQL Server Database for the Data Source of a Data Access Page

Data access pages can have only two kinds of data sources: Access database files and SQL Server databases. This chapter focuses on the use of Access database files. However, you can also have a SQL Server database act as the data source for a page. It's possible to designate a SQL Server database as the source for a page even when you're authoring the page from an Access database file.

When you create a blank data access page, Access automatically assigns the local database as the source. If you're working from an Access database file and you want a SQL Server database to serve as the page's data source, click the Page connection properties control on the Field List. This opens a Data Link Properties dialog box. On the dialog box's Provider tab, select Microsoft OLE DB Provider For SQL Server. Complete the Connection tab for an Access project's Data Link Properties dialog box. Figure 14-15 shows the two tabs that designate the NorthwindCS database on the cabSony1 SQL server as the data source for a data access page.

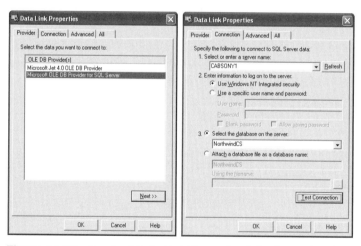

Figure 14-15   A pair of Data Link Properties tabs for setting the data source of a data access page to the NorthwindCS database.

When working with SQL Server data sources, you don't need to set the path to a database with UNC notation. This is because a SQL Server database specifies the connection to a data source in terms of the server name and the database's name on the server.

Next, add another bound span control to the Products_CategoryID section that counts the number of product records within a category. You initially get this control from the Toolbox. Next, select the new bound span control, and open its Properties dialog box to the Data tab. Use the drop-down list for the *ControlSource* setting to designate *ProductID*. Then select dscCount from the *TotalType* setting. These two settings cause the bound span control to count the number of unique *ProductID* values within each category. On the Other tab, update the *Id* setting to *bspCountOfProductID*. Then select the label for the new bound span control. Change its *InnerText* value on the Other tab of its Properties dialog box to *Count of Products* and its *Id* setting to *bspCountOf-ProductID_Label*. In the Products-CategoryID section, adjust the size and position of the bound span control and its label until you get the results you want. In doing so, you might find it useful to set the *TextAlign* property of the bound span control to *left*. The setting is available on the Format tab of the control's Properties dialog box.

The last task is to add a computed field that tells the report user whether it's time to reorder a product. The report uses an expression that returns *Yes* whenever *UnitsInStock* is less than *ReorderLevel*. Otherwise, the expression returns *No*.

Before adding a new bound span control for the calculated field in the Products section of the report, rearrange the text box controls so that those for *ProductName* and *UnitsInStock* appear on the first row and the text box for *ReorderLevel* appears in the second row along with the new bound span control. Type the following expression into the *ControlSource* property for the bound span control. Notice that it relies on a familiar *Immediate If* statement.

```
ReorderNow: IIf(UnitsInStock<ReorderLevel,"Yes","No")
```

Next, change the *InnerText* setting for the bound span control's label to Reorder? This property assignment cryptically asks the question, "Is it time to reorder?" The expression on the bound span control's *ControlSource* property answers this question. Also, assign *bspReorderNow* to the control's *Id* setting. This *Id* setting will demonstrate its usefulness with the code sample in the next section.

Complete the application with the normal resizing and repositioning. You might also want to assign a title for the page. In HTML, you set this property to determine the contents of the browser's title bar when it opens a page. You will also notice the property when you examine a data access page in Page view. To assign a value to the page's *Title* property, click the page's title bar in Design view. Then open the Properties dialog box. On the Other tab, type a name that reflects the page's purpose or role, such as *dapCalculatedFields*. Finally, save the page with UNC notation that designates its connection to the database file. A completed version of the report is available with this book's companion content in the dapCalculatedFields.htm file.

The report in Figure 14-16 illustrates the outcome of the enhancements to the dapExpandCategoryIDForProducts data access page presented in Figure 14-13. Notice that the labels describing the products within a category show the name of the category rather than a *CategoryID* code number. In addition, users can tell how many products are in a category without opening that category to get the information from the inner navigation bar. Finally, the report computes whether it's time to reorder a product and displays the results with a Yes or No.

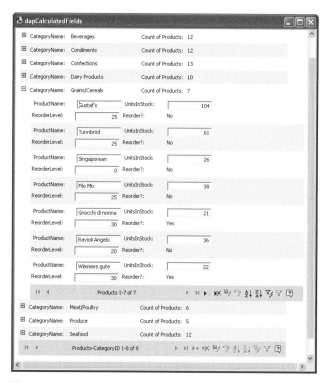

Figure 14-16   With calculated fields, you can dramatically improve the ease of interpreting an interactive report.

Applying Conditional Formatting to a Report

As improved as the report in Figure 14-16 is over the one in Figure 14-13, if there was a long list of products within a category, it might be difficult to see which products need a new order. One way to resolve this is to apply a bold font selectively to the computed value for reordering. The event procedure in this section applies a bold font to those products with a value of *Yes*, which serves as an answer to the question about whether it's time to reorder. Figure 14-17 shows another version of the report (dapExpandReportandFormat) with conditional formatting of bold for products with a *bspReorderNow* value of *Yes.* See how much easier it is now to tell which products need a new order?

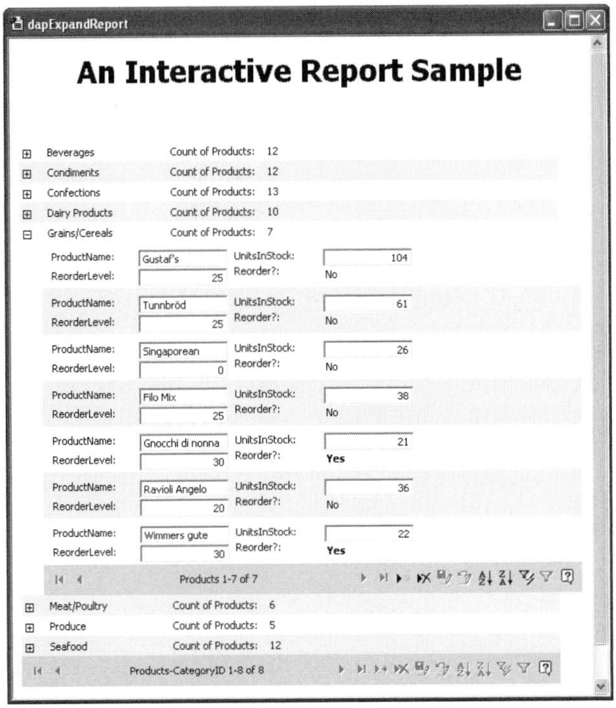

Figure 14-17   You can improve readability by implementing conditional formatting with an event procedure for the data source control in a data access page.

This improved readability results from an event procedure for the page's data source control. Each time a user opens a child section of a report, the data source control on the page reloads the page. The data source control (MSODSC) is a top-level object in the data model for a page. The following event procedure fires when the data source control for the report page finishes reloading in response to a user opening the products within a category. The procedure loops through the sections on a page. The *NextSibling* property allows the procedure to advance from one section of a report to the next. When any HTML controls fall within a section that has a value of *RecordLevel* greater than *UnitsInStock*, the procedure assigns a bold font to the *bspReorderNow* control.

```
<SCRIPT event=DataPageComplete(dscei) for=MSODSC language=vbscript>
<!--
'Highlight items that are almost out of stock
```

```
dim sect
dim dscconst
dim bandHTML

'Check that event fired for DataPage in the Products GroupLevel
if (dscei.DataPage.GroupLevel.RecordSource = "Products") then
    set dscconst = MSODSC.Constants
    set sect = dscei.DataPage.FirstSection

    'Go through the sections of the event's DataPage object
    do
        'Want to ignore the caption section
        if (sect.Type = dscconst.sectTypeHeader) then
            set bandHTML = sect.HTMLContainer

            'Conditional formatting on the bspReorderNow control.
            'Change the text to bold if the ReorderLevel is
            'greater than UnitsInStock.
            if (CInt(bandHTML.children("ReorderLevel").innerText) > _
                CInt(bandHTML.children("UnitsInStock").innerText)) _
                Then
                bandHTML.children("bspReorderNow").style.fontweight _
                    = "bold"
            end if
        end if
        set sect = sect.NextSibling
    loop until (sect is nothing)
end if
-->
</SCRIPT>
```

You type the script similarly to the way described earlier in this chapter for the *onchange* event procedure. Open the Script Editor. Select the Script Outline view of the Document Outline window. Then expand the events for MSODSC, which represents the data source control object on a page. Double-click the *DataPageComplete* event. This opens the shell for the event procedure. Finally, copy the body of the event procedure into the shell.

Programming Data Access Pages with VBA

You can program solutions with data access pages at several different levels. This section explores solutions based on VBA, the *AllDataAccessPages* collection, the *DataAccessPage* object, and selected methods of the *DoCmd* object. Programmatic manipulation of data access pages by using VBA can serve multiple administrative needs.

Enumerating Data Access Pages and Their Properties

The *AllDataAccessPages* collection works like the *AllForms* and *AllReports* collections. Its members are not database objects, but rather *AccessObject* objects. These objects are available whether or not a data access page is open. The *AllDataAccessPages* collection lets you track the full set of all data access pages associated with a database. The following short VBA procedure inventories all the data access pages associated with the *CurrentProject* object of an Access database file or an Access project, and the procedure notes whether the pages are open.

The *FullName* property of an *AccessObject* object in the *AllDataAccessPages* collection has a special meaning. Recall that pages are not stored as objects in the database file; they are separate HTML files. The location of the pages can be anywhere on a LAN. The *FullName* property indicates the path and filename for a data access page. The next procedure lists all the pages in a project and itemizes them by their *Name* and *FullName* properties. The *Name* property value is the shortcut for the data access page that appears in the database window.

```
Sub ListMyPages()
Dim obj1 As AccessObject

'Iterate through the members of the AllDataPages collection.
'Print link name, whether its page is loaded, and
'the address at which the link points.
For Each obj1 In CurrentProject.AllDataAccessPages
    Debug.Print "Link name: " & obj1.Name
    Debug.Print String(5, " ") & "Is loaded: " & obj1.IsLoaded
    Debug.Print String(5, " ") & "Link address: " & obj1.FullName
    Debug.Print
Next obj1

End Sub
```

Because the *AllDataAccessPages* collection has a limited number of properties, you are likely to need the *DataAccessPages* collection to get more information about the data access pages associated with a database. While the *AllDataAccessPages* collection belongs to the *CurrentProject* object shown in the preceding sample, the *DataAccessPages* collection belongs to the *Application* object. In addition to this distinction, data access pages belong to the *DataAccessPages* collection only when they are open. Therefore, you must open a data access page before you can reference it as a member of the *DataAccessPages* collection. Since proper applications restore settings to the way they were before their operation, you should close any data access pages that you opened to make them members of the *DataAccessPages* collection.

The following procedure prints the links, the path and filename for the page links, and the data source specification for selected data access pages. The first two items are available from the *AllDataAccessPages* collection. However, the last item requires an excerpt from the connection string for a member of the *DataAccessPages* collection. The data source specification within the *ConnectionString* property for a *DataAccessPages* member starts with the string *"Data Source"* and ends with the first semicolon after *"Data Source"*. If you create a new copy of a database with the most recent data, it's possible that some of your data access pages will reference an incorrect, older version of that database. You can put the called procedure in the following sample within a loop and go through the data access pages in the *CurrentProject* object. The previous sample illustrates this type of design. When you have just a few objects to report on, you can speed up your application by referencing just a subset of items with indexes, as the following code illustrates.

> **Note** If you change the target files in the first procedure, save it to avoid a file-locking error. The sample needs an exclusive lock on the current database, and it cannot make the lock if uncommitted changes exist.

```
'Save module after updating dapName settings
Sub CallPrintDAPConnectionString()
Dim dapName As String

'Pass the name of two data access page links
'for lookup of target properties
dapName = "dapMenuPage"
PrintDAPConnectionString dapName
dapName = "dapProducts"
PrintDAPConnectionString dapName

End Sub


Sub PrintDAPConnectionString(dapName As String)
Dim bol1 As Boolean
Dim str1 As String
Dim int1 As Integer
Dim int2 As Integer

bol1 = True
```

```
'If file is not loaded, set boll to False
If CurrentProject.AllDataAccessPages(dapName).IsLoaded = False Then
    DoCmd.OpenDataAccessPage dapName, acDataAccessPageBrowse
    boll = False
End If

'Print target for page link and data source for page at
'which the link points
str1 = DataAccessPages(dapName).ConnectionString
int1 = InStr(str1, "Data Source")
int2 = InStr(int1, str1, ";")
Debug.Print CurrentProject.AllDataAccessPages(dapName).Name
Debug.Print String(5, " ") & "Link points at " & _
    CurrentProject.AllDataAccessPages(dapName).FullName
Debug.Print String(5, " ") & "Data file for page points at " & _
    Mid(str1, int1, int2 - int1)

'If file was initially closed, close it again
If boll = False Then
    DoCmd.Close acDataAccessPage, dapName, acSaveNo
End If

End Sub
```

Creating and Deleting Data Access Pages

If you programmed data access pages much with Access 2000, you might have noticed the *CreateDataAccessPage* method. This method belonged to the *Application* object, and it enabled the creation of new, blank data access pages as well as new links to existing data access pages. If you look for this method with the Object Browser in Access 2003, you will not see it. The method still exists, but it generates a run-time error. Happily, it's relatively easy to program around the run-time error. Access 2003 retained the *acDataAccessPage* argument for the *DeleteObject* method. This method is handy for discarding page links that you no longer need as well as relinking existing pages with new data access pages.

The following pair of VBA procedures shows the new technique for using the *CreateDataAccessPage* method for making a new data access page file and linking to it in the current project. Recall that a data access page for an Access project has three important characteristics. First, it is a standalone Web page. Second, it must have a data source control that specifies a relationship to a data source. Third, it's the target of a link inside an Access database file or Access project that points at the standalone Web page.

The *CreateDataAccessPage* method takes two arguments. The first of these is for the path and filename of the standalone Web page. Your specification for this first argument doesn't require an extension. Therefore, you should not end it with .htm. The method automatically appends the correct extension to the file for the data access page. The second argument takes a Boolean variable assignment. An assignment value of True causes the method to create a new data access page file. A value of False is appropriate when you're creating a new link for an existing standalone page. When you invoke the method, it opens a blank data access page in memory. You must provide a memory variable for the return value from the method. Failing to do so generates a compile-time error. You can give the variable an *AccessObject* data type.

After invoking the *CreateDataAccessPage* method as described, you will generate a run-time error. In my tests of the method, the most common result was error 13, with a description of Type Mismatch. If I ran the procedure successively without erasing the previously created data access page, I also generated error 2023. This error can occur when your application tries to create a data access page file that already exists.

The sample application that follows includes traps and fixes for both of the errors that I encountered. Other errors are logged to the Immediate window before a normal exit. The sample application sets the filename and path for the data access page in the first procedure. By default, the connection string for the page points at the current project's connection. In addition, the connection string uses letters to denote drives. The second procedure combines the arguments for the filename and the path for the *CreateDataAccessPage* method and invokes the method. This procedure also includes error traps. One of these traps is for the case in which the application tries to write over an existing data access page. When the application detects this error, it invokes a third procedure to delete the old file and then retries the *CreateDataAccessPage* method. Notice that the called procedure removes both the page link with the *DeleteObject* method and the file to which it links with the *Kill* statement. The other error trap is for the type mismatch error. This is the normal result of trying to create a new data access page with the method. Although the method generates a run-time error, it successfully creates a new page with a data source control set to the database for the current project. The page resides in memory. Therefore, when the second procedure traps this error, it saves the page in memory and closes the page. This completes the task.

After the second (and optionally the third) procedure performs its tasks, control returns again to the first procedure. At this point, the new data access page exists, but it has a connection string specified with driver letters, which may not work well for a community of users that can use the same drive letter to point at different physical drives. The main procedure therefore calls the *setUNCSting* procedure. This procedure reopens the page and assigns it a connection string with a UNC syntax before resaving and closing the page.

```
Sub CallNewDataAccessPageForNewPage()
Dim dapName As String
Dim dapPath As String
```

```vbnet
'Set parameters for page and link
dapName = "dapfoo3"
dapPath = "c:\inetpub\wwwroot\pmall\"

'Create page with default connection string
NewDataAccessPage dapName, dapPath

'Call any intermediate processing if desired

'Set UNC connection
SetUNCString dapName

End Sub


Sub NewDataAccessPage(dapName As String, dapPath As String)
On Error GoTo NewPageTrap
Dim dapPathFile
Dim dap1 As AccessObject

'Concatenate path and file for CreateDataAccessPage method
dapPathFile = dapPath + dapName

'Create new data access page and wipe old copy
'if it exists
Set dap1 = CreateDataAccessPage(dapPathFile, True)

NewPageExit:
'This normal exit path is not strictly necessary because
'procedure does not end normally
Exit Sub

NewPageTrap:
If Err.Number = 2023 Then
'Delete old version of page, if it already exists
    DeleteDap dapName, dapPath
    Resume
ElseIf Err.Number = 13 Then
'Save page and close page, to finish method
    DoCmd.RunCommand acCmdSave
    'debug.Print currentproject.dataaccesspages(dapName).
Else
'Print out error number and description otherwise
    Debug.Print Err.Number, Err.Description
End If

End Sub
```

(continued)

```
Sub DeleteDap(dapName As String, dapPath As String)
Dim dapPathFile
Dim dap As AccessObject

'Specify file to delete with extension
dapPathFile = dapPath + dapName + ".htm"

'First delete link in Database window
DoCmd.DeleteObject acDataAccessPage, dapName

'Next kill file for data access page
Kill dapPathFile

End Sub


Sub SetUNCString(dapName)

'Open target page
DoCmd.OpenDataAccessPage dapName, acDataAccessPageBrowse

'Re-write connection string with UNC syntax
'to point at Chapter14.mdb in the Chapter14 path
'on the cabSony1 computer
str1 = DataAccessPages(dapName).ConnectionString
int1 = InStr(str1, "Data Source")
int2 = InStr(int1, str1, ";")
DataAccessPages(dapName).ConnectionString = _
    Left(str1, int1 - 1) & _
    "Data Source=\\cabSony1\Chapter14\Chapter14.mdb" & _
    Right(str1, Len(str1) - int2 + 1)

'Save and close page
DoCmd.RunCommand acCmdSave
DoCmd.Close

End Sub
```

Basing Data Access Pages on Access Forms and Reports

Data access pages were a popular new feature back when I was explaining the benefits of Access 2000 in the seminars I gave throughout the United States. The attendees told me they liked data access pages because they had the look and feel of Access forms and reports. Data access pages were viewed as relatively familiar and easy to develop. Perhaps the most common question asked by seminar registrants was, "Is there any automatic way to base a data access page on an existing Access form or report?" At the time, when only Access 2000 was available, the answer was no—however, it changed to yes when Access 2002 was introduced, and Access 2003 offers the same benefit. Although the conversion process is not perfect in every case, it's always automatic.

The process for automatically creating a data access page works for both Access forms and reports. In addition, you can do so both manually and programmatically. To perform the process manually, select either an Access form or report in the Database window and choose File, Save As. Access responds by opening a Save As dialog box. In the drop-down list control on the dialog box, select Data Access Page. In the New Data Access Page dialog box, designate a folder and name for the new data access page based on the form or report. Then click OK to save the data access page in memory to disk.

You can achieve results comparable to the File, Save As command by using the *DoCmd* object's *OutputTo* method. Using the programmatic solution to base data access pages on forms and reports has a couple of advantages over the manual technique. First, the programmatic approach makes it easy to process sets of forms and reports to data access pages in one step. Second, by learning to use the programmatic solution, you can offer this capability to users of your custom solutions.

When outputting a data access page based on a form or a report, you will typically specify as many as four arguments for the *OutputTo* method. The first argument is an intrinsic constant for either a form (*acForm*) or a report (*acReport*), depending on the type of Access object on which you base your data access page. The second argument is a string denoting the name of the Access form or report that serves as the basis for the new data access page. The third argument is another intrinsic constant (*acFormatDAP*) to specify that the method will generate a data access page. This is necessary because the *OutputTo* method can generate many different types of output, including text files, Excel workbooks, ASP, XML files, and more. The fourth argument represents the name of the path and file that will store the new data access page.

When you create a data access page with the *OutputTo* method, you're responsible for archiving any existing files that have the same name as your new data access page. If you specify a name for your new page that's identical to one that already exists in the same path, Access silently copies over the old file. You're also responsible for creating a link in the project that points at the file for the new data access page. This sample points a link at a new page. If you already have a link pointing at the new data access page based on the page's filename, Access creates another link with the same name, except it appends an underscore and a sequential number to the link's name. You can use manual or programmatic techniques to ensure that the new link is correct. For example, you can delete the old link if it exists.

To demonstrate automating the creation of a data access page based on an Access form, I used the AutoForm Wizard to generate an Access form named *frmOrderDetails* for the *Order Details* table. This form is available in the Access database file for this chapter (Chapter14.mdb). Next, I ran the following procedure to create a data access page based on the form and a link to the new page. The procedure has three parts. The first part creates the new page with the *OutputTo* method. The second part creates a link for the page in the Database window for the Access database file. The third part uses the link to open the page based on the form and changes its connection string to a UNC style before saving and closing the page.

```
Sub dapfrmOrderDetails()
Dim dap As AccessObject
Dim dapPath As String

'Create a new data access page in dapPath based on
'the frmOrderDetails form
dapPath = _
    "c:\inetpub\wwwroot\pmall\dapfrmOrderDetails.htm"
DoCmd.OutputTo acForm, _
    "frmOrderDetails", _
     acFormatDAP, _
     dapPath

'This code creates a link in the current project to the
'data access page at dapPath
On Error Resume Next
Set dap = _
CreateDataAccessPage(dapPath, False)
If Err.Number = 13 Then
    DoCmd.RunCommand acCmdSave
    DoCmd.Close
End If

'Set UNC connection
SetUNCString "dapfrmOrderDetails"

End Sub
```

Figure 14-18 shows the original Access form and its data access page representation inside an Access window. The original form in the upper-left portion of the screen translates perfectly into a data access page. There are even some extra touches in the lower right corner. For example, both the original form and its representation on a data access page have a record selector with the same kind of functionality. You can also view the total number of records in both forms and move among them with navigator controls. The data access page offers enhanced functionality, such as filtering and sorting. However, you can programmatically or manually restrict the availability of these capabilities to the form on the data access page.

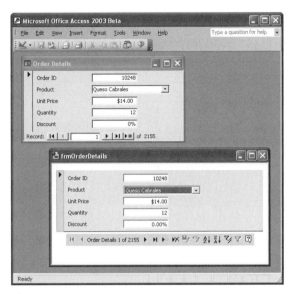

Figure 14-18   Automatically generated data access pages can have the same look and feel as Access forms.

Although this approach is promising, it has a couple of limitations. First, a subform in a main/subform combination doesn't get translated; the *OutputTo* method generates just the main form. Second, bound graphic images do not translate from Access forms to their data access page counterparts. You can use the technique discussed in the "Managing Images on a Data Access Page" section earlier in this chapter to display images tied to data values for forms generated automatically by the *OutputTo* method.

As mentioned in Chapter 6, you can represent parent-child data relationships with nested sections in Access reports. This lets you display the same kind of information found in a main/subform. Figure 14-19 shows an excerpt from the report *rptProductsWithinCategories*. As you can see, the report lists products within categories. For each category, the report shows the *UnitsInStock* and *ReorderLevel* field values.

The following VBA procedure shows how to convert the report shown in Figure 14-19 into an interactive report on a data access page. As you can see, the changes are minor in relation to the earlier sample for converting a form to a data access page. The code still must perform three main functions. Access automatically recognizes the source object as a form and the nesting in the original report. With the same basic syntax, Access adjusts to the input changes and creates a new output in the style of an interactive report.

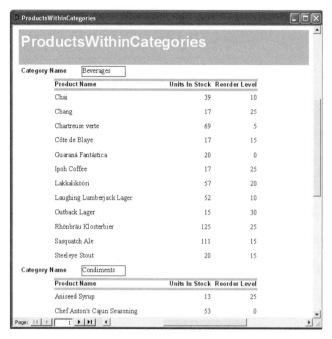

Figure 14-19 An Access report with a nested relationship for showing how the *OutputTo* method can generate a data access page with an interactive report style.

```
Sub daprptProductsWithinCategories()
Dim dap As AccessObject
Dim dapPath As String

'Create a new data access page in dapPath based on
'the rptProductsWithinCategories report
dapPath = _
    "c:\inetpub\wwwroot\pma11\" & _
    "daprptProductsWithinCategories.htm"
DoCmd.OutputTo acReport, _
    "rptProductsWithinCategories", _
    acFormatDAP, _
    dapPath

'This code creates a link in the current project to the
'data access page at dapPath
On Error Resume Next
Set dap = _
CreateDataAccessPage(dapPath, False)
If Err.Number = 13 Then
    DoCmd.RunCommand acCmdSave
```

```
    DoCmd.Close
End If

'Set UNC connection
SetUNCString "daprptProductsWithinCategories"

End Sub
```

Figure 14-20 shows a slightly edited version of the automatically created interactive report based on the report in Figure 14-19. Notice that the report uses a caption area above the data values to label the values for products within a category. This caption area is a special kind of header section, just like those discussed in the "Getting Started with Forms on Data Access Pages" section and elsewhere throughout this chapter. As attractive and efficient as this report is, it could benefit from some of the techniques demonstrated for computed fields earlier. I moved the category name legend in Design view so that it does not overlap with the Expand control (the plus sign [+]) on the interactive report. I also added meaningful labels to the two navigator bars. You can do this by selecting the descriptor in each bar and then updating its *RecordsetLabel* property on the Data tab. It takes at least two clicks to select the label for a navigator bar. First, you select the bar. Then you select the label on the bar. Revise the *RecordsetLabel* property on the Data tab of the label's Properties dialog box. After making these and any other changes you want, you can save the interactive report just like any other data access page.

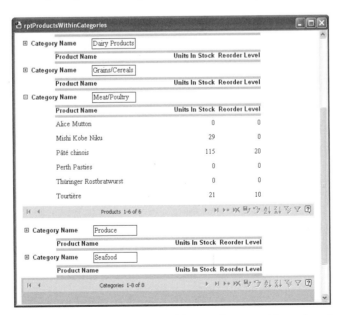

Figure 14-20   A slightly edited interactive report based on the Access report in Figure 14-19.

Office 2003 Web Components

Three Office 2003 Web Components ship with Office 2003: the Spreadsheet, Chart, and PivotTable list components. You can use them on data access pages to enhance their functionality. The data access page is actually driven by a fourth Office 2003 Component called a Data Source Component. You apply this component by managing data access pages as we have discussed throughout this chapter. If a site has a license that permits intranet distribution, the site administrator can configure browsers under the license to automatically download and configure Office 2003 Web Components the first time they load a page using a component.

Office Spreadsheet Sample

Figure 14-21 shows one use of a spreadsheet component (or control) on a data access page in a browser (see dapSalesGrowth.htm in this book's companion content). Controls on the page show the *CategoryName*, *ProductName*, and *ProductSales* fields for the *Sales By Category* query in the sample database. The query is excerpted from the Northwind database sample. This query computes sales by product in 1997 for each product. The query lists the category ID and name of each product along with its sales.

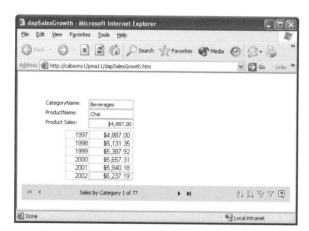

Figure 14-21   The spreadsheet component on this data access page uses sales from the database for 1997 to project sales through 2002 in a browser.

The sample in Figure 14-21 extends the basic query by projecting sales from 1997 through 2002. First, an event procedure copies the current value of the *ProductSales* control from the page to a spreadsheet cell. Then formulas in the component apply a progressive series of growth rates to sales starting with

1998. These rates increase sales from one year to the next. While the growth rates are the same for all products, the actual sales levels vary between products because the 1997 sales are different for each product. Finally, to protect the formulas in the current session from damage, you can lock selected spreadsheets to block users from inadvertently changing them. This is a minor issue since the correct values reappear on the next load of the page. (Clicking Refresh on the browser does not restore the original values.)

You can add a spreadsheet component to the data access page based on the *Sales by Category* query in the same way that you add any other control from the Toolbox. Access sequentially numbers controls of each type as it adds them to a page. Therefore, the first spreadsheet added in a session has the name spreadsheet0. You can override this setting by opening a spreadsheet component's Properties dialog box and making an assignment to the *Id* property for the component.

In addition to a Properties dialog box, Office Web Components have a Commands And Options dialog box. You can cause the dialog box to appear by right-clicking the spreadsheet in Design view and selecting Commands And Options from the menu. This dialog box lets you set and examine specialized properties for a component. For example, you can choose to remove the row and column headers to make the spreadsheet component's appearance integrate more tightly with the rest of the page. The sample in Figure 14-21 made these and other adjustments to the spreadsheet through its Commands And Options dialog box.

The following script shows the event procedure that transfers the current value of the contents in the *productsales* text box to the spreadsheet—in particular, cell B1. The code is for the *onrowenter* event of the *document*. The *document* is an object that denotes the page, and the *onrowenter* event fires when new values are available on the object. This is similar to the current event for Access forms because it signals that new data is ready for an object. This event fires when a user first loads a page or moves between the records behind form controls. Each time the event fires, the procedure copies the current value of the *productsales* text box to the cell in row 1 and column 2 of the Sheet1 worksheet. By default, a spreadsheet component initially has three worksheets. You can add extra ones and add and remove the tab control for showing the active worksheet within a spreadsheet component.

```
<SCRIPT event=onrowenter for=document language=vbscript>
<!--

spreadsheet0.Worksheets("Sheet1").cells(1,2) = productsales.value

-->
</SCRIPT>
```

Figure 14-22 shows the Design view of the data access page in Figure 14-21. In the current figure, cell B2 is selected on Sheet1. This is one row below the row populated by the preceding event procedure. In addition, the Commands And Options dialog box for the spreadsheet component appears. The Formula tab on this dialog box displays any formula for the currently selected cell. In this instance, the formula computes the value in cell B2 so that it is 5 percent greater than the value in cell B1. Cells B3 through B6 contain formulas that yield progressively larger values than those from the preceding years. As you can see from the values in column A, these rows represent successive years.

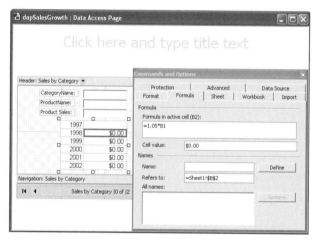

Figure 14-22   The Design view of the data access page from Figure 14-21 with the Commands And Options dialog box for its spreadsheet component.

Office Chart Sample

The sample in this section builds on the preceding one by adding an Office 2003 Chart component that charts the values in the spreadsheet. The chart shows a graphical depiction of how sales grow over time for each product. Figure 14-23 shows a product with its spreadsheet projections in a browser window. In addition, a graphical depiction of the projections appears on the right side of the page. The 3-D line chart dynamically updates each time the values in the spreadsheet change. Recall that these values change whenever the user navigates to a new product. The companion content for this chapter makes this data access page available as dapSalesGrowthChart.htm.

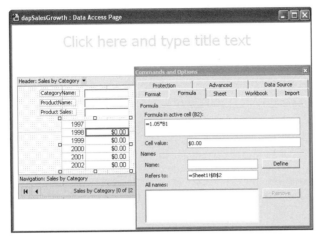

Figure 14-23   The Office 2003 Chart component on a data access page accepts values from a Spreadsheet component that changes its sales projections when a user moves off the current record.

To add a Chart component to your data access pages, select it from the Toolbox and then drag it to the area on your page where you want the chart. Click inside the Microsoft Office Web Component placeholder to launch the Commands and Options Builder. This builder lets you specify a data source for the chart and designate ranges in the data source for the chart to display. Figure 14-24 depicts a data access page after the addition of a chart and the selection of Spreadsheet0 as the data source for the chart. As you can see from the Data Source tab, the next step is to designate the specific ranges for the chart. In the chart shown in Figure 14-23, this includes a Category Labels range that runs along the horizontal axis and a Values range that plots against the vertical axis.

The Data Range tab opens after you click the Ranges button on the Data Source tab. Click the Add button on the Data Range tab. This creates a new data series for the chart. In this example, the builder types *Series1* as the Series name. Specify the Category Labels range with this string: *"Sheet1!$A$1:$A$6"*. The cell values in the Category Labels range appear along the horizontal axis of your chart. Next, designate the Values range with *"Sheet1!$B$1:$B$6"*. The cells in the Values range plot against the chart's vertical axis. Finish specifying the chart by selecting the Type tab. Click Line to display the different types of line charts from which you can choose. Then highlight the 3D Line option. Since this completes the specification, close the builder dialog box.

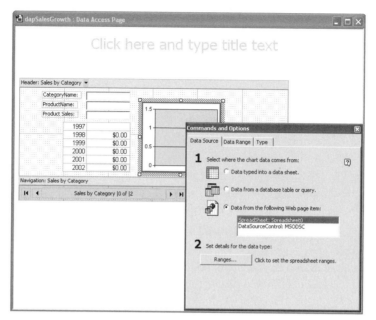

Figure 14-24 The initial Commands And Options dialog box for specifying the data source for a Chart component.

After making these selections for your chart, the line will appear flat. This is because you are in Design view. Therefore, there are no values to plot. Switch into Page view to see your chart with data. Notice how the values in the 3-D line chart change when you move to a new record. This happens because the spreadsheet values revise and the spreadsheet is, in turn, dependent on the *productsales* text box.

Creating and Using Office PivotTable Lists

The PivotTable list control lets users sort, group, filter, outline, and report data. It can also work with data from more providers than a normal data access page or other Office XP Web Components can. For example, you can apply a Pivot-Table list control to Jet and SQL Server databases. You can also apply it to any ODBC data source, multidimensional data cubes, and nontraditional data sources, such as Outlook Search results. A particularly powerful feature of the PivotTable list control is that when you base a Chart control on a PivotTable list control, the chart behaves like a PivotChart. This enables filtering and analytical capabilities, including summing, adding, and averaging numeric quantities. Developers can set up a PivotTable list and let users work within the confines of a data environment without forcing them to know a data structure and a query language to extract results.

You add a PivotTable list control to a data access page from the Toolbox. By default, the control connects to the data source for the page on which it resides. You can override this default connection by right-clicking the control and choosing Commands And Options. On the Data Source tab of the Commands And Options dialog box, click Edit. In the Select Data Source dialog box, double-click Connect To New Data Source, highlight Other/Advanced for the kind of data source to which you want to connect, and click Next. This presents the Provider tab of a Data Link Properties dialog box with the full list of OLE DB providers to which you can connect your PivotTable list control. Since one of these is the OLE DB Provider For ODBC Drivers, the list of data source types to which you can connect includes any source with an ODBC driver. Complete the other tabs to specify your connection to a data source besides the one for the data access page.

You can build a PivotTable list control with the same general techniques that you use within Access forms. (See Chapter 7.) Figure 14-25 shows a Pivot-Table list control under construction within a data access page. The PivotTable list control already has a *CategoryName* field in the drop row area, and the *ProductName* field is about to be dropped within the *CategoryName* field. By subsequently dragging the *ProductSales* field to the detail drop area, the resulting pivot table will display total sales by product within the category.

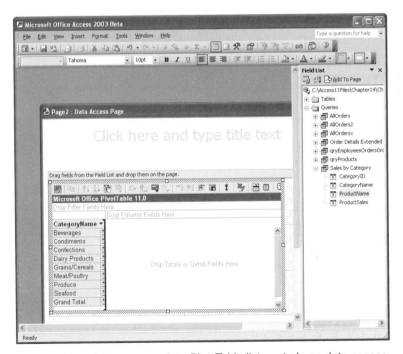

Figure 14-25   You can populate PivotTable list controls on data access pages as you would within normal Access applications.

Users can browse data access pages with PivotTable list controls and perform any desired analysis that you enable. For example, Figure 14-26 shows two different analyses in a browser window for the same basic PivotTable list control with the *CategoryName*, *ProductName*, and *ProductSales* fields on a data access page. The top browser window shows *ProductSales* aggregated by *CategoryName*. The bottom browser window presents a list of *ProductSales* by *ProductName* filtered by the Meat/Poultry category. Both PivotTable displays rely on the *Sales by Category* query that serves as the source for the PivotTable list control behind both browser windows.

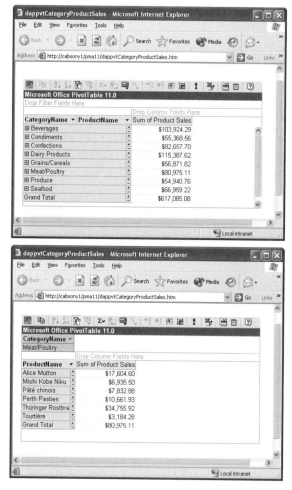

Figure 14-26   A pair of different browser windows illustrates some of the variety that users can generate from the same PivotTable list control.

Pivot tables are typically used by financial, operational, and decision-support analysts. An Access developer's job often involves setting up the data source for the PivotTable list control, such as the *Sales by Category* query for the two displays in Figure 14-26, and assign it to a PivotTable list control as described earlier. You can also set up a starter report in a PivotTable list control to introduce users to the resources that it exposes. You can create a starter report from a page's Design view with simple graphical techniques (a programmatic approach is demonstrated in the next section). Click the Help button for a review of how these techniques work. The power of a report based on a pivot table is that a user can easily modify the report without help from a developer. By putting the PivotTable list control on a Web page, you increase its availability to prospective users so that they can create their own report variations even when they are unable to physically connect to a LAN.

You can add a Chart control to a data access page and designate a Pivot-Table list control as its source. This process is easy for developers and flexible for users who are comfortable with analysis using pivot tables and pivot charts. Pivot charts are easier to design than charts on a spreadsheet, because you don't have to type in spreadsheet cell ranges as you do when basing a Chart component on a Spreadsheet component. You simply designate the PivotTable list control as a source and then graphically lay out any fields in the chart. It hardly matters what fields you put where because the point of a pivot chart is that users can modify these fields.

Figure 14-27 shows a pivot chart on the same Web page as the PivotTable list from the preceding sample. Notice there is a filter for products in the Meat/Poultry category. When you add an item to the detail drop area in a pivot chart, the control automatically aggregates it. You cannot plot an unaggregated field with a pivot chart. The control does not allow it. Notice also that the PivotTable list and PivotChart controls are in sync. When Access created the aggregate to plot product sales, it also updated the PivotTable list and added total and grand total values.

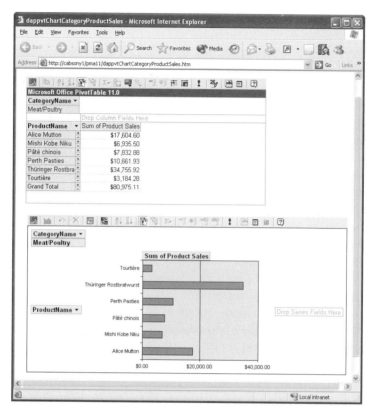

Figure 14-27 A pivot chart tied to a PivotTable list control.

Programming a PivotTable List Control from FrontPage

The Spreadsheet, Chart, and PivotTable Office Web Components do not require a data access page to function. Using FrontPage, you can insert any of these three Office Web Components on an ordinary Web page. Using the Microsoft Script Editor, you can program the operation of any Office Web Component. An advantage of this approach is that you can run these Web pages with Internet Explorer 4 while data access pages require a minimum of Internet Explorer 5. In addition, programming the object models for the Office Web Components lowers security barriers to the operation of a Web page, as compared to using the manual design interface for the Office Web Components. You can learn more about the object models for the Office Web Components from selected Help files (.chm) in the local resources folder of the following path \Program Files\Common Files\Microsoft Shared\Web Components\11\. For computers with an English-language Office 2003 installation, the local resources folder is 1033.

The sample for this section demonstrates how to automatically populate a PivotTable list control on a Web page. In addition, the sample performs an aggregation and hides the details used to compute the aggregations. Figure 14-28 displays the PivotTable list control along with its Field List on a page in a browser. The page reports the number of customers in each country from the *Customers* table in the Northwind.mdb file. Because the data source for the control is the *Customers* table, a user can respecify from a browser the participation of any field in a row, column, or filter drop area. Attempting to open this page on a Windows XP computer with the default security settings will raise a security fault that blocks the display of the page if you designed the page with the manual design techniques described in the "Creating and Using Office PivotTable Lists" section of this chapter. However, programming the solution as demonstrated here allows the page to show with the default Windows XP security settings.

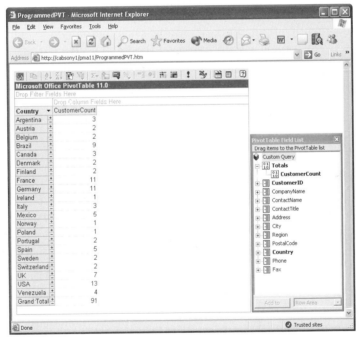

Figure 14-28   A programmed PivotTable list control with its Field List open.

The first step using FrontPage to design a page like the one in Figure 14-28 is to add a new Web page with a PivotTable list control to a Web site. You can begin by choosing File, New to open the Task Pane. Click the Blank Page link in the New Page section of the New Task Pane to open an empty page. From the tab controls below the page, select the Design tab. Then choose Insert, Web Component to open the Insert Web Component dialog box. Select the Spreadsheets And Charts item in the Components Type list on the left side of the dialog box. Double-click the Office PivotTable item from the Choose A Control list on the right to add the control to the page. The double-click also closes the dialog box. At this point, your page is likely to have a name such as new_page_1.htm, and the page's title is new_page_1. Choose File, Save As to create a more meaningful filename and title for the page. Enter a name, such as ProgrammedPVT, in the File Name box on the Save As dialog box. This revises the page's filename to ProgrammedPVT.htm and its title to ProgrammedPVT. The default name for the PivotTable list control in the code behind the page is PivotTable1.

Now that you have a PivotTable list control on a blank page, you are ready to program it. Choose Tools, Macro, Microsoft Script Editor to open the IDE behind the Web page. If the Document Outline window does not show, choose View, Other Windows, Document Outline. From the Script Outline view of the Document Outline window, double-click the *onload* event for the window object. This opens a script block in the head section of the code for the Web page with the shell for an *onload* event procedure that fires as soon as the page loads. The complete script follows. The script's role is to connect the PivotTable list control to the *Customers* table in the Northwind database and to format the page so that it looks like the display in Figure 14-28.

The *onload* event procedure has five short blocks of code. No additional custom code is necessary to prepare the Web page with its PivotTable list control for display.

- The first block specifies an ADO connection string for the Northwind.mdb file and assigns the string to the *ConnectionString* property for the *PivotTable1* object. Recall that the *PivotTable1* object represents the PivotTable list control on the page.

- The second code block instantiates and opens an ADODB *Recordset* object that points at the *Customers* table in the Northwind.mdb file. This block also assigns the recordset to the *DataSource* property of the *PivotTable1* object.

- The third block assigns the *Country* field to the row drop area and the *CustomerID* field data drop areas within the PivotTable list control. The *ptView* object represents the active view of the PivotTable list control. The *InsertFieldset* method for the view object of a *PivotTable* object enables the assignment of fields to drop areas within the PivotTable list control.

■   The event procedure's fourth section designates a variable (*Customer-IDCnt*) for an aggregate function that counts the number of *CustomerID* values within each country. Then the code assigns the variable to the data drop area.

■   The closing code section invokes the *HideDetails* method for the *ActiveData* object within PivotTable1. This hides the *CustomerID* values when the Web page opens. The count of *CustomerID* values remains visible.

```
Sub window_onload

Dim strConn
Dim rst1
Dim strSource
Dim ptView

'Assign connection string to PivotTable1
strConn = "Provider=Microsoft.Jet.OLEDB.4.0;" & _
    "Data Source=C:\Program Files\Microsoft " & _
    "Office\Office11\Samples\Northwind.mdb"
PivotTable1.ConnectionString=strConn

'Assign recordset to PivotTable1
set rst1 = CreateObject("ADODB.Recordset")
strSource = "SELECT * FROM Customers"
rst1.Open strSource, strConn
PivotTable1.DataSource=rst1

'Assign Row and Data drop areas
set ptView = PivotTable1.ActiveView
ptView.RowAxis.InsertFieldset ptView.Fieldsets("Country")
ptView.DataAxis.InsertFieldset ptView.Fieldsets("CustomerID")

'Develop CustomerID count and assign to Data drop area
set ptConstants = pivotTable1.Constants
set CustomerIDCnt = ptView.AddTotal("CustomerCount", _
    ptView.Fieldsets("CustomerID").Fields(0), _
    ptConstants.plFunctionCount)
ptView.DataAxis.InsertTotal CustomerIDCnt

'Hide details to show just CustomerID count
PivotTable1.ActiveData.HideDetails


End Sub
```

Summary

This chapter provides a succinct introduction to Web techniques based on data access pages, Office Web Components, and FrontPage. These three technologies are a natural extension of your Access development capabilities and enable you to easily create powerful Web solutions. Much as an Access database file (.mdb file) or Access project (.adp file) acts as a repository for different kinds of objects in a single project, a Web site managed by FrontPage can play a similar role for the files in a Web application. In addition, FrontPage offers powerful development and formatting capabilities of its own. This chapter examines the use of FrontPage with data access pages and Office Web Components.

Data access pages are an important technology because they enable you to create forms and reports on the Web for your Access and SQL Server databases. Furthermore, data access pages have a look and feel that is similar to Access forms and reports. This will make your clients feel right at home when they use your solutions on the Web. In some cases, you can actually copy existing Access forms and reports to data access pages with little or no editing. Because of security and client browser requirements, data access pages might be best suited to intranet solutions or Internet solutions that run on a virtual private network.

Office Web Components offer spreadsheet, chart, and pivot table controls that can exist on data access pages or on standalone Web pages. While data access pages must be developed from Access, you can create solutions with the spreadsheet, chart, and pivot table components from Access or FrontPage. The same IDE that you use to code event procedures for data access pages also works for standalone Web pages with Office Web Components. While the Office Web Components offer a convenient graphical user interface, you may occasionally find that you obtain more flexibility and less exposure to security faults that block page display by using code behind a page instead of manual development techniques.

15

XML and Access

Extensible Markup Language (XML) technologies have gained widespread acceptance in the computing industry in large part because the XML structure is particularly suitable for sending content over the Internet. This merit makes it likely that XML will play an even greater role in future computer innovations. Access developers who want to position themselves for new computer initiatives are wise to learn about XML technologies and using Access with these technologies.

XML is a syntax for representing any source, including data in Access database objects. XML documents have a simple format for representing data that is based on text, custom tags, and attributes. Related technologies, such as XML schemas for specifying structure in XML documents and XSLT (XML Stylesheet Language Transformations) for formatting and transforming XML documents, further enhance the power that XML can bring to your solutions.

This chapter introduces you to XML technologies, particularly XML technologies that work well with Access, including XML document syntax, XML schemas, and XSLT. You'll learn about the structure of XML documents and the broad range of sources that you can represent as XML. For example, you can expose Jet database tables, SQL Server views, XML schemas, and XSLT as XML documents with XML syntax. In addition, the chapter demonstrates how to program Microsoft Core XML Services (MSXML) from Access. MSXML offers a COM-based model for processing XML documents.

The first section offers an overview of selected XML technologies to facilitate your understanding of Access 2003 built-in XML features. You'll learn enough about XML tags and elements to read an XML document created by the Access *ExportXML* method. In addition, you'll gain sufficient mastery of XSD schemas to construct an Access table based on an XML document. The Access *ImportXML* method performs this function. A discussion of XSLT highlights the capability of this technology for representing data from an XML document in a table on a Web page.

The chapter's second and third sections feature manual and programmatic techniques for exporting, importing, and showing the contents of Access database objects via XML. The second section features manual techniques. You'll learn menu items and dialog box design elements for creating and processing XML documents. You'll also learn how to transport data over the Internet from Access databases via XML. The third section illustrates how to automate selected manual techniques. In addition, you'll learn how to process XML documents in ways not possible through the Access menus and dialog boxes. This is accomplished by showing you how to extend the built-in Access XML functionality with a basic understanding of XML technologies.

Introduction to XML Technologies

XML is a hot topic among system developers—especially the designers of Windows and Office. Applications developers, including those who create solutions with Access and the other Office packages, typically are in the early stages of learning about XML and the benefits it can bring to their solutions. A reason for this distinction between system and application developers may be the rapid proliferation of XML technologies and a lack of appreciation of how to use those technologies from Access and the other Office solutions. Access 2003 is XML-oriented and should help Access application developers to start using XML to enhance the solutions that they create for clients.

This section introduces three XML technologies that you can use with Access 2003 and other packages in Office 2003. First, this section examines XML document syntax. Knowledge of this syntax will help you read and process XML documents that can contain Access data. Second, the section shifts the focus to XSD schemas. XSD stands for XML Schema Definition. The XSD schema is an industry standard for specifying the structure of XML documents. For example, you can designate the data types for values in an XML document, as well as specify the primary key for an XML document based on an Access table. XSD schemas are XML documents, except their content is a statement about the structure of another XML document containing data. Third, the section acquaints you with XSLT, a language for manipulating the format of XML documents via style sheets and transformations. XSLT is based on XML syntax.

The following URL takes you to an especially useful reference within MSDN with a description of MSXML 4.0: *http://msdn.microsoft.com/library /default.asp?url=/library/en-us/xmlsdk/htm/xslt_starter_78s4.asp*. The site provides a thorough review of XML technologies, including starter kits for XML, XSD schemas, and XSLT.

The World Wide Web Consortium (W3C) is the premier destination for publications defining standards for XML and its related technologies. To learn more about the wealth of resources available from the W3C, go to its home page (*http://www.w3.org/*) and browse the list of technologies on its left border.

XML Document Syntax

XML is a text-based format for representing data. The data can be from Access databases, Excel workbook files, and Word documents, plus many other sources. XML documents are powerful because of their flexibility. Like HTML, XML embeds content within tags. XML syntax offers a hierarchical system for representing the content of documents. However, because you can specify your own tags, XML is adaptable to any source material. Also, XML has more rigid syntax conventions than those for HTML. These syntax conventions provide the basis for a consistent set of rules for retrieving content from an XML document, even when the tags used in one document are radically different from the tags used in another document. When a document follows the syntax rules, XML literature refers to the document as well-formed. For an XML parser to read an XML document, it must be well-formed. Microsoft Internet Explorer browsers include parsers for XML documents. If you attempt to view an XML document that is not well-formed, the browser reports an error in the document syntax. Otherwise, you will see the XML document contents in Internet Explorer.

> **Note**   Unless you are going to author XML documents from scratch, you do not need to know the rules for constructing a well-formed document. Those seeking a precise definition of what makes an XML document well-formed can find it at *http://www.w3.org/TR/2000/REC-xml-20001006#dt-wellformed.*

An XML document consists of declarations, tags, and attributes. In the declaration area, which is sometimes called the prolog, you declare a document to be consistent with a specific version of XML syntax. The current XML version is 1.0. You can also specify namespaces and other references that help to refine the definition of an XML document. For example, the prolog can denote namespaces that define tags used in an XML document. You can also denote a schema that specifies structure for the content in an XML document. Additionally, you can designate an XSLT file that includes code to reformat the representation of the data in an XML document.

You can represent data values within an XML document with tags that define elements and attributes that function similarly to properties for elements. An element nearly always has a start tag and an end tag. A start tag embraces the element's name in angle brackets (<elementname>). Between any start tag and end tag, you can include the text representation for a value. You can denote the element's end tag with a forward slash just before the element name (</elementname>). Start and end tags can occur one or more times within a document. An XML document requires a root set of tags—one just after the declaration and prolog for a document and the other as the last tag in the document. If the outermost start and end tags with data occur just once, then these tags satisfy the requirement for a root set of tags. Otherwise, you can specify another element with an arbitrary name to serve as the root element for the XML document. The other elements nest within the root element. XML syntax permits multiple levels of element nesting within an XML document. This nesting feature is one of the strengths of XML data representations. In ADO, you represent a join between customers and orders as a single rowset. In XML, you can represent the orders for a customer nested within that customer. This nesting better represents the internal structure of the data.

The following document, which is available as MyShippersWith-Elements.xml in the companion content for this chapter, shows a representation of the values from the *Shippers* table in the Northwind.mdb file with tags denoting elements. All other XML documents created for this chapter are also available in the companion materials for the chapter. You can create and edit a document such as MyShippersWithElements.xml from your favorite text editor (I like Notepad.exe). The declaration in the first line designates the document as an XML document version 1.0. The starting *<dataroot>* tag has a matching tag (*</dataroot>*) on the last line of the document; *<dataroot>* and *</dataroot>* are the root tags for the document. Within the dataroot element are three repeating *Shippers* elements. Nested with each *Shippers* element are a set of elements containing column values from the *Shippers* table.

```
<?xml version="1.0" ?>
<dataroot>
<Shippers>
<ShipperID>1</ShipperID>
<CompanyName>Speedy Express</CompanyName>
<Phone>(503) 555-9831</Phone>
</Shippers>
<Shippers>
<ShipperID>2</ShipperID>
<CompanyName>United Package</CompanyName>
<Phone>(503) 555-3199</Phone>
</Shippers>
```

```
<Shippers>
<ShipperID>3</ShipperID>
<CompanyName>Federal Shipping</CompanyName>
<Phone>(503) 555-9931</Phone>
</Shippers>
</dataroot>
```

Attributes also facilitate the representation of data values in an XML document. Recall that you can think of attributes as properties of an element. You designate attributes as name-value pairs. An equal sign delimiter (=) separates the name from the value and attribute values must appear within quotation marks. The convention is to use double quotation marks, but single quotation marks are also acceptable. It is most common to see single quotation marks as attribute value delimiters when the value contains one or more double quotation marks within it. The MyShippersWithAttributes.xml document that follows shows the syntax for using attributes to represent the values in column values from the *Shippers* table, which is the same source for the preceding XML document.

This XML document sample also illustrates how to close an element without a distinct end tag. Notice that the start *Shippers* tag with the column values for each of the first two *Shippers* elements ends with a closing slash. This closing slash represents the end tag. The third *Shippers* element in the document shows the syntax with a distinct closing tag for the element. Either design practice is acceptable.

```
<?xml version="1.0" ?>
<dataroot>
<Shippers ShipperID="1" CompanyName="Speedy Express"
Phone="(503) 555-9831" />
<Shippers ShipperID="2" CompanyName="United Package"
Phone="(503) 555-3199" />
<Shippers ShipperID="3" CompanyName="Federal Shipping"
Phone="(503) 555-9931" ></Shippers>
</dataroot>
```

Figure 15-1 shows the MyShippersWithElements.xml and MyShippersWithAttributes.xml documents in a browser. The Internet Explorer browser has a built-in XML document viewer, which is based on its parser for XML syntax. Notice that the viewer automatically indents nested elements. For example, the *Shippers* element is indented relative to the *dataroot* element. Within the MyShippersWithElements.xml document, the *ShipperID*, *CompanyName*, and *Phone* elements are indented for each *Shippers* element. This indenting feature with Internet Explorer improves the clarity of a document's structure relative to viewing the same document in a basic text editor, such as Notepad. On the other hand, Internet Explorer does not enable the editing of an XML document unless you invoke the View, Source command, and save your changes. However, when choosing View, Source from a browser, the document's tags appear without any automatic indenting. Notice that elements in an XML document that have other elements within them appear with expand/contract controls to their left. All the controls in Figure 15-1 are fully expanded so they appear with a minus sign (–). However, you can collapse the nested elements by clicking the control. In a collapsed state, the control appears with a plus sign (+). The Internet Explorer XML document viewer converts all rows in MyShippersWithAttributes.xml document to a format with an embedded end tag, instead of the mixed use of the embedded end tag for the first two rows and an explicit end tag for the last row (as in the original document).

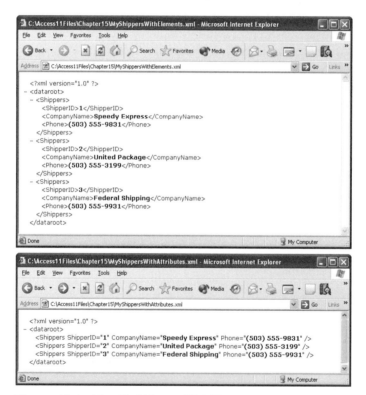

Figure 15-1 The MyShippersWithElements.xml and MyShippers-WithElements.xml documents in a browser.

There are many other features you could learn about XML documents. I highlight three aspects of XML document syntax that should improve your ability to read the XML documents that you encounter. In addition, you can use these guidelines to create your own XML documents.

By now you should have the idea that formatting an XML document is a lot like programming. Therefore, there are tags for marking text as a comment in a document so that it is readable to the human eye, but it is not parsed along with the rest of the text in a document. There are two common uses for the block comment marker. First, to add a comment to a document that provides information about its purpose, author, original date, or similar kind of content. Second, you can bound regular content in block comment markers to remove the content from the parsed version of a document. This is helpful for debugging the document's structure. The syntax for a comment marker appears next.

```
<!-- text to be commented out of a document can be on 1+ lines ‡
```

There are five special characters that are routinely represented by escape sequences in XML documents. These characters have special meaning to the parser. Therefore, using the escape sequence allows you to designate one of the characters without having the parser misinterpret your content. For example, the open angle bracket (<) denotes the start of a tag, but it also represents the less than sign. If you mean the less than sign, then you should use the special escape sequence (<) rather than the open angle bracket (<). The following table shows the five escape sequences you can encounter in XML documents.

Meaning	Escape sequence
< (less than)	&lt;
> (greater than)	&gt;
& (ampersand)	&amp;
' (apostrophe or single quotation marks)	&apos;
" (double quotation marks)	&quot;

CDATA sections are another formatting convention that you are likely to discover in some XML documents. Like the escape sequences in the preceding table, CDATA sections enable you to represent any special markup characters in an XML document so that the parser does not interpret them as standard markup. The difference is that a CDATA section applies to a whole block of code rather than a single character. In this sense, a CDATA section acts like an element in an XML document. In addition, you do not need to use escape sequences for special characters, such as <. The start of a CDATA section is indicated with <![CDATA[. Denote the end of a CDATA section with]]>. Nothing between the starting and ending delimiters is parsed by an XML reader. Instead, it passes through as is. A CDATA section cannot include its start nor its end delimiters. In addition, there are no escape sequences to represent them.

The SpecialMarkupSamples.xml file illustrates the syntax for representing special characters with either escape sequences or a CDATA section. The document also illustrates the syntax for a block comment marker. Figure 15-2 shows the document in a browser.

```
<?xml version="1.0" ?>
<dataroot>
<!-- example with escape sequence -->
<message> a &lt; b</message>
<!-- example with CDATA section -->
<![CDATA[ a < b ]]>
</dataroot>
```

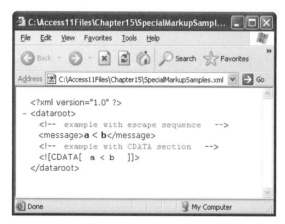

Figure 15-2   Either escape sequences or CDATA sections can be used to represent special markup characters in an XML document.

XSD Schemas

Recall that a schema specifies the structure of an XML document. Since an XML document can reflect a table from an Access database file, you can think of a schema as a table definition that you see in the Design view for a table. The difference is that Design view represents the table through a graphical UI and the XSD schema reflects the structure of the document in XML code. Yes, the language for expressing XSD schemas is XML. This feature is one of the strengths of XSD schema versus alternative means of representing the structure of XML documents.

As you spend time learning about XML, you are likely to encounter three different formats for describing the structure of an XML document. A Document Type Definition (DTD) is an early way of representing the structure of XML documents that differs from schemas. The language for expressing DTDs is

Extended Backus-Naur Form (EBNF). It is not important that you know more about EBNF other than that it is not XML. This means that document authors have to master another language just to express the structure of their XML documents. In addition, DTDs are not smart about the demands of a database, such as a rich data type structure. Schemas get around both of these weaknesses of DTDs and add other benefits, such as easy extensibility and self-documenting capabilities.

There are actually two types of schemas for XML documents. Microsoft took the initiative in defining a schema model for XML documents before the formal approval of a standard by the W3C. This early implementation of schemas for XML documents has the name XDR schema for XML-Data Reduced schema. Microsoft implemented this early schema in Internet Explorer 5 and version 2.0 of Microsoft XML Core Services (MSXML 2.0). Shortly after the W3C adopted a standard for expressing XML schemas in XSD language, Microsoft switched its support to XSD schemas. The XSD schema standard is implemented in MSXML 4.0 and Internet Explorer 6.0.

> **Note**   Subsequent to the release of MSXML 4.0, Microsoft released MSXML 5.0, which added support for inline XSD schemas in XML documents instead of requiring a separate XSD schema file from the structure of the XML document that it supports.

When working with XML documents and Access, your XML documents will typically refer to three external schemas. The standard schema for all XML documents is the W3C XSD schema standard at *http://www.w3.org/2001/XMLSchema*. XML documents created with Access typically refer to a schema with a URN (Uniform Resource Name) of *schemas-microsoft-com:officedata*. URNs specify the name and source for a document rather than the exact location of a resource on the Web as with a URL. In addition, your schema will contain information derived from the Access database object, such as a table, query, or form that serves as the basis for an XML document. The schema name frequently is the same as the XML document, except that its file has an .xsd extension instead of the .xml extension used for the XML document.

Figure 15-3 shows an XML document based on the *Shippers* table in an Internet Explorer browser. This document was generated through the Access UI. The *Shippers* table was imported, along with the *Customers* and *Orders* tables, to the Chapter15.mdb file from the Northwind.mdb file. The *<dataroot>*

tag is immediately after the declaration tag for the XML document. Within the *<dataroot>* tag, three attributes point to XSD schemas for the document. These schemas can define elements and attributes in the remainder of the Shippers.xml file. The Shippers.xsd schema file appears in the same folder as the Shippers.xml document file. You can refer to schemas in other folders and at Web-based URLs as well. To refer to a file-based URL, use the following format: *file://DriveLetter://path/filename.fileextension.*

Figure 15-3   The Access UI creates XML documents that use attributes in the root tag for an XML document to refer to XML schemas.

The attributes in the dataroot denote namespaces. In XML, namespaces are collections of pre-defined tags and attributes. Generally, you point a reference to a namespace with the *xmlns:namespaceprefix*, such as *xmlns:od* to point at the *shemas-microsoft-com:officedata* namespace. If any item (tags or attributes) in the XML document explicitly represents types from the *schemas-microsoft-com:officedata namespace*, then you should precede the item with the prefix representing the namespace, which is *od* in this case. You can designate a default namespace of schema types by using the *xsi:noNamespaceSchemaLocation* attribute. The namespace at *http://www.w3.org/2001/XMLSchema-instance* is the implementation of the W3C XSD Schema standard. The *xsi:noNamespaceSchemaLocation* attribute points at the location of the XSD schema file to look up any element or attribute in a document that does not have a prefix. It is normal for XML documents created with the Access UI. You will sometimes find a namespace for a custom schema referenced with the *xsi:schemaLocation* attribute, instead of the *xsi:noNamespaceSchemaLocation* attribute. Documents that always use a namespace prefix before tags and attributes in an XML document require this attribute for pointing at a custom XSD schema.

Authoring XSD schemas can be detailed work that is easily subject to error. Access developers are not likely to be writing their own schemas, and Access 2003 has no built-in tools to simplify the task. An Access developer is more likely to read a schema to understand the structure of the contents within an XML document. The following listing shows the XSD schema, Shippers.xsd, for XML document Shippers.xml depicted in Figure 15-3. Like the XML document, the XSD schema was created automatically for the *Shippers* table with a few clicks in the Access UI. Viewing the schema in a browser improves its readability by automatically indenting nested elements. When working with a schema listing from Notepad, such as the one that follows, I often draw connecting lines on the left edge of a listing between matching tags to improve the readability of a schema document.

```xml
<?xml version="1.0" encoding="UTF-8"?>
<xsd:schema xmlns:xsd="http://www.w3.org/2001/XMLSchema" xmlns:od="urn:schemas-
microsoft-com:officedata">
<xsd:element name="dataroot">
<xsd:complexType>
<xsd:sequence>
<xsd:element ref="Shippers" minOccurs="0" maxOccurs="unbounded"/>
</xsd:sequence>
<xsd:attribute name="generated" type="xsd:dateTime"/>
</xsd:complexType>
</xsd:element>
<xsd:element name="Shippers">
<xsd:annotation>
<xsd:appinfo>
<od:index index-name="PrimaryKey" index-key="ShipperID " primary="yes"
unique="yes" clustered="no"/>
</xsd:appinfo>
</xsd:annotation>
<xsd:complexType>
<xsd:sequence>
<xsd:element name="ShipperID" minOccurs="1" od:jetType="autonumber" od:sql-
SType="int" od:autoUnique="yes" od:nonNullable="yes" type="xsd:int"/>
<xsd:element name="CompanyName" minOccurs="1" od:jetType="text" od:sql-
SType="nvarchar" od:nonNullable="yes">
<xsd:simpleType>
<xsd:restriction base="xsd:string">
<xsd:maxLength value="40"/>
```

(continued)

```
</xsd:restriction>
</xsd:simpleType>
</xsd:element>
<xsd:element name="Phone" minOccurs="0" od:jetType="text" od:sqlSType="nvar-
char">
<xsd:simpleType>
<xsd:restriction base="xsd:string">
<xsd:maxLength value="24"/>
</xsd:restriction>
</xsd:simpleType>
</xsd:element>
</xsd:sequence>
</xsd:complexType>
</xsd:element>
</xsd:schema>
```

There are two broad design features worthy of your attention in the XSD schema that shows in the listing for Shippers.xsd. First, the schema is obviously an XML document. Therefore, learning about XSD schema can build on the knowledge that you already have about XML syntax. Second, the XML document defining the schema uses prefixes for tags and attributes. In this case, the schema uses two standard collections of types denoted by *xsd* for the W3C schema standard and *od* for the contents of the *schemas-microsoft-com:office-data* URN.

The preceding schema listing defines two complex types. A complex type is a type that references at least one other type for a tag or an attribute. The first type or element is the *dataroot* type. This type builds on two other types—the *Shippers* element and the *generated* attribute type. The *Shippers* type is a complex type that nests within the *dataroot* type, whose tag is the root tag for the Shippers.xml document. The schema's structure allows an unlimited number of *Shippers* elements (*maxOccurs="unbounded"*) within the *dataroot* element. However, the schema specifies that a *Shippers* element is not required (*minOccurs="0"*) for the XML document to be valid. The generated attribute is formatted with a native *dateTime* data type from the W3C standard for XSD schemas; notice the *xsd* prefix for the *dateTime* data type name.

The *Shippers* element definition includes several sections. First, it defines the primary key for the document within the *appinfo* element. The tag structure for this process is interesting because *appinfo* has an *xsd* prefix, but the *index* element, nested within the *appinfo* element, has an *od* prefix. In addition, the index element has a series of attributes that should be familiar to most experienced Access developers, except for one—*clustered*. This attribute applies exclusively to SQL Server databases, and its availability confirms that you can create XML documents based on an Access project referencing a SQL Server database containing one or more tables. The *clustered* attribute is true when the rows are physically sorted on a storage device in the order of the primary key or index.

The *Shippers* element is complex because its definition depends on several other elements, including but not restricted to the index for the document's primary key. Three of these other elements are the *ShipperID*, *CompanyName*, and *Phone* elements. These element definitions appear within *<xsd:sequence>* and *</xsd:sequence>* tags. These tags maintain the order of the elements in the XML document according to their order in the XSD schema. Other XSD schema elements operate on groups of nested elements differently, such as allowing just one element from a group to appear in a document (*choice*) or allowing all nested elements to appear in any order (*all*). The definitions for the *ShipperID*, *CompanyName*, and *Phone* attribute have both *od:JetType* and *od:SQLType* attribute specifications, which again confirms that you can create schema for XML documents based on Jet as well as SQL Server databases. In fact, the schema is interpretable by an Access database file pointing at a Jet database or an Access project pointing at a SQL Server database. The three elements (*ShipperID*, *CompanyName*, and *Phone*) have *minOccurs* attribute settings, which in this context specify whether an element value is required for a *Shippers* element. A value of 1 denotes a required value, and a value of 0 indicates an optional value. Both the *CompanyName* and *Phone* element definitions include an *xsd:Simple* element for defining a special constraint. In this case, the number of characters in the text field.

XSLT

One of the advantages of XML documents is that you can read them without a special reader. After all, the data is in text format. This is not true for either Jet or ADO. In spite of the inherent readability of XML, the actual format of the text values is often awkward to read. This is where XSLT can come in handy. With XSLT, you can select, transform, and reformat the layout of values from an XML document.

XSLT is a rule-based programming language that is XML-based. This means that the XML knowledge that you acquired in the prior reviews of XML documents and XSD schemas applies to XSLT as well. XSLT is a reasonably rich programming language, and it is distinct in syntax and operation from most languages that Access developers know already. Therefore, it represents special challenges as you add it to your suite of tools. Nevertheless, there are some easy opportunities to adapt XSLT in Access applications.

As you begin to migrate to XSLT, I urge you to think in terms of recycling and tweaking XSLT code samples that do much of what you want done. This section demonstrates this approach. First, I describe and demonstrate the operation of a Hello, World! sample from the MSDN site (*http://msdn.microsoft.com /library/default.asp?url=/library/en-us/xmlsdk/htm/xslt_starter_2uhw.asp*). Then I adapt and extend the sample to illustrate how you can modify its output and run it from an Access form. While this demonstration is not based on a database, it does show you how to use XSLT with an Access form. In the "Programmatically Using XML from Access 2003" section, I will revisit XSLT and show you how to programmatically format Access tables for output in HTML pages. The sample in this section even opens the HTML page automatically.

> **Note** The samples developed for this section, as in most of the rest of the book, were tested and evaluated with Windows XP and Internet Explorer 6. This combination makes MSXML 4.0 available. XSLT relies on parsing capabilities provided through MSXML 4.0. It is recommended that you deploy MSXML 4.0 before attempting to run the samples in this section.

Presenting and Demonstrating the Hello, World! XSLT Sample

When reformatting an XML document with XSLT, you will need a target XML document to transform and an XSLT program to implement the new format. In addition, you need to tell the XML parser that it should use the XSLT program, which typically resides in a separate file from the XML document. The Hello World! sample resides in a couple of files—hello.xml and hello.xsl.

The hello.xml file appears below. Notice that it has an xml-stylesheet element with an href attribute that points at the hello.xsl file. The syntax for this element is similar to that used for tying an XML document to an XSD schema. In this case, the link is to the file with the XSLT program (hello.xsl). If you commented out the xml-stylesheet element, the file appears in a browser as an ordinary XML file with a comment. However, with the xml-stylesheet element uncommented, the XML file's appearance in a browser is transformed by the hello.xsl file.

```
<?xml version="1.0"?>
<?xml-stylesheet type="text/xsl" href="hello.xsl"?>
<hello-world>
  <greeter>An XSLT Programmer</greeter>
  <greeting>Hello, World!</greeting>
</hello-world>
```

Figure 15-4 shows the hello.xml with and without commenting for the xml-stylesheet element. The top window in the figure shows the hello.xml with comment markup surrounding the *xml-stylesheet* element. Notice that the file has just two elements with data values and that the *greeter* element with a value of An XSLT Programmer appears before the *greeting* element with a value of Hello, World! The bottom window shows the hello.xml file with the comment markup removed for the xml-stylesheet element. There is no markup for the element values. In addition, the *greeting* element value appears before the *greeter* element value. Also, the XSLT formatted version of the XML file adds a new word, from, before rendering the *greeter* element value.

Figure 15-4 The hello.xml file rendered before and after transformation by an XSLT file.

The following script shows the hello.xsl file that transforms the appearance of the XML document from the top window in Figure 15-4 to the bottom window in the figure. Notice that the listing commences with the declaration of an XML document, which confirms that XSLT is an XML-based syntax. The root node for the document with the XSLT program is the *xsl:stylesheet* element. An attribute for this node points at the W3C XSLT standard. Next, the *xsl:template* element specifies a template for the overall formatting of the hello.xml file contents. The *match* attribute for this element points at the *hello-world* element in the hello.xml file. The template applies to the elements nested within the hello-world element. The template lays out an HTML page. The H1 heading font in the page body formats the *greeting* element value. Instead of directly referencing the *greeter* element, the XSLT code applies a template with an *apply-template* element that designates another template through its select attribute. This attribute points at the *greeter* template. The *greeter* template precedes the value of the *greeter* element with from, and the template also applies an *H2* font setting and an italics font style. The *xsl:value of* element designates a value to display. The element's *select* attribute specifies the value to display. In this case, the period (.) denotes the template's name, which is *greeter*.

```
<?xml version="1.0"?>
<xsl:stylesheet
     xmlns:xsl="http://www.w3.org/1999/XSL/Transform"
     version="1.0">
  <xsl:template match="/hello-world">
     <HTML>
       <HEAD>
         <TITLE></TITLE>
       </HEAD>
       <BODY>
          <H1><xsl:value-of select="greeting"/></H1>
          <xsl:apply-templates select="greeter"/>
       </BODY>
     </HTML>
  </xsl:template>
  <xsl:template match="greeter">
     <DIV><H2><I>from
         <xsl:value-of select="."/></I></H2>
     </DIV>
  </xsl:template>
</xsl:stylesheet>
```

Extending and Running an XSLT Sample from an Access Form

The extension and adaptation of the Hello, World! sample from the preceding section involves a slightly modified XML document (CustomHelloWorld.xml) and a similarly modified XSLT file (CustomHelloWorld.xsl). The XML document and XSLT program replace the *greeter* element with a corresponding *message* element. In addition, the called template (*greeter*) is dropped because the application transforms the text before invoking the XSLT program. However, the new XSLT program retains the same formatting for font size and italics. The CustomHelloWorld.xsl file contents appear next.

```
<?xml version="1.0"?>
<xsl:stylesheet
      xmlns:xsl="http://www.w3.org/1999/XSL/Transform"
      version="1.0">
  <xsl:template match="/hello-world">
      <HTML>
        <HEAD>
          <TITLE></TITLE>
        </HEAD>
        <BODY>
          <H1><xsl:value-of select="greeting"/></H1>
          <DIV><H2><I>
              <xsl:value-of select="message"/></I></H2>
          </DIV>
        </BODY>
      </HTML>
  </xsl:template>
</xsl:stylesheet>
```

The novel aspect of the extension is the use of an Access form to gather input that, in turn, populates element values. The code behind the form writes out an XML file as a textstream object to a file that holds the XML document (CustomHelloWorld.xml). Before persisting the textstream object to a file, the code inserts the contents of three text boxes on the form (frmWriteXMLToHT-MLWithXSLT). A click event procedure for a button on the form opens the Cus-tomHelloWorld.xml file, which displays as an HTML page in the pma11 Web site initially developed in Chapter 14. Figure 15-5 shows the form with some sample content in its text boxes, and Figure 15-6 reveals the page that displays when the user clicks the Show HTML button on the form.

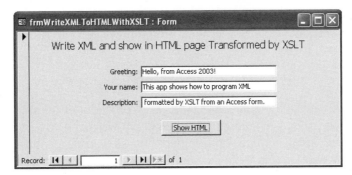

Figure 15-5   An Access form used to collect values for writing an XML document.

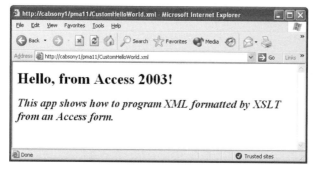

Figure 15-6 A browser displaying the XML document generated by the click event procedure for the button on the form in Figure 15-5.

For me, the magic of this application is in the click event procedure for the button on the form. The writing of a text file is a major factor in conjuring this magic. The text file is in the format of an XML document and reflects the current values in the text boxes. The application achieves this result through the use of the *FileSystemObject* class. Your VBA project requires a reference to the Microsoft Scripting Runtime to use the *FileSystemObject* class. The *str1* variable contains the script for the XML document. The string expression for *str1* copies values of text boxes into the script. Then the procedure uses a *FileSystemObject* instance (*fso1*) to persist the *tso1* textstream instance that contains the string variable representing the XML document to a text file. The application persists the XML document to CustomHelloWorld.xml at the pma11 Web site. To run this application, you need pma11 on your intranet or you need to designate another Web site that is on your intranet. Before setting the *tso1* and *fso1* instances to nothing, the procedure invokes the *FollowHyperlink* method for a URL pointing at CustomHelloWorld.xml. This opens a browser session with the XML document formatted by the XSLT program in CustomHelloWorld.xsl. The complete listing for the click event procedure appears next.

> **Note** To make the *cmdShowHTML_Click* procedure work properly in your computing environment, you probably will need to update the *strServer* variable value, and perhaps the *strWebsite* variable value, for a Web server and Web site conveniently available to you.

```
Private Sub cmdShowHTML_Click()

Dim str1 As String
Dim fso1 As New Scripting.FileSystemObject
Dim tso1 As Scripting.TextStream
Dim strGreeting As String
Dim strName As String
Dim strDescription As String
Dim strMessage As String
Dim strFilePathName As String
Dim strServer As String
Dim strWebsite As String
Dim strURL As String

'Copy text box values for insertion in XSLT code
strGreeting = Me.txtGreeting
strMessage = Me.txtYourName & " " & Me.txtDescription

'Copy saved text box values into xml script
str1 = "<?xml version='1.0'?> " & _
    "<?xml-stylesheet type='text/xsl' href='CustomHelloWorld.xsl'?> " & _
    "<hello-world>" & _
    "   <message>" & strMessage & "</message>" & _
    "   <greeting>" & strGreeting & "</greeting>" & _
    "</hello-world>"

'Save xml script to a file
strFileNamePath = _
    "C:\Inetpub\wwwroot\pma11\CustomHelloWorld.xml"
Set tso1 = _
    fso1.CreateTextFile(strFileNamePath, True)
tso1.Write str1
tso1.Close

'Open browser to saved xml file
strServer = "cabsony1"
strWebsite = "pma11"
strURL = "http://" & strServer & "/" & _
    strWebsite & "/CustomHelloWorld.xml"
Application.FollowHyperlink strURL, , True

'Clean up objects
Set tso1 = Nothing
Set fso1 = Nothing

End Sub
```

Manually Using XML from Access 2003

This section aims to give you a hands-on feel for creating and using XML documents based on tables and other database objects in an Access database file or an Access project. You will see how Access can generate both XML documents and their matching XSD documents. In addition, you'll learn how to use these documents in other Access applications, with e-mail, and in browsers.

Exporting, Importing, and Presenting an Access Table

In this section, you are shown how to export, import, and present the *Shippers* table from an Access database as an XML document. The *Shippers* table is convenient for demonstrations because it has few rows and columns. The examples in this section provide step-by-step instructions for generating an XML document based on the *Shippers* table and importing that document into another Access application to create a faithful copy of the table's contents and structure. You also learn how to display the data in a tabular format in the XML document within a browser. The section closes with an example that attaches an XML document and its matching XSD schema to an e-mail message. This example suggests how you can readily mail Access data across the Internet and have another Access application on another continent recreate both the table values and structure. Though the examples in this section use the *Shippers* table, the guidelines apply to any Access table.

Generating XML Files

The Access UI offers an exceptionally easy means of creating XML documents and XSLT transforms that are suitable for presentation on the Web. You can base the XML documents on tables and queries, as well as the data behind forms and reports in Access database files and Access projects. To export a table as an XML document, such as the *Shippers* table in Chapter15.mdb, select the table in the Database window. Then choose File, Export. From the Export dialog box for the selected object, designate a destination folder via a selection from the Save in drop-down box. Next, select XML from the Save as type drop-down box. This selection causes Access to populate the File name text box with the name of the object highlighted in the Database window. If you select the *Shippers* table, clicking Export eventually creates a file named Shippers.xml. However, you can specify a different file name for the XML document by modifying the default entry in the File name drop-down box. Clicking Export on the dialog box presents the Export XML dialog box with selected check boxes for Data (XML) and Schema of the data (XSD); see Figure 15-7. Access does not select by default the third check box, which is Presentation of your data (XSL). Clicking OK on the Export XML dialog box creates files based on your selections.

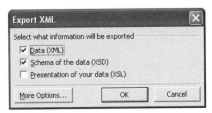

Figure 15-7   The Export XML dialog box for creating XML files based on Access database objects, such as tables, queries, forms, and reports.

The set of selections is richer than it might appear from a casual examination of Figure 15-7. In addition to creating an .xml file with the contents of the selected database objects, the default selections also create an .xsd file with the XSD schema for the selected object in the Database window when you invoke the File, Export command. The "XSD Schemas" section in this chapter presents and describes the files for an XML document and XSD schema based on the *Shippers* table.

Clicking the Presentation Of Your Data (XSL) check box will add two additional files to those created when you click OK on the Export XML dialog box. One of these files will have an XSLT program; the file's default name for the *Shippers* table will be Shippers.xsl. The other file will be an HTML file with an .htm extension (Shippers.htm). To view this file in a browser, you must use Internet Explorer 6+. This is because opening the HTML page requires MSXML 4.0+ on the computer, which installs along with Internet Explorer 6+. If a client does not have Internet Explorer 6 on a workstation, you have two alternatives. First, you can save the generated files to a Web site, such as pma11. Choose the LAN location for an intranet Web site, or save the files to a local folder and then upload them to your Web site on a remote Web server. After selecting the Presentation of your data (XSL) check box on the Export XML dialog box, click More Options. Then select the Presentation tab. Select the Server (ASP) check box. Then click OK. The Server (ASP) selection causes the XSLT transform to run on the Web server and return HTML to the browser through an .asp file named after the selected object in the Database window (for example, Shippers.asp). The second option is to install Internet Explorer 6+ on the workstation that needs to open the .htm file created by the standard process. This option installs MSXML 4.0+ on the local workstation. You can obtain the most recent Internet Explorer download at *http://www.microsoft.com/windows/ie /downloads/default.asp*.

There are a few other options for controlling the output from the File, Export command for XML files. These options typically will not have a critical impact on the use of your XML files, and the default settings are appropriate for most circumstances.

Importing XML Documents

One reason for exporting XML documents based on Access database objects is so that you can import them into other Access database files and Access projects. XML documents store the data and much of the structure associated with Access tables. In addition, creating XML documents based on queries as well as the data behind forms and reports gives you a snapshot of the data in those objects at a moment in time—namely, the moment when the XML document was generated.

It is important to understand that an XML document is a text file with tags and the tags can have attributes. Because XML documents are text files, you can import them into any application that can open a text file. In Figure 15-3 you saw that an Internet Explorer browser can import an XML document for viewing. The Internet Explorer browser brings special benefits, including automatic indenting for nested elements and collapse/expand controls for hiding and exposing document details. However, you can also read XML documents with other packages that can read text files. Just as you can use the Notepad utility program to create XML documents (mentioned in the "XML Document Syntax" section of this chapter), you can also use Notepad to open XML documents for viewing. The "XSD Schemas" section demonstrates how a schema appears in Notepad—after opening the XML document, you can view it, edit it, and save changes.

Access can store the XSD schema file along with the XML document file from an Access database file or an Access project. This feature enables another Access database file to open an XML document and re-create the data source associated with the document. This includes the values and the structure, including the data types, the primary key, and any indexes. While reading an XML document and showing its values as text is useful, capturing its value along with its structure is substantially more beneficial. Recall that XSD schema created by Access represent data values with Jet and SQL Server data types. Therefore, you can pass data between Access and SQL Server in either direction by exporting an XML document with its XSD schema from one application, for example an Access project, and importing the document and schema into another application, such as an Access database file.

Because XML is text, it passes through Internet firewalls, whereas an Access database file and an ADO object, such as a recordset, are blocked by many firewalls. The ability of XML files to pass through firewalls allows you to post an XML document file along with its XSD schema file to a Web site so that remote users can download it and reconstruct the source data in Access. You can also send an XML document and its XSD schema file through e-mail as attachments to one or more recipients. Because you often will be passing relatively small text files, data transfer via XML can be faster than transferring a whole database just for one or two small tables.

To demonstrate the XML Import capability, start a new Access database file or Access project that can connect to the XML document and XSD schema file. In the companion content for this chapter, you'll find a Chapter15Receive.mdb and Chapter15Receive.adp. If you use an .adp file, recall that you must connect it to a SQL Server or MSDE 2000 database. You can use the Chapter15ReceiveSQL.mdf file in the companion content for this chapter to achieve this task—see Chapter 11 for details on how to do this. Once you gain local access to the XML document file and the XSD schema file, you can start to create a table based on the XML document by choosing File, Get External Data, Import. Use the Look in drop-down box to point the Import dialog box at the folder containing the XML document and XSD schema files. Select XML from the Files of type drop-down box. Then simply double-click the XML document file to open the Import XML dialog box. If you click Options, Access expands the dialog box to show three possible ways of processing the XML document and XSD files (see Figure 15-8). The default option is to create a new table with the name of the XML document and populate the table with data from the XML document. You can also choose to import the structure without the data or to append the data to an existing table. If you want to create a new table based on the contents of the XML document, just click OK. Otherwise, select a check box for one of the other two options before clicking OK.

Figure 15-8   The Import XML dialog box for importing the XML document created in the "Generating XML Files" section.

These steps work the same for importing an XML document and its XSD schema into an Access project, with one exception. At the conclusion of importing the XML document into a SQL Server table, Access presents the error message explaining the *Identity* property was not set. Actually, this behavior is by design. SQL Server does not necessarily let a user write values into an *Identity* field. This ability depends on the permissions associated with a login or user account, but Access cannot ensure the permissions are valid for all users (see Chapter 13 for more details about SQL Server security). Therefore, Access turns off the *Identity* property and presents an error message. In addition, Access creates an *ImportErrors* table to make the error description readily available for viewing. One workaround for this problem is to turn the *Identity* property back on. You can do this by opening the table in Design view and selecting the column that had the *Identity* property turned off during the importing process. Next, change the *Identity* property setting on the Column tab to Yes. Either accept the default Identity Seed and Identity Increment settings or override them with whatever values your application requires. In order to make these design changes to the table, your login and/or user account must have permission.

Viewing the XML as a Table in a Browser

When you select the Presentation of your data (XSL) check box in the Export XML dialog box, Access creates two additional files—namely, an .xsl file and an .htm file. In the case of exporting the *Shippers* table with the default settings, the two extra files have names of Shippers.xsl and Shippers.htm. If you have Internet Explorer 6.0 or later installed on your computer, you can open the Shippers.htm file by choosing the File, Open command, and then navigating to the .htm file. A table appears in your browser (see Figure 15-9). For many viewers, this is a substantial improvement in readability over the layout for a standard XML document (see Figure 15-3).

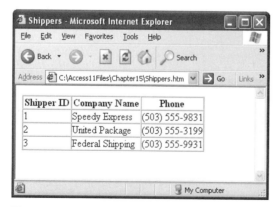

Figure 15-9 The Shippers.htm file generated by the Access File, Export command in an Internet Explorer 6.0 browser.

There is one problem with the default settings for representing an XML document as a table on a Web page. The .htm file opens properly only in Internet Explorer 6.0 or later browsers (even Internet Explorer 5.0 browsers on Windows 2000 Server computers cannot open the file properly). That's because the .htm file requires software installed on a computer along with Internet Explorer 6.0 or later. The "Generating XML Files" section of this chapter describes how to create another presentation version of the XML document that runs on a Web server and downloads HTML. If you were working with the *Shippers* table, you would navigate to Shippers.asp instead of Shippers.htm. The .asp file must reside in a Web site running on a Microsoft Internet Information Services Web server (the only place .asp files run). You can deploy the .htm file to any folder on a computer.

Exporting Related Tables

To demonstrate how to export tables in relationships, I used a Microsoft Access file type to import the *Orders* and *Customers* tables from the Northwind database to the Chapter15.mdb file. Recall that the *Shippers* table was already in Chapter15.mdb. Use the Relationships window to adjust the relationships among the three tables to match those in the Northwind database. After your adjustments, the *Customers* table and the *Shippers* table will be in a many-to-many relationship with the *Orders* table serving as a junction table between the other two tables. As a consequence of this design, the *Shippers* table will be in a one-to-many relationship with the *Orders* table. In other words, one shipper can deliver multiple orders.

By exporting the *Shippers* table with the *Orders* table that depends on it, you can see how the Access XML processing capabilities handle a one-to-many relationship. Start by selecting the *Shippers* table. Then choose File, Export. In the Export Table dialog box, designate an appropriate folder for the .xml and .xsd files, such as C:\Access11Files\Chapter15. Select XML as the file type. Override the *Shippers* default name with *ShippersOrders*. Click Export to open the Export XML dialog box. Next, click More Options. Access automatically selects the Shippers check box on the Data tab, but it does not select the Orders check box. Click this check box to select it so that the *Shippers* and *Orders* tables populate the XML document that Access generates. Notice there is an expand control next to the *Orders* table. Leave the control alone for now. A subsequent example will demonstrate its role. Click OK to close the Export XML dialog box and generate the ShippersOrders.xml and ShippersOrders.xsd files.

If you open the ShippersOrders.xml file, the first element you see after the dataroot element is the *Shippers* element. Nested below this element are the

ShipperID, CompanyName, and *Phone* elements for the Speedy Express shipper, whose *ShipperID* element value is 1. Nested below these elements are a series of elements for the orders shipped via Speedy Express. The first set of elements based on the *Orders* table have an *OrderID* element value of 10249, and the next set of elements based on the *Orders* table have an *OrderID* element value of 10251. Notice there is a gap in *OrderID* numbers. This is because the elements for the order with an OrderID of 10250 nests below the *Shippers* element with a *ShipperID* element value of 2 for the United Package shipper.

The nesting of *Orders* elements within *Shippers* elements reflects the one-to-many relationship between the *Shippers* table and the *Orders* table. This is a common XML document feature that some developers find preferable to relational views of one-to-many relationships. In a relational view, all the data from the *Shippers* table and the *Orders* table appear in a single datasheet. There is no natural break in the design of the datasheet when the orders for one shipper stop and the orders for the next shipper begin.

Exporting the Data Behind a Form

In addition to exporting XML documents based on Access tables, you can also use the File, Export command to create XML documents based on the data behind forms and reports. The best way to understand how to create an XML document based on the data behind an Access form may be to follow the steps for creating an XML document based on a typical form. You use the same steps as for creating an XML document based on a report, but before invoking the File, Export command, you start by selecting a report instead of a form.

Figure 15-10 shows a main/sub form generated with the help of the Auto-Form tool on the Database toolbar. This form is available in Chapter15.mdb as *frmCustomersOrders.* As you can see, the form presents data from the *Customers* and *Orders* table. I shifted the sub form view to the right and adjusted its column widths to highlight that the sub form also exposes *CompanyName* column values in its *Shipvia* column. Therefore, the *frmCustomersOrders* form also has data behind it from the *Customers, Orders,* and *Shippers* tables. Since there are no filters in this AutoForm tool–generated form, the form contains all the data from the tables behind it.

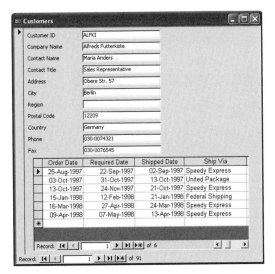

Figure 15-10   The *frmCustomersOrders* form used to demonstrate the process for creating an XML document based on the data behind a form.

Begin to create an XML document based on the data behind *frmCustomers-Orders* by selecting the form in the Database window and choosing File, Export. Next, designate a destination folder for the XML document, such as C:\Access11Files\Chapter15. If you do not mind naming the XML document after the form (namely, frmCustomersOrders.xml), click Export. Otherwise, revise the file name drop-down box on the Export Form dialog box before clicking Export. Click More Options on the Export XML dialog box and select the Data tab. Notice that Access selects the *Customers* table by default. Then click the expand control for the *Orders* table. Next, click the expand control for [Lookup Data] to expose the *Shippers* table. With all tables exposed, select the *Orders* and *Shippers* tables so that all three tables are selected on the Data tab. Finally, click OK to create the XML document and its corresponding XSD schema.

If you open the frmCustomersOrders.xml file in a browser, you can see the *Orders* elements nested within *Customers* elements. Furthermore, the nested *Orders* elements correspond to those for the *Customers* elements making the orders. If you navigate the browser to the bottom of the *frmCustomers-Orders*.xml file, you can see the three *Shippers* elements based on the rows in the *Shippers* table. These rows do not nest within any other elements. Instead, they trail the last *Orders* element for the last *Customers* element. The *Shippers* elements have the same level of indentation as the *Customers* elements in the document. This indicates that the values from the *Shippers* and *Orders* tables are at the same hierarchical level in the document, though the *Shippers* elements have no elements nested within them.

Programmatically Using XML from Access 2003

In this section, you'll learn programming techniques for working with Access and XML documents. Some of these techniques revolve around critical Access *Application* object methods for exporting database objects as XML documents from Access database objects and Access projects, as well as importing XML documents into tables in Access database files and Access projects. Other techniques demonstrate basic MSXML programming techniques for retrieving whole XML documents, portions of XML documents, and even revising XML documents. A third area of functionality relates to presenting Access database objects exported as XML documents in a browser using built-in programming techniques. You'll also learn custom extensions of the built-in techniques that enable you to readily create custom representations of XML documents based on objects from either .mdb or .adp files.

Creating and Processing XML for an Access Table

Exporting an XML document based on an Access table normally involves exporting two files—one containing the data as an XML document and the other containing the XML schema for the XML document. The XML data file has an .xml extension, and the XML schema file has an .xsd extension. Through an extensive array of arguments, the *ExportXML* method for an Access *Application* object can create the .xml and .xsd files, as well as perform a wide variety of other functions for generating XML. As you are getting started, you'll need a few of the arguments that this section covers. To complete the transfer of the data from an Access table from one Access file (either an .mdb or an .adp file) to another, you need to invoke the *ImportXML* method for the Access *Application* object in the document that reconstructs the Access table from the XML document and schema. Subject to the limitations noted in the "Manually Using XML from Access 2003" section of this chapter, you can use XML to freely exchange Access data between any pair of Access database files or Access projects.

Exporting the XML for a Table with the *ExportXML* Method

To export a table with the *ExportXML* method, you need to specify four arguments. Two arguments designate the table, one argument specifies the name of the path and file for the XML document, and the one remaining argument denotes the name of the path and file for the XML schema. You can specify the arguments positionally or by name. The *ExportXMLForShippersTable* procedure demonstrates the syntax that uses names to specify arguments; this procedure is available in Chapter15.mdb. The *ObjectType* argument designates the type of database object that can serve as the source for an XML document. The following code sample uses the *acExportTable* constant to designate a table as a source for the XML document. The *DataSource* argument is a string value with the name of the table. Depending on the *ObjectType* argument value, the *DataSource* argument can name a table, a query, a form, a report, or a SQL Server stored procedure, view, or user-defined function.

> **Note**   Use the Object Browser to examine the arguments and intrinsic constants for selected argument values with the *ExportXML* method. For example, the browser reports the following intrinsic constant names for specifying the *ObjectType* argument: *acExportForm*, *acExportFunction*, *acExportQuery*, *acExportReport*, *acExportServerView*, *acExportStoredProcedure*, and *acExportTable*.

```
Sub ExportXMLForShippersTable()
Application.ExportXML _
    ObjectType:=acExportTable, _
    DataSource:="Shippers", _
    DataTarget:="C:\Access11Files\Chapter15\Shippersp1.xml", _
    SchemaTarget:="C:\Access11Files\Chapter15\Shippersp1.xsd"
End Sub
```

After invoking the *ExportXMLForShippersTable* procedure, Access adds a pair of files to the C:\Access11Files\Chapter15 folder on your computer. Make sure the folder exists prior to invoking the procedure or change the path in the *DataTarget* and *SchemaTarget* arguments. The procedure uses file names of Shippersp1.xml and Shippersp1.xsd so that it will not overwrite files created manually from earlier examples in this chapter.

Viewing and Manipulating an XML Document

Before importing an XML document exported from another Access database file or Access project, it can be useful to examine or even modify the XML document so that the document writes properly to a new database object or appends to an existing one. If the source database object for an XML document and schema match the name of a database object into which you create a new database object based on the XML document, then the new imported object appears with a number after it. For example, if you attempt to create a new *Shippers* table into a database that already has a *Shippers* table, the *ImportXML* method creates a new table named *Shippers1* based on the XML document. There are several workarounds for this situation. Three possible solutions include: erasing the old data before appending the new data to a database object; appending the new data to existing data in a database object; and editing the XML document and schema so that the *ImportXML* method creates a new table with a different name. In any event, two capabilities are helpful. One is to view the contents of an XML document, and the other is to update the contents of an XML document.

Your applications can view and manipulate an XML document through MSXML. As mentioned earlier, MSXML installs automatically with Internet Explorer 6.0, which installs along with Windows XP. You can learn more about MSXML version 4.0 installation and redistribution at this URL:

http://msdn.microsoft.com/library/default.asp?url=/library/en-us/xmlsdk /htm/sdk_intro_6g53.asp?frame=true.

When running procedures in an Access module that utilize MSXML, you will need a reference to a version of MSXML. Office 2003 makes available MSXML 5.0. From the References dialog box, you can create a reference for MSXML 5.0 by browsing to MSXML5.DLL in the \Program Files\Common Files\Microsoft Shared\Office11 folder.

MSXML offers a means of viewing and manipulating an XML document via a traditional COM object model interface. Since VBA can reference COM objects, you can use MSXML to process XML documents created by the *ExportXML* method. The following samples apply the *DOMDocument* and the *IXMLDOMNodeList* objects. The *DOMDocument* object is the top-level pointer at an XML source, such as an XML document or an XML schema. You can use this object to point at any file comprised of XML, such as an XML document, an XML schema, or even an XSLT program. You can use the *DOMDocument* object to retrieve and create all other XML objects in an XML source. The *DOMDocument* is an in-memory representation of an XML source. Any XML source is a hierarchical collection of nodes. Nodes within an XML source consist of elements, attributes, *CDATA* sections, and other components within an XML source.

The pair of procedures in the next listing read an XML document file into memory, and then print the in-memory version of the document to the Immediate window. These procedures, as well as the other procedures in this section, are in Chapter15Receive.mdb. The next pair of procedures depend on a reference to MSXML 5.0 and a global declaration and instantiation of a *DOMDocument* object. In fact, other samples in this section rely on the prior existence of the reference and *DOMDocument* object. The syntax for the global declaration and instantiation is on the next line.

```
Dim doc1 As New MSXML2.DOMDocument50
```

The first procedure in the next listing specifies the name of the path and file for an XML document and passes that value to the second procedure. In this case, the target XML document file is the XML document generated in the preceding section—namely, Shippersp1.xml in the C:\Access11Files\Chapter15\ path. The second procedure, a function procedure, loads the XML document into the *doc1* variable in memory as a *DOMDocument* object. Next, the second procedure assigns the *doc1* memory variable to the function's name so that the XML document becomes available through the function call in the first procedure. By isolating the reading of the XML document in a function procedure, this simple application makes it easy to reuse the code for reading an XML document into the *doc1* variable in other procedures. When focus returns to the first procedure, the sample prints the XML property for the XML document. This property returns the whole document in this case because it applies to a *DOMDocument* object. This kind of application is useful when you want to review the content of an XML document, including all its tags.

```
'Requires reference to Microsoft XML, v5.0 as
'well as a global declaration and instantiation
'of doc1 as a MSXML2.DOMDocument50 object
Sub PrintXML()
Dim str1 As String
str1 = "C:\Access11Files\Chapter15\Shippersp1.xml"
'Print in-memory doc object
Debug.Print ReadXML(str1).XML
End Sub

Function ReadXML(strToXML As String)
'Load XML file into doc object
doc1.Load strToXML
'Return doc1 object
Set ReadXML = doc1
End Function
```

Although the printout of the XML in an XML document is informative because it includes all the tags along with their values, the tags can be distracting. It is sometimes more useful to present just the column values for each row delimited by something, such as a blank line, to separate rows of column values. The next listing illustrates one approach to this task. The sample application consists of three procedures, one of which is the *ReadXML* function procedure described in the preceding sample. Therefore, the next listing shows just two procedures. The application prints to the Immediate window the contents of each column for successive row values from the Shippersp1.xml document. In between successive rows, the sample prints a blank line. Figure 15-11 displays the output. While the listing applies to the Shippersp1.xml file, it can process the contents of any table from an Access database file or an Access project via the *ExportXML* method or a manual technique for creating an XML document based on an Access database object. The sample returns the values of elements. Therefore, if your XML document stores its values in attributes, such as MyShippersWithAttributes.xml from the "XML Document Syntax" section of this chapter, you should modify the sample.

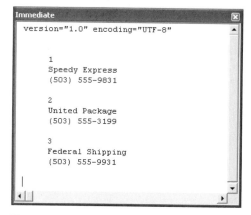

Figure 15-11 The Shippersp1.xml tag values printed as sets of column values to the Immediate window.

The *CallParseAllNodesInATable* procedure performs two functions. First, it populates the *doc1* variable by calling the *ReadXML* function with an XML document argument based on the string value in *str1*. In the sample listing, the *str1* variable points at a path and file for an XML document. Change this for any document that you want to print. Next, the *CallParseAllNodesInATable* procedure invokes the *ParseAllNodesInATable* procedure. The first procedure passes a list of nodes for the whole document by applying the *childNodes* method to the doc1 variable. The *ParseAllNodesInATable* procedure accepts its argument with a variable named nodelist that has an *IXMLDOMNodeList* type.

The second procedure has a novel design because it successively calls itself whenever it discovers a node with child nodes, except for the first node. Actually, the procedure performs multiple tests for each node. First, if the current node has a length of more than two nodes to its final element, the procedure prints a blank line. This works well for the XML document based on the *Shippers* table because each *Shippers* element has three nodes below it for

ShipperID, *CompanyName*, and *Phone* values. The feature represents a limitation of the application, which will print a blank row only between the column values of successive rows when there are at least three column values in a table. Next, the procedure starts a loop to iterate through all the nodes in the current node list. When first called, the node list consists of the declaration node and any nodes before the first *Shippers* element. Each *Shippers* element contains three nodes in the node list below it. When the procedure finds the beginning of a node list below a *Shippers* element, the procedure iterates through the nodes in the list with a *For...Each* loop. If the current node has children, then it is not one of the column values in a *Shippers* element. Therefore, the procedure calls itself with an argument of child nodes for the current node. In this way, the procedure can return all the child nodes for each *Shippers* element. Similarly, the procedure can return all the nodes within the elements, marking all rows of any XML document created with the *ExportXML* method.

> **Note**   The *ParseAllNodesInATable* procedure uses a Static declaration to track values of *bolChild* between successive calls of the procedure by itself.

```
Sub CallParseAllNodesInATable()
Dim str1 As String
str1 = _
    "C:\Access11Files\Chapter15\Shippersp1.xml"
ReadXML (str1)
ParseAllNodesInATable doc1.childNodes
End Sub

Sub ParseAllNodesInATable(ByVal nodelist As MSXML2.IXMLDOMNodeList)

Dim nod1 As IXMLDOMNode
Static bolChild As Boolean

'Skip a line if nodes in a list is greater than 1
'and function started processing child nodes (rows)
'for root node
If nodelist.length > 1 And bolChild = True Then
    Debug.Print
End If

'Loop through nodes; if node has child nodes get
'the child nodes and call function iteratively
```

(continued)

```
For Each nod1 In nodelist
    If nod1.hasChildNodes = True Then
        bolChild = True
        Call ParseAllNodesInATable(nod1.childNodes)
    Else
        If bolChild = True Then
            Debug.Print Space(5) & nod1.nodeTypedValue
            bolChild = False
        Else
            Debug.Print nod1.nodeTypedValue
        End If
    End If
Next nod1

End Sub
```

The *ReviseShipperIDValues* procedure that appears next updates *ShipperID* values in the XML document created in the preceding section. The procedure commences by reading the XML document and creating a list of nodes that includes all the *ShipperID* values from the document. The *getTag-ElementsByTag* method extracts just the nodes with *ShipperID* values from the XML document. Recall that these *ShipperID* values are 1, 2, and 3. The procedure adds 3 to each *ShipperID* value by using the *nodeTypedValue* property for the node. This property represents the value according to the schema for the document, which assigns an *Autonumber* type to the node. Although the *ShipperID* nodes have an *Autonumber* type, you can modify their values within an XML document. After updating the *ShipperID* values, the procedure closes by saving the in-memory representation to the file from which it came.

```
Sub ReviseShipperIDValues()
Dim str1 As String
Dim nlt1 As MSXML2.IXMLDOMNodeList
Dim nod1 As IXMLDOMNode

'Read table in Shippersp1.xml document
str1 = "C:\Access11Files\Chapter15\Shippersp1.xml"
ReadXML (str1)

'Return just the ShipperID values
Set nlt1 = doc1.getElementsByTagName("ShipperID")

'Increment ShipperID values by 3
For Each nod1 In nlt1
    nod1.nodeTypedValue = nod1.nodeTypedValue + 3
Next nod1
```

```
'Save the XML document with new ShipperID values
doc1.Save str1

End Sub
```

Importing an XML Document as an Access Table

The *ImportXMLXSD* procedure (see the next listing) shows the syntax for three different ways to import an XML document, Shippersp1.xml, into an Access database file. Before running the procedure, delete all previously created tables from Chapter15Receive.mdb. The procedure resides in the same .mdb file. The procedure invokes the *ImportXML* method with two different argument sets. Actually, the first argument is always the same. It is the name of the path and file for an XML document that the *ImportXML* method will use as a source for populating an Access table. The second argument is what makes the two invocations inside a *Do* loop different from the one invocation outside the loop. The two invocations inside the loop specify that the *ImportXML* method should append the data in the XML document. The difference is that one deletes any prior data from a previously existing *Shippers* table, and the other does not delete any prior data from the *Shippers* table already in the database. The third invocation of the method occurs outside the *Do* loop. In this instance, the syntax attempts to add a new table to the database named Shippers that contains the data in the XML document. If a *Shippers* table already exists, this invocation of the method will generate a new version of the table named *Shippersx*, where *x* represents an integer denoting the version number for the table after the initial version.

The *ImportXMLXSD* procedure starts by invoking the *OpenSchema* method for the connection of the current project to return a recordset of metadata about tables in the database for the project. The *Do* loop mentioned earlier iterates through the rows of the recordset to find a row with a *Table_Name* column value equal to *Shippers*. If it finds such a row, it means the database already has a *Shippers* table. In this case, the procedure follows one of three courses of action based on user replies to two questions presented by invoking the *MsgBox* function. Two nested *If* statements handle the logic for offering these options. The first *MsgBox* function explains that the table already exists, but asks if the user wants to append the data anyway. The attempt to append the data might not succeed for rows in the XML document with the same *ShipperID* value as a row in the previously existing *Shippers* table. If the user replies No to the first prompt, a second prompt asks if the procedure should copy the existing data over the existing data in the *Shippers* table. If the user replies Yes to this second prompt, an *ElseIf* clause for the inner *If* statement within the *Do* loop deletes all rows in the *Shippers* table before appending the values from the

XML document into the table. This append operation will succeed so long as the table structure matches the one specified in the XML schema for the XML argument. If the user replies No to the second prompt, the procedure does not attempt to update the *Shippers* data with the contents of the XML document.

> **Note**   A simple error trap allows the procedure to exit gracefully from errors. For example, if a user attempts to add data from the Shippersp1.xml document without erasing the prior data, the procedure presents an error message without losing control. The user can rerun the procedure and erase the prior values if desired.

No matter which option a user selects within the inner *If* statement in the *Do* loop, the sample exits the procedure if a version of the *Shippers* table already exists. On the other hand, if the database for the current project does not contain a *Shippers* table, the logic transfers control to the last formulation of the *ImportXML* method. This method creates a *Shippers* table based on the XML schema for the XML document and populates the table with values from the XML document.

```
Sub ImportXMLXSD()
On Error GoTo ImportTrap
Dim rst1 As ADODB.Recordset

'Search for Shippers table in current project, and
'append new data if it already exists or
'copy new data over existing data or
'ignore new data
Set rst1 = _
    CurrentProject.Connection.OpenSchema(adSchemaTables)
Do Until rst1.EOF
    If rst1("Table_Name") = "Shippers" Then
        If MsgBox("Table already exits.  Do you want " & _
            "append XML data?", vbYesNo) = vbYes Then
            Application.ImportXML _
                "C:\Access11Files\Chapter15\Shippersp1.xml", _
                acAppendData
        ElseIf MsgBox("Table already exits.  Do you want " & _
            "copy XML data over existing data?", vbYesNo) = _
            vbYes Then
            CurrentProject.Connection.Execute _
                ("DELETE * FROM Shippers")
            Application.ImportXML _
```

```
                "C:\Access11Files\Chapter15\Shippersp1.xml", _
                acAppendData
        Else
            MsgBox "Exiting without changing anything.", vbInformation
        End If
        Exit Sub
    End If
    rst1.MoveNext
Loop

'Insert structure and data for Shippers table
Application.ImportXML _
    "C:\Access11Files\Chapter15\Shippersp1.xml", _
    acStructureAndData

'Clean up objects and exit
rst1.Close
Set rst1 = Nothing
Exit Sub

'Present error description in a message box
ImportTrap:
MsgBox Err.Description

End Sub
```

It is not uncommon in database applications to have to append new data to a table without deleting existing data. One way to demonstrate this capability with the current resources is to alter the Shippersp1.xml document after populating the *Shippers* table with the document. You can run the *ReviseShipperID-Values* procedure to make the *ShipperID* values different than those initially created for the Shippersp1.xml document by the *ExportXML* method. Then rerun the *ImportXMLXSD* procedure and select the first prompt to append the data. These actions will extend the initial *Shippers* table so that the table contains six rows with *ShipperID* values from 1 through 6. The second attempt to append rows succeeds because the primary key values are different than those already in the table.

Exporting a Parameter Query and Importing Its Data

Parameter queries are a convenient mechanism for allowing users to interact with an application at run time. Your applications can point the *ExportXML* method at a parameter query. When a user invokes the application to export an XML document and its schema, the *ExportXML* method can pass along the parameter query prompt for one or more parameter values. After the user responds to any parameter query prompts, the *ExportXML* method can compose an XML document and matching schema based on the result set from the run time–supplied parameters. You can handle this task more elegantly by creating ADO *Parameter* objects and managing the assignment of values to the objects at run time. See Chapter 4 for more discussion and samples illustrating how to do this.

The following SQL script shows an Access parameter query. Chapter15.mdb contains this query; the query's name is *CustomersOrdersFilter*. The query joins select columns from the *Customers* and *Orders* tables. At run time, the query prompts for a customer code. This is a five-character field corresponding to a *CustomerID* column value in the *Customers* table. Since one customer can have many orders, the query can return multiple rows when the user designates a single customer.

```
SELECT Customers.CustomerID, Orders.OrderID, Orders.OrderDate, Orders.ShippedDa
te, Orders.Freight, Orders.ShipVia
FROM Customers INNER JOIN Orders ON Customers.CustomerID=Orders.CustomerID
WHERE (((Customers.CustomerID)=[Customer Code?]));
```

When an application refers to the *CustomersOrdersFilter* query in the *DataSource* argument for the *ExportXML* method, the procedure presents the query's prompt. Since the *DataSource* argument names a query, the *ObjectType* argument should be set to *acExportQuery*. The *ExportCustomersOrdersFilter* procedure below illustrates the syntax for creating an XML document and an XML schema named, respectively, CustomersOrdersFilter.xml and CustomersOrdersFilter.xsd. The procedure resides in Chapter15.mdb. If you run this procedure repeatedly and supply different parameter values, it will overwrite the XML document and schema each time.

```
Sub ExportCustomersOrdersFilter()

Application.ExportXML _
    ObjectType:=acExportQuery, _
    DataSource:="CustomersOrdersFilter", _
    DataTarget:="C:\Access11Files\Chapter15\CustomersOrdersFilter.xml", _
    SchemaTarget:="C:\Access11Files\Chapter15\CustomersOrdersFilter.xsd"

End Sub
```

When you use the *ImportXML* method to import the result set from a parameter query, your application retrieves the result set for the most recent invocation of the parameter query. In essence, the process captures the result set just as if it were a table. The *ImportXMLForQuery* procedure to follow illustrates the syntax for capturing the result set from the *CustomersOrdersFilter* parameter query invoked by the *ExportCustomersOrdersFilter* procedure. The *ImportXMLForQuery* procedure, which resides in Chapter15Receive.mdb, will create a new table each time you invoke it, because the procedure has its second argument set to *acStructureAndData*. By creating a second procedure that is identical, except that it replaces the second argument value with *acAppendData*, you can append new data from successive invocations of the parameter query to the existing table. This kind of design is particularly appropriate when you need to successively add new data from different time periods. You can run the procedure exporting XML at the end of each day, week, month, or quarter. The procedure importing XML can run with *acAppendData* as its second parameter on all occasions, except the first time when the application creates the design for the table and initially populates it with data.

```
Sub ImportXMLForQuery()
Application.ImportXML _
    "C:\Access11Files\Chapter15\CustomersOrdersFilter.xml", _
    acStructureAndData
End Sub
```

Creating .HTM Files to Show Exported XML

One cool feature about the *ExportXML* method is that it will create an .xsl file and an .htm file that taps the .xsl file. Specify the .xsl file with the *ExportXML* method's *PresentationTarget* argument. Whenever you specify the *PresentationTarget* argument, you also must assign a value to the *ObjectType* and *DataSource* arguments. Recall that the *DataSource* argument designates an .xml file containing the XML document. The .htm file generated by the *ExportXML* method contains a script that writes over itself. The script requires a version of MSXML on the client workstation to support use of the *Load* method. The code inside the script transforms the contents of the .xml file for display in a browser according to the code inside the .xsl file. When users attempt to open the .htm file, they automatically invoke the script that displays all the column values stored in the XML document.

The *ExportXMLForShippersTableInBrowser* procedure illustrates the syntax for the *PresentationTarget* argument. Notice that the argument points to an .xsl file in the same folder as the .xml file. The use of the *SchemaTarget* argument in this context is optional. That's because the primary purpose of the procedure is to generate the files to view the contents of the .xml file in a browser with an HTML table instead of the tagged format that is characteristic of XML documents. The *ExportXMLForShippersTableInBrowser* procedure generates four files. Three are specified in the arguments for the *ExportXML* method. The fourth file has an .htm extension and a filename that matches the .xml file. This .htm file contains the script described in the preceding paragraph.

```
Sub ExportXMLForShippersTableInBrowser()

Application.ExportXML _
    ObjectType:=acExportTable, _
    DataSource:="Shippers", _
    DataTarget:="C:\Access11Files\Chapter15\Shippersp2.xml", _
    SchemaTarget:="C:\Access11Files\Chapter15\Shippersp2.xsd", _
    PresentationTarget:="C:\Access11Files\Chapter15\Shippersp2.xsl"

End Sub
```

The HTML table that appears when a user opens the Shippers2.htm file in a browser is the same as the one shown in Figure 15-9. Refer back to that illustration to note a couple of features of the table. First, it shows data for all the columns. Second, it has very basic formatting. You can create your own .xsl file with more elaborate formatting that shows just selected columns. Then, with a slightly edited version of the script in the .htm file generated by the *ExportXML* method, you can cause the .htm file to open with the custom formatting in your .xsl file as well as any column selection that you specify. When modifying automatically generated files, I find it convenient to create new versions of the .xsl and .htm files with custom code. It is easy to reuse the .xml generated by the *ExportXML* method.

The following listing shows the XSLT script for the Shippersp21.xsl file. This file contains my custom transformation for showing the Shippersp2.xml file in a browser. The script contains two template elements. The first template lays out the overall format for the HTML page. Notice that it contains opening and closing *HTML* tags. This template references the XML document's root node in its *match* pattern (match = "/"). Within the BODY section of the HTML page, the XSLT code designates a table with two columns—one with a heading of *Shippers* and the other with a heading of *Phone*. The *Shippers* heading is for the *CompanyName* element values in the XML document. A *STYLE* tag in the *HEAD* section of the HTML page designates a background color of gray for the table heading. The second template references the *Shippers* element in the XML source. This second template specifies the values to extract for the columns in the table, as well as the formatting for those columns. For example, in the first column it shows the *CompanyName* element from the *Shippers* elements within the XML source and the *Phone* element in the second column. In addition, *Phone* column values will appear with bold and italic font settings, but the *CompanyName* column values will show with the default font settings for the HTML page. Conspicuous by its absence is the *ShipperID* element. The values for this element will not appear in browsers using this transformation for the Shippersp2.xml file.

```xml
<?xml version="1.0"?>
<xsl:stylesheet
      xmlns:xsl="http://www.w3.org/1999/XSL/Transform"
      version="1.0">
  <xsl:template match="/">
      <HTML>
        <HEAD>
          <TITLE></TITLE>
          <STYLE>TH { background-color: Gray }</STYLE>
        </HEAD >
        <BODY>
          <TABLE border='1' style='width:300;'>
            <TR><TH colspan='2'>Shippers</TH></TR>
            <TR><TH>CompanyName</TH><TH>Phone</TH></TR>
            <xsl:apply-templates select = 'dataroot' />
          </TABLE>
        </BODY>
      </HTML>
  </xsl:template>
  <xsl:template match="Shippers">
    <TR>
      <TD><xsl:value-of select = 'CompanyName' /></TD>
      <TD><B><I><xsl:value-of select = 'Phone' /></I></B></TD>
    </TR>
  </xsl:template>
</xsl:stylesheet>
```

Now that we have a custom .xsl file, we also need an .htm file that applies the transformation in the .xsl file to the .xml file generated by the *ExportXML-ForShippersTableInBrowser* procedure. One especially easy way to compose the required .htm file is to edit the .htm file generated by the procedure and save the edited file with a new name, such as Shippersp21.htm. In fact, all you have to do is edit one line. The following script shows this line in bold font. The original version of the line passed Shippersp2.xsl as an argument to the *Load-DOM* procedure. The edited version passes the new custom XSLT transformation, which resides in Shippersp21.xsl. This file should reside in the same folder as the .xml document.

As you can see, the script in .htm consists of three procedures. The *ApplyTransform* procedure is the main procedure that starts whenever a user loads a new copy of the page in a browser. This procedure invokes the two other procedures. The first of these instantiates a version of MSXML. Next, the procedure uses the instance of MSXML to load the Shippersp2.xml and

Shippersp21.xsl files into memory. In its final line, the *ApplyTransform* procedure invokes the *Write* method of the *Document* object for the HTML page to write the .xml file transformed by the .xsl file over the script.

> **Note** The script in the .htm file wipes itself out after loading. This is why you have to reload the page to reflect a change in your XSLT transformation. You cannot simply refresh the page, because the script to apply a new XSLT transformation is no longer available after a page loads.

```
<HTML xmlns:signature="urn:schemas-microsoft-com:office:access">
<HEAD>
<META HTTP-EQUIV="Content-Type" CONTENT="text/html;charset=UTF-8"/>
</HEAD>
<BODY ONLOAD="ApplyTransform()">
</BODY>
<SCRIPT LANGUAGE="VBScript">
    Option Explicit

    Function ApplyTransform()
        Dim objData, objStyle

        Set objData = CreateDOM
        LoadDOM objData, "Shippersp2.xml"

        Set objStyle = CreateDOM
        LoadDOM objStyle, "Shippersp21.xsl"

        Document.Open "text/html","replace"
        Document.Write objData.TransformNode(objStyle)
    End Function

    Function CreateDOM()
        On Error Resume Next
        Dim tmpDOM

        Set tmpDOM = Nothing
        Set tmpDOM = CreateObject("MSXML2.DOMDocument.5.0")
        If tmpDOM Is Nothing Then
            Set tmpDOM = CreateObject("MSXML2.DOMDocument.4.0")
        End If
```

```
   If tmpDOM Is Nothing Then
      Set tmpDOM = CreateObject("MSXML.DOMDocument")
   End If

   Set CreateDOM = tmpDOM
End Function

Function LoadDOM(objDOM, strXMLFile)
   objDOM.Async = False
   objDOM.Load strXMLFile
   If (objDOM.ParseError.ErrorCode <> 0) Then
      MsgBox objDOM.ParseError.Reason
   End If
End Function
```

```
</SCRIPT>
</HTML>
```

Figure 15-12 shows the table in a browser generated by Shippersp21.htm invoking Shippersp21.xsl to transform Shippersp2.xml. You can best appreciate the impact of the custom XSLT file by contrasting Figure 15-12 with Figure 15-9. Recall that Figure 15-9 shows the *Shippers* table with the standard XSLT transformation provided by Access. The custom XSLT selects a subset of the columns, which exclude *ShipperID*, and it applies special formatting in the table header area as well as in the *Phone* column.

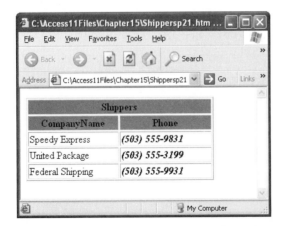

Figure 15-12   The table that appears when a browser opens Shippersp21.htm.

Summary

The chapter has three major sections. In the first section, you gain exposure to core concepts for XML documents, XSD schemas, and XSLT—particularly as they relate to Access data and built-in Access XML capabilities. The next section explores manual techniques for processing Access data with XML. The section begins with a series of demonstrations showing you how to represent an Access table as an XML document. You also learn how to import that table into another Access database file or Access project. In addition, you learn how to show the data in a browser. The chapter also notes that you can attach .xml and .xsd files to e-mail messages for transport over the Internet instead of downloading them from a Web server. The second section further illustrates how to prepare data from related tables in Access databases, as well as the data from behind Access forms, for transport over the Internet. The third section demonstrates how to program selected examples presented in the second section, as well as how to perform tasks with XML documents not possible through the Access UI. For example, you learn how to select a subset of the elements from an XML document and how to update element values in an XML document.

Index

Symbols

Numerics

A

Rick Dobson

Rick Dobson, Ph.D., is an author and trainer who specializes in Microsoft Access, Microsoft SQL Server, Microsoft Visual Basic .NET, and Web technologies. A Microsoft Certified Professional, he is a big fan of programmatic solutions, particularly those that involve VBA, Visual Basic .NET, ADO, Microsoft ADO.NET, Jet SQL, T-SQL, and SQL-DMO.

Rick is the author of five other books on Access and SQL Server. This sixth book on Microsoft databases is the third edition of his book on programming Microsoft Access. Other recent books by Rick include *Programming Microsoft Visual Basic .NET for Microsoft Access Databases* and *Programming Microsoft SQL Server 2000 with Microsoft Visual Basic .NET*. He also writes for leading computer resources, such as *SQL Server Magazine*, MSDN, the Microsoft Developer Network (*www.msdn.microsoft.com*), and *Smart Access*.

Rick and his wife, Virginia, jointly run their business, CAB, Inc. (*www.cabinc.net*). Rick's work targets intermediate and advanced Access, SQL Server, and Web developers, while Virginia focuses on Access power users and beginning developers. She has been a regular columnist and contributor for *www.smartcomputing.com*, *Microsoft OfficePro,* and other publications.

CAB operates *www.programmingmsaccess.com* and related developer seminars. The ProgrammingMSAccess.com Web site features code samples, live demonstrations, tutorials, FAQs, and links to other online resources for Access and SQL Server developers. The annual seminars attract database developers and administrators from large and mid-size organizations, including Ford Motor Company, EDS, Prudential Financial, the U.S. Navy, and Panasonic. You can contact Rick at rickd@cabinc.net.

Learning solutions for *every* software user

Microsoft Press® creates comprehensive learning solutions that empower everyone from business professionals and decision makers to software developers and IT professionals to work more productively with Microsoft® software. We design books for every business computer user, from beginners up to tech-savvy power users. We produce in-depth learning and reference titles to help developers work more productively with Microsoft programming tools and technologies. And we give IT professionals the training and technical resources they need to deploy, install, and support Microsoft products during all phases of the software adoption cycle. Whatever technology you're working with and no matter what your skill level, we have a learning tool to help you.

Microsoft®

microsoft.com/mspress

Get a **Free**
*e-mail newsletter, updates,
special offers, links to related books,
and more when you*

register online!

Register your Microsoft Press® title on our Web site and you'll get
a FREE subscription to our e-mail newsletter, *Microsoft Press
Book Connections.* You'll find out about newly released and upcoming
books and learning tools, online events, software downloads, special
offers and coupons for Microsoft Press customers, and information
about major Microsoft® product releases. You can also read useful
additional information about all the titles we publish, such as detailed book descriptions, tables of contents and indexes, sample
chapters, links to related books and book series, author biographies,
and reviews by other customers.

Registration is easy. Just visit this Web page and fill in your information:

http://www.microsoft.com/mspress/register

Microsoft
